SILMAN'S CHESS ODYSSEY

Other Siles Press books by Jeremy Silman

The Complete Book of Chess Strategy (1998)
The Amateur's Mind, 2nd Edition (1999)
The Reassess Your Chess Workbook (2001)
Pal Benko (2003)
Silman's Complete Endgame Course (2007)
How to Reassess Your Chess, 4th Edition (2010)

SILMAN'S CHESS ODYSSEY

Cracked Grandmaster Tales, Legendary Players, *and* Instruction and Musings

International Master

Jeremy Silman

SILES PRESS LOS ANGELES

First Edition

10 9 8 7 6 5 4 3 2 1

Printed in the United States.

Library of Congress Cataloging-in-Publication Data
Names: Silman, Jeremy, author.
Title: Silman's chess odyssey : cracked grandmaster tales, legendary players, and instruction and musings /
by International Master Jeremy Silman.
Identifiers: LCCN 2021052979 |
ISBN 9781890085247 (paperback) ISBN 9781890085551 (ebook)
Subjects: LCSH: Chess. | Chess--Tournaments. | Chess players. |
Chess--Miscellanea.
Classification: LCC GV1445 .S55 2022 | DDC 794.1--dc23/
eng/20211109
LC record available at https://lccn.loc.gov/2021052979

Cover design by Wade Lageose for Lageose Design

SILES PRESS
a division of Silman-James Press
www.silmanjamespress.com
info: silmanjamespress.com

To Shintaro Katsu (the real man) who created a blind man. Would it work? Yes! Zatoichi the Swordsman won, and tons of Zatoichi-love went all over the world.

The first film was 1962, and after that, everyone wanted to see the movies. Who wouldn't!? A man that couldn't see but could cut your head off with his sword if he wanted to!

So why did I dedicate this book to Zatoichi? Because his films are wonderful. I watch all the Zatoichi movies over-and-over again. And you should have the magic too.

CONTENTS

LIST OF GAMES

Part Three — Portraits and Stories

PREFACE

As I sit down to write this preface I find myself at a loss for words. Why? I've been writing about chess for over fifty years (as well as teaching and playing), but every paragraph I start to write seems as if I've written or said it a thousand times before.

I ask myself what are my current thoughts on chess. For starters, computer chess engines are monsters. Humans have no way to beat them, and they will get better and better.

Chess for me continues to be a part of everyday as I must feed my habit? I very much enjoy the game when I play blitz against other masters. Sadly, several of my close friends (my chess posse) have died: Igor Ivanov, Walter Browne, Pal Benko, Steve Brandwein (I can still hear Steve chanting, "I came, I ate, and I left"), and John Grefe, and I miss there banter. I enjoy teaching (if the student is really engaged) and I have a handful of students. But mostly I love, love, love chess books.

Recently published books such as Davorin Kuliasevic's *How to study Chess on your Own*. Caruana's *Ruy Lopez*. And *Bobby Fischer and His World*. There are endless chess books to read and reread and players to read about and games to study.

I love chess history. For example, Gioacchino Greco—he was the best chess player in the world circa 1620. You must look at his games (see part four)! Greco was a master of tactics, positional play, and openings—he did everything! If Greco knew "imbalances" (which I created) he would be a chess god. As for Philidor (in the 1700s), Greco would destroy him.

World Champion Emanuel Lasker became interested in Go after being introduced to it by his namesake Edward Lasker, probably in 1907 or 1908. After that Emanuel and Edward were invited to meet a Go master at a Japanese Club. Emanuel loved it and created Go meetings at his house.

Years ago, after looking at Lasker's games, I decided to play Go (along with chess). Now I just play chess, and only on rare occasions do I will take out the Go set.

And I am constantly amused by the endless stories. One of my favorites is the account Steinitz wrote following his physical battle with the hard-drinking Joseph Henry Blackburne (who was also known as the Black Death).

"After a few words Blackburne pounced upon me and hammered at my face and eyes with fullest force about a dozen blows...but at last I had the good fortune to release myself from his drunken grip, and I broke the windowpane with his head, which sobered him down a little."

I laugh every time I look at this, as I hope you will do when you read some of the stories squeezed in between the history and instruction within these pages.

There are so many sides to chess: You can have fun with it. You can study for long hours every day and become a strong player (that was my path). You can be a bad player, but just love the game and feel joy when you sit down at the board. You can be a five-year old kid (boy or girl), or a ninety year old that plays everyday.

I hope that every chess player will find some part of this book that speaks to them.

Jeremy Silman
December 2021

ACKNOWLEDGMENTS

I'd like to express my gratitude to John Donaldson, Holly Lee, Tony Saidy, and Ash Warren for looking over my manuscript.

A special thank you to Irwin Fisk for finding the photographs that he took some forty-five years ago of the historic Lone Pine tournaments.

And a thank you to the Marshall Chess Club and Frank Brady; the Cleveland Public Library's John G. White Collection; and the Mechanics' Institute, San Francisco for the use of photos from their archives.

PART ONE

Cracked Grandmaster Tales

All chess players and fans have their favorite chess heroes—they watch their play and go over their games. But are they in touch with the human side of these legends? Are they aware of the sad or crazy or funny or sweet moments that go on behind the scenes—some fun, some unfortunate?

These cracked grandmaster tales are all incidents I witnessed or was a part of—information straight from the "horse's mouth." Keep your eyes open, you'll see trickery, lots of humor, and more.

CRACKED GRANDMASTER TALES

1

Rosendo Balinas and the Cup of Honey

Grandmaster Rosendo Balinas (1941-1998), a Filipino, was the world's strongest Asian player in the '60s to the mid-'70s (Eugenio Torre eventually took the "best Asian player throne"). He earned his grandmaster title when he won a powerful tournament in Odessa with an undefeated 10-4 score. He beat a lot of great players during his career, including Bent Larsen, Lev Polugaevsky, and Luděk Pachman.

During the Lone Pine tournament of 1979 I was paired with Balinas. I was pleased with the pairing since playing any grandmaster was a rush—if I won, great. If I lost, I would view it as a learning experience. The game started in quiet fashion.

Rosendo Balinas vs. Silman, Lone Pine 1979

1.c4 c5 2.Nf3 Nf6 3.Nc3 d5 4.cxd5 Nxd5 5.g3 g6 6.Bg2 Bg7 7.0-0 0-0 8.Qb3 Nc7 9.d3 Nc6

At this point Balinas placed a thermos filled with hot tea on the table. Then he put a big cup of honey next to it.

I expected him to take a bit of honey and mix it in with the tea, but instead he shocked me! He took the tea, poured it into the honey (which turned into a thick goo) and then drank every bit of it. Appalled, I noticed that his eyes immediately glazed over as the sugar hit his brain. Then, smiling, he continued the game.

10.Na4?

The Knight isn't happy on the side, and the opening up of the h1-a8 diagonal won't have any negative effect on Black's position.

10...b6 11.Bg5

Another dubious move.

11...Bg4

Black wants total control over the d4-square.

12.Rfe1 Ne6 13.Be3 Bxf3 14.exf3

14.Bxf3 Ned4 15.Bxd4 Nxd4 16.Qd1 Nxf3+ 17.exf3 Qd7 is also horrible for White (black's Bishop is superior to white's Knight, and white's pawn structure is a disaster).

14...Ned4

I looked at my opponent again and noted that he was completely out of it. In fact, I wouldn't have been surprised if he passed out and fell on the floor.

15.Qd1 Nb4 16.a3??

White's position was awful, but this literally forces me to wipe him out. I felt sorry for Mr. Balinas, but in the war-game known as chess one can't take any prisoners.

16...Nxd3

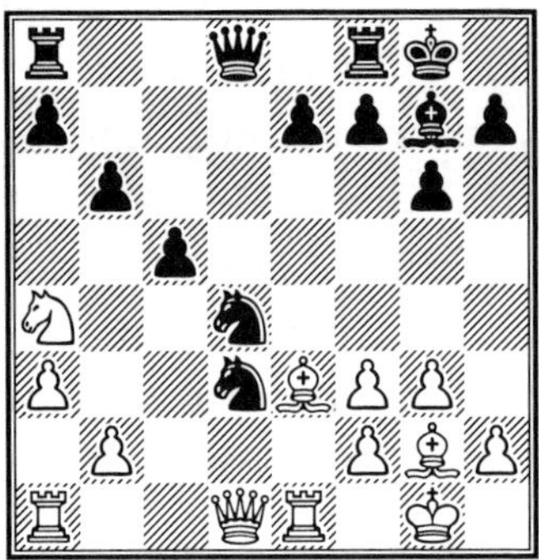

He should have resigned here. The rest is nothing less than spouting blood.

17.Bxd4 Bxd4 18.Re2

18.Qxd3 Bxf2+ picks up white's Queen.

18...b5 19.Nc3 Nxb2 20.Qc2 Na4 21.Nxb5 Bxa1 22.Qxa4 a6 winning white's Knight. 0–1.

A horrible game, and one that gave me no pleasure in winning.

I should add that some years later, when I was in bad shape, he got revenge after I sacrificed all my pieces (for more or less nothing). When the opponent is ill or out of sorts, the healthy player smells blood and goes for the kill! Clearly, professional chess is a cruel game and not for the faint of heart!

Igor Ivanov at the 1988 New York Open (Photo: GHF).

2

Igor Ivanov and the Game that Wasn't a Game

Though Balinas' sugar-bomb is beyond understanding, I have seen many strong players fall victim to alcohol. One grandmaster that suffered from this blight was Igor Vasilyevich Ivanov (1947-2005). This very sweet, kind man, was an extremely strong player—his victory over Anatoly Karpov in 1979 makes that clear. We were friends (we occasionally studied together), and we played nine times (two wins for him, one for me, and six draws). However, my one victory is nothing to be proud of, and I don't view it as a win at all.

Igor came to the board in a state of near coma. Unfortunately, he was an avid worshiper of the god Bacchus. Sitting (kind of) in his chair, he rested his head, in his hands on the table and stayed in that position. Whenever I made a move, he would slowly raise his hand, grab something, and after making the move his hand would crash back onto the table.

Igor Ivanov vs. Silman, San Mateo Rapid 1989

1.c4 e5 2.Nc3 Nf6 3.g3 Bb4 4.Bg2 0-0 5.d3 Re8 6.Bd2 c6 7.Nf3 h6 8.0-0 d5?

I wasn't able to concentrate and was distraught about playing Igor since he was "ill." I was thinking about offering a mercy draw (with the idea of dragging him to his hotel room so he could sleep it off) but my last move was a mistake and, with hardly any thinking, he dashed out.

[clockwise from top left]
Igor Ivanov and Jerry Hanken; Silman warms his hands; Ivanov and SIlman shake before battle; Silman and Ivanov during the game that ended in a draw. Death Valley, December 1986 (Photos: GHF).

9.Nxd5!

So much for pity. Now I'm worse and offering a draw would be insulting.

9...Nxd5 10.cxd5 Bxd2 11.dxc6??

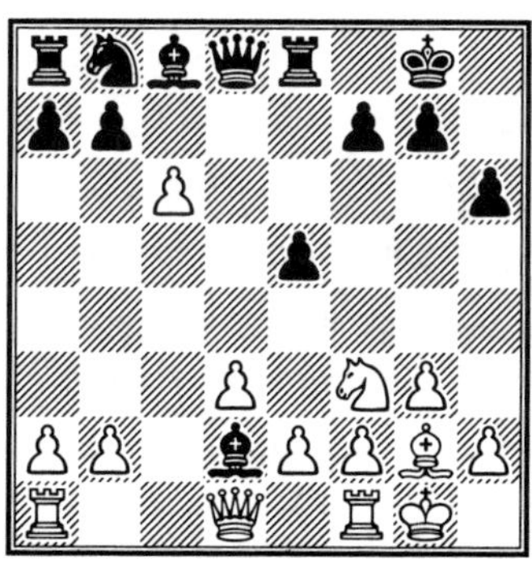

11.Nxd2! cxd5 12.Qb3 was strong. Instead, he blunders away a piece!

11...Ba5 12.Nxe5 Nxc6 13.Nxc6 bxc6 14.Bxc6 Bh3 15.Qa4?

Hanging more stuff.

15...Rxe2 16.Qd1 Bxf1 17.Kxf1 Re1+ 18.Qxe1 Bxe1 19.Bxa8 Bxf2 20.Kxf2 Qxa8 21.Rd1 Qd5 22.d4 Qxa2 23.Rd2 Qd5, 0–1.

Igor laughed as he resigned, but I felt horrible about "the game that wasn't a game" and him drinking himself into a stupor.

I also remember Igor playing in the U.S. Championship (in Long Beach). I watched as he (shades of Balinas!) took out his thermos of hot tea (or was it coffee?) and, as he started pouring it into the cup, he looked up and smiled at his opponent. Then he looked down and realized that he had poured the scalding liquid onto his hand! Leaping up, Igor started dancing around the room in a frenzy, screaming, "Hot! Hot! Hot!"

Allow me to share the following tribute to Igor, written by the great Boris Spassky.

3

A Tribute to Igor Ivanov by Boris Spassky

Igor Ivanov and I shared a similar fate. Neither of us could adapt to the socialist paradise. Both of us received our living strength from Imperial Russia, which had over 1,000 years of culture. Igor was lucky and received a good musical education from his mother who died when he was only fourteen years old. She dreamed to see him as a good pianist and cellist, but his passion was to become a professional chess player. Fortunately, Igor was very talented at chess.

As an artistic personality Igor was living like a careless bird, flying from one place to another, playing chess and piano and singing Russian romances. He did not have the persistence which is so important for getting the grandmaster's title. Igor did not care about himself and became a grandmaster only a few months before his death. He could have easily gotten it twenty years ago!

In 1979, Igor won a famous game against Anatoly Karpov. As a consequence of this victory, Colonel Baturinsky, *Schach Fuehrer* of the USSR, gave him a chance to participate in the Capablanca Memorial in Havana the following year. This was the first and the last invitation which he received from the "generous colonel." Coming back from Havana to Moscow, the plane of the Soviet company Aeroflot made a stop in Gander, Newfoundland. Igor asked for political asylum and the socialist paradise lost one of its most talented masters.

Every time our chess diagonals crossed, I was very glad to meet Igor. Both of us liked the Russian operatic romances. We especially enjoyed the great bass singer Feodor Shaliapin and the beautiful soprano Nadezda Obuhova. We reminisced about our chess teacher from the Palace of Pioneers, Alexander Cherepkov, who is now eighty-six years old, and of course we talked of St. Petersburg.

Igor did not have any illusions about communists or perestroika. It is easy to change the state's flag and emblem, but it is not possible to change a head or a conscience. It takes decades.

Igor's professional life in the West was difficult. He played many tournaments with small prizes and really needed the grandmaster's title to get the invitations for the big events. The country where he started his new chess life, Canada, is not for chess. Both its chess leaders in the early 1980s—Kevin Spraggett and Igor Ivanov—had to move to another area: Kevin to Europe and Igor to the USA. In his new homeland, he won nine Grand Prix titles, which was a great accomplishment.

Igor was lucky to meet his wife Elizabeth who gave him everything, and he was very grateful to her. The last part of his life, Igor settled with her in St. George, Utah, where he headed a chess school and almost became a "balanced American." He liked his friends, his wife, children, animals, music, and adventures. Two cats, Petrushka and Sasha, played an important role in his life. Igor liked to give concerts where he played piano and sang. He was good-natured and people liked him for his excellent sense of humor.

We played in the last round in the Interzonal in Toluca, Mexico in 1982. Igor needed a point for the grandmaster title, and I a point to qualify for the Candidates. Igor defended his inferior position like an ancient Greek hero and made a draw! Nether of us needed a draw! After the game, we looked at each other with open mouths. Friendship is friendship, but sport is sport.

Last October, Igor being very ill, wanted to meet his friends one last time. Thanks to his good friend Alan Crooks he was able to come to Reno but was only able to play two games.

Igor left this world courageously: no complaints, no regrets, just hiding his pain. Before saying good-bye, we pretended we would meet again, but our eyes were very sad: we knew that in this life we had met each other for the last time. Igor left us on November 17, 2005.

I will have warm feelings for Igor forever.

—Boris Spassky, San Francisco October 5, 2006

Walter Browne and the Curse of the Faulty Glasses

Grandmaster Browne had come to the Sunnyvale tournament full of confidence. He felt that sub-par eyesight was hindering his performances and he had just bought glasses. Claiming that he was finally able to see, he drew me in an early round and, after winning a couple games, faced Dennis Waterman who, in those days, was a formidable opponent. Here is my game against Browne:

Walter Browne vs. Silman, Sunnyvale 1974

1.e4 c5 2.Nf3 Nc6 3.d4 cxd4 4.Nxd4 g6 5.Nc3 Bg7 6.Be3 Nf6 7.Bc4 Qa5 8.0–0 0–0 9.Nd5 Nxd5 10.exd5 Ne5 11.Bb3 d6 12.h3 Qa6 13.Bg5 Re8 14.Re1 Bd7 15.c3 Rac8 16.Qd2 Bf6 17.Bh6 b5

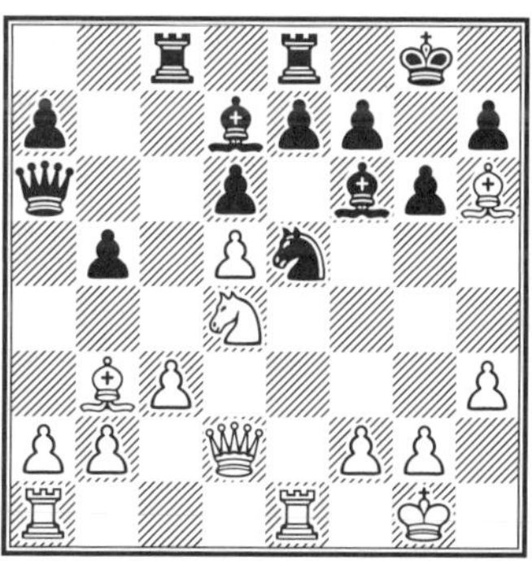

18.Re4 Qb7 19.Bg5 Bg7 20.Rae1 a5 21.f4 a4 22.fxe5 dxe5 23.Nf3 axb3 24.axb3 f6 25.Bh6 Bxh6 26.Qxh6 Qxd5 27.Rxe5 fxe5 28.Ng5 Rc6 29.Qxh7+ Kf8 30.Rf1+ Bf5 31.Qh6+ Kg8 32.Qh7+ Kf8 33.Qh6+, ½–½.

I was friends with both these gentlemen and, as luck would have it, my game was next to theirs (I was sitting beside Walter). Waterman, playing Black, had noticed my draw against Browne and decided to try the same opening:

[above] Dennis Waterman, late 1970s;

[below] Walter Browne, late 1980s (Photo: GHF).

Walter Browne vs. Dennis Waterman, Sunnyvale 1974

1.e4 c5 2.Nf3 Nc6 3.d4 cxd4 4.Nxd4 g6 5.c4 Bg7 6.Be3 Nf6 7.Nc3 Ng4 8.Qxg4 Nxd4 9.Qd1 Ne6 10.Rc1 d6 11.Bd3 Bd7 12.0–0 Bc6 13.Qd2 Qa5 14.Bb1 Qh5 15.Nd5 g5

Claiming the e5-square for Black's pieces. A typical concept in this opening.

16.f3 Be5 17.g3 Rg8 18.Qf2 Bf4 19.Kh1 Bxe3 20.Qxe3 f6 21.f4? gxf4 22.gxf4 Kd7 23.f5 Ng5 24.c5 Nf7 25.Nf4 Qh6 26.Qb3 Rg7 27.cxd6 Nxd6 28.Qe6+ Ke8 29.Rxc6 bxc6 30.e5 Rb8 31.b3 Rb4!

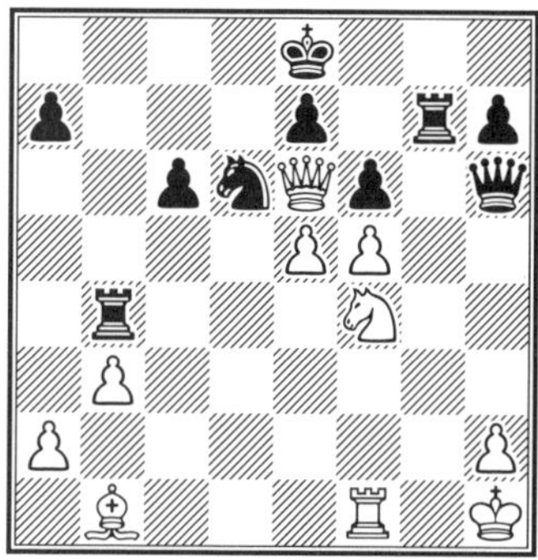

32.exd6 Rxf4

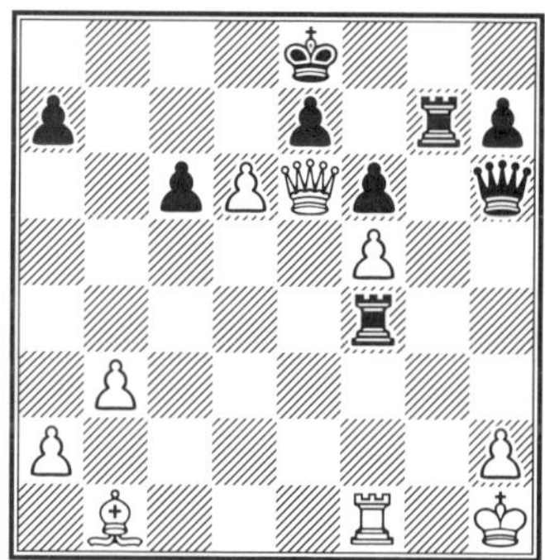

33.Re1?!

Browne could have forced a draw by perpetual check with the simple 33.Qc8+ Kf7 34.Qe6+. However, White refused the draw since 33.Re1 looks like a killer (the threat is 34.Qc8+ Kf7 35.Rxe7 mate).

After playing 33.Re1 Browne's face showed complete confidence and he was waiting for Black to resign when the 6'4" Waterman leapt on his chair, screamed "Woo hoo! Woo hoo!" as he lifted the Queen way up into the sky, and then descended with it as the "woo hoo" continued to fill the room. At that moment Browne realized that it wasn't Waterman that was getting mated, but Browne! A strangled "No!" burst out of his mouth, and he physically reached up to prevent black's Queen from landing on h2. Alas, the downward momentum was too much to stop and Waterman smashed the Queen onto h2, knocking the pawn off the table.

33...Qxh2+!, 0-1

Since 34.Kxh2 Rh4 mate.

Browne, in shock, yelled "My eyes! My eyes!" Then he stormed out of the room. Browne's new glasses were found in a garbage can a short time later.

Walter Browne was one of the most exciting chess players in the world. But many people don't know that Walter was also a world-class poker player and Scrabble player.

Dennis Waterman (he lived in Vegas at that time) was another all-around great game player. He was 2400-strength at chess, a magnificent Scrabble player, one of the world's finest backgammon players, an accomplished Go player, and also a world-class poker player.

When those two came face to face you knew fireworks would ensue. Sure enough, Browne, Waterman and I were at a huge New Year's party and I was watching them battle away on the Scrabble board. Suddenly they started to argue, punches were thrown, and, well, there was never a boring moment when Browne and Waterman got together.

5

Miguel Najdorf and the Dirty Trick

Every chess player knows the name Najdorf. Fischer's and Kasparov's favorite opening (1.e4 c5 2.Nf3 d6 3.d4 cxd4 4.Nxd4 Nf6 5.Nc3 a6) is named after him, and this "animated" individual has countless tales attributed to him. In fact, he was one of the most likable, lively, and crazy players in the history of chess.

When I got paired with the great Miguel in Lone Pine 1976, I was over the moon. Who wouldn't be happy if they got to play Najdorf?

Miguel Najdorf vs. Silman, Lone Pine 1976

1.d4 Nf6 2.c4 e6 3.Nf3 d5 4.Nc3 Be7 5.e3 0–0 6.Bd3 b6 7.b3 Bb7 8.0–0 Nbd7 9.Bb2 Ne4 10.Qe2 a6 11.Rad1 Bb4 12.Nb1 Bd6 13.Ne5 f5 14.f3 Ng5 15.Nd2 c5 16.Nxd7 Qxd7 17.dxc5 Bxc5 18.f4 Nf7 19.Nf3 Qe7 20.Nd4 Nd6 21.cxd5 Bxd5 22.Rc1 a5 23.Nc2 Ne4 24.Rfd1 Rfd8 25.Bc4 Nf6 26.Nd4 Rac8 27.h3 Bxc4 28.Rxc4 Rd5 29.Kh2 Re8 30.Qf3

Black has a very comfortable position, and though I didn't know what his last move did, I was intent on figuring out its purpose. However, after a bit

"Why are you looking at me, little boy?" Najdorf vs. Silman Lone Pine, 1976.

of a think I looked up and stared at my opponent (I had plenty of time on the clock and decided to indulge myself). I was thinking, "Wow, I'm actually playing Najdorf. How cool is that? What can be better than this!?"

At that moment Najdorf looked me in the eye and screamed (so everyone in the whole room could hear it), "Why are you looking at me, little boy? Why are you looking at me?"

I freaked out and wanted to leave the board as quickly as possible. I bashed down 30...Ne4 and quickly rushed away. Unfortunately, White's 30.Qf3 was a trap and though just about everything would be fine for me (30...Qd7 is probably best), my move walked right into his landmine.

30...Ne4??

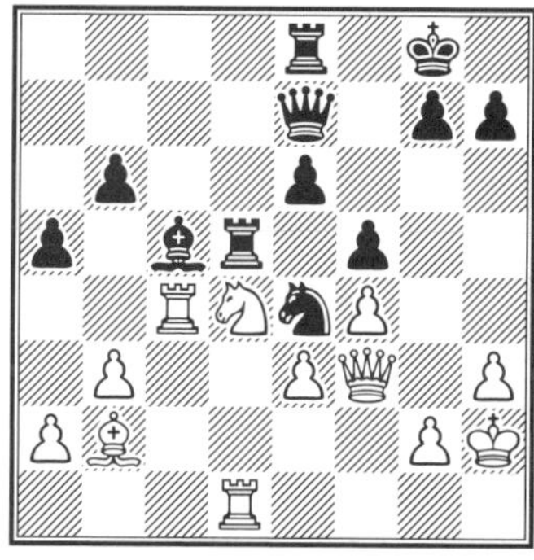

This blunder takes me from a nice, very safe position to an immediate loss. When I returned to the board I saw Najdorf's reply. It just took a glance for me to realize that I had botched the game.

[left] Pal Benko circa 1950; [right] Miguel Najdorf mid-1960s.

31.Nxf5! Qd7?

This makes things even worse but I was still on tilt. Better was 31...Rxf5 but after 32.Qxe4 I'm a pawn down for nothing.

32.Nxg7 Rxd1 33.Nxe8 Qxe8 34.Qxd1 Qg6 35.Qf3 Nd2 36.Qa8+ Bf8 37.Rc8 Nf1+ 38.Kg1, 1–0. Absolutely horrible!

I resigned, signed the scoresheets, and glared at Najdorf in an unfriendly manner. Seeing that I was angry, he got up, walked around the table, put his arm on my shoulder, and said, "It happens to everybody. Don't let it get to you. Let's go and look at some of the games together and try to figure out what's going on!"

Najdorf had a magical way of calming anyone down. For the rest of the tournament, at some point during each of his games, Najdorf would come to my table, drag me near, and ask, "How am I doing? Is my position okay?"

It was simply impossible to be mad at him.

6

More Najdorf Fun

Some people feel that Najdorf wouldn't resort to the gremlin-like antics I related above. The fact was he did such things all the time. If anyone else acted that way, the opponent would go berserk with rage. But when Najdorf did it, the "victim" just rolled his eyes, perhaps raved for a moment to let off steam, and then all would be well. He was a once-in-a-lifetime personality and the people around him took this stuff in stride.

Pal Benko wrote the following about Najdorf:[1]

> Once, Najdorf asked an opponent if he was playing for a win. The guy said, "No, I'm not. Would you like a draw?" When Najdorf refused, his opponent became very irate and wanted to now why he asked if he was playing for a win in the first place. Najdorf said, "I was just wondering."
>
> It must be understood that Najdorf was an incredibly nice guy, but he would use every trick in the book to win. During our third game, we adjourned in a position where I was up a pawn in a Rook endgame. I didn't have a chance to analyze the position, and was thinking about a move when we resumed on the next day. Suddenly he looked at me, his face showing pain and some outrage at the same time, and he said, "How can you do this to an old man like me? How can you play this out? I analyzed all night and it's a dead draw! A dead draw! I guarantee it. In fact, I'll bet you a thousand dollars it's a draw! A thousand dollars!"
>
> I ignored him and tried to think but he wouldn't shut up, he just kept gibbering on and on. Finally I just gave him the draw, anything to get some quiet. Then I went upstairs to my room and looked at the position. Instantly I saw that it was easily winning for me—he had been lying through his teeth. So I rushed downstairs and confronted him.
>
> "Why did you lie to me like that? What in hell is wrong with you? Why didn't you let me think?"
>
> He just smiled, put his arm around me and said "Don't worry about it. Come on, I'll take you out to a nice nightclub!"
>
> How can you stay mad at a guy like that?"

1 Pal Benko and Jeremy Silman, *Pal Benko: My Life, Games and Compositions.* Los Angeles: Siles Press, 2003.

[above left] Petrosian and Tal, Curaçao 1962 (Photo: RIchard Cantwell);
[above right] John Fedorowicz, New York Open 1988 (Photo: GHF).

[clockwise from left] Tigran Petrosian, Lone Pine 1978; Yasser Seirawan, Lone Pine 1977; Jack Peters, Lone Pine 1976; Tigran Petrosian Lone Pine 1978. (Photos: Irwin Fisk.)

7

Tigran Petrosian Hunts Me Down

When I was in my early teens my chess heroes were Emanuel Lasker, Alexander Alekhine, Tigran Petrosian (who took the world championship from Botvinnik in 1963), and Bobby Fischer. Of course, meeting Lasker and Alekhine was impossible, but a child can dream and I had high hopes that someday, against all odds, I would meet Petrosian and Fischer.

Lone Pine 1976 was the event that allowed me to finally see Petrosian face to face. I was in the skittles room where several grandmasters were analyzing a game. A particular position was bothering them all, and there was no consensus as to what was really going on. Then Petrosian walked in, looked at the position for ten to fifteen seconds, tossed out a subtle positional move, and left.

The grandmasters stared at the move for a while and suddenly realized that Petrosian had solved it!

This was also the tournament where Petrosian played a masterpiece against Jack Peters. The King-walk from one side of the board to the other stands out:

Tigran Petrosian vs. Jack Peters, Lone Pine 1976

1.c4 Nf6 2.Nc3 c5 3.g3 Nc6 4.Bg2 e6 5.Nf3 Be7 6.d4 d5 7.cxd5 Nxd5 8.0–0 0–0 9.Nxd5 exd5 10.dxc5 Bxc5 11.a3 a5 12.Ne1 d4 13.Nd3 Bb6 14.Bd2 Re8 15.Rc1 Bg4 16.Re1 Rc8 17.h3 Bf5 18.Qb3 Be4 19.Bxe4 Rxe4 20.Qb5 Na7 21.Rxc8 Nxc8 22.Bg5 Qd6 23.Rc1 Na7 24.Qf5 Re8 25.Bf4 Qd8 26.Rc2 Nc6 27.h4 h6 28.Qb5 Na7 29.Qf5 Nc6 30.Kf1!

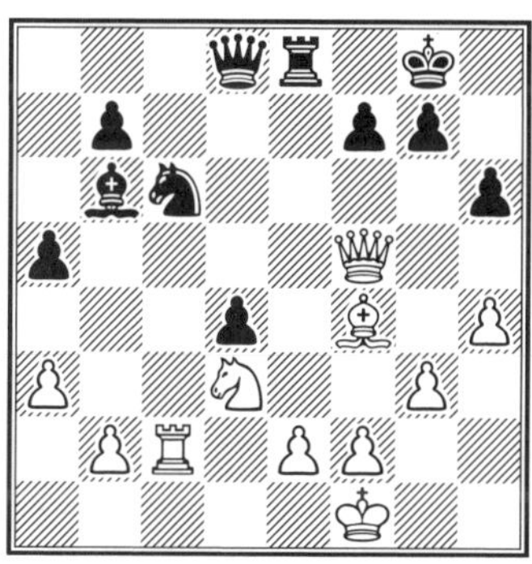

The start of a long march.

30...Re6 31.Qb5 Na7 32.Qb3 Nc6 33.h5 Ne7 34.Ke1 Nd5 35.Qb5 Nf6 36.Kd1 Nd5 37.Be5 Ne7 38.g4 Nc6 39.Bg3 Na7 40.Qb3 Nc6 41.Kc1 Re4 42.f3 Re3 43.Kb1 Ne7 44.Bh4 Qd6 45.Bxe7 Rxe7 46.Rc8+ Kh7 47.Rf8 Qc7 48.f4 Bc5 49. Qd5 Re5 50.Rxf7, 1–0.

I was a mere bystander for Petrosian's skittles appearance, and after watching his game against Peters I thought I was the closest I'd ever come to the great Tigran. Cut to my game against John Fedorowicz, which featured no fewer than three exchange sacrifices.

Silman vs. John Fedorowicz, Lone Pine 1976

1.e4 c5 2.Nf3 d6 3.d4 cxd4 4.Nxd4 Nf6 5.Nc3 g6 6.Be3 Bg7 7.f3 0–0 8.Qd2 Nc6 9.Bc4 Bd7 10.Bb3 Rc8 11.0–0-O Ne5 12.Bg5 Nc4 13.Bxc4 Rxc4 14.Nb3 Rxc3

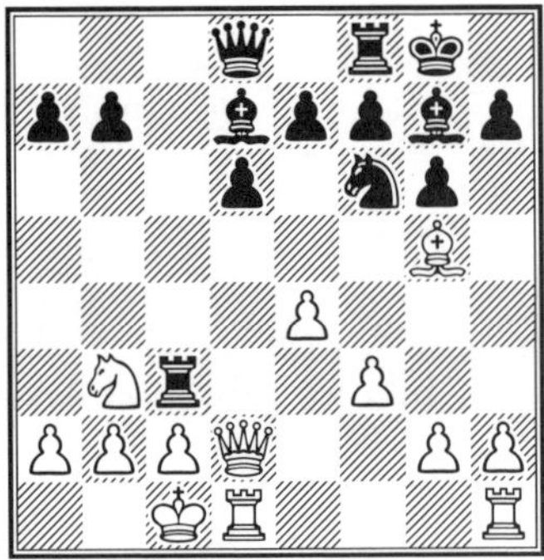

The first exchange sacrifice of the game.

15.bxc3 Be6 16.e5 Ne8 17.Bh6 Bxe5

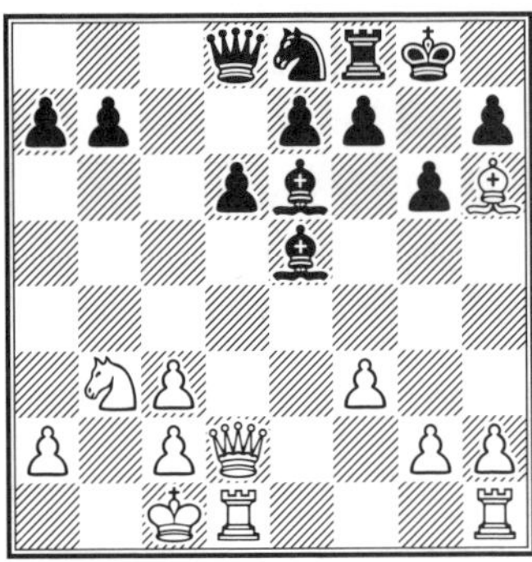

The second exchange sacrifice!

18.Bxf8 Kxf8 19.Rhe1 Bf6 20.Rxe6

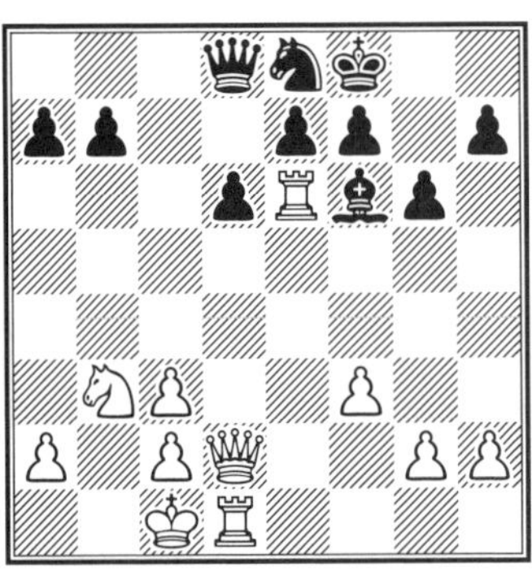

The third exchange sacrifice!

20...fxe6 21.Qe3 Qc8 22.Rd3 Nc7 23.Nd4 a6 24.f4 Kg8 25.Qh3 Nd5 26.Qxe6+ Qxe6 27.Nxe6 Nxc3 28.Kd2 Nxa2 29.Rb3 b5 30.Nc7 b4 31.Nd5!?

31.Nxa6 should win —Petrosian.

31...a5 32.Nxf6+ exf6 33.Rd3?

33.Re3! —Petrosian.

33...Nc3 34.Ke3

34.Rxd6?? Ne4+.

34...d5 35.Kd4 Kf7 36.Re3 a4 37.Re1 a3 38.Kc5 a2 39.Ra1 Ke6 40.Kxb4 Ne2 41.g3 Nd4 42.Rxa2 Nf3 43.c3 d4 44.Rf2 Ne1 45.Re2+, 1-0.

Okay, it was an interesting game but no big deal. HOWEVER—

I was walking around the tournament hall an hour or two after the game ended when, to my amazement, Petrosian rushed up to me and started talking about the endgame in the Fedorowicz game (he didn't care about the exchange sacrifices; all he cared about was the endgame). We chatted about the ins and outs of that endgame, and then he asked if I would like to find some private place and analyze it! Ahhh, heaven! Pure delight! Literally a dream come true.

We spent a long time analyzing every detail. Then he said he had to go, and that seemed to be that. During that session he pointed out that I should have played 31.Nxa6, which would win handily. We also looked at the actual game (31.Nd5) but he seemed dissatisfied about something.

The next day he again rushed up to me and dragged me to our analysis hide-out. This time he criticized my thirty-third move (33.Rd3), which seemed so natural and good when I played it he recommended 33.Re3 followed by my King rushing forward.

Finally, after my inferior 33.Rd3 Nc3 34.Ke3 he asked why Black didn't simply push the a-pawn. We put some serious time into that (he was sticking my King all over the place), and he eventually decided that the game was a likely draw after 34...a4 35.Kf3!!, which is a move I would never have found (35.Rxd6?? b3! 36.Rd8+ Kg7 37.cxb3 axb3 38.Rb8 b2 39.Rxb2 Nd1+ wins for Black).

Analysis of 34…a4.

34...a4!

Instead of Fed's 34...d5?? blunder. Now White's the one playing for a draw and he has to be very careful.

35.Rxd6??

35.Kf3!! was found by Petrosian after a long search. After 35...a3 36.Rxd6 Nb5 37.Rd1 (37.Rb6?? a2 38.Ra6 Na3 wins for Black.) 37...Kf7 38.Ke3 Ke6 39.Kd3 Kd5 the game should be drawn.

Silman vs. Vassily Smyslov, Frank Thornally looks on, Lone Pine 1976.

Vassily Smyslov and John Grefe, Lone Pine 1976 (Photo: Irwin Fisk).

35...b3! 36.Rd8+ Kg7 37.cxb3 axb3 38.Rb8 b2 39.Rxb2 Nd1+ winning the Rook and the game.

This time he was far more satisfied and that ended our interactions. I'll always cherish the memory of those two analysis sessions.

8

Vassily Smyslov and the Psychic Premonition

Lone Pine 1976 had to be the greatest tournament I ever played in due to my interactions with Petrosian, Najdorf, and the seventh world champion Vassily Smyslov. The pairings were posted in the evening, and when I saw who my opponent would be I was—well, let's just say—extremely excited.

Dennis Waterman (we helped each other prepare during the event) told me to study Smyslov's favorite systems which is not an easy thing to do since Smyslov played a lot of different openings. I sat down to study the books I had brought when, suddenly, I had a profound "psychic flash:"

Me: "He's not going to play any of his usual openings. In fact, he's going to play something he's never played before."

Dennis: "Very funny. Now open those books so we can figure out what you should do against his stuff."

Me: "No, I'm serious. He's going to play 1.e4 c5 2.Nf3 e6 3.d4 cxd4 4.Nxd4 a6 5.Bd3 and now 5...g6."

Dennis: "Are you feverish? Everyone knows that 5...g6 is a beginner move. Nobody in their right mind plays that. It's awful."

Me: "It might be awful, but he's going to play it!"

Dennis shook his head in disgust and walked out out of the room. Opening the one book that covered the position after 5.Bd3 I noted that Dennis was right —the move 5...g6 was indeed considered to be moronic and one line was given to show just how bad Black's game was after that move. Having full faith in my "vision" of Smyslov's play, I memorized the analysis and went to bed.

The next day Waterman watched the initial moves so he could give me a "You should have listened to me!" look. The game followed the moves I expected, and after 1.e4 c5 2.Nf3 e6 3.d4 cxd4 4.Nxd4 a6 5.Bd3 Smyslov blitzed out the "awful" 5...g6, Waterman's mouth fell to the floor, and feeling very "full-of-myself" I played the book's recommendation.

Just as Dennis had warned, what I had read was total garbage and Smyslov wiped me off the board (In fact, he hardly sat down during the game, usually walking when it was his move, tossing his reply at me while he was standing, and

[clockwise from top] Vassily Smyslov with his cat, 2002; Alla Kushnir, 1975 (Photo: Courtesy of Mechanics' Institute, San Francisco); Maia Chiburdanidze, World Championship, Las Vegas 1999 (Photo: GHF); Pal Benko and István Bilek; Larry Evens, Lone Pine 1976 (Photo: Irwin Fisk).

walking away again!). Afterwards 5...g6 became all the fashion, and our game appeared in magazines and books showing how White should NOT play!

Silman vs. Vassily Smyslov, Lone Pine 1976

1.e4 c5 2.Nf3 e6 3.d4 cxd4 4.Nxd4 a6 5.Bd3 g6 6.Nc3 Bg7 7.Be3 Nc6 8.Nb3 d5 9.exd5 exd5 10.Bc5 b6 11.Ba3 Nge7 12.0–0 0–0 13.Ne2 Qc7 14.c3 Ne5 15.Nbd4 Nc4

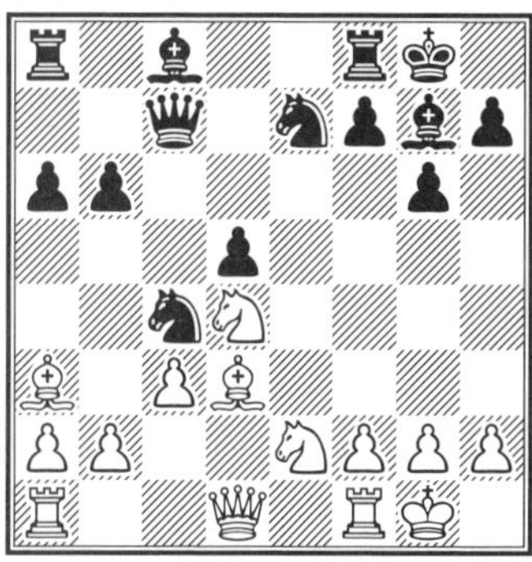

16.Bxc4 dxc4 17.Qa4 Bd7 18.Qb4 Rfe8 19.Qd6 Qb7 20.Rfe1 Nd5 21.Nf4 Nf6 22.f3 g5 23.Nfe2 Nd5 24.Qg3 h6 25.Qf2 b5 26.Ng3 b4 27.cxb4 Nxb4 28.Rxe8+ Rxe8 29.Ndf5 Nd3 30.Qd2 Qb6+ 31.Kf1 c3 32.bxc3 Bb5, 0-1. The guy thrashed me.

The moral of this story: Sometimes a spirit might tell you the future, but that doesn't mean it's a future you want to experience!

9

Thrashed by Alla Kushnir

Alla Kushnir played three title matches against the Women's World Champion Nona Gaprindashvili, losing all three (though the last one was a super close four wins, five losses, and seven draws). The second strongest woman in the world, Kushnir was allowed to leave the Soviet Union for Israel with the stipulation that she would forgo the next women's championship cycle (1973-1975).

Arriving at Lone Pine (from Israel), Kushnir was the only female player in the tournament! In those days, men weren't used to losing to women (times have changed!), and quite a lot of the players were spooked at the possibility that they would get paired with Kushnir since she was obviously extremely strong. That honor was given to Grandmaster Larry Evans in the first round.

Alla Kushnir vs. Larry Evans, Lone Pine 1975

1.d4 Nf6 2.c4 c5 3.d5 e6 4.Nc3 exd5 5.cxd5 d6 6.Nf3 g6 7.Bg5 Bg7 8.e3 h6 9.Bh4 0-0 10.Nd2 b6 11.Be2 Ba6 12.a4 Qe7 13.0-0 Bxe2 14.Qxe2 Nbd7 15.f4 Rfe8 16.Rae1 Nf8 17.e4 Qd7 18.Qf3 N6h7 19.Nc4 Bxc3 20.bxc3 f6 21.f5

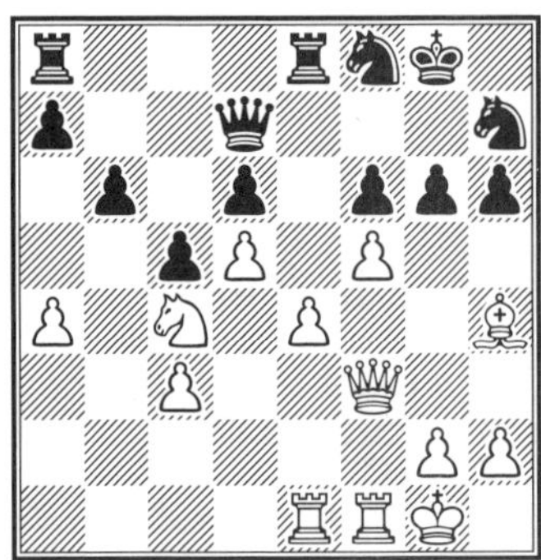

12...g5 22.Bg3 Qxa4 23.Nxd6 Re7 24.e5 Rxe5 25.Bxe5 fxe5 26.f6 Qd7 27.Nf5 Kh8 28.Nxh6 Re8 29.Qh5 e4 30.Nf7+ Kg8 31.Nh6+ Kh8 32.c4 e3 33.Nf5 a6 34.Ne7 b5 35.Rxe3 bxc4 36.Qf7, 1-0.

She thrashed him! Not a good start for Evans, but he showed his strength of mind by fighting back and ending up in second place behind Vladimir Liberzon.

As luck (or bad luck?) would have it, I was paired with her too.

Silman vs. Alla Kushnir, Lone Pine 1975

1.e4 c5 2.c3 e6 3.d4 d5 4.e5 Nc6 5.Nf3 Qb6 6.a3 c4 7.g3 Bd7 8.Bh3 h6 9.0-0 Nge7 10.Nbd2 Na5 11.Rb1 g5 12.Bg2 0-0-0 13.h4 g4

My opening didn't turn out as I had hoped and Black has an excellent game, though White is still alive and kicking.

14.Ne1 h5 15.Bh1 Nf5 16.Ng2 Bh6 17.Re1 f6 18.Nf1 Rdf8 19.exf6 Rxf6 20.Bxh6 Rhxh6 21.Nfe3 Nd6 22.Nf4 Rxf4!?

True to her aggressive style, she gives up an exchange to rip open the position of my King. The safer 22...Qd8 was superior, when I would prefer Black.

23.gxf4 Qd8 24.f5!

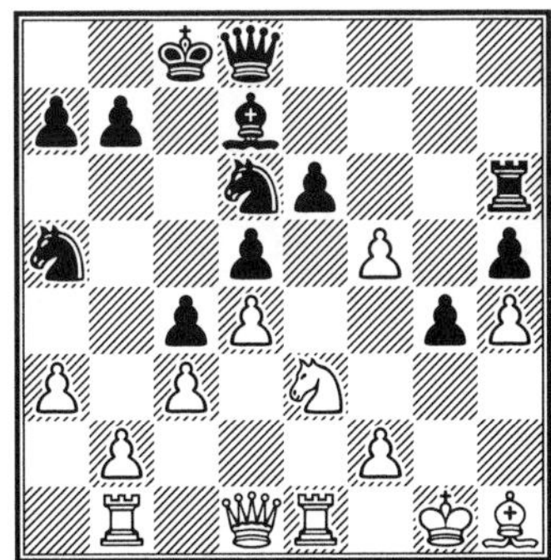

A strong move that undermines d5.

24...Qxh4 25.fxe6 Bxe6 26.Ng2?!

I was already having trouble with the clock. 26.Nxd5?? loses to 26...g3, but 26.Qc2 Qg5 27.Nxd5 g3 is complicated. Best might be 26.Bg2! Rf6 27.Qe2 when Black's attack seems to be failing. The rest features inaccurate play by both sides, which usually means mutual time pressure is at work.

26...Qf6 27.Qd2 Bf5 28.Rbd1 Be4 29.Qf4 Qg7 30.Nh4 Rf6 31.Qh2 Qg5 32.Bg2 Nc6 33.Re3 Ne7 34.Rde1 Nef5 35.Bxe4?

Missing 35.Nxf5 Qxf5 36.f3 Bxf3 [36...gxf3?? 37.Bh3] 37.Re5 Qc2 with a very tense battle to follow.

35...Nxe4 36.Rxe4 dxe4 37.Qe5 Nxh4, 0-1.

She played well and deserved to win. Games like that (with time pressure blunders plaguing both sides) are seen all the time and the person with the better nerves usually triumphs. In this game she outplayed me, then we both made mistakes, and after the smoke cleared she was the last person standing. When you lose a game like this all you can do is tip your hat, congratulate the opponent, and do your best in the next game.

After beating me in round six, she wiped out Grandmaster Bilek in round seven!

[top] Isaac Kashdan, captain of the Tel Aviv Olympiad 1964 with Pal Benko, Donald Byrne (smoking the cigarette) Arthur Bisguier, and William Addison (Photo: Beth Cassidy); [middle] Isaac Kashdan and Sammy Reshevsky inbetween rounds at Lone Pine, 1979 (Photo: Irwin Fisk); [bottom] Arnold Denker, Joe Reinhardt, and Herman Steiner, 1946.

Alla Kushnir vs. István Bilek, Lone Pine 1975

1.d4 g6 2.c4 Bg7 3.Nf3 d6 4.g3 Nd7 5.Bg2 a6 6.0-0 c5 7.Nc3 Ngf6 8.e4 0-0 9.e5 Ne8 10.dxc5 dxe5 11.Be3 Nc7 12.Qd2 f5 13.Rad1 e4 14.Ng5 h6 15.Ngxe4!!

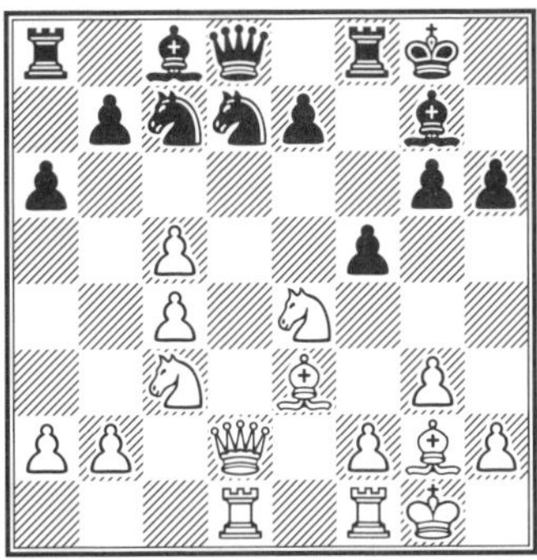

15...fxe4 16.Bh3 Rf5 17.Bxf5 gxf5 18.Bxh6 Qf8 19.Bxg7 Qxg7 20.f3 exf3 21.Rxf3 Nf8 22.Nd5 Nxd5 23.cxd5 e5 24.Rc1 a5 25.Rb3 a4 26.Rb6 a3 27.b4 f4 28.Qg2 Bf5 29.Re1 Rd8 30.d6

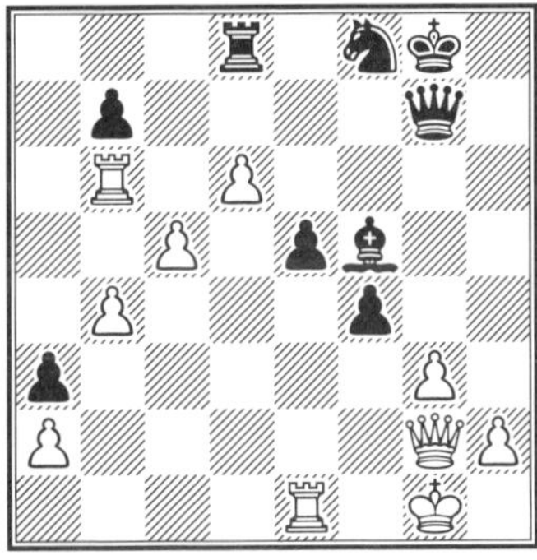

30...Rd7 31.gxf4 Qxg2+ 32.Kxg2 Rg7+ 33.Kf2 Be6 34.Re3 Bd5 35.Rg3 exf4 36.Rxg7+ Kxg7 37.b5 Nd7 38.c6 Nxb6 39.d7, 1–0.

Kushnir had a very good tournament, winning the three games previously mentioned, losing three (to Grandmasters Benko, Biyiasas, and Forintos), and drawing grandmasters Reshevsky, Csom, and Robatsch (she made a quick draw with International Master Martz in the final round).

In 1978 she tried one final time to play for the Women's World Championship. Facing Maia Chiburdanidze, Kushnir lost a fourteen game match by 4-3 (7 draws) and promptly retired from chess! As it turned out, Chiburdanidze was a monster and she went on to take Gaprindashvili's title and kept it until the advent of the amazing Chinese woman Xie Jun who took her title in 1991.

Lyudmila Belavenets (who won the USSR women's championship in 1975) said that Kushnir (after retiring from chess) totally severed ties and communication with all her chess acquaintances and friends. With chess out of the way, Kushnir immersed herself into academia, becoming a world-renowned archaeologist and professor of numismatics (the study of ancient coins and currency).[1]

She died in Tel Aviv in 2013 at the age of seventy-one.

10

The Hidden Three-Time Repetition

When I was a kid someone gave me a book titled, *If You Must Play Chess* by two-time (1945 and 1946) U.S. Champion Grandmaster Arnold Denker. Denker was famous for his wild attacking style and tactical genius, and the games in his book literally popped with energy. I read it from cover to cover.

About seven years later I found myself in an interesting situation. I was paired with Mr. Denker during Lone Pine 1975. I was delighted to play him, but instead of him attacking like a maniac, he played a quiet positional game, systematically outplayed me, and achieved a dead won position.

Arnold Denker vs. Silman, Lone Pine 1975

1.Nf3 c5 2.e4 Nc6 3.d4 cxd4 4.Nxd4 g6 5.Nc3 Bg7 6.Be3 Nf6 7.Be2 0-0 8.Nb3 d6 9.Qd2 Be6 10.Rd1 Na5 11.0-0 Rc8 12.f3 Bc4? 13.e5 Ne8 14.Nxa5 Qxa5 15.Bxc4 Rxc4 16.Nd5 Qd8 17.Bg5 f6 18.exf6 exf6 19.Bf4

And Black is (quite deservedly!) getting stomped.

I realized that I had played like an idiot and that my opponent had played extremely well, but the world keeps turning and I decided that if I was going to go down I would hold on like grim death and make him earn it. Indeed, as the game went on he started making mistakes and eventually I had turned a lost position into an inferior one that, after I went through more suffering, could probably be held.

19...Rf7 20.b3 Rc8 21.c4 b6 22.Rfe1 Bf8 23.Re6 Ng7 24.Re2 g5 25.Be3 Nf5 26.Bf2 Qd7 27.Qd3 Ne7 28.Rde1 Ng6 29.Bd4 Bg7 30.Bb2 Rd8 31.Qe3 Ne5 32.Bxe5 dxe5 33.Rd1 Qe6 34.Red2 Rfd7 35.Kf1 Kh8 36.Ke2 Bf8 37.Nc3 Bc5 38.Rxd7 Rxd7 39.Qe4 Rxd1 40.Kxd1 a5 41.Qd5 Qf5 42.Ne4 Bd4 43.Qd8+ Kg7 44.Qe7+ Kg6 45.Qe8+ Kg7 46.Qe7+ Kg6

At this point Denker realized that the position had occurred twice. Since a third repetition of this position would be a draw, he moved his King to e2.

47.Ke2 Qf4

1 According to Batgirl.

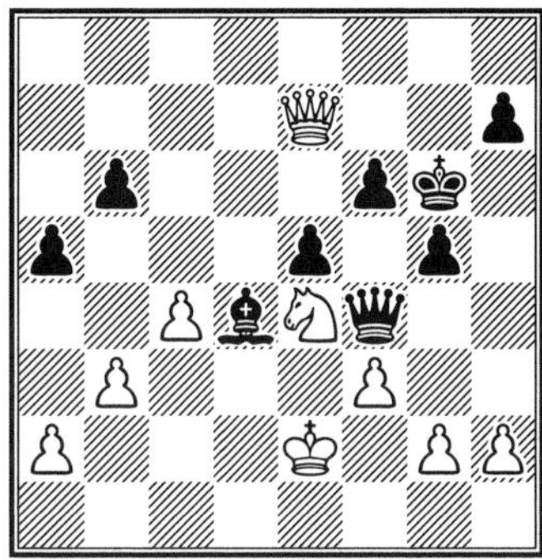

Denker relaxed since he no longer had to worry about a draw by three-time repetition because not only is his King on e2 instead of d1, but black's Queen is now on f4 instead of f5. However, instead of sitting for a long think, he decided to gain lots of time on the clock by playing a few random moves.

48.Qe8+ Kg7 49.Qe7+ Kg6 50.Kd1?

Here I announced my intention to play 50...Qf5 with a draw by three-time repetition. Denker said it wasn't a three-time rep and that I was lying! Horrified by his accusation, I got up and asked grandmaster Isaac Kashdan (the director and a close friend of Denker) to deal with our problem, I explained that I was going to repeat the position for the third time with my next move and thus claimed the draw, and Denker once again whined:

"He's lying Kash! He's lying!" Kashdan, in *true* professional style said:

"Okay Arnold" and walked away! I had to physically drag Kashdan back to the board and demonstrate each repetition before he finally accepted reality.

50...Qf5, ½–½.

Kashdan looked at his friend, and muttered, "Sorry Arnold."

Denker then pulled Reshevsky to the board and said, "I was winning, Sammy, I was winning!" And I just walked away from the whole mess.

After that, things became a bit uncomfortable when we played. We butted heads in four more games, with him drawing one and me winning three. In one game he picked up a Rook, realized he was hanging stuff, put it back and then denied he touched it (there were, as is often the case, no witnesses). In another, he got so upset when his position started to deteriorate that he kept kicking me under the table.

11

Tal in Disneyland

After winning the 1988 World Blitz Chess Championship in St. John, New Brunswick and pocketing the $50,000 first prize, Mikhail Tal (the eighth world chess champion) decided to make a visit to Los Angeles and give a couple of simultaneous exhibitions. As he was leaving his hotel in St. John to go to the airport, he walked into a glass wall splitting his head open (which required several stitches). Fortunately, a messed up forehead and a little pain couldn't contain his adventurous spirit, and (with a police escort) he caught his flight and made it to the City of Angels (looking like death warmed over, I might add).

Realizing that his time was very limited, I decided to make the one day we had together memorable. First stop was lunch at the Hotel Bel-Air. Owned by the Sultan of Brunei , it was filled with history—the hotel was a common place to stay for the likes of Judy Garland, Bette Davis, Lauren Bacall, Paul Newman, Audrey Hepburn, and on and on it goes. We enjoyed a lovely outdoor brunch with all the trimming, including peacocks walking about in the garden. The fact that Ric Ocasek (of The Cars) was sitting next to us with a couple of young ladies added to the ambiance.

Next stop was Disneyland, and Tal was completely captivated! We did as many rides as possible, but he fell in love with the Pirates of the Caribbean and insisted we go on it a second time. Everything was going well until I opened my mouth and started talking about some cutting edge opening lines. Mistake! Suddenly he blurted out an endless stream of variations (often twenty-plus moves deep, and all of it without sight of a board) at warp speed and, to my shame, I couldn't keep up with him. He would stop, glare at me, then continue with more variations ending in, "So, what do you think?"

Help!

Fortunately, he took it all in stride, found the Disneyland store and, as he stuck one thing after another in his shopping cart for his family back in Russia, he happily sang some Russian "shopping song", his face shining with satisfaction.

Then it was on to Labate's Chess Center for Tal's simul.

The Magician from Riga died less than five years later, in 1992 at the age of fifty-five.

[top] Mikhail Tal and Silman about to enter Disneyland; [insert middle] Finding the way to Pirates of the Caribbean;
[above] Tal during his simul Labate's Chess Center; Anaheim, California, Ed Labate looks on; [bottom] Tal at work (Photos: GHF).

[top] Thirteen-year-old Sofia and eleven-year-old Judit Polgar; and [middle] Judit and Silman ready to start their game at the New York Open, 1988; [bottom] Silman raves while Judit and Yaz look on. Third Amber Tournament, Le Metropole Palace, Monte Carlo 1994. (Photos: GHF).

12

Silman Draws a Little Girl

The New York Open 1988. I was paired with the most popular player in the event, eleven-year-old Judit Polgar. She was holding her own against strong opposition (including grandmasters) and I was supposed to be her latest victim. What made things particularly unpleasant was that dozens of Judit fans were watching and they wanted blood—MY blood! Of course, I was older, more experienced, and I fully expected to win.

Judit Polgar vs. Silman, New York 1988

1.e4 c5 2.Nf3 Nc6 3.d4 cxd4 4.Nxd4 Nf6 5.Nc3 d6 6.Bc4 Qb6 7.Nb3 e6 8.Be3 Qc7 9.f4 Be7 10.Qe2 0–0 11.0–0–0 a6 12.g4 b5 13.Bd3 Nb4 14.g5 Nxd3+ 15.Rxd3 Nd7 16.Bd4 Re8 17. Qh5 Bb7 18.Rh3 Nf8 19.f5

A typical Sicilian. She wants my King's head, and I'll either counter on the queenside or center, or simply defend and push her attack back.

19...e5

Chasing white's Bishop off that dangerous diagonal. I was worried about 19...exf5 20.Bxg7 Kxg7 21.Nd4 Kh8 22.Nxf5 though 22...d5 23.Nh6 Qf4+ 24.Kb1 dxe4 seems to be okay for Black.

20.Be3

20.f6! was probably better.

20...b4 21.g6?!

Judit fears nothing, but this actually loses. 21.Nd5 was correct.

21... fxg6 22. fxg6 hxg6?!

Sigh. 22...bxc3 wins for Black. I was scared of 23.gxh7+ Kh8 24.Qf7 Nd7?? (I missed 24...Ne6! 25.Qxe6 Bxe4 which refutes White's play.) 25.Rg1 Bf6 26.Bh6 which wins for White.

23.Qh8+ Kf7 24.Rf1+?!

24.Rf3+ is correct since 24...Ke6 can now be met by 25.Qh3 mate.

24...Ke6

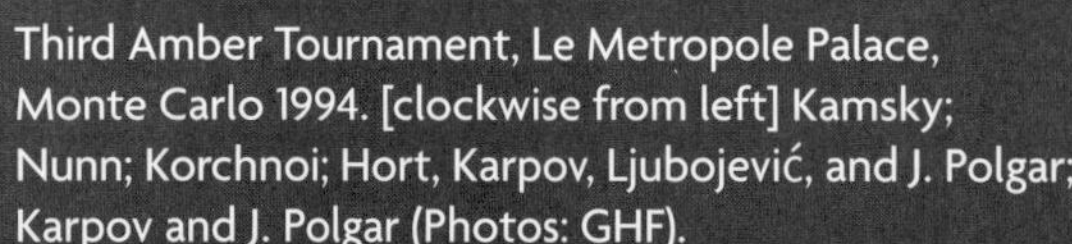

Third Amber Tournament, Le Metropole Palace, Monte Carlo 1994. [clockwise from left] Kamsky; Nunn; Korchnoi; Hort, Karpov, Ljubojević, and J. Polgar; Karpov and J. Polgar (Photos: GHF).

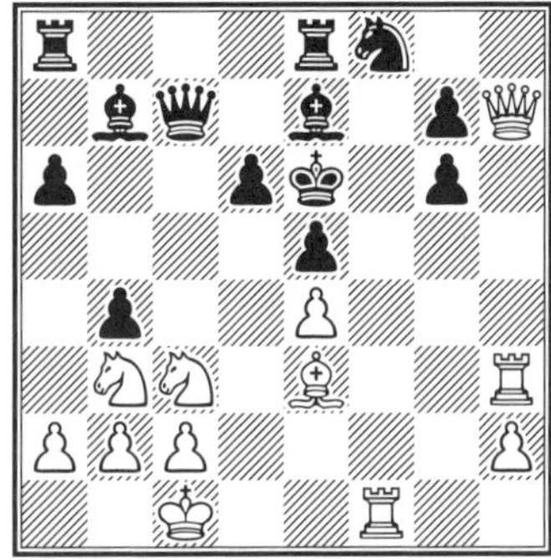

25.Nd5 Bxd5 26.Qg8+ Kd7 27.Qxd5 Qc6

27...Ne6! left Black in good shape.

28.Rf7

We both missed 28.Nc5+! Kc7 29.Rf7 Qxd5 30.exd5 dxc5 31.Bxc5 with a nice initiative.

28...Ne6, ½–½.

Nowadays, I would have played on since Black is doing well. However, the game was hard on my nerves (especially with the hostile crowd surrounding me) so I was happy to draw and escape the masses!

Afterwards we rushed to the skittles room to analyze the game. I expected a quiet, shy little girl that would listen intently to my "grown up" ideas. Instead, she took over the analysis! Her hands tossed the pieces here and there with amazing authority, and her comments made it clear that she was the one that fully expected to win and I was somehow fortunate to have survived!

It was only then that I realized that she was going to rock the chess world.

13

How *Not* to Eat Dessert

The 1990s. I was enjoying Venice when I realized there was a tournament that I promised to visit. Leaping in my car, I drove nonstop to the Principality of Monte Carlo, known for its amazing ocean views, world famous casinos, and (most importantly to me) the Third Melody Amber tournament. This super-strong event was sponsored by the Dutch businessman and lover of chess, Joop van Oosterom. He named it after his daughter.

I was there for just a couple days, which were filled with analysis with Karpov and other chess greats, and a very nice visit with my dear friend Yasser Seirawan (among other things we agreed to work together on his *Play Winning Chess* series). Great stuff, but this tale is all about dessert.

I was enjoying the buffet at the restaurant of the five-star Le Metropole Palace (the tournament site) with the players and other tournament guests. At one point a Russian player, frustrated that he couldn't find a waiter, got up and walked over to the dessert trolley. Giving the room one final look for help, he stuck his whole hand in the huge bowl of pudding and ladled it onto his plate! I couldn't believe my eyes (I had intended to order that dessert, but I quickly changed my mind!). Things continued to devolve. Seeing his friend successfully making the dessert trolley his own, another Russian got up, walked up to the trolley, and stuck his hand in the same bowl!

Ever since then I've done my best to avoid buffets and, in particular, dessert trolleys.

14

A Lesson in Indian Chess

This story has nothing to do with grandmasters, but I think it is enjoyable.

Though Europe embraced castling in the fifteenth and sixteenth centuries, India stuck to its own version—no castling allowed and a pawn can't move two squares on its first move—for quite a while (until as late as the nineteenth century!) I had heard that some Indian players still stick to the old rules, but I didn't believe it. However, while in Delhi (in December of 2006) I was checking out various shops and noticed several chess sets on display in one of them.

I was going to walk by but my wife and friends insisted I enter. The owner showed me the sets and before I knew it challenged me to a game. I thanked him and tried to escape, but my compatriots wouldn't take no for an answer. Giving in, I quickly set up the pieces and the game was on!

1.e3

I smiled and thought, "This guy is awful. The game won't last long."

1...e5

My opponent looked at me as if I were a complete imbecile and said, "That's illegal. Pawns can only move one square at a time. You don't know Indian chess, do you?"

I shook my head, shrugged, and put the pawn back on e7. My opponent once again spoke: "No, no! Touch move! You must put the pawn on e6."

1...e6 2.g3 e5

I was stubborn.

3.Bg2 Nf6 4.Nh3 d6

Learning the rules in Delhi, December 2006.
"The King does a Knight leap!"
My opponent points, as if to say,
"That *is* the way a King castles!"
(Photos: GHF).

After this move my opponent spoke again:

"You do know how to move your King, right?" My first thought was, Oh god, what's he going to say next? He continued:

"The King can move like a Knight once in a game. You really need to learn how to play this game."

I thought he was cheating and I blurted out, "Give me a break! I intend to move my bishop to e7 and then castle."

He glared at me again. "Tsk. There's no such thing. You either move your King one square in any direction or you use your one-time-only Knight move."

I started laughing. "Really? You're joking, right?"

His stony look made it clear that he was dead serious.

5.b3 c6

I was very happy with this move. I thought, "If you can't beat them, join them!"

6.Bb2

Now, with a huge smile, I moved my King to c7, making use of the "king can move like a Knight once in a game" rule. black's King does the impossible.

6...Ke8-c7!!!

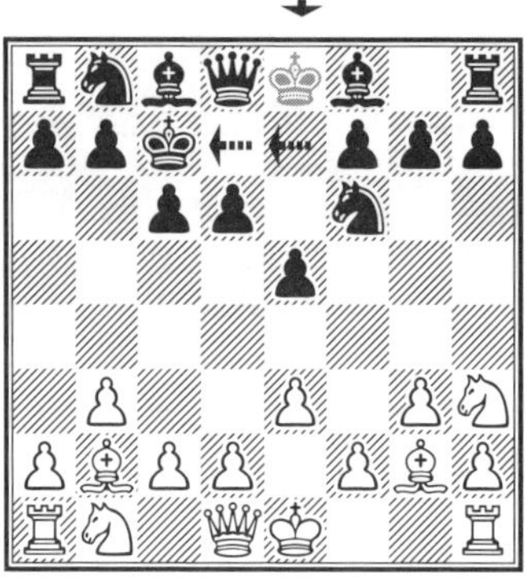

"The King does a Knight leap!"

Our eyes locked, he smiled, and the game continued. After I won, I left thinking that the gentleman was making things up and toying with me. Imagine my surprise when, a few months later, I read that in the old "Indian Chess" the King CAN move like a Knight once in a game (!), that castling isn't allowed, and that pawns can only move one move at a time even if the pawn hasn't moved (no two-move rule).

Live and learn!

15

How I Became a Simultaneous Villain

Chess professionals have different philosophies when it comes to giving simultaneous exhibitions. Emanuel Lasker, for example, had fun, took chances, and didn't take the games seriously. He expected to lose quite a few simul games, and he was happy to do so since it made the victors and the audience happy. Many other players (in Lasker's time as well as today) see simultaneous exhibitions in the same way.

The other kind of simultaneous player wants to win every game, and he takes the whole thing very seriously indeed. He views it as a competition—many vs. one. And that is also perfectly okay.

I gave my first "serious" simultaneous exhibition in 1976 in Berkeley. At the time I was living a typical Haight Ashbury existence (my novel, *Autobiography of a Goat*, will give you more insight into what I mean) and I arrived at the exhibition in bad shape. At first I was doing very well in all the games, but suddenly I hit a wall and I started making one horrible move after another—suffice to say it was awful (I don't remember the exact number, but it was something like fifteen losses and fifteen wins).

The next day I woke up, looked at the *San Francisco Chronicle*, and to my horror noticed the following headline: SILMAN'S SIMULTANEOUS DISASTER!

After that unpleasant experience I swore to take each simultaneous exhibition seriously, and as such, rarely lost a game.

Fast forward to 1989. I was playing in Wijk aan Zee, a memorable tournament: Anand wiped me out in table tennis again and again; Fedorowicz chased me around town after suffering through the great beer caper; my hardcover edition of Klaus Kinski's memoir (*All I Need Is Love*) had vanished into the maw of several grandmasters who demanded I loan it to them; and I was asked to join various grandmasters and international masters in a series of simultaneous exhibitions against children (something like forty per simul). I won the first thirty-nine fairly fast, but one kid was quite good and was holding on like grim death. He offered a draw, I refused, and eventually I prevailed.

A while later the tournament organizers and all the GMs and IMs that did the simuls got together for a dinner and discussions about the exhibitions. The main organizer took the microphone. It went something like this:

"Ladies and gentlemen, thank you all for your participation. Let's see how everyone did: Grandmaster so-and-so won thirty-seven, drew one, and lost two."

Everyone applauded.

"International Master so-and-so won thirty-four and lost six."

Massive applause.

And it went on and on like that, with everyone losing at least one game.

Then they mentioned my result:

"Jeremy Silman won every game, forty to zero."

Endless boos and jeers! I was stunned. Why was I being booed? It turned out that all the titled players were supposed to lose at least one game, but nobody told me. And so a simultaneous villain was born—a chess pariah, an untouchable. I wandered from Euro-village to Euro-village and in every one people threw trash at me or beat me with sticks. Life became a living hell. Then, as I stood on the precipice on a particularly large mountain, I—

Okay, okay. I wasn't a pariah. Nobody hit me with sticks. Yes, the boos were real, I did indeed drown under the waves of public humiliation, but life goes on and lessons are learned.

A word of warning. If you play me in a simultaneous exhibition don't expect me to show mercy. I still try as hard as possible to win every game.

16

The Greatest Chess Storyteller of All Time

Growing up I had lots of chess heroes. However, the ones that were still alive were Tal, Fischer, Petrosian, and Bent Larsen (now, sadly, all deceased). Naturally I studied all their games and followed every event they were in.

I mentioned how I was lucky enough to meet Tal and Petrosian, and though I only saw Fischer from afar (never speaking face to face with him) I did have some strange/unfortunate "Fischer moments" (e-mail and a disturbing phone call from Bobby to Benko's apartment in Budapest while we were waiting to meet him for dinner) that I don't wish to get into.

The fourth hero was the amazing Danish Grandmaster Bent Larsen and I was very fortunate to meet him when he visited Southern California in 1988. During the mid-'60s (where he won tournament after tournament ahead of the world's finest players) it wasn't clear who was the best non-Soviet player in the world—Fischer or Larsen. All conjecture ended when Fischer beat Larsen 6-0 in their 1971 Candidates semifinal match.

To give you a glimpse as to how strong Larsen was, he beat Petrosian 2-0 in the legendary Second Piatigorsky Cup. Here is one of those games:

Bent Larsen late 1988 (Photos: GHF).

Bent Larsen vs. Tigran Petrosian, Santa Monica, Second Piatigorsky Cup 1966

1.e4 c5 2.Nf3 Nc6 3.d4 cxd4 4.Nxd4 g6 5.Be3 Bg7 6.c4 Nf6 7.Nc3 Ng4 8.Qxg4 Nxd4 9.Qd1 Ne6 10.Qd2 d6 11.Be2 Bd7 12.0–0 0–0 13.Rad1 Bc6 14.Nd5 Re8 15.f4 Nc7 16.f5 Na6 17.Bg4 Nc5 18.fxg6

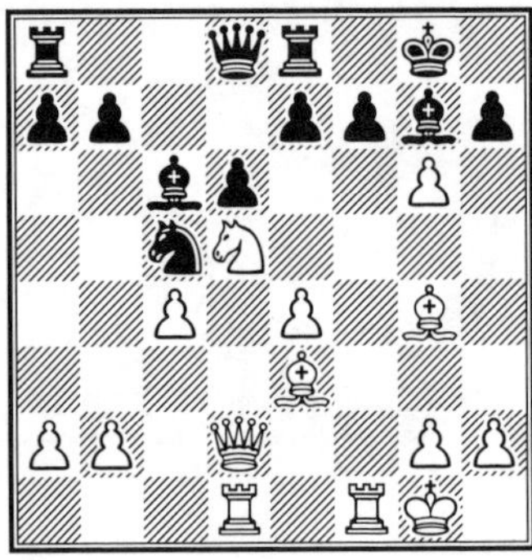

18...hxg6 19.Qf2 Rf8 20.e5 Bxe5 21.Qh4 Bxd5 22.Rxd5 Ne6 23.Rf3 Bf6 24.Qh6 Bg7 25.Qxg6!! Nf4 26.Rxf4 fxg6 27.Be6+ Rf7 28.Rxf7 Kh8 29.Rg5 b5 30.Rg3, 1–0.

Larsen also beat Tal in a 1969 Candidates match by a dominating score of 5½–2.½.

Bent Larsen wasn't just one of the world's best chess players, he was also one of the world's finest chess writers. He wrote with energy, wit, authority, and depth. I view his book, *Larsen's Selected Games of Chess* (later reprinted under the title *Bent Larsen Master of Counter-Attack*", and then expanded by New In Chess with the title: *Bent Larsen's Best Games*), to be one of the best chess books ever.

Ed Labate and I spent several hours with Bent at a restaurant, and the "great Dane" regaled us with one incredible story after another. It was one of those experiences that you don't want to ever end.

Bent eventually discussed his match with Fischer. He was still angry that Fischer had ("illegally") been given a berth in the 1970 Interzonal (Benko gave his spot to Bobby Fischer). Fischer won that event with 15 wins, 1 loss, and 7 draws (3½ points ahead of the field), while Larsen tied for second with Geller and Hübner (15 points out of twenty-three games). Fischer's one defeat: Bent Larsen!

I was sad to hear that he was still upset about Fischer's "illegal" spot, and that he never really got over his 6-0 defeat in the Candidate Matches. The fact is Larsen fought to win every game, was incredibly combative in his play, so he had nothing to be ashamed of. Nevertheless, it's impossible for a proud and supremely confident man who truly felt he was the best in the world to accept a 6-0 drubbing, and (though he had some impressive successes in the early to mid-1970s)

he was never able to regain the same high level he repeatedly showed before the match.

Here's one of the stories Larsen told me during that dinner:

> Grandmaster Friedrich Sämisch [1896-1975] had just gotten married and, after the honeymoon, the newlywed couple returned to Samisch's home. Hoping to relax after the festivities, his wife was cooking a nice dinner when Samisch noticed a letter on the floor. It turned out that it was an invitation to a very strong tournament, so Samisch told his wife that he had to participate and off he went (the dinner still cooking!), leaving her behind.
>
> Two months later he returned, his two huge travel cases in tow. His wife rushed up to him, delirious with joy. She told him to relax, that she would make him a welcome-home meal, and he could tell her all about his adventures. Samisch sat back, happy to be reunited with his bride. Then he noticed a letter on his desk. It had been sent a couple of weeks earlier and it was inviting him to a wonderful event with many of the world's best players.
>
> Leaping up, he said, "Another invitation. If I leave now I can just make it!"
>
> Since his bags were still closed and had everything he needed, he grabbed them, gave his wife a kiss, and rushed out. Two months later he returned home only to find that he no longer had a wife.

Larsen and I stayed in touch after the dinner, and I did my best to persuade him to write more books. Unfortunately, the work we discussed never materialized, and in 2010 he died in Buenos Aires at the age of seventy-five.

17

A Cold War Moment

Bratislava, Slovakia, 1993. I was the head of the American delegation for the World Youth Chess Championships. The person in charge acted like the Cold War was still alive, and felt he could rule with an iron fist. When I arrived (to the usual total chaos), I found that the organizers had used popsicle-sticks on the wall charts to show the coaches' and players' names, plus various delegations were complaining about outrageous fines that were being handed out.

I noticed that Pal Benko's name was on top of the American popsicle ladder (signifying that he was the head of the delegation). I told Mr. Cold War that he had made a mistake and that I was in charge of the American teams, with Benko taking up the rest of the coaching responsibilities. Mr. Cold War said, "This is a serious matter! We have to give you a fine of $1,000 since it will take time to fix this error!"

I looked him in the eye, took Pal's popsicle-stick off the board, placed mine on top and Benko's below me, smiled and said, "Problem solved!" Then I walked away.

The coaches and players stayed in hotels paid for by the USCF, but we had a problem. The USCF, having forgotten to pay for Benko's accommodations in advance, had promised to wire the money to cover the bill, but this hadn't happened. When we realized that Benko had been sent adrift by our federation, I contacted them—once again they promised that the wire would be there shortly.

Days passed, Mr. Cold War did his best to make everyone's life a misery, and poorer teams stuffed relatives into their rooms (five or six people inside a space designed for two). The actual players would go down for breakfast (which was free for the participants), where they would fill backpacks with food for those hiding in the rooms.

In the meantime, the hotel was freaking out due to Benko's inability to pay his bill (credit cards were rare in Slovakia and the hotel refused to accept them), and it became clear that the USCF, which was incredibly incompetent in those days (hopefully they've improved) had screwed us again.

Finally, the next to last day, and payment past due, I was forced to enact a scene right out of an old spy movie: At four in the morning, a cab pulled up to the curb two blocks from the hotel and patiently waited. I quietly lead a lone figure through the hotel's empty halls and out the back door. Having successfully made our exit without incident, I dragged the horrified grandmaster to the waiting cab, which then whisked him over the border to the safety of the Vienna airport. Mission accomplished—a successful escape! When the organizers eventually re-

Pal Benko and Silman, 1999 (Photo: GHF).

alized that something was amiss, I just played dumb and shrugged my shoulders. Such intrigue wasn't part of the job description, but a coach has to be ready for any eventuality!

18

Welcome to Provo

Provo, Utah, 1973 is where I first got to know Dennis Waterman. It's quite rare to remember the first thing someone ever said to you, but oddly enough I recall my first words with Dennis. After finishing a game, I went to the skittles area and saw some guy (Waterman) beating up various players at blitz:

Me: "Can I play the winner?"
Waterman: "I only play people that are good!"

An ominous start, but we hung out together after that and became lifelong friends. Later that year, after I graduated high school, I moved to San Francisco to play chess, and I slept on Waterman's floor.

At the Provo tournament: Waterman was paired with a gentleman named Isaacson. Dennis and I were chatting on the stage before the game began. A local player told us to shut up (though no games were in progress) and suddenly he went berserk and threw a solid (heavy) glass ashtray at our heads! Somehow it flew between us (a direct blow could have been fatal) and smashed against the wall with a thud. Welcome to Provo indeed! Then Dennis, a bit shaken up, sat down and played following game:

Dennis Waterman vs. Doug Isaacson, Provo 1973

1.e4 c5 2.Nf3 Nc6 3.d4 cxd4 4.Nxd4 Nf6 5.Nc3 e5 6.Ndb5 d6 7.Bg5 a6 8.Bxf6 gxf6 9.Na3 Be6 10.Bc4 Rc8 11.Bxe6 fxe6 12.Nc4 b5 13.Ne3 Nd4 14.0-0 h5 15.Ne2 Nxe2+ 16.Qxe2 Ke7 17.a4 Bh6 18.axb5 Bxe3 19.fxe3 axb5 20.Ra7+ Rc7 21.Qf3 Rh6 22.Rfa1 Kf7 23.Ra8 Qd7 24.Qg3 Rg6 25.Rf8+ Kxf8 26.Qxg6 Qf7 27.Qh6+ Ke7 28.Ra8 d5 29.Qh8 Rd7 30.Qc8 f5 31.Qc5+, 1-0.

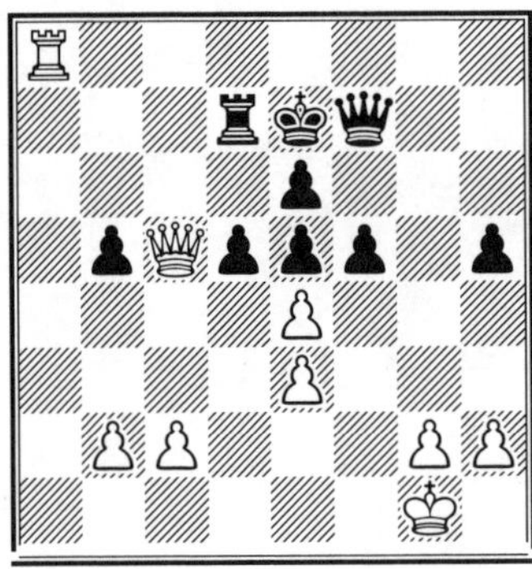

Since 31...Kf6 (31...Rd6 32.Ra7+) 32.Rf8 picks up black's Queen.

Waterman wrote: "In the final position Black is losing his Queen. The symmetrical pawn formation is accentuated by the cross in the middle of the board. Not only is the King being crucified, we also have the Holy Trinity atop the cross."

Okay Dennis, if you say so.

19

Celebrities Gone Wild

Day One: 1988 and I just landed in Mazatlan, Mexico. Though the main course was the World Thirty-Minute Championships (packed with the best players in the world), we had arranged a side event that had various actors and singers and songwriters ready to do battle against other Hollywood types. I was the director.

Most of us flew together, and when we looked for our transportation to the resort we were shocked to find a tank and several military trucks filled with armed soldiers! Apparently they feared that we would be abducted.

The event proved memorable. Some highlights:

Day Two: My celebrity crew wanted to go to Señor Frog's, which was the hot club in town. I mentioned this to the organizers and, after a few minutes, several

Top photo: [front] James Komack (producer), Wendy Starbuck (event organizer), Gene Scherer (actor), [second row] Lew Ayres (actor), Dr. Joseph Wagner, Marina Dlugy, Hiram Strait (magician), William Smithers (actor), Gerry Goffin (lyricist), [back row] Grandmaster Max Dlugy, Eric Estrada (actor), International Master Jeremy Silman, Grandmaster Walter Browne.
Middle photo: Silman with the Polgar sisters: Sophia, Susan, and Judit.
Bottom photo: Morgan Fairchild, Claude Akins, Gene Scherer, and the Polgar sisters: Sophia, Judit, and Susan Mazatlan 1988. (Photos: Irwin Fisk).

police cars pulled up, loaded us in their vehicles, and rushed us to the club. There was a two-block line, but the police walked by it, took us in, and then looked for a table. Everything was packed. No tables were available. Once again our trusty police escort took over. Going to the largest table, they ordered everyone there to leave at once. In a blink, the table problem was taken care of!

I was sitting next to an attractive young woman and, after I downed a beer, when the music began playing and people started dancing I got up, took her hand, and said, "Let's dance!" She put her mouth to my ear and whispered, "My husband owns this club and most of this town. If he sees you dancing with me he'll have you killed."

So much for dancing!

Day Three was quiet, but Day Four wasn't: After the first few days I ran into a surprising problem: One of my celebrities (a male) had been stealing chess clocks. He denied it but when I entered his room there they were. Once again I went to the organizers, gave them back the clocks, and explained that one of my celebrities was insane.

Day Five: Two of my male celebrities (I started thinking of these guys as gremlins) got drunk, found where the room of an extremely famous grandmaster was, and (with me in tow trying to stop them) pushed the door in only to find that the grandmaster wasn't dressed. I apologized, dragged them out, and then I... Yes, you guessed it! I went to the organizers and apologized for my people's behavior.

After that things cooled down (the winner of the celebrity event leapt into a fountain to celebrate his victory). Nevertheless, though it ended well, I made a point to never do another celebrity event!

20

Arthur Dake and the Nosey Chess Politicians

Grandmaster Arthur Dake (1910-2000) was a remarkable man. A merchant seaman who traveled to various Asian nations (Japan, China, etc.) at the young age of sixteen, he played in his first chess tournament (the New York State Championship) at age twenty and came in third (which was quite an amazing result). He followed this up by winning the Marshall Chess Club championship and then he did even better by tying for first in the Antwerp team matches with Akiba Rubinstein and Frederick Yates. Incredibly, by 1931 (age twenty-one) he was viewed as one of America's finest players!

To make it clear how strong this man was, he played in the sixth chess Olympiad (his fellow team members were Frank Marshall, Reuben Fine, I. A. Horowitz, and Abraham Kupchik) and scored a mind-blowing 13 wins, no losses, and 5 draws!

California Chess Congress, Pasadena 1932: Arthur Dake vs Alexander Alekhine (Dake won their game, Alekhine won the tournament).

As good as those results where, I would guess his chess career highlight would be his victory over the World Chess Champion, Alexander Alekhine:

Arthur Dake vs. Alexander Alekhine, Pasadena 1932

1.e4 c6 2.d4 d5 3.exd5 cxd5 4.c4 Nf6 5.Nc3 Nc6 6.Nf3 Be6 7.c5 g6 8.Bb5 Bg7 9.Ne5 Qc8 10.Qa4 Bd7 11.0-0 0-0 12.Bf4 a6 13.Bxc6 bxc6 14.Rfe1 Nh5 15.Bd2 Ra7 16.Re2 Be8 17.Rae1 f5 18.Nf3 Nf6 19.Rxe7 Rxe7 20.Rxe7 f4 21.Bxf4 Ne4 22.Be5 Bh6 23.Nxe4 dxe4 24.Ng5

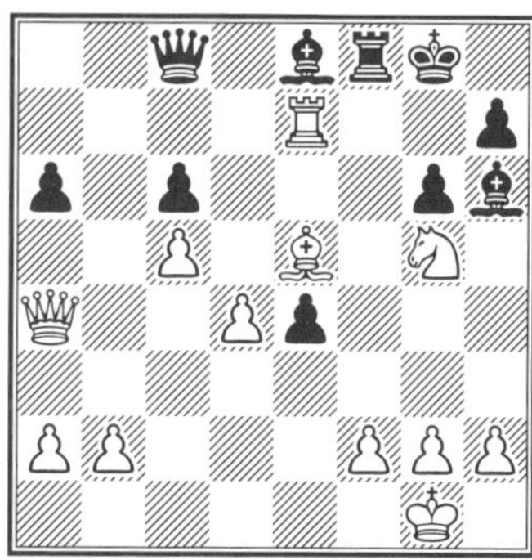

24...Qf5 25.Qb3+ Bf7 26.Nxf7 Rxf7 27.Rxf7 Qxf7 28.Qb8+ Qf8 29.d5 e3 30.f4 Qxb8 31.Bxb8 Kf7 32.dxc6 Ke8 33.b4 g5 34.g3 gxf4 35.gxf4 Kd8 36.a4 Kc8 37.Bd6 Bg7 38.Kf1, 1–0.

When I was paired with Grandmaster Dake at the 1987 U.S. Open, I was facing a seventy-seven-year-old man. Though I was very happy to play a legend, I also understood his glory days were decades behind him. In other words, I thought I would easily win. (Thanks to the database, I now see that he was still beating and drawing 2300 and 2400 players in the '70s and '80s. Impressive!).

A few minutes before the game started a couple of well-known chess politicians approached me. The conversation went like this:

Politician: "Jeremy, we would like you to draw your game against Dake."

Me: "I'm glad you would like that, but it's not going to happen. I'm sure Dake also wants to go for the win."

Politician: "Mr. Dake doesn't know about this. It's between us."

Me: "It's between you. I have no interest in this nonsense. Now let me play my game."

I walked away.

After the first twenty moves went by, I took a little stroll while Dake was thinking. The two idiots approached me again.

Politician: "You're trying to beat him! Don't do that! Offer a draw."

Me: "Yes, I am trying to beat him, but he's also trying to beat me! In fact, he's playing well. He doesn't need your help."

The two politicians watched the whole game closely. When the game became boring and a draw was agreed, Dake and I chatted a bit about the opening and middlegame, and that was that. He was a gentleman throughout. I have to admit that I'm delighted that I don't have to listen to the self-serving gibberish of chess politicians anymore, which includes the unsavory people running FIDE.

Arthur Dake vs. Silman, U.S. Open 1987

1.e4 c6 2.d4 d5 3.exd5 cxd5 4.Bd3 Nc6 5.c3 g6 6.Bf4 Bg7 7.h3 Bf5

White's line, which was a favorite of Fischer's, isn't that exciting so I decided to create an imbalance in the pawn structure, create some complications, and see if my opponent could handle the heat.

8.Bxf5 gxf5 9.Ne2 Nf6 10.Qd3 Qd7 11.Ng3 e6 12.Nd2

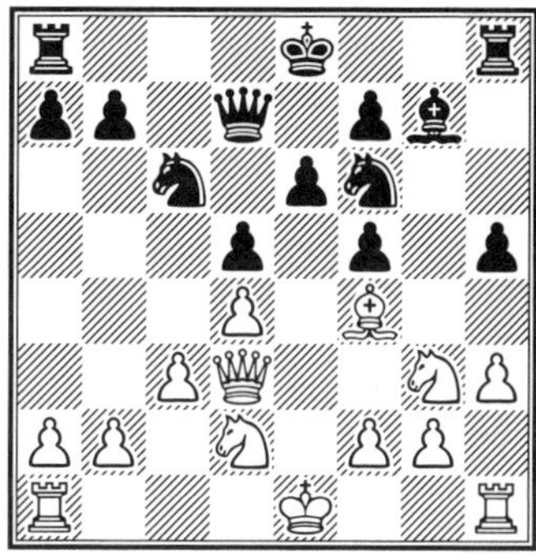

h5 13.h4 Ng4 14.f3 Nf6 15.Nb3 Ne7 16.Qe3 Kf8 17.Nc5 Qc6 18.Nd3 Nd7 19.Ne2 Ng6 20.Bg5 f6 21.Ndf4 Kf7 22.Nxg6 Kxg6 23.Bf4 Kf7 24.0-0 Nf8 25.Qd3 Ng6 26.g3 Rac8 27.Rac1 Bf8 28.Kf2 Bd6 29.Bxd6 Qxd6 30.Qe3 Rc6 31.Nf4 Nxf4 32.Qxf4 Qxf4 33.gxf4 b5 34.Ke3, ½-½.

21

George Koltanowski Does Me a Favor

Grandmaster George Koltanowski (1903-2000) is known to many chess fans as a strong player who played against Colle, Horowitz, Rubinstein, Tarrasch, Grünfeld, Euwe, Spielmann, Yates, Tartakower, Maróczy, Alekhine, Fine, Keres, Menchik, Vidmar, Flohr, Sultan Khan, Kashdan, Sämisch, and many more legendary figures.

However, his real claim to fame was his incredible skill at blindfold chess. Vying for the top "blindfold guru" title against Réti and Alekhine, he surpassed them in 1937 by playing thirty-four games simultaneously without seeing any of the boards.

His other record was playing fifty-six consecutive blindfold games with only ten-seconds a move! His score of fifty wins and six draws is simply amazing.

I met Koltanowski in 1975 when he called me and asked if I could come to his condo (we both lived in San Francisco). Of course I could! Once there his wife gave me some tea, we chatted a bit, and then he told me why I was invited: It turned out that a big invitational tournament in Mexico City was being held (much of it to be televised) and Koltanowski was asked to pick one player to represent the United States (the other participants were from South America and Cuba).

The USCF wanted him to pick a New Yorker, but Koltanowski decided that I should get the invitation. This was a wonderful thing for a twenty-one-year-old, and I instantly accepted.

Months later I boarded a plane and made myself at home in Mexico City's Olympic Village (for some reasons dozens of soldiers with rifles constantly patrolled the place).

The day after my arrival, I was feeling half dead, a doctor was called, and I was told that I had a 103° temperature. A real pity! But the show must go on, so off I went to the gorgeous building that housed the event.

I started out well and halfway through (still with a high fever and still in a haze) I was in first place with a 4-1 score. Here's my game from the first round.

Silman vs. Carlos Escondrillas, Mexico City 1975

1.e4 e5 2.Nf3 Nc6 3.Bb5 a6 4.Ba4 Nf6 5.0-0 Be7 6.Re1 b5 7.Bb3 d6 8.c3 0-0 9.h3 h6 10.d4 Re8 11.Nbd2 Bf8 12.Nf1 Bd7 13.Ng3 Na5 14.Bc2 g6 15.b3 c5 16.Be3 Nc6 17.d5 Ne7 18.Qd2 Kh7 19.Bxc5

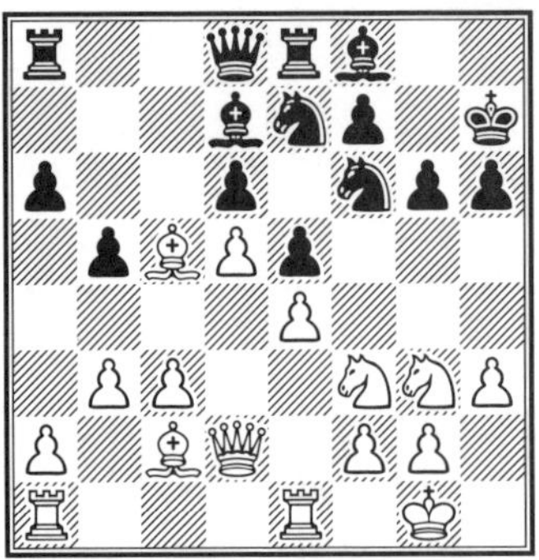

When you have a high fever you're not afraid of anything!

19...dxc5 20.Nxe5 Kg8 21.c4 Bg7 22.f4 Nh7 23.Rad1 b4 24.Rf1 a5 25.Nf3 a4 26.e5 axb3 27.axb3 Ra2 28.e6 Bxe6 29.dxe6 Qxd2 30.exf7+ Kxf7 31.Rxd2 Rea8 32.Rff2 Ra1+ 33.Kh2 Nf8 34.f5 gxf5 35.Nxf5 Nxf5 36.Bxf5 Bf6 37.Rd6 R8a6 38.Rd5 R6a5 39.g4 Kg7 40.Kg3

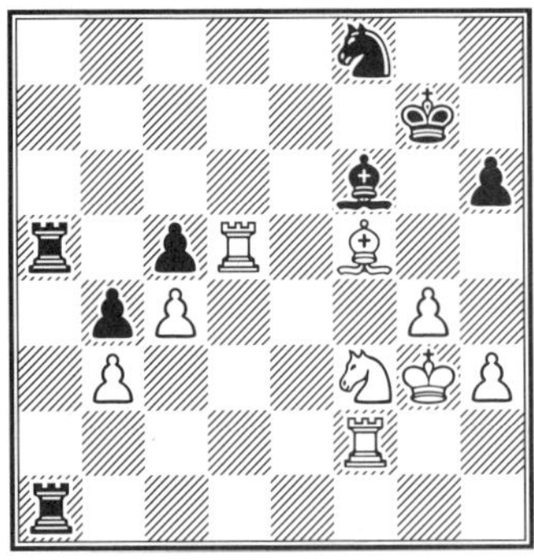

40...R1a3 41.Bc2 Ra1 42.h4 Be7 43.Ne5 R5a2 44.Rf7+ Kg8 45.Rxe7 Rxc2 46.Nf3 Rc3 47.g5 hxg5 48.Rxg5+ Kh8 49.Re8 Rg1+ 50.Kf4 Rxg5 51.Nxg5 Kg8 52.h5 Rc1 53.Rc8 Rf1+ 54.Ke5 Kg7 55.Ne6+ Nxe6

George Koltanowski, (Photo: Courtesy of the World Chess Hall of Fame).

56.Kxe6 Rf6+ 57.Ke5 Rh6 58.Rxc5 Rxh5+ 59.Kd6 Rh3 60.Rb5 Rxb3 61.c5 Kf6 62.c6 Rd3+ 63.Kc7, 1–0.

Dictators and presidents and other powerful people were watching this event and insisted that I come to their tournaments (I apparently gave them the impression that I was good, which was clearly not the case!).

And here I made a fatal mistake. My fever vanished and I was 100% healthy! From that point on I played like a moron, drawing one game and losing three in the four games that followed. Suddenly all the powerful people viewed me as a leper (the rich and powerful don't like failure!), and I decided that I was going to win the last game no matter what.

I was Black and the first sixteen moves had been seen before in the games of Euwe, Unzicker, Ólafsson, Spassky, and others.

Jorge Rovira Mas vs. Silman, Mexico City 1975

1.d4 Nf6 2.c4 e6 3.Nc3 Bb4 4.e3 c5 5.Nf3 0-0 6.Bd3 d5 7.0-0 Nc6 8.a3 Bxc3 9.bxc3 dxc4 10.Bxc4 Qc7 11.Bd3 e5 12.Qc2 Re8 13.Nxe5 Nxe5 14.dxe5 Qxe5 15.f3 Be6 16.Re1 Rad8

A known position. White has the center pawns and the two Bishops while Black has plenty of space and active pieces.

At this point my opponent offered a draw. I immediately said no. He gave me a look that said, "This guy is an idiot."

George Koltanowski.

All the other games finished quickly, leaving us alone on the stage. And I played and played and played, much to my opponent's consternation. Nevertheless, I had real chances to win but, of course, flubbed it.

17.Rb1 Qd5 18.Bb5 Bf5 19.Qb2 Bxb1 20.Bxe8 Nxe8 21.Qxb1 b6 22.e4 Qc4 23.Qc2 Rd3 24.Re3 Rd6 25.Kf2 Nc7 26.Qe2 Qb3 27.Rd3 Rxd3 28.Qxd3 Ne6 29.f4 c4

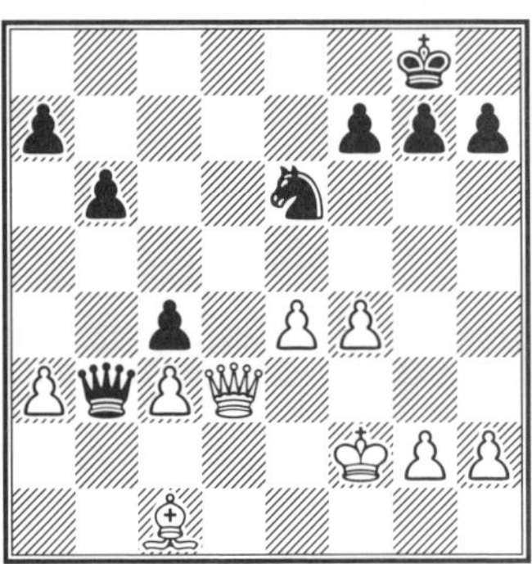

30.Qd2 h6 31.Ke3 Nc5?

31...Qb1! leaves White in serious trouble.

32.Qd8+ Kh7 33.Bd2 Qb1 34.Qd5 Qg1+ 35.Kf3 Qf1+ 36.Kg3 f6 37.Qf5+ Kg8 38.Be3 Qd3 39.Kf3 Qd1+ 40.Kg3 Qd3 41.Kf3 Na4 42.Qc8+ Kf7 43.Qc7+ Kg6 44.f5+ Kh7 45.Qf7 Qd1+, ½–½

Finally I accepted reality and offered a draw. He jumped up and berated me: "Yes, of course! Of course! Last rounds are made for draws! Don't you know that? They are made for draws! Stupid gringo, stupid gringo!"

After I returned home it took me a full week to get the words "stupid gringo" out of my head.

Though I only ended with an even score, I always felt that I was in Koltanowski's debt for his kindness in giving me that rare opportunity.

22

Carlos Castaneda and the Penthouse Suite

I first read Castaneda's magnificent book, *The Teachings Of Don Juan*, when it appeared in 1968, and as the years went by I read all the other books in the series (if you enjoy the thought of alternative realities then you'll love these books). So, what does a mystic like Mr. Castaneda have to do with chess? Not much, but his intervention helped a nineteen-year-old man and, through that young man, me.

The year was 1976. The adventure started with a visit to San Francisco's Mechanics' Institute (home of the oldest chess club in the United States) where this fellow, David, approached me, introduced himself, and said that he'd heard about my upcoming drive from San Francisco to Toronto where I'd play in the Canadian Open. He asked if he could go along, and though he didn't have any money, he had a millionaire uncle that had a penthouse suite in Toronto and I would be welcome to stay there since the uncle would be in Europe for a couple months.

Warning bells went off! "No money?" "A millionaire uncle?" "I could stay in the millionaire's luxurious pad if I drove him?" I was waiting for him to offer me a great deal on a bridge.

My first inclination was to say, "No!". Instead I asked him where he came from and he told me the following (much shortened here) story:

> I just came from Oregon. I was trapped in an insane asylum and managed to escape. It was late at night and very dark, and after running as far and fast as I could, I found myself standing next to a highway. I tried to get a lift, but nobody stopped, UNTIL, one guy pulled over, said, "I'm heading for Portland. If that's okay then hop in."
>
> I jumped at the chance and was blown away when I realized that the driver was Carlos Castaneda! He told me he was going to lecture there and we hit it off pretty well.

Once again I added up the impossibility of it all: No money, a millionaire uncle's penthouse suite in exchange for a long ride, an asylum (and, he never told me why he was in there). I made a quick glance to make sure he wasn't carrying a long knife, and final salvation by Carlos Castaneda. He wanted me to be the next brick in his imaginary castle.

Then I realized that my life had been even more improbable, and if I was to be David's next brick in his reality than why the hell not? I said, "Yes," and, a couple weeks later he appeared at the agreed upon spot and off we went (two other chess players also came along for the ride), my old jalopy wheezing every inch of the way.

It was an eventful drive, including a breakdown on the Detroit freeway during rush hour (if you've ever broken down in Detroit you'll understand how horrifying it was). But the most interesting moment occurred when we were on top of the Rocky Mountains. I was completely burned out and my companions insisted I stop driving. I gave the keys to one of the guys, crawled into the backseat, and just as the new driver started the car I got a flash of impending doom! I leapt up and screamed, "Stop the car! If we drive down there we'll die!"

They told me that I was delirious and I had to shut up, but I wasn't going to be denied. I insisted that our lives were on the line and, finally, they agreed to open the hood and show me that all was well. But all wasn't well. The cap to the brake-fluid was off and there wasn't a drop left. We wouldn't have survived a drive down the extremely steep mountain road.

We finally reached Toronto and David led us to his uncle's place. I expected him to rush off or admit that he made everything up, but instead we pulled up to a magnificent, very upper-crust multi-story apartment building. We followed David to the entrance, rang the bell, and the doorman came out and said (looking at David with fondness), "Ah, it's absolutely wonderful to see you again sir."

Moments later we were all in the penthoused suite—more than enough rooms for four people, pure luxury, views of the city. Everything David promised turned into reality.

You might be asking, "Where's the chess?"

Well, on the day before the final round I went to check out my car, which was in the building's garage. My heart skipped a beat when I saw that someone had stolen my car battery. At this point I was pretty much broke and intended to make my way to Chicago where I'd stay with Dennis Waterman (who was now a bigwig in the Chicago commodities market). But I didn't have enough money to buy a new battery (I barely had enough cash to pay for gas). One of the guys who drove with us and was staying in the penthouse suite was a well-known grandmaster. Seeing my predicament, he said, "I need a draw in the last round to win a good deal of money. You're well known as an opening theoretician, so if you can give me some new analysis I'll pay for the battery.

And so everything worked out. The grandmaster was successful, I had a brand new car battery, David was safe and sound in pure luxury, and I managed (on fumes) to wend my way to Chicago. Carlos Castaneda died in 1998, but I often thank him (in my mind) for saving the mysterious David and turning a very long drive into something much more.

PART TWO

Legendary Players

As a twelve-year-old kid I fell in love with another world. I became enamored with chess and its history. I bought my first chess book, and I looked at it every day. Then another book and after that, another and another. People thought I was crazy, but I couldn't stop!

My first chess god was Alexander Alekhine, whose tactics blew me away! Next was Adolf Anderssen and the Immortal Game. Then I read about Zukertort (it sounded like something to eat), and so it went on and on

My favorite (yes, I do have a favorite!) was (and still is) Emanuel Lasker. This man had it all—tactics, endgame mastery, master of chess psychology, attack, and was World Champ for twenty-seven amazing years!

I've chosen eleven chess legends to present here (not to say there aren't other legends), some household names and some lesser known, that interest me and therefore want to pass on for others to enjoy.

1

ADOLF ANDERSSEN

Mr. Slice and Dice!

Adolf Anderssen (1818-1879) was born in the Prussian Imperial city of Breslau (now Wrocław, Poland). He learned how to play chess at the age of nine, and acquired much of his chess understanding by going over all of the games of the legendary Louis-Charles Mahé de La Bourdonnais vs. Alexander McDonnell match. (Note: Cary Utterberg's book on the match, *De La Bourdonnais versus McDonnell,*[1] is a fantastic read.)

A professor of mathematics, Anderssen was known as a good-natured man who lived most of his life with his mother and his sister.

---

1 Cary Utterberg, *de La Bourdonnais versus McDonnell, 1834*. Jefferson, NC: McFarland & Company, 2005.

Steinitz wrote: "Anderssen was honest and honorable to the core. Without fear or favor he straightforwardly gave his opinion, and his sincere disinterestedness became so patent....that his word alone was usually sufficient to quell disputes...for he had often given his decision in favor of a rival..."

Here's an early game:

Tassilo von Heydebrand und der Lasa vs. Adolf Anderssen, Breslau match (3) 1846

1.e4 c5 2.d4 cxd4 3.Nf3 Nc6 4.Bc4 e6 5.Nxd4 Bc5 6.Nf3 Nge7 7.Nc3 0-0 8.a3 Ng6 9.0-0 f5 10.exf5 Rxf5 11.Bd3 Rh5 12.g4 Rh3 13.Kg2 Rxf3 14.Kxf3

14.Qxf3 loses to 14...Nh4.

14...Qh4 15.Kg2 Nce5 16.h3 b6 17.Bxg6 hxg6 18.Bf4 Bb7+ 19.f3

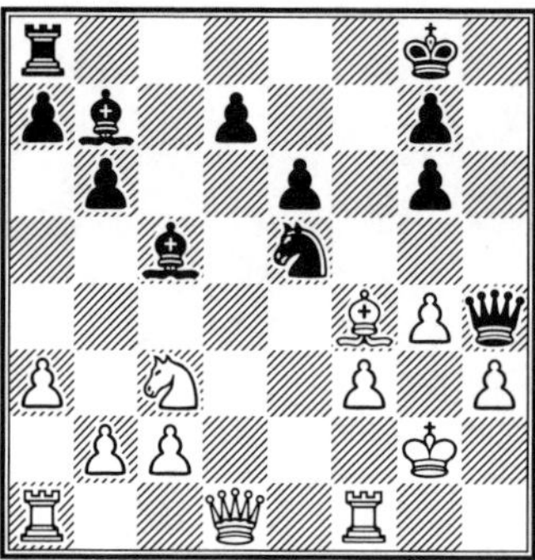

19...Nxf3 20.Rxf3 Qf2+, 0-1.

Adolf Anderssen vs. Daniel Harrwitz, Breslau match (1) 1848

1.e4 e5 2.Nf3 Nc6 3.d4 exd4 4.Bc4 Bc5 5.c3 Nf6 6.e5 d5 7.Bb5 Ne4 8.cxd4 Bb4+ 9.Bd2 Bxd2+ 10.Nbxd2 0-0 11.Bxc6 bxc6 12.0-0 f5 13.Rc1 Qe8 14.Qc2 Rb8 15.Nb3 Rb6 16.Nfd2 Qh5 17.f3 Nxd2 18.Qxd2 f4 19.Nc5

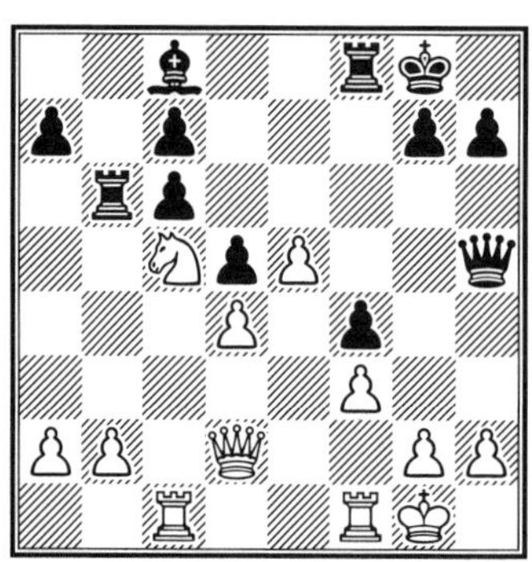

White's Knight dominates the Bishop. Now White's plan is to put pressure against Black's weak queenside pawns.

Adolf Anderssen, Pierre Charles Fournier de Saint-Amant, and Daniel Harrwitz (Image: Courtesy of the Cleveland Public Library's John G. White Collection).

19...Qg6 20.Rfe1 Be6 21.Rc3 Qe8 22.Ra3 Bf5 23.b3

Also playable is 23.Rxa7 Qb8 24.Qa5 Rxb2 25.Qxc7 Qxc7 26.Rxc7, but White decides to avoid any complications.

23...a6

23...Qb8 24.e6.

24.Rxa6 Rxa6 25.Nxa6 Qc8 26.Nc5 Be6 27.a4 g6 28.a5 Re8 29.a6 Qb8 30.Ra1 Qa7 31.Qb4 Kf7 32.Qb7 Qb6 33.a7 Qxb7 34.Nxb7 Ra8 35.Nd8+ Ke7 36.Nxe6 Kxe6 37.b4, 1-0.

A smooth positional victory.

Setting aside the previous positional game, Anderssen was a living example of the romantic style. He played in many tournaments and matches, but he always had to carefully ponder whether or not to travel to a chess event since, though his position in the university allowed him to be financially solvent, leaving for other countries would only be worthwhile if he managed to win a prize.

Fortunately, he did very well. This gave him confidence, and for much of the 1850s and 1860s he was widely viewed as the best player in the world.

His first international tournament was the London International in 1851. He was invited but wasn't sure he should go due to the expenses such a trip would incur. Fortunately, the main organizer of this event was none other than Howard Staunton, and he guaranteed the money for Anderssen (I always thought Staunton was a curmudgeon, but I might have to change my view due to his kindness in this instance). The event was based on mini-matches and Anderssen dominated the event, even crushing Staunton (4-1, no draws).

Ernst Falkbeer vs. Adolf Anderssen, Berlin match 1851

1.e4 e5 2.Nf3 Nc6 3.c3 d5 4.Bb5 dxe4 5.Nxe5 Qd5 6.Qa4 Nge7 7.f4 exf3 8.Nxf3 Bd7 9.0-0 0-0-0 10.d4 Qh5 11.Bf4 Kb8 12.Be2 Nd5 13.Bd2 Bd6 14.Qd1 Nf4 15.Bxf4 Bxf4 16.Nbd2 Ne5

16…g5!

17.dxe5 Bc6 18.h3 Be3+ 19.Kh2

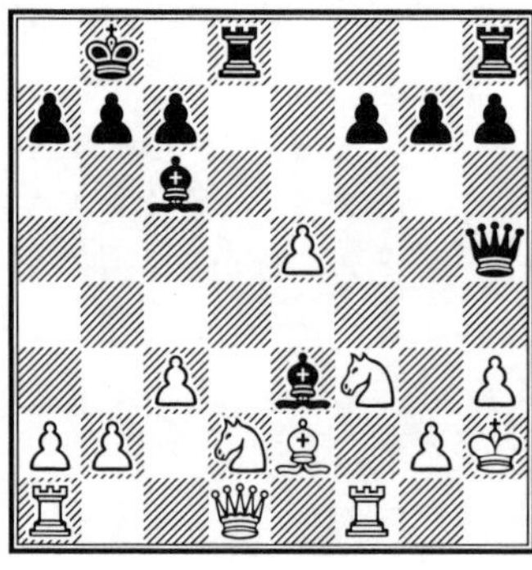

19…Bxf3?

19…Bxd2! 20.Nxd2 Qg5.

20.Bxf3 Qxe5+ 21.Kh1 Rxd2 22.Qb3 Bb6 23.Qxf7 Rhd8 24.Rae1 Qg3 25.b4 c6 26.Re8 Bc7 27.Rxd8+ Rxd8 28.Kg1 Qh2+ 29.Kf2 Bb6+ 30.Ke1 Qg3+ 31.Ke2 Qe5+ 32.Be4 Qxe4, 0-1.

Here are some typical eviscerations:

Eduard Jeney vs. Adolf Anderssen, Germany 1851

1.e4 e5 2.Bc4 Nf6 3.Qf3 Bc5 4.h3 0-0 5.d3 c6 6.Nc3 d5 7.Bb3 Bb4 8.Bd2 Be6 9.Nge2 a5 10.a3 Bxc3 11.Bxc3 Nbd7 12.Ng3 d4 13.Bd2 Bxb3 14.cxb3 Qb6 15.b4 axb4 16.Bxb4 c5 17.Bd2 Qxb2 18.Ke2 Rxa3 19.Rab1 Qa2 20.Rxb7 c4 21.Rd1 Rxd3 22.Qf5 Nc5 23.Rc7 c3 24.Nf1 Qa6 25.Ke1 cxd2+ 26.Nxd2

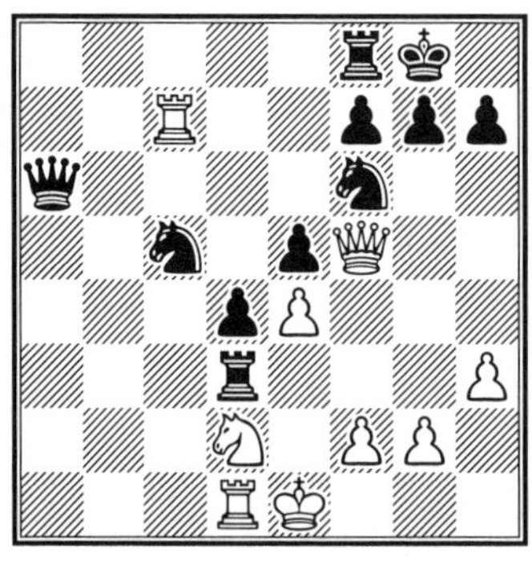

26...Rxd2 27.Rxd2 Nd3+ 28.Kd1 Qa1+ 29.Ke2 Nf4+ 30.Qxf4 exf4 31.f3 Qg1 32.Kd3 Qe3! 33.Kc2 Rb8 34.Rd3 Qe2 35.Rd2 Qe1 36.Rd1 d3+, 0-1.

Johann Löwenthal vs. Adolf Anderssen, London match (8) 1851

1.e4 e5 2.Nf3 Nc6 3.Bb5 Nf6 4.d3 Bc5 5.0-0 Nd4 6.Nxd4 Bxd4 7.c3 Bb6 8.Bg5 h6 9.Bh4 c6 10.Bc4 g5 11.Bg3 d6 12.h3 h5 13.d4 h4 14.Bh2 Qe7 15.Nd2 g4 16.dxe5 dxe5 17.hxg4 Nxg4 18.Be2 Rg8 19.Nc4 Bc7 20.Qd2 b5 21.Ne3 Qg5 22.Bxg4 Bxg4 23.f3 Bb6 24.Rae1 Rd8 25.Qf2 Bh3 26.f4

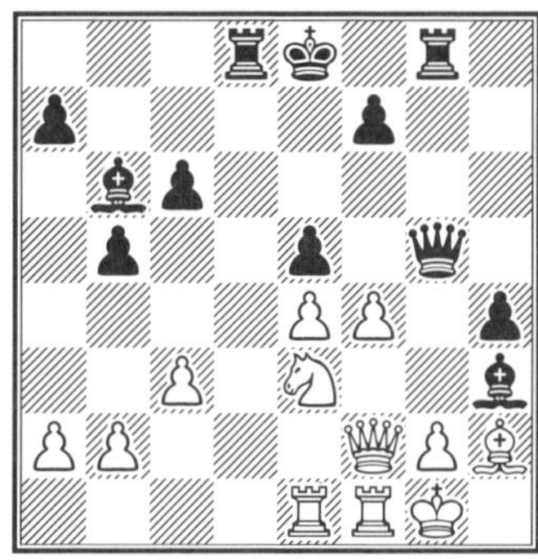

26...Qxg2+ 27.Qxg2

27.Nxg2 Rxg2+.

27...Bxe3+

Other winners were 27...Bxg2 and 27...Rxg2+.

28.Rxe3 Rxg2+ 29.Kh1 Rxh2+ 30.Kxh2 Bxf1, 0-1.

Johann Löwenthal vs. Adolf Anderssen, London match (6) 1851

1.e4 e5 2.f4 exf4 3.Bc4 Qh4+ 4.Kf1 g5 5.Nc3 Bg7 6.d4 Ne7 7.e5 f6 8.Ne4 Rf8 9.Qe2 Nbc6 10.Nf3 Qh5 11.exf6 Bxf6 12.c3 g4 13.Ng1 d5 14.Nxf6+ Rxf6 15.Bb5 f3 16.Qe5 fxg2+ 17.Kxg2 Qf7 18.Bxc6+ bxc6 19.Be3 Bf5 20.Re1 Be4+ 21.Kg3

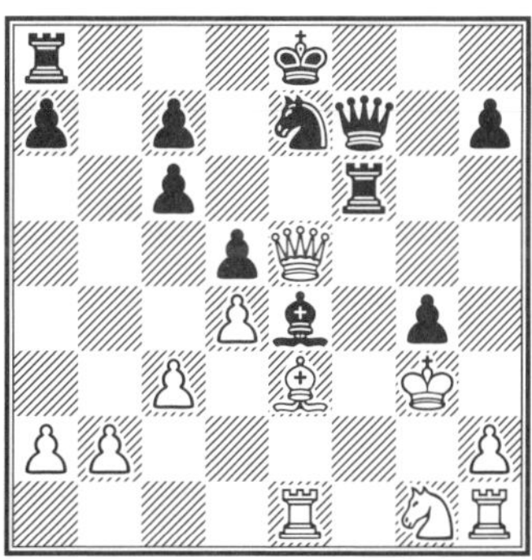

21...Rf3+ 22.Nxf3 Qxf3+ 23.Kh4 Qh3+ 24.Kg5 h6+

24...Kd7; 24...0-0-0.

25.Kf6 Qh4+ 26.Bg5 Qxg5+ 27.Qxg5 hxg5 28.Rhg1 Kd7 29.Kf7

29.Kxg5 Bf3.

29...Rh8 30.Re2 Nf5 31.Kf6 Rg8 32.Kf7 Nh6+ 33.Kf6 Rg6+ 34.Ke5 Re6, 0-1.

Adolf Anderssen vs. Adolf Zytogorski, London 1851

1.e4 e5 2.Nf3 Nc6 3.Bc4 Nf6 4.Ng5 d5 5.exd5 Na5 6.Bb5+ c6 7.dxc6 bxc6 8.Be2 Bd6 9.Nc3 Bf5 10.d3 0-0 11.0-0 Rc8 12.a3 Bb8 13.b4 Nb7 14.Nge4 Bxe4 15.dxe4 Qc7 16.f4 Rcd8 17.Qe1 Rfe8 18.f5 Qb6+ 19.Kh1 Nd6 20.Bg5 Kf8 21.Bxf6 gxf6 22.Qh4 Ke7 23.Rad1 a6 24.Rd3 Rg8 25.Na4 Qc7 26.Nc5 a5 27.Rfd1 axb4 28.axb4 Ba7 29.Ne6! Qb6 30.Nxd8 Rxd8 31.Qe1

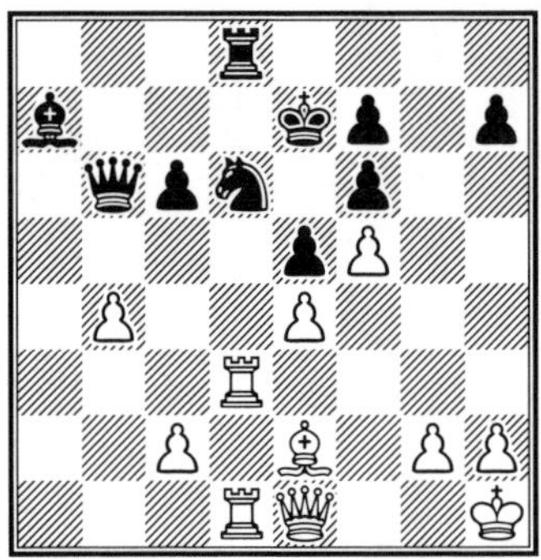

There were many winning moves: 31.g4, 31.c3, 31.Bf3, etc.

31...Nxe4??

31...Qf2 was best, though Black would still be completely lost.

32.Rxd8 Nf2+ 33.Qxf2 Qxf2 34.R1d7, 1-0.

Lionel Kieseritzky vs. Adolf Anderssen, London knockout 1851

1.e4 c5 2.b3 Nc6 3.Bb2 e6 4.Nf3 d6 5.d4 cxd4 6.Nxd4 Bd7 7.Bd3 Nf6 8.0-0 Be7 9.Nd2 0-0 10.c4 Ne5 11.Qe2 Ng6 12.f4 e5!

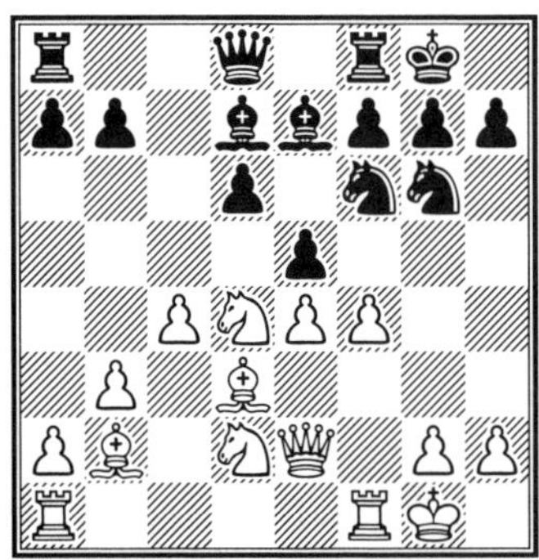

13.fxe5 dxe5 14.Nc2 Bc5+ 15.Kh1 Bg4 16.Nf3 Nf4 17.Qd2 Nxd3, 0-1.

The Immortal Game

This well-known game, which was played for fun during a rest period of the actual tournament, is one of the most famous games of all time. After the game, Kieseritzky was so impressed that he immediately telegraphed the moves to his Parisian chess club.

Adolf Anderssen vs. Lionel Kieseritzky, London 1851

1.e4 e5 2.f4 exf4 3.Bc4 Qh4+ 4.Kf1 b5 5.Bxb5 Nf6 6.Nf3 Qh6 7.d3 Nh5 8.Nh4 Qg5 9.Nf5 c6 10.g4 Nf6 11.Rg1 cxb5 12.h4 Qg6 13.h5 Qg5 14.Qf3 Ng8 15.Bxf4 Qf6 16.Nc3 Bc5 17.Nd5 Qxb2 18.Bd6 Bxg1

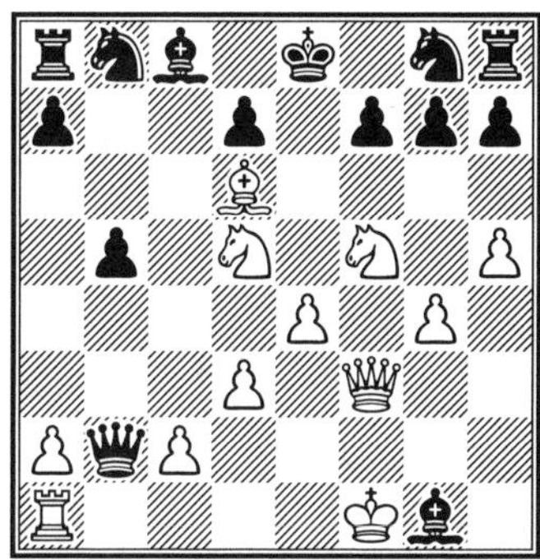

19.e5!!

19.Re1 was crushing, but why protect your Rook when you can "wow" everyone in the building?

19...Qxa1+ 20.Ke2 Na6

20...Ba6 21.Nc7+ Kd8 22.Nxa6 Qc3 23.Bc7+ Qxc7 (23...Kc8 24.Nd6 mate) (23...Ke8 24.Nd6+ Kf8 25.Qxf7 mate) 24.Nxc7 Nc6 25.Nxa8 with an easy win.

21.Nxg7+ Kd8 22.Qf6+ Nxf6 23.Be7, 1-0.

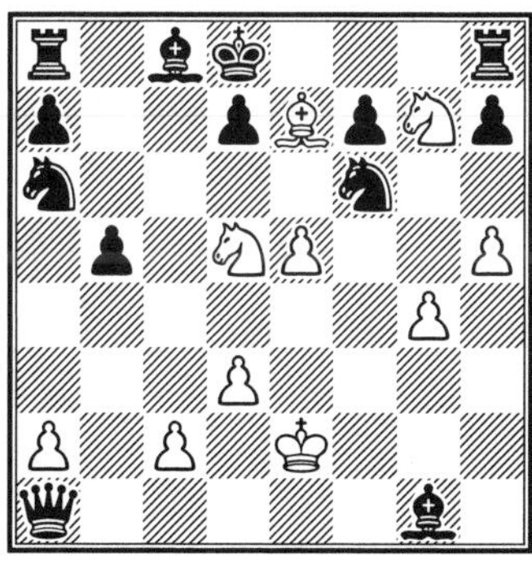

The Evergreen

A year later Anderssen pulled another rabbit out of his hat—this game was described by Wilhelm Steinitz as, "An evergreen in the laurel crown of the departed chess hero."

I like this more than the Immortal Game since both sides were trying to mate the other at the same time!

Adolf Anderssen vs. Jean Dufresne, Berlin 1852

1.e4 e5 2.Nf3 Nc6 3.Bc4 Bc5 4.b4 Bxb4 5.c3 Ba5 6.d4 exd4 7.0-0 d3 8.Qb3 Qf6 9.e5 Qg6 10.Re1 Nge7 11.Ba3 b5? 12.Qxb5 Rb8 13.Qa4 Bb6 14.Nbd2 Bb7 15.Ne4 Qf5? 16.Bxd3 Qh5

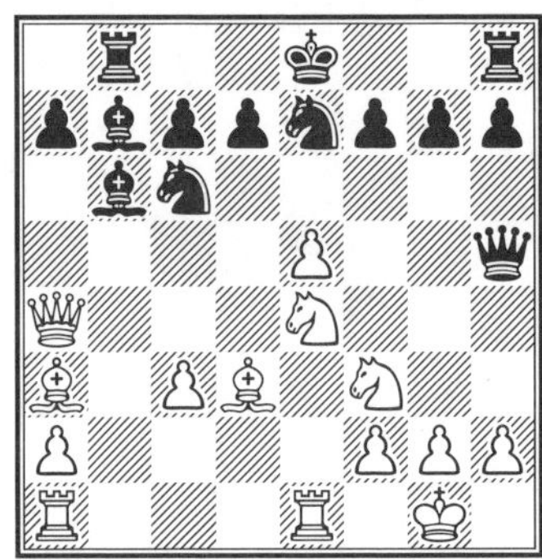

17.Nf6+!?

White has all sorts of moves that would win easily: 17.Ng3, 17.Rad1 and many more. However, in those days "beauty" was more important than "boring" (aka safe and sound) play. Thus, there was no way Andersson could ignore throwing the kitchen sink at his opponent. 17.Nf6+!? takes an easy win and turns it into a slight plus. But it's pretty and exciting and boils the spectators' blood. Best was 17.Rad1 (17.Ng3 and other moves also fry Black.) 17...0-0 18.Ng3 Qh6 19.Bc1 Qe6 20.Ng5 Qh6 21.Bxh7+ Kh8 22.Bc2 and it's over since White will play Nxf7 next move when the c1-bishop will chop off black's Queen: 22...Kg8 23.Nxf7 Qe6 24.Ng5 (Black's poor Queen only has one square to go to!) 24...Qh6 25.Bb3+ Kh8 26.Nf7+ and black's Queen will leave the chessboard.

17...gxf6 18.exf6 Rg8!

Suddenly white's King is in danger. I can imagine what the crowds were saying; some would insist that White is winning while others would say that Black is going to take off Anderssen's head. I wouldn't be surprised if a fistfight broke out!

19.Rad1!?

A "quiet" move that sets up a beautiful finish. However, 19.Rad1 gave up all his advantage, while 19.Be4 (so, so boring!) retained an edge. Anyway, who cares about truth when you're reaching for immortality?

19...Qxf3??

Dufresne, as if he was a lemming, happily leapt over the cliff. He could have saved himself with 19... Qh3 (19...Bd4 20.cxd4 Qxf3 21.Be4 Rxg2+ 22.Kh1 Rxh2+ 23.Kxh2 Qxf2+, =) 20. Bf1 Qf5 (Everything else loses.) 21.Kh1 Black wins after 21.fxe7 Qxf3. 21... Qxf6 22. Bxe7 Nxe7 23. Rxd7 Kf8 24. Rexe7 Qxf3 25. Qa3 Qxg2+ 26. Bxg2 Bxg2+ 27. Kg1 Bh3+, draw. I have to admit that this would have been an exciting finish!

20.Rxe7+!

At this point the spectators were swooning. Which side is going to be mated?

20...Nxe7

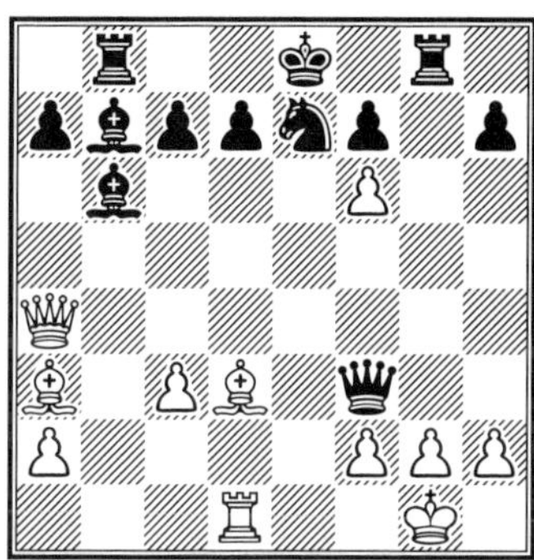

20...Kd8 black's King can run but it can't hide! 21.Rxd7+! Kc8 (21...Kxd7 22.Bf5+ Ke8 23.Bd7+ Kd8 24.Bxc6+ with mate in 3 more moves.) 22.Rd8+ (You just don't see chess like this anymore!) 22... Nxd8 (22...Kxd8 23.Bf5+ Qxd1+ 24.Qxd1+ Nd4 25.Bh3 when White will gobble up the d4-Knight [or go Be7+ first] when the black King will be a target for the rest of the game) 23.Qd7+! Kxd7 24.Bf5+ Kc6 (24...Ke8 25.Bd7 mate) 25.Bd7 mate.

21.Qxd7+! Kxd7 22.Bf5+ Ke8 23.Bd7+ Kf8

23...Kd8 24.fxe7 mate.

24.Bxe7, 1-0.

One of Anderssen's "endless" match opponents was Carl Mayet, who wasn't close to Adolf's level. The following two games are examples of this:

Adolf Anderssen vs. Carl Mayet, Berlin match (1) 1851

1.e4 e5 2.Nf3 Nc6 3.Bc4 Bc5 4.b4 Bxb4 5.c3 Ba5 6.d4 exd4 7.0-0 d3 8.Ng5 Nh6 9.e5 Nxe5 10.Re1 Qe7 11.f4 Bb6+ 12.Kh1 Nhg4 13.Nh3 d6 14.Bxd3 0-0 15.fxe5 Nxe5 16.Nf4 c6 17.Nd2 g5 18.Qh5 f5 19.Bc4+ Kg7

19...d5 20.Nxd5 cxd5 21.Bxd5+ Kh8 22.Nf3 Bc7 23.Bxg5 Qd7 (23...Qg7 24.Nxe5 Bxe5 25.Bh6 and Black can resign.) 24.Nxe5 Qxd5 25.Ng6+ Kg7 (25...Kg8 26.Ne7+) 26.Qh6+ Kf7 (26...Kg8 27.Qxf8 mate) 27.Qxh7 mate.

20.Nf3 h6

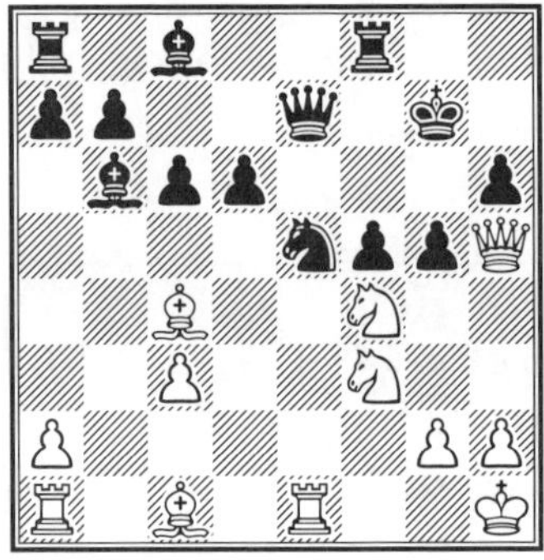

20...gxf4 21.Bxf4 Bc7 22.Nxe5 dxe5 23.Rxe5 Qf6 (23...Bxe5 24.Qh6+ Kh8 25.Bxe5+ Qxe5 26.Qxf8 mate) 24.Rae1 Kh8 25.Re7 Qg6 26.Bxc7 Qxh5 27.Be5+ Rf6 28.Bxf6 mate.

21.Nxe5

The second best move, which is also completely crushing. However, even better was 21.Rxe5 Qf6 (21...dxe5 22.Qg6+ Kh8 23.Qxh6+ Qh7 24.Ng6+ mate.) 22.Re7+ Qxe7 (22...Kh8 23.Ng6+) 23.Qg6+ Kh8 24.Qxh6+ Qh7 25.Ng6 mate.

21...Qf6 22.Ng4 fxg4

22...gxf4 23.Re7+ Kh8 (23...Qxe7 24.Qxh6#) 24.Nxf6 Rxf6 25.Qe8+.

23.Re7+, 1-0.

23...Kh8 (23...Qxe7 24.Qg6+ Kh8 25.Qxh6+ Qh7 26.Ng6 mate) 24.Ng6+ Qxg6 25.Qxg6 and mate in two.

Adolf Anderssen vs. Carl Mayet, Berlin match (2) 1851

1.e4 e5 2.Nf3 Nc6 3.Bc4 Bc5 4.b4 Bb4 5.c3 Ba5 6.d4 exd4 7.0-0 d3 8.Ng5 Nh6 9.e5 Bb6 10.Kh1 Nxe5 11.Re1 d6 12.f4 Ng4 13.Nh3 0-0 14.fxe5 Nxe5 15.Bg5 Qe8 16.Qh5 Qc6 17.Bb3 Bg4 18.Qh4 h5 19.Nd2 Rae8 20.Nf4 Qxc3 21.Ne4 Qd4 22.Nxh5 Bxh5 23.Qxh5 d2 24.Nf6+!

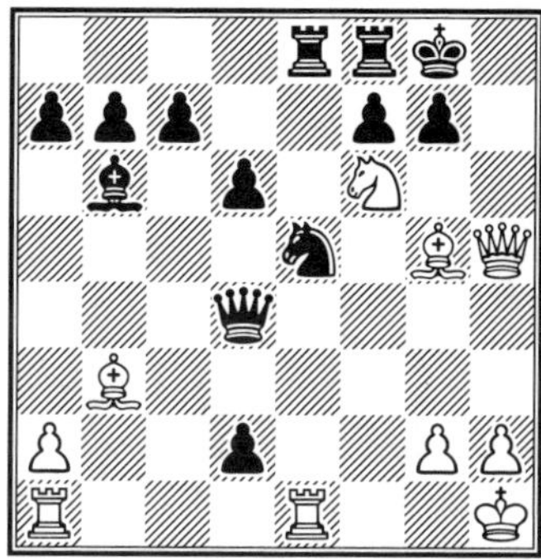

24.Bxd2 should win, though Black can fight with 24...Nd3 25.Rf1 Qxe4 26.Bxf7+ Rxf7 27.Qxf7+ Kh7 28.Rf3 Nf2+ 29.Rxf2 Bxf2 30.Qxf2 etc. White's 24.Nf6! is infinitely superior.

24...gxf6 25.Bxf6 dxe1Q+ 26.Rxe1 Qh4

26...Ng6 27.Qxg6 mate.

27.Qxh4 Ng6 28.Qg3 Rxe1+ 29.Qxe1 d5 30.Bxd5 c6 31.Bb3 Bd8 32.Qg3 Bxf6 33.Qxg6+ Bg7 34.h4, 1-0.

I must say something about Anderssen being considered the best player in the world during the 1850s and 1860s. It just so happened that there was a rather large "blip on the 'best player' radar." That "blip" is named Paul Morphy!

I'm sure that Anderssen thought he could beat Morphy, and I even think that Anderssen was slightly superior than Morphy in raw tactics. The problem was that Morphy (also a romantic), who was obviously ahead of his time, didn't take foolish risks and only went for blood when it was sound to do so.

Anderssen was quite different in that he was often in trouble in his quest to smash his opponents in brutal ways and was only saved by relying on his incredible tactical skills. In other words, they were both tactical geniuses, but Morphy had a sound foundation while Anderssen, like most of the players in his day, would charge wildly into battle.

Three world champions comment on Morphy's style:

Emanuel Lasker:

> Morphy discovered that the brilliant move of a master is essentially conditional not on a sudden and inexplicable realization, but on the placing of the pieces on the board.

Capablanca:

> He did not look for complicated combinations, but he also did not avoid them, which really is the correct way of playing. His main strength lay not in his combinative gift, but in his positional play and general style.

Schachkampf in Paris zwischen Anderssen und Morphy.

Adolf Anderssen vs. Paul Morphy, Paris 1858 (Image: Courtesy of the Cleveland Public Library's John G. White Collection).

Smyslov:

> Morphy's play was captivated by freshness of thought and inexhaustible energy. His harmonious positional understanding and deep intuition would have made Morphy a highly dangerous opponent even for any player of our times.

A match was arranged in Paris between Anderssen and Morphy. Anderssen claimed that he was badly out of practice while Morphy got the flu. Typically for that time, Morphy was treated with leeches, which in turn created a serious loss of blood. When the actual chess began, Anderssen was badly beaten by the score of two wins, two draws, and seven defeats. When asked about his defeat, Anderssen admitted that Morphy was the stronger player and that he was fairly beaten. Anderssen also attested that in his opinion, Morphy was the strongest player ever to play the game, even stronger than the famous French champion De La Bourdonnais.

Adolf Anderssen vs. Paul Morphy, Paris 1858

1.e4 e5 2.f4 exf4 3.Nf3 g5 4.h4 g4 5.Ne5 Nf6 6.Nxg4 d5 7.Nxf6+ Qxf6 8.Qe2 Bd6 9.Nc3 c6 10.d4

From this point on White had a superior position and he never let it go.

10...Qxd4 11.Bd2 Rg8 12.exd5+ Kd8

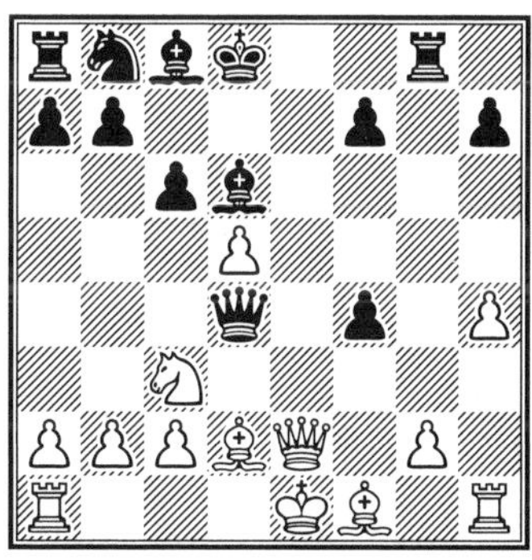

13.0-0-0 Bg4 14.Qe4 Qxe4 15.Nxe4 Bxd1 16.Nxd6 Bh5 17.Bxf4 cxd5 18.Nxb7+ Ke7 19.Bb5 Rxg2 20.Re1+ Kf6 21.Re8 Bg6 22.Nd6 Nc6 23.Rxa8 Rxc2+ 24.Kd1 Nd4 25.Re8 Bh5+ 26.Ke1 Nf3+ 27.Kf1 Rxb2 28.Be2 Rxa2 29.Bg5+ Nxg5 30.hxg5+ Kxg5 31.Re5+ Kf6 32.Rxh5, 1-0.

Anderssen had no gripe about Morphy, but he was extremely upset by Morphy's fans, as shown in his following words:

> It was impossible for Morphy to express an opinion on this subject, as I did not go to Paris to get a certificate of ability. Those who surrounded the American, however, seemed to think that they flattered me most when they

> said, "How high an opinion Morphy had of your play, and that he considered you the strongest of all opponents he had met till now. But to be reckoned stronger than a Löwenthal, I consider next door to nothing.

After Anderssen was defeated by Morphy, he rested from chess and returned to his job of teaching. Then a few years later he jumped back into the world of chess.

The 1860s were very good for Anderssen, who was still at his peak and won several important tournaments and was successful in most of his matches. However, new players were appearing, such as Ignatz Kolisch, Steinitz, and Zukertort. Anderssen was viewed as the best player in the world again (Morphy had retired from chess) but those other guys were getting better and better.

Anderssen played two matches with Kolisch, with the first one (in 1860) drawn (five wins, five losses, one draw), and the other (in 1861) barely won by Anderssen (four wins, three losses, and two draws).

A casual match in 1862 against Steinitz was won by Anderssen (two wins, one loss), and they played another match (considered the first official contest for the World Championship) in 1866 which was won by Steinitz, with eight wins and six losses (by the time the match ended both players had beaten each other to pulp).

Johannes Zukertort, who was rising fast, lost to Anderssen in 1868 (eight wins, three losses, one draw). However, Zukertort won a revenge match in 1871 (just two wins for Anderssen, five losses, no draws). At this point it was clear that youth (Steinitz and Zukertort—Kolisch was out of the picture since he quit serious chess after he won a very strong tournament in Paris 1867) mixed with an older Anderssen, made the future clear (as is the case in all sports).

Okay, perhaps it wasn't clear! When all the young guys were ready to take over, Anderssen kept winning tournaments in the 1860s and even in the 1870s!

Anderssen's Best Tournament Results

London International (1851): First.

London Chess Club Tournament (1851): First.

London International (1862): First.

Aachen (1868): Tied for first/second with Max Lange

Hamburg (1869) Tied for first/second with Paulsen.

Barmen (1869): First.

Baden-Baden (1870): First ahead of Steinitiz (Anderssen won both games against Steinitz), Neumann, Blackburne, Paulsen.

After this, age started to weaken him. His two best results in major tournaments in that period were:

Vienna International (1873): Third.

Leipzig (1877): Paulsen was first, Anderssen tied second/third with Zukertort

Anderssen's Most Important Matches

In the 1800s matches were common, and Anderssen played many. The ones that stand out in his prime years (no casual games included) were:

Win over Ernst Falkbeer (1851): 4 wins, 1 loss, 0 draws.

Win over Johann Löwenthal (1851): 5 wins, 4 losses, 0 draws.

Win over Daniel Harrwitz (1858): 3 wins, 1 loss, 2 draws.

Defeated by Paul Morphy (1858): 2 wins, 7 losses, 2 draws.

Win over Jean Dufresne (1859): 4 wins, 0 losses, 0 draws.

Tied with Ignatz Kolisch (1860): 4 wins, 4 losses, 1 draw.

Win over Ignatz Kolisch (1861): 4 wins, 3 losses, 2 draws.

Tied with Louis Paulsen (1862): 3 wins for both, two draws.

Defeated by Wilhelm Steinitz (1866): 6 wins, 8 losses, no draws.

Win over Johannes Zukertort (1868): 8 wins, 3 losses, 1 draw.

Ignatz Kolisch vs. Adolf Anderssen, London 1861

1.e4 c5 2.Nf3 e6 3.d4 cxd4 4.Nxd4 Nf6 5.Bd3 Nc6 6.Be3 d5 7.exd5 exd5 8.0-0 Bd6 9.h3 h6 10.c4 0-0 11.Nc3 Be5 12.Nf3 Bxc3 13.bxc3 Be6 14.cxd5 Nxd5 15.Qd2 Qf6 16.Nd4 Ne5 17.Bc2 Rfd8 18.Nxe6 fxe6 19.Bd4

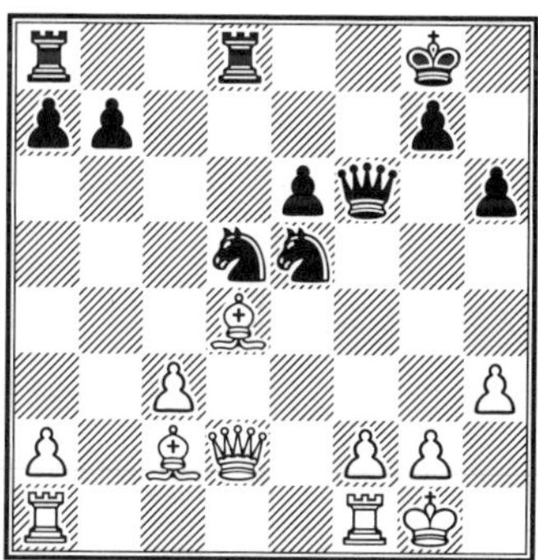

19...Nxc3!

19...Nf3+ is very tasty, but it will end up with a draw: 20.gxf3 Nf4 21.Bxf6 Rxd2 22.Be5 Ne2+ 23.Kh2 Rxc2 24.Rad1 Rf8 (24...Rxa2 25.Rd7 can only be good for White.) 25.Rd7 Rf7 26.Rfd1 g5 27.R1d2 (27.Rxf7 Kxf7 28.Rd7+ Kg6 29.Rxb7 Rxa2 favors Black.) 27...Rxd2 28.Rxd2 , =.

20.Qxc3

20.f4 Rxd4 21.Qxc3 (21.Qxd4?? Ne2+) 21...Nc4 with an edge for Black.

20...Rxd4 21.Rae1 Rc4 22.Qxe5?!

22.Qd2, =.

22...Qxe5 23.Rxe5 Rxc2 24.Rxe6 Rxa2 25.Re7 b5 26.Rc1 Rf8 27.Rcc7 Rfxf2 28.Rxg7+ Kf8 29.Rxa7 Rxg2+ 30.Rxg2 Rxa7 31.Rg6??

31.Rb2.

31...Rg7, 0-1.

Wilhelm Steinitz vs. Adolf Anderssen, London 1862

1.e4 e5 2.Nc3 Bc5 3.Bc4 Nf6 4.d3 d6 5.Nf3 Nc6 6.0-0 Bg4 7.Be3 a6 8.Kh1 Ba7 9.Rg1 h6 10.h3 Bh5 11.g4 Bg6 12.Ne2 d5 13.exd5 Nxd5 14.Bxa7 Rxa7 15.d4 Nb6 16.Bb3 h5 17.g5 Qd7

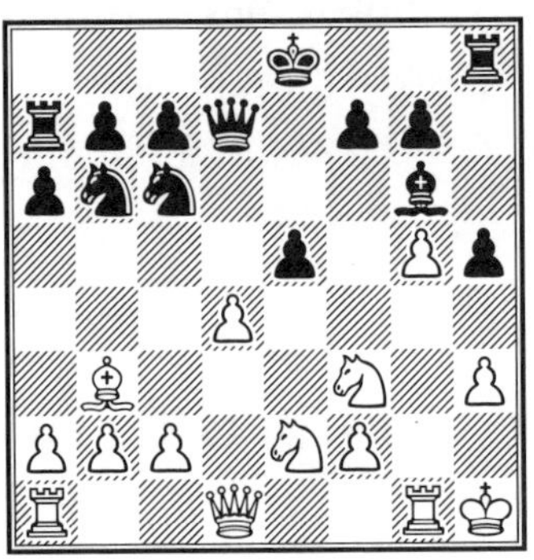

18.Kh2 exd4 19.Nexd4 Qd6+ 20.Kg2 0-0 21.Ne2 Qc5 22.Re1 Raa8 23.Nf4 Rad8 24.Qe2 Nd4 25.Qe7 Qc6 26.Re3 Nxf3 27.Rxf3 Be4 28.g6 Bxf3+ 29.Kg3 Nd5 30.gxf7+ Kh8 31.Bxd5 Bxd5, 0-1.

Jakob Rosanes vs. Adolf Anderssen, Breslau 1862

1.e4 e5 2.f4 d5 3.exd5 e4 4.Bb5+ c6 5.dxc6 Nc6 6.Nc3 Nf6 7.Qe2 Bc5 8.Nxe4 0-0 9.Bxc6 bxc6 10.d3 Re8 11.Bd2 Nxe4 12.dxe4 Bf5 13.e5 Qb6 14.0-0-0 Bd4 15.c3 Rab8 16.b3 Red8 17.Nf3

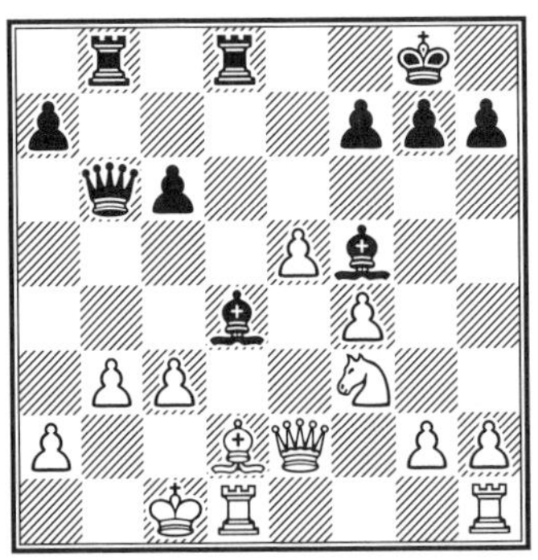

Qxb3! 18.axb3 Rxb3 19.Be1 Be3+, 0-1.

In the strong tournament Baden-Baden 1870, everyone played two games against everyone else. Anderssen was losing in both games against Steinitz (who came in second, half a point behind first place Anderssen), but somehow turned the tables and won both! Here's Anderssen (after Steinitz botched it) ripping his opponent limb by limb!

Wilhelm Steinitz vs. Adolf Anderssen, Baden-Baden 1870

1.e4 e5 2.Nc3 Bc5 3.f4 d6 4.Nf3 Nf6 5.Bc4 c6 6.fxe5 dxe5 7.Qe2 Nbd7 8.d3 b5 9.Bb3 a5 10.a3 Qb6 11.Nd1 a4 12.Ba2 0-0 13.Ne3 Ba6 14.Nf5 b4 15.axb4 Qxb4+ 16.c3 Qa5 17.Ng5 Rad8 18.Qf3 Qb6 19.Bb1 a3 20.b4 Bxb4 21.cxb4 Qxb4+ 22.Ke2 a2 23.Bd2 Qb5 24.Rxa2 Nc5 25.Rxa6 Qxa6 26.Bb4 Rb8 27.Bxc5 Rb2+ 28.Ke3 Qa5 29.Rd1 Qxc5+

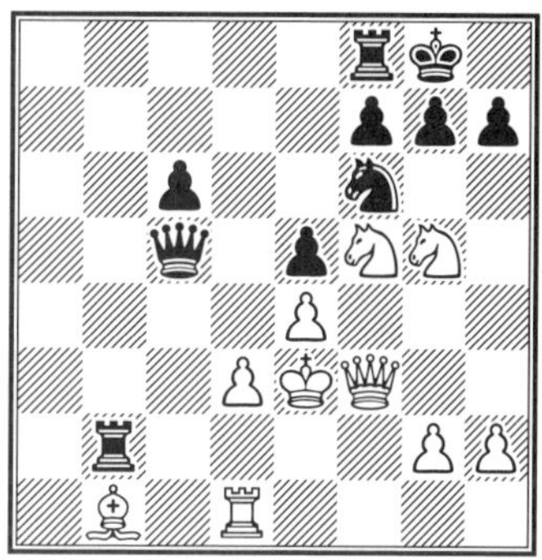

30.d4 exd4+ 31.Kf4 h6 32.Nh3 Re8 33.Qd3 g5+ 34.Kf3 g4+ 35.Kg3 Rxe4 36.Qf1 Qe5+ 37.Kh4 gxh3+ 38.Kxh3 Rb3+ 39.g3 Rf4 40.Nxh6+ Kf8 41.Qc4 Rh4+ 42.Kg2

42.Kxh4 Qh5 mate.

42...Rxh2+ 43.Kxh2 Qxg3+ 44.Kh1 Qh3+ 45.Kg1 Rg3+, 0-1.

It's funny that Steinitz was a crazed attacker in his youth, but he had trouble with Adolf Anderssen, who was an even better attacker. As years went by and chess was changing, Anderssen made changes too. Steinitz became a positional player, and Anderssen couldn't deal with that. During Anderssen's final years, he to embraced positional ideas, though he was always looking to cut off his opponent's head with a tactic.

Anderssen vs. Paulsen is a good way to end this portrait. Anderssen played a splendid positional game mixed with all sorts of little tactics. They say that you can't teach an old dog new tricks, but Anderssen, the king of tactics, was trying hard to make those changes. I wonder how good he could have become if he continued honing his positional skills. Unfortunately, ill-health dragged him down, and at the age of sixty, he was gone.

Adolf Anderssen vs. Louis Paulsen, Vienna 1873

1.e4 e5 2.Nf3 d6 3.d4 exd4 4.Qxd4 Nc6 5.Bb5 Bd7 6.Bxc6 Bxc6 7.Bg5 Nf6 8.Nc3 Be7 9.0-0-0 0-0 10.Rhe1 Re8 11.Kb1 Bd7 12.Bxf6 Bxf6 13.e5 Be7 14.Nd5 Bf8 15.exd6 cxd6

15...Bxd6 16.Nxc7 Rxe1 17.Nxe1 Qxc7 18.Qxd6.

16.Rxe8 Bxe8 17.Nd2 Bc6 18.Ne4 f5 19.Nec3 Qd7 20.a3 Qf7 21.h3 a6 22.g4 Re8 23.f4 Re6 24.g5 b5 25.h4 Re8 26.Qd3 Rb8 27.h5 a5

27...Qxh5 28.Qxf5.

28.b4 axb4 29.axb4 Qxh5 30.Qxf5 Qf7 31.Qd3 Bd7 32.Ne4 Qf5 33.Rh1

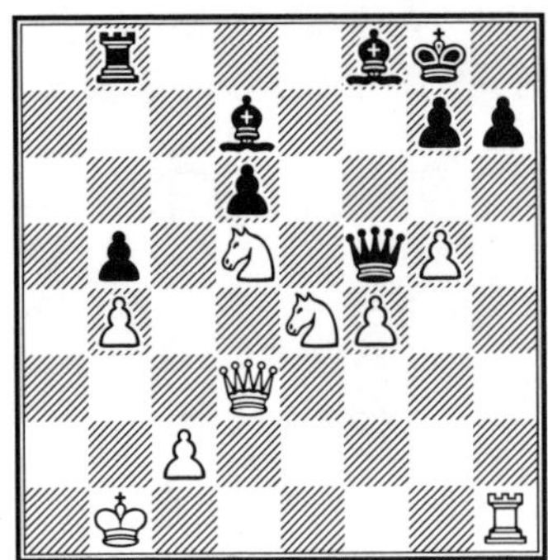

33...Re8

33...Be6 34.Rh4 Kh8 (34...Qxd5 35.Nf6+ gxf6 36.Qxh7 mate) (34...Bxd5 35.Nf6+) 35.Ne3.

34.Nef6+ gxf6 35.Nxf6+ Kf7 36.Rxh7+ Bg7 37.Rxg7+ Kxg7 38.Nxe8+ Kf8 39.Qxf5+ Bxf5 40.Nxd6 Bd7 41.Ne4 Kg7 42.Ng3 Kf7 43.f5 Ke7 44.Kc1 Kd6 45.g6 Be8 46.Kd2 Kd5 47.Kd3 Ke5 48.Ke3 Kd5 49.Kf4 Kc4 50.Ne4 Kxb4 51.Nd6 Bc6 52.f6 Kc3 53.Nxb5+ Bxb5 54.f7, 1-0.

Anderssen's final tournament, Paris International (1878), had him in sixth place. He died of a heart attack in 1879 at the age of sixty.

2

IGNATZ KOLISCH

Unknown Tactical Monster

Baron Ignatz von Kolisch (1837-1889) was born in the Austrian Imperial city of Pressburg (which today is Bratislava, Slovakia). While a young man, he was the private secretary of the Russian Prince Sergey Urusov (who was a close friend of Leo Tolstoy!). Kolisch eventually got involved in banking when he met Albert Salomon von Rothschild, and after that, the sky was the limit.

I was wondering how Kolisch first got interested in the game when it struck me that Prince Urusov, ten years older than Kolisch and a very strong player

(International Master level!), most likely took him under his wing and became (aside from his employer) his chess teacher. This makes a lot of sense, though I have no proof that this is true. Even so, Kolisch had a deep love for opening gambits, and Urusov was the creator of the Urusov gambit (1.e4 e5 2.Bc4 Nf6 3.d4). In other words, it is quite possible that Urusov's infatuation with gambits is what influenced Kolisch to embrace the same love affair.

Batgirl's[1] take on my teacher/student theory:

> I'm not sure I could make the stretch of Urusov being Kolisch's teacher, but most certainly, being associated with the brothers Urusov and traveling in their circles, which included the best chess players in Russia, he must have had a huge impact and influence on Kolisch's embracing of chess.
>
> Kolisch also strongly influenced Prince Dadian when they met in Hamburg, Germany in 1867. There Dadian met Thomas Wilson Barnes, the man with the best record against Morphy, who instructed him, but Kolisch was the man at that time and he and Dadian, basically a novice with a lot of money, played many games. That Dadian won a Muzio against Kolisch at that time probably says more about Kolisch's tact than Dadian's nascent talent.

Though Kolisch could play strong positional chess and excellent endgames when he had too, his style was mainly dedicated to violent attacks and slashing tactical takedowns. He was a genius in this form of chess, but often went too far in his search for thrills and beauty. In fact, at times his games incorporated a bit of gambling in that he "threw the dice" in the hopes that his opponents would drown in the not-quite-sound complications he created. I have to admit that most of his gambles paid off, and that he was able to defeat other opponents from beginning to end.

Except for a few offhand games, Kolisch only played serious chess from 1860 to 1868. A multimillionaire, businessman, writer, and chess patron, he gave up serious play after 1868 (at thirty years old) and devoted himself to business.

One might think that someone who only played for a few years couldn't have made much of an impression in the chess world, but nothing could be further from the truth. Chessmetrics had Kolisch as the number one player in the world in 1867, number two in 1862, number three in 1860 and 1863, and number four in 1861! His highest Chessmetrics rating was a flabbergasting 2785!

I decided to share his games and his life because he's someone few people have heard of, even though he was one of the strongest players of the ninetieth century. And there is another reason why I delved into this gentleman's past as unlike many players whose lives were ones of desperation, with barely sufficient means, or complete poverty, Kolisch seems to have been successful in every endeavor he embraced.

1 Batgirl is a highly respected and much followed chess history columnist on chess.com.

His first exposure to serious chess was in 1860 (at twenty-three years old), and what a year it was! He literally went from an unknown to one of the top five players in the world—all in the span of a few months! His 1860 match with Adolf Anderssen ended in a tie, both sides winning five games, with only one draw.

One of the funniest things about this match is that both players were known berserkers, and Kolisch, instead of trying to pull Anderssen's teeth by using positional methods, went *mano-a-mano* (literally hand-to-hand) with him. For example, as White he dared toss the King's Gambit at Anderssen three times (winning all three games)! Evidently, this crazy "go for his throat" strategy worked!

Cambridge (1860): Kolisch won the event. Kolisch was a tactical and attacking genius, but he could also handle himself in positional or endgame situations.

Manchester (1860): Eight game match vs. John Owen. Owen's highest Chessmetrics rating was 2533, and he was number five in the world in 1862. Their match ended in a tie, 4 to 4 (no draws!).

London (1860): Eleven game match vs. Thomas Barnes. Keep in mind that Steinitz pointed out that Barnes had the best score of anyone in off-hand games vs. Morphy, so Kolisch's demolition of Barnes by a score of 10 to 1 (with no draws!) had to be a shock. Barnes' highest Chessmetrics rating was an impressive 2570, which gives you some insight into just how strong Kolisch was.

Bristol (1861): Fourth British Chess Association Congress. Kolisch was knocked out in the first round after losing 1 to 2 (1 loss and 2 draws) to Louis Paulsen (who went on the win the event). Chessmetrics has Paulsen in the world number one and two spots for several years, with a high rating of 2785, so the young Kolisch's defeat was nothing to be ashamed of.

London (1861): Nine game match vs. Adolf Anderssen. A very close back and forth affair, they were tied after eight games, with Anderssen winning the final game (4 wins, 3 losses, 2 draws). Anderssen was one of the best players in the world from 1850 to 1879 (Chessmetrics has Anderssen as the world number one in 1857, with an all time high rating of 2690).

London (1861): Thirty-one game match vs. Louis Paulsen. An epic tussle, with Paulsen taking it by a nose with a 16 to 15 score (7 wins, 6 losses, 18 draws)!

St. Petersburg (1862): Eight game match vs. Ilya Shumov. Kolisch won 6-2 (no draws). The odd thing about this match was that Kolisch lost the first two games, apparently took his face out of the vodka bottle, and then reeled off 6 straight wins! Shumov's highest Chessmetrics rating was 2492.

St. Petersburg (1862): Four game match vs. Sergey Urusov. The match was tied, 2 to 2 (no draws). Urusov (whom I postulated might have been Kolisch's teacher) had a Chessmetrics rating of 2485.

Paris (1864): Eight game match vs. Philip Hirschfeld. After six games, Kolisch was down two games with two to play, but he got his act together and won the last two to tie the match four to four (with no draws). Chessmetrics had Hirschfeld as number six in the world in 1864, with a high rating of 2547.

Paris (1864): Eight game match vs. Samuel Rosenthal. Rosenthal had a high Chessmetrics rating of 2615 though he was just starting out in 1864. Though never as strong as Kolisch, the final result of seven to one (with no draws) must have been an ego-slap of epic proportions.

Paris (1867): A powerhouse tournament filled with a myriad of top players. Fortunately for Kolisch it was held during his prime, and he came in clear first place ahead of Szymon Winawer (Chessmetrics rating: 2658), Wilhelm Steinitz (Chessmetrics rating: 2834), Gustav Neumann (Chessmetrics rating: 2713), Jules Arnous de Rivière (Chessmetrics rating: 2581) and many others. He had a win and a draw vs. Steinitz.

Ignaz Kolisch vs. Leopold Epstein, Paris 1857

1.e4 c5 2.d4 e6 3.Bd2 cxd4 4.Nf3 Nc6 5.c3 dxc3 6.Bxc3 h6 7.Bc4 Bb4 8.0-0 Nf6 9.a3 Bxc3 10.Nxc3 a6 11.Ba2 d6 12.Re1 0-0 13.Re3 Qc7 14.Rd3 Rd8 15.Qd2 b6 16.Rd1 Ne8 17.Nh4

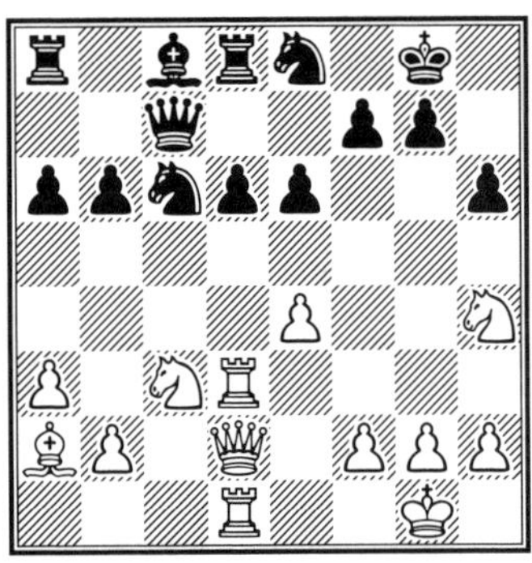

17...Bb7 18.Rg3 Kh7 19.f4 Ne7 20.f5 exf5 21.exf5 f6 22.Ng6 Nxg6 23.fxg6+ Kh8 24.b4 a5 25.Rh3 d5 26.Rxh6+ gxh6 27.Qxh6+ Kg8 28.Nxd5 Qg7 29.Nxf6+, 1-0.

Giuseppe Mandolfo vs. Ignaz Kolisch, Trieste 1858

1.e4 e5 2.Bc4 Nf6 3.Nc3 c6 4.d3 b5 5.Bb3 a5 6.a4 b4 7.Na2 d5 8.exd5 cxd5 9.Nf3 Nc6 10.Qe2 Bg4 11.0-0 Bc5 12.Bg5 h6

12...0-0 was much better.

13.h3 h5 14.hxg4 hxg4 15.Nxe5 Nd4 16.Qe1 Ne4! 17.Bxd8

Now White gets destroyed.

17...Ng3!

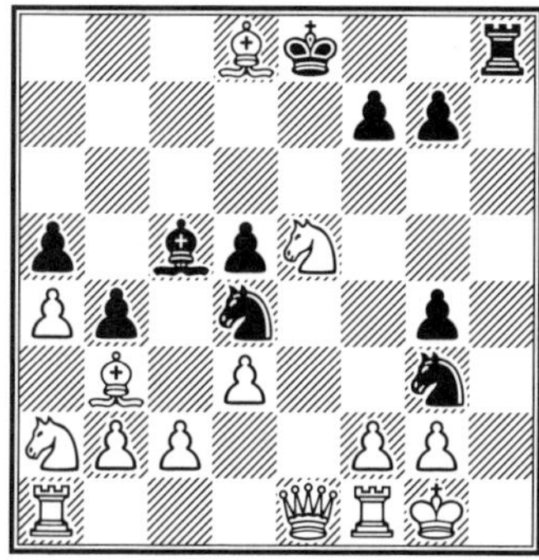

18.Nc6+ Nde2+ 19.Qxe2+ Nxe2+, 0-1.

The next game with the white King going all over the place, will blow your mind!

Ignaz Kolisch vs. Adolf Anderssen, Paris 1860

1.e4 e5 2.f4 exf4 3.Nf3 g5 4.h4 g4 5.Ne5 h5 6.Bc4 Rh7 7.d4 f3 8.gxf3 d6 9.Nd3 Be7 10.Be3 Bxh4+

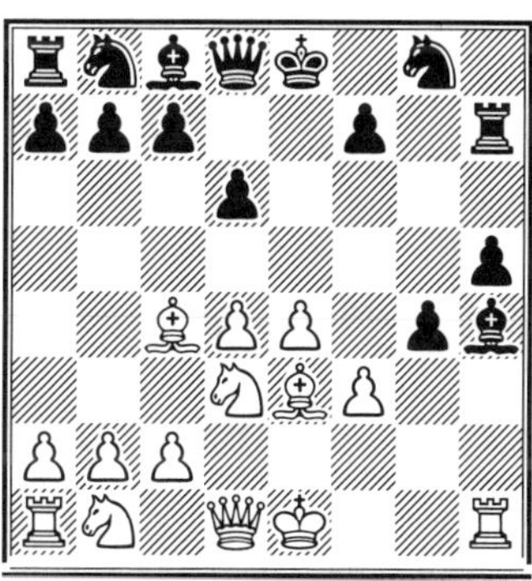

Now the white King will show his skill.

11.Kd2! Bg5 12.Nc3 Bxe3+ 13.Kxe3! Qg5+ 14.f4 Qg7 15.e5 Bf5 16.Nb5 Na6 17.exd6 0-0-0 18.Ne5 cxd6 19.Nxf7 Re8+ 20.Kd2! Kb8 21.Nfxd6 Rf8 22.Qe2 Bg6 23.Rae1 Nb4 24.f5 Qh6+ 25.Kc3, 1-0.

William Steinitz vs. Ignaz Kolisch, Paris 1867

1.e4 e5 2.f4 exf4 3.Nf3 g5 4.Bc4 Bg7 5.0-0 d6 6.d4 h6 7.g3 g4 8.Ne1 f3 9.c3 Ne7

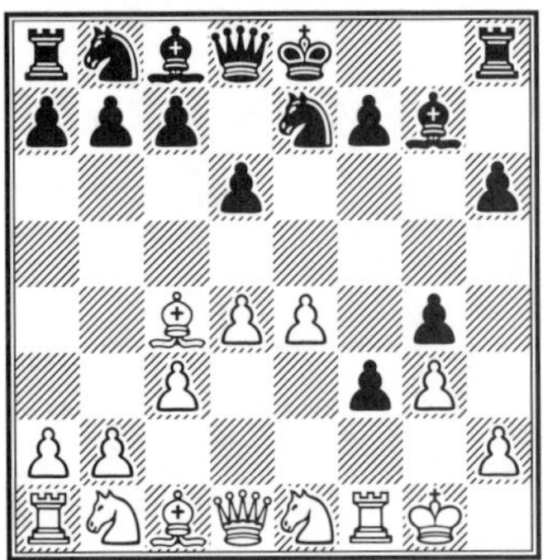

10.h3

10.Nxf3 gxf3 11.Qxf3 and anyone can win.

10...h5 11.Nxf3 gxf3 12.Qxf3 Bxh3 13.Qxf7+ Kd7 14.Qxg7 Bxf1 15.Bxf1 Qg8 16.Bh3+ Kd8 17.Qxg8+ Rxg8 18.Bf4 Nd7 19.Na3

Better was 19.Nd2.

19...Nf6 20.Be6 Rg6 21.Re1 h4 22.e5 Nh5 23.exd6 Nxf4 24.dxe7+ Ke8 25.Bf5 Rxg3+ 26.Kh1 Nd5 27.Nb5 a6 28.Be4 axb5 29.Bxd5 c6 30.Bg2 Rg7 31.d5 Nxe7 32.Rf1 cxd5 33.Bxd5 Rd8 34.c4 bxc4 35.Bxc4 Rd2 36.b4 Re4 37.Bf7+ Ke7 38.Bb3 Ree2 39.Ra1 Rh2+ 40.Kg1 Rdg2+ 41.Kf1 h3, 0-1.

Unfortunately, being a true gentleman, a business mogul, a chess genius, and/or having all the money in the world can't save you when your time has come. Kolisch died of kidney failure (in 1889) at only fifty-two years of age.

The Death of Baron Ignatz Kolisch[1]

By Wilhelm Steinitz

We deeply regret to learn the death of this celebrated master which occurred on the first of May, at the age of fifty-two years. Ignatz Kolisch was born at Pressburg in the year 1837, and made his first appearance in Vienna Chess circles at the age of nineteen. He showed his remarkable genius in contests with masters like Hamppe and Jenay with whom he held his own albeit his youth. In 1859, he made his debut as a European celebrity by defeating Harrwitz in two off-hand games at the Cafe de la Regence, and in the same year he proceeded to England where he encountered successfully some of the strongest English players, notably the late Mr. Barnes who had made the best score against

1 Originally published in a 1889 issue of *Chess Monthly*.

Morphy in off-hand games but whom Kolisch defeated by the extraordinary score of twelve to one.

In 1860, Kolisch won the first prize in the tournament of the British Chess Association held at Cambridge, Stanley taking second place. In the same year his celebrated match with Louis Paulsen for ten games up, which is one of the most remarkable on record, was arranged. Kolisch lost at first five games to one, but with firm tenacity he drew game after game, occasionally adding a win to his score, until at last the match was given up as drawn, Paulsen standing only seven to six with no less than nineteen draws.

In the Bristol Tournament of 1861, the two players met again in the final round for first and second prizes and this time Paulsen won both games. In the same year Kolisch played a match with Anderssen for the first four games, which was won by the Prussian master by the odd game. Sometime after he defeated Shumov at St. Petersburg and Rosenthal decisively in matches. In the year 1867 Kolisch achieved his greatest triumph in the Paris Tournament where he won the chief prize offered by the late Emperor Napoleon III, Winawer coming out second, Steinitz third, and Neumann fourth.

In consequence of this success he challenged Morphy, who was at the time on a visit to Paris, for a match, but the great American master declined the contest, on the ground it is said, that Kolisch had been defeated by Anderssen and Paulsen, who had not taken part in the Paris Tournament, but over whom, he, Morphy, had achieved a decided success. It is much to be deplored that this contest which surely would have been a most interesting one did not come off, and we can only add, according to the views prevalent in our time, that Kolisch was fully entitled to offer his challenge, and provided that he otherwise proposed fair terms, Morphy was bound to accept the challenge or to abdicate any claims to the championship.

After his great victory in Paris, Kolisch retired altogether from direct match and tournament play and only took part as a leader for the Austrian side in the consultation match of two games by telegraph and correspondence between London and Vienna which commenced in 1872, and after a duration of twenty months, ended by one game and a draw in favor of England whose games were conducted by Messrs. Steinitz and [William Norwood] Potter.

For several years before the Paris Tournament and up to the time of his death, Kolisch devoted himself to financial speculations which turned out most successful, and he realized a large fortune especially during his residence in Paris from 1873 to 1880. In the latter year he returned to Vienna and shortly afterward received the Baron title of one of the German principalities. He, however, never relinquished his love for the game which had given him the first start in life, and the chess world is indebted solely to his influence for the organization of the Baden Tournament in 1870.

He was also, along with Baron Rothschild of Vienna, the main promoter of the two Vienna Tournaments of 1873 and 1882, and he liberally contributed to the funds of those tournaments, as well as to the London Chess Congress of 1883, and to other chess institutions of a similar description. As a player Kolisch chiefly belonged during his short and brilliant career to the old school and he was gifted with most remarkable powers of originality, brilliancy and depth of combination that made him one of the most skillful and ingenious generals in the conduct of the kingside attack that ever appeared in the chess arena.

In giving large odds to inferior players he hardly ever had an equal, and some of his games at the odds of a Knight or Rook belong to the finest on record. In his match and tournament play he showed some indications of the circumspective style which tends to hold the balance all over the board and seizes the slightest advantage at any point, but in that respect he was a little inferior to his great opponent Louis Paulsen who may be regarded as one of the first pioneers of the modern school. Kolisch was however, undoubtedly superior to Paulsen in the final tactics on the kingside and for brilliancy and originality of conception combined, his style would only yield the palm to Anderssen of all the opponents whom he encountered in matches. To sum up his record, he must be regarded as inferior to Paulsen as a match player whilst his chief victory in Paris cannot place him on an equal rank as a tournament player with Anderssen who three times in succession, namely: in London 1851, London 1862, and Baden 1870 bore off first honors against much stronger teams than Kolisch encountered in Paris. But it should be stated on the other hand that Kolisch had very little theoretical knowledge and that his original powers chiefly sustained his remarkable success which records his name undoubtedly among the greatest masters of the age.

3

JOHANNES ZUKERTORT

Master of Dynamics

Johannes Zukertort was born September 7, 1842 in Lublin, Poland. It's always interesting to wonder what a person will eventually become—a life in the military perhaps, a businessman, will he struggle to survive, a doctor or lawyer, or will he be an artist of some sort? Anything and everything is possible after that first breath is taken. I suspect though, that few parents would guess, "chess player!"

To be fair, Johannes Zukertort was, at least at first, far more than a chess player. Zukertort himself was quite clear in his early accomplishments: he earned a medical degree in 1866 (other sources say it was 1865) at the University of Breslau; he served in the medical corps in 1866 for the German army; he fought in many battles (including the Franco-Prussian war of 1870-71) and was awarded several medals (including the Order of the Red Eagle and the Iron Cross); he was an accomplished swordsman; and he was highly skilled in games like dominoes, whist, and of course chess. An extremely impressive list, but that wasn't enough! He also claimed that he was from aristocratic descent (his mother was a baroness) and that he was fluent in fourteen languages. One is left wondering if he had a cape and could fly.

Though I admit to being skeptical, I'm sure some of this was reality, some was padded, and some was probably total nonsense. We'll never know—I think it's been verified that he spoke fluent German, Polish, and Yiddish by the age of eleven, and he clearly spoke fluent English later in life, so his talent for languages is obvious. But the mere fact that he made these claims (and in the case of chess, backed it up!) tells us he was a man of great imagination, more than a little ego, a high degree of intelligence, and (as proved by his chess style) an abundance of creativity.

The Building of a Chess Player

Zukertort learned how to play chess at the advanced age of nineteen (in Breslau, Germany, which is now Wrocław, Poland). Like all total beginners, he was terrible (his first tournament was a handicap event where he lost every game, though he got Queen odds in all of them), but like all champions, he refused to stay that way. The great Adolf Anderssen lived in Breslau, and somehow they became friends (If you're serious about chess, hanging out with the world's best player is as good as it gets!). Zukertort claimed to have played 6,000 games against Anderssen (initially he gave Zukertort Knight odds), but whether it was 200 or 6,000, it all amounted to the same thing: vast and quick improvement! When he moved to Berlin in 1867 he was an extremely strong player, though still inferior to Anderssen and Steinitz.

In 1871 Zukertort beat the aging Anderssen 5 to 2 in a match (Anderssen, having won the Baden-Baden tournament in 1870 ahead of Steinitz, proved that he was still a chess powerhouse), but it's still unclear whether it was a serious contest or just games between friends. Nevertheless, the victory gave him worldwide notoriety and that led to an offer (in 1872) from St. George's Chess Club to move to England. It went well, and Zukertort and England proved to be a good match.

Zukertort was still inferior to Steinitz, but he did what he did best: patiently learning and improving.

Tournament and Match Highlights

(1878): Equal first with Winawer whom he defeated in a playoff match 3-1. Ahead of Blackburne, Mackenzie, Bird, Anderssen, and many others.

(1883): First ahead of Steinitz, Blackburne, and Chigorin.

(1880): Match victory over Rosenthal, 12½-6½.

(1881): Match victory over Blackburne, 9½- 4½.

These fine results, and the death of Anderssen in 1879, led to the popular view (after the 1883 London event) that Zukertort was the best player on Earth or, at worst, second to Steinitz. And so, in 1886, these two giants of chess played a match (held in New York, St Louis, and New Orleans) to determine who would become the first official chess champion of the world.

Some might think that a match is a match, and the superior player will win. But there are always other factors involved, and in this case the "other factors" were enormous:

- Steinitz had better nerves than Zukertort (a big plus for Steinitz).
- They played this match at £400 a side (that's around $50,000 today!), and due to their financial circumstances whoever lost would be bankrupt. I would think both players would be completely freaked out. Here superior nerves are a huge advantage.
- Zukertort's health (due to poverty and a sense of isolation) had been sliding for quite a while, and his "interest" in laudanum (a potent tincture containing 10% powdered opium, including the alkaloids morphine and codeine) didn't bode well.

Let's quote Henry Bird:

> Steinitz and Zukertort actually played for £400 a side, a sum neither party could afford to lose, even thought they could tax their chess supporters for it. Any chance of a return match which Zukertort so much desired, became impossible... There is too much reason to fear that the result of this match, and Zukertort's sensitiveness to supposed coolness towards him afterwards, mainly contributed to cause his premature break up and untimely end. I always advised him before the match, in justice to himself, to stipulate for a time limit of twenty or twenty-five moves an hour, and not to play for more than £100 a side, the previous extreme maximum for the greatest matches, happy for him if he had observed this rule; as he himself admitted.

As if the script had been written ahead of time, Zukertort took a commanding 4-1 lead, and then Steinitz cast off the heebie-jeebies and started to play better while poor Zukertort completely collapsed. The final score was 10-5 with five draws in favor of Steinitz.

Zukertort was a great player when serious dynamic possibilities were present, but he was relatively weak when subtle and/or slow strategy was called for.

On the other hand, give Zukertort dynamics (the aggressive potential in any given position or move) and he was an untamable storm! Here's an example:

Johannes Zukertort vs. Joseph Blackburne, London 1883

1.c4 e6 2.e3 Nf6 3.Nf3 b6 4.Be2 Bb7 5.0-0 d5 6.d4 Bd6 7.Nc3 0-0 8.b3 Nbd7 9.Bb2 Qe7 10.Nb5 Ne4 11.Nxd6 cxd6 12.Nd2 Ndf6 13.f3 Nxd2 14.Qxd2 dxc4 15.Bxc4 d5 16.Bd3 Rfc8 17.Rae1 Rc7 18.e4 Rac8 19.e5 Ne8 20.f4 g6 21.Re3 f5 22.exf6 Nxf6 23.f5 Ne4 24.Bxe4 dxe4 25.fxg6 Rc2 26.gxh7+ Kh8

26...Kg7 27.h8=Q+! Kxh8 28.Rh3+ Kg8 29.Qh6 forces mate since 29...Qg7 is met by 30.Qxe6+, and 29...Rxg2+ loses to 30.Kh1! Rxh2+ 31.Rxh2 e3+ 32.d5! Bxd5+ 33.Kg1.

27.d5+ e5

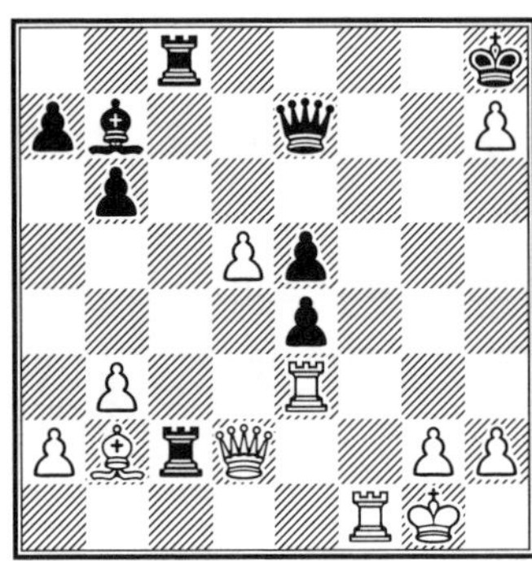

27...Rxb2 28.Qxb2+ e5 29.Rxe4 is easy for White.

28.Qb4!! R8c5

28...Qxb4 29.Bxe5+ Kxh7 30.Rh3+! Kg6 31.Rf6+ Kg5 32.Rg3+ Kh5 33.Rf5+ Kh6 34.Bf4+ Kh7 35.Rh5 mate; 28...Re8 29.Rf8+ Qxf8 30.Bxe5+ Qg7 31.Bxg7+ Kxg7 32.Qd6 and Black is doomed.

29.Rf8+! Kxh7

29...Qxf8 30.Bxe5+.

30.Qxe4+ Kg7 31.Rg8+!

The actual game went 31.Bxe5+ which is also a game ender: 31...Kxf8 32.Bg7+ Kg8 (32...Qxg7 33.Qe8 mate) 33.Qxe7.

31...Kxg8 32.Qg6+ Qg7 33.Qe8+ Qf8 34.Rg3+ Kh7 35.Qg6+ Kh8 36.Bxe5+

36.Qh5+ and 36.Rh3+ also mate.

36...Qg7 37.Qxg7, 1-0.

Johannes Zukertort vs. Vincenz Hruby, Vienna 1882

1.c4 e6 2.e3 Nf6 3.Nf3 d5 4.d4 b6 5.Be2 Bb7 6.0-0 Be7 7.Nc3 0-0 8.Bd2 c5 9.Rc1 cxd4 10.Nxd4 Nc6 11.Nxc6 Bxc6 12.Bf3 Rc8 13.cxd5 Nxd5 14.Nxd5 Bxd5 15.Rxc8 Qxc8 16.Bxd5 exd5 17.Bc3 Rd8 18.Qa4 Qd7 19.Qa6 Bd6 20.Rd1 f6 21.g3 Be5 22.Bd4 h5 23.Qe2 Qf5 24.Bxe5

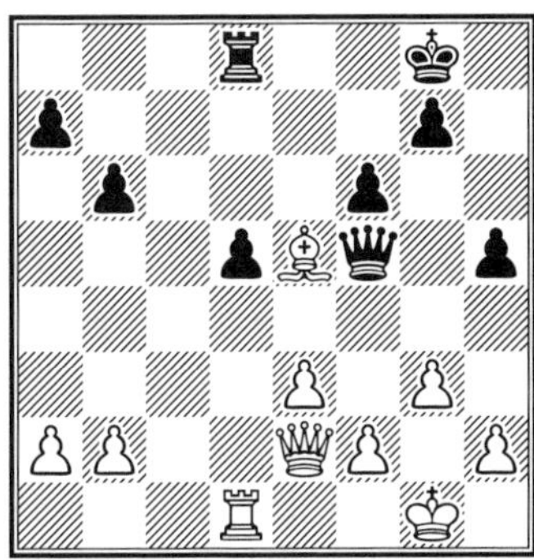

24... fxe5?!

Black should have tried 24...Qxe5 though the defense is far from easy after 25.Rd4 when a buildup like Qd1 followed by e3-e4 is very annoying.

25.e4 Qf7 26.exd5 Rxd5 27.Rxd5 Qxd5 28.Qxh5 Qd4 29.Qe2 Kf7 30.Kg2 Ke6 31.h4 Qd5+ 32.Qf3 Qxa2 33.Qg4+ Kf7 34.Qf5+ Kg8 35.Qxe5 and White, who is now a pawn up, went on to win the game.

Johannes Zukertort (blindfolded) vs. Siegmund Oppler, Posen 1862

1.e4 e5 2.Nf3 Nc6 3.Bc4 Bc5 4.b4 Bb6 5.b5 Na5 6.Nxe5 Nh6 7.d4 d6 8.Bxh6 dxe5 9.Bxg7 Rg8 10.Bxf7+ Kxf7 11.Bxe5 Qh4 12.Qf3+ Ke8 13.Bg3 Qg5 14.d5 Bd4 15.c3 Bf6 16.Nd2 Bg4 17.Qd3 c6 18.bxc6 bxc6 19.f4 Qg7 20.e5 Qe7 21.d6 Qe6 22.0-0 Bg7 23.f5 Qf7 24.e6 Qf6 25.Ne4 Qh6 26.d7+ Kd8

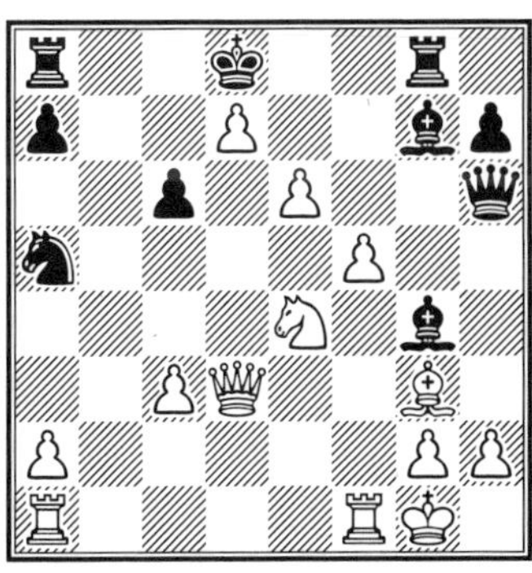

27.Bc7+! Kxc7 28.Qd6+ Kb7

28...Kd8 29.e7 mate.

29.Rab1+

Of course, 29.Rfb1+ is the same as 29.Rab1+, while 29.Qb4+ is also mate after 29...Kc7 30.Qxa5+ Kb7 and now White has to choose which Rook should lower the boom.

29...Ka6

29...Nb3 30.Rxb3+ Ka6 31.Qa3 mate.

30.Nc5, 1-0.

Adolf Anderssen vs. Johannes Zukertort, Paris 1878

1.e4 e5 2.Nf3 Nc6 3.Bb5 Nf6 4.d3 d6 5.Bxc6+ bxc6 6.Nc3 g6 7.h3 Bg7 8.Be3 c5 9.g4 h5 10.g5 Ng8 11.Ne2 Ne7 12.c3 Be6 13.Nd2 Qd7 14.h4 Qb5 15.Qc2 Rb8 16.b3 Qa5 17.f3 0-0 18.Rd1 Rfd8 19.0-0 Rd7 20.d4 cxd4 21.cxd4 Qb6 22.Qd3 exd4 23.Nxd4 Bxd4 24.Bxd4 c5 25.Bf2 Nc6 26.f4 d5 27.Qb1 d4 28.f5 gxf5 29.exf5 Bd5 30.Ne4 Ne5 31.Bg3 Ng4 32.Rf4 Bxe4 33.Qxe4 Qb7 34.f6 Ne3 36.Rd2 Qxe4 36.Rxe4 Rbd8 37.Bf2 Nd5 38.Re5 a5 39.Rc2 d3 40.Rd2 Nc3 41.Re1 Rd5 42.Kg2 Kh7 43.Bg3 a4 44.Bc7 R8d7 45.Ba5 Ne2 46.Rdd1 axb3 47.axb3

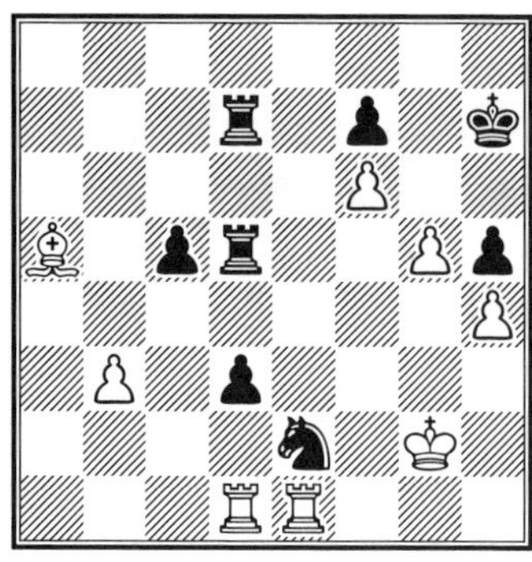

47...c4! 48.Kf2

48.Bb4 c3 was also easy for Black.

48...Rf5+

Also winning was 48...Rxa5 49.Rxe2 Rf5+ 50.Ke1 c3.

49.Kg2

49.Ke3 Rxa5.

49...Rxa5, 0-1.

4

SIEGBERT TARRASCH

Renaissance Man

Siegbert Tarrasch was born in Germany, March 5, 1862. Parents always dream that their children would be special, but Tarrasch really was! He excelled in school and, after that (in 1880), he moved to Halle, studied medicine, and opened up his own flourishing, medical practice. He loved medicine, he loved helping his patients, but he also had another love (other than his family)—chess.

Like many people, Tarrasch had a job and played chess whenever he could. But unlike other casual chess players Tarrasch was one of the best in the world. When 1889 rolled around Tarrasch *was* the best player in the world! He dominated, winning four powerful tournaments in Breslau 1889, Manchester 1890, Dresden 1892, and Leipzig 1894. And then, when everyone thought the dream would continue forever, a man named Emanuel Lasker turned everything upside down by beating Steinitz in a 1894 match, and taking the World Championship.

However, Tarrasch was still amazing—he was the second best player in the world. Okay, Tarrasch still thought he was the best in the world. He was also a great chess writer, using Steinitz's ideas but making them easier to understand to the masses (control the center, bishop pair, space, and mobility).

But time goes by and in the early 1900s powerful new players like Rubinstein, Nimzowitsch, Capablanca, and Alekhine started to take over.

I must say that, in the legendary St. Petersburg 1914 chess tournament (this was the preliminaries), Tarrasch did very well. Capablanca was first (8 points), Lasker (who was very rusty) and Tarrasch were tied (6½), followed by Alekhine and Marshall (6).

During the final double-round event, Lasker managed to toss away his cobwebs and magnificently win first (with 13½), Capablanca was second (13), Alekhine third (10), Tarrasch was forth (8½), and Marshall fifth (8).

Tarrasch was still playing tournaments through 1932 (quite well!). However the young bucks (mentioned above) were too much for him. He died in 1934.

Siegbert Tarrasch vs. Dr. Josef Noa, Hamburg 1885

1.e4 e6 2.d4 d5 3.Nc3 Nf6 4.e5 Nfd7 5.Nce2 c5 6.c3 Nc6 7.f4 cxd4 8.cxd4 Bb4+ 9.Bd2 Qb6 10.Nf3 0-0 11.Bxb4 Qxb4+ 12.Qd2 Nb6 13.Nc3 Rd8 14.Nb5 Bd7 15.Nd6 Rab8 16.Rc1 Qxd2+ 17.Kxd2 Nc8 18.Nb5 a6 19.Nc3 N8e7 20.Bd3 Rbc8 21.b3 Nb4 22.a3 Nbc6 23.b4 h6 24.h4 Nb8 25.Ke3 Rc7 26.Rc2 Rdc8 27.Rhc1 Kf8 28.g4 Be8 29.Nd2 Nd7 30.Nb3 Nb6 31.Nc5 Nc4+

This game shows Tarrasch's endgame and tactic skills.

32.Bxc4 dxc4

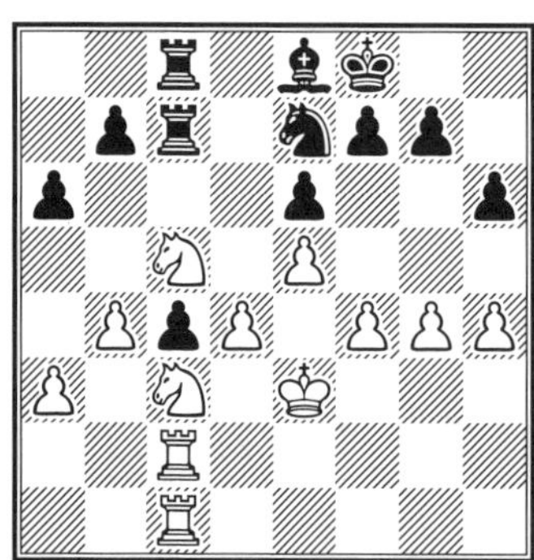

33.N5e4 b5 34.Nd6 Rb8 35.f5 Bd7 36.Rf2 Nd5+ 37.Nxd5 exd5 38.g5 h5 39.Rcf1 Kg8 40.g6 f6 41.Re2 Bc6 42.Rfe1 Rd8 43.Kf4 fxe5+ 44.Rxe5! Kf8

44…Rxd6 45.Re8+ Bxe8 46.Rxe8 mate.

45.Nf7 Re8 46.Ng5 Rce7??

46...Rxe5 47.dxe5 Re7 48.f6 gxf6 49.exf6 Rxe1 50.Nh7+ Ke8 51.f7+ Kd7 52.f8=Q Rf1+ 53.Kg5 Rxf8 54.Nxf8+ Ke7 55.g7 Kf7 56.Kh6 Kg8 57.Ng6.

47.Nh7+, 1-0.

It's a forced mate: 47…Kg8 48.Rxe7 Rc8 49.f6 Rf8 50.Nxf8 Kh8 51.fxg7+ Kg8 52.Nh7 Bd7 53.Nf6 mate.

Siegbert Tarrasch vs. Isidor Gunsberg, Frankfort 1887

1.e4 e6 2.d4 d5 3.Nc3 dxe4 4.Nxe4 Nf6 5.Bd3 Nbd7 6.Be3 Nxe4 7.Bxe4 Nf6 8.Bd3 Bd7 9.Nf3 Bd6 10.0-0 Ng4 11.Bg5 f6 12.Bd2 Qe7 13.h3 Nh6 14.c4 c6 15.b4 0-0-0 16.Re1 Bxb4 17.Rb1 Bxd2 18.Qxd2 Kb8 19.c5 Bc8 20.Rb3 Qc7 21.Reb1 Ka8 22.Rb6 e5 23.R1b4 Rhe8 24.dxe5 fxe5 25.Ra4 e4 26.Qa5 Qb8 27.Bxe4 Bf5

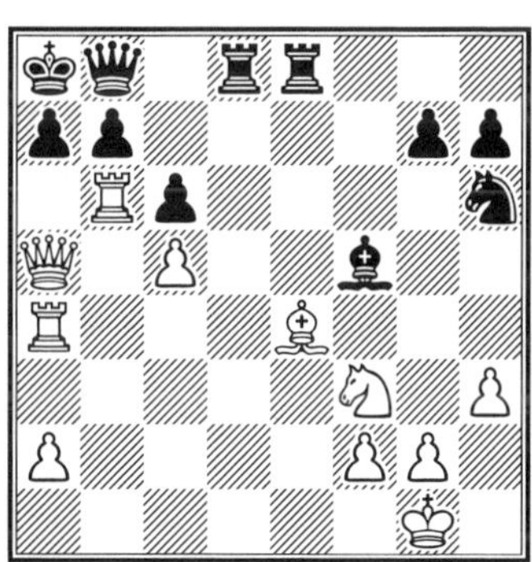

28.Ra6!

The only move, but it wins!

28…Rd1+ 29.Ne1 Rxe1+ 30.Qxe1 Bxe4

30...Rxe4 31.Rxe4 bxa6 32.Re8 Bc8 33.Qe4 Qb7 34.g4 Qd7 35.Re7 Qd5 36.Qxd5 cxd5 37.Rxg7.

31.Rxe4 Rxe4 32.Qxe4 bxa6 33.Qxc6+ Qb7 34.Qe8+ Qb8 35.Qe4+ Qb7 36.c6 Qc7 37.Qe8+ Qb8 38.Qd7 Qb1+ 39.Kh2 Nf5 40.c7, 1-0.

Louis Paulsen vs. Siegbert Tarrasch, Nuremberg 1888

1.e4 e6 2.d4 d5 3.e5 c5 4.c3 Nc6 5.Nf3 Qb6 6.Bd3 cxd4 7.cxd4 Bd7 8.Be2 Nge7 9.b3 Nf5 10.Bb2 Bb4+ 11.Kf1 Be7

11...0-0 12.g4 Nh6 13.Rg1 f6 14.exf6 Rxf6 15.g5 Rxf3! 16.Bxf3 Nf5.

12.g3 a5 13.a4 Rc8 14.Bb5 Nb4 15.Bxd7+ Kxd7 16.Nc3 Nc6 17.Nb5 Na7 18.Nxa7 Qxa7 19.Qd3 Qa6!

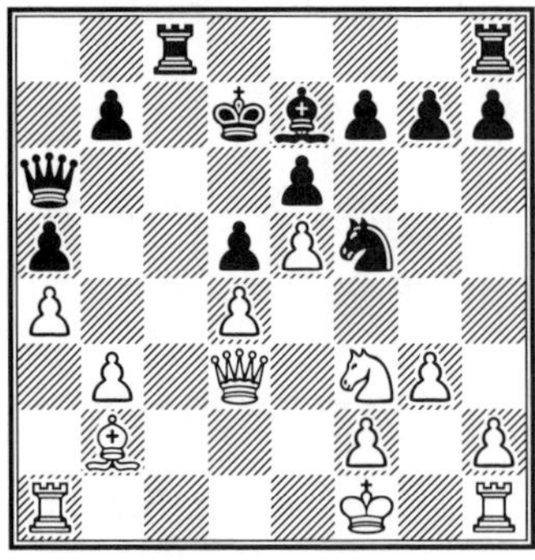

So far we have seen Tarrasch's tactical skills. Now let's look at Black's positional skills.

20.Qxa6 bxa6 21.Kg2 Rc2 22.Bc1 Rb8 23.Rb1 Rc3 24.Bd2 Rcxb3 25.Rxb3 Rxb3 26.Bxa5 Rb2 27.Bd2 Bb4 28.Bf4 h6 29.g4 Ne7 30.Ra1 Nc6 31.Bc1 Rc2 32.Ba3 Rc4 33.Bb2 Bc3 34.Bxc3 Rxc3 35.Rb1 Kc7 36.g5 Rc4 37.gxh6 gxh6 38.a5 Ra4 39.Kg3 Rxa5 40.Kg4 Ra3 41.Rd1 Rb3 42.h4 Ne7 43.Ne1 Nf5 44.Nd3 a5 45.Nc5 Rc3 46.Rb1 Nxd4 47.Na6+ Kd8 48.Rb8+ Rc8 49.Rb7 Ke8 50.Nc7+ Kf8 51.Nb5 Nxb5 52.Rxb5 Ra8 53.f4 a4 54.Rb1 a3 55.f5 a2 56.Ra1 Ra4+ 57.Kh5 Kg7 58.fxe6 fxe6 59.Rg1+ Kh8 60.Ra1 Kh7 61.Rg1 a1=Q 62.Rg7+ Kh8, 0-1.

Johannes Minckwitz vs. Siegbert Tarrasch, Leipzig 1888

1.e4 e6 2.d4 d5 3.exd5 exd5 4.Nf3 Nf6 5.Bd3 Bd6 6.0-0 0-0 7.Nc3 c6 8.Ne2 Qc7 9.Ng3 Bg4 10.h3 Be6 11.Nf5 Bxf5 12.Bxf5 Nbd7 13.Bg5 Ne4 14.Bxd7 Qxd7 15.Be3 f5 16.Qd3 Rae8 17.Rae1 h6 18.Nh2 Qc7 19.Nf3 Qf7 20.Rc1 b5 21.b3 g5 22.c4 bxc4 23.bxc4 g4!

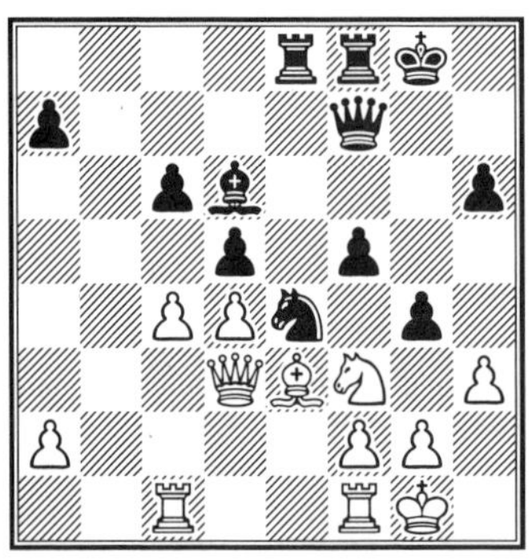

24.hxg4

24.Ne5 Bxe5 25.dxe5 gxh3 26.Bf4 hxg2 27.Kxg2 Qg6+ 28.Kh2 Qh5+ 29.Qh3 Qxh3+ 30.Kxh3 d4 31.f3 Nc5 32.Rcd1 Rf7 33.Rh1 (33.Rxd4 Ne6 wins) 33...Kh7 34.Kg3 Re6 35.Rxd4 Rg6+ 36.Kf2 Ne6 winning.

24...fxg4 25.Ne5

25.Nd2 Qh5 26.g3 Bxg3 27.fxg3 Nxg3.

25...Qh5! 26.cxd5 Bxe5 27.dxe5 g3 28.fxg3 Nxg3 29.Rf3 Rxf3 30.gxf3 Rf8 31.f4 Ne2+! 32.Kf2 Nxf4 33.Rg1+ Kh8 34.Bxf4 Rxf4+ 35.Ke1 Qxe5+, 0-1.

Theodor von Scheve vs. Siegbert Tarrasch, Dresden 1892

1.d4 d5 2.Nf3 c5 3.c3 e6 4.Bf4 Qb6 5.Qc2 cxd4 6.cxd4 Nc6 7.e3 Bd7 8.Nc3 Rc8 9.Be2 Nf6 10.0-0 Be7 11.a3 Nh5 12.Bg3 Nxg3 13.hxg3 0-0 14.Bd3 g6 15.Kh2 Na5 16.Ne5 Be8 17.Rh1 f6 18.Nf3 Nc4 19.Rab1 Qa5 20.Bxc4 Rxc4 21.Qd2 Bf7 22.Ra1 Rfc8 23.g4 b6 24.g3

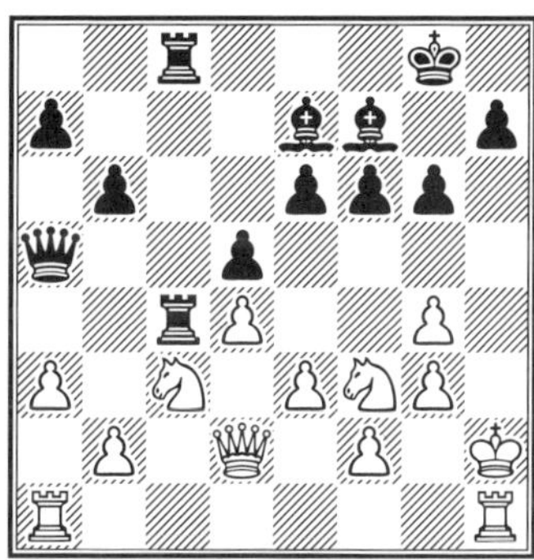

Have a look at a smooth, positional kill. Note that Black has two Bishops and will soon take over the queenside too.

24...g5!

An important move. Now Black's f7-Bishop can move to g6 where it rules the b1-h7 diagonal.

However, if Black didn't play 24...g5, White would play g4-g5. Why would g4-g5 be good? Because White would block Black's f7-Bishop and white's kingside Knight can land on the e5 hole.

25.Ng1?!

Better moves were 25.Qe2 or 25.Qd3 or 25.Qe1, though Black would still be on top.

25...b5 26.Nge2 Qb6 27.Kg2 a5 28.Ra2?

This can't be good! However, there was a reason (good or bad): by playing Ra2 it will "scare" Black to play ...b5-b4 when axb4 opens up the a-line.

28…Qc6

White is already busted.

29.Qd1

Since White played 28.Ra2, he might have continued with 29.Rha1.

29…Bg6

It's clear that Black is winning since his two Bishops and pressure on the queenside is too much for White to deal with.

30.Qa1

White decided to double on the a-line, hoping that Black would play 30…b4. Unfortunately, Black played 30…b4 anyway and crushed White.

30…b4 31.axb4 axb4 32.Ra6 Qe8!

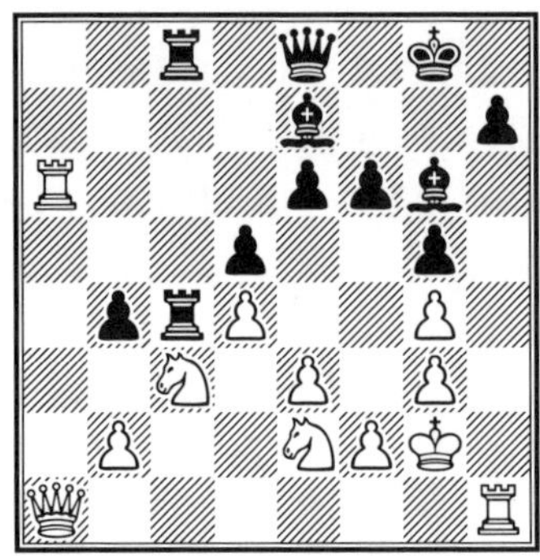

33.Rxe6

33.Nd1 doesn't help: 33…Be4+ 34.f3 Bd3. Anyway, after 33.Rxe6 Black rolled over poor von Scheve.

33…bxc3 34.Nxc3 Qd7 35.Rb6 Bd8 36.Ra6 Qxg4 37.f3 Qf5 38.e4 dxe4 39.fxe4 Qg4 40.Qe1 Rxd4 41.Ra7

After this, various mates float about. You might want to see if you can find them.

41…Bxe4+ 42.Kg1 Bb6, 0-1.

You can learn a lot from this positional game.

Emanuel Schiffers vs. Siegbert Tarrasch, Leipzig 1894

1.e4 d5 2.exd5 Qxd5 3.Nc3 Qa5 4.d4 Nf6 5.Bd3 Bg4 6.f3 Bh5 7.Nge2 c6 8.0-0 e6 9.Ne4 Nbd7 10.Bf4 Nxe4 11.fxe4 Bg6 12.c3 e5 13.b4 Qc7 14.Bg3 Bd6 15.Qc2 0-0 16.a4 Rfe8 17.Rae1 a5!

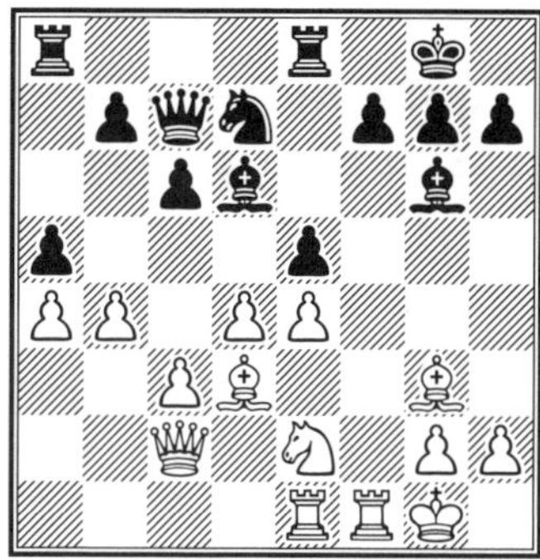

This weakens White's a4-pawn (making it a weakness) and if 18.b5 then 18...c5 is very strong. After 17...a5 White is in serious trouble. Another good move was 17...Nf6.

18.Qb3 axb4 19.cxb4 Nf6

Tarrasch once said: "Chess is a terrible game. If you have no center, your opponent has a freer position. If you do have a center, then you really have something to worry about!"

20.dxe5 Bxe5

Now Black owns the e5-square, while the a4-pawn and e4-pawn are weak.

21.Nf4 Rad8

Another move is 21...Bxe4! 22.Nh5 Nxh5 23.Bxe5 Rxe5 24.Rxe4 Nf6 25.Rxe5 Qxe5 and Black is much better due to the extra pawn.

22.Nxg6 hxg6 23.Bc4 Bxg3 24.hxg3

24.Qxg3 Qxg3 25.hxg3 Rd4 26.e5 Rxc4 27.exf6 Rxe1 28.Rxe1 Rxb4 and Black should win.

24...Re5 25.a5

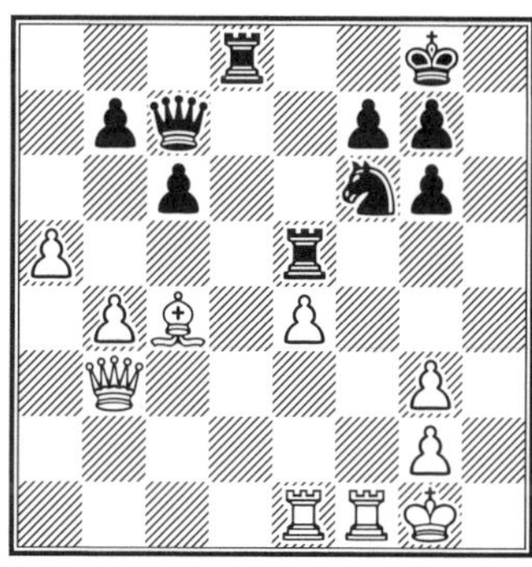

25...b5!

Looking at this move, you would think that it wasn't doing much. However, it really is a monster of a move that wins the game! Why is 25...b5 so good? Because ...b5 opens up the g1-a7 diagonal when white's King will be in serious trouble.

26.axb6

26.Bd3 Qa7+ 27.Rf2 Ng4, 0-1.

26...Qxb6+ 27.Qe3 Qxb4 28.Ba2 Ng4 29.Rxf7 Kh7

Getting off the a2-g8 diagonal.

30.Qe2 Qd4+, 0-1.

31.Rf2 Rf8 (31...Rxe4 is another knockout) 32.Rf1 Rxf2 33.Rxf2 Re4 34.Qd2 Qxd2 35.Rxd2 Re1 mate.

Siegbert Tarrasch vs. Harry Pillsbury, Budapest 1896

1.e4 e5 2.Nf3 Nc6 3.Bb5 Nf6 4.0-0 Nxe4 5.d4 Nd6 6.dxe5 Nxb5 7.a4 d6 8.axb5 Nxe5 9.Re1 Be7 10.Nxe5 dxe5 11.Qxd8+ Kxd8 12.Rxe5 Bd6 13.Re2 Bf5 14.Be3 Re8 15.Nc3 b6 16.Rd2 Kc8

What is White's best move, and is White crushing Black, or is White just a bit better, or is Black better, or is Black in trouble? Good luck!

17.Bxb6!

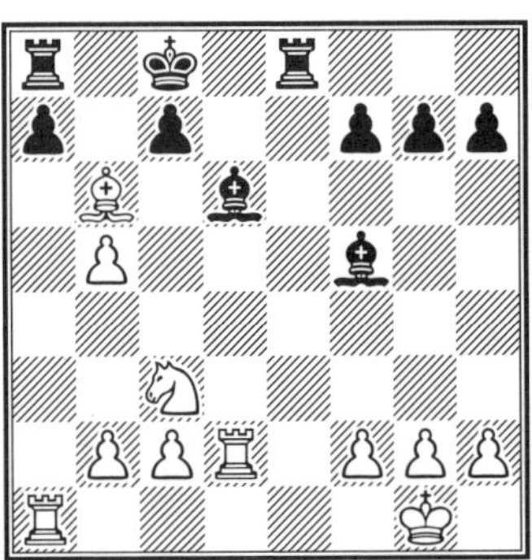

A great move, but White only gets a small plus. However, that's typical; you play the best moves and see if your opponent can hold on.

17...Bxh2+

Better was 17...Ba3!, which is a hard move to see! 18.bxa3 (18.Ba5 Bxb2 19.Rad1 Bxc3 20.Bxc3 and the game should end in a draw thanks to the opposite bishops.) 18...axb6 19.a4 with just a little bit for White.

18.Kxh2 cxb6 19.Nd5 Kb7

And now.

20.Nb4

Leaves White with a small and annoying advantage. In the actual game 20.Ne3 Be6 when the game is equal, but Tarrasch managed to outplay Pillsbury and Tarrasch won anyway.

Siegbert Tarrasch vs. Simon Alapin, Marseille 1903

1.e4 e6 2.d4 d5 3.Nc3 dxe4 4.Nxe4 Bd7 5.Nf3 Bc6 6.Bd3 Nf6 7.Ng3 h5 8.Qe2 h4 9.Ne4 h3 10.g3 Qd5 11.c4 Qh5? 12.d5!

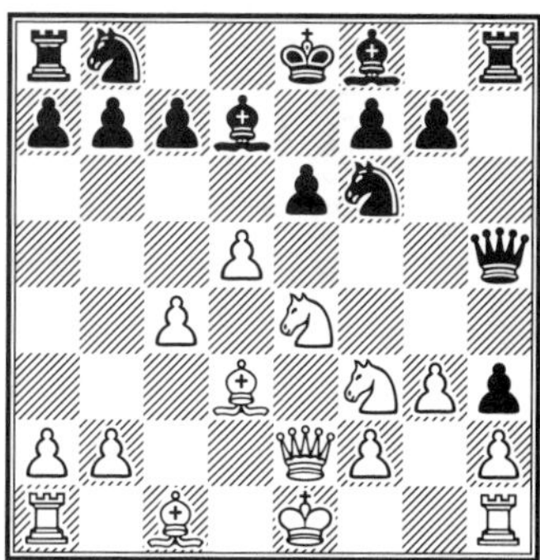

White's pieces are better and central pawns also help. But if you don't make use of it, then you're opponent can turn the table.

12...Bd7?

12...Bb4+ 13.Kf1 Ng4 14.Bf4 e5 15.Neg5 etc.

13.g4!

Black realizes that his King and Queen are in trouble.

13...Nxg4

13...Qxg4 14.Rg1 Qh5 15.Rg5 Qh6 16.Re5 Qg6 17.Nxf6+ Qxf6 18.Bg5 and black's Queen is lost.

14.Ng3 Bb4+ 15.Kf1 Nxh2+ 16.Rxh2 Qg4 17.Bf5, 1-0.

Once again, black's Queen will die.

In the 1908 World Championship match (Emanuel Lasker vs. Siegbert Tarrasch), the players were introduced and Tarrasch clicked his heels, bowed stiffly, and said, "To you, Dr. Lasker, I have only three words, 'check and mate.'" Then he left the room.

Emanuel Lasker vs. Siegbert Tarrasch, World Championship (3) 1908

1.e4 e5 2.Nf3 Nc6 3.Bb5 a6 4.Ba4 Nf6 5.0-0 Be7 6.Re1 b5 7.Bb3 d6 8.c3 Na5 9.Bc2 c5 10.d4 Qc7 11.Nbd2 Nc6 12.h3 0-0 13.Nf1 cxd4 14.cxd4 Nxd4 15.Nxd4 exd4 16.Ng3 Nd7 17.Bb3 Qb6 18.Nf5 Bf6 19.Bf4 Ne5 20.Bd5 Ra7 21.Qb3 Rc7 22.g4

Lasker played 22.g4? allowing Tarrasch to take over the game.

22...g6 23.Nh6+ Kg7 24.g5 Bd8 25.Qg3

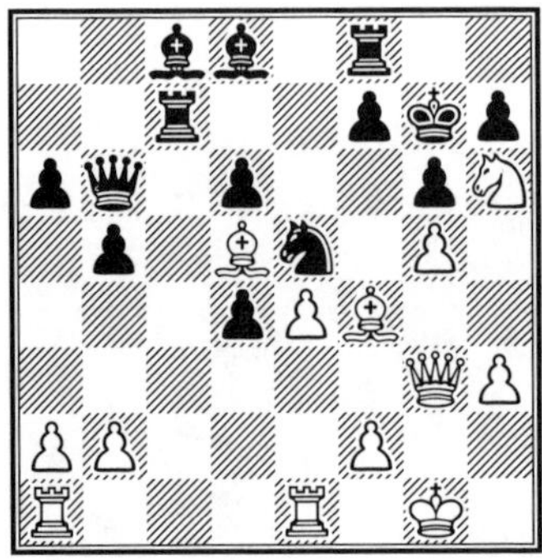

25...f6 26.Nf5+?! Kh8 27.Nh4 fxg5 28.Bxg5 Bxg5 29.Qxg5 d3

29...Rc2 was also good.

30.Kh1 Rc2

And White should have resigned. However, Lasker fights to the end, so here it is:

31.Re3 Rfxf2 32.Ng2 d2 33.Rg1 Rc1 34.Qe7 Rxg1+ 35.Kxg1 d1Q+ 36.Kxf2 Qf3+ 37.Ke1 Qa5+

I am sure that Lasker, and the spectators, were enjoying the splatter.

38.Rc3 Bxh3 39.Qxd6 Qaxc3+

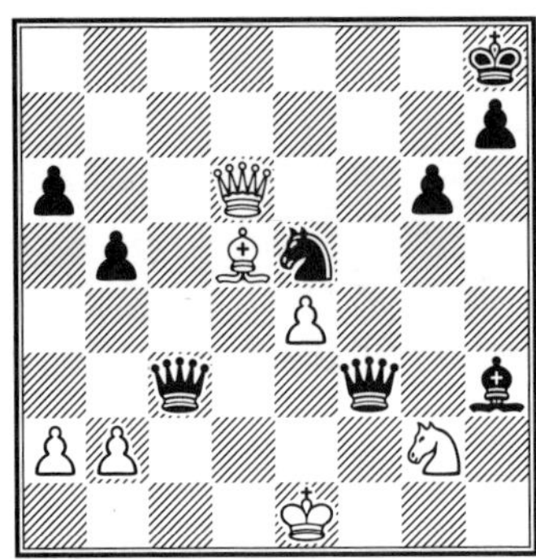

You don't see something like this very often.

40.bxc3 Qxc3+ 41.Ke2 Qc2+ 42.Ke3 Qd3+ 43.Kf4 g5+ 44.Kxg5 Nf7+, 0-1.

The match ended with 8 wins for Lasker, 3 wins for Tarrasch, and 5 draws.

Tarrasch was the best player in the world for a few years (and continued to be second best for quite a while), but it's never forever. There is always a young, energetic player somewhere who will rule the chess world and be anointed as the next chess god.

5

WILHELM STEINITZ

Behold the Austrian Morphy!

Whenever chess players get together and talk about top players of the past, someone will open their mouth and spew out nonsense about the first World Champion. My favorite is: "If Steinitz were playing today he wouldn't even have a 2200 rating."

Really?

From 1866 to 1894, this guy was far stronger than any other player who ever lived (with the exception of Morphy, though Morphy never played anyone as strong as Steinitz!). After 1894, until his death in 1900, he ran into several debilitating problems: old age, mental and physical illness, and new players who learned how to play proper chess by following Steinitz's teachings.

Looking at his prime games, Steinitz was a fantastic tactician (modern high grandmaster level), he had an amazingly creative mind, and his understanding of positional chess was, in the 1870s, light-years ahead of everyone.

Steinitz, born in 1836, learned to play chess at age twelve. He fell in love with the game and by 1861 he was the Vienna City champion. Due to his desire to attack, attack, and attack some more, he was nicknamed "the Austrian Morphy."

Following are three games with Carl Hamppe, who was Vienna's finest player before Steinitz became boss. First I will show you an absolutely brilliant game played by Mr. Hamppe and Mr. Meitner known as the Immortal Draw:

Carl Hamppe vs. Philipp Meitner, Vienna 1870

1.e4 e5 2.Nc3 Bc5 3.Na4 Bxf2+ 4.Kxf2 Qh4+ 5.Ke3 Qf4+ 6.Kd3 d5 7.Kc3 Qxe4 8.Kb3 Na6 9.a3 Qxa4+!! 10.Kxa4 Nc5+ 11.Kb4 a5+ 12.Kxc5

12.Kc3 d4+ 13.Kc4 b6 14.c3 Be6+ 15.Kb5 Ne7 16.Qf3 Kd7 17.Bc4 c6+ 18.Qxc6+ (18.Kxb6 Na4+ 19.Kb7 Rhb8 mate) 18...Nxc6 19.Bxe6+ fxe6 20.Kc4 a4 21.b4 axb3 22.a4 Kd6 23.Ba3 b5+ 24.axb5 Ra4+ 25.Bb4 Na5 mate.

12...Ne7

Threatening ...b6+ followed by ...Bd7 mate.

13.Bb5+ Kd8

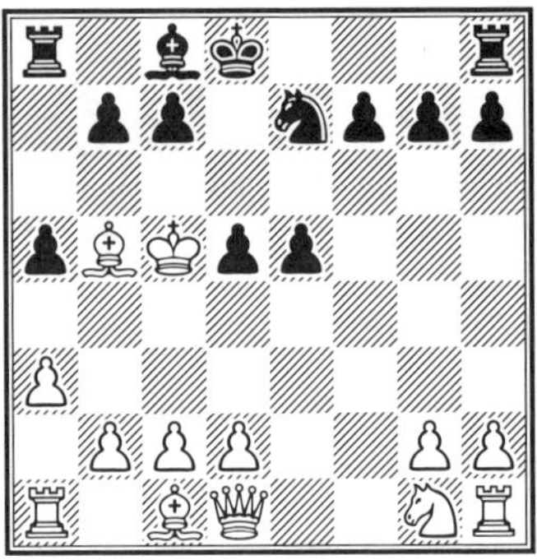

14.Bc6!! b6+

14...bxc6?? and white's King is suddenly safe.

15.Kb5 Nxc6 16.Kxc6 Bb7+! 17.Kb5

17.Kxb7?? Kd7! 18.Qg4+ Kd6! and ...Rhb8 will mate white's King.

17...Ba6+ 18.Kc6

18.Ka4?? Bc4! followed by ...b5 mate.

18...Bb7+ ½-½.

One might think that Carl Hamppe was a chess powerhouse, but look a the following games and you'll see a young Steinitz rip Hamppe to bits.

Carl Hamppe vs. Wilhelm Steinitz, Vienna 1859

1.e4 e5 2.Nc3 Nf6 3.f4 d5 4.exd5 Nd5 5.fxe5 Nxc3 6.bxc3 Qh4+ 7.Ke2 Bg4+ 8.Nf3 Nc6 9.d4 0-0-0 10.Bd2 Bf3+ 11.gxf3

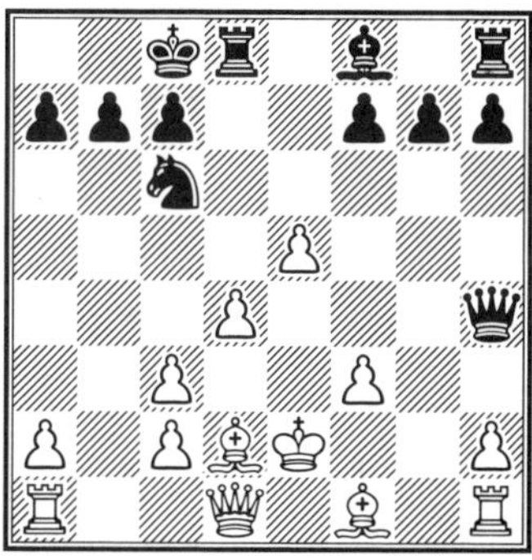

11...Nxe5 12.dxe5 Bc5 13.Qe1 Qc4+ 14.Kd1 Qxc3 15.Rb1 Qxf3+ 16.Qe2 Rxd2 17.Kd2 Rd8+ 18.Kc1 Ba3+ 19.Rb2 Qc3 20.Bh3+ Kb8 21.Qb5 Qd2+ 22.Kb1 Qd1+ 23.Rxd1 Rxd1, 0-1.

Carl Hamppe vs. Wilhelm Steinitz, Vienna 1860

1.e4 e5 2.Nc3 Nc6 3.Bc4 Bc5 4.d3 d6 5.Nge2 Be6 6.0-0 Nf6 7.Bg5 Qd7 8.Nd5 Bxd5 9.exd5 Ne7 10.Nc3 Bd4 11.Bxf6 gxf6 12.Ne4 Qf5 13.Bb5+ Kf8 14.c3 Bb6 15.a4 a5 16.Bc4 Qg6 17.Kh1 f5 18.Nd2 f4 19.Ne4 f5 20.Nd2 h5 21.Qf3 Kg7 22.d4 Qg4 23.dxe5 dxe5 24.Rae1 Ng6 25.Ba2 e4 26.Qh3 f3 27.Nc4 Nf4 28.Qxg4+ hxg4 29.gxf3

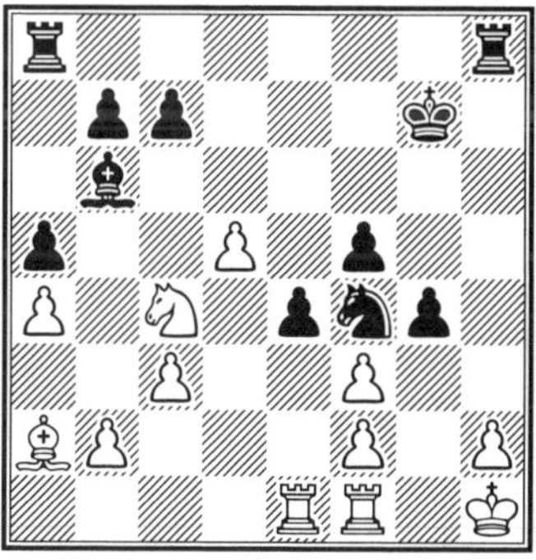

29...g3! 30.fxg3

30.Nxb6 Rxh2+ 31.Kg1 Nh3 mate.

30...Rxh2+! 31.Kxh2 Rh8, 0-1.

Steinitz again plays Mr. Meitner (the other player who made the Immortal Draw come true). Steinitz eviscerates his opponent:

Wilhelm Steinitz vs. Philipp Meitner, Vienna 1860

1.e4 e5 2.Nf3 Nc6 3.d4 exd4 4.Bc4 Bc5 5.0-0 Nf6 6.e5 d5 7.exf6 dxc4 8.Re1+ Be6 9.Ng5 Qd5 10.Nc3 Qf5 11.g4 Qxf6 12.Nd5 Qd8 13.Rxe6+ fxe6 14.Nxe6 Qd7 15.Qe2 Be7 16.Ndxc7 Kf7 17.Qxc4 Ne5 18.Qb3 Qd6 19.f4 Nxg4 20.Ng5+ Kg6 21.Qd3+ Kh5 22.Qh3+ Kg6 23.Qxg4

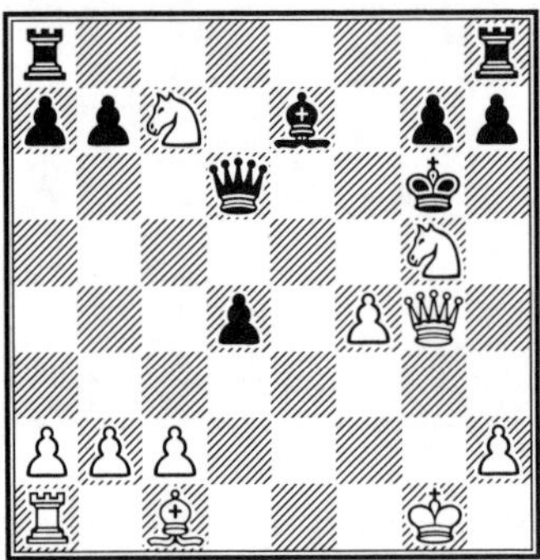

Another bomb is 23.f5+ Kxf5 24.Qd3+ Kf6 25.Ne4+.

23...Qb6 24.Nge6+ Kf6 25.Qg5 Kf7 26.Qg7, 1-0.

Wilhelm Steinitz vs. Max Lange, Vienna match 1860

1.e4 e5 2.Nf3 Nc6 3.d4 exd4 4.Bc4 Qe7 5.0-0 Ne5 6.Nxe5 Qxe5 7.c3 c5 8.f4 Qf6 9.e5 Qb6 10.Kh1 Be7 11.f5 d5 12.Bxd5 Nh6 13.f6 Bf8 14.Bxh6 gxh6 15.Bxf7+ Kxf7

15...Kd8 16.Na3 Be6 17.cxd4.

16.Qh5+ Ke6 17.Qe8+ Kd5

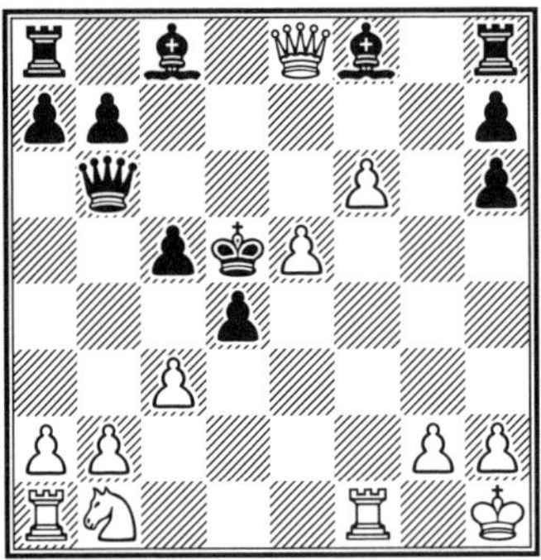

18.cxd4

The best way to drag the enemy King to its death was 18.c4+! Kxc4 19.b3+ Kd3 20.Qh5 Ke4 21.e6 Bxe6 22.Re1+ Kd3 (22...Kf4 23.g3 mate) 23.Qe2 mate.

18...Be6

18...cxd4 was better, though White was winning anyway.

19.Nc3+ Kc4 20.d5 Rxe8 21.Rf4+ Kd3 22.Rd1+ Kc2 23.Rf2, 1-0.

Wilhelm Steinitz vs. Thomas Barnes, London 1862

1.e4 c5 2.Nf3 e6 3.Be2 g6 4.0-0 Bg7 5.Nc3 a6 6.e5 f5 7.b3 Nh6 8.Na4 Qc7 9.Ba3 Bf8 10.d4 b6 11.dxc5 bxc5 12.Qd2 Nf7 13.Qc3 Nc6 14.Rfe1 Nfxe5 15.Nxe5 Nxe5 16.Bc4 Nxc4 17.Qxh8 Nxa3 18.Qxh7 Qc6 19.Rad1 d5 20.Nb6 Qxb6 21.Qxg6+ Kd8 22.Qf6+ Kc7 23.Qxf8 Qd6 24.Qg7+ Bd7 25.c4 d4

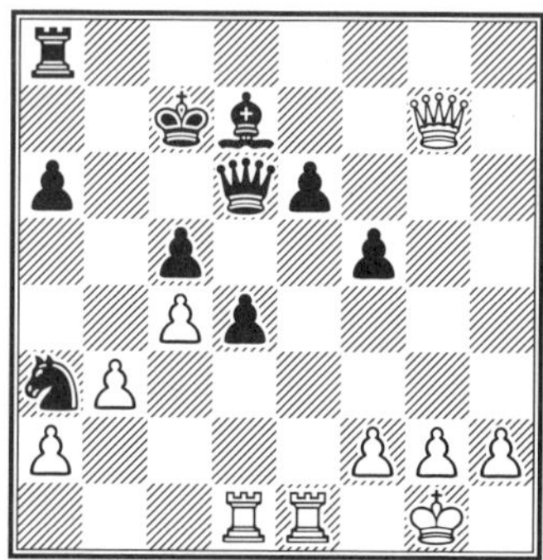

26.b4!

Makes the d4-pawn vulnerable and also allows an eventual c4-c5.

26...Nc2

26...cxb4 27.h4 a5 28.c5 Qf8 (28...Qxc5 29.Rxd4) 29.Qxd4.

27.bxc5 Qxc5 28.Rxe6! Qf8 29.Qe5+ Kc8 30.Rb1 Nb4 31.Rf6 Qe8 32.Qc5+ Nc6 33.Rf8, 1-0.

Wilhelm Steinitz vs. Augustus Mongredien, London 1862

1.e4 d5 2.exd5 Qxd5 3.Nc3 Qd8 4.d4 e6 5.Nf3 Nf6 6.Bd3 Be7 7.0-0 0-0 8.Be3 b6 9.Ne5 Bb7 10.f4 Nbd7 11.Qe2 Nd5? 12.Nxd5 exd5 13.Rf3 f5 14.Rh3 g6 15.g4 fxg4

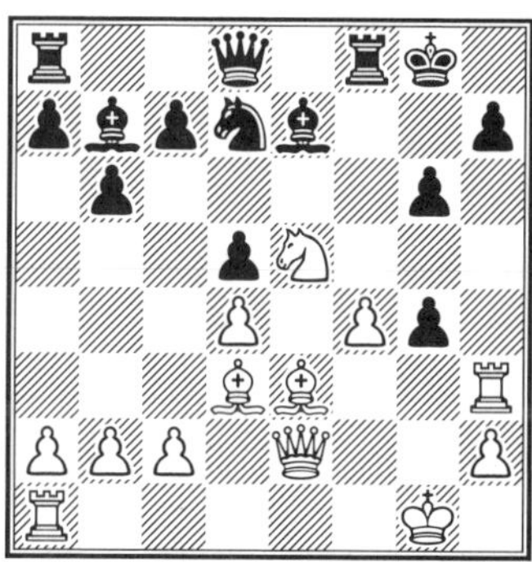

16.Rxh7!!

16.Qg4 is supposed to be an easier win, but 16.Rxh7 also wins.

16...Nxe5

16…Kxh7 (16…Nf6 17.Rh6) 17.Qxg4 Nf6 18.Qxg6+ Kh8 19.Qh6+ Kg8 20.Kh1 wins.

17.fxe5 Kxh7 18.Qxg4 Rg8

18…Qe8 19.Qh5+ Kg7 20.Qh6+ Kg8 21.Bxg6 Rf7 22.Kh1 Bf8 23.Qh5 Bg7 24.Rg1 Kf8 25.Rg3! with the threat of 26.Bxf7 Qxf7 27.Rf3 winning black's Queen.

19.Qh5+ Kg7 20.Qh6+

20.Qxg6+?? Kh8 and Black wins.

20...Kf7 21.Qh7+ Ke6

21...Rg7 22.Bxg6+ Kf8 23.Qh8+ Rg8 24.Bh6 mate.

22.Qh3+ Kf7 23.Rf1+

23.e6+! Ke8 24.Qh7 and Black gets mated in a few moves.

23...Ke8 24.Qe6 Rg7 25.Bg5

25.Bh6 is also crushing.

25...Qd7

25...Bc8 26.Qc6+ Bd7 27.Qxg6+ Rxg6 28.Bxg6 mate.

26.Bxg6+ Rxg6

26...Kd8 27.Rf8+ Qe8 28.Rxe8 mate.

27.Qxg6+ Kd8 28.Rf8+ Qe8 29.Qxe8, 1-0.

The next game was an exhibition game where Steinitz gave Queen's Rook odds.

Wilhelm Steinitz vs. Rock, London 1863

1.e4 e5 2.Nf3 Nc6 3.Bc4 Bc5 4.b4 Bxb4 5.c3 Ba5 6.d4 exd4 7.0-0 Nf6 8.Ba3 Bb6? 9.Qb3 d5 10.exd5 Na5 11.Re1!

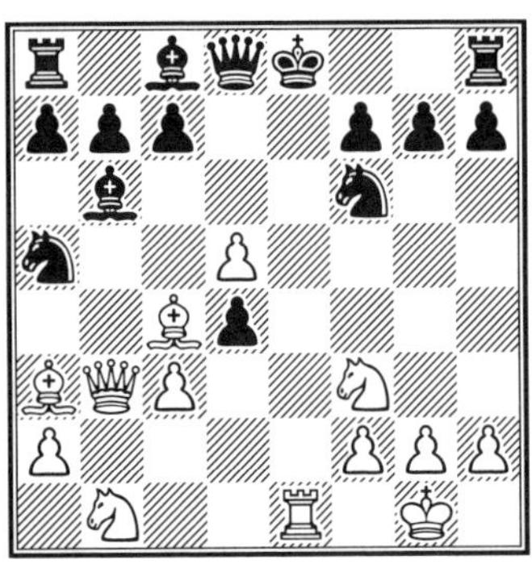

Be6 12.dxe6! Nxb3 13.exf7+ Kd7 14.Be6+ Kc6 15.Ne5+ Kb5 16.Bc4+ Ka5 17.Bb4+ Ka4 18.axb3, 1-0.

Wilhelm Steinitz vs. Augustus Mongredien, London match 1863

1.e4 g6 2.d4 Bg7 3.c3 b6 4.Be3 Bb7 5.Nd2 d6 6.Ngf3 e5 7.dxe5 dxe5 8.Bc4 Ne7 9.Qe2 0-0 10.h4 Nd7 11.h5 c5 12.hxg6 Nxg6 13.0-0-0 a6 14.Ng5 Nf6

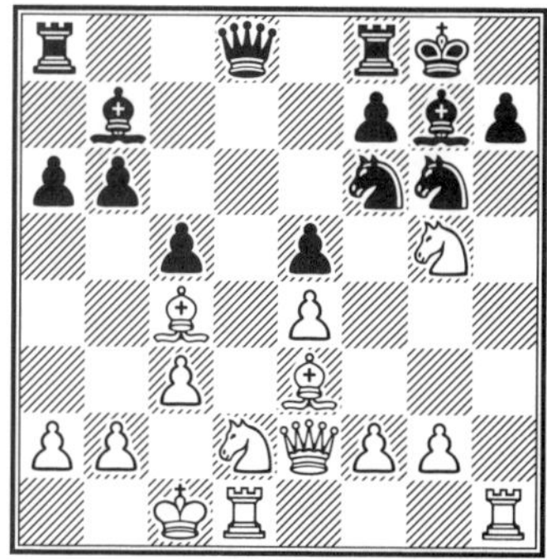

15.Nxh7! Nxh7

15...b5 16.Nxf6+ Qxf6 17.Qh5 Rfe8 18.Bd5 Bxd5 19.Qh7+ Kf8 20.exd5 and White is winning.

16.Rxh7

Another way to bring down Black's kingside wall is 16.Qh5 Nf6 17.Qxg6 Qc8 (hoping for ...Qg4) 18.Rh7! Ne8 (18...Nxh7 19.Bh6) 19.Rdh1 and mate in 3.

16...Kxh7 17.Qh5+ Kg8 18.Rh1 Re8 19.Qxg6 Qf6 20.Bxf7+ Qxf7 21.Rh8+ Kh8 22.Qxf7, 1-0.

Wilhelm Steinitz vs. Frederic Deacon, London match (7) 1863

1.e4 e5 2.f4 exf4 3.Nf3 g5 4.h4 g4 5.Ne5 Nf6 6.Bc4 d5 7.exd5 Bd6 8.d4 Nh5 9.Nc3 Qe7 10.Bb5+ Kd8 11.0-0 Bxe5 12.dxe5 Qxe5 13.Re1 Qf6 14.Qe2 c6 15.dxc6 bxc6 16.Ne4 Qxh4 17.Bxf4 Nxf4 18.Qd2+ Bd7 19.Qxf4

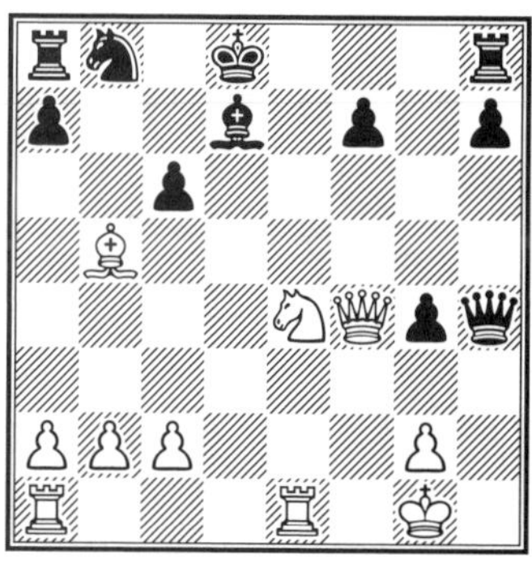

[eft] Adolf Anderssen;

[below] Emanuel Lasker vs. Wilhelm Steinitz, (left to right) Adolf Anderssen, Paul Morphy, Johannes Zukertort, and Louis Paulsen (Images: Courtesy of the Cleveland Public Library's John G. White Collection).

19...cxb5 20.Nd6 Be6 21.Rad1 Nd7 22.Nxf7+ Ke7

22...Bxf7 23.Qxf7.

23.Qd6+ Kxf7 24.Qxe6+, 1-0.

The 1866 match against Anderssen went back and forth, and was an extremely intense battle with King's Gambits and Evans Gambits drawing blood from both sides. Interestingly, Anderssen tossed in two Sicilians and won both. After twelve games the match was tied. Realizing that Anderssen might win the match, Steinitz pushed away the crazy juice (in other words, he stopped the addiction of tactics and nothing but tactics) and decided to play a solid setup, only going after an attack after long preparations. Due to this, he won the match. In retrospect, this was a precursor of Steinitz' future positional change.

Adolf Anderssen vs. Wilhelm Steinitz, London match (13) 1866

1.e4 e5 2.Nf3 Nc6 3.Bb5 Nf6 4.d3 d6 5.Bxc6+ bxc6 6.h3 g6

The idea is to fianchetto his dark-squared Bishop and eventually start a kingside attack with ...f7-f5.

7.Nc3 Bg7 8.0-0 0-0 9.Bg5 h6 10.Be3 c5

Freezing the center so he can play on the kingside.

11.Rb1

Oddly, after all the gambits, both sides are playing carefully and thoughtfully. The old rule: "The best way to beat a wing attack is a counterattack in the center."

11...Ne8

Preparing his ...f7-f5 plan.

12.b4 cxb4 13.Rxb4

Trying to break the center open with d3-d4.

13...c5

Steinitz says, "No!"

14.Ra4?!

The Rook is not happy on a4. Better was 14.Rb3 when 14...Be6 is answered by 15.Nd5.

14...Bd7 15.Ra3 f5

It's clear that Steinitz had a clear, long-term plan while Anderssen didn't.

16.Qb1 Kh8 17.Qb7 a5 18.Rb1 a4 19.Qd5 Qc8 20.Rb6 Ra7 21.Kh2 f4

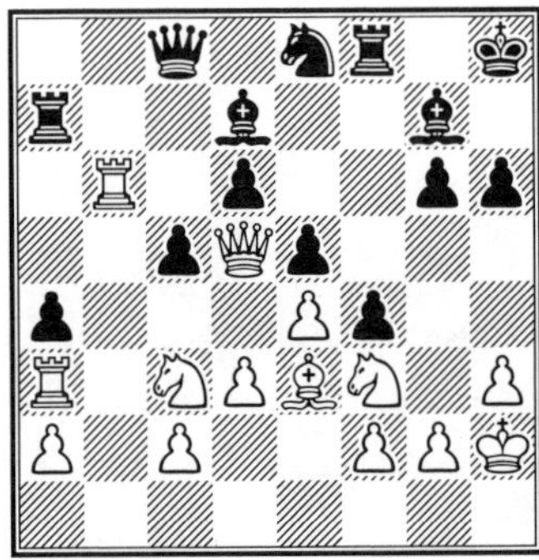

The attack starts in earnest and an attacker like Anderssen isn't a very good defender.

22.Bd2 g5 23.Qc4 Qd8 24.Rb1 Nf6 25.Kg1 Nh7 26.Kf1 h5 27.Ng1 g4 28.hxg4 hxg4

White is lost.

29.f3 Qh4 30.Nd1 Ng5 31.Be1

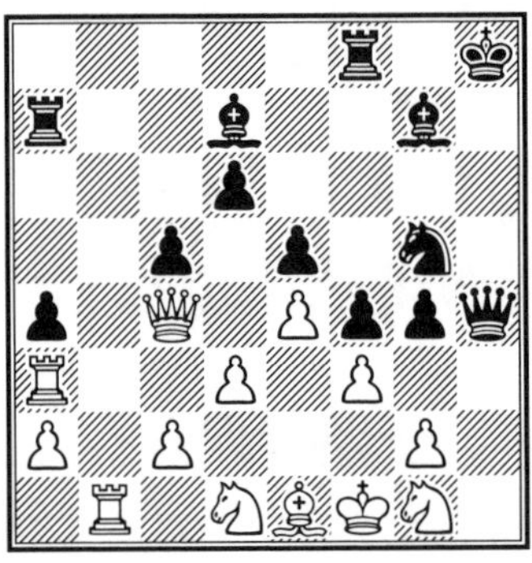

31...Qh7 32.d4 gxf3 33.gxf3 Nh3

33...Qh1 was stronger, intending ...Bh3+.

34.Bf2 Nxg1 35.dxc5 Qh3+ 36.Ke1 Nxf3+ 37.Rxf3 Qxf3 38.Nc3 dxc5 39.Bxc5 Rc7 40.Nd5 Rxc5 41.Qxc5 Qxe4+ 42.Kf2 Rc8 43.Nc7 Qe3+, 0-1.

Looking at Steinitz' matches from 1860 to 1870, you realize that he never lost a serious match. As for his tournaments during this period, he did well, but nothing spectacular. Clearly, he thrived in matches, and he held onto his "kill, kill, kill" style throughout this decade. He did indeed deserve the name of the "Austrian Morphy"!

Steinitz Matches in the 1860s

Steinitz vs. Eduard Jeney (1860): 2-2.

Steinitz vs. Max Lange (1860): 3-0.

Steinitz vs. Heinrich Strauss (1860): 3-0.

Steinitz vs. Reiner (1860): 3-0.
Steinitz vs. Serafino Dubois (1862): 5½-3½.
Steinitz vs. Joseph Blackburne (1862/63): 8-2.
Steinitz vs. Frederic Deacon (1862/63): 7½-3½.
Steinitz vs. Frederic Deacon (1862/63): 5½-1½.
Steinitz vs. Augustus Mongredien (1863): 7-0.
Steinitz vs. Valentine Green (1863/64): 8-1.
Steinitz vs. James Robey (1865): 4-1.
Steinitz vs. Adolf Anderssen (1866): 8-6.
Steinitz vs. Henry Bird (1866): 9½-7½.
Steinitz vs. George Fraser (1867): 4-2.

Steinitz's Tournaments in the 1860s

London (1862): Anderssen first, Paulsen second, Owen third, Dubois and McDonnell tied fourth/fifth, Steinitz sixth.

Dublin (1865): Steinitz first.

Dundee (1867): Newmann first, Steinitz second.

Paris (1867): Kolisch first, Winawer second, Steinitz third.

Steinitz Changes the Chess World

When Wilhelm Steinitz stepped into 1870 he was still tossing tactics here and there, not fearing anything at all. He was also coming up with various new opening ideas. One of these (eventually named the "Steinitz Gambit") called for white's King to remain in the center by moving his King to e2 (though it might go here or there later), and White will also be down a pawn.

Why would anyone play this? Here are the reasons:

- White gets a strong pawn center.
- White will likely regain the pawn.
- And White will gain time by attacking Black's vulnerable Queen.

The Steinitz Gambit wasn't easy to deal with, and eventually it faded away like all the other interesting but not quite workable ideas. Nevertheless, Steinitz demonstrated an extremely creative, original mind, and after a couple years went by, he literally changed chess as it was, dragging everyone into a whole new understanding of what the game could and would be.

Wilhelm Steinitz vs. Louis Paulsen, Baden-Baden 1870

1.e4 e5 2.Nc3 Nc6 3.f4 exf4 4.d4 Qh4+ 5.Ke2 d6 6.Nf3 Bg4 7.Bxf4 0-0-0

7...Bxf3+ 8.Kxf3.

8.Ke3

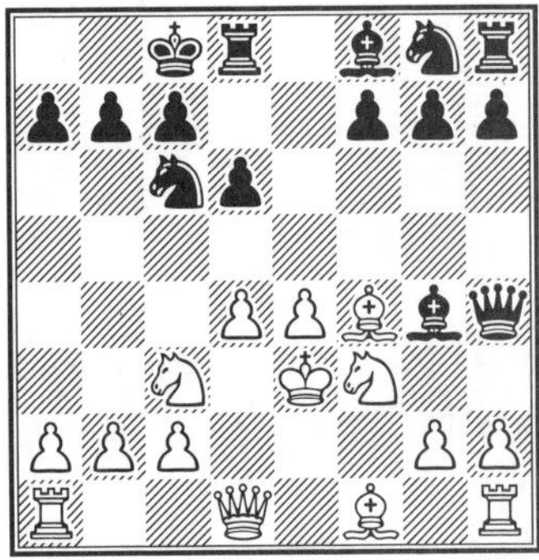

Yes! The King is a fighting piece!

8...Qh5

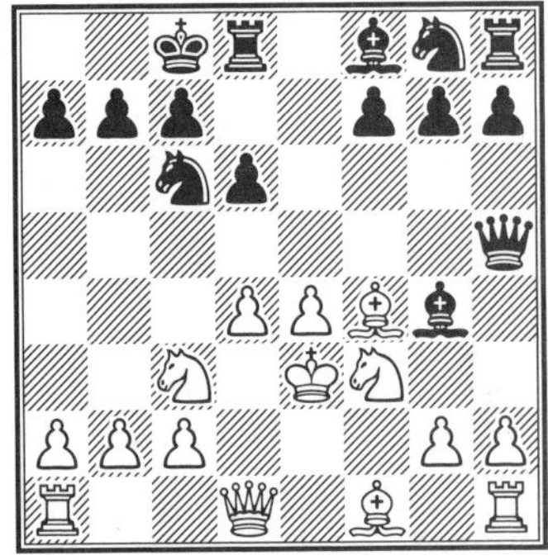

9.Be2 Qa5 10.a3 Bxf3 11.Kxf3!

11.Bxf3 g5 12.Bg3 Bg7.

11...Qh5+ 12.Ke3 Qh4 13.b4 g5 14.Bg3 Qh6 15.b5 Nce7 16.Rf1 Nf6 17.Kf2 Ng6 18.Kg1

White has a winning position!

18...Qg7 19.Qd2 h6 20.a4 Rg8

21.b6!

White sacrifices a pawn so that a4-a5 will rip open Black's pawn cover.

21...axb6 22.Rxf6!

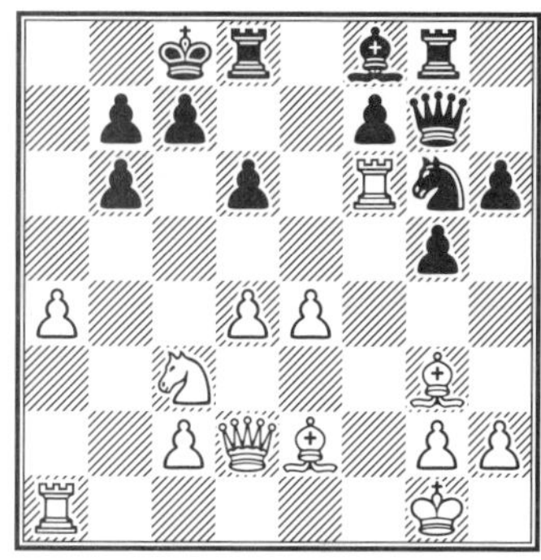

22.a5 was also very strong.

22...Qxf6 23.Bg4+ Kb8 24.Nd5 Qg7 25.a5 f5

25...b5 26.a6.

26.axb6 cxb6 27.Nxb6 Ne7 28.exf5 Qf7 29.f6 Nc6 30.c4 Na7 31.Qa2 Nb5 32.Nd5 Qxd5 33.cxd5 Nxd4 34.Qa7+ Kc7 35.Rc1+ Nc6 36.Rxc6, 1-0.

In 1873 Steinitz "officially" showed the world his new chess ideas; he morphed from attacker to positional player (in general, other players at the time didn't have a plan, they just tried to find a killing tactic). This gave Steinitz a huge edge over his opponents since he was able to build his position, only attacking when the position called for it. The next game is an early one in which Steinitz demonstrated his new chess paradigm.

Louis Paulsen vs. Wilhelm Steinitz, Baden-Baden 1870

1.e4 e5 2.Nf3 Nc6 3.Nc3 g6 4.Bc4 Bg7 5.d3 d6 6.Bg5 Qd7 7.a3 h6 8.Bh4 g5 9.Bg3 Nge7 10.h4 g4 11.Nd2 h5 12.Nd5 Nxd5 13.Bxd5 Ne7 14.Bb3 f5 15.exf5 Nxf5 16.Nf1 c6 17.c3 Qc7

Black not only frees his light-squared Bishop, it also intends to move the Queen to b6 where it puts pressure on b3, b2, and f2.

18.Qe2 Qb6 19.Ba2 Bd7 20.0-0-0 0-0-0 21.f3 Nxg3 22.Nxg3 d5

Now Black has two Bishops and a strong pawn center. He also intends to place a Rook on the f-file. However, White has a plan that might save, if Steinitz allows it.

23.Kb1 Bf8!

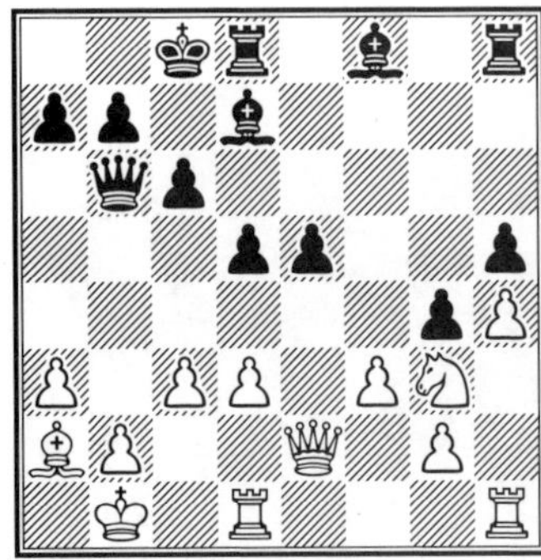

This move tells White that Black has all the time in the world to maximize his pieces. The idea of 23...Bf8 is to defend e5 by ...Bd6 and threaten ...e5-e4 threatening white's Knight. White stops that obvious threat and implements his own plan.

24.Ka1 Bd6 25.Nf1 Rdf8 26.Nd2 Rh6 27.c4

Now we see White's plan! Black's d5-pawn is under attack, and if Black plays 27...dxc4 then Bxc4 not only frees white's Bishop, it also gives a fantastic square on e4 for white's Knight.

27...Be6

Black doesn't give White the e4-square. Now Black's center is solid and White's pieces are still hemmed in.

28.Nb3 gxf3

Creating a weak pawn (a target!) on f3.

29.gxf3

Threatening to win a piece by c4-c5.

29...Bc7

Stopping White's obvious threat.

30.Nd2

A cute try was 30.Rc1 when the thematic 30...Rhf6 (beating on f3) is met by31.Nc5 when 31...Qxc5? 32.cxd5 would make White happy.

30...Rhf6 31.Rc1

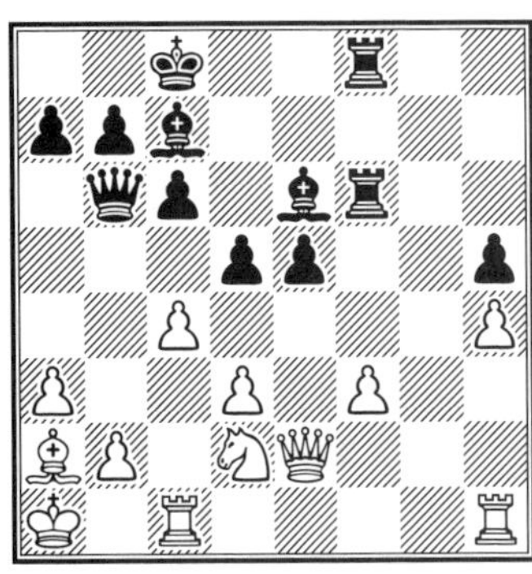

31...Kb8 32.cxd5 cxd5 33.Rhg1 Bd6

White's passive pieces haven't been able to find active diagonals or squares. In the meantime White has weak pawns on d3, f3, and h4.

34.Rg5 Bf7 35.Nb1 Qd4 36.Nc3 a6

Once again, White has nothing to do, while White's weaknesses are (d3, f3, h4) are ready to fall.

37.Rg7 Be6, 0-1 (time).

In the early 1870s Steinitz was still depending on brutal attacks (the Austrian Morphy remained a part of him), but his opponents didn't realize that he was soon to rip reality apart with a chess paradigm shift that would change chess forever.

Zukertort who had been living in Berlin for several years moved to London, much improved and ready for bear!

Wilhelm Steinitz vs. Johannes Zukertort, London 1872

1.e4 e5 2.Nc3 Nc6 3.f4 exf4 4.d4 Qh4+ 5.Ke2 d5 6.exd5 Bg4+ 7.Nf3 0-0-0 8.dxc6 Bc5 9.cxb7+ Kb8 10.Nb5 Nf6 11.Kd3 Qh5 12.Kc3 Bxd4+ 13.Nbxd4 Qc5+ 14.Kb3 Qb6+ 15.Bb5 Bxf3 16.Qxf3 Rxd4 17.Qc6 Qa5 18.c3 Rd6 19.Qc4 a6 20.Ba4 Nd5 21.Ka3 g5 22.b4 Qb6 23.Qd4 Qxd4 24.cxd4 Nb6 25.Bb2 Nc4+ 26.Kb3

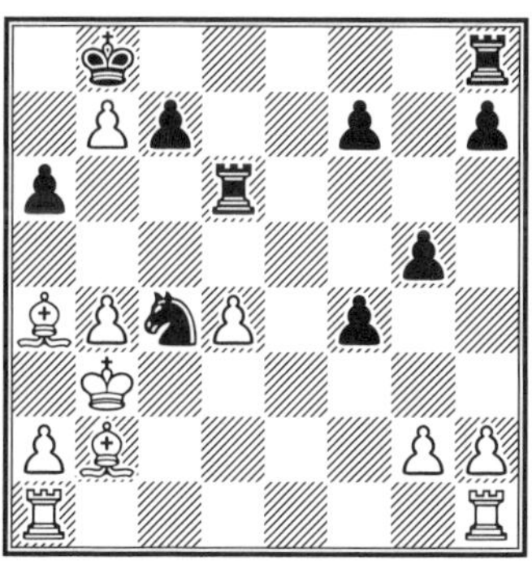

26...Nxb2 27.Kxb2 Rxd4 28.Kc3 Rhd8 29.Rad1 R4d6 30.Rxd6 Rxd6 31.Rd1 Rf6 32.Bc2 Kxb7 33.Bxh7 Kb6 34.h3 f3 35.gxf3 Rxf3+ 36.Rd3 Rf2 37.a4 a5 38.bxa5+ Kxa5 39.Rd5+ Kb6 40.a5+ Ka7 41.Bd3 Rf3 42.Rxg5 Rxh3 43.Rf5 Rh7 44.Rc5 f5 45.Rxf5 Re7 46.Rg5 Rd7 47.Re5 Rg7 48.Re8 Rg1 49.Be4 Rc1+ 50.Kb4 c5+ 51.Kb5, 1-0.

Zukertort was clearly outplayed in the above game, so they arranged a match, Steinitz won that too by the score of 9-3 (seven wins for Steinitz, one win for Zukertort, and four draws), and off they went into the embrace of history. I should add that, in 1872, Steinitz didn't worry about Zukertort (as the results in 1872 proved). However, Zukertort was one of those guys that never quit, and he got better and better as the years went by until he became a very serious opponent indeed.

The next game is from their 1872 match. Steinitz dominated Zukertort when he played various gambits (King's Gambit, Evans Gambit), as well, he smoothly wiped out Zukertort when he demonstrated his positional skills. It soon became clear that Steinitz was superior in every part of the game:

Wilhelm Steinitz vs. Johannes Zukertort, London match (12) 1872

1.d4 f5 2.g3 Nf6 3.Bg2 e6 4.Nf3 Be7 5.0-0 0-0 6.c4 Qe8 7.Nc3 d5 8.Ne5 c6 9.b3 Ne4 10.Bb2 Nd7 11.Nd3 Ndf6 12.Qc2 Bd6 13.Nxe4 fxe4 14.Ne5 Bxe5 15.dxe5 Ng4 16.h3 Nh6 17.g4 Qe7 18.f3 exf3 19.exf3 Bd7 20.f4 Qc5+ 21.Kh1 b5 22.Rad1 bxc4 23.Bd4 Qe7 24.bxc4 a5 25.Qf2 Rfc8 26.Bc5 Qe8 27.Rfe1 Rab8

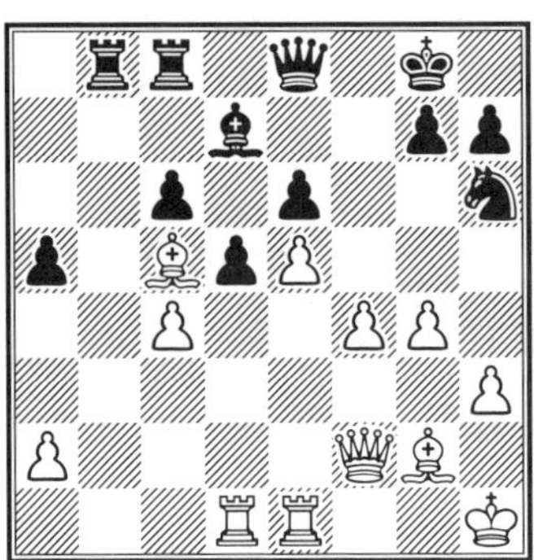

28.f5 exf5 29.e6 Bxe6 30.cxd5 fxg4 31.Rxe6 Qh5 32.dxc6 g3 33.Qd4 Nf5 34.Qd5 Kh8 35.Re5, 1-0.

This next game from the London match presents a painful look at poor Zukertort.

Wilhelm Steinitz vs. Johannes Zukertort, London match (2) 1872

1.e4 e5 2.Nf3 Nc6 3.Bc4 Bc5 4.b4 Bxb4 5.c3 Ba5 6.d4 exd4 7.0-0 dxc3 8.Qb3 Qf6 9.Bg5 Qg6 10.Nxc3 Bxc3 11.Qxc3 Nf6 12.Bd3 0-0 13.Rae1 b5 14.e5 Nd5 15.Qc2 Qh5 16.a3 h6 17.Bd2 Nde7 18.Re4 Ng6 19.Rfe1

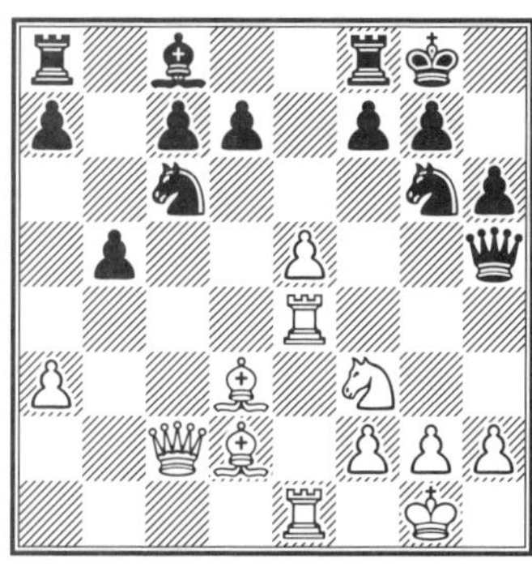

19...Bb7 20.g4 Qh3 21.R1e3 f5 22.exf6 Rxf6 23.Bf1 Qxf3 24.Qb3+ d5 25.Rxf3 Rxf3 26.Qxf3 dxe4 27.Qxe4 Nge5 28.f4 Nc4 29.Qe6+ Kh8 30.Bc3 N6e5 31.Bxc4, 1-0.

A Complete Player

This game against Anderssen opened up the positional floodgates, and Steinitz became the first complete chess player ever (some might claim that Morphy was also a complete player, but I don't believe it).

Steinitz created many new ideas in the openings, and his tactical skills were always waiting to cut off his opponent's head. He had excellent endgame skills, good defensive skills (in those days "defensive skills" were dirty words), and his buildup of calm strategic plans left his opponents in the dark.

As can be expected, when someone turns what you know into ashes (chess and everything else), you find that criticism will pour down on you. In Steinitz's case some of the old school called him cowardly, but after he wiped them out using both positional and tactical acumen, most of the haters shut up, and others (like Anderssen) became believers and embraced it!

Adolf Anderssen vs. Wilhelm Steinitz, Vienna 1873

1.e4 e5 2.Nf3 Nc6 3.Bb5 a6 4.Ba4 Nf6 5.d3 d6 6.Bxc6+ bxc6 7.h3 g6 8.Nc3 Bg7 9.Be3 Rb8 10.b3 c5 11.Qd2 h6 12.g4

White has just played 12.g4 intending to castle long and then wipe Black out with a kingside attack. How would you deal with this?

12...Ng8!

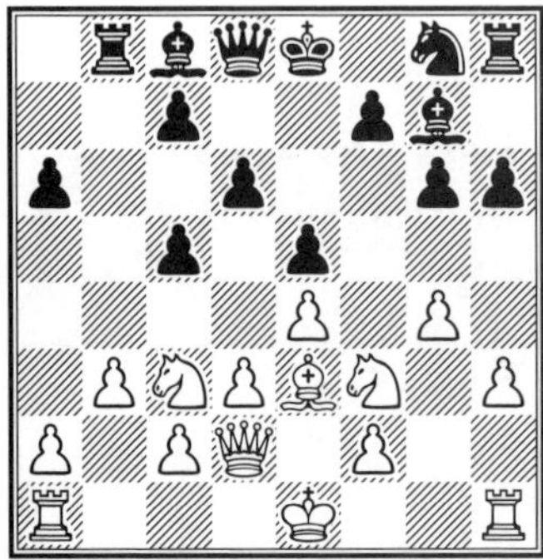

Another excellent move is 12...h5 13.g5 Nh7 when White's attack is already snuffed out. The idea behind Black's 12...Ng8 is clear, and I'll discuss it in two more moves.

13.0-0-0 Ne7 14.Ne2 Nc6

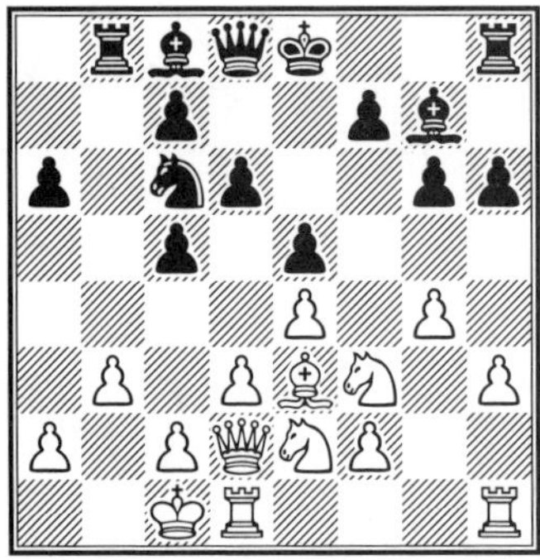

Pure positional mastery! Black has moved his Knight from f6-g8-e7-c6-d4. This takes time, but the fact that the center is closed allows the Knight's journey to an improved square.

So, how does Black stand? He stands very well since White's hope for kingside attack is already dead (g4-g5 is answered by ...h5. If White plays Rdg1 followed by h3-h4-h5, Black just plays ...g6-g5 when the Kingside is locked. In the meantime Black will play ...Nd4, ...a6-a5-a4 when the only one that's attacking in Steinitz. Note that if White plays f2-f4 at some point, Black can chop on f4 when Black's dark-squared Bishop reigns supreme on the a1-h8 diagonal.

15.Qc3?

An ugly move. White didn't want to play 15.c3 since that weakens White's queenside pawn structure (Black would react by ...a6-a5-a4). Probably 15.Kb1 and when Black plays ...a6-a5 White would play a2-a4, shoring up his King position.

15...Nd4 16.Nfg1 0-0 17.Ng3

17.Qd2 Kh7.

17...Be6 18.N1e2 Qd7 19.Bxd4

A painful decision, but black's Knight was a monster.

19...cxd4 20.Qb2

Another ugly Queen move, though White's position is already bad.

20...a5 21.Kd2

21.a4 Qc6 (Threatening both 21...Rxb3 or 21...Bxb3.) 22.Kd2 (22.Kb1 is met by 22...Qc5, 23...Rb4, 24...Rfb8 followed by a sacrifice on b3.) 22...Qxa4 and Black is winning.

21...d5 22.f3 Qe7 23.Rdf1 Qb4+

Black had many good choices: 23...a4, 23...c5, etc. However, you can only play one move and 23...Qb4+ is fine.

24.Kd1 a4 25.Rh2 c5 26.Nc1 c4

White is getting destroyed.

27.a3 Qe7 28.b4 c3 29.Qa1

White's Queen is entombed.

29...Qg5 30.Rff2 f5

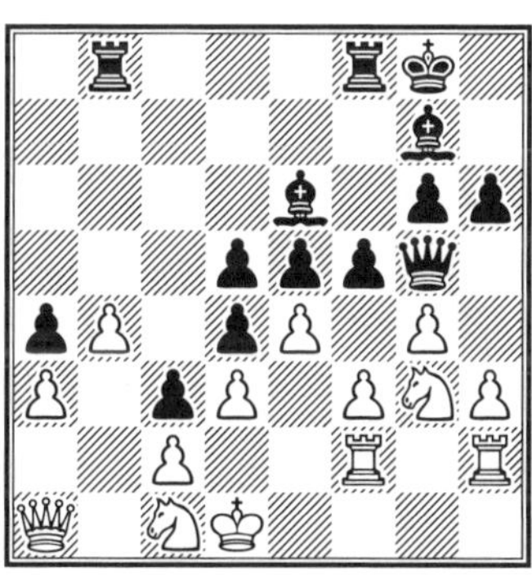

Amazing. Black owns the queenside, the center, and now he wants to kingside too! Notice how calmly Black has placed his pieces and pawns on the best squares. The rest is Steinitz mopping up.

31.exf5 gxf5 32.h4 Qg6 33.Nxf5 Bxf5 34.gxf5 Rxf5 35.Ne2 Rbf8 36.Qa2 Qf7 37.Rh3 Kh7 38.Ng1 Bf6 39.Ke2 Rg8 40.Kf1 Be7 41.Ne2 Rh5 42.f4 Bxh4 43.Rff3 e4 44.dxe4 Qg6 45.Ng3 Bxg3, 0-1.

I should call attention to the fact that in 1870 Steinitz wiped out Blackburne (who was then considered one of the best players in the world) with the score of 5½-½. Wanting revenge, another match was put together in 1876, and this time Steinitz dominated with a score of 7-0.

[top] Johannes Zukertort vs. Wilhelm Steinitz; [bottom] Emanuel Lasker vs. Wilhelm Steinitz (Photos: Courtesy of the Cleveland Public Library's John G. White Collection).

The next years were busy ones, with Steinitz winning several tournaments and many matches (he was viewed as unbeatable in matches). He also gave many simultaneous and blindfold exhibitions. The big change, though, was his writing for a famous British sports magazine (*The Field*), and due to his work as a chess correspondent and his desire to study chess as deeply as he could, he quit playing in tournaments for ten years.

Steinitz obviously had a lot of things on his plate, but he was a chess player and chess players always crave to play in tournaments. So, in June of 1882, he once again embraced his love affair with the chess pieces and returned to the fold, playing in Vienna (he tied for first with Winawer). Next, was a strong event in London (Zukertort came in first, Steinitz came in second, and Blackburne and Chigorin followed at third and fourth).

This wasn't the same Zukertort that he played in 1872, Zukertort was now extremely strong.

It was obvious that Steinitz really enjoyed writing, and when he lost his post at *The Field* in October 1883, he moved to the United States and created his own magazine called *International Chess Magazine*.

Steinitz had thought of himself as being World Champion after beating Anderssen in their 1866 match, and defeating Zukertort in their 1872 match solidified his dominance. Due to this, many chess fans accepted that he was "The Man" in chess. However, others just didn't believe it. With the resurgence of Zukertort (he had fantastic results during the years when Steinitz wasn't playing), and with some fans claiming that Zukertort was the real champion, both players knew that there had to be a reckoning.

Matches During this Period

Steinitz vs. Joseph Blackburne (1870): 5½-½

Steinitz vs. Johannes Zukertort (1872): 9-3

Steinitz vs. Blackburne (1876): 7-0

Steinitz vs. Dion Martinez (1882): 3 wins, 1 loss, 3 draws

Steinitz vs. Dion Martinez (1882): 7-0

Steinitz vs. Philipp Meitner (1882): 5-0

Steinitz vs. Alexander Sellman (1882): 2 wins, no losses, 3 draws

Steinitz vs. Celso Golmayo (1883): 8 wins, 1 loss, 1 draw

Steinitz vs. George Mackenzie (1883): 3 wins, 1 loss, 2 draws

Steinitz vs. Dion Martinez (1883): 9 wins, no losses, 2 draws

Steinitz vs. Alexander Sellman (1885): 3-0

Tournaments During this Period

Baden-Baden (1870): Anderssen first, Steinitz second.

London (1872): Steinitz first ahead of Blackburne and Zukertort.

Vienna (1873): Steinitz first ahead of Blackburne, and Anderssen.

Vienna (1882): Steinitz and Winawer tied first/second ahead of Mason, Mackenzie, Zukertort, and others. Steinitz won the playoff, 2-1.

London (1883): Zukertort first, Steinitz second ahead of Blackburne and Chigorin.

The First Official World Chess Champion

1886 was an epic year. Though past players had been viewed as the World Champion, there never was an official title. Now the two best players in the world (Zukertort and Steinitz) would butt heads and fans of both players were forced to accept that the victor was the real deal.

The match was played in three cities: New York, St. Louis, and New Orleans (in honor of Morphy, who died in 1884). It started badly for Steinitz, who won the first game but then lost four games in a row.

Johannes Zukertort vs. Wilhelm Steinitz, World Championship (1) 1886

1.d4 d5 2.c4 c6 3.e3 Bf5 4.Nc3 e6 5.Nf3 Nd7 6.a3 Bd6 7.c5

White plays for queenside space. Does Black have anything?

7...Bc7 8.b4 e5!

Black counters in the center. Always make sure you have something that gives you positive play.

9.Be2

Such an obvious move, but White should have opened the center with 9.dxe5 Nxe5 (9...Nh6!? 10.Nd4 Bxe5 is interesting.) 10.Nd4 Bd7 (10...Nh6!?) with chances for both sides.

9...Ngf6

9...e4 was better. However, both players were confident about their wing attacks.

10.Bb2 e4

Black changes the landscape again. Before it was White's queenside space vs. Black's kingside space. Now Steinitz closes the center but gains kingside space. Note how Black's dark-squared Bishop is now ruler of the h2-b8 diagonal while 10...e4 blocks white's dark-squared Bishop (on b2).

11.Nd2 h5!

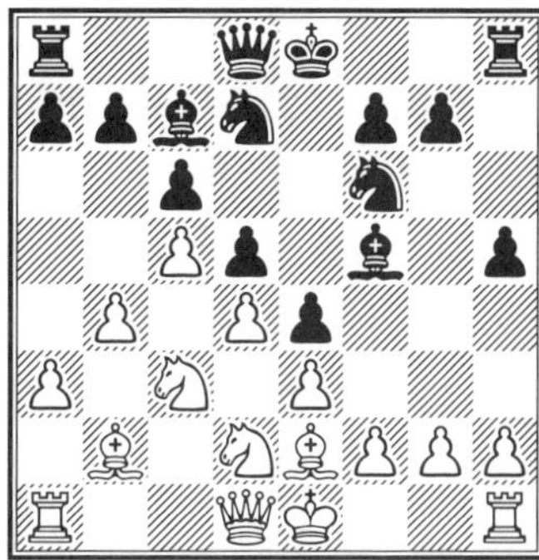

The race is on! White intends to wipe you Black's queenside, while Black intends to crash through on the kingside. Both sides need to play with energy since passive play will, in the long run, lead to disaster.

12.h3 Nf8

The Knight wasn't doing much on d7, so Black brings it into the battle by moving it to f8 and then g6 and h4. Another thematic plan was 12...Ng8 followed by 13...Qg5.

13.a4 Ng6 14.b5

White starts his "I'm going to rule over the whole queenside!" plan.

14...Nh4 15.g3

Not many players would retreat by 15.Bf1.

15...Ng2+!?

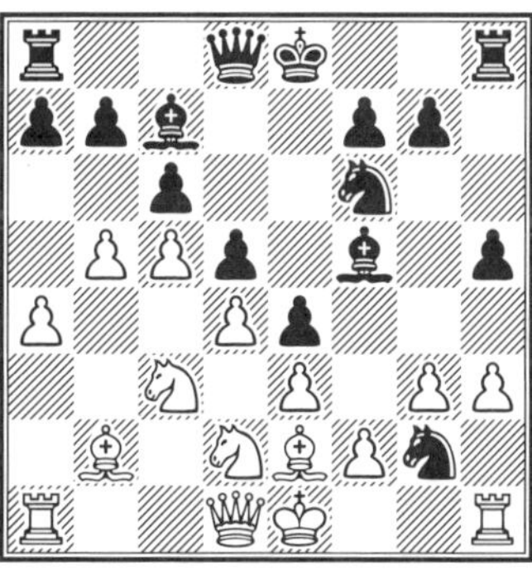

Steinitz goes all in! 15...Ng6 was good since white's kingside pawns are vulnerable, but Steinitz had something else in mind.

16.Kf1 Nxe3+

Forced.

17.fxe3 Bxg3

So much for mutual wing attacks. white's King is stuck on the kingside without any pawn protection, so White will have to put all his energy into coming up with a defensive setup.

18.Kg2 Bc7 19.Qg1?!

Defense was difficult way back in Steinitz' time and it's still tough today. 19.Qf1 and 19.Nf1 would have kept the result a mystery.

19...Rh6 20.Kf1 Rg6 21.Qf2 Qd7 22.bxc6 bxc6 23.Rg1

The "tricky" 23.Nb5?? loses right away after 23...Bxh3+ 24.Ke1 Bg3.

23...Bxh3+ 24.Ke1 Ng4! 25.Bxg4 Bxg4

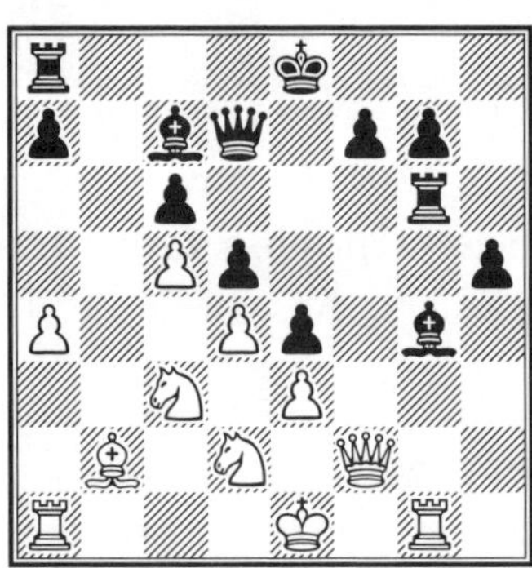

White is busted. Here is why:

✦ White's King, which will be hunted down forever, will always be wandering the board like Caine.

✦ Black isn't behind in material anymore since he now has 3 pawns for the piece.

26.Ne2 Qe7

Black had many tasty choices: 26...Rf6 (perhaps best), 26...Rb8, etc.

27.Nf4 Rh6

27...Rf6 screams to be played.

28.Bc3 g5 29.Ne2 Rf6 30.Qg2 Rf3! 31.Nf1

Of course, 31.Nxf3?? exf3 is Armageddon for White.

31...Rb8 32.Kd2 f5

Visually it's eye candy (and it does the job). However, 32...Qf6 was a killer, while 32...Bh3 also ends the game: 33.Qxg5 Qxg5 34.Rxg5 Rf2 35.Re1 Rb3 winning a piece (Black threatens to take on e2 when the c3-Bishop will be undefended. If White tries to run from the b3-Rook by 36.Ba1 then 36...Ba5+ and 36...Rd3+ are both game over).

33.a5 f4

The rest of the game was agony for White.

34.Rh1 Qf7 35.Re1 fxe3+ 36.Nxe3 Rf2 37.Qxf2 Qxf2 38.Nxg4 Bf4+ 39.Kc2 hxg4 40.Bd2

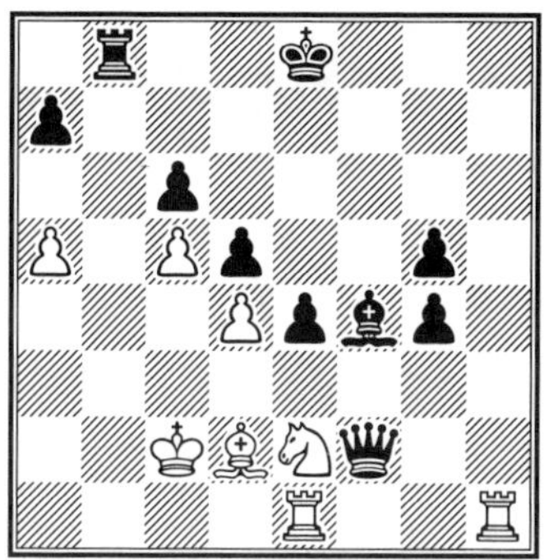

40... e3

I have to mention that Zukertort had created a trap: 40...Bxd2 41.Refl Qxe2?? (41...Qxf1 42.Rxf1 Bxa5 leaves Black with four extra pawns and an easy win. However, sometimes people play quickly, often to their detriment!) 42.Rh8+ Ke7 43.Rh7+ Ke8 (or 43...Ke6) 44.Rh8+, draw by perpetual check.

41.Bc1 Qg2 42.Kc3 Kd7 43.Rh7+ Ke6 44.Rh6+ Kf5 45.Bxe3 Bxe3 46.Rf1+ Bf4, 0-1.

After losing four games in a row, giving Zukertort a four to one lead, you would think that Steinitz would be depressed and Zukertort would be dancing in the street. Instead, Steinitz demonstrated his enormous willpower while Zukertort collapsed. Steinitz rolled over him by winning nine more games, losing only one, and drawing five. The final score was a dominating ten wins for Steinitz, five for Zukertort, and five draws (12½-7½).

The ninth game of the match shows that Steinitz's positional skills were just too much for Zukertort.

Johannes Zukertort vs. Wilhelm Steinitz, World Championship (9) 1886

1.d4 d5 2.c4 e6 3.Nc3 Nf6 4.Nf3 dxc4 5.e3 c5 6.Bxc4 cxd4 7.exd4 Be7 8.0-0 0-0 9.Qe2 Nbd7 10.Bb3 Nb6 11.Bf4 Nbd5 12.Bg3 Qa5 13.Rac1 Bd7 14.Ne5 Rfd8 15.Qf3 Be8 16.Rfe1 Rac8 17.Bh4 Nxc3 18.bxc3 Qc7

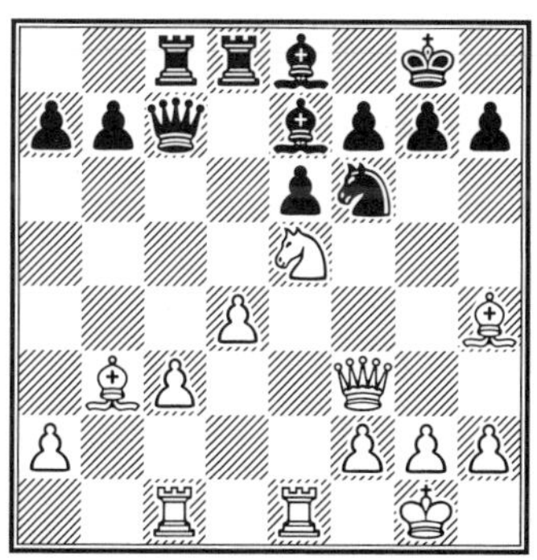

19.Qd3

Emanuel Lasker's 19.Bg3! Bd6 20.c4 would have kept the game percolating: 20...Nd7 21.c5 (or 21.Nxd7 Qxd7 22.d5 exd5 23.cxd5 when White has a passed pawn, but being able to push it is another matter.) 21...Bxe5 and now 22.Rxe5! creates a bit of fun: 22...Nxe5 23.Bxe5 Qe7 when White has good compensation, but not more.

19...Nd5 20.Bxe7 Qxe7 21.Bxd5?

Trading minor pieces helps Black. Also, Zukertort thought that his Knight would be much stronger than Steinitz' bishop. As the game shows, Zukertort was wrong.

21...Rxd5 22.c4 Rdd8 23.Re3?

He can't stop dreaming of a mating attack. Once again, he's wrong. The rest of the game shows Steinitz completely outplaying his opponent.

23...Qd6

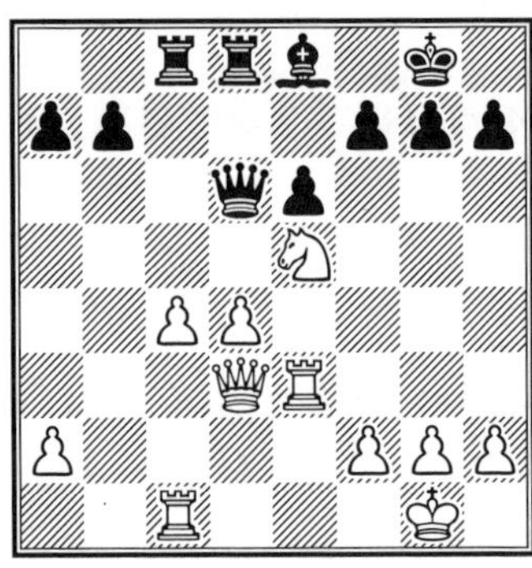

24.Rd1 f6 25.Rh3 h6 26.Ng4 Qf4 27.Ne3 Ba4 28.Rf3 Qd6 29.Rd2 Bc6 30.Rg3 f5 31.Rg6 Be4 32.Qb3 Kh7 33.c5 Rxc5 34.Rxe6 Rc1+ 35.Nd1 Qf4 36.Qb2 Rb1 37.Qc3 Rc8 38.Rxe4 Qxe4, 0-1.

After the match Zukertort was a total wreck. Thomas Seccombe, in an article about the gutted challenger, had this to say:

> He returned from the States a broken-down man. His nerves seemed overstrained, an impediment in his speech was noticeable, and he had not the energy to rouse himself from a kind of mental torpor.

Tim Harding, in his excellent book *Eminent Victorian Chess Players*[1] wrote:

> It seems likely that he had already suffered a minor stroke." I have to agree with Mr. Harding. In fact, I asked Doctor Saidy if Zukertort's symptoms pointed to a stroke, and he felt it was a very real possibility.

Clearly, Zukertort needed rest and lots of time to recuperate (if recuperation was at all possible). Unfortunately, he was now penniless and if he didn't play he

1 Tim Harding, *Eminent Victorian Chess Players: Ten Biographies*. Jefferson, NC: McFarland & Company, 2012.

wouldn't make any money. Thus he played and, in general, did horribly. It was very clear that Zukertort was no longer the same man that he was before the Steinitz match. Oddly, in his final event (in 1888) he got off to a good start, but became ill (he suffered a cerebral hemorrhage), fell into unconsciousness in the hospital, and died the next day—he was only forty-five years old.

Though Zukertort had supporters and friends, his final years were lived in poverty and ill health. I feel he was a lonely man, fueled by his desire to reach the height of chess perfection. Once he was unable to do so, his flame burned out.

After this match Steinitz was challenged for the World Championship several times. But life isn't just chess, and when Flora, his twenty-one year old daughter, died in 1888, he was gutted. Then in 1892, his wife Caroline Golder (they married in 1865) and constant companion died from hepatitis at the age of forty-five.

As for the matches, he played a World Championship match against Mikhail Chigorin in 1889. Steinitz joked that "it would be a match between an old master of the new school and a young master of the old school." Steinitz was fifty-two years old during the match, while Chigorin was thirty-eight. Steinitz beat Chigorin (10½-6½). Amazingly, there was only one draw!

After that he played a World Championship match against Isidor Gunsberg (Steinitz won (10½-8½).

After the Gunsberg match, another match against Chigorin was held in 1892. It was as close as close could be. After twenty-one games it was tied, and then Steinitz won the last two games, winning the match.

Steinitz, low on money (he was always low on money) and getting old, accepted a challenge in 1893 from a twenty-five-year-old man named Emanuel Lasker. Who would have known that Lasker was going to be one of the greatest players in the history of chess?

The match was made in 1894 and Lasker won, 12-7 (ten wins, five losses, four draws).

Emanuel Lasker vs. Wilhelm Steinitz, World Championship (17) 1894

1.e4 e5 2.Nf3 Nc6 3.Bc4 Bc5 4.d3 Nf6 5.Nc3 d6 6.Be3 Bb6 7.Qd2 Na5 8.Bb5+ c6 9.Ba4 Bxe3 10.fxe3 b5 11.Bb3 Qb6 12.0-0 Ng4 13.Rae1 f6 14.h3 Nh6 15.Ne2 Nxb3 16.axb3 0-0

Black is a bit better already. That's not a surprise since Lasker wasn't a great opening master. However, how Steinitz positionally outplayed Lasker is extremely impressive. The problem for White is that Steinitz is going to play on the queenside, and the center isn't a friend to Lasker either. That leaves passive defense (not Lasker's cup-of-tea!) or a kingside attack, which is also hard to do.

17.Ng3 a5 18.d4 Nf7 19.Qf2 Ra7 20.Rd1 a4 21.b4

Lasker could have tried 21.Nh5 but after 21...Kh8 22.Qg3 Rg8 White's attack will lead to nothing while Black is ready to crash through on the queenside.

21...Qc7

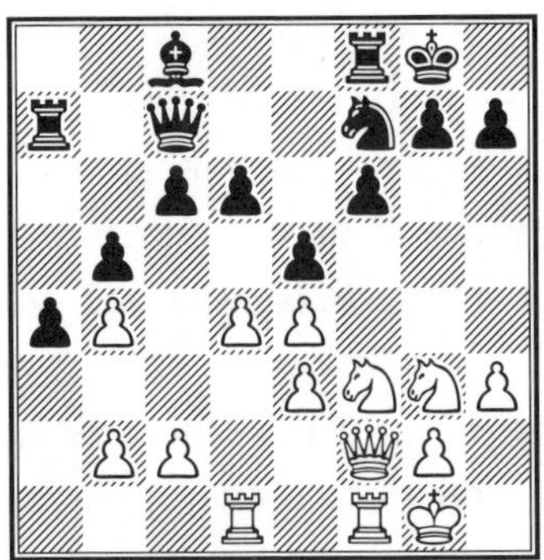

22.Ne1? c5 23.Qd2 Be6 24.d5 Bd7 25.Ra1 cxb4 26.Qxb4 Rc8 27.Qd2 Qc4 28.Rf2 Ng5 29.Qd3 Rac7

The young Lasker caves and starts to embrace passivity and pure defense. His only way to hold off his opponent was 22.Rd3! when 22...c5 is met with 23.Rc3. Black still has an edge, but White has good chances to draw. 22...c5 23.Qd2 Be6 24.d5 Bd7 25.Ra1 cxb4 26.Qxb4 Rc8 27.Qd2 Qc4 28.Rf2 Ng5 29.Qd3 Rac7

Also strong is 29...Bxh3 30.Qxc4 Rxc4 31.gxh3 Nxh3+ 32.Kg2 Nxf2 33.Kxf2 g6 and White is probably lost, but he might have thought that he could win without going into complications?

30.h4 Nf7 31.Qxc4 Rxc4 32.Rd2 g6 33.Kf2 Nd8

Bringing more artillery to the queenside.

34.b3 R4c7 35.Rdd1 Nb7 36.Rdb1 Kf7 37.Ke2 Ra8 38.Kd2 Na5 39.Kd3 h5 40.Ra2 Raa7 41.b4 Nc4 42.Nf3 Ra8 43.Nd2 Nb6 44.Rf1 Rac8 45.Nb1 Ke7 46.c3 Nc4 47.Raf2 Na3!

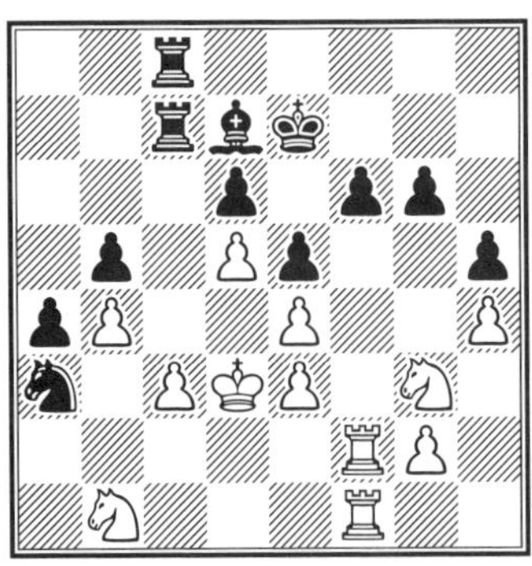

A pretty finish.

48.Ne2

William Steinitz commemorative stamp sheet, Chad, 1983.

48.Rxf6 Nxb1 49.Rf7+ Kd8 50.Rf8+ Be8 51.Rxb1 Rxc3+ 51.Ke2 Rc2+ 52.Kf3 Rc1 53.Rb2 R8c2 and the game is over since Black's passed a-pawn is ready to march to a1.

48...Nxb1 49.Rxb1 Bg4 50.Rc1 Rc4 51.Rc2 f5, 0-1.

The only move is 52.Ng3 when 52...Bd1! (or 52...fxe4+ 53.Kd2 Bd7-e8-f7xd5) 53.Rc1 Bb3 54.Kd2 (54.exf5 Rg4 55.f6+ Kf7 56.Nf1 Bxd5 wins) 54...Rf8 (54...a3 is also game over) 55.Rcf1 a3 and White is doomed. A fine positional game by Steinitz.

Naturally, Steinitz wanted revenge, so another match was arranged (the sixth official World Championship match) in 1896. But aging doesn't stop, and Steinitz wasn't close to his prime. To make it worse, Lasker was better than before. Though old, he still was a force to be reckoned with. For example, in the powerful St. Petersburg tournament (won by Lasker) Steinitz came in second, ahead of Tarrasch, Pillsbury, and Chigorin.

That must have given Steinitz some confidence, but in the next tournament, Nuremberg, Steinitz came in sixth, while Lasker once again came in first.

Wilhelm Steinitz vs. Georg Marco, Nuremberg 1896

1.d4 d5 2.c4 e6 3.Nc3 c6 4.e4 dxe4 5.Nxe4 Nf6

This line was rather new at that time, which explains why 5...Nf6 (which gives White a comfortable edge) was played instead of the modern, very sharp, 5...Bb4+ 6.Bd2 (6.Nc3 c5 is another interesting line.) 6...Qxd4 7.Bxb4 Qxe4+ 8.Be2. I should add that, though 5...Nf6 isn't considered the best, some strong players still give it a try now and then.

6.Nxf6+ Qxf6 7.Nf3 Bb4+ 8.Bd2 Bxd2+ 9.Qxd2 Nd7

One might think that Black is fine due to the early exchanges. However, that's not quite correct because White has more central space and, when Black eventually plays ...c6-c5, White will have a queenside pawn majority. All this gives White a small but annoying plus.

10.0-0-0 0-0 11.Qe3

Stopping Black from playing ...e6-e5.

11...c5

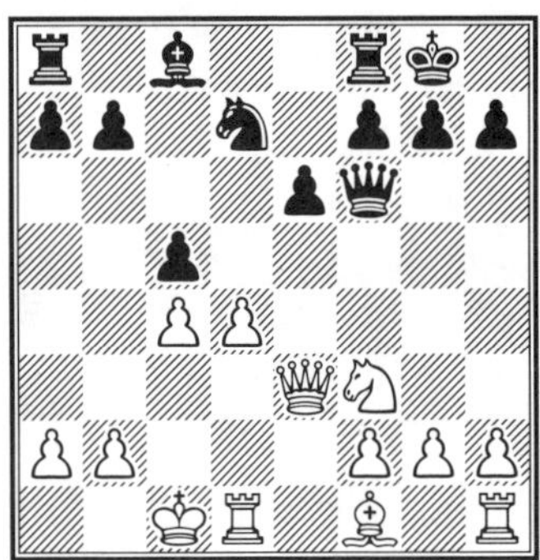

12.dxc5

Some readers might ask, "Why doesn't White play 12.d5 and get a passed pawn." The problem is that after 12.d5 exd5 13.cxd5 white's King is a bit airy and the c8-Bishop is now free to fly down the c8-h3 diagonal. 13...Qd6 followed by 14...Nf6 is very comfortable for Black, while 13...Nb6 is also good: 14.Qe5 (14.Qxc5 loses to 14...Bf5 when white's King is stuck on the c-file and ...Rac8 is ready to splatter White's position. 14.Bd3 Nxd5 also favors Black: 15.Bxh7+ [not 15.Qe4 Qh6+] 15...Kxh7 16.Rxd5 b6 followed by 17...Be6 when black's Bishop is better than white's Knight, while Black is the one with the queenside pawn majority.) 14...Rd8 15.Qxf6 gxf6 16.d6 Be6 and the a2-pawn is attacked and the d6-pawn will fall via ...Nc8 or ...Nd5 followed by ...Rxd6.

12...Qf5 13.Bd3 Qxc5 14.Rhe1 Qc7

I don't like this move since White is ahead in development and his pieces are aiming at black's King. 14...Qxe3+ was the prudent choice when White is better, but Black has very good drawing chances.

15.Ne5

Steinitz wants that endgame, and though the trades give White a win/draw with no worries about losing, I still think Black should go for it.

15...Re8?!

This makes it a bit harder for himself. Black should have traded with 15...Qxe5 16.Qxe5 Nxe5 17.Rxe5 b6 (and not 17...f6? 18.Rc5 e5 19.Be4 and White should win this position.) 18.b3 g6 19.Be4 Rb8 20.Bf3 Bb7 21.Bxb7 Rxb7 22.Kb2 Rc8 followed by ...Kg8-f8-e7, and Black should have good chances to hold.

16.Kb1 Nf8?

Black tosses away his last chance to go into the endgame.

17.c5! f6 18.Nc4

Now it's clear that the middlegame is much better than the endgame for White.

18...e5?

Black had to try 18...Bd7 followed by ...Bc6, though he would still be in very bad shape. Now White has a winning position thanks to his spacial advantage, his control of the d-file, the black King's vulnerability, and White's superior pieces.

19.Nd6 Re7 20.f4 Bd7 21.f5!

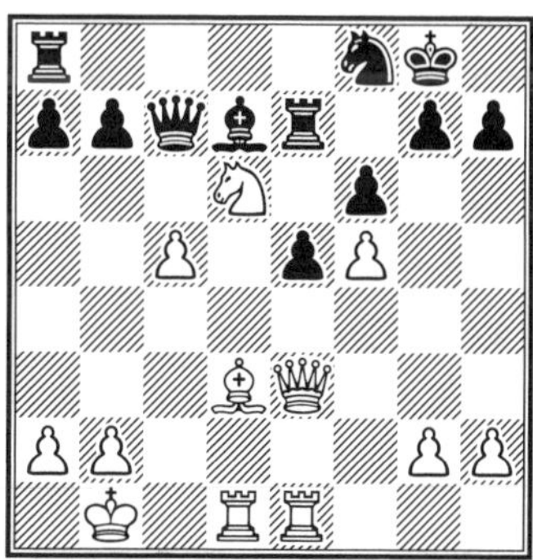

Taking more space, depriving Black's pieces of the e6-square, and also prepping for a pawn attack with g2-g4-g5.

21...Bc6 22.Bc4+ Kh8 23.g4 b6 24.g5 fxg5 25.Qxg5

For poor Marco, the rest must have been like watching an enormous tsunami heading straight for you and knowing that nothing could stop it.

25...h6 26.Qh5 bxc5 27.Nf7+ Kh7 28.Ng5+ Kh8 29.f6 gxf6 30.Qxh6+ Nh7 31.Nxh7 Rxh7 32.Qxf6+ Rg7 33.Rxe5, 1-0.

The second Lasker match was held in November, and it was stopped when Steinitz became ill. The score was ten wins for Lasker, two for Steinitz, and five draws. Four weeks later he was sent to a psychiatric clinic.

One source claimed that he went "hopelessly mad."

Another source had this to say: "Just four weeks after the match, Steinitz lost his mind and had to seek psychiatric help. Lasker, on the other hand, took a three year long break from chess, devoted himself to mathematical studies and went on to hold the title longer than anyone else in history (twenty-seven years)."

And yet another reported, "Shortly after the match, Steinitz had a mental breakdown and was confined for forty days in a Moscow sanatorium, where he played chess with the inmates."

I very much like what I.A. Horowitz wrote about this match:

> One is of two minds about the second Lasker–Steinitz match: On the one hand it is tempting to assert that it should never have been played at all. Steinitz was then over sixty years old and in poor health physically, and had driven himself close to nervous collapse through trying to regain the prestige he had lost in losing the title. On the other hand, had Lasker denied him the opportunity to regain the crown he had worn for so long, it would have been considered, and rightly so, the rankest injustice. Perhaps it is sensible, therefore, to look on the second match as one of those sad things that, for better or worse, just had to happen.

The Matter of Defense

A lot of people have criticized Steinitz for his defensive, "I dare you to hurt me" stance. The fact is, he did walk into some horrific over-the-board situations. Sometimes he held on and won, and other times he was mashed into sludge. A stubborn man, I think he enjoyed the challenge.

Certainly, he sometimes went overboard (and sometimes over, over, OVER-board) trying to defend dangerous situations. The Evans Gambit with Black was one of his favorites. In the following game Steinitz makes his point and wins:

Andres Clemente Vasquez vs. Wilhelm Steinitz, Havana match 1888

1.e4 e5 2.Nf3 Nc6 3.Bc4 Bc5 4.b4 Bxb4 5.c3 Bc5 6.d4 exd4 7.cxd4 Bb4+ 8.Kf1 Na5 9.Bd3 c6 10.a3 Be7 11.e5 d5 12.Nc3 Nh6 13.Ne2 Nf5 14.g4 Nh4 15.Nxh4 Bxh4 16.Nf4 g6

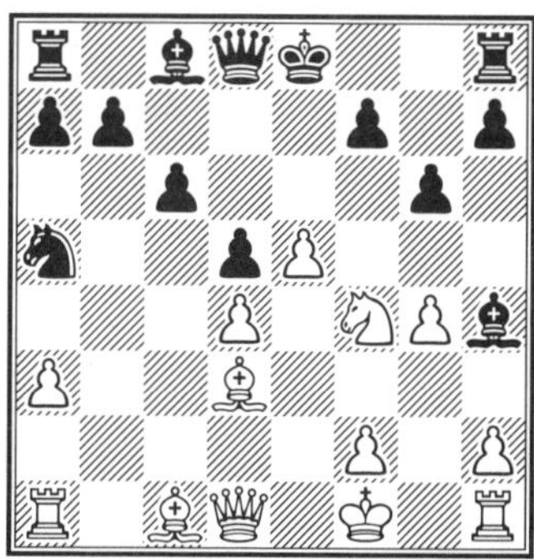

17.Ng2 h5 18.h3 Be7 19.gxh5 Rxh5 20.Nf4 Rh4 21.e6 Bxe6 22.Nxe6 fxe6 23.Bxg6+ Kd7 24.Rb1 Qh8 25.Qa4 Bd8 26.Be3 Bb6 27.Ke2 Rf8 28.Qb4 Nc4 29.Rbg1 Qf6 30.Rh2 Qf3+ 31.Kd3 Rxd4+, 0-1.

Steinitz completely outplayed Mr. Vasquez. Here is another example of his standing tall in the face of an enemy attack.

Mikhail Chigorin vs. Wilhelm Steinitz, World Championship (5) 1889

1.e4 e5 2.Nf3 Nc6 3.Bc4 Bc5 4.b4 Bxb4 5.c3 Ba5 6.0-0 Qf6 7.d4 Nge7 8.Bg5 Qd6 9.Qb3 0-0 10.Rd1 Bb6 11.dxe5 Qg6 12.Qa3 Re8 13.Nbd2 d6 14.exd6 cxd6 15.Bf4 Bc5 16.Qc1 Bg4 17.Bg3 Rad8

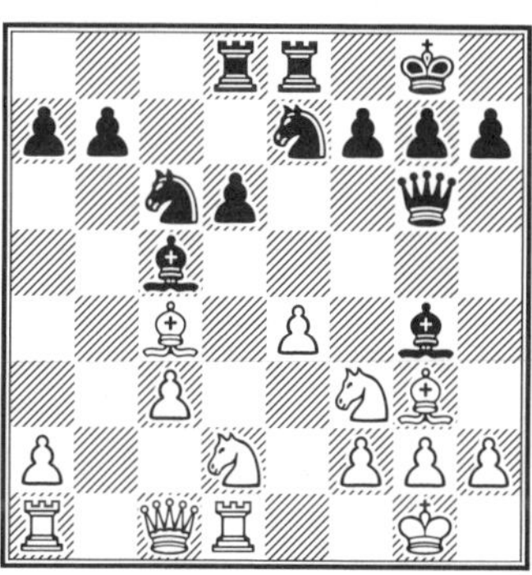

18.h3 Bxf3 19.Nxf3 Qxg3 20.Kh1 Qg6 21.Rd3 Qf6 22.Qd2 Ng6 23.Ng5 Nce5 24.Rf3 Nxf3 25.Bxf7+ Qxf7 26.gxf3 Qc4, 0-1.

As for Steinitz' hardheaded desire to prove he could defend anything—well, he absorbed a lot of unnecessary pain, the following is a typical debacle:

Isidor Gunsberg vs. Wilhelm Steinitz, World Championship (2) 1891

1.e4 e5 2.Nf3 Nc6 3.Bc4 Bc5 4.b4 Bxb4 5.c3 Ba5 6.0-0 Qf6 7.d4 Nh6 8.Bg5 Qd6 9.d5 Nd8 10.Qa4 Bb6 11.Na3 c6 12.Be2 Bc7 13.Nc4 Qf8 14.d6

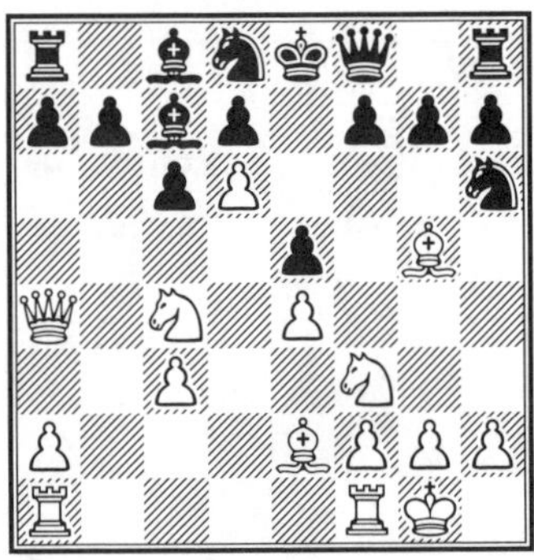

14...Bxd6 15.Nb6 Rb8 16.Qxa7 Ng4 17.Nh4 Ne6 18.Bxg4 Nxg5 19.Nf5 Ne6 20.Rfd1 Bc7 21.Na8 Rxa8 22.Qxa8 Kd8 23.Rxd7+ Kxd7 24.Rd1+, 1-0.

God, that had to hurt!

I will end with one of Steinitz' most celebrated games. Some denizens on the web have said that this game "has been analyzed to death" and that it's "lost its luster." Really? I've gone over this game many times and I never tire of it. It was a thing of beauty when it was played, it's still a thing of beauty now, and it will always be a thing of beauty.

Wilhelm Steinitz vs. Curt von Bardeleben, Hastings 1895

1.e4 e5 2.Nf3 Nc6 3.Bc4 Bc5 4.c3 Nf6 5.d4 exd4 6.cxd4 Bb4+ 7.Nc3 d5 8.exd5 Nxd5 9.0-0 Be6 10.Bg5 Be7 11.Bxd5 Bxd5 12.Nxd5 Qxd5 13.Bxe7 Nxe7 14.Re1 f6 15.Qe2 Qd7 16.Rac1 c6

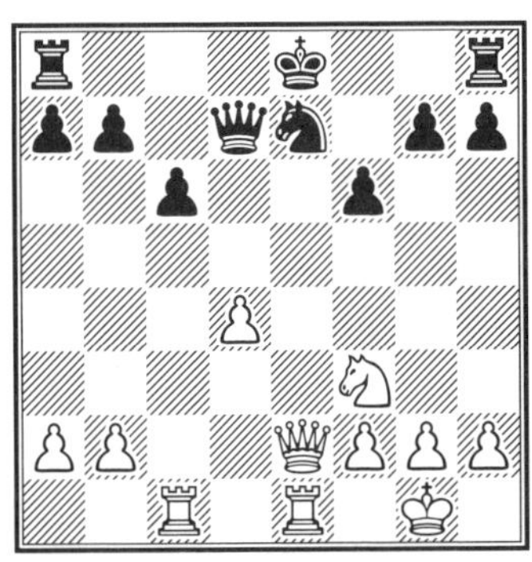

17.d5! cxd5 18.Nd4 Kf7 19.Ne6 Rhc8 20.Qg4 g6 21.Ng5+ Ke8

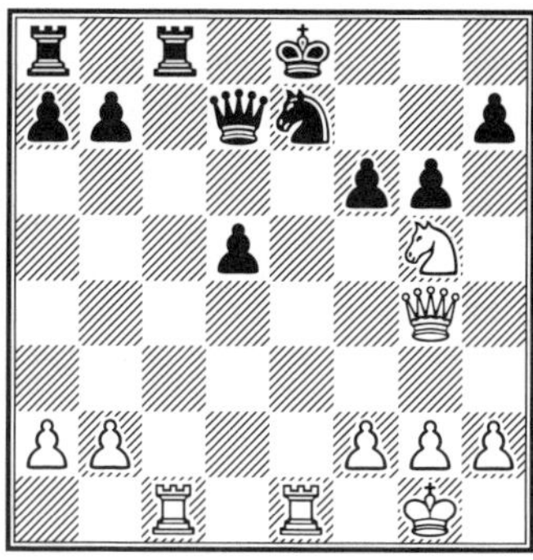

22.Rxe7+! Kf8

- 22...Qxe7 23.Rxc8+ Rxc8 24.Qxc8+ Qd8 25.Qxd8+ Kxd8 26.Nxh7 Ke7 27.h4 Kf7 28.f4 Kg7 29.Nxf6 Kxf6 30.g4.
- 22...Kxe7 23.Re1+ Kd6 24.Qb4+ Rc5 (24...Kc6 25.Rc1#) (24...Kc7 25.Ne6+ Kb8 26.Qf4+) 25.Re6+ Qxe6 26.Nxe6 Kxe6 27.Qxc5.

23.Rf7+ Kg8 24.Rg7+ Kh8 25.Rxh7+

At this point von Bardeleben got up and left the tournament hall without resigning.

Here's the end.

25...Kg8 26.Rg7+ Kh8 27.Qh4+ Kxg7 28.Qh7+ Kf8 29.Qh8+ Ke7 30.Qg7+ Ke8 31.Qg8+ Ke7 32.Qf7+ Kd8 33.Qf8+ Qe8 34.Nf7+ Kd7 35.Qd6, 1-0.

Matches from 1886-1900

Steinitz vs. Johannes Zukertort (1886): First official World Championship match 12½-7½

Steinitz vs. Andres Vasquez (1888): 5-0.

Steinitz vs. Celso Golmayo (1888): 5-0.

Steinitz vs. A. Ponce (1888): 4-1.

Steinitz vs. Mikhail Chigorin (1889): Second official World Championship match 10½-6½ (only one draw!).

Steinitz vs. Isidor Gunsberg (1890/91): Third official World Championship match 10½-8½.

Steinitz vs. Mikhail Chigorin (1892): Fourth official World Championship match 12½-10½.

Steinitz vs. Emanuel Lasker (1894): Fifth official World Championship match 12-7 (Steinitz must have done an about face when he saw Lasker win a strong tournament in New York with a 13-0 score!).

Steinitz vs. Alfred Ettlinger (1894): 10-0.

Steinitz vs. Emanuel Schiffers (1896): 6½-4½.

Steinitz vs. Emanuel Lasker (1896-97): Sixth official World Championship match 12½-4½.

Tournaments from 1894-1900

New York (1894): Steinitz first ahead of Albin and Pillsbury.

Hastings (1895): Pillsbury first, Chigorin second, Lasker third, Tarrasch fourth, Steinitz fifth.

St. Petersburg (1895/96): Lasker first, Steinitz second, Pillsbury third, Chigorin fourth.

Nuremberg (1896): Lasker first, Maróczy second, Pillsbury and Tarrasch tied third/fourth, Janowski fifth, Steinitz sixth.

Vienna (1898): Tarrasch and Pillsbury tied for first/second, Janowski third, Steinitz fourth.

Cologne (1898): Amos Burn first, W. Cohn, Charousek, and Chigorin tired second thru fourth, Steinitz fifth.

London (1899): Emanuel Lasker first, Janowski, Pillsbury, and Maróczy tied for second thru fourth, Schlechter fifth, Blackburne sixth, Chigorin seventh, Showalter eighth, Mason ninth, W. Cohn tenth, and Steinitz eleventh.

Wilhelm Steinitz died penniless in 1900.

6

EMANUEL LASKER

A Positional and Tactical Mystery

In general, when one asks what any World Champion's strengths were/are, it's fairly easy to give a somewhat educated answer. Steinitz: the first master of positional chess. Alekhine: dynamic, combinative genius. Capablanca: endgame mastery and positional elegance. Tal: attack and tactics. Lasker: endgame mastery, the first chess psychologist. But, when discussing Lasker, is that the whole story?

Warning! Emanuel Lasker is my favorite chess player, so I'm going to lay it on a bit thick!

- Was Emanuel Lasker really that good at the endgame? Yes. In fact, he's easily in the list of the top five best endgame players ever.
- What was Lasker's chess psychology? He saw chess as a fight, and he entered that fight without any fear whatsoever. He knew how to turn up the heat, and where other players would crack, he would stand tall and, invariably, come out the victor.
- And let's not forget his defensive prowess. Where nobody (back then or now) was Lasker's superior in the endgame, he's (in my opinion) the greatest defensive player ever. Simply put, he saved positions that even the greatest modern players wouldn't have been able to save.

Those amazing attributes alone might explain why he retained the World Championship for an outrageous twenty-seven years! But what if I told you that he had another specific chess talent, one that was just as pronounced as his massive endgame skills? Lasker had the ability to calculate extremely deeply, and he had an imagination that led to him seeing things that others would never find. This means that he was able to come up with delightful combinations, just like all the other great tacticians.

Lasker used this talent to find defenses that no other human would even think of. He used this talent to create chaotic tactical tidal waves (like Tal did), which drowned one opponent after another. He used this talent to find endgame ideas that are now well known, but had never been seen before Lasker found them over the board! And he used this talent to create defensive setups that even modern computers are incapable of seeing.

I could give examples of all these things, but I'll keep it simple and just concentrate on his use of basic tactics.

The following double Bishop sacrifice had never been seen before Lasker played it in this game.

Emanuel Lasker vs. J. H. Bauer, Amsterdam 1889

1.f4 d5 2.e3 Nf6 3.b3 e6 4.Bb2 Be7 5.Bd3 b6 6.Nf3 Bb7 7.Nc3 Nbd7 8.0-0 0-0 9.Ne2 c5 10.Ng3 Qc7 11.Ne5 Nxe5 12.Bxe5 Qc6 13.Qe2 a6 14.Nh5! Nxh5

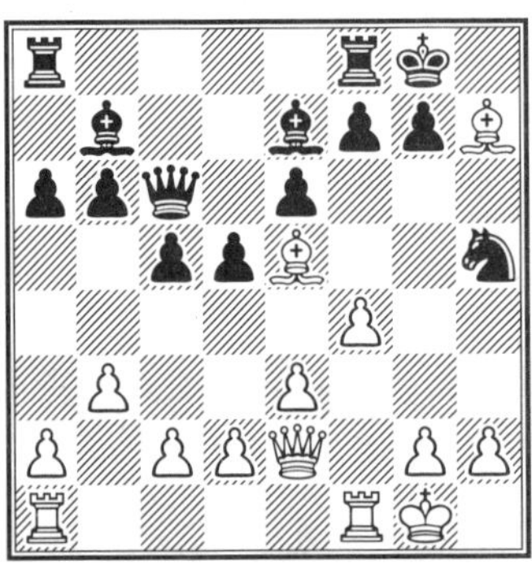

14...c4 15.Nxf6+ Bxf6 (15...gxf6 16.Bxh7+ Kh8 [16...Kxh7 17.Qh5+ Kg7 18.Qg4+ Kh6 19.Rf3 fxe5 20.Rh3+ Bh4 21.Rxh4 mate] 17.Qh5 Kg7 [17...Rg8 18.Bg6+ Kg7 19.Qh7+ Kf8 20.Qxf7 mate] 18.Qg5+ Kxh7 19.Qh4+ Kg6 20.Qg4+ Kh7 21.Rf3 fxe5 22.Rh3+ Bh4 23.Rxh4 mate.) 16.Bxh7+ Kxh7 17.Qh5+ Kg8 18.Bxf6 gxf6 19.Rf3 Rfd8 20.Qh6 and mates.

15.Bxh7+! Kxh7

15...Kh8 16.Qxh5 Bg5 17.Bg6+ Bh6 18.Qxh6+ Kg8 19.Qxg7 mate.

16.Qxh5+ Kg8 17.Bxg7!

Ripping away the last shred of pawn protection from the black King.

17...Kxg7

17...f6 18.Rf3 (18.Bh6 also mates.) 18...Qe8 (18...Rf7 19.Qh8 mate) 19.Qh8+ Kf7 20.Qh7 Qb8 21.Qh5+ Kg8 22.Rg3 and mates.

18.Qg4+ Kh7 19.Rf3 e5

Hopeless, but it's the only way to prevent mate.

20.Rh3+ Qh6 21.Rxh6+ Kxh6 22.Qd7 Bf6 23.Qxb7

And White easily won the game.

It's very important to understand that tactics aren't just used for mating attacks. Tactics also allow positional ideas to come to fruition and make technical endgames far easier to play.

Scha/Schneppe/Schone vs. Lasker/Ked/Wolff, Berlin consultation game 1890

1.e4 e5 2.Nf3 Nc6 3.Bb5 Nf6 4.0-0 Nxe4 5.d4 Nd6 6.Bxc6 dxc6 7.dxe5 Nf5 8.Qxd8+ Kxd8 9.Bg5+ Ke8 10.Nc3 h6 11.Bd2 Be7 12.Ne2 Be6 13.b3 Rd8 14.Rad1 Bd5 15.Ne1 c5 16.c4 Bc6 17.Nc2 Be4 18.Ne3 Nd4 19.Nf4 Bg5 20.Nfd5 c6 21.f4 Bh4 22.Ba5 b6 23.Nxb6 axb6 24.Bxb6

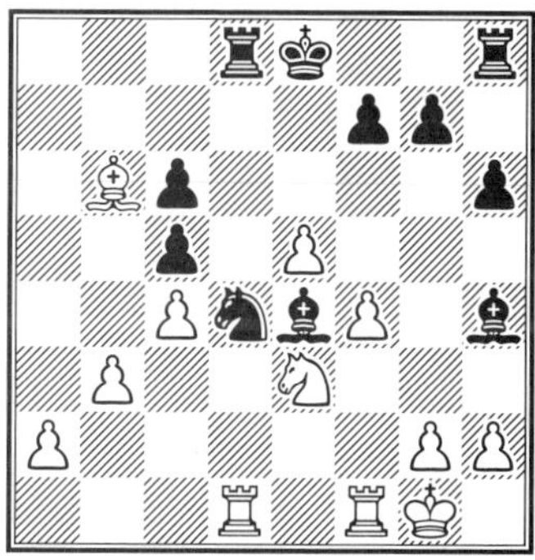

24...Ne2+!

24...Ra8 was also strong, but Lasker's move was by far the best.

25.Kh1 Rxd1 26.Rxd1

Better was 26.Nxd1 though 26...Kd7! 27.Bxc5 Ke6 is also winning for Black.

26...Nxf4 27.Bxc5 Nd3, 0-1.

The double threat of 28...Nxc5 and 28...Nf2+ ends the game.

In our next position, Lasker (who was sixty-six years old at this point!) understood that a pedestrian move like 34...R2d4 wouldn't give him anything after 35.Ne4 Qh5 36.Qe2=. So he came up with the idea of sacrificing his Queen for a Rook, Knight and pawn. In 1934 such a sacrifice was unheard of, but (like the double Bishop sacrifice) it became normal after this game.

Max Euwe vs. Emanuel Lasker, Zurich 1934

1.d4 d5 2.c4 e6 3.Nc3 Nf6 4.Bg5 Nbd7 5.e3 c6 6.Nf3 Be7 7.Qc2 0-0 8.a3 Re8 9.Rc1 dxc4 10.Bxc4 Nd5 11.Bxe7 Qxe7 12.Ne4 N5f6 13.Ng3 c5 14.0-0 cxd4 15.Nxd4 Nb6 16.Ba2 Rb8 17.e4 Rd8 18.Rfd1 Bd7 19.e5 Ne8 20.Bb1 g6 21.Qe4 Ba4 22.b3 Bd7 23.a4 Nd5 24.Bd3 Rbc8 25.Bc4 Bc6 26.Nxc6 bxc6 27.Rd3 Nb4 28.Rf3 Rc7 29.h4 Rcd7 30.h5 Qg5 31.Re1 Rd4 32.hxg6 hxg6 33.Qe2 Rd2 34.Qf1 Nc2!!

34...R2d4 35.Ne4 Qh5 36.Qe2, =.

35.Ne4 Qxe5!

The point of 34...Nc2.

36.Nf6+ Qxf6 37.Rxf6

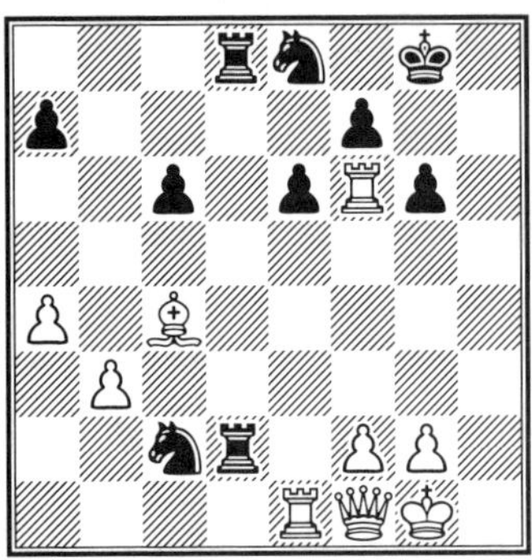

37...Nxf6

Black is better after this, but extremely interesting is the super complex 37...Nxe1!? 38.Rf4 (38.Rxe6! is the best defense: 38...fxe6 39.Bxe6+ Kg7 40. Qa6 Black is better, but his open King mixed with white's nimble Queen and active Bishop has to give White counterplay (I'll let someone else come up with an assessment!]) Lasker [wisely!] didn't want to touch any of this and preferred the far more manageable path he took in the game.) 38...Rd1! (Much better, and far more surprising, than regaining the Queen by 38...Nf3+ 39.Rxf3 Rd1 when 40.Rc3 targets the weakness on c6 and keeps White very much in the game.) 39.Be2 Ra1! 40.Rc4! (40.Kh2? Nc2 wins for Black.) 40...Rd2! 41.Kh2! (and not 41.Rxc6?? Rxe2 42.Qxe2 Nf3 mate!) 41...Nf3+ 42.gxf3 Rxf1 43.Bxf1 Rxf2+ 44.Bg2 Nf6 45.Rxc6 and though Black is obviously better, White's queenside majority and long range Bishop would seem to make a Black win tough to achieve. However, "would seem" and reality are often two different things, and 45...Rb2! 46.Ra6 Nh5 (46...Nd5 allows 47.Kg3) 47.Kg1 Nf4 places White in a desperate situation. 48.Bf1 (48.Bh1 has to be bad.) 48...Rxb3 49.Rxa7 Rxf3 doesn't inspire the White side with confidence.

38.Rc1?!

It's understandable that White didn't want to give back the Queen, all the more so since 38.Re2 Rd1 39.Rxc2 Rxf1+ 40.Kxf1 leads to a pawn down endgame against one of the greatest endgame players of all time. Nevertheless, this is the path Euwe should have taken. After 38.Rc1 Lasker sweeps Euwe off the board.

38...Ne4 39.Be2 Nd4 40.Bf3 Nxf2 41.Qc4 Nd3 42.Rf1 Ne5 43.Qb4 Nexf3+ 44.gxf3 Ne2+ 45.Kh2 Nf4+ 46.Kh1 R2d4 47.Qe7 Kg7 48.Qc7 R8d5 49.Re1 Rg5 50.Qxc6 Rd8, 0-1.

Nothing can be done about the threat of ...Rh8 mate.

The game is all the more impressive when you realize that his opponent, Max Euwe, took the World Championship from Alekhine one year later!

Let's enjoy a few more Lasker tactics.

Francis Joseph Lee vs. Emanuel Lasker, London 1899

1.e4 e5 2.Nf3 Nc6 3.Bb5 a6 4.Ba4 Nf6 5.d3 d6 6.c3 b5 7.Bc2 g6 8.a4 Bb7 9.Nbd2 Bg7 10.Nf1 d5 11.Qe2 0-0 12.Ng3 Qd6 13.0-0 Rfe8 14.h3 Na5 15.Bd2 c5 16.Rfd1 Qc7 17.Qe1 c4 18.d4 Nxe4 19.Nxe4 dxe4 20.Nxe5 Bxe5 21.dxe5 Qxe5 22.Be3 Nc6 23.b3 Na5 24.b4 Nc6 25.Rd7 Re7 26.Rdd1 Rd8 27.Rxd8+ Nxd8 28.axb5 axb5 29.Qd2 Ne6 30.h4 Bc6 31.Ra6 Rd7 32.Qe1 Bb7 33.Ra5 f5 34.g3 f4 35.gxf4 Nxf4 36.Bd4 Qf5 37.Qe3

[top] Emanuel Lasker circa 1890s; [bottom] Lasker vs. Gustavus Reichhelm 1892 (Photos: Courtesy of the Cleveland Public Library's John G. White Collection).

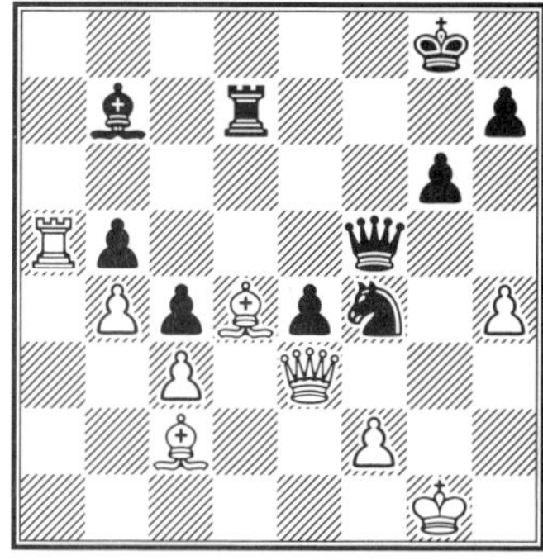

37...Rxd4!

The start of a long, very pleasing combination. An alternative was 37...Qg4+ 38.Kf1 Qg2+ 39.Ke1 Qg1+ 40.Kd2 Ng2 41.Qe2 e3+ 42.fxe3 Bf3 and it's all over.

38.cxd4

38.Qxd4 Ne2+— King and Queen fork one.

38...Qg4+ 39.Kf1 Qg2+ 40.Ke1 Qg1+ 41.Kd2 c3+! 42.Qxc3

42.Kxc3 Nd5+ — King and Queen fork two.

42...Qxf2+ 43.Kd1 e3 44.Bb3+ Kg7 45.d5+ Kh6 46.Qe1 Bc8!, 0-1.

White resigned since 47.Qxf2 exf2 promotes the f-pawn.

Emanuel Lasker vs. Jacques Mieses, Leipzig match (1) 1889

1.d4 f5 2.c4 c5 3.dxc5 Qa5+ 4.Nc3 Qxc5 5.e4 fxe4 6.Nxe4 Qc7 7.Nh3 g6 8.Nf4 Bg7 9.Nd5 Qd8 10.Bg5 Bxb2 11.Nd6+ Kf8 12.Qf3+ Bf6 13.Bxf6 Nxf6 14.Nxf6 exf6 15.Qd5 Qe7+ 16.Kd2 Kg7 17.Re1 Qf8 18.h4 h5 19.Rh3 Nc6 20.Rhe3 Qd8

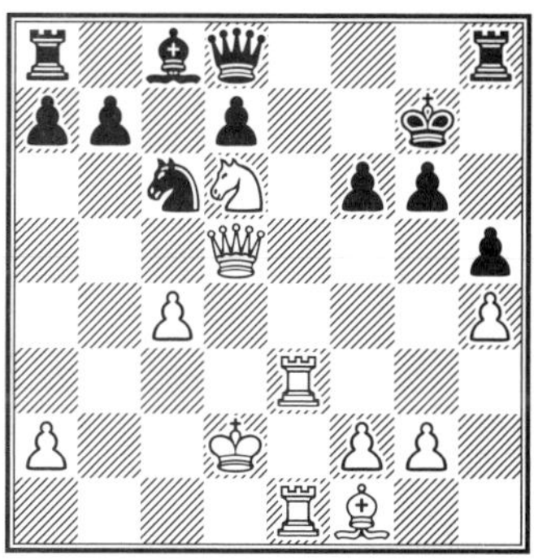

21.Qf7+

In the actual game White went for a piece up endgame via 21.Re8 Rxe8 22.Rxe8 Qa5+ 23.Qxa5 Nxa5 24.Rxc8 Rxc8 25.Nxc8 and, for some reason, Black didn't resign and instead hung out until move 37 before finally giving up.

21...Kh6 22.Qxg6+!! Kxg6 23.Rg3+ Kh7 24.Bd3+ f5 25.Bxf5+ Kh6 26.Nf7, 1-0.

Albin Reif vs. Emanuel Lasker, Hauptturnier 1889

1.f4 e5 2.fxe5 f6 3.exf6 Nxf6 4.Nf3 d5 5.e3 Nc6 6.Bb5 Bd6 7.Bxc6+ bxc6 8.0-0 0-0 9.b3 Ng4 10.h3 Qf6!

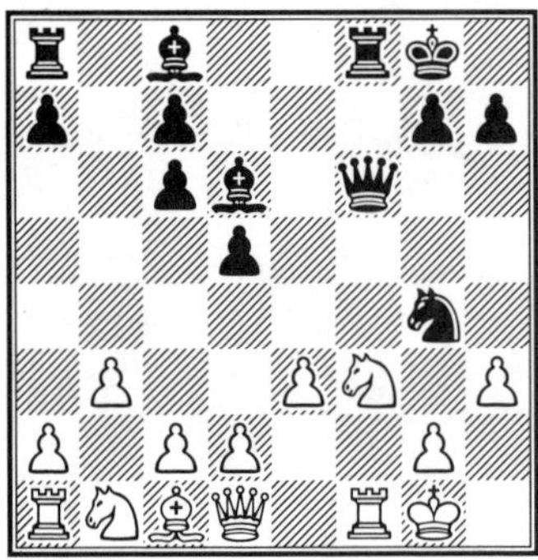

The mark of a great player. Instead of reacting to White's threat, Black makes one of his own!

11.c3?

11.hxg4 Qxa1 12.Nc3 Bb4; 11.Nc3 was best when 11...Nxe3! 12.dxe3 Qxc3 is clearly better for Black.

11...Nh2! 12.Rf2

The actual game ended quickly: 12.Nxh2 Bxh2+ 13.Kxh2 Qxf1, 0-1.

12...Bxh3!!

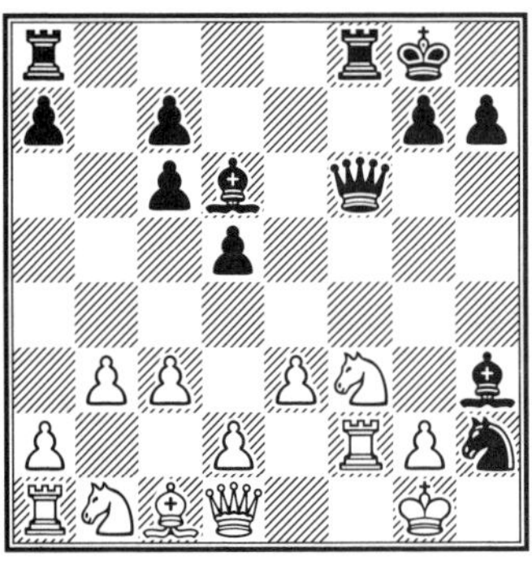

13.gxh3 Nxf3+ 14.Kh1

14.Kg2 Nh4+ mates in a couple moves.

14...Qh4 15.Rxf3 Rxf3 16.Qxf3 Rf8, 0-1.

Okay, the next game is a bit different since I'm highlighting a possible variation (with Lasker's side losing) that lower rated players will enjoy. I also give the real game, and also best play for both sides showing how Lasker would have created maximum chaos in an effort to save a bad position. (Since Lasker won, the chaos must have worked!).

Rudolf Loman vs. Emanuel Lasker, Amsterdam 1889

1.e4 e5 2.Nf3 Nc6 3.Bb5 a6 4.Ba4 Nf6 5.0-0 d6 6.Nc3 b5 7.Bb3 Bg4 8.h3 Bh5 9.d3 Nd4 10.Kh2 g5 11.g4

Lasker, no doubt deciding that his opponent didn't deserve any respect at all, played the wild (and unsound) 10...g5 last move. By breaking the pin White has forced Lasker to either retreat and accept the loss of the g5-pawn or go for the gusto by sacrificing on g4 (which was Lasker's intention all along).

11...Nxg4+ 12.hxg4 Bxg4

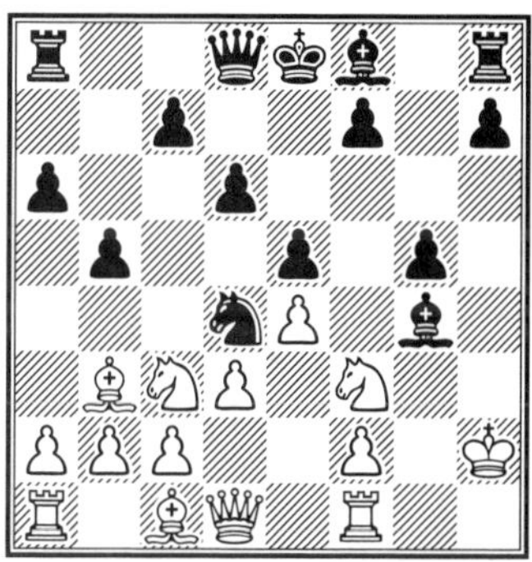

13.Nxe5!

In the game White was simply out-calculated by Lasker: 13.Bxf7+ Kxf7 14.Nxg5+ Qxg5 15.Bxg5 Bxd1 and it was only here that White noticed that 16.Raxd1 would be met by 16...Nf3+ 17.Kg2 Nxg5 with an extra piece. White chose 16.f4 instead, but after the coldblooded 16...Bg4 17.fxe5+ Kg6 18.Bf6 Bg7 19.Rf4 h5 20.Raf1 Raf8 White was soon forced to resign.

13...Bxd1??

Lasker wouldn't have fallen for this. Instead he would have created maximum chaos by 13...Nxb3 14.Qxg4 Nxa1 15.Bxg5 Qc8 16.Qf4 dxe5 17.Qxe5+ Qe6 18.Qxh8 Kd7 19.f4 (19.Rxa1?? Bd6+ wins the white Queen.) 19...Nxc2 though after 20.Nd5 Lasker would have been in bad shape.

14.Bxf7+ Ke7 15.Nd5, 1-0.

Emanuel Lasker vs. Abraham Mocatta, London simultaneous exhibition 1891

1.e4 e5 2.Nf3 Nc6 3.Bb5 Nf6 4.0-0 Nxe4 5.d4 Nd6 6.Bxc6 bxc6 7.dxe5 Nb7 8.Ng5 Nc5 9.Re1 Ne6 10.h4 Be7 11.Qf3 Bxg5 12.hxg5 Nxg5 13.Qg3 h6 14.f4 Ne6 15.Nc3 Qe7 16.f5 Ng5 17.f6 Qe6 18.Bxg5 hxg5 19.Ne4 g6 20.Nxg5 Qc4 21.Rad1 Qc5+ 22.Re3 Qxc2 23.Rde1 Qc4

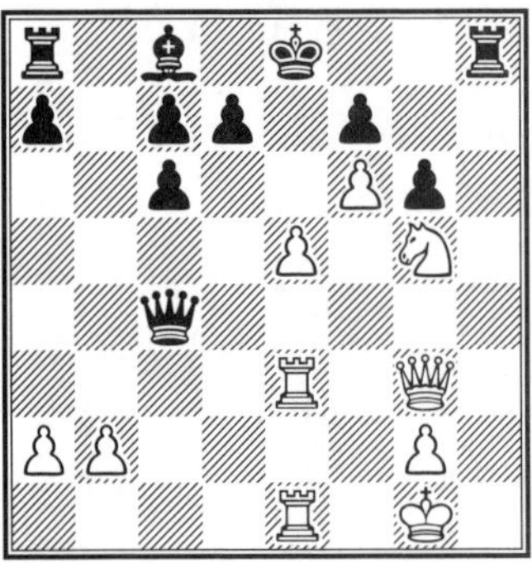

24.e6!! dxe6

24...fxe6 25.Nxe6! dxe6 26.Qxg6+ Kd8 27.Qg7 Re8 28.Rd1+ and Black has to resign.

25.Qxc7 Bd7

25...0-0 26.Qh2! forces mate.

26.Rd1

This mates faster than the flashy 26.Nxe6!

26...Rd8 27.Qd6, 1-0.

I find that many players are not aware of Lasker's outstanding tactical prowess. I already mentioned his various chess skills but now I want to point out the general nature of his tactics—sure, you'll find the usual crushing attacks, but you'll also notice that he uses tactics as a means to make positional plans blossom, defensive strategies work, and endgame concepts flow in perfect order. If you look closely at Tal's tactical explosions you'll see they are very different than Lasker's. Tal's were all about blowing you off the board. Lasker often used tactics to highlight more subtle but no less important things.

What Lasker's games remind us of is that tactical building blocks don't necessarily lead to attacks. For example, a pin can be the backbone of a lovely combination, but often a pin works its magic in calmer ways. In the following example Lasker has the better game and begins making use of a number of pins. White missed his best defense and drowned under wave after wave of pins. One of the most important building blocks of tactics is the simple, "obvious," undefended or inadequately defended piece. In fact, a combination isn't feasible without the presence of an undefended or inadequately defended piece, or without a vulnerable King.

The next game between Steinitz and Lasker is an example that shows what can happen if your pieces aren't properly protected. Training your eye to see this kind of thing is critically important; it allows you to avoid losing stuff in this fashion and it also allows you to punish those that aren't as careful.

William Steinitz vs. Emanuel Lasker, World Championship (16) 1894

1.d4 d5 2.c4 e6 3.Nc3 Nf6 4.Bg5 Be7 5.Nf3 Nbd7 6.e3 0-0 7.c5 Ne4 8.Nxe4 dxe4 9.Bxe7 Qxe7 10.Nd2 Nf6 11.Nc4 b6 12.b4 Nd5 13.Qb1 f5 14.Ne5 a5 15.Nc6 Qg5 16.h4 Qf6 17.cxb6 f4 18.Qxe4 fxe3 19.f3 Bb7 20.b5 Bxc6 21.bxc6 cxb6 22.Bd3 Qh6 23.g3 Rac8 24.Rc1 Rc7 25.0-0 Rd8 26.f4 Qg6 27.Qxg6 hxg6 28.Bxg6 Ne7 29.Be4 Rxd4 30.Bf3 Nf5 31.Rfe1 Kf7 32.Rb1 Nxg3 33.Rxb6 Nf5 34.Rb7 Rxb7 35.cxb7 Rb4 36.Rc1 Nd4 37.Kg2 Rb2+ 38.Kg3 Rxb7!

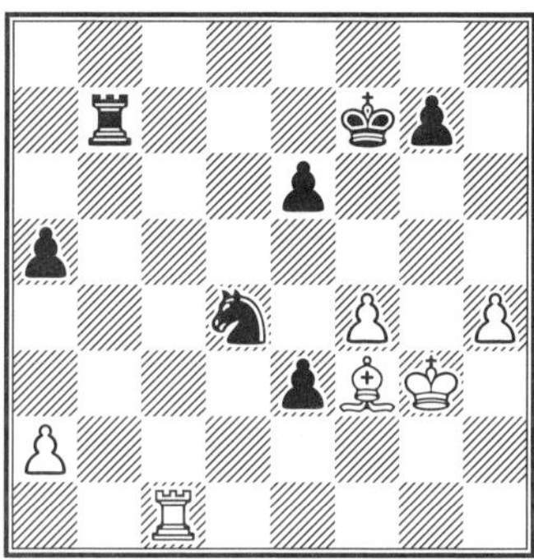

The point of Black's earlier check. 38...Nxf3? 39.Rc7+ Kg6 40.Kxf3 isn't what Black had in mind.

39.Bxb7 Ne2+ 40.Kf3 Nxc1 41.Kxe3 Nxa2

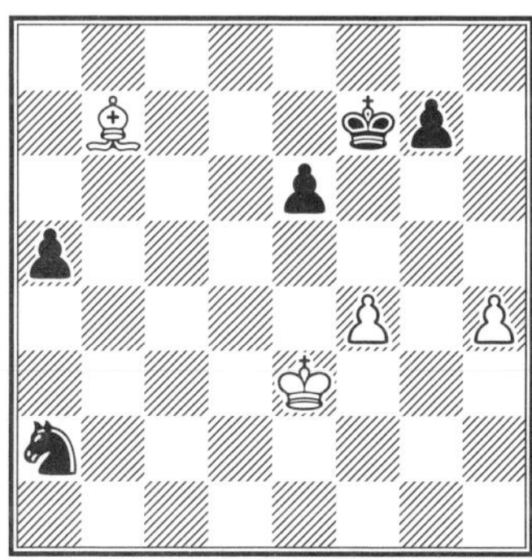

42.Kd4?

Perhaps taken aback by Black's little forking combination, White misses 42.f5! Nb4 (42...exf5 43.Bd5+ picks up black's Knight and draws easily) 43.fxe6+ Kxe6 44.Kd4 with a theoretical draw.

42...Kf6 43.Kc5 Nc3

And White was suddenly getting run over. The rest of the game was easy thanks to Lasker's peerless technique:

44.Kc4 Ne2 45.Kb5 Nxf4 46.Kxa5 Ng6 47.h5 Nf4 48.Bf3 Kf5 49.Kb4 e5 50.Kc3 e4 51.Bd1 e3 52.Bf3 Kg5 53.Kc2 Kh4 54.Kd1 Kg3, 0-1.

Emanuel Lasker vs. Alfred Ettlinger, New York match (4) 1893

1.e4 b6 2.d4 Bb7 3.Bd3 g6 4.Nf3 Bg7 5.c3 e6 6.Na3 Ne7 7.Bf4 0-0 8.h4 f5 9.e5 Nd5 10.Bg5 Qe8 11.Qd2 a6 12.h5 gxh5 13.Rh3 Ne7 14.0-0-0 Bxf3 15.Rxf3 Ng6 16.Rh1 h4 17.Rfh3 Nc6 18.g3 Rf7 19.gxh4 Bf8 20.h5 Nh8 21.Bf6 h6 22.Rg1+ Kh7 23.Qf4 Bg7 24.Bxf5+

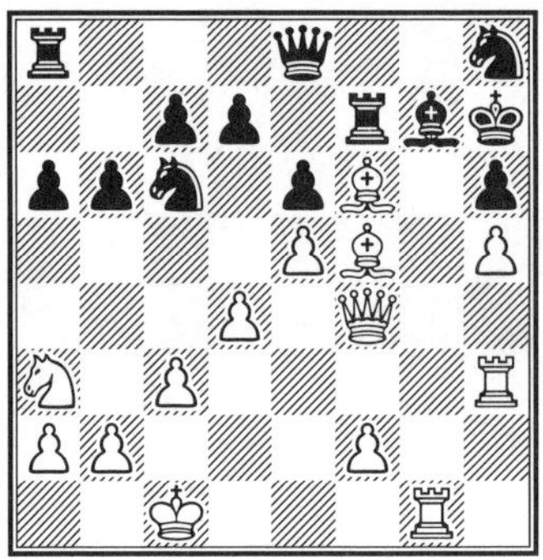

Equally good is 24.Rhg3 Bxf6 25.Bxf5+ exf5 26.Qxf5+ Ng6 27.Qxg6+ Kh8 28.Qxh6+ Rh7 29.Qxf6+ Rg7 30.Qxg7 mate.

24...exf5 25.Qxf5+ Kg8 26.Rhg3 Qe6 27.Qh7+!! Kf8

27...Kxh7 28.Rxg7+ Rxg7 29.Rxg7 mate.

28.Qxh8+!, 1-0.

28...Bxh8 29.Rg8 mate.

William de Visser vs. Emanuel Lasker, New York 1893

1.e4 e5 2.Nf3 Nc6 3.d4 d5 4.exd5 Qxd5 5.dxe5 Qxd1+ 6.Kxd1 Bg4 7.Bf4 0-0-0+ 8.Nbd2 Bc5 9.Ke1 Nb4 10.Rc1 Nxa2 11.Rd1 Nb4 12.Rc1 f6 13.Ne4 Bb6 14.exf6 Nxf6 15.Nxf6 gxf6 16.Be2 Bf5 17.Bd1 Rhe8+ 18.Kf1

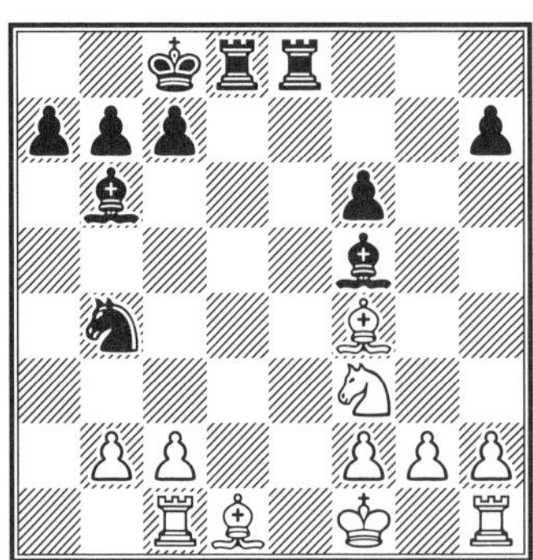

18...Nxc2! 19.Bxc2

In the game White played 19.g4 but he went down fast after 19...Bxg4.

19...Bxc2 20.h4

20.Rxc2 Rd1+ 21.Ne1 Rdxe1 mate.

20...Bd3+ 21.Kg1 Re2

And after Black chops on b2 or f2 he'll be two pawns up with an easy win.

Emanuel Lasker vs. Leon Labatt, U.S. (simultaneous exhibition) 1893

1.e4 e6 2.d4 d5 3.Nc3 Nf6 4.e5 Nfd7 5.f4 c5 6.dxc5 Bxc5 7.Qg4 0-0 8.Bd3 f5 9.Qh3 Rf7 10.g4 g6 11.gxf5 gxf5 12.Nf3 Nf8 13.Bd2 Bd7 14.0-0-0 Na6 15.Ng5 Rg7

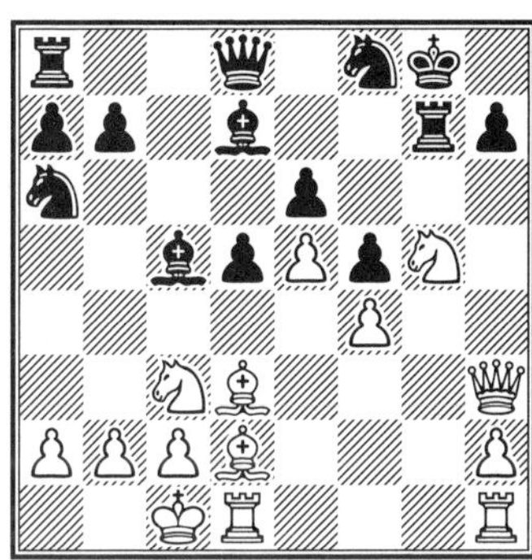

16.Bxf5 exf5 17.Nxd5 Nc7 18.Ba5 b6 19.e6 Ncxe6 20.Bc3 Nxg5 21.fxg5 Qe8 22.Rhe1 Qf7 23.Nf6+ Kh8 24.Nxd7

24.Nh5 is also crushing.

24...Nxd7 25.g6!

Lovely. The h-pawn is pinned and the g7-Rook is pinned.

25...Qxg6 26.Rxd7 Rg8 27.Bxg7+ Rxg7 28.Rd8+ Rg8 29.Qc3+ Qg7 30.Ree8 Bd4

30...Qxc3 31.Rxg8 mate.

31.Rxg8+ Qxg8 32.Qxd4, 1-0.

After winning the World Championship, many players still didn't think Lasker was the best. The Hastings tournament of 1895 which was stuffed with every top player on Earth—including Lasker, Tarrasch, Steinitz, Chigorin, Pillsbury, Teichmann—was a chance for Lasker to show his superiority. Unfortunately he had just gotten over typhoid fever and was still quite ill. Nevertheless, he still showed his enormous strength in many games.

Emanuel Lasker vs. David Janowski, Hastings 1895

1.d4 d5 2.c4 e6 3.Nc3 Nf6 4.Bg5 Be7 5.Nf3 0-0 6.e3 b6 7.Rc1 Bb7 8.cxd5 exd5 9.Bd3 c5 10.0-0 Nbd7 11.dxc5 Nxc5 12.Bb1 Rc8 13.Bf5 Ne6 14.Bh4 Kh8 15.Ne5 Qe8 16.Qf3 Ng8 17.Bg3 Nh6 18.Bb1 f6 19.Nd3 Qd7 20.Qd1 Rfd8 21.Nf4 Nxf4 22.Bxf4 g5 23.Bg3 Bf8 24.Qd3 f5 25.Ne2 Bg7 26.Nd4 Rf8 27.Rxc8 Qxc8 28.Qd2 Rf7 29.Rc1 Qe8 30.h4 gxh4 31.Bxh4 Bc8 32.Bg3 Ng4 33.Nb5!

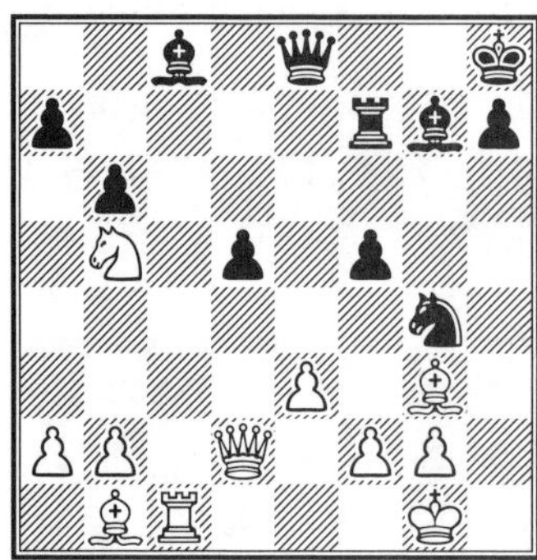

Using two tactical tools: a fork threat on d6 and the vulnerability of the inadequately defended Bishop on c8.

33...Rf8 34.Nd6 Qe6 35.Rxc8 Rxc8 36.Bxf5!, 1-0.

William Pollock vs. Emanuel Lasker, Hastings 1895

1.e4 e5 2.Nf3 Nc6 3.Bc4 Bc5 4.b4 Bb6 5.c3 d6 6.a4 a6 7.a5 Ba7 8.b5 axb5 9.Bxb5 Nf6 10.a6 0-0 11.d3 Ne7 12.axb7 Bxb7 13.Na3 d5 14.0-0 Ng6 15.exd5 Nxd5 16.Qe1 Qf6 17.Bg5 Qf5 18.Nc2 Nxc3!

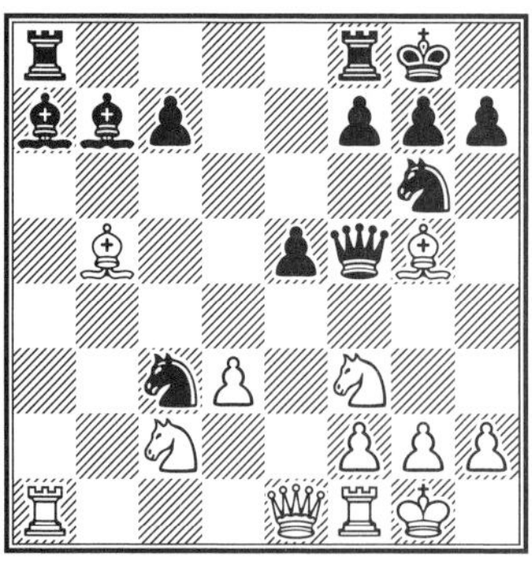

Freeing the b7-Bishop's diagonal and taking advantage of the g5-Bishop's inadequately defended state.

19.Rxa7

19.Qxc3 Bxf3 leaves the g5-Bishop out to dry: 20.Qd2 Qg4 21.Ne1 Bb7 with an extra pawn and two monster Bishops raking down the a7-g1 and b7-h1 diagonals.

19...Bxf3!

Better than 19...Rxa7 20.Ne3 Qe6 21.Qxc3.

20.Ne3 Qxg5 21.Rxa8 Rxa8 22.Qxc3 Nf4

The dual threat of 23...Nxg2 and 23...Ne2+ ends the game.

23.Ra1 Ne2+, 0-1.

I don't think Black (in the following game) had any idea that he was about to be caught, gutted, and devoured.

Emanuel Lasker vs. Carl Walbrodt, Hastings 1895

1.e4 e5 2.Nf3 Nc6 3.Bb5 Nf6 4.0-0 Be7 5.Nc3 d6 6.d4 exd4 7.Nxd4 Bd7 8.Nde2 0-0 9.Ng3 Ne5 10.Bxd7 Qxd7 11.b3 Rad8 12.Bb2 Nc6 13.Nf5 Qe6 14.Re1 Ne5 15.f4 Ng6 16.Nd5

Black could quietly resign here.

16...c6 17.Nfxe7+

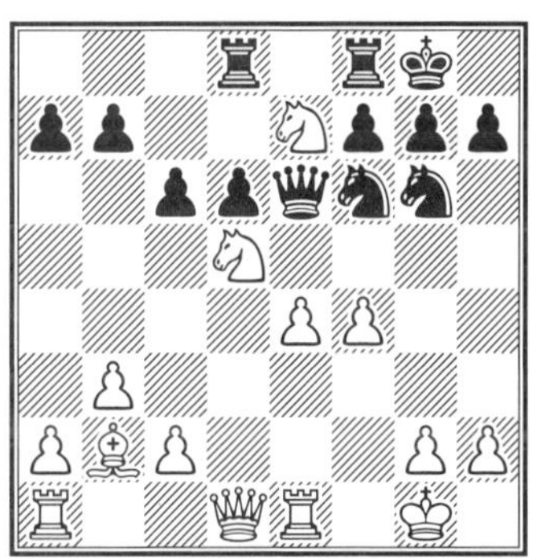

17...Nxe7 18.f5 Nxf5

18...Qd7 19.Nxf6+ gxf6 20.Qh5 d5 21.Bxf6 Qd6 22.Qh6

19.Nxf6+ gxf6 20.exf5 Qxf5 21.Rf1 Qe4 22.Bxf6 Rde8 23.Rf3 h5 24.Rg3+, 1-0.

Emanuel Lasker vs. Harry Pillsbury, Hastings 1895

1.e4 e5 2.Nf3 Nc6 3.Bb5 g6 4.d4 exd4 5.Nxd4 Bg7 6.Nxc6 bxc6 7.Bc4 Ne7 8.Nc3 d6 9.0-0 Be6 10.Bg3 0-0 11.Be3 c5 12.Bxe6 fxe6 13.Qd2 Rb8 14.Rab1 Nc6 15.b3 Qh4 16.f3 Nd4 17.Ne2 Be5 18.f4 Nxe2+ 19.Qxe2 Bxf4 20.Bxf4 Rxf4 21.Rxf4 Qxf4 22.Rf1 Qe5 23.Qa6

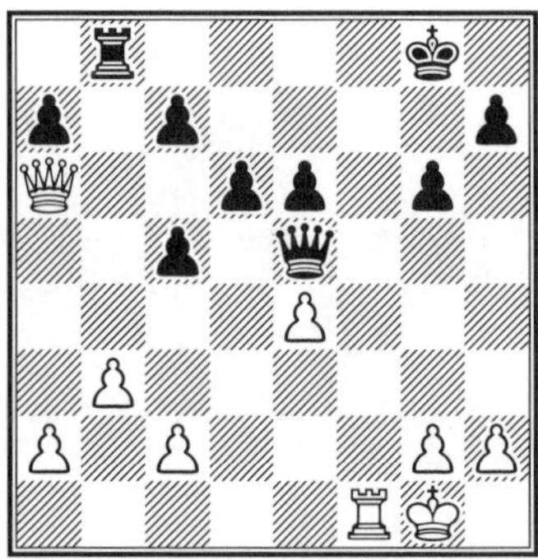

23...Qd4+ 24.Kh1 Qxe4 25.Qxa7 Qb7 26.Qa4 c6 27.Qe4 Qd7 28.a4 e5 29.h3 Rb4 30.Qe1 e4 31.a5 d5 32.a6 Qe7 33.Qg3 e3 34.Ra1 Qf6 35.Re1 d4 36.a7 Qd8 37.Ra1 Qa8 38.Qd6 Rb7 39.Qxc6 e2 40.Qxb7!, 1-0.

Pillsbury resigned here.

Although Lasker beat Pillsbury in Hastings, Pillsbury ended up winning first prize, with second going to Chigorin (Lasker was third).

Oddly, in St. Petersburg 1895/96, where only four players played six games against each other, Pillsbury beat Lasker two games to one with two draws, but this time Lasker won the event by beating Steinitz (three wins, one loss, two draws) and Chigorin (four wins and two draws) while Pillsbury came in third!

Let's take a look at a Pillsbury win from St. Petersburg:

Emanuel Lasker vs. Harry Pillsbury, St. Petersburg 1895/96

1.e4 e5 2.Nf3 Nf6 3.Nxe5 d6 4.Nf3 Nxe4 5.d4 d5 6.Bd3 Be7 7.0-0 Nc6 8.Re1 Bg4 9.c3 f5 10.Qb3 0-0 11.Bf4? Bxf3 12.gxf3 Ng5 13.Kg2 Qd7 14.Qc2? Ne6! 15.Bc1 Bd6 16.Nd2 Rae8 17.Nf1 Nexd4!

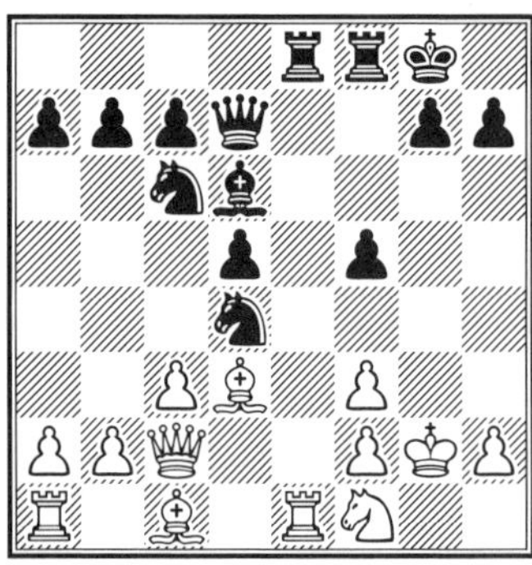

Taking advantage of White's undefended Rook on e1.

18.Qd1 Rxe1 19.Qxe1 Nxf3! 20.Kxf3 f4!

Allowing black's Queen to penetrate on the h3-c8 diagonal. 20...Ne5+ was also strong.

21.Qd1 Ne5+ 22.Ke2

22.Kg2 f3+ 23.Kh1 Qh3 24.Ne3 Ng4 25.Qg1 Nxh2 mates.

22...Qg4+ 23.Kd2 Qxd1+ 24.Kxd1 Nxd3

And Black easily won.

25.Ke2 Ne5 26.f3 Re8 27.b3 Ng4+ 28.Kd2 Ne3 29.Bb2 Ng2 30.h3 Bc5 31.Nh2 Bf2 32.c4 dxc4 33.bxc4 h5, 0-1.

Sadly, Pillsbury died young, at thirty-three, from syphilis. His score against Lasker was a fantastic five wins, five losses, four draws.

To quote Alekhine:

> Pillsbury aspired for the candle of his life to burn constantly at both ends. Wine, women, and not harmless songs, but strong cigars—this was Pillsbury's principle in life.
>
> Lasker was my teacher, and without him I could not have become whom I became. The idea of chess art is unthinkable without Emanuel Lasker.

Mikhail Chigorin vs. Emanuel Lasker, St. Petersburg 1895/96

1.e4 e5 2.Nf3 Nc6 3.Bc4 Bc5 4.b4 Bxb4 5.c3 Bc5 6.0-0 d6 7.d4 Bb6 8.a4? **Nf6 9.Bb5 a6 10.Bxc6+ bxc6 11.a5 Ba7 12.dxe5 Nxe4 13.Qe2?** **d5 14.Nd4?** **Nxc3!**

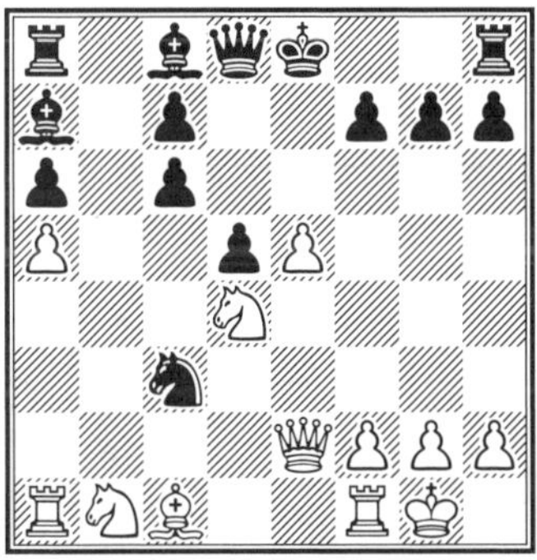

It turns out that White's d4-Knight was inadequately defended!

15.Nxc3 Bxd4 16.Qd3 c5 17.Qg3 Be6 18.Bg5 Qd7 and Black won.

Finally one more game from St. Petersburg—this game is one of the greatest of all time. It features moments of incredible brilliance, time trouble errors, frayed nerves, missed opportunities, and an incredible end by Lasker who finally drags his prey down. Play over it as if it were a movie, and let the emotional intensity of the violent battle wash over you.

Harry Pillsbury vs. Emanuel Lasker, St. Petersburg 1895/96

1.d4 d5 2.c4 e6 3.Nc3 Nf6 4.Nf3 c5 5.Bg5 cxd4 6.Qxd4 Nc6 7.Qh4 Be7 8.0-0-0 Qa5 9.e3 Bd7 10.Kb1 h6 11.cxd5 exd5 12.Nd4 0-0 13.Bxf6 Bxf6 14.Qh5 Nxd4 15.exd4 Be6 16.f4 Rac8 17.f5

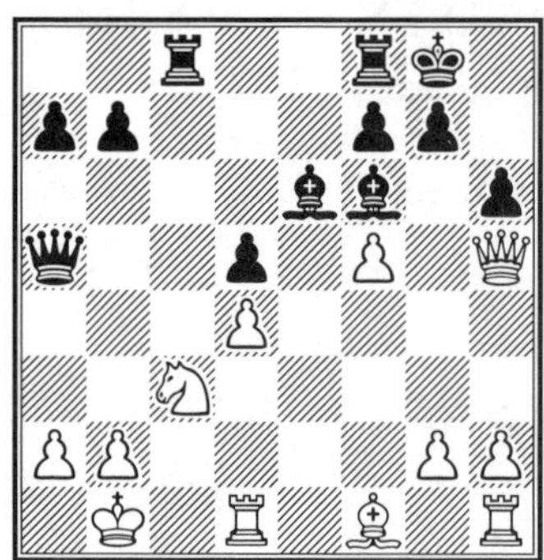

17...Rxc3!! 18.fxe6

18.bxc3 Qxc3 19.Qf3 was a better defense, but Black retains a monster attack with 19...Bxf5+!! (19...Qxf3 20.gxf3 Bxf5+ gives Black a superior endgame.) 20.Qxf5 Qb4+ 21.Ka1 Bxd4+ 22.Rxd4 Qxd4+ 23.Kb1 Re8 24.Bd3 g6 25.Qh3 Re6 26.Bc2 Rb6+ 27.Bb3 a5 and the threat of ...a5-a4 is more than annoying.

18...Ra3!! 19.exf7+ Rxf7 20.bxa3 Qb6+ 21.Bb5! Qxb5+ 22.Ka1 Rc7? 23.Rd2 Rc4 24.Rhd1?

24.Re1! Qa5 25.Re8+ Kh7 26.Qf5+ g6 27.Re7+! (27.Qxf6?? Rc1+ 28.Kb2 Qc3 mate) 27...Bxe7 28.Qf7+ Kh8 29.Qe8+ with a perpetual check. Analysis by Kasparov.

24...Rc3? 25.Qf5 Qc4 26.Kb2?

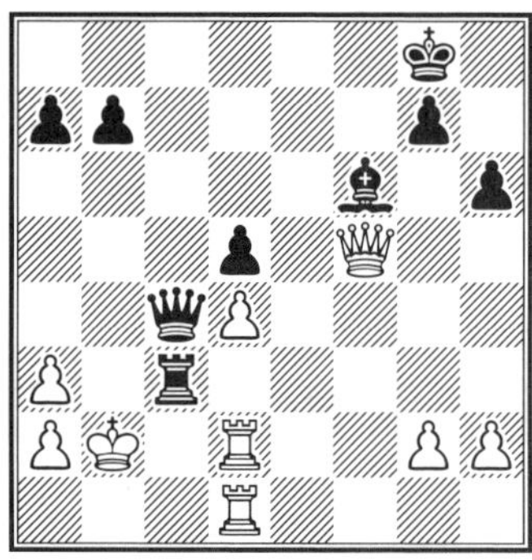

26...Rxa3!!

I wonder if Pillsbury could believe his eyes—here the horror comes again!

27.Qe6+ Kh7 28.Kxa3??

28.Qf5+ Kg8!! (28...Kh8 only draws.) 29.Kb1 (29.Qe6+ Kh8) 29...Bxd4!! 30.Re1 (30.Qe6+ Kh8 31.Qe8+ Kh7; 30.Rxd4 Qxa2+ 31.Kc1 Rc3+ 32.Qc2 Rxc2 mate) 30...Qb4+ 31.Kc1 Qc3+ 32.Qc2 (32.Rc2 Qxe1 mate.) 32...Qa1+ 33.Qb1 Rc3+ 34.Rc2 Be3+ 35.Rxe3 Qxb1+ 36.Kxb1 Rxe3 with a winning endgame.

28...Qc3+ 29.Ka4 b5+ 30.Kxb5 Qc4+ 31.Ka5 Bd8+ 32.Qb6 Bxb6, 0-1.

I've pointed out that Lasker's tactics are a bit different than tactics by Tal or Kasparov or Alekhine. In fact, when you take a long look at Lasker's games, you realize that tactics are the fuel that drives all his other world class chess talents, including endgame and defense.

The following game shows how Lasker mixes simple positional concepts with careful calculation. There aren't any combinations here, and you won't find any attack or any explosions. Yet his "hidden" tactical eye is all reaching and all seeing under the quiet tapestry that he weaves.

Emanuel Lasker vs. Stepan Levitsky, Moscow (simultaneous exhibition) 1896

1.e4 e5 2.Nf3 Nc6 3.Bb5 Nf6 4.0-0 Nxe4 5.d4 Be7 6.Qe2 Nd6 7.Bxc6 bxc6 8.dxe5 Nb7 9.Nc3 0-0 10.Re1 Nc5 11.Be3 Ba6 12.Qd2 Ne6 13.Rad1 d5 14.exd6 cxd6 15.Nd4 Nxd4 16.Bxd4 d5 17.Qe3 Bd6 18.Bc5 Bxc5 19.Qxc5 Qb6 20.Na4

20.Qxb6? axb6 deprives the Knight of the c5-square.

20...Qxc5 21.Nxc5 Bc8 22.Re2 Bf5 23.c3 Rfe8

Black isn't able to dislodge the Knight: 23...Rab8 24.f3 Rb5 25.b4 a5 26.a4 Rbb8 27.Rd4.

24.Rde1 Kf8?

Playing into Lasker's hands. Black should have swapped off one Rook and kept the other by 24...Rxe2 25.Rxe2 Rb8 26.f3 h5.

25.Rxe8+ Rxe8 26.Rxe8+ Kxe8 27.f3

White's next step is to bring his King to d4. Black will do his best to stop this from happening.

27...Ke7 28.Kf2 Kd6 29.b4 Ke5

29...a5?? 30.Nb7+ wins the a-pawn.

30.Ke3 g5

Stopping f3-f4+, which would force the black King away and give d4 to White's monarch.

31.a3

Lasker's in no hurry, so he makes slight improvements and also goofs about a bit to lull his opponent into a false haze of safety. 31.a3 gets the pawn off the light square, making it safe from the enemy Bishop.

31...h5 32.Nb7 Bd7 33.g3 f6 34.Nc5 Be8

34...Bf5 35.f4+ gxf4+ 36.gxf4+ Kd6 37.Kd4 and White has succeeded in taking over the d4-square.

35.Nd3+ Kf5

He should have held tough with 35...Kd6 and hoped White couldn't find a way to break through.

36.Kd4 g4 37.f4 Bd7 38.Nc5 Bc8

Everything up to this point has been "autopilot" for Lasker. No calculation was necessary, just good old positional knowhow. However, now the second World Champion did have to calculate since he knew that endgames featuring pawn races can be tricky.

39.b5!

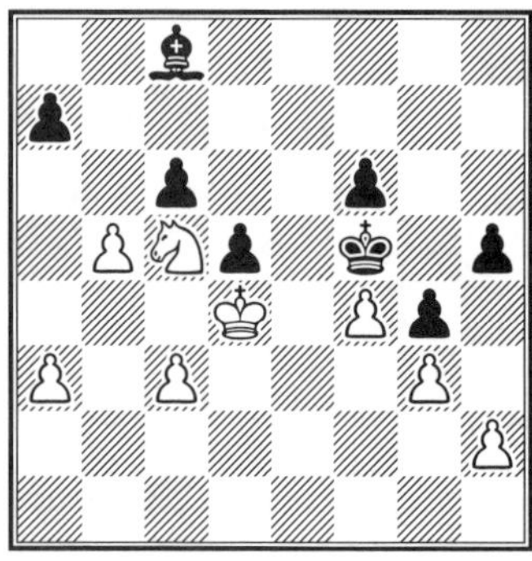

Here Lasker, being a huge fan of rock 'n' roll, followed his favorite rock group's philosophy to "break on through to the other side."

39...cxb5 40.Kxd5 a6 41.Kd6 h4 42.Kc7 hxg3 43.hxg3 Be6

Lasker understood that his Knight is keeping black's King from moving to e4-f3xg3 when the g3-pawn will sprint to the finish line. When deciding to take this path (on move 39) he rejected 44.Nxa6?? Ke4 45.Nc5+ Kf3 46.Nxe6 Kxg3 and the game will be drawn (e.g. 47.Kc6 Kf2 48.f5 g3 49.Nf4 Kf3 50.Nh3 g2 51.Kxb5 Kg3 52.Ng1 Kf2 53.Nh3+ Kg3 54.Ng1 Kh2 55.Nf3+ Kg3, etc.).

He also rejected 44.Kb6 Bc4 45.Kxa6?? b4+ (DISCOVERED CHECK!) when Black wins, and 44.Kb6 Bc4 45.Nxa6 Ke4 when Black wins again!

That leaves 44.Nxe6 as the main option, but then black's King (after it recaptures on e6) can finally make a dash to the g3-pawn. In this kind of situation, White needs to have everything calculated to perfection.

Emanuel Lasker 1896
(Photo: Courtesy of the Cleveland Public Library's John G. White Collection).

44.Nxe6! Kxe6 45.Kc6!

The only move, nothing else wins.

45...Kf5 46.Kd5!

The only move, again nothing else wins.

46...a5 47.Kd4!

And another move where nothing else wins. For example: 47.Kc5 Ke4 48.Kxb5 Kf3 49.c4 Kxg3 50.c5 Kxf4 51.c6 g3 52.c7 g2 53.c8Q g1=Q.

47...Ke6 48.Kc5!, 1-0.

Black resigned since White wins the race after 48...Kf5 49.Kxb5 Ke4 50.c4 Kf3 51.c5. This shows us that calculation isn't always necessary when you have a position's basic blueprint already in your head (in this case, controlling the c5- and d4- squares so your Knight and King can live on them). However, when calculation is called for, it's often to avoid enemy tricks (as in the discovered check) and find a path (sometimes a very subtle path—and sometimes the only path!) to victory. Thus knowing basic tactical building blocks (I'm once again referring to the discovered check) not only allows you to use them against your opponent, but to avoid being victimized by them too.

Lasker and J. S. Ryan (Photo: Courtesy of the Cleveland Public Library's John G. White Collection).

Emanuel Lasker vs. NN, Moscow (simultaneous exhibition) 1896

1.e4 e5 2.Nf3 Nc6 3.Bb5 Nf6 4.d4 Nxe4 5.Qe2 Nd6 6.Bxc6 bxc6 7.dxe5 Nb7 8.Nc3 Be7 9.b3 0-0 10.Bb2 Nc5 11.0-0-0 a5 12.Nd4 Ba6 13.Qg4 Qe8 14.Nf5 Ne6 15.Ne4 Kh8 16.Nf6 Bxf6 16.Nf6!!

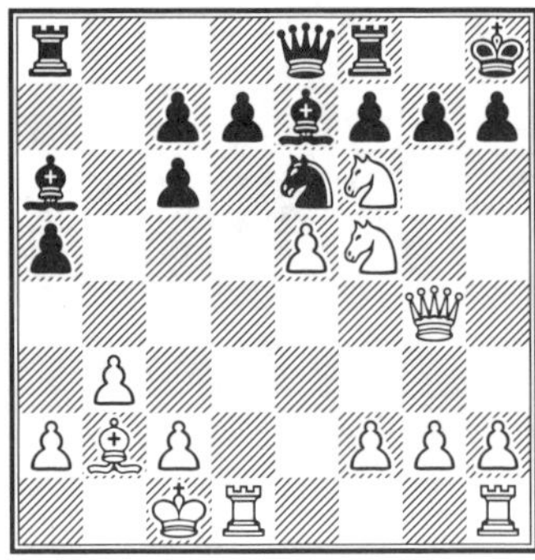

16...Bxf6

16...Qd8 17.Rxd7.

17.exf6 g6 18.Ne7 Rg8 19.h4 Rb8

19...h5 20.Nxg6+! Rxg6 21.Qxg6! fxg6 22.f7+.

20.h5 g5 21.Ng6+!!, 1-0.

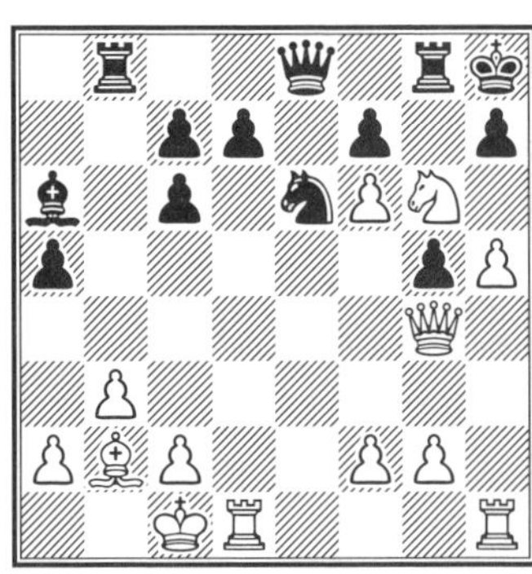

Moritz Porges vs. Emanuel Lasker, Nuremberg 1896

1.e4 e5 2.Nf3 Nc6 3.Bb5 Nf6 4.0-0 Nxe4 5.d4 Be7 6.Qe2 Nd6 7.Bxc6 bxc6 8.dxe5 Nb7 9.b3 0-0 10.Bb2 d5 11.exd6 cxd6 12.Nbd2 Re8 13.Rfe1 Bd7 14.Ne4 d5 15.Ned2 Ba3 16.Be5 f6 17.Qa6 fxe5 18.Qxa3 e4

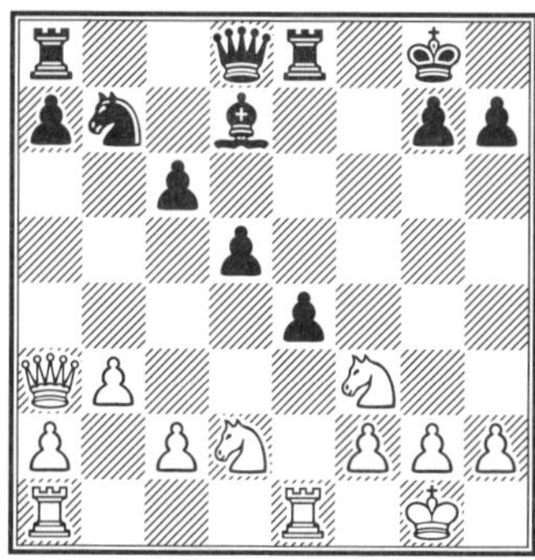

19.Nd4 Qf6 20.c3 Rf8 21.f3 Qg5 22.Qc1 Nc5 23.Nf1 Qg6 24.Re3 Nd3 25.Qd1 Nf4 26.Ng3 h5 27.Nde2 Nxg2! 28.Kxg2 exf3+ 29.Rxf3 Bh3+! 30.Kxh3 Qg4+ 31.Kg2 Qxf3+ 32.Kg1 h4 33.Nh1 Qe3+ 34.Kg2 h3, 0-1.

William Steinitz vs. Emanuel Lasker, Nuremberg 1896

1.e4 e6 2.d4 d5 3.Nd2 c5 4.dxc5 Bxc5 5.Nb3 Bb6 6.exd5 Nf6 7.Bb5+ Bd7 8.Bxd7+ Qxd7 9.c4 exd5 10.c5 Bc7 11.Nf3 Nc6 12.0-0 0-0 13.Nbd4 Nxd4 14.Qxd4 Rfe8 15.Be3 Re4 16.Qd3 Rae8 17.Rfd1 h6 18.a3 Qg4

White is gobbling up Black's queenside, while Black is building on the other wing. Which strategy will win out?

19.b4 g5 20.Qc3 Qf5 21.Qd3 Qg6 22.Qb5 Qh5 23.Qxb7

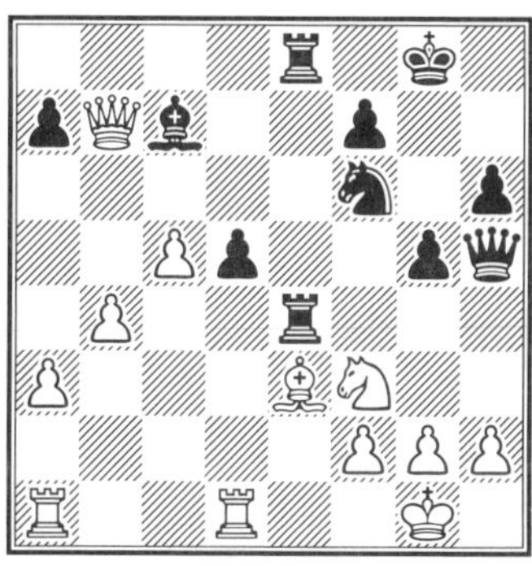

23...Bxh2+!

Devastating. Black wins by force.

24.Nxh2 Rh4 25.f3 Rxh2 26. Qc7 Rh1+ 27.Kf2 Qh4+ 28.Qg3 Qxg3+ 29.Kxg3 Rxd1 30.Rxd1 Rxe3

Black was a piece up and won easily.

Richard Teichmann vs. Emanuel Lasker, Nuremberg 1896

1.e4 e5 2.Nf3 Nc6 3.Bb5 Nf6 4.0-0 Nxe4 5.d4 Be7 6.Qe2 Nd6 7.Bxc6 bxc6 8.dxe5 Nb7 9.b3 0-0 10.Bb2 d5 11.Nd4 Qd7 12.Nd2 c5 13.N4f3 Qf5 14.Rac1 c6 15.Rfe1 a5 16.a4 Nd8 17.Nf1 Ne6 18.Ng3 Qg6 19.Qd2 h5 20.Ne2 Qf5 21.Ba3 Re8 22.Qe3 h4 23.h3 Ba6 24.Kh1 d4 25.Qd2 Red8 26.Neg1 Nf4 27.Bxc5

In this position (which favors Black) White thought he saw a neat tactic based on the piece sacrifice 27.Bxc5. Show how Lasker refuted it.

27...Bxc5 28.Nxh4

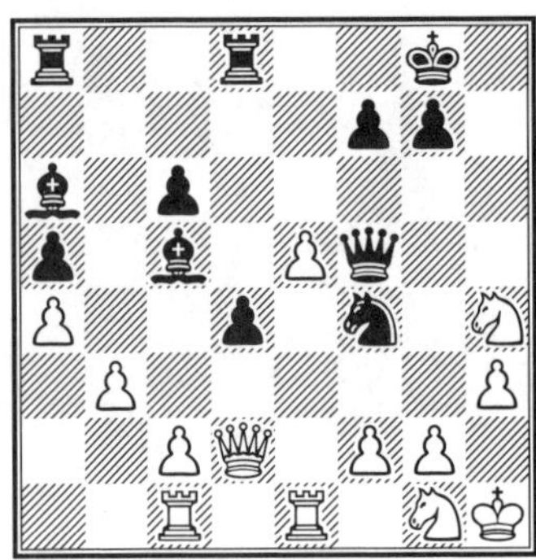

28...Qg5!

28...Bb4? 29.Qxb4 Qh5 30.Qd2 Qxh4 31.g3.

29.Ngf3

29.Re4 fails to 29...Nxh3!

29...Bb4!

Everything else is good for White.

30.Qxb4 Qxh4!

Everything else is at least equal for White. I suspect that Teichmann missed this move.

31.Qd2 Qh6

The only good move.

32.Re4 Ne6

And Black, who is up a piece, went on to win the game.

Emanuel Lasker vs. Emil Schallopp, Nuremberg 1896

1.d4 d5 2.Nf3 Nf6 3.c4 e6 4.Nc3 Be7 5.Bf4 0-0 6.c5 b6 7.b4 a5 8.a3 Ne4 9.Nxe4 dxe4 10.Ne5 f6 11.Nc4 axb4 12.axb4 Rxa1 13.Qxa1 Nc6 14.Qc3 Nxd4 15.e3 Nf5 16.Nd2 Bb7 17.c6 Bxc6 18.Qxc6 Bxb4 19.Qc2 Qd5

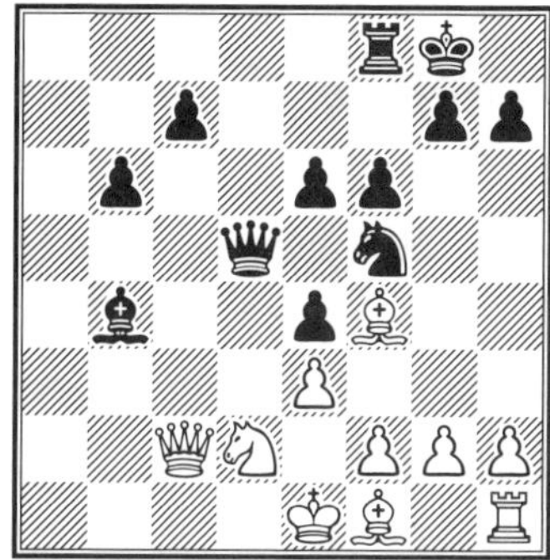

Black has sacrificed a piece for three pawns, a huge lead in development, and a strong attack. It look's like Lasker is doomed. Will his legendary defensive skills and tactical powers save him?

20.Bc4!! Bxd2+ 21.Ke2! Qd7

In the actual game Black played 21...Qc6 when 22.Kxd2 Rd8+ 23.Ke2 didn't leave him with enough compensation for the sacrificed piece.

22.Qxe4!

22.Qxd2 is also strong; 22.Rd1?? misses 22...Nd4+!! 23.exd4 Bxf4.

22...Kh8

White threatened both 23.Bxe6+ and 23.Qxf5.

23.Bxe6 Qb5+

23...Nd6 24.Bxd7 Nxe4 25.Bc6 wins a piece.

24.Bc4 Qb4 25.Bd3! g6 26.Qxb4 Bxb4 27.Bxc7 Bc5 28.Rb1 followed by 29.Bxb6 with an extra pawn in the endgame.

Emanuel Lasker vs. Georg Marco, Nuremberg 1896

1.d4 d5 2.c4 e6 3.Nc3 Nf6 4.Nf3 Be7 5.e3 0-0 6.Bd3 b6 7.cxd5 exd5 8.0-0 Bb7 9.b3 Ne4 10.Ne2 Bd6 11.Bb2 Nd7 12.Rc1 Qf6 13.Qc2 Qh6 14.Ng3 Nxg3 15.hxg3 Nf6 16.Rfe1 Rae8 17.Nd2 Ng4 18.Nf1 f5 19.Re2 g6 20.Bc3 Nf6 21.f3 Nh5 22.Be1 Qg5 23.Bb5 c6

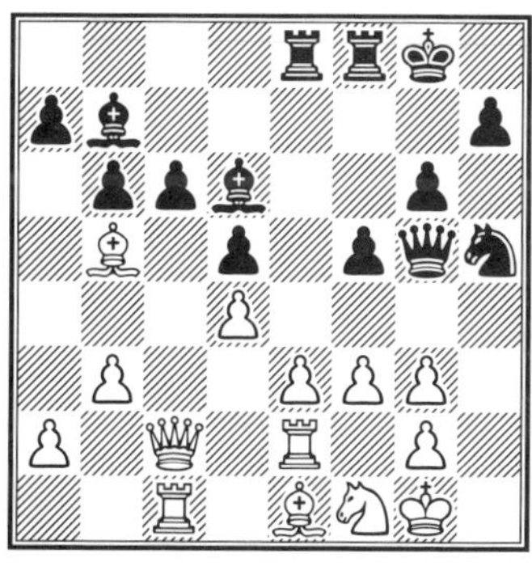

Lasker has a slight disadvantage. How did he spice things up and turn "worse" to "equal with a big dollop of interesting?"

24.Bxc6!!

24.Bd3? Nxg3 25.Nxg3 Bxg3 26.Bxg3 Qxg3 leaves Black with a pawn more.

24...Rc8 25.Bxb7 Rxc2 26.Bxd5+ Kh8 27.Rexc2 f4!

Best. 27...Nxg3 runs into 28.f4; 27...Bxg3 gives White the initiative after 28.Bb4 Rd8 29.Rc8. One line goes: 29...a5 30.Be6! axb4 (30...Kg7 31.R1c7+ wins.) 31.Rxd8+ Qxd8 32.Rc8 Qxc8 33.Bxc8 with a winning endgame.

28.e4 fxg3 29.e5 and white's Rook, Bishop and pawn and the potential power of White's two connected passed pawns give him full compensation for the Queen. Marco, shocked that his superior position turned into this, crashed and burned and lost quickly.

Emanuel Lasker vs. Siegbert Tarrasch, Nuremberg 1896

1.e4 e5 2.Nf3 Nc6 3.Bb5 a6 4.Bxc6 dxc6 5.Nc3 Bc5 6.d3 Bg4 7.Be3 Qd6 8.Bxc5 Qxc5 9.Qd2 Bxf3? 10.gxf3 Ne7 11.0-0-0 Ng6 12.Qe3! Qxe3+ 13.fxe3 Rd8 14.Ne2 f6 15.Rhg1 Kf7 16.Rdf1 Rhe8 17.Ng3 Nf8 18.f4 c5?? 19.Nh5!

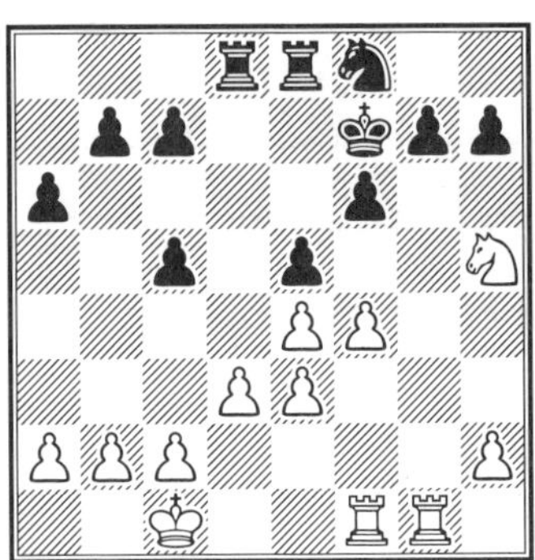

Everything else was indeed equal, but this wins!

19...g6

Everything else is worse:

- 19...Ng6 20.f5.
- 19...Ne6 20.f5 Ng5 21.h4.

20.fxe5!

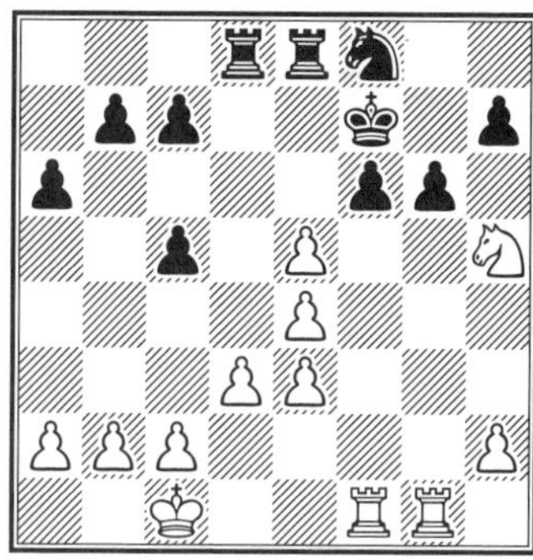

White's point. Now Black is busted.

20...Rxe5 21.Nxf6, 1-0.

When he was a pawn down. Lasker's incredible technique chewed him up, spit him out, and easily took home the full point.

A Taste of History

I always try to instill a love of chess history in my writing. History tells us that the lives of many chess greats were full of color and drama, joy and trauma, epic failures, and unbelievable successes. You'll get a small taste of this here. For those who are simply bored by the subject, just go right to the positions. However, if you read on you might discover that there is indeed more to chess than pieces and a board.

At this point I want to look at Lasker's play right after he lost his title, and point out something that many chess fans don't think about very often: how non-chess factors often lead to bumpy results.

In Lasker's case, his result at Hastings 1895 was marred by his run in with typhoid fever (illness is a common result killer!), and his play in his match with Capablanca was influenced not only by Capablanca's magnificent play (Lasker praised his opponent's genius after the match), but by the stifling Cuban heat which Lasker wasn't able to deal with.

Age also reared its ugly head—Lasker was fifty-two years old and past his prime, while Capablanca, twenty years younger, was at his very best. It must be admitted, at that time, Capablanca was slightly the stronger player. As the old saying goes, "time and tide wait for no man." To me, the fact that a prime Capablanca was only slightly the stronger player says volumes about Lasker's level during his peak years.

Another "illness" that can rip the wings off a high-flying chess professional is, unsurprisingly, love. Unlike Capablanca, who was a renowned ladies' man, Lasker didn't appear to have much to do with women. This changed in 1902 when he visited a gentleman by the name of Ludwig Metzger (he was an editor of a well-known newspaper (the *Berliner Lokalanzeiger*). Mr. Metzger and his wife were famous for their parties, which usually featured poets, writers, musicians, painters, and other creative people.

In this case a young lady named Martha Kohn was also invited (she wrote for Metzger's paper), and was told by Mrs. Metzger that she wanted to introduce her to a gentleman that had just won the World Chess Championship. Martha was unimpressed, and said:[1]

> Your enthusiastic recommendations of this person rouse in me nothing but deep ingratitude. I understand nothing of mathematics, and I think chess must be terribly boring. No, my dear, he is not for me and my tastes, and so I would not be to his taste either.

According to Martha's memoirs, she had just finished saying these things when Lasker appeared, walked up to Mrs. Metzger, and was introduced to Martha. She thought him withdrawn, but quickly realized that there was far more to Mr. Lasker than she had supposed. Indeed, Lasker wasn't "dry" at all—his humble nature and his deep knowledge of many subjects won her over and they quickly became close friends. It turned out that Martha and her husband, Emil (who was an invalid and quite ill), were also big party givers, and after their initial meeting Lasker became a regular guest at their home.

We get a clear understanding of just how enamored Lasker was of Martha when, right before he left for a tournament in America, he introduced his new friend to his mother (Rosalie Lasker), and said:

> It is my hope that these two beings, whom I love more than anything on earth, should become friends!

When left alone with Rosalie, Martha said:

> Honored lady—he really does not know me all that well; if he did, he would not have presented me to his mother, but to the devils themselves!"

Rosalie replied:

> Oh, Emanuel knows exactly what he's saying; if he says it, then that's what he thinks!

After that, it turned into something akin to an old Hollywood movie. Lasker would write Martha fawning letters, one letter read:

> I need only to think of Europe for your face to appear before me. For me, Europe and yourself are one and the same.

But since she was married, and since Lasker was friends with her husband

1 Quotations on this page and the next from: Dr. J. Hannak, trans. by Heinrich Fraenkel, *Emanuel Lasker: The Life of a Chess Master*. New York: Simon & Schuster, 1959.

Emil, he kept his desires hidden as best he could. He was madly in love with Martha, but he could never out and out say it.

The Hollywood movie scenario got more heated when Emil's health got worse and worse. She remained by her husband's side, Lasker was supportive and continued to visit, and life went on.

I bring all this up because such long-lived emotional turmoil has to take its toll on one's chess. Indeed, we can see Lasker crack a bit when a World Championship match vs. Siegbert Tarrasch finally was arranged. Lasker dominated the match, but at one point his play worsened. It turned out that being so close to Martha (the match was held in Munich and Düsseldorf while Martha, and Lasker's brother Berthold, lived in Berlin) and not being able to see her had driven him into a deep depression. Finally he cracked and wrote,

> Do come at once, come as my guardian angel, or I might lose the whole match!

As it turned out, Martha very much would have liked to help her friend, but didn't want to leave Emil alone. In the end, it was Emil himself who took command and told Martha:

> We can't leave him in the lurch, Martha. You get on the next train to Munich, and Berthold had better go too. It will make all the difference for Emanuel."

The next day she was in Munich, Emanuel's depression vanished, and he went on to win the match eight wins to three.

Siegbert Tarrasch vs. Emanuel Lasker, Munich, World Championship (4) 1908

1.e4 e5 2.Nf3 Nc6 3.Bb5 Nf6 4.0-0 d6 5.d4 Bd7 6.Nc3 Be7 7.Re1 exd4 8.Nxd4 Nxd4 9.Qxd4 Bxb5 10.Nxb5 0-0 11.Bg5 h6 12.Bh4 Re8 13.Rad1 Nd7 14.Bxe7 Rxe7 15.Qc3 Re5 16.Nd4 Rc5

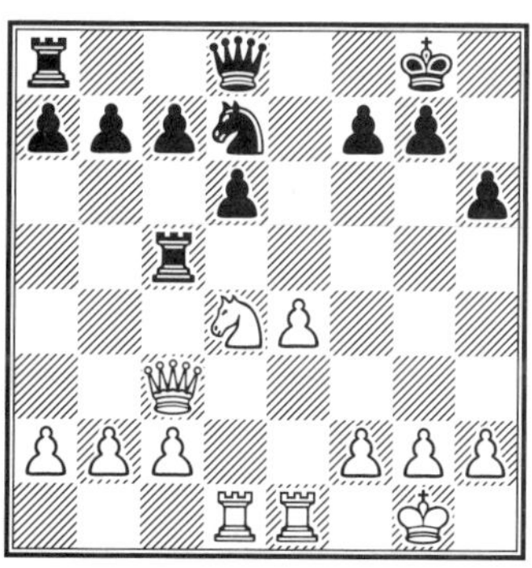

17.Qb3 Nb6 18.f4 Qf6 19.Qf3 Re8 20.c3 a5 21.b3 a4 22.b4 Rc4

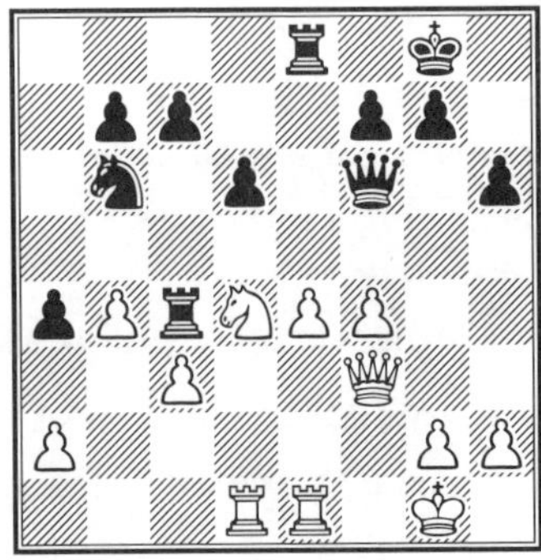

23.g3 Rd8 24.Re3 c5 25.Nb5 cxb4 26.Rxd6 Rxd6 27.e5 Rxf4

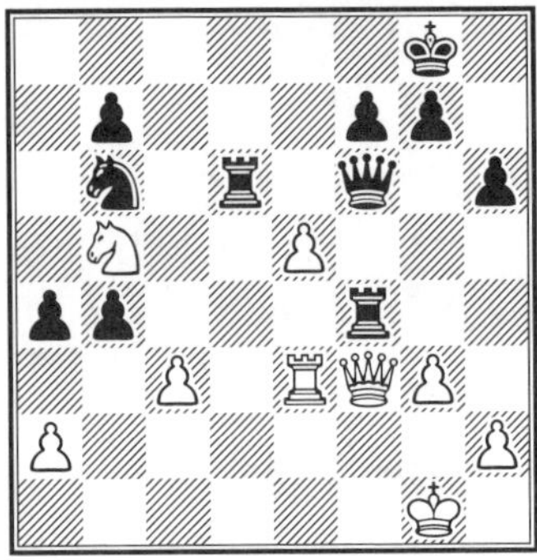

28.gxf4 Qg6+ 29.Kh1 Qb1+ 30.Kg2 Rd2+ 31.Re2 Qxa2 32.Rxd2 Qxd2+ 33.Kg3 a3 34.e6 Qe1+ 35.Kg4 Qxe6+ 36.f5 Qc4+ 37.Nd4 a2 38.Qd1 Nd5 39.Qa4 Nxc3 40.Qe8+ Kh7 41.Kh5 a1Q, 0-1.

Emanuel Lasker vs. Siegbert Tarrasch, Munich, World Championship (11) 1908

1.e4 e6 2.d4 d5 3.Nc3 Nf6 4.Bg5 Bb4 5.exd5 Qxd5 6.Nf3 c5 7.Bxf6 gxf6 8.Qd2! Bxc3 9.Qxc3 Nd7 10.Rd1 Rg8 11.dxc5 Qxc5 12.Qd2 Qb6 13.c3 a6 14.Qc2 f5 15.g3 Nc5 16.Bg2 Qc7 17.Qe2 b5 18.0-0 Bb7 19.c4 b4! 20.Qd2 Rb8 21.Qh6

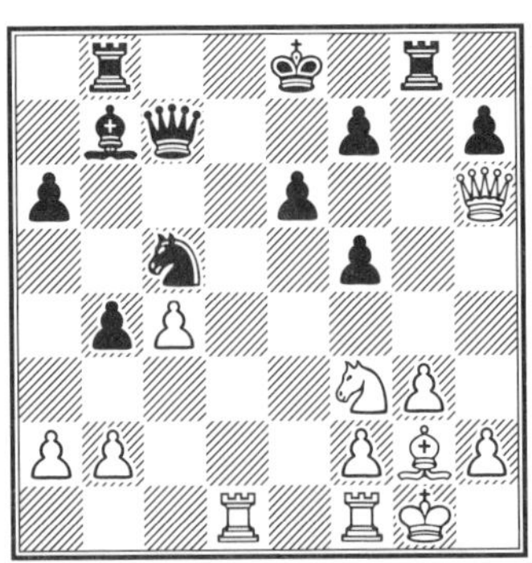

Black has a nice Knight on c5 but his kingside weaknesses and, most importantly, his insecure King will lead to a rapid defeat.

21...Bxf3 22.Bxf3 Qe5 23.Rfe1 Qxb2 24.Qf4 Rc8 25.Qd6 f6 26.Bh5+

26.Rxe6+ Kf7 27.Qe7+ wins, but 26.Bh5+ is more accurate.

26...Rg6 27.Bxg6+

The immediate 27.Rxe6+ is equally good.

27...hxg6 28.Rxe6+!, 1-0.

This kind of emotional roulette repeated itself in his World Championship match with Carl Schlechter (held in Vienna and Berlin). Lasker was looking forward to seeing Martha, but instead of a joyous reunion he was immersed in horror—Emil had died. Martha was, grieving, and Lasker made a point of staying away while she dealt with her loss.

A year later he proposed, and after pondering whether she could actually handle a chess player's lifestyle of non-stop travel, she accepted and they were married.

Returning to Lasker's triumphant first place finishes:

St. Petersburg (1895/96): First ahead of Steinitz, Pillsbury, and Chigorin.

Nuremberg (1896) ahead of Maróczy, Pillsbury, Tarrasch, Janowski, Steinitz, Schlechter, and many others.

There followed:

Moscow (1897/97): World Championship rematch vs. Steinitz, which Lasker dominated 10-2 with just 3 draws.

London (1899): First place (4½ points ahead of the second place finisher!).

Paris (1900): First place (2 points ahead of Pillsbury, who took second).

After Paris, Lasker didn't play in many tournaments, and he took long periods of time away from chess.

Cambridge Springs (1904): Tied for second place behind Frank Marshall (Marshall's greatest success).

Trenton Falls (1906): First place.

New York, **Philadelphia**, **Washington D.C.**, **Baltimore**, **Chicago**, and **Memphis** (1907): World Championship match with Frank Marshall, which was a wipeout (8-0 with 7 draws).

Düsseldorf and **Munich**(1908): World Championship match with Tarrasch (8-3 with 5 draws).

Emanuel Lasker aboard ship, a chess player's lifestyle of non-stop travel, ship bound for a tournament. (Photo: Courtesy of the Cleveland Public Library's John G. White Collection.)

Traveling exhibition created by the Emanuel Lasker Society.

St. Petersburg (1909): Mini-match with Speijer (2-0 with 1 draw).

Paris (1909): Mini-match with Janowski (2-2, no draws).

Paris (1909): Match with Janowski (7-1 with 1 draw).

St. Petersburg (1909): Tied for first with Rubinstein.

Vienna and **Berlin** (1910): World Championship match with Schlechter (1 win, 1 loss, 8 draws).

Berlin (1910): World Championship match with Janowski (8-0, 3 draws).

St. Petersburg (1914): First place ahead of Capablanca, Alekhine, Tarrasch, Marshall, Rubinstein, Nimzowitsch, and others.

Berlin (1916): Rematch with Tarrasch (a blowout, 5 wins, no losses, 1 draw).

Berlin (1918): First place ahead of Rubinstein, Schlechter, and Tarrasch.

Havana (1921): World Championship match with Capablanca (no wins, 4 losses, 10 draws).

It's interesting to note that after winning the World Championship, Lasker won every tournament and match except Hastings 1895, Cambridge Springs 1904, and finally the Capablanca match.

And here, in the twilight of Lasker's career, we see something remarkable. After his loss to Capablanca, the chess world felt that Lasker was more or less "done"—considering his age and the advent of a new kind of chess player that advocated a hypermodern approach. Lasker took some time away from the game, instead concentrating on math, philosophy, bridge, and other pursuits. Then, at the age of fifty-four he accepted an invitation to play at the extremely strong Mährisch Ostrau event, which was stacked with young talent like Réti, Grünfeld, Euwe, Tartakower, Bogoljubov, and Spielmann (Tarrasch, Rubinstein, and others were also present). Could the old warhorse deal with this "new" kind of chess?

When the smoke cleared, Lasker had confounded his critics once again by taking clear first (8 wins, no losses, 5 draws) a point ahead of second place Réti.

Réti was having an incredible tournament, and in the end the game between them decided everything.

I'll quote *Emanuel Lasker: The Life of a Chess Master:*[1]

> Frau Martha Lasker, as usual, sat in a quiet corner not too near the board but within her husband's sight, busy with her knitting. From time to time she would send Emanuel a cup of coffee or a cigar, for ever since, at a certain great tournament, a stranger had offered him an opium-scented cigar. After that, Lasker would never touch a cigar unless it was handed to him by his wife. From time to time, while his opponent was thinking, he would walk over to his wife

1 Dr. J. Hannak, trans. by Heinrich Fraenkel, *Emanuel Lasker: The Life of a Chess Master.* New York: Simon and Schuster, 1959.

for a brief whispered chat. He did so as his momentous game against Réti was reaching the critical stage.

"How is it?" she asked. "People say your position is not so good."

"Do they?" said Lasker with a smile.

"Well, I'm not particularly worried about it; in fact, I rather like it." And, of course, he did win the game.

One year later, at the age of fifty-five, Lasker decided to give it another go. This time the tournament (the legendary New York 1924 event) was outrageously strong, with Capablanca, Alekhine, and Réti being the favorites. This was a double round robin with eleven players (thus twenty games in all). One would think that such a long, strong, grueling tournament would be much too much for the event's old man. Yet, another miracle: Lasker dominated the tournament with thireteen wins, six draws, and only one defeat (to Capablanca)! Capablanca came in second (1½ points) behind the old lion, followed by Alekhine, Marshall, Réti, Maróczy, Bogoljubov, Tartakower, Yates, Edward Lasker, and Janowski.

In 1925 the fifty-six-year-old Lasker played in Moscow. This was Bogoljubov's greatest victory, but Lasker came in clear second, once again ahead of Capablanca (who was third) and a lineup of the world's best players.

This event was his last serious tournament, and h e probably wouldn't have played again if the rise of the German fascists hadn't stripped him of every penny he had (both he and his wife were Jewish). Broke, he played in four more tournaments: Zurich 1934, Moscow 1935, Moscow 1936, and Nottingham 1936.

Lasker's result in Moscow 1935 stunned the world. The 66-year-old Lasker (who was undefeated) came in third behind Botvinnik and Flohr (he drew them both), ahead (again!) of Capablanca (whom he beat!) and other top players.

Unfortunately Lasker wasn't the same superman in his final two events. Both tournaments were very, very strong. He was sixth out of ten in Moscow 1936, and eighth out of fifteen in Nottingham 1936. Realizing that he no longer had the magic juice, he never played in another tournament.

Emanuel Lasker vs. José Raúl Capablanca, Moscow 1935

1.e4 e6 2.d4 d5 3.Nc3 Bb4 4.Nge2 dxe4 5.a3 Be7 6.Nxe4 Nf6 7.N2c3 Nbd7 8.Bf4 Nxe4 9.Nxe4 Nf6 10.Bd3 0-0 11.Nxf6+ Bxf6 12.c3 Qd5 13.Qe2 c6 14.0-0 Re8 15.Rad1 Bd7 16.Rfe1 Qa5 17.Qc2 g6 18.Be5 Bg7 19.h4! Qd8 20.h5 Qg5 21.Bxg7 Kxg7 22.Re5 Qe7 23.Rde1 Rg8 24.Qc1! Rad8 25.R1e3 Bc8 26.Rh3 Kf8 27.Qh6+ Rg7 28.hxg6 hxg6 29.Bxg6!

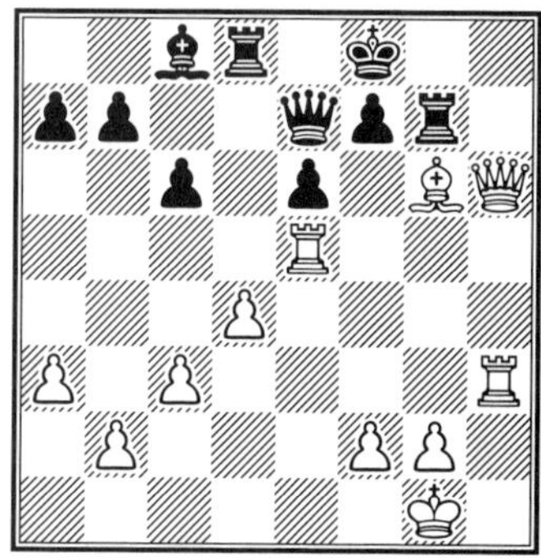

29...Qf6

29...fxg6 30.Qh8+ Kf7 (30...Rg8 31.Rf3+) 31.Rf3+.

30. Rg5!! Ke7

30...Rd5 31.Rxd5 cxd5 32.Qh8+ Ke7 33.Qxc8 Qxg6 34.Qc7+ wins since 34...Ke8 (34...Kf6 35.Rf3+ Kg5 36.Rg3+) 35.Rh8+ Rg8 36.Qc8+ are both game over.

31.Rf3 Qxf3

31...Rxg6 32.Rxf6 Rxh6 33.Rxh6; 31...Rh7 32.Qxh7 Qxg5 33.Rxf7+.

32.gxf3

And White easily earned the full point.

There is so much more to tell about Lasker's life including the many adventures and hardships that brought about his move to Russia, and then his final move to New York.

Emanuel Lasker died in 1941 in New York City (a charity patient at the Mount Sinai Hospital). He was seventy-two. After his death, Martha told his friends: "The world of chess has lost much; I have lost all."

Martha died a year later.

I've made it clear that I'm not by any means impartial on the subject of Lasker. Let's look at the opinions of others:

José Raúl Capablanca:

> That he was a great master of the endgame is an indisputable truth; in fact, I have never known a more skilled master. But he was also the deepest and most resourceful of any I have ever met.

Alexander Alekhine:

Lasker's mastery precisely in .the endgame—especially in a complex, rather than a purely technical endgame_stood for at least two decades at an unreachable height.

Mikhail Tal:

The greatest champion ever was Emanuel Lasker, of course. He was an amazing tactician, who could win what seemed like completely hopeless games.

Anatoly Karpov:

The kings of the past—Lasker and Capablanca especially—almost never studied openings. They were such geniuses—and they knew it—that they could deal with any unpleasantness over and board, and they showed this in practice.

Vladimir Kramnik:

In my view, it was Lasker who invented contemporary chess. When you look at Steinitz's games, you understand: they reek of a bygone age. Whereas with Lasker, there are a lot of games where you might say an absolutely contemporary chess player played them.

Mikhail Chigorin vs. Emanuel Lasker, London 1899

1.e4 e6 2.Qe2 Nc6 3.Nc3 e5 4.g3 Nf6 5.Bg2 Bc5 6.d3 d6 7.Bg5 h6 8.Bxf6 Qxf6 9.Nd5 Qd8 10.c3 Ne7 11.Nxe7 Qxe7 12.0-0-0 Bd7 13.f4 0-0-0 14.Nf3 Bb6 15.Rhf1 f6 16.Kb1 Rhe8 17.f5 Ba4 18.Rc1 Kb8 19.Nd2 a6 20.Bf3 Ba7 21.h4 Rc8 22.Nc4 Red8 23.Ne3 Be8 24.Rfd1 Bf7 25.c4 c6 26.Rc2 Bd4 27.Rdc1 Qc7 28.Nd1 Qa5 29.Nc3 b5 30.b3 Rd7 31.cxb5 axb5 32.Nd5 Kb7 33.g4 Rdd8!

Defending c8 and thus threatening the Knight.

34.Ne7

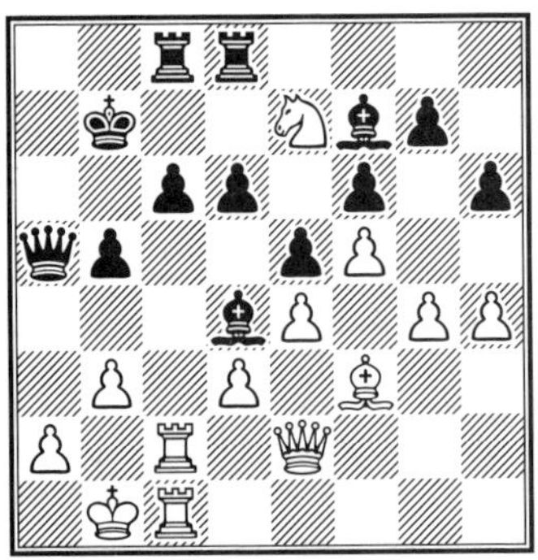

34...Bxb3! 35.Nxc8 Rxc8 36.Qd2 Qa3 37.Rh1 Ra8 38.Rh2 Bxa2+!

38...Bxc2+ 39.Qxc2 Ra4! is also crushing.

39.Rxa2 Qb3+ 40.Kc1

40.Rb2 Bxb2 41.Qxb2 Qxd3+ 42.Rc2 Qxf3 with an attack and three extra pawns.

40...Rxa2 41.Qxa2 Be3+ 42.Qd2

42.Rd2 Qxa2.

42...Qxd3, 0-1.

42...Qc3+ is also a stone cold winner.

Géza Maróczy vs. Emanuel Lasker, London 1899

1.d4 d5 2.Nf3 Nf6 3.c4 e6 4.e3 c5 5.Nc3 Nc6 6.a3 dxc4 7.Bxc4 a6 8.0-0 b5 9.Be2 cxd4 10.exd4 Bb7 11.b4 Be7 12.Bb2 0-0 13.Bd3 Qb6 14.Ne4 a5 15.bxa5 Nxa5 16.Nxf6+ Bxf6 17.Ne5 Rad8 18.Qc2 h6 19.Be4 Bxe5!

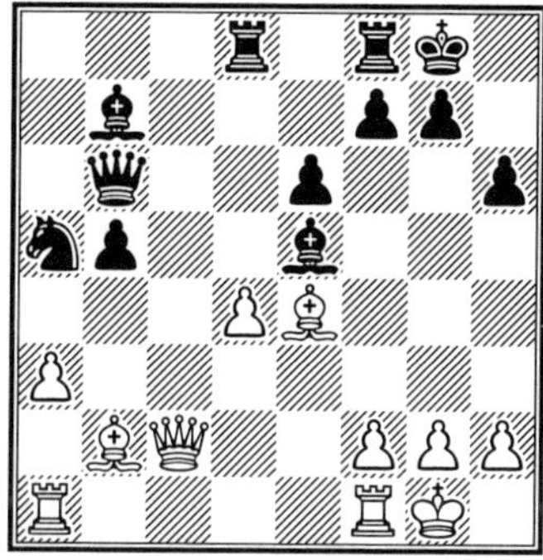

20.dxe5 Bxe4 21.Qxe4 Nb3 22.Qb4 Nxa1 and the game is over.

NN vs. Emanuel Lasker, Budapest (simultaneous exhibition) 1900

1.e4 e5 2.Nf3 Nc6 3.d4 exd4 4.Bc4 Bc5 5.0-0 Nf6 6.Bg5 d6 7.Bb5 h6 8.Bh4 Bg4 9.Nbd2 g5 10.Bxc6+ bxc6 11.Bg3 h5 12.h3 Bxf3 13.Nxf3 g4 14.hxg4 hxg4 15.Nxd4 Qd7 16.Re1 Nh5 17.Nf5 0-0-0 18.Qxg4 Rdg8 19.Qf3 Rh7 20.Rad1 Rg6 21.Kf1 Rf6 22.Be5 Rg6 23.Qc3 dxe5!!

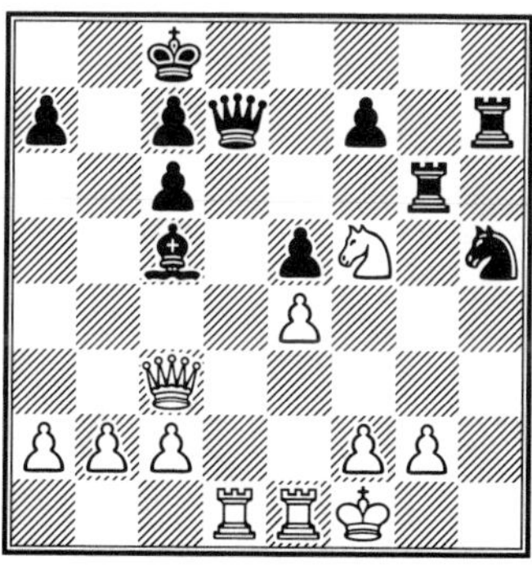

24.Rxd7??

White could draw with 24.Qxc5 Nf4 25.Qf8+ Kb7 26.Qb4+ with a perpetual check.

24...Nf4! 25.Rd8+ Kxd8 26.Rd1+

26.Ng3 Rxg3!

26...Bd4

26...Kc8?? 27.Ke1.

27.Rxd4+

27.Ke1 Rh1+ 28 Kd2 Bxc3+.

27...exd4 28.Qxd4+ Rd6!!, 0-1.

Emanuel Lasker vs. NN, (simultaneous exhibition) 1900

1.e4 e5 2.f4 exf4 3.Nf3 g5 4.h4 g4 5.Ng5 h6 6.Nxf7 Kxf7 7.d4 d5 8.Bxf4 dxe4 9.Bc4+ Kg7 10.Be5+ Nf6 11.Rf1 Be7 12.Qe2 Nc6 13.Nd2 Nxd4 14.Qxe4 Nc6 15.Bc3

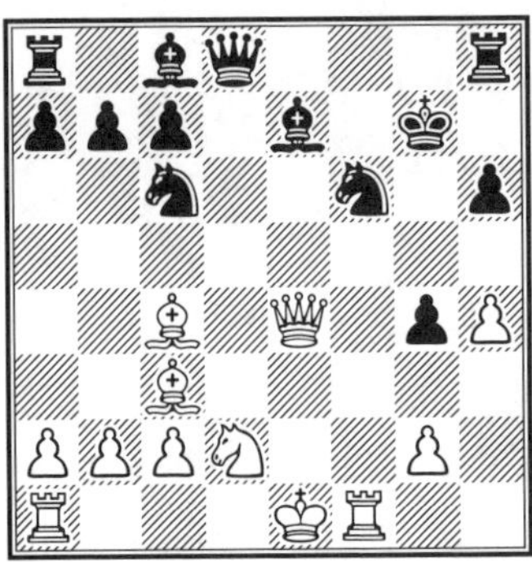

Rf8 16.0-0-0 Qe8 17.Bd3 Rh8 18.Qf4 Qf7 19.Ne4 Rf8 20.Ng5 Qg8 21.Qe4 Kh8 22.Nh7! Qg7 23.Nxf6 Bxf6 24.Rxf6! Rxf6 25.Qe8+ and mate next move.

Emanuel Lasker vs. Richard Teichmann, St. Petersburg 1909

1.e4 e5 2.Nf3 Nc6 3.Bb5 a6 4.Ba4 Nf6 5.0-0 Be7 6.Qe2 b5 7.Bb3 d6 8.c3 0-0 9.d4 exd4 10.cxd4 Bg4 11.Rd1 d5 12.e5 Ne4 13.Nc3 Nxc3 14.bxc3 f6 15.h3 Bh5 16.g4 Bf7 17.e6! Bg6 18.Nh4 Na5 19.Nxg6 hxg6 20.Bc2 f5 21.Kh1 Bd6 22.gxf5

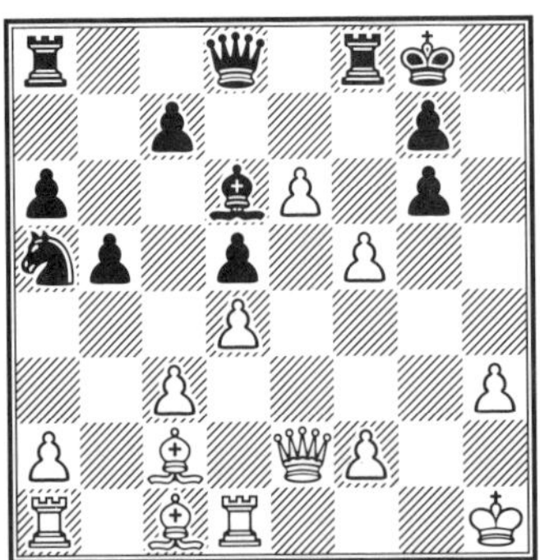

22...Qh4

22...gxf5 23.Rg1 Rg1 leaves White with a strong attack.

23.Qf3 gxf5 24.Rg1 f4 25.Rg4 Qh6 26.e7!! Bxe7 27.Bxf4 Qe6

Here Black resigned without waiting for White's reply.

28.Rxg7+! Kxg7 29.Rg1+ Kf7 30.Qh5+ Kf6 31.Qg6, 1-0.

David Janowski vs. Emanuel Lasker, World Championship 1909

1.e4 e5 2.Nf3 Nc6 3.Nc3 Nf6 4.Bb5 Bb4 5.0-0 0-0 6.d3 d6 7.Bg5 Nxc3 8.bxc3 Ne7 9.Bc4 Ng6 10.Nh4 Nf4 11.Bxf4 exf4 12.Nf3 Bg4 13.h3 Bh5 14.Rb1 b6 15.Qd2 Bxf3 16.gxf3 Nh5 17.Kh2 Qf6 18.Rg1 Rae8 19.d4 Nh8 20.Rb5 Qh6 21.Rbg5 f6 22.R5g4 g6

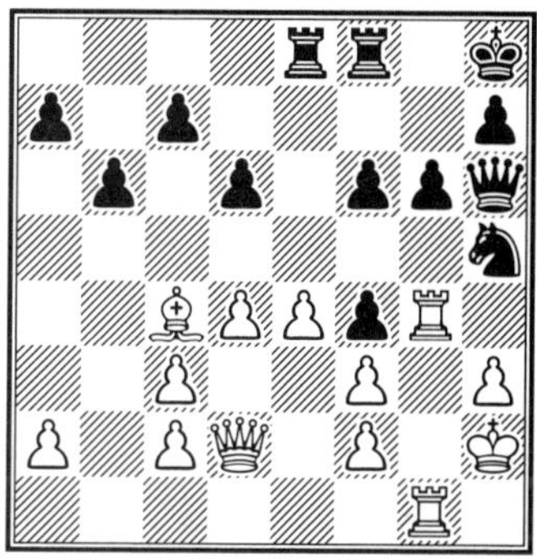

23.Bd3 Re7 24.c4 Ng7 25.c3 Ne6 26.Bf1 f5 27.R4g2 Rf6 28.Bd3 g5!

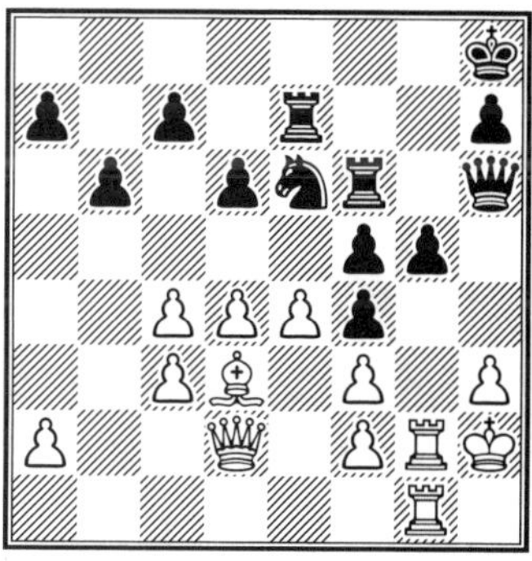

29.Rh1 g4 30.Be2 Ng5 31.fxg4 f3 32.Rg3 fxe2, 0-1.

Emanuel Lasker vs. Frank Marshall, St. Petersburg 1914

1.e4 e5 2.Nf3 Nf6 3.Nxe5 d6 4.Nf3 Nxe4 5.Qe2 Qe7 6.d3 Nf6 7.Bg5 Be6 8.Nc3 Nbd7 9.0-0-0 h6 10.Bh4 g5 11.Bg3 Nh5 12.d4 Nxg3 13.hxg3 g4 14.Nh4 d5

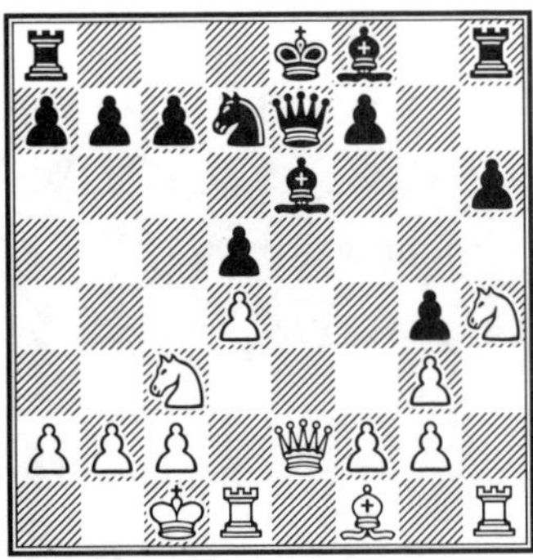

15.Qb5! 0-0-0 16.Qa5! a6

16...Kb8 17.Nb5.

17.Bxa6!! bxa6 18.Qxa6+ Kb8 19.Nb5 Nb6 20.Rd3 Qg5+ 21.Kb1 Bd6 22.Rb3 Rhe8 23.a4! Bf5 24.Na7!

24.Nxf5 followed by 25.a5 and the immediate 24.a5 also win.

24...Bd7 25.a5 Qd2 26.axb6 Re1+ 27.Ka2 c6 28.Nb5! cxb5 29.Qa7+

Black resigned here.

29...Kc8 30.Qa8+ Bb8 31.Qa6, 1-0.

Emanuel Lasker vs. Erich Cohn, St. Petersburg 1909

1.e4 e5 2.Nf3 Nc6 3.Bb5 Nf6 4.0-0 Be7 5.Nc3 d6 6.d4 Bd7 7.Bg5 exd4 8.Nxd4 0-0 9.Bxc6 bxc6 10.Qd3 Ng4 11.Bxe7 Qxe7 12.Rae1 Qh4 13.Nf3 Qh5 14.h3 Ne5 15.Nxe5 Qxe5 16.f4 Qc5+ 17.Kh2 Be6 18.b3 f5 19.e5 d5 20.Na4

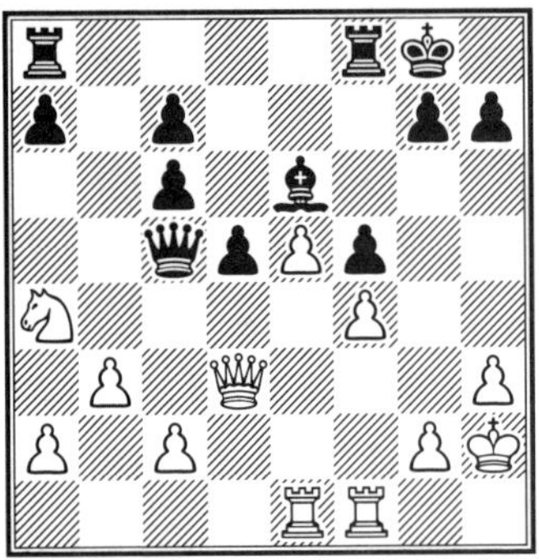

White plays to "win" the c5-square, which turns his Knight into a monster.

20...Qe7 21.Qd4

Moves like 21.Qa6 and 21.Qc3 are also good, but Lasker's choice is the most human, and the smoothest.

21...Rfb8 22.Nc5 a5 23.a3!

When the Knight will be permanently enshrined on c5 by b3-b4. White now has a positionally winning game, and Black quickly collapsed and lost.

Emanuel Lasker vs. David Janowski, World Championship 1910

1.d4 d5 2.c4 e6 3.Nc3 c5 4.cxd5 exd5 5.Nf3 Be6 6.e4 dxe4 7.Nxe4 Nc6 8.Be3 cxd4 9.Nxd4 Qa5+ 10.Nc3 0-0-0 11.a3 Nh6 12.b4 Qe5 13.Ncb5 Nf5 14.Rc1 Nxe3 15.fxe3 Qxe3+ 16.Be2

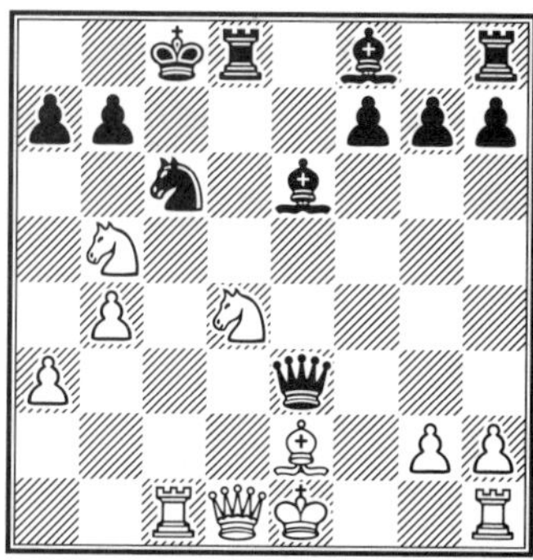

16...Be7 17.Rc3 Bh4+ 18.g3 Qe4 19.0-0 Bf6 20.Rxf6! gxf6 21.Bf3 Qe5 22.Nxa7+ Kc7 23.Naxc6 bxc6 24.Rxc6+ Kb8 25.Rb6+ Kc8 26.Qc1+

26.Qc2+ Kd7 27.Qa4+ also wins.

26...Kd7 27.Nxe6 fxe6 28.Rb7+ Ke8 29.Bc6+, 1-0.

Key Moments In Time—Lasker's Last Stand

The legendary Emanuel Lasker became the second World Chess Champion in 1894 when he took the title from Wilhelm Steinitz—Lasker kept the title until 1921 when, at the age of fifty-two, he succumbed to the much younger Capablanca.

Lasker was also a philosopher and a world class mathematician—he earned his doctorate in math in 1902 and published a theorem which, even today, is critically important for the ins and outs of algebra and algebraic geometry (you can look up "zeros of simultaneous polynomials," but your head might explode if you do).

Looking at his tournament and match records, one might think that it was all clear sailing for Lasker. But there was one moment when that twenty-seven-year reign (a record that almost certainly will never be broken) was in serious jeopardy. His opponent was the extremely strong Austrian player, Carl Schlechter.

Schlechter was born in 1874, and it was clear that he was a solid master in the 1890s (a tie match against David Janowski, another tied match against Simon Alapin), and a world class grandmaster from 1900 onwards (he showed the world that he was the real deal when he crushed Janowski in 1899 with a score of six wins, one loss, and three draws).

Schlechter was a great player, he wasn't very exciting. In fact, he was known as a draw master.

Since the World Champion has to (now and then) accept challenges, Lasker decided to give Schlechter a shot at the title. I'm sure Lasker wasn't worried since their record was three wins for Lasker and one win for Schlechter (with a few draws). However, Lasker wisely arranged the match to be a battle of thirty games, which would pretty much toss luck out the window.

Unfortunately, nobody believed that Schlechter had a chance, so funding fell through and Lasker had to accept a ten-game match instead of the desired thirty.

The first four games were drawn. The fifth game, though, turned the chess world on its head!

Carl Schlechter vs. Emanuel Lasker, World Championship (5) 1910

1.e4 e5 2.Nf3 Nc6 3.Bb5 Nf6 4.0-0 d6 5.d4 Bd7 6.Nc3 Be7 7.Bg5 0-0 8.dxe5 Nxe5 9.Bxd7 Nfxd7 10.Bxe7 Nxf3+ 11.Qxf3 Qxe7 12.Nd5 Qd8 13.Rad1 Re8 14.Rfe1 Nb6 15.Qc3 Nxd5 16.Rxd5 Re6 17.Rd3 Qe7 18.Rg3 Rg6 19.Ree3 Re8 20.h3 Kf8 21.Rxg6 hxg6 22.Qb4 c6

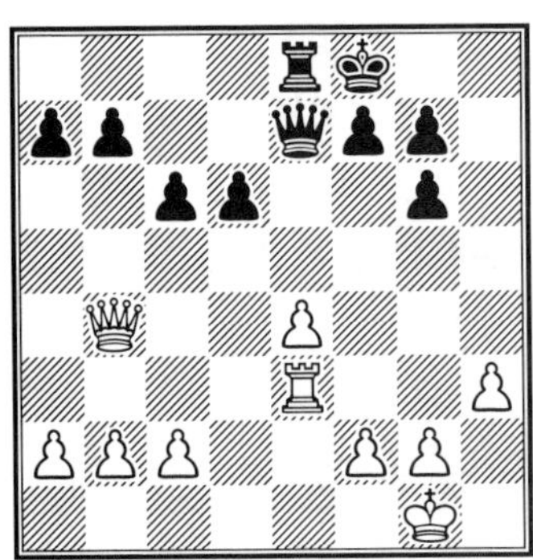

23.Qa3 a6 24.Qb3 Rd8 25.c4 Rd7 26.Qd1 Qe5 27.Qg4 Ke8 28.Qe2 Kd8 29.Qd2 Kc7 30.a3 Re7 31.b4 b5 32.cxb5 axb5 33.g3 g5 34.Kg2 Re8 35.Qd1 f6 36.Qb3 Qe6 37.Qd1 Rh8 38.g4 Qc4 39.a4 Qxb4 40.axb5 Qxb5 41.Rb3 Qa6 42.Qd4 Re8 43.Rb1 Re5 44.Qb4 Qb5 45.Qe1 Qd3 46.Rb4 c5 47.Ra4 c4 48.Qa1 Qxe4+ 49.Kh2 Rb5?!

Lasker has outplayed his opponent and is now winning. Simplest is 49...Kd7 50.Ra7+ Ke8 moving the King to safety of the kingside when Black's c- and d-pawns will prove decisive.

50.Qa2! Qe5+ 51.Kg1 Qe1+ 52.Kh2 d5 53.Ra8 Qb4?!

53...Qe5+ and 53...Rb7 both give Black very good winning chances.

54.Kg2

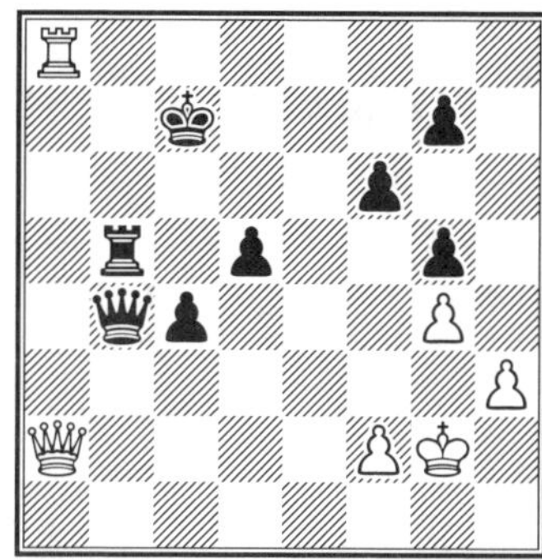

54...Qc5⁇

A horrible blunder that could easily have changed chess history. Far better was 54...c3 when Black retains good chances for victory. Now, after 54...Qc5, White wins by force.

55.Qa6 Rb8 56.Ra7+ Kd8 57.Rxg7 Qb6 58.Qa3 Kc8 59.Qf8+, 1-0.

59...Qd8 is met by 60.Qc5+ Qc7 61.Qc7 mate.

In game six Lasker had a superior position, but Schlechter did what he does best—he defended and managed to draw.

Game seven saw Lasker, playing Black, emerging from the opening with an edge. Schlechter desperately sacrificed a Bishop in a multi-piece endgame. Lasker missed the best continuation, Schlechter brilliantly offered a Rook (which couldn't be taken), Black still had an advantage, Lasker botched it and was even a bit worse, then Lasker was a bit better, and when the smoke cleared Schlechter had escaped with another draw.

Carl Schlechter vs. Emanuel Lasker, World Championship (7) 1910

1.e4 c5 2.Nf3 Nc6 3.d4 cxd4 4.Nxd4 Nf6 5.Nc3 g6

5...g6 is known to be poor nowadays, but Sicilian opening theory was still in its infancy at that time.

6.Bc4 d6 7.Nxc6 bxc6 8.e5 Ng4 9.e6 f5 10.0-0 Bg7 11.Bf4 Qb6 12.Bb3 Ba6 13.Na4 Qd4 14.Qxd4 Bxd4 15.c4 0-0 16.Rad1 Bf6 17.Rfe1 g5

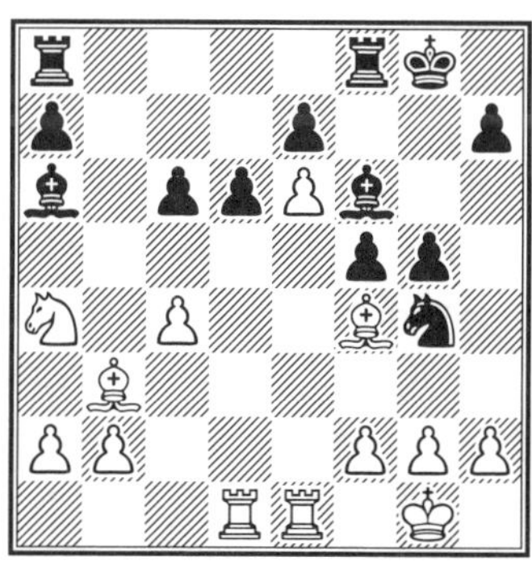

18.Bxd6!?

Incredibly brave and very creative! 18.Bc1 or 18.Bd2 are the sane choices, when Black is better, but White is fighting the good fight. One possible line is 18...Bd4 (18...Ne5!?) 19.Re2 h6 20.h3 Ne5 21.Bb4 c5 22.Bxc5 dxc5 23.Rxd4 Nf3+ 24.gxf3 cxd4 25.Nc5 Bc8 26.Rd2 Rd8 27.Bc2 f4 28.Be4 Rb8 29.b3 Rb6 30.Bd5.

18...exd6 19.Rxd6 Be5

19...Ne5 was probably better.

20.c5!

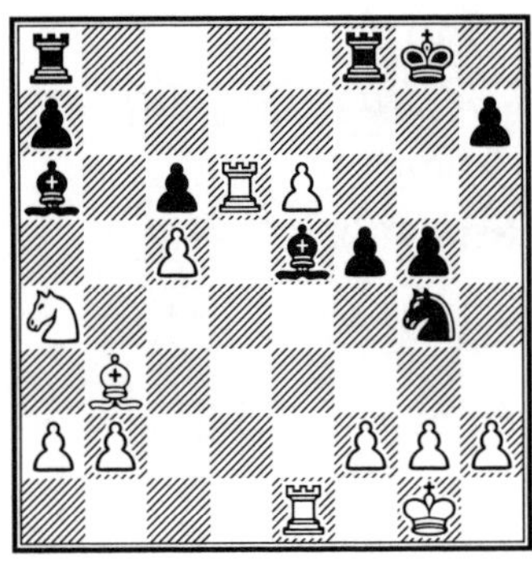

These guys are fighting tooth and nail!

20...Rfe8 21.g3 Bf6 22.Rxc6 Bb7?

22...Bb5 retains an advantage for Black.

23.Rc7 Be4 24.Nc3 Bxc3 25.bxc3 Ne5 26.Rd1 Nf3+ 27.Kf1 Nxh2+ 28.Ke1 Nf3+ 29.Ke2 Ne5 30.Rdd7! f4! 31.Rg7+ Kh8 32.Rxg5 Bd3+ 33.Kd1 fxg3 34.fxg3 Ng6 35.Rd5 Be4 36.Rd6 Bf5 37.Bd5 Rab8 38.c6 Nf8 39.Rb7 Rbc8 40.e7 Ng6 41.Bf7 Rxe7 42.Bxg6 Bg4+ 43.Kc1 Re1+ 44.Kb2 hxg6 45.Rxg6 Bf5 46.Rf6 Be4 47.Rxa7 Rb1+ 48.Ka3 Bxc6, ½-½.

An incredible game!

I don't know why, but this Schlechter was anything but dull. It seems that he went into this match with a do-or-die mentality. I think Lasker was stunned, and it took him a while to realize that his opponent wanted buckets and buckets of blood.

Game eight was also a battle, but it too ended in a draw.

Game nine was another Sicilian (1.e4 c5 2.Nf3 Nc6 3.d4 cxd4 4.Nxd4 Nf6 5.Nc3 e5 6.Nb3 Bb4 7.Bd3 d5) and another advantage for Lasker (who was playing Black). However, the "drawing master" continued to play like a man who just ate twenty pounds of sugar, and he went after Lasker with all his might. Lasker didn't break, though, and he tried everything possible to win. However, a draw was agreed on move sixty-five.

And now Lasker had to face the fact that he might lose his title. Many historians think that Schlechter had to win by two points to take the World Championship. However, I don't believe it. I think that Schlechter felt that his win in game five was pure luck and, since he didn't want to win the title in such a "shameful way" (most players, even in those days, would not think like that, but Schlechter would), he decided to go all out to win so he could take the championship in a honorable manner.

My view that the "two-point advantage" is rubbish seems to be proved by a letter Lasker wrote to the *New York Evening Post* two days before the final game: "The match with Schlechter is nearing its end and it appears probably that for the first time in my life I shall be the loser. If that should happen, a good man will have won the World Championship."

And so the tenth and final game was played, with Schlechter wanting to win "honestly" and Lasker having to win to save his title. Both players were exhausted, stressed, but completely ready to fight to the last pawn.

Emanuel Lasker vs. Carl Schlechter, World Championship (10) 1910

1.d4 d5 2.c4 c6 3.Nf3 Nf6 4.e3 g6 5.Nc3 Bg7 6.Bd3 0-0 7.Qc2 Na6 8.a3 dxc4 9.Bxc4 b5 10.Bd3 b4 11.Na4 bxa3 12.bxa3 Bb7 13.Rb1

White is clearly better.

13...Qc7 14.Ne5?!

The tension is going to affect both players, and this Knight move shows that Lasker has the yips. Simply 14.0-0 retained a pronounced opening plus.

14...Nh5?

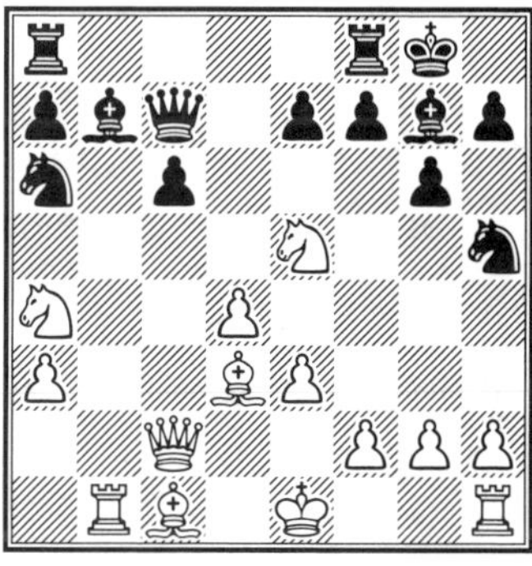

I don't understand this move.

15.g4?

Lasker goes all in, but why? Just 15.f4 (or 15.0-0) leaves Black in bad shape.

15...Bxe5 16.gxh5?!

16.dxe5 Ng7 17.0-0 retained a significant advantage.

16...Bg7 17.hxg6 hxg6 18.Qc4 Bc8 19.Rg1

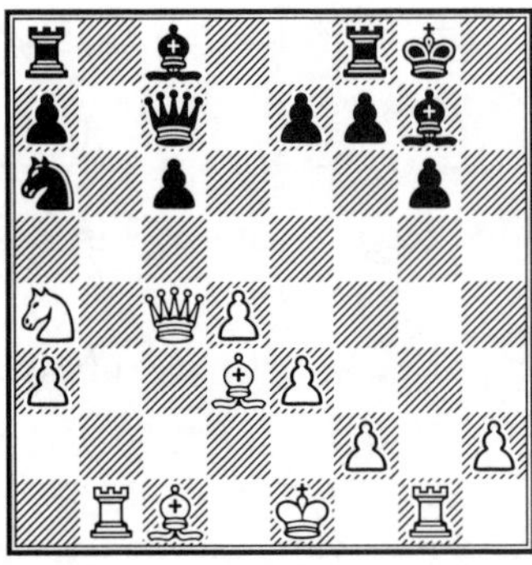

I would prefer 19.h4 followed by 20.h5. Here's what Lasker had to say about him keeping his King in the center: "When so much is riding on a single game, that both players should be in a heightened state is understandable. My fantasy veered toward the adventurous. Had this position arisen in the beginning the match, I would probably have refrained from such an idea."

19...Qa5+?

Black wrongly fears Rxg6: 19...Qxh2 20.Rxg6 Nc7 and Black is right back in the game.

20.Bd2 Qd5 21.Rc1 Bb7 22.Qc2 Qh5 23.Bxg6?

After all the brilliant chess that was played in the other games, it's clear that both players are completely freaked out. The only question is, "Who will crack first?" 23.Qb3 hitting b7 and creating a pin along the a1-g8 diagonal, was much stronger.

23...Qxh2 24.Rf1 fxg6 25.Qb3+ Rf7 26.Qxb7 Raf8 27.Qb3 Kh8 28.f4 g5

28...e5!? might be a bit better, when 29.dxe5 Rd8 30.Qb2 Qh4+ gives Black at least a draw and perhaps a chance at more.

29.Qd3 gxf4 30.exf4 Qh4+

30...Nc7! was better, protecting the Knight and swinging it around to d5 where it can take part in the attack against white's King.

31.Ke2

31.Kd1 might be more accurate since it allows white's King to find a home on c2.

31...Qh2+ 32.Rf2 Qh5+ 33.Rf3 Nc7

Finally the Knight gets into the battle.

34.Rxc6

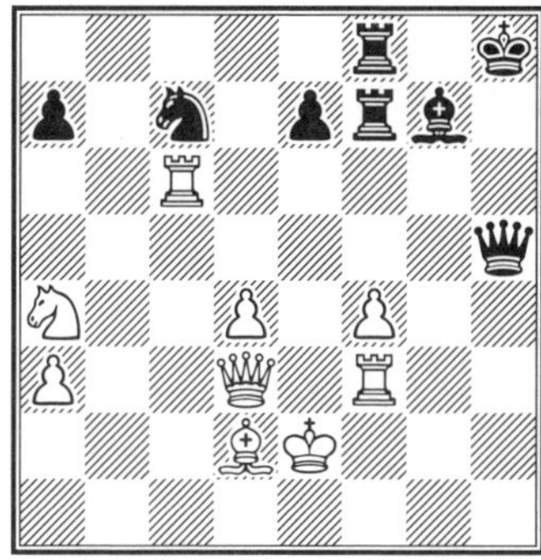

34.Rh1 Qxh1 35.Rh3+ Qxh3 36.Qxh3+ Kg8 37.Nc5 Rd8 offered mutual chances. I'm sure Lasker saw this, but felt that Rxc6 was more complicated and gave Black more chances to make a mistake. Indeed, here's what Tarrasch had to say, "Unbelievable! With destruction facing him at every turn, Lasker uses this opportunity to grab a pawn. It is like a general under fire, lighting a cigar."

34...Nb5 35.Rc4

35.Ke1 is the best move IF a draw is fine for White. However, a draw is NOT okay for Lasker, so he had to play 35.Rc4 and hope the Gods would be kind.

35...Rxf4?!

35...Qg4, claiming that Black has a significant advantage (other tries are 35...Nd6 and 35...Rd8). The idea of 35...Qg4 is to avoid Rc5 hitting black's Queen and b5-Knight at the same time. It also avoids some lines where Rh3 might embarrass the black Queen on the h-file. And finally, the maneuver (after 35...Qg4) ...Rf7-f5-h5-h2/h3/h1 is possible. Schlechter's exchange sacrifice looks promising, but it actually tosses away Black's advantage.

36.Bxf4 Rxf4 37.Rc8+ Bf8 38.Kf2

Black has obvious compensation for the exchange sacrifice, but the best he can get is a draw. That's all that Black needs so the exchange sacrifice, if followed up correctly, will hand Schlechter the title.

38...Qh2+ 39.Ke1

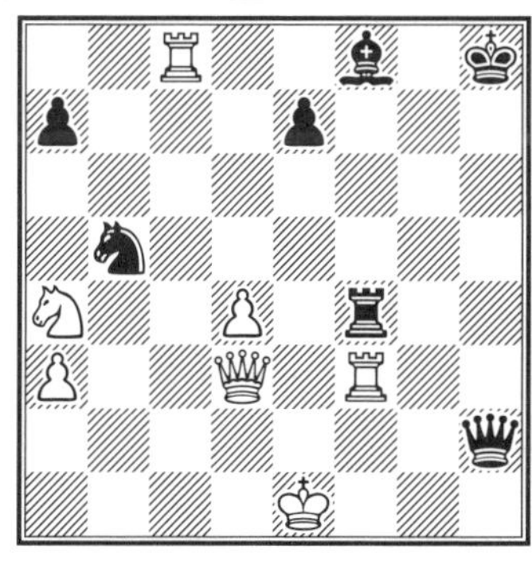

39...Qh1+⁈

Poor Schlechter cracks! Now he's on the brink of defeat. 39...Qh4+ would have drawn.

40.Rf1 Qh4+ 41.Kd2 Rxf1 42.Qxf1 Qxd4+ 43.Qd3 Qf2+ 44.Kd1 Nd6 45.Rc5

45.Rb8, keeping an eye on the f3-bishop, might have been more accurate.

45...Bh6

45...Bg7 was better.

46.Rd5 Kg8

46...Qa2 47.Nc5 is very good for White.

47.Nc5 Qg1+

47...Qg2 not allowing white's King off the first rank, seems better.

48.Kc2 Qc1+ 49.Kb3 Bg7 50.Ne6

50.Rg5 was very strong. Of course, White's choice, though not as strong as 50.Rg5, is hard to resist.

50...Qb2+⁈

50...Qb6+ offered more resistance. Kasparov gave the following line: 51.Kc2 Qb2+ 52.Kd1 Qa1+ 53.Ke2 Qb2+ 54.Kf3 Qf6+ 55.Nf4 Nf7 and in light of White's exposed King, it is not clear if he can win.

51.Ka4 Kf7 52.Nxg7 Qxg7 53.Qb3 Ke8 54.Qb8+ Kf7 55.Qxa7 Qg4+ 56.Qd4

Centralizing his pieces.

56...Qd7+ 57.Kb3 Qb7+ 58.Ka2 Qc6 59.Qd3 Ke6 60.Rg5 Kd7 61.Re5 Qg2+ 62.Re2 Qg4 63.Rd2 Qa4 64.Qf5+ Kc7 65.Qc2+ Qxc2+ 66.Rxc2+ Kb6 67.Re2 Nc8 68.Kb3 Kc6 69.Rc2+ Kb7 70.Kb4 Na7 71.Kc5, 1-0.

Lasker retained his title by the skin of his teeth!

They played two more times (both games were played in 1918). Lasker won one and drew the other. Unfortunately, Schlechter died on December 27, 1918. With World War I raging, food was hard to come by. Poor Schlechter had no food to eat and no coal to heat his house. He starved to death, too proud to ask for help.

Einstein on Lasker

I'll give Albert Einstein the last word on Lasker and present his foreword to *Emanuel Lasker: The Life of a Chess Master:*[1]

1 Dr. J. Hannak, trans. by Heinrich Fraenkel, *Emanuel Lasker: The Life of a Chess Master.* New York: Simon & Schuster, 1959.

Emanuel Lasker was undoubtedly one of the most interesting people I came to know in my later life. We owe a debt of gratitude to those who have troubled to acquaint contemporary and future generations with his life-story. For few indeed can have combined such a unique independence of personality with so eager an interest in all the great problems of mankind.

I am no chess player myself, so I am not in a position to admire his mental powers in the sphere of his greatest intellectual achievements; indeed I have to confess that I have always disliked the fierce competitive spirit embodied in that highly intellectual game.

I met Emanuel Lasker in the house of my old friend Alexander Moszkowski, and I came to know him well during the many walks we took together, discussing ideas on a variety of subjects. It was a somewhat unilateral discussion in which, almost invariably, I was in the position of listener for it seemed to be the natural thing for this eminently creative man to generate his own ideas rather than adjust himself to those of someone else.

Whenever we met I seemed to detect a somewhat tragic note in his personality, in spite of a fundamentally optimistic inclination to always seek some positive meaning in life. His mind which had that exceptional elasticity characteristic of chess players was imbued with chess to such an extreme that he could never quite rid himself of the spirit of the game, even while dealing with philosophical and human problems. Nevertheless, I had the impression that to him chess was a means of livelihood rather than the real object of his life.

What he really yearned for was some scientific understanding that beauty peculiar to the process of logical creation, a beauty from whose magic spell on one can escape who has ever felt even its lightest influence. Spinoza's material life and economic independence were based on the grinding of lenses; in Lasker's life chess played a similar part. But Spinoza was luckier, for his business was such as to leave his mind free and independent; whereas master-chess grips its exponent, shackling the mind and brain, so that the inner freedom and independence of even the strongest character cannot remain unaffected. This I became aware of whenever I talked to Lasker or read one of his philosophical books. Of these I was most interested in his *Philosophie des Unvollendbar*, a highly original work and very revealing of its author's personality.

Finally, I should like to add a word of explanation as to why I never attempted, either in writing or in conversation, to deal with Lasker's criticism of the theory of relativity. Since even in this biography, with the emphasis on the man and the chess player rather than the scientist, a slight reproach seems noticeable in the passage mentioning that essay, I had better say a word about it.

Lasker's keen analytical brain had immediately and clearly recognized that the entire problem hinged on the constancy of the velocity of light in empty space. He clearly saw that, once such constancy was admitted, the relativisation of time was unanswerable, whether one liked it or not (and he did not like it at all). What then was to be done? He tried to emulate what Alexander the (so called) "Great" did when cutting through the Gordian knot.

Lasker's argument could be summarized thus: No one has any direct and immediate knowledge about the velocity of light in absolutely empty space; for even interstellar space contains a certain if infinitesimal quantity of matter, and this applies even more to space from which the air has been pumped by imperfect human agencies. Who then can presume to deny that the velocity of light in absolutely empty space would be infinite?

This is the gist of Lasker's argument, and it could be answered in this way: True enough, no one can tell from any direct and experimental knowledge precisely how light would move in absolutely empty space. But it is virtually impossible to think of any reasonable theory of light based on the notion that infinitesimal traces of matter, while influencing the velocity of light to a remarkable extent, would yet remain almost independent of the density of such matter.

Pending the proposition of such a theory, which, incidentally, would have to accord with well known optical phenomena in almost empty space, any physicist must consider this particular Gordian knot to be still unraveled and unravellable, unless he is content with the existing extent of the unraveling. And the moral? A keen brain and a powerful mind is no substitute for the deft touch of nimble fingers. However, I rather liked Lasker's stubborn intellectual independence, a most rare quality in a generation whose intellectuals are almost invariably mere camp-followers. And so I let the matter rest.

I am glad that the readers of this sympathetic biography will get to know a man who was so strong a personality and yet so sensitive and lovable a person. As for myself, I shall remember with gratitude the pleasing conversations I enjoyed with that incessantly eager, truly independent and yet most modest of men.

—Princeton, N.J., October 1952

7

FRANK MARSHALL

How to Build a Chess Champion

Let's talk about Frank Marshall. This man was U.S. Chess Champion from 1909 to 1936. A man who beat Emanuel Lasker once and Capablanca twice. A player who feared no one, which allowed him to win many tournaments against world class competition. An American hero who dared dream of being World Chess Champion.

Born in New York City in 1877, his family moved to Montreal, Canada, when Frank was eight and stayed there for eleven years. Unlike today's extremely young grandmasters, Marshall took quite a while to "cook." He wasn't recognized as a proven master until 1899 when in, his early twenties, he won a tournament in London. This immediately gave him, as Marshall put it, an "international reputation".

Fifteen Year Old Marshall Challenges Steinitz and Pillsbury (1893-1894)

Okay, those games were simultaneous exhibitions. And yes, Pillsbury was also blindfolded. In fact, both were given a sleeping tincture (a Mickey Finn) which made the two chess greats fall unconscious from time to time.

What? My wife tells me that there wasn't any tincture! Oh well, I guess playing many opponents at the same time, with Pillsbury blindfolded to boot, was more than enough odds.

Though Marshall got odds, these games were still very important for the young Marshall and for those who want to understand him. Aside from playing such famous players (he must have been extremely excited!), these games show just how much he depended on attack and tactics (you can see his tactical talent bubbling out with every move), apparently without any positional skills at all.

Wilhelm Steinitz vs. Frank Marshall, Montreal (simultaneous exhibition) 1893

1.e4 e6 2.d4 d5 3.Nd2 Ne7 4.Bd3 Nbc6 5.c3 Ng6 6.Nb3 e5 7.Qe2 Be6 8.Nf3 Bd6 9.exd5 Bxd5 10.dxe5 0-0??

Marshall couldn't stop himself! Now 11.exd6 Re8 12.Be3 Nf4 gives Black an attacking setup, but both 13.Qf1 and 13.Bxf4 Bxf3 14.gxf3 Rxe2+ 15.Bxe2 refutes it. However, Steinitz didn't want his rabid opponent to have any chances at all.

11.Bxg6

Marshall, in his delightful book *My Fifty Years of Chess*[1] (though many suspect it was ghostwritten by Fred Reinfeld) wrote: "Steinitz smiled a little at my inexperience as he upset all my plans with this move, winning a piece outright and skillfully avoiding my attack."

11...Re8 12.Bc2

12.Bg5 was even stronger.

12...Nxe5 13.Nxe5 Rxe5 14.Be3 Qh4

Hoping for 15.0-0?? Rxe3 16.fxe3 (16.g3 Rxe2 17.gxh4 Rxc2 is game over) 16...Qxh2+ 17.Kf2 Bg3 mate.

1 Frank J. Marshall, *My Fifty Years of Chess*. New York: Chess Review, 1942. (Later published under the title *Marshall's Best Games of Chess*.)

15.0-0-0

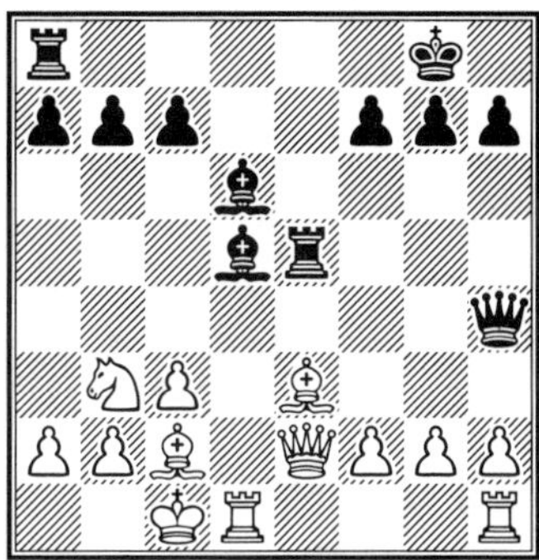

I read Marshall's book when I was thirteen years old, and when I looked at this game I remember laughing when I saw Marshall's next move.

15...Qa4

The guy only has one thing on his mind! The Queen-leap to h4 on move fourteen and, when white's King castles queenside, leaping again to a4, seemed extremely funny. I still laugh when I see this.

16.Kb1 Rd8 17.f4 Bc4 18.Qf3 Ra5 19.Nxa5 Qxa2+ 20.Kc1 Qa1+ 21.Bb1 Qxa5 22.Qe4 Ba2 23.Qxh7+ Kf8 24.Rd4 c6 25.Rhd1 Qc7 26.Qh8+, 1-0.

Pillsbury gave a simultaneous exhibition too, with the added difficulty of playing blindfolded at the same time!

Harry Pillsbury (blindfold) vs. Frank Marshall, Montreal 1894

1.d4 d5 2.c4 Nf6 3.cxd5 Qxd5

It's clear from the Steinitz and Pillsbury games that Marshall didn't know much about openings. Instead, he made it up with pure ferocity!

4.Nc3 Qd8 5.e4 e5 6.d5 Bd6 7.f4? exf4

Marshall wrote: "White loses a pawn without any compensation. Pillsbury was taking chances as he was playing against an inexperienced youth. Or he may have been giving me an opportunity. Masters sometimes do that in simultaneous exhibitions."

8.Nf3 Bg4 9.Bd3 Nh5 10.0-0 Bc5+ 11.Kh1 Qf6 12.Ne2

White didn't want to play this move but if 12.Bd2 then 12...Ng3+! wins on the spot.

12...g5

Of course Marshall would play this. Better though, was 12...Nd7 with ...0-0-0 to follow.

13.Qc2 Bb6 14.Bd2 Rg8 15.e5 Qh6 16.a4

The safer move was 16.Bf5 when White is better.

16...Ng3+ 17.Nxg3 fxg3 18.Bc3 Bxf3 19.gxf3 g4

Another typical Marshall, "don't stop until he's dead" move. However, 19... Na6 (yes, development is important) is better, while 19...Bf2 is also good for White after 20.Rxf2 gxf2 21.Qxf2 Nd7 when 22.Bf5 and 22.e6 turns the tables for White, who is now the attacker.

20.f4?

An easy move to make, especially if you're blindfolded and playing other boards at the same time. 20.Qg2 was winning for White.

20...Bf2 21.Rxf2 gxf2 22.Qxf2 g3

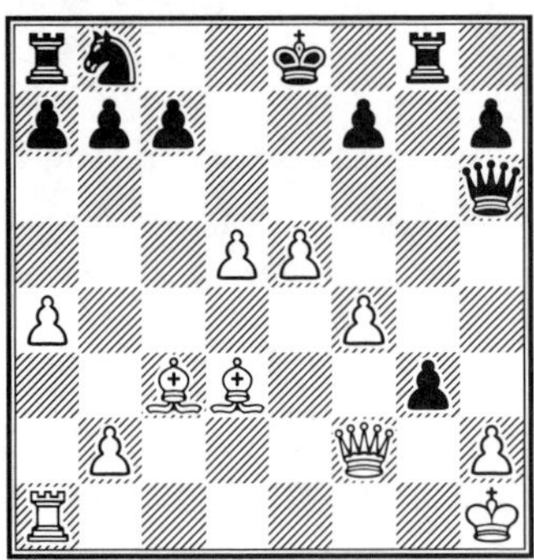

Marshall never stops!

23.Qd2?

23.Rg1! was correct. Pillsbury, who was also a great tactician, would have seen this move right away in normal circumstances. However, multiple opponents and a blindfold covering your eyes makes it hard to make good decisions: 23...gxf2?? (23...Nd7 24.Rxg3 Rxg3 25.Qxg3 0-0-0 gives both sides chances.) 24.Rxg8+ Ke7 25.Bb4+ Kd7 (25...c5 26.dxc6+ Ke6 27.cxb7) 26.Bf5+ and Black has to resign.

23...Nd7

Now Black is in charge.

24.e6 fxe6 25.dxe6 Nc5 26.Bc4 Rd8 27.Qg2 Ne4 28.Rf1 Rd1!

I'm sure Marshall was ecstatic when he played this move.

29.Be1

29.Rxd1 Nf2+ 30.Kg1 gxh2+ 31.Kxf2 Rxg2+ 32.Kxg2 Qg6+ and White loses material: 33.Kxh2 Qh5+ followed by ...Qxd1. OR, 33.Kf2 Qc2+ 34.Rd2 Qxd2+ 35.Bxd2 h1=Q.

29...Rxe1 30.Rxe1 Nf2+ 31.Kg1 gxh2+ 32.Kxf2 Rxg2+ 33.Kxg2 Qxf4 34.Be2 and White resigned without waiting for a reply. The game might have continued in this way: 34...Qd2, 0-1 and 34...Qe4+ 35.Kxh2 Qh4+ 36.Kg2 Qxe1, 0-1.

Marshall considered this 1899 game "one of my earliest brilliancies!"

Frank Marshall vs. Dr. Johannes F. Esser, London 1899

1.e4 e5 2.Nf3 Nc6 3.Bc4 Nf6 4.d4 exd4 5.0-0 Ne4 6.Re1 d5 7.Bxd5 Qxd5 8.Nc3 Qd8 9.Re4+ Be7 10.Nxd4 Nxd4 11.Rxd4 Bd7 12.Bf4 Qc8 13.Nd5 Bd8 14.Qh5 0-0 15.Bxc7! Be6

15...Bxc7 16.Ne7+ Kh8 17.Qxh7+ Kxh7 18.Rh4 mate.

16.Bxd8 Bxd5

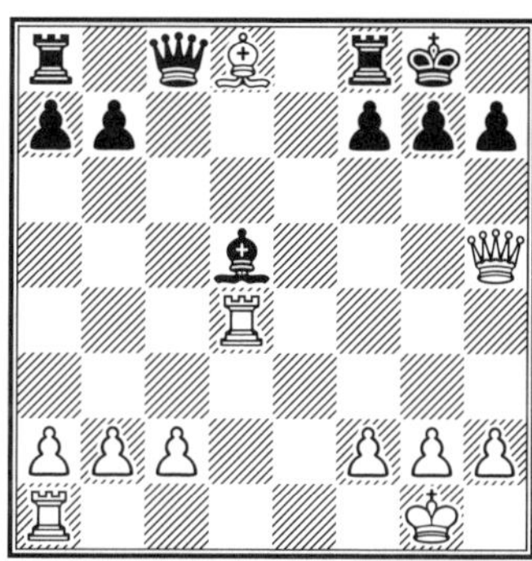

16...Qxd8 17.Rad1 Bxd5 18.Rxd5 with a winning game.

17.Bf6! Qc6

17...gxf6 18.Qxd5 Qxc2 19.Qxb7 Rab8 20.Qxa7 Qxb2 21.Rad1 Ra8 22.Qe7 and black's King isn't happy. 22...Qb6 23.Rd6 etc.

18.Bxg7 Kxg7 19.Qxd5 Qxc2 20.Qe5+

20.Rg4+ Kh8 21.Qe5+ f6 22.Qe7 was also a killer. Here's the rest of the game after 20.Qe5+:

20...f6 21.Qe7+ Kg6

21...Kh8 or 21...Rf7 both lose to 22.Rg4+.

22.Rh4

22.Rd7 and 22.Rg4+ are better. But at this point Marshall saw an easy win and just did it.

22...Kg5

Black goes into lemming mode.

23.Qg7+ Kxh4 24.Qh6+ Kg4 25.h3+ Kf5 26.Qxh7+, 1-0.

After his excellent performance at London, Marshall had some ups and downs, but his result in the Paris 1900 event (May 17 to June 20) was very good. Marshall tied for third with Géza Maróczy (12 points). Pillsbury came in second (12½ points), and Emanuel Lasker was first (14½). Other players below the top four were Amos Burn, Mikhail Chigorin, Carl Schlechter, Georg Marco, Jacques Mieses, Jackson Showalter, and David Janowski (born Dawid, but David is now commonly used). The highlight of the tournament was Marshall's win over Lasker!

Frank Marshall vs. Emanuel Lasker, Paris 1900

1.d4 d5 2.c4 e6 3.Nc3 Nf6 4.Bg5 c6 5.e4 dxe4 6.Nxe4 Bb4+ 7.Nc3 c5 8.a3 Bxc3+ 9.bxc3 Qa5 10.Bd2 Ne4 11.Nf3 Nxc3 12.dxc5 Nxd1 13.Bxa5 Nb2 14.a4 Bd7 15.c6 Bxc6 16.Ne5 Be4 17.Bc3

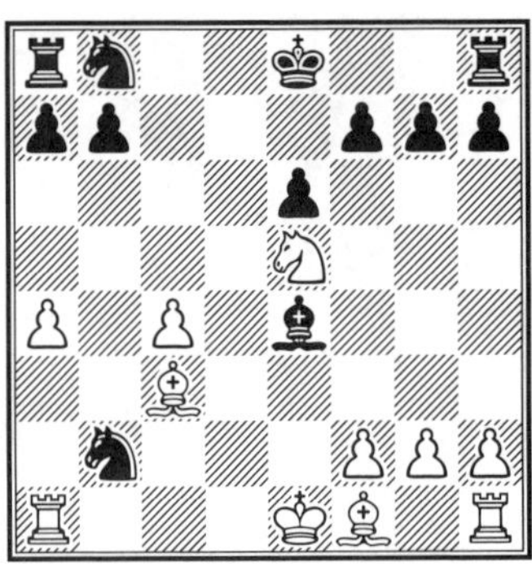

17...f6 18.f3 Bc2 19.Kd2 Nxa4 20.Kxc2 Nxc3 21.Nd3 Nd5 22.cxd5 exd5 23.Nc5 b6 24.Bb5+ Kf7 25.Na4 Nc6 26.Nc3 Rhc8 27.Rhd1 Ne7 28.Kb2 Rc7 29.Bd3 a5 30.Na4 Rc6 31.Rac1 Rb8 32.Rxc6 Nxc6 33.Rc1 Ne5 34.Rc7+ Ke6 35.Bb5 g5 36.Ra7 d4 37.Ra6 Kd5 38.Kc2 Rb7 39.Ra8 Nc6 40.Kd2 Nb4 41.Rd8+ Ke5 42.Nb2 Rc7 43.Nc4+ Kf5 44.Rxd4 Rc5 45.Be8 Rd5 46.Ne3+ Ke5 47.Nxd5 Kxd4 48.Nxb4 axb4 49.Bf7 f5 50.Bg8 h5 51.Bf7 h4 52.h3 b5 53.Be8 Kc4 54.Bd7 b3 55.Bxf5 Kb4 56.Bd3 b2 57.Kc2 Ka3 58.Kb1, 1-0.

Marshall played the endgame well, but it might surprise you to know that he was actually very skilled in that phase of the game.

Marshall's notes to the next game (from Paris 1900) are hilarious! Thus, I'll let him entertain us with moves and prose:

Frank Marshall vs. Amos Burn, Paris 1900

[Marshall]: "Britisher Amos Burn was a very conservative player and liked to settle down for a long session of close, defensive chess. He loved to smoke his pipe while he studied the board. As I made the second move, Burn began hunting through his pockets for his pipe and tobacco.

1.d4 d5 2.c4 e6 3.Nc3 Nf6 4.Bg5 Be7

"Not much thought needed on these moves, but Burn had his pipe out and was looking for a pipe cleaner.

5.e3 0-0 6.Nf3 b6 7.Bd3 Bb7 8.cxd5 exd5

"He began filling up his pipe. I speed up my moves.

9.Bxf6 Bxf6 10.h4

"Made him think on that one—and he still didn't have the pipe going."

10...g6 11.h5 Re8 12.hxg6 hxg6

"Now he was looking for matches.

13.Qc2 Bg7 14.Bxg6!

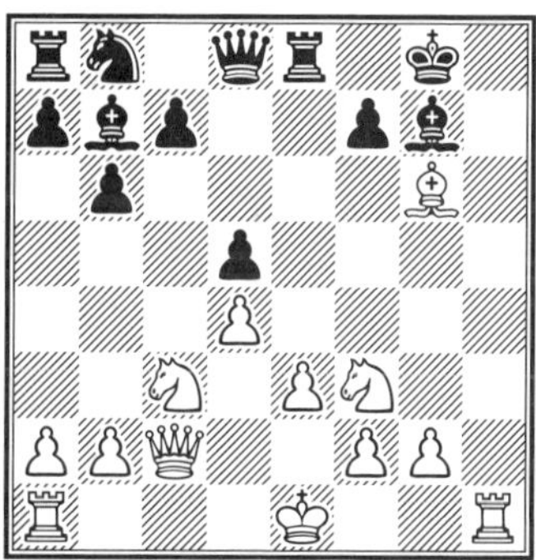

14...fxg6

"He struck a match, appeared nervous. The match burned his fingers and went out.

15.Qxg6 Nd7 16.Ng5 Qf6 17.Rh8+!, 1-0.

"Poor Burn. I think I swindled him out of that one. If he could only have got that pipe going, it might have been a different story. He took it good naturally and we shook hands. Then his pipe went out."

Marshall followed up with a tournament in Monte Carlo. One would expect that after his London 1899 triumph and after Paris 1900, Marshall would continue to show that he was "the man." Instead, he failed to live up to expectations, tying for eighth and ninthth with Gunsberg. Janowski won the tournament with an impressive (10-3) result while von Scheve, Chigorin, and Schlechter tied for second through fourth with excellent (9-4) results.

Here's a game where Marshall outplayed Blackburne and then fell apart on move seventeen:

Joseph Blackburne vs. Frank Marshall, Monte Carlo 1901

1.c4 e5 2.Nc3 Nc6 3.g3 Nf6 4.Bg2 Bc5 5.d3 0-0 6.Nf3 d6 7.h3 Be6 8.Bg5 h6 9.Bxf6 Qxf6 10.Ne4 Bb4+ 11.Kf1 Qe7 12.a3 f5 13.Ned2 Bc5 14.b4 Bb6 15.Rc1 Bf7 16.Ne1 Rae8 17.Nb3 f4

17...e4 18.dxe4 fxe4 19.c5 dxc5 20.bxc5 Na5 21.Nxa5 Bxa5 gave Black a winning position. Not a difficult sequence.

18.g4 Be6?!

18...a5 gives Black a safe and superior position.

19.c5

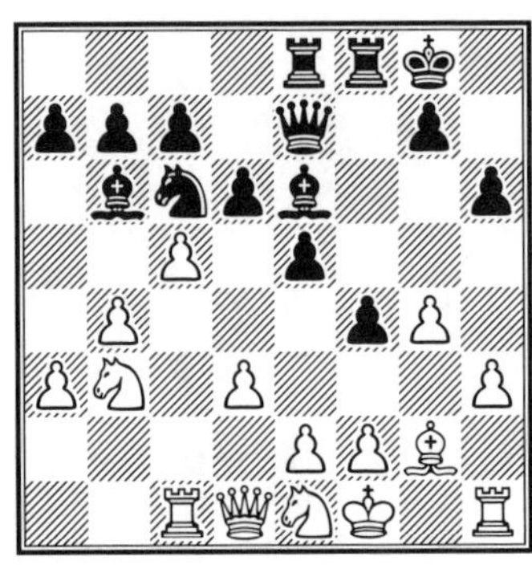

16...Qf7 20.Rb1 dxc5 21.bxc5 Ba5??

21...Na5, =.

22.Bxc6 bxc6 23.Nxa5 and White, now a piece up, went on to win.

The next tournament (in Buffalo) saw Marshall completely collapse, coming in fifth from six players (seven losses, one draw, two wins against last-place finisher Louis Karpinski). Pillsbury won the event, 2½ points ahead of second/third-place finishers Delmar and Napier. In fact, it seems to me Marshall was probably ill since he played so horribly. Here's an example from Buffalo:

Frank Marshall vs. Eugene Delmar, Buffalo 1901

1.e4 e5 2.f4 Bc5 3.Nf3 d6 4.d4 exd4 5.Bd3 Nc6 6.0-0 Bg4 7.h3 Bxf3 8.Qxf3 Nf6 9.a3 a5 10.Kh1 h5 11.e5

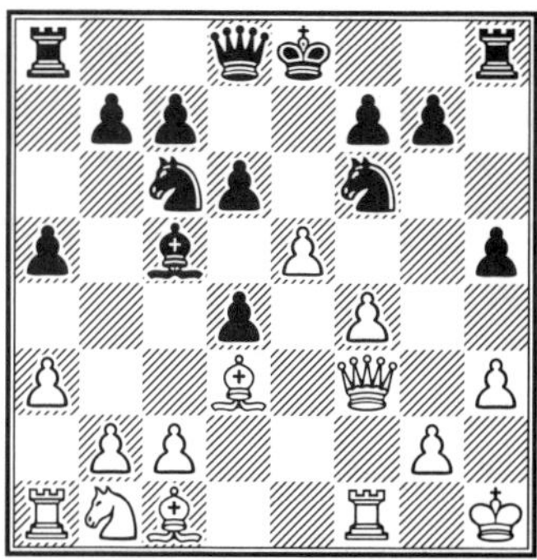

11...dxe5 12.fxe5 Nxe5 13.Re1 Qe7 14.Bf4?? Nxf3, 0-1.

After his poor result in Monte Carlo 1901, Marshall gave it another try. Once again he came in ninth behind Maróczy (first), Pillsbury and Janowski (second/third), Teichmann (fourth), Schlechter and Tarrasch (fifth/sixth), Wolf (seventh), and Chigorin (eighth). However, his ninth place put him ahead of eleven other players, and his form was far better than his earlier disasters.

Here's a victory against Carl Schlechter with Marshall playing the gambit which has his name (Marshall Gambit).

Frank Marshall vs. Carl Schlechter, Monte Carlo 1902

1.d4 d5 2.c4 e6 3.Nc3 c6 4.e4 dxe4 5.Nxe4 Bb4+ 6.Bd2 Qxd4 7.Bxb4 Qxe4+ 8.Be2 Nd7 9.Nf3 c5 10.Bc3 Ngf6 11.Qd6 Qc6 12.Qg3 0-0 13.Rd1 Nh5 14.Qh4 g6 15.Rxd7 Qxd7 16.g4

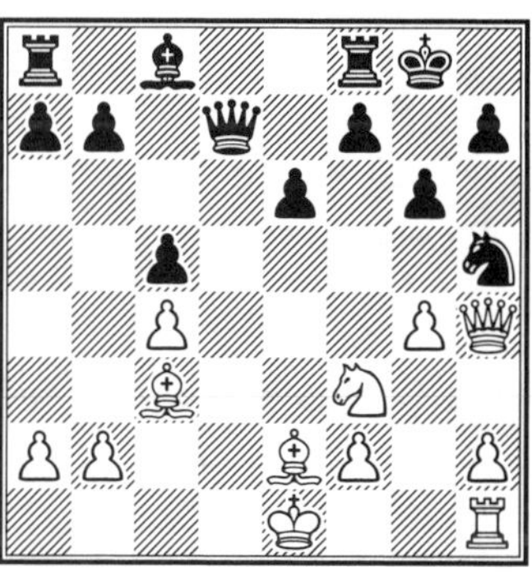

16...Qd8 17.gxh5 Qxh4 18.Nxh4 e5 19.hxg6 hxg6 20.Rg1 Re8 21.Nf3 f6 22.Rxg6+ Kf7 23.Rg3 Bd7 24.Nd2 Rh8 25.Ne4 b6 26.Rf3 f5 27.Bxe5 Rh4 28.Nd6+, 1-0.

It seems to me that Marshall rebuilt himself in 1902—the London matches helped him get back on track and give him some much needed confidence.

In a six-game match against William Ward, Marshall won 4-2 with no draws.

In a five-game match against Teichmann, Marshall won 2 and lost none.

This game highlighted his positional skills, and it also showed him that every game he played didn't have to be tactics, tactics, and more tactics.

Frank Marshall vs. Richard Teichmann, London match (5) 1902

1.d4 d5 2.c4 e6 3.Nc3 c6 4.e4 dxe4 5.Nxe4 Bb4+ 6.Nc3 c5 7.a3 Ba5 8.Nf3 cxd4 9.Qxd4 Qxd4 10.Nxd4 Bxc3+ 11.bxc3 a6 12.Bf4 f6 13.Bd6 e5 14.Nc2 Ne7 15.Ne3 Nbc6 16.Nd5 Nxd5 17.cxd5 Ne7 18.c4 Bf5 19.Be2 Kd7 20.Bb4

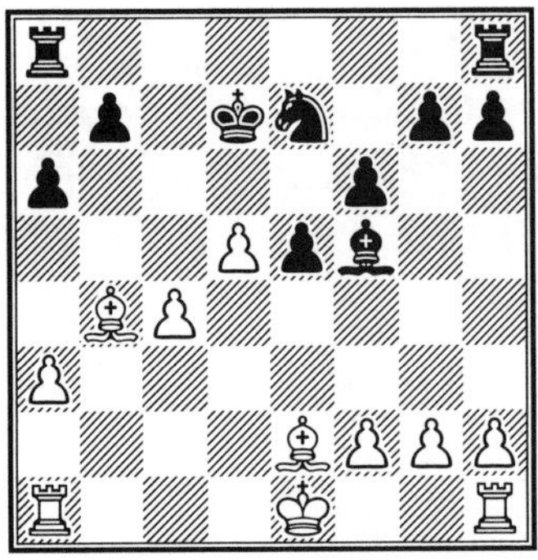

20...a5 21.Bxe7 Kxe7 22.0-0 b6 23.f4 exf4 24.Rxf4 Bg6 25.Ra2 Kd6 26.Rb2 Rab8 27.Rf3 Bh5 28.Rfb3 Bxe2 29.Rxe2 Kc5 30.Re4 Rhd8 31.Rb5+ Kd6 32.Re6+ Kc7 33.Rc6+, 1-0.

Here's Marshall in his most vicious form.

Rudolf Loman vs. Frank Marshall, London match (1) 1902

1.e4 e5 2.Nf3 Nf6 3.Nxe5 d6 4.Nf3 Nxe4 5.Nc3 d5 6.Qe2 Be7 7.Nxe4 dxe4 8.Qxe4 0-0 9.Be2 Re8 10.0-0 Bd6

Though Black is a pawn down, he has more than enough compensation.

11.Qd3 Nc6 12.c3 Qf6 13.Bd1 Bf5 14.Qc4 Qg6

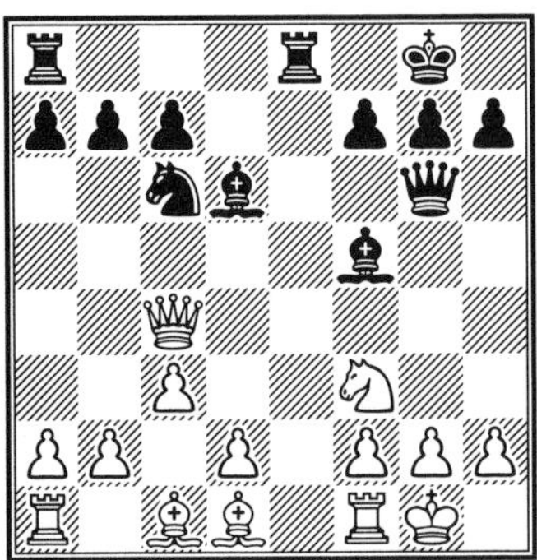

15.Qh4 Bd3 16.Re1 Rxe1+ 17.Nxe1 Re8 18.f3 Qh6 19.Qxh6 Rxe1+ 20.Kf2 Rf1+ 21.Ke3 gxh6, 0-1.

DSB Kongress (1902): The Deutscher Schachbund (DSB Kongress) was another letdown. Marshall shared ninth/tenth with Rudolf Swiderski. Janowsky was first, Pillsbury second, and Henry Atkins was third.

Monte Carlo (1903): Siegbert Tarrasch finished first, Géza Maróczy second, Harry Nelson Pillsbury was third (Marshall got a win and draw against Pillsbury in this tournament.), and Marshall ended up in ninth place.

I'm seeing a pattern here! He came in ninth in Monte Carlo 1901, 1902, and 1903, and ninth/tenth in the DSB Kongress 1902. What does this mean? It means that he was still growing as a player, and better things were yet to come.

The following game was against Colonel Moreau who came in last with a score of no wins, no draws, twenty-six losses! So why am I showing this game? For two reasons: This kind of King's Gambit is very rare, and Marshall announced mate in eleven after Black's twentieth move!

Frank Marshall vs. Col. Moreau, Monte Carlo 1903

1.e4 e5 2.f4 exf4 3.Nf3 g5 4.Bc4 g4 5.0-0 gxf3 6.Qxf3 Qf6 7.e5 Qxe5 8.Bxf7+ Kd8 9.d4 Qxd4+ 10.Kh1 Bh6 11.Bd2 Qg7 12.Bb3 Nc6 13.Bc3 Ne5 14.Qd5 d6 15.Rd1 Bd7 16.Ba4 Bc6 17.Bxc6 bxc6 18.Qxe5 Qg4 19.Na3 Kd7 20.Nc4 f3

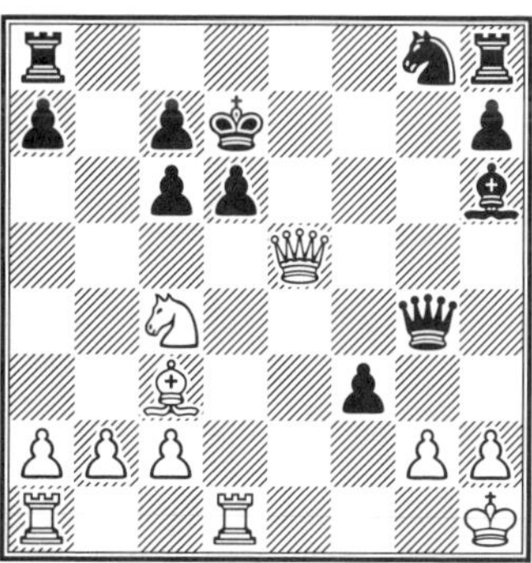

Marshall announced mate in eleven moves, though it was nine instead!

21.Rxd6+ cxd6 22.Qxd6+ Kc8 23.Qxc6+ Kd8 24.Rd1+ Ke7 25.Qd6+ Ke8 26.Re1+ Kf7 27.Ne5+ Ke8 28.Ng6+ Kf7 29.Nxh8, 1-0.

Vienna Gambit Tournament (1903): Chigorin won first place, Marshall was second, Marco third, and Pillsbury fourth, and the rest were Mieses, Maróczy, Teichmann, Swiderski, Schlechter, Gunsberg.

The next game was played in the Vienna Gambit tournament of 1903. Players were required to start with 1.e4 e5 2.f4 exf4. I would guess that playing in such an event would be great fun for everyone—players and spectators alike!

The game shows that Marshall was a bit of a gambler, sometimes ignoring the best move for more interesting, tactical ideas.

Mikhail Chigorin vs. Frank Marshall, Vienna 1903

1.e4 e5 2.f4 exf4 3.Bc4 d5 4.Bxd5 Qh4+ 5.Kf1 g5 6.g3 Qh6 7.Nc3 Nf6 8.d4 Nc6 9.Kg2 Bd7 10.h4 Rg8 11.Nf3 gxh4 12.Ne2 h3+ 13.Kf1

Black has a winning advantage and moves like 13...0-0-0, 13...Nb4, 13...Ne7 and others should wipe White out. However, I think Marshall fell in love with 13...fxg3 which sacrifices his Queen so he can create two connected pawns on the 6th rank.

13...fxg3 14.Bxh6 g2+ 15.Kg1 Bxh6 16.Qd3 Ng4 17.Rxh3 Be3+ 18.Kxg2

18.Qxe3 Nxe3 19.Rxh7, with equal changes.

18...Nf2+ 19.Rg3 Rxg3+ 20.Kxg3 Nxd3

Marshall keeps bashing away, though the position is equal.

21.cxd3?

Better was 21.Bxc6 bxc6 22.cxd3 with quite an interesting position.

21...Nb4 22.Rf1?

More tripled pawns! 22.Ne5 was the way to go, though Black now has an edge.

22...Nxd5 23.exd5

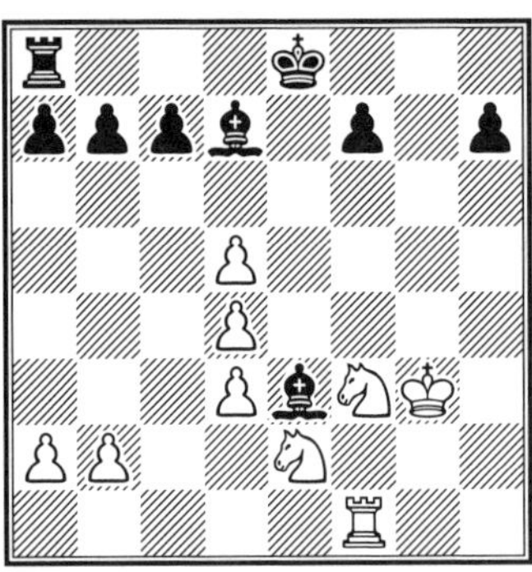

23...Ke7

23...f6, taking away the e5 and g5 squares from the f3-knight and, in various lines the black King can move to d7, e7, or f7.

24.Ne5 Rg8+ and Black eventually got the full point.

Here's another example of the insanity that lurks in the King's Gambit.

Géza Maróczy vs. Frank Marshall, Vienna 1903

1.e4 e5 2.f4 exf4 3.Bc4 d5 4.Bxd5 Qh4+ 5.Kf1 g5 6.d4 Bg7 7.Nc3 Ne7 8.Nf3 Qh5 9.h4 h6 10.Qd3 Nbc6 11.Ne2 Bd7 12.Qb3 Nxd5 13.exd5 Ne7 14.Qxb7 0-0 15.c3

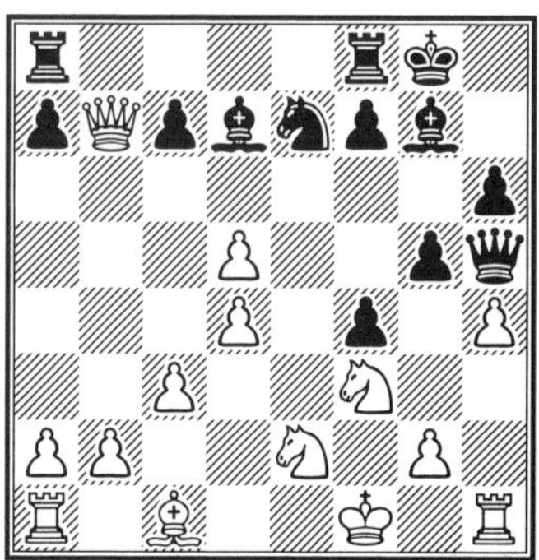

15... Rab8 16.Qxa7 Bb5 17.Qc5 Bxe2+ 18.Kxe2 g4 19.d6 gxf3+ 20.gxf3 Nf5 21.dxc7 Ng3+ 22.Kd2 Qxf3 23.Re1 Rbe8 24.Rxe8 Rxe8 25.Kc2 Qe4+ 26.Kb3 Qb7+ 27.Kc2 Qe4+ 28.Kb3 Qb7+ 29.Kc2 Bf8 30.Qc4 Re2+ 31.Bd2 Rxd2+ 32.Kxd2 Qxb2+ 33.Kd1 Qxa1+ 34.Kc2 Nf5 35.Qa4 Ne3+, 0-1.

Harry Pillsbury vs. Frank Marshall, Monte Carlo 1903

1.d4 d5 2.c4 c6 3.Nf3 Nf6 4.Nc3 Ne4 5.e3 e6 6.Bd3 f5 7.Ne5 Qh4 8.Qc2 Nd7 9.0-0 Bd6 10.f4 g5 11.Nf3 Qh5 12.Bxe4 fxe4 13.Nxg5 Nf6 14.Qe2 Qg6 15.c5 Bc7 16.Kh1 h6 17.Nh3 Rg8 18.Bd2 b6 19.b4 bxc5 20.bxc5 Ba6 21.Qf2 Bxf1 22.Rxf1 Rb8 23.Bc1 Ba5 24.Nd1 Kd7 25.Rg1 Qh5 26.Qc2 Rg7 27.Ndf2 Rbg8 28.Qd1 Qxd1 29.Nxd1 Rb8 30.g3 Ng4 31.Rg2 Rb1 32.Rc2 Rg8 33.Kg2 Bd2!

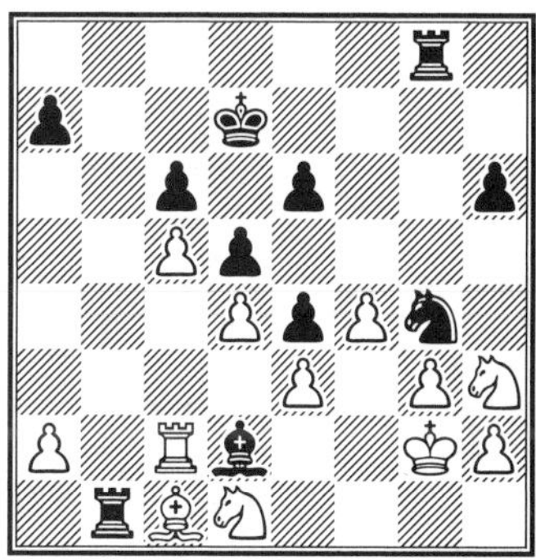

[Marshal]: "Thus the white Bishop comes to an inglorious end. The simplifying text prepares a decisive return of the exchange, after which Black's command of the seventh, plus a passed e-pawn, wins easily."

34.Bxd2 Rxd1 35.Rb2 Rb8! 36.Rxb8 Rxd2+ 37.Kg1 Rd1+ 38.Kg2 Nxe3+ 39.Kf2 Ng4+ 40.Kg2 Rd2+ 41.Kg1 e3 42.Rb1 e2 43.Nf2 e1Q+ 44.Rxe1 Nxf2 and Black won.

Monte Carlo Rice Gambit (1904): In this six-player double-round tournament. Marshall tied for first with Swiderski. Mieses finished third, Marco fourth and von Scheve fifth. Forgács[1] came in last.

Monte Carlo (1904): This six-player double-round event immediately followed the Rice tournament. Marshall came in third, but the top three, Maróczy (7½), Schlechter (7), and Marshall (6½) were close to each other and far ahead from the last three.

Marshall's form had been all over the place, but his last few tournaments showed that he was a whole new Marshall—or was he? It was expected that the World Champion (Lasker) was almost certainly going to win at Cambridge Springs, could Marshall keep up his form and finish in the top five (of sixteen players)? Nobody could have guessed that the Cambridge Springs tournament would be his greatest achievement!

Cambridge Springs (1904): Marshall won the event with an amazing (and undefeated) score of 13-2 (one of his four draws was with Lasker). Lasker tied for second/third with Janowski (with 11 points), and the rest (including Marco, Showalter, Schlechter, Chigorin, and Pillsbury.) were way behind.

In many peoples' minds, his clear improvement and winning this event propelled him from a flawed but exciting tactician to a potential World Champion!

Frank Marshall vs. Harry Pillsbury, Cambridge Springs 1904

1.d4 d6 2.e4 Nf6 3.Nc3 g6 4.f4 Bg7 5.e5 dxe5 6.fxe5 Nd5 7.Nf3 Nc6 8.Bc4 e6 9.Bg5 Nxc3 10.bxc3 Ne7 11.0-0 h6 12.Bf6 Bxf6 13.exf6 Nf5 14.Qe2 Qxf6 15.g4

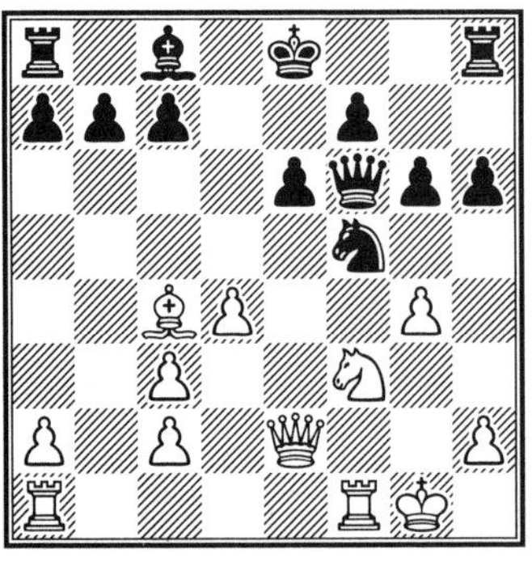

1 Leó Forgács (1881-1930) was a Hungarian master who played under the name Fleischmann until 1908. He is given only as Forgács in this book to avoid confusion.

15...Nd6 16.Ne5 Qe7 17.Bd3 0-0 18.Rf2 Kg7 19.Raf1 Bd7 20.Rf6 Rg8 21.Nxg6 Qxf6 22.Rxf6 Kxf6 23.Qe5, 1-0.

So, how do you build a chess champion? Talent, hard work, and an incredible amount of perseverance.

Sylvan Beach (1904): Marshall played in four player double round tournament. He won all the games. More importantly, he played with authority.

Frank Marshall vs. Kenneth Howard, Sylvan Beach 1904

1.d4 d5 2.c4 e6 3.Nc3 c5 4.cxd5 cxd4 5.Qxd4 Nf6 6.e4 exd5 7.exd5 Be6 8.Bb5+ Bd7 9.d6 Nc6 10.Qd3 Be6 11.Bf4 a6 12.Bxc6+ bxc6 13.Nf3

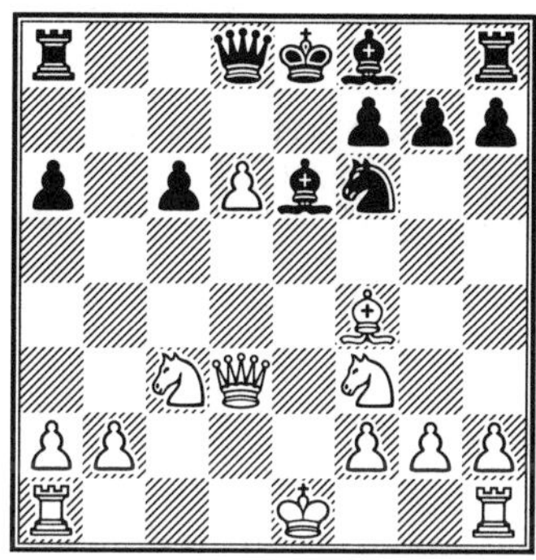

13...Qb6 14.0-0 Rd8 15.Rfe1 Nh5 16.Rad1 Qb7 17.Be5 Nf6 18.Bxf6 Rxd6 19.Nd4 gxf6 20.Ne4 c5 21.Nxd6+ Bxd6 22.Nxe6, 1-0.

USA Congress (1904): Ten players, Marshall continued his impressive turnaround by mowing his opponents down, winning the tournament with 8 wins and 1 draw.

Marshall's play had clearly improved; he no longer rushed (okay, sometimes he couldn't resist), he built up his position in a calm, logical manner, and he mixed all that with his desire to rip everyone opponent to bits.

Frank Marshall vs. Louis Uedemann, USA Congress 1904

1.d4 d5 2.c4 e6 3.Nc3 Nf6 4.Bg5 Be7 5.e3 c6 6.Nf3 Nbd7 7.Bd3 dxc4 8.Bxc4 Nd5 9.Bxe7 Qxe7 10.e4 Nxc3 11.bxc3 0-0 12.0-0 Rd8 13.e5 Nf8 14.Rb1 b6 15.Nd2 Nd7 16.f4 g6 17.Ne4 b5 18.Bb3

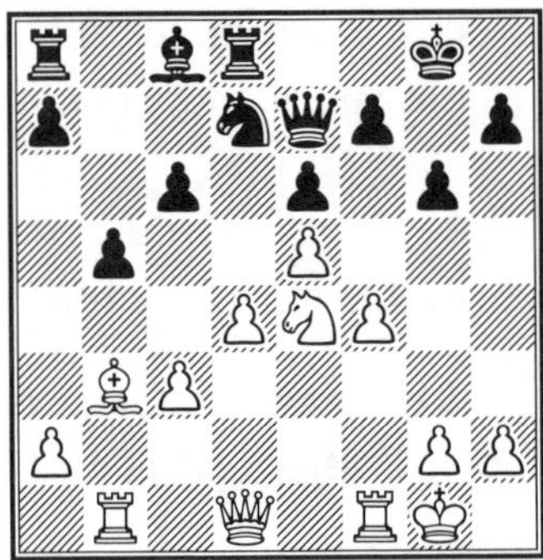

18...Nb6 19.Nf6+ Kg7 20.Qg4 Nd5 21.Bxd5 exd5 22.Qg5 Rh8 23.Nh5+ Kf8 24.Qh6+ Ke8 25.f5 Qf8 26.Nf6+ Kd8 27.Qxf8+ Rxf8 28.Nxh7 Rh8 29.Ng5 Ke8 30.fxg6 fxg6 31.Nf7 Rh7 32.Nd6+ Ke7 33.Rf6 Rg7 34.Rbf1 Be6 35.Nb7 Rc8 36.Nc5 Bf5 37.h3 Rc7 38.g4 Bd7 39.Rd6 Rh7 40.Rxg6 Rxh3 41.Rg7+, 1-0.

Fighting for the World Championship

Frank Marshall was on top of the world after his total domination of the Cambridge Springs 1904 tournament. The world wanted to know if he was really that good. Marshall, a fearless competitor, leapt into battle.

Marshall vs. Janowski, Match Two (1905):Marshall and David Janowski had previously played a match in 1899, with Janowski winning 3-1. Their match in 1905 was, for Marshall, revenge. Now much stronger than he was in 1899, Marshall won (8 wins, 5 loses, 4 draws).

Both players had to put up $500 ($13,500 in 2021 dollars) for the match, which wealthy supporters provided.

Frank Marshall vs. David Janowski, match (13) 1905

1.d4 d5 2.c4 e6 3.Nc3 c5 4.cxd5 exd5 5.Nf3 Nc6 6.Bg5 f6!?

6...Be7 is the move that most sane people would play, but neither White or Black are sane. Thus 6...f6 starts a series of moves that rip open his king-side pawn structure to win White's pawn on d4.

7.Bf4 g5 8.Bg3 g4 9.Nd2 Nxd4??

I'm sure Marshall started to drool after this move! The correct continuation was 9...cxd4! 10.Nb5 Kf7 when both sides have chances: 11.Nc7 Rb8 12.Qb3 (If White wanted to draw he might try 12.Nb5, but that would be a mistake: 12...Bf5! 13.Bxb8 Qxb8 and Black has a serious initiative.) 12...Ne5 13.Rc1 Ne7 and chaos reigns!

10.e3

And suddenly Black is in big trouble.

10...Nc6 11.h3

One of several strong moves.

11...h5

Of course, 11...gxh3 12.Qh5+ has to be avoided.

12.hxg4 Bxg4 13.Qb3 Nb4 14.Bb5+?

A tempting move, but 14.a3! is very hard to deal with: 14...c4 15.Nxc4! dxc4 16.Bxc4 Nd3+ 17.Kf1 with a winning attack.

14...Bd7?

14...Kf7! keeps Black in the game: 15.Nxd5 Nxd5 16.Bc4 (16.e4 is also good) 16...Nge7 17.e4 Bh6 when White is a bit better, but anything can happen.

15.a3 c4 16.Nxc4 Nd3+ 17.Ke2 dxc4

17...Nc5 18.Qc2 Kf7 19.Rad1 and I don't think Black will survive.

18.Bxc4!?

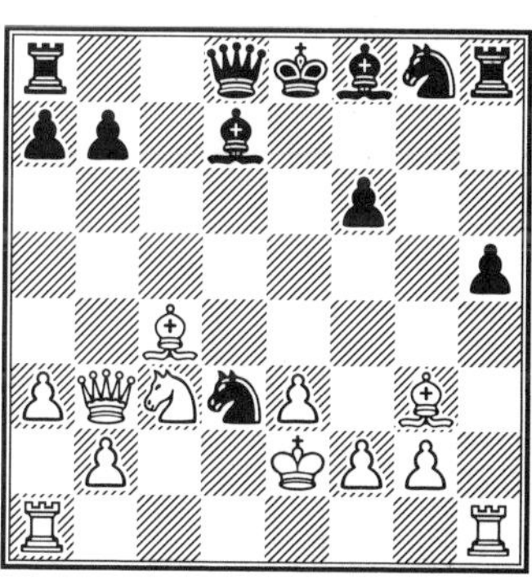

18.Qxc4 a6 19.Qe6+ Be7 20.Bxd7+ Qxd7 21.Qxd7+ Kxd7 22.Rad1 Ke6 23.Rxd3 with an extra pawn, better piece placement, and a superior pawn structure.

18...Nc5 19.Qc2

19.Qa2 Nh6 20.Rad1 with a winning attack.

19...Ne7

Stopping Qg6+. Another way to do that is 19...f5 but Black won't be singing happy tunes when he makes it: 20.Rad1 Nf6 21.Rh4! (21.Bh4 Rh6)

21...Be7 (21...Nce4 22.Nxe4 fxe4 23.Rxe4+ Nxe4 24.Qxe4+ Qe7 25.Qg6+ Kd8 26.Bb5 Rh6 27.Qg8 Rc6 28.Bxc6 bxc6 29.Bh4 Qxh4 30.Qxf8+ Kc7 31.Qxa8 and it's time for Black to resign.) 22.b4! Rc8 23.bxc5 Rxc5 24.Rhd4 and White has a winning position.

20.Rad1

20.Rhd1 is more accurate.

20...Qb6?

20...Rc8 is better.

21.Rd6

Even better was 21.b4 when 21...Ne6 (21..Be6 22.Nb5) fails to 22.Rxd7! Kxd7 23.Rd1+ Ke8 24.Rd6, winning.

21...Bc6 22.Rhd1 Bg7 23.b4 h4

23...Nd7 24.Re6 Nf8 (24...Kd8 25.Na4) 24...Nf8 25. Rxe7+ Kxe7 26.Bd6+ Ke8 27.Nd5 Bxd5 28.Rxd5, and again White wins.

24.bxc5 Qxc5 25.Ne4?!

The game should be over, but 25.Ne4 makes things a bit harder for White. 25.Nd5 was the straightforward way to finish off his opponent: 25...Bxd5 (25...hxg3 26.Nc7+ Kf8 27.Rd8+ Be8 28.Ne6+ Kf7 29.Nxc5+ Nd5 30.Bxd5+ Kf8 31.Ne6+ Kf7 32.Nd4+ Ke7 [32...Kf8 33.Qc5 mate] 33.Qc7+ Kf8 34.Qf7#) 26.R6xd5 Qc8 27.Rd8+ Qxd8 28.Rxd8+ Rxd8 29.Bc7 Rd7 30.Be6, and White wins

25...Qh5+! 26.f3 hxg3 27.Qd3

27.Qd2! Kf8 28.Qb2 Qe5 (28...Rh6 29.Rd8+ Rxd8 30.Rxd8+ Be8 and now both 31.Qxb7 and 31.Qb4 win.) 29.Rd8+ Rxd8 30.Rxd8+ Be8 31.Qxb7 (31.Qxe5 fxe5 30.Nd6 Bf6 31.Rxe8+ Kg7 34.Rxh8 Kxh8 35.Nxb7 and White has an extra pawn and a better pawn structure.) 31...Rh2 32.Qd7 Qb2+ (32...Rxg2+ 33.Kd3 Nd5 34.Rxe8+ Qxe8 35.Qxd5) 33.Nd2 Rxg2+ 34.Kf1 Rf2+ 35.Kg1 Qc1+ 36.Bf1 Kf7 37.Qxe8+ Ke6 38.Rd7 Bf8 (38...Qc5 39.Bc4+) 39.Rxa7 Rxd2 (39...Qxd2 40.Bc4+ Ke5 41.Rxe7+ and Black will be mated in a few moves.) 40.Qxf8 and black's King is too vulnerable.

27...Kf8

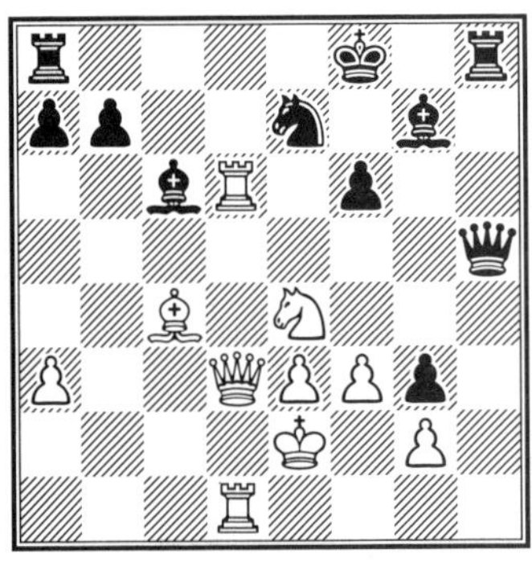

28.Rd8+?

A pity. Marshall put so much work into this game and now he tosses away some of his advantage. Correct was 28.Qc3! Qe5 (28...Rh6 29.Rd8+ Rxd8 30.Rxd8+ Be8 31.Qb4 Qh1 32.Qb5 Qxg2+ 33.Kd3 Qf1+ 34.Kc2 Rh2+ 35.Nd2) 29.Rd8+ Rxd8 30.Rxd8+ Be8 31.Nd6 winning.

28...Rxd8 29.Qxd8+ Be8 30.Nd6 Nc6 31.Qc8 Qe5!

31...Qg6 32.Bd3! (The bishop heads for e4 where it protects white's King and makes Bxc6 possible.) 32...f5! (32...Qh5 33.Be3 Qe5 34.f4 Qe7 [34...Qh5+ 35.Bf3 Qg6 36.f5 Ne7 37.Qe6 wins] 35.Bxc6 bxc6 36.Nxe8) 33.Bxf5 Ne7 34.Bxg6 Nxc8 35.Nxe8 Rh2 and now 36.f4 and 36.Rg1 gives White winning chances.

32.Be6 Nd8 33.Nxe8 Qxe6 34.Rxd8 Qxc8 35.Rxc8 Rh2?

35...Ke7! 36.Rc7+ Kxe8 37.Rxg7 Rh2 38.Rxg3.

36.Nd6+ Ke7 37.Nf5+ Kd7 38.Rg8 Ke6 39.e4 Bh6 40.Nxh6?!

I don't like this move. Instead, 40.Rxg3 makes more sense since the Knight seems to me to be better than black's Bishop.

40...Rxh6 41.Rxg3 Rh1 42.f4 Ra1 43.Rb3 b6 44.Kf3 Rf1+ 45.Kg4 Re1 46.Kf3 Rf1+ 47.Ke3 Re1+ 48.Kd4 Rd1+ 49.Rd3 Rg1 50.g3 Re1 51.Rc3 Kd6

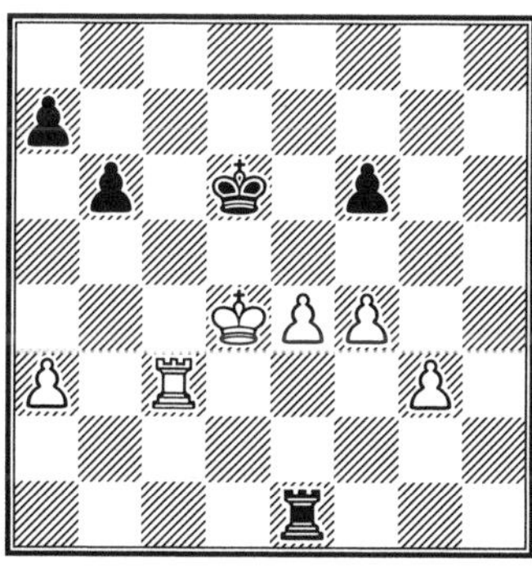

Both players must have been exhausted here; White trying to find a way to break through, and Black defending and defending and defending (yes... sleep...sleep...sleep). Now Marshall, who probably just wanted to get it over with, lashed out.

52.e5+??

Now it's a simple draw.

52...fxe5+ 53.fxe5+ Kd7??

Why? The obvious 53...Rxe5 shares the point: 54.Rc6+ Kxc6 55.Kxe5 b5 56.g4 a5 57.g5 Kd7 58.Kf6 b4 59.axb4 axb4 60.g6 b3 61.g7 b2 62.g8=Q b1=Q, draw.

54.Kd5 Rd1+ 55.Ke4 Re1+ 56.Re3 Rg1 57.Kf5 Rf1+ 58.Kg6 Ke6??

58...Rg1 still hangs on. After 58...Ke6? Black is lost.

59.g4 b5 60.g5 Rb1 61.Kh7 Rh1+ 62.Kg7 Rb1 63.g6 a5 64.Kg8 b4 65.axb4 axb4 66.Rh3 Kxe5 67.Rd3 b3 68.g7 b2 69.Rd2 Kf5 70.Kf7, 1-0.

A thrilling battle.

Ostend (1905): A fourteen player tournament with two games against everyone. Maróczy was first with 19½ points, Janowski and Tarrasch tied for second/third, Schlechter fourth, Marco and Teichmann tied for fifth/sixth, Burn, Marshall, and Leonhardt all tied for seventh/ninth, and Wolf, Alapin, Blackburne, Chigorin, and Taubenhaus finished in the cellar.

Frank Marshall vs. Amos Burn, Ostend 1905

1.e4 e5 2.Nf3 Nc6 3.Bc4 Bc5 4.c3 Nf6 5.d4 exd4 6.cxd4 Bb4+ 7.Kf1 Nxe4

7...d5 would give Black a very comfortable game.

8.d5 Ne7 9.Qd4 Nf6 10.Bg5 Ng6 11.Nbd2 h6 12.Re1+ Kf8

12...Be7 13.Bxf6 gxf6 14.d6 cxd6 15.Qxf6 Rf8 16.Ne4 Bxf6 17.Nxd6 mate.

13.Bd3 Be7 14.Bxg6 hxg5

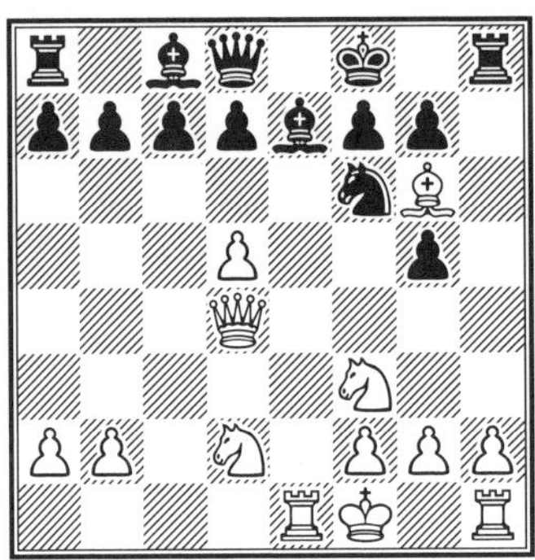

14...fxg6 15.Ne5 Qe8 16.Qd3 hxg5 17.Nxg6+ Kf7 18.Nf3 Rh5 19.Rxe7+ Qxe7 20.Nxe7 Kxe7 21.Qg6 Kf8 22.Ne5. Analysis by Marshall.

15.Ne5 fxg6 16.Nxg6+ Kf7 17.Rxe7+ Kxg6 18.Qd3+ Kh6 19.h4 g4

19...Qxe7 20.hxg5+ Kxg5 21.Nf3+ Kg4 (21...Kf4 22.g3+ Kg4 23.Qg6+ Kxf3 24.Qf5 mate. 22.Qg6+ Kf4 23.g3+ Kxf3 24.Qf5 mate. Analysis by Marshall.

20.h5 Nxh5 21.Qf5, 1-0.

The end might have gone like this: 21...g6 22.Rxh5+ gxh5 23.Qf6.

Barmen Masters (1905): Another strong tournament (sixteen players), and this time Marshall did well. Janowski and Maróczy tied for first/second, while Marshall came in clear third. Players below included: Ossip Bernstein, Schlechter, Berger, Chigorin, Wolf, and Leonhardt.

Nuremberg (1905): The seventeen game match between Siegbert Tarrasch and Marshall was serious stuff! After beating Janowski in his match, Marshall was full of confidence and challenged Tarrasch. Marshall got pasted, winning just 1 game, losing 8, and drawing 8.

It seems that Marshall was unable to deal with a world-class positional player who had tons of experience. Another (big!) problem was Marshall's openings, he was often worse with both colors, and if he did get an advantage Tarrasch would calmly stabilize his position.

Frank Marshall vs. Siegbert Tarrasch, Nuremberg match (7) 1905

1.e4 e5 2.Bc4 Nf6 3.Nc3 Bc5 4.d3 d6 5.Na4 Bb6 6.Nxb6 axb6 7.f4 Be6 8.Bxe6 fxe6 9.fxe5 dxe5 10.Nf3 Nc6 11.0-0 0-0 12.a3 Qd6 13.Be3 Ng4 14.Qe2 Nxe3 15.Qxe3 Nd4 16.Nxd4 Qxd4 17.Qxd4 exd4

I'm surprised that a draw wasn't agreed here. Instead they dithered around.

18.Rxf8+ Kxf8 19.Rf1+ Ke7 20.Rf4 Ra5 21.Kf1 Rc5 22.Rf2 Rb5 23.b3 Rh5 24.h3 b5 25.b4 Rg5 26.Rf4 e5 27.Rf2 Rg6 28.Rf5 Re6

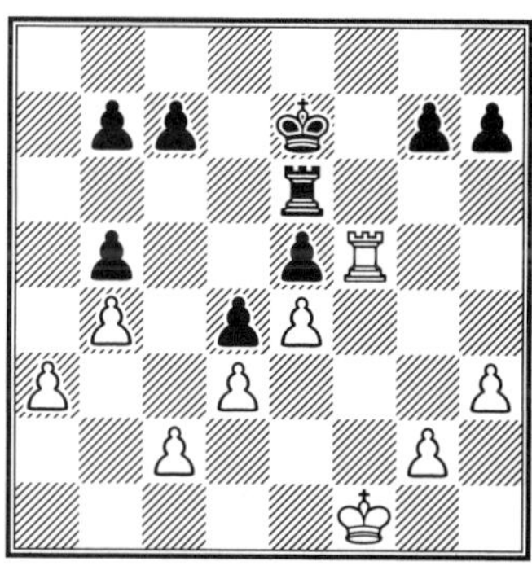

It's still a dead draw, but Marshall, thinking there was no danger, got himself into a bit of trouble.

29.Ke2?

29.Rh5 had to be played when 29...h6 30.Ke2 kills all danger since ...g6 hangs the h6-pawn. There's a lesson here: In chess you have to be careful with every single move. If not, one little inaccuracy can turn a happy face into pure hell.

29...g6

Ooops! Suddenly White has some problems.

30.Rf1

30.Rg5?? Kf6 31.Rg3 Ra6 32.Rf3+ Ke7 is a nightmare since the a3-pawn will fall.

30...Ra6 31.Ra1 b6 32.Kd2 Ra4 33.c3?

Marshall continues to miss the proper defensive moves. Correct was 33.g4 when 33...c5 34.bxc5 bxc5 35.Rb1 Ra5 36.Kc1 (white's King will protect the a3-pawn with Kb2) 36...Kf6 (Threatening ...Kg5) 37.h4 and, since black's King can't penetrate on the kingside the game is drawn.

33...c5 34.cxd4?!

34.Kc2 might be a bit better, but White would still suffer.

34...cxb4?

Tripled pawns! 34...exd4! 35.bxc5 bxc5 36.Rb1 Ra5 is winning for Black: 37.Kc2 Kd6 38.Kb3 Ke5 39.Rf1 c4+ 40.dxc4 bxc4+ 41.Kxc4 Rxa3 42.Rf7 Rc3+ 43.Kb4 Kxe4 44.Rxh7 (44.Re7+ Kd3) 44...Rc6 Intending 45...Rd6 followed by rushing the d-pawn to d1.

35.dxe5 Ke6 36.d4

White's last stand was 36.Kc2 bxa3 37.Kb3 Rd4 38.Kxa3 Rxd3+ 39.Kb4 when we get a very interesting position after 39...Rd2. Can White survive? Probably not.

36...bxa3 37.Kc3 a2 38.g4 g5 39.Kd3 b4 40.Kc4 b3+ 41.Kxb3 Rxd4 42.Rxa2 Rxe4 43.Ra6 Re3+ 44.Kc2 Rxh3 45.Rxb6+ Kxe5 46.Rb4 Re3 47.Kd2 Re4, 0-1.

I would guess that Marshall lost all hope after this defeat. Tarrasch won the match, 8 wins, 1 loss, and 8 draws.

However, Marshall was still improving while the much older Tarrasch was getting weaker and weaker each year and by 1910 Marshall was clearly the superior player.

New York (1906): Marshall had a four game match against Albert Fox. It was a rout (three wins for Marshall, one draw).

Frank Marshall vs. Albert Whiting Fox, New York match (2) 1906

1.d4 d5 2.c4 e5 3.dxe5 Bb4+ 4.Bd2 Bxd2+ 5.Nxd2 d4 6.Ngf3 Ne7 7.Nb3 c5 8.e3 dxe3 9.Qxd8+ Kxd8 10.Nxc5 exf2+ 11.Kxf2 Nbc6 12.Bd3 Kc7 13.h3 b6 14.Na4 Be6 15.Rhd1 Rad8 16.Nc3 Kb8 17.b3 h6 18.Be4 Rxd1 19.Rxd1 Rd8 20.Rd6 Rxd6 21.exd6 Kc8 22.dxe7, 1-0.

Smooth as can be. He ate his opponent up in one gulp.

Ostend (1906): The unique format of this event was never repeated: It started with five stages of thirty-six players. After that first stage twenty-four players remained. Then another stage whittled it down to sixteen players, then the next stage also had sixteen players, and finally the last stage had nine players (you could call them survivors!). When it was over, Carl Schlechter was first, Maróczy second, and Akiba Rubinstein third. Marshall took seventh place.

Since this whole tournament gives me a headache, I'll share Marshall's exciting game against Swiderski and that will be that!

Rudolf Swiderski vs. Frank Marshall, Ostend 1906

1.d4 d5 2.Nf3 c5 3.e3 Nf6 4.Nbd2 Nc6 5.Be2 Bf5 6.dxc5 e5 7.Bb5 Qc7

7...Bxc5 is probably better, when 8.Nxe5 Qc7 9.Nxc6 bxc6 10.Bd3 when 10...Bg4 gives Black interesting compensation for the sacrificed pawn (central kingside space, more development, more active pieces).

8.b4 Be7 9.Bb2 Nd7 10.a3 0-0 11.c4 Bd3 12.Qb3 e4

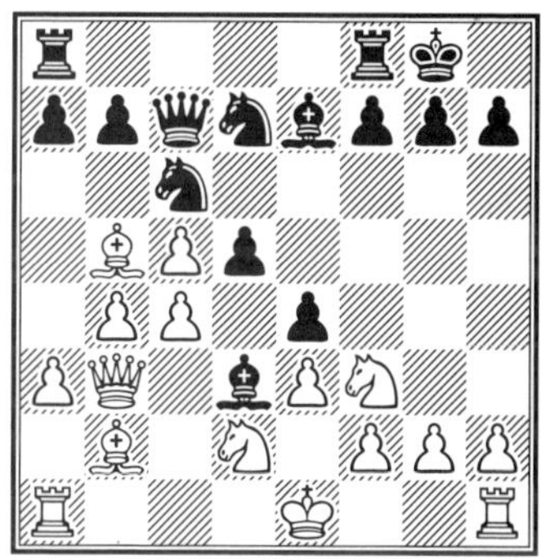

13.cxd5

Marshall thought that this was a prepared line from Swiderski. Spielmann won a game as Black after 13.Bxc6 bxc6 though he needed help from his opponent. It seems that Swiderski was right; 13.cxd5 is very good for White, while 13.Bxc6? Qxc6! 14.cxd5 Qg6 15.d6 Bxd6, though a bit better for White, is interesting.

13...Bxb5 14.Nxe4 Nce5 15.Bxe5

15.d6 Nd3+ 16.Kd2 Bxd6 17.Nxd6 Ba6 is probably good for White but I suspect Marshall would be happy. Another bother for Black is 15.Nxe5 Nxe5 16.d6 Nd3+ 17.Kd2 Bxd6 18.Nxd6 which looks similar with 15.d6, but the trade of a pair of Knights seems to make it even better.

15...Nxe5 16.d6 Nd3+ 17.Kd2 Qc6 18.dxe7

Marshall thought that this was an error, saying that 18.Nc3 would win. But is that true? Let's take a look: 18.Nc3! (Probably best) 18...Bf6 19.Nxb5

Nxf2 20.Nbd4 Bxd4 21.exd4 (21.Nxd4 Qxg2 22.Rhg1 Qxh2 23.Nf3 Qh5 and White is better but Black is still doing his best to keep the chaos chugging!) 21...Nxh1 22.Rxh1 Rae8 and we have another good position for White, while Black would enjoy the crazy unknown.

18...Qxe4 19.exf8=Q+ Rxf8 20.Nd4?

Many a man has fallen in the face of tactical rain falling on their heads. It turns out that 20.a4! is best (20.Rhf1 Rd8 21.Nd4 Nxc5! 22.bxc5 Rxd4+! 23.exd4 Qxd4 24.Kc2 Ba4): 20...Rd8 21.Nd4 Rxd4 (Yahhhoooo!) 22.exd4 Qxd4 23.Qc3 Qxf2+ 24.Kd1 Bc4. This looks like Black is doing well, but 25.Rb1! (not 25.Qxc4?? Nb2+ picking up white's Queen.) stops the fork on b2 and leaves Black in trouble.

20...Nxf2

Now Black is cooking! White has to be very careful which means, due to the complexity, that White will melt in Black's flames.

21.Rhg1?

21.Nxb5 Nxh1 22.Rg1 Nf2 23.Nd6 Qe5, =.

21...Rd8 22.Raf1

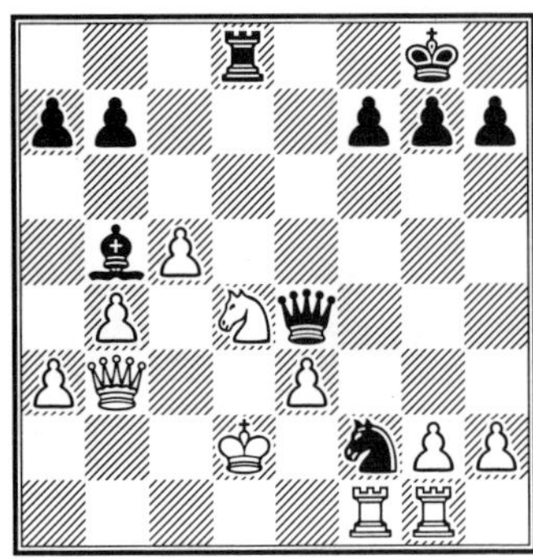

22...Rxd4+!

This has turned into a mugging rather than a chess game.

23.exd4 Qxd4+ 24.Kc1 Qa1+ 25.Qb1 Qc3+ 26.Qc2 Qxa3+ 27.Kd2 Qxb4+ 28.Ke3 Ng4+ 29.Kf3 Nxh2+, 0-1.

Play might continue: 30.Kg3 Qg4+ 31.Kf2 (31.Kxh2 Qh4 mate) 31...Qf4+ 32.Ke1 Nxf1 when Black has a large material advantage and a crushing attack.

DSB Kongress (1906): Another triumph for Marshall! Seventeen players, and he won nine games and drew seven. Unbeaten first place always soothes a chess player's soul. In this case, he got some revenge since Tarrasch could only come in equal ninth thru eleventh, while Janowski came in sixteenth!

Apparently there were some very strange rules (if you can call them rules) about the time limits:

> If the game is finished within the first session (usually 9AM until 2PM), then no time violation has happened; if the game is continued, then the tournament director will decide after the end of the game whether some player exceeded the time limit. A small exceedance—say 5 minutes—has no implications; a considerable exceedance causes a penalty of 1 M (Mark) per minute. A player, who disturbs the tournament by playing too slow (i.e., an exceedance of 30 minutes), will also get a warning. Three warnings cause the elimination from the tournament, and the player will not be invited again.

If that isn't insane, nothing is!

This next game shows Marshall's skills to perfection.

Frank Marshall vs. Erich Cohn, Nuremberg, DSB Kongress (2) 1906

1.d4 d5 2.c4 e6 3.Nc3 c5 4.cxd5 exd5 5.Nf3 Nf6 6.Bg5 Be6 7.e4 cxd4 8.Bb5+ Nbd7 9.Nxd4 Bb4 10.e5 h6 11.exf6 Bxc3+ 12.bxc3 hxg5 13.Nxe6 fxe6 14.fxg7 Rg8 15.Qh5+

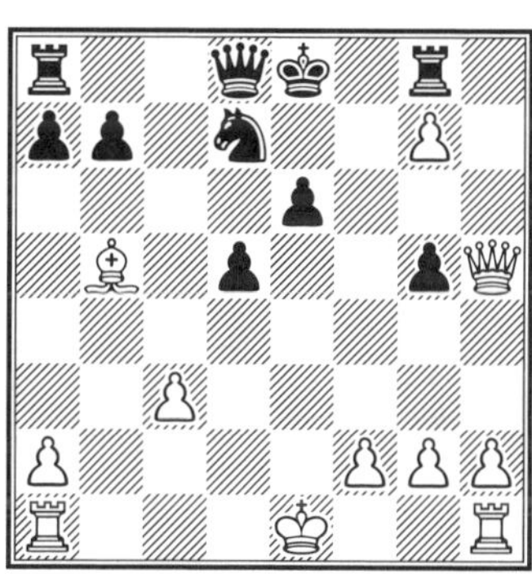

15...Ke7 16.Qxg5+ Kf7 17.Qh5+ Ke7 18.0-0 Rxg7 19.Rfe1 Nf6 20.Qh3 Qd6 21.Bd3 Rag8 22.g3 Ng4 23.Bf5 Ne5 24.Bxe6 Rf8 25.Qh4+ Rf6 26.Bxd5 Qxd5 27.Qd4 Ke6

27...Kd6 28.Rxe5.

28.Rad1, 1-0.

Frank Marshall vs. Heinrich Wolf, Nuremberg, DSB Kongress (14) 1906

1.d4 d5 2.c4 dxc4 3.Nf3 Nf6 4.Nc3 a6 5.e3 e6 6.Bxc4 c5 7.0-0 Nc6 8.a3 Qc7 9.Qe2 b5 10.Ba2 Bb7 11.dxc5 Bxc5 12.b4 Bd6 13.Bb2 0-0 14.Rac1 Rad8 15.Bb1

As usual, Marshall takes aim at black's King. However, black's Bishops are also aiming at white's King! So, who will be first to start bombing the king-side?

15...Ba8

A wasted move.

16.Ne4

Marshall, of course, goes right at his opponent.

16...Nd5

Better was 16...Nxe4 when 17.Bxe4 h6 18.Bxc6 Bxc6 19.Nd4 Bxh2 20.Kh1 Rxd4 21.Bxd4 Bd6 22.Rfd1 and Black doesn't have enough compensation for his loss of material.

17.Neg5!

White wins an exchange with 17.Nxd6 Rxd6 (17...Qxd6 18.Bxh7+! Kxh7 19.Ng5+ Kh6 20.Qg4 with a winning attack.) 18.Be5, etc. In Marshall's notes he didn't even mention alternatives to 17.Neg5 (Aside from 17.Nxd6, 17.Nc5 is also very strong.). That tells me that Marshall, looking at 17.Nxd6 and 17.Nc5, thought, "Yeah, they are good moves, but I want to mate that guy and 17.Neg5 is the way to do it!"

17...g6

17...h6 18.Qc2 g6 19.Nxe6, wins.

18.Nxh7! Kxh7 19.Ng5+ Kg8

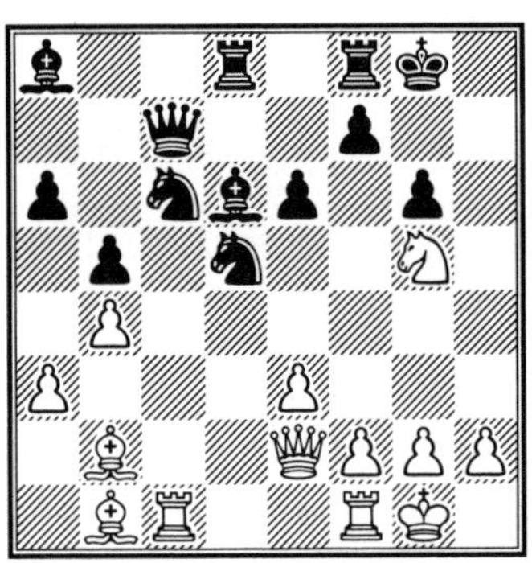

20.Qh5 f6 21.Bxg6 Rd7 22.Nxe6 Rh7 23.Bxh7+

Sometimes you have too many good options. This is a case in point. 23.Qg4, 23.Qxh7+, 23.Nxc7 are also lethal.

23...Qxh7 24.Qxh7+ Kxh7 25.Nxf8+ Bxf8 26.Rfd1 Nce7 27.e4 Nb6 28.Rc7 Kg8 29.Bxf6

29.Rd8 is also crushing.

29...Ng6 30.Rd8, 1-0.

Marshall was in great form in this tournament, and his fans were delighted! Maybe he would be World Champion after all!?

The World Chess Championship! (1907)

Emanuel Lasker (thirty-eight years old) vs. Frank Marshall (twenty-nine years old).

It's going to happen!!!! I can't wait. Marshall is coming into the tournament with a lot of confidence since he beat Lasker in Paris 1900. Bets go all over the world! Men and women faint at the sight of these two chess gods.

Rules:

- The agreed upon dates are January 26 to April 8, 1907.
- The match will be played in New York, Philadelphia, Washington DC, Baltimore, Chicago, and Memphis.
- Draws don't count and the winner is the first to get eight wins. Pretty simple.

It's starting! At last it's starting! Okay—

LET'S GET READY TO RUMMMMMBLLLE!!!!

"Arrrrghhh"—the American fans were crying in the streets! Why did Marshall get wiped off the map (Lasker crushed him with eight wins, no losses, seven draws)? Well, the following tidbit might (or might not) explain some of it:

In his autobiography, Marshall only said one thing about his match with Lasker: "Tedious play aimed at wearing down my opponent is averse to my nature."

But there was a bit of information that most don't know: Back on December 30 1906 *The Philadelphia Inquirer* reported:

> Mr. Marshall in a letter states that he has just been in a bad train wreck [on December 15th], which occurred at Donaldsonville, LA. His train while traveling at a high rate of speed collided with a freight. Mr. Marshall, though badly bruised and shocked, escaped with a sprained ankle and cut head. Mr. Marshall, in view of his accident and the nervous shock, expects to cancel several of his Southern engagements and returns at once to New York. It is not expected, however, that he will be prevented from playing his match with Dr. Lasker, which, in all probability, will begin the middle of January.

The match began, and I believe that Marshall was still reeling from the accident (physically or emotionally) and wasn't at his best. However, let's be honest: Emanuel Lasker and (eventually) Capablanca, were light-years ahead of all the other players. And Marshall's dreams of being World Champion were exactly that—a dream. This doesn't mean that Marshall wasn't a very strong player, he was easily in the top ten in the world. But nobody could touch Lasker at this point in his career.

Marshall had to be happy in game three of this match since all his pieces were active. This meant that he would be trying to create a kingside attack against

Lasker's King. What Marshall didn't fully understand was that Lasker had a universal style. In other words, Lasker was a master of the endgame, possessed amazing tactical and calculation skills, had solid openings, was the first player to use psychology, and could attack or defend at the highest level. In a nutshell, Lasker was better than Marshall in every phase of the game.

Lasker outplayed Marshal in the following game. When he didn't get much in the opening Lasker looked for a way to get his opponent to overreach, and knowing Marshall wouldn't be able to resist, he offered him an attack.

Frank Marshall vs. Emanuel Lasker, World Championship match (3) 1907

1.d4 d5 2.c4 e6 3.Nc3 Nf6 4.Bg5 Be7 5.e3 Ne4 6.Bxe7 Qxe7 7.Bd3 Nxc3 8.bxc3 Nd7 9.Nf3 0-0 10.0-0 Rd8 11.Qc2 Nf8 12.Ne5 c5 13.Rab1 Qc7 14.Qb3?!

14.Rfc1 b6 15.cxd5 exd5 16.Qa4, +=.

14...b6 15.cxd5 exd5 16.Qa4 Bb7 17.Qd1 Rd6 18.Qg4 Re8 19.Qg3 Rde6 20.Bf5 R6e7 21.f4

I don't like f4.

21...Bc8 22.Bxc8 Rxc8 23.Qf3 Qd6 24.Rfc1?

I don't like this too!

24...Rec7 25.h3? h6?!

25...cxd4 26.exd4 f6.

26.Kh2

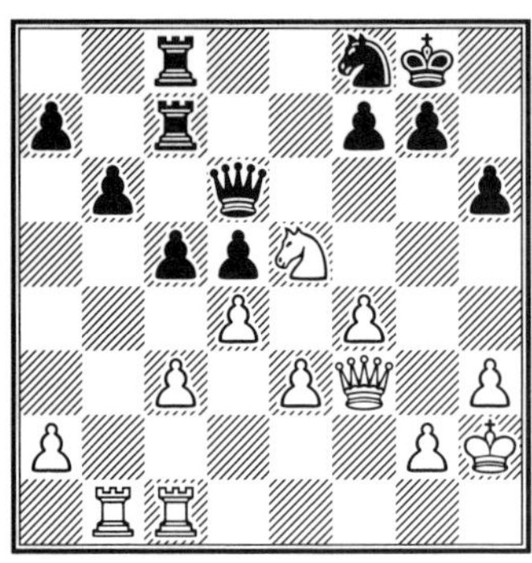

26...Nh7

26...Nd7 is better.

27.Qh5? Nf6 28.Qf5 cxd4 29.exd4 Ne4

29...Qe6 is better since Black's pawn positions are better.

30.Nxf7 Rxf7 31.Qxc8+ Rf8 32.Qb7 Qxf4+ 33.Kg1 Qg5? 34.Kh2 Qg3+ 35.Kg1 Nd2 36.Qxd5+ Kh8 37.Kh1 Nf3 38.gxf3 Qxh3+ 39.Kg1 Qg3+ 40.Kh1 Rf4 41.Qd8+?! Kh7 42.Rf1 Rf5, 0-1.

Marshall resigned in view of 43.Qe8 Qh4+ 44.Kg2 Rg5.

Marshall had defeated Lasker in Paris years earlier, but after that Marshall never beat Lasker in a serious tournament or match game again. Not counting draws, their life score in serious tournaments and matches was twelve wins for Lasker and one for Marshal.

What do you do when you've failed to win the world chess championship and, more important, you've realized that the biggest title will never be yours?

Well, you play chess of course!

Yes, the top players dream of becoming the World Champion, but you don't get into the game for that. You play because it's part of you and, quite simply, you love it.

Frank Marshall had good times and bad times, but he always looked for the next tournament, new opening ideas, and improvement in all phases of the game. And when he won a game by a beautiful attack—*that* was what he lived for.

Ostend (1907): An interesting and strong tournament. There were six players, and each had to play four games against the others. Tarrasch took first (Marshall drew three games against Tarrasch and lost one), Schlechter was second, Marshall and Janowski tied for third/fourth, Burn was fifth, and Chigorin sixth.

Frank Marshall vs. Amos Burn, Ostend (14) 1907

1.d4 Nf6 2.Nf3 d6 3.Bf4 Nbd7 4.e3 g6 5.Bd3 Bg7 6.Nbd2 0-0 7.h4 Re8 8.h5 Nxh5

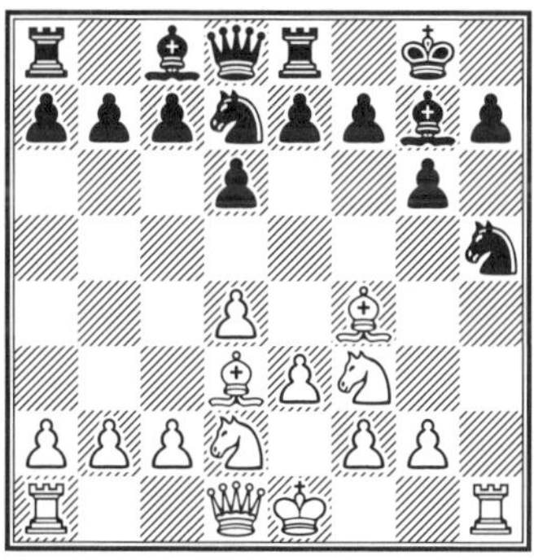

9.Rxh5 gxh5 10.Bxh7+ Kxh7??

10...Kf8! favors Black.

11.Ng5+ Kg6 12.Ndf3 e5 13.Nh4+ Kf6 14.Nh7+ Ke7 15.Nf5+ Ke6 16.Nxg7+

One move faster is 16.d5+ Kxf5 17.Qxh5+ Ke4 18.Qf3+ Kf5 19.g4+ Kg6 20.Qe4+ f5 21.Qxf5 mate.

16...Ke7 17.Nf5+ Ke6 18.d5+ Kxf5 19.Qxh5+ Ke4 20.0-0-0, 1-0.

In Marshall's day, if any chess player heard the word "swindle" they immediately thought of Marshall. Marshall was famous for finding himself in bad (often hopeless) positions, but when that occurred magic appeared: Marshall tossed whatever pieces he had left at his opponent and, lo and behold, the opponent's brain melted as tactic after tactic left Marshall with another victory.

Here's a typical example:

Frank Marshall vs. Mikhail Chigorin, Ostend (13) 1907

1.d4 d5 2.Nf3 e6 3.Bf4 Nf6 4.e3 Bd6 5.Bg3 c6 6.Bd3 Bxg3 7.hxg3 Nbd7 8.Nbd2 Qc7 9.Qe2 c5 10.c3 c4 11.Bc2 b5 12.e4 dxe4 13.Nxe4 h6 14.Nfg5 Bb7 15.0-0-0 0-0 16.f4 Rab8 17.a3 a5 18.Nd2 Bd5 19.Nge4 b4 20.axb4 axb4 21.Nxf6+ Nxf6 22.Qe5 Qa5 23.Nxc4 Qa6

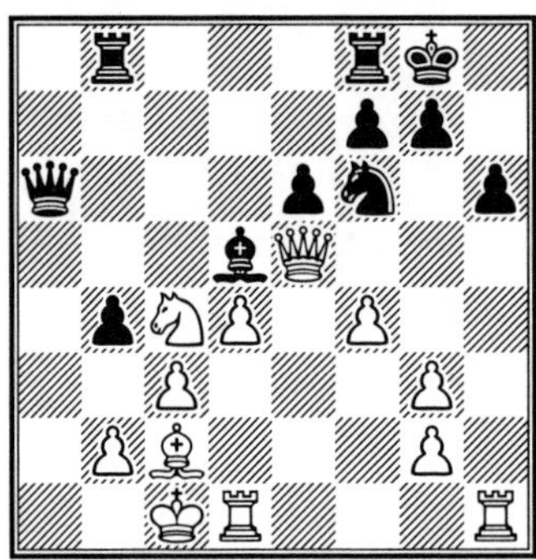

White is off-the-chart dead since the c4-Knight is ready to be captured and white's King is about to be brutalized. So, what would you do if you were Marshall? Well, that's easy:

24.Rxh6

24.Ne3 Qa1+ 25.Bb1 (25.Kd2 Qxb2 26.c4 Ne4+ 27.Ke1 Qc3+ 28.Ke2 Nxg3+, 0-1.) 25...bxc3, 0-1.

24...bxc3 25.Rdh1

Spooking Black with the threat of Rh8 mate.

25...gxh6

25...Qa1+ is even better: 26.Bb1 gxh6 27.Rxh6 cxb2+ and it's mate in 13.

26.Rxh6 cxb2+?!?

This loses. 26...Qa1+ 27.Bb1 cxb2+ forces mate: 28.Kc2 (28.Kd1 Qxb1+; 28.Kd2 Ne4+) 28...Be4+ 29.Kd2 Qxb1 30.Qg5+ Bg6 31.f5 Qc1+ 32.Ke2 Qxg5, 0-1. It's mate in six.

27.Kd2 Ne4+ 28.Bxe4 Bxe4 29.Qh8, 1-0.

Marshall had positional skills too; it's just that he preferred whack-a-mole chess. When he did play positionally, he was always on the lookout for a segue into an attack. The following game shows this philosophy in perfection:

Frank Marshall vs. Carl Schlechter, Ostend (17) 1907

1.d4 d5 2.c4 e6 3.Nc3 c5 4.cxd5 exd5 5.Nf3 Nc6 6.Bg5 Be7 7.Bxe7 Ngxe7 8.e3 0-0 9.dxc5 Qa5 10.Bd3 Qxc5 11.0-0 Be6 12.Rc1 Qb6 13.Na4 Qb4 14.h3 h6 15.a3 Qd6 16.Nc5 Rab8 17.Qe2 Bf5 18.Bxf5 Nxf5 19.Rfd1 Nfe7 20.e4 b6 21.e5 Qd8 22.Ne4

White is better, but when Black played...

22...Qc8⁇

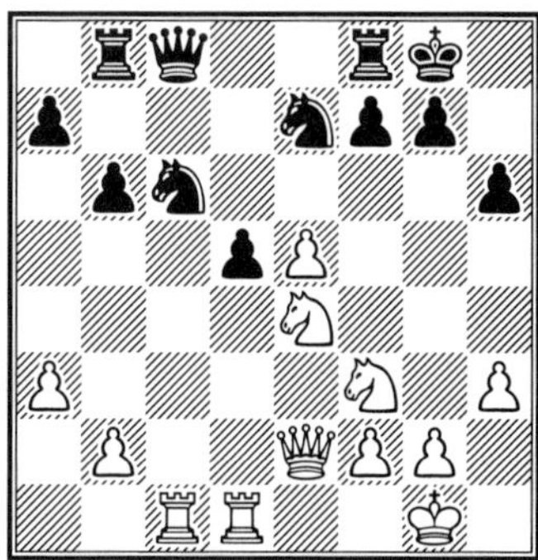

Marshall immediately went into overdrive.

23.Nf6+ gxf6 24.exf6 Ng6?

Black had to play 24...Qe6 though White gets a winning endgame: 25.Qxe6 fxe6 26.fxe7 Nxe7 27.Re1 Rf6 28.Rc7 and Black is lost.

25.Qd2 Qf5 26.Qxh6 Qxf6 27.Rxc6! Qxb2

Allowing a nice finish. 27...Qg7 was a must, but it was so hopeless that Black just ignored it: 28.Qxg7+ Kxg7 when both 29.Rc7 and 29.Rxd5 will leave White with two extra pawns.

28.Rd4! Qb1+ 29.Kh2 Qf5 30.Rg4!, 1-0.

A sacrifice on g6 will end the game.

Karlsbad (1907): A very strong group of twenty players! Marshall didn't do very well, although he finished ahead of many legends. Akiba Rubinstein first, Géza Maróczy second, Paul Saladin Leonhardt third, Aron Nimzowitsch and Carl Schlechter tied for fourth/fifth, Milan Vidmar sixth. Marshall tied for eleventh/twelfth, ahead of Spielmann, Tartakower, Chigorin, Janowski, and others.

Vienna (1908): Twenty players, nineteen games, Maróczy, Schlechter, and Duras tied for first (14 points). Rubinstein was fourth, and Marshall, Leonhardt, and Mieses tied for ninth/eleventh. By the way, last place (with just 1½ points) was Richard Réti!

Frank Marshall vs. Richard Réti, Vienna 1908

1.e4 e5 2.Nf3 Nc6 3.Nc3 Nf6 4.Bb5 Bb4 5.0-0 0-0 6.d3 Bxc3 7.bxc3 d6 8.Bg5 Qe7 9.h3 Nd8 10.Bc4 Be6 11.Nd2 h6 12.Be3 d5 13.exd5 Nxd5 14.Bxd5 Bxd5 15.d4

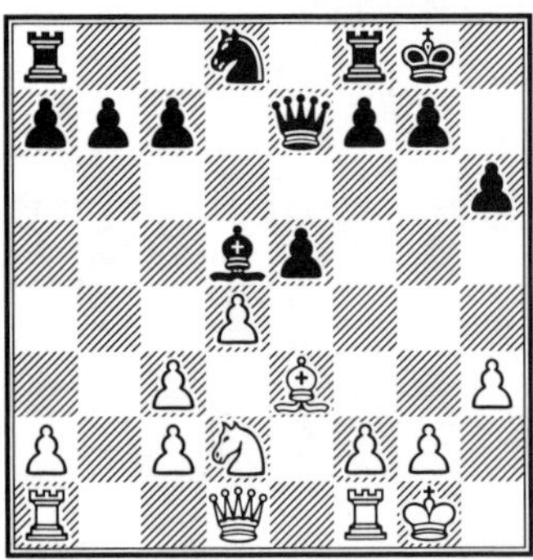

15...exd4 16.cxd4 f5 17.Re1 Qf7 18.c4 Bxc4 19.Nxc4 Qxc4 20.d5 Rf7?

20...Nf7 was correct.

21.Rc1 Qb5 22.Bf4 c6 23.d6 c5 24.Qd5 Rc8 25.Re7

25.Rcd1 was also powerful.

25...Qc6 26.d7 Ra8 27.Re8+ Kh7 28.Qxc6 bxc6 29.Rd1 a6 30.Bc7 Ra7 31.Rxd8, 1-0.

Jacques Mieses vs. Frank Marshall, Vienna 1908

1.e4 e6 2.d4 d5 3.Nc3 c5 4.Nf3 Nc6 5.Be3 Nf6 6.exd5 exd5 7.dxc5 Be7 8.Be2 0-0 9.0-0 Re8 10.h3 Bf5 11.a3 a5 12.Na4 Qc7 13.Qc1 Rad8 14.Bd3 Ne4 15.Nd2

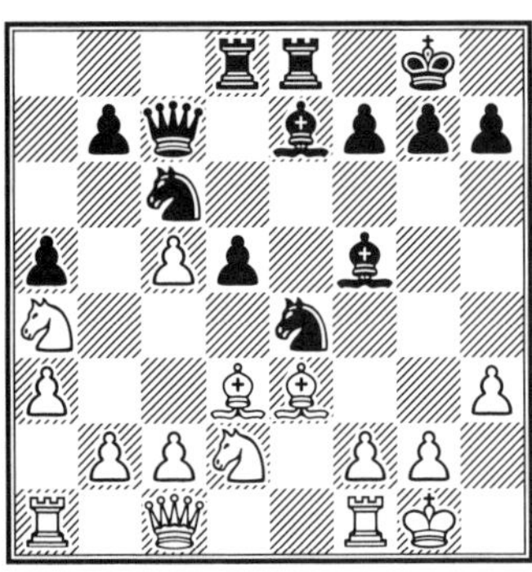

15...Qe5 16.Re1 Qf6 17.Bxe4 dxe4 18.Nf1 Qg6 19.Ng3 h5 20.Nxf5 Qxf5 21.b4 Ne5 22.Bf4 Ng6 23.Be3 Nh4 24.Bf4 Qg6 25.Bg3 Bg5 26.Qb1 Rd2

Other crushing moves were 26...e3 and 26...Nf3+.

27.Qb3 e3 28.Qc3 exf2+ 29.Bxf2 Be3, 0-1.

DSB-16 Kongress (1908): Marshall again won a tournament with no losses. His score (11½-3½) put him (1½) ahead of second place Georg Salwe. Spielmann took third.

Frank Marshall vs. David Przepiórka, Düsseldorf, DSB Kongress (8) 1908

1.d4 d5 2.c4 e6 3.Nc3 c5 4.cxd5 exd5 5.Nf3 Nc6 6.g3 cxd4 7.Nd4 Bc5 8.Nb3 Bb4 9.Bg2 Nge7 10.0-0 Be6 11.Bg5 f6 12.Bd2 0-0 13.a3 Bd6 14.Nb5 Bf7 15.Nxd6 Qxd6 16.Rc1 d4 17.Bf4 Qd8 18.Nc5 b6 19.Nb7 Qd7 20.Nd6

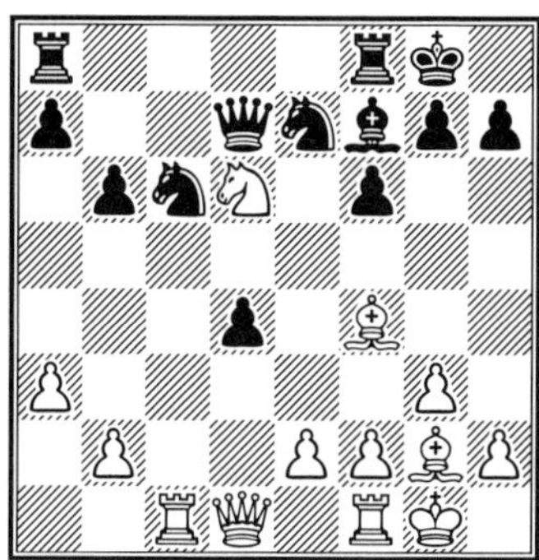

White has a small edge, but Marshall manages to make it very, very big!

20...Bd5?

Black should have played 20....g5 21.Nxf7 gxf4 22.Nh6+ Kg7 23.Nf5+ Kg6 24.Bxc6 Nxc6 25.Rxc6 Qe4 26.Qc2 Qxc2 27.Rxc2 and White still has an edge, but not more than that.

21.Bxd5+ Nxd5 22.Qb3 Nce7 23.Nb5 Kh8 24.Bd6 Rad8??

24...Rfc8, though White would have a clear advantage.

25.Rfd1 Rfe8 26.Rxd4

26.Bxe7 Qxe7 27.Rxd4 is more or less the same thing.

26...a6 27.Bxe7 Qxe7 28.Rxd5, 1-0.

Play might have gone: 28...axb5 29.Rxd8 Rxd8 30.Qxb5 and White has two extra pawns.

Smooth, wasn't it? It's amazing how calm, technical skills often win games in what looks like a simple manner. Marshall always loved tactical play, but as he grew older, and as he got more and more experience, he started to appreciate positional chess too.

[left] Frank Marshall with wife Caroline and son Frank Jr, circa 1907; [below] Marshall vs. Jackson W. Showalter. Showalter had regained the U.S. Champion title in 1906 on Harrry Pillsbury's death. Marshall took the title from Showalter in this 1909 match (Photos: Courtesy of the Marshall Chess Club).

Lodz (1908): Akiba Rubinstein, Marshall, and Salwe. Each played an eight game match with the others. When the smoke cleared Rubinstein won (with 9½), Marshall (8), and Salwe (6½).

Warsaw (1908): This eight game, hard-fought, match pitted Marshall vs. Akiba Rubinstein. Rubinstein won (3 wins to 2 with 3 draws). Since Rubinstein was the second-best player on Earth, Marshall's result was good. The sixth game was going well for Marshall but he wasn't able to break through. Eventually it equaled out, though Marshall kept slogging along, still remembering his long-gone advantage.

Berlin (1908): A ten game match Marshall vs. Jacques Mieses, Marshall won five games, Mieses won four, with one draw. Marshall won the last game!

Frank Marshall vs. Jacques Mieses, Berlin match (1) 1908

1.d4 d5 2.c4 e6 3.Nc3 c5 4.cxd5 exd5 5.Nf3 cxd4 6.Nxd4 Nc6 7.Bf4 Bb4 8.e3 Nge7 9.Rc1 0-0 10.Be2 Bd6 11.Bg3 Nxd4 12.Qxd4 b6 13.Bd3 Bb7 14.Bxd6 Qxd6 15.0-0

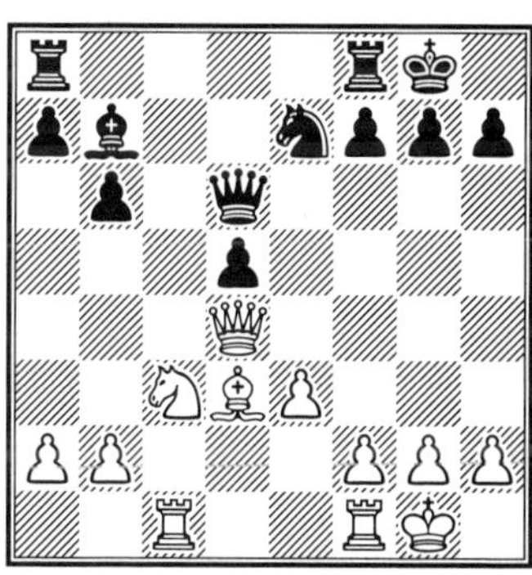

15...Rfc8 16.Nb5 Qd7 17.Rxc8+ Bxc8 18.Rc1 Nc6 19.Qh4 g6 20.Qf6 Nb4 21.Rc7 Qe6 22.Qd8+ Kg7 23.Nd6 Bb7 24.Nxf7, 1-0.

Jacques Mieses vs. Frank Marshall, Berlin match (10) 1908

1.e4 e5 2.Nc3 Nf6 3.g3 Nc6 4.Bg2 Bc5 5.d3 d6 6.Na4 Bg4 7.f3 Be6 8.Ne2 Qd7 9.h3 Nd4 10.Nxc5 dxc5 11.Nxd4 Qxd4 12.f4 c4 13.f5 Bd7 14.Qe2 cxd3 15.Qxd3 Qxd3 16.cxd3 Bb5 17.d4 exd4 18.e5 Nd7 19.a4 Ba6 20.b4 c6 21.Bf4 0-0 22.0-0-0 d3 23.Rhe1 Nb6 24.a5 Na4 25.Kd2 Nb2 26.Ra1 Rad8 27.Kc3 d2 28.Bxd2 Rd3+ 29.Kc2 Rxg3 30.Rg1 Nc4 31.Bf4 Ne3+ 32.Kb3 Bc4+ 33.Kc3 Nd1+ 34.Kd4 Rd8+

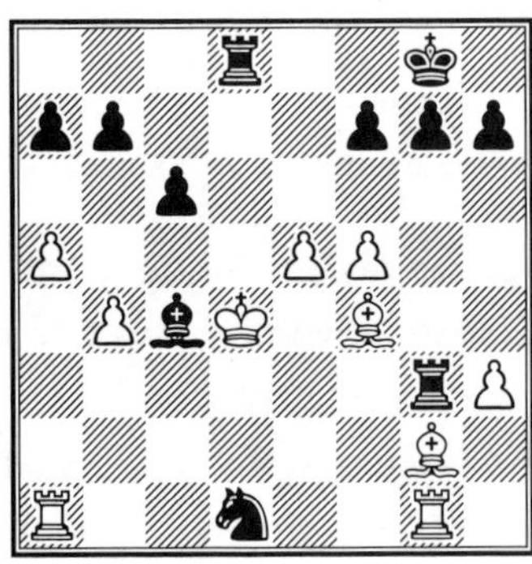

35.Kc5

35.Ke4 gets mated by 35...Nf2 mate, 35...Bd3 mate, and 35...Nc3 mate.

35...Rc3

35...Rxg2 is also strong, but 35...Rc3 is even better.

36.Rc1

Stopping an instant mate.

36...Bb5+ 37.Rxc3 Nxc3

Threatening ...Na4 mate.

38.Ra1 Nd5! 39.Bg3 Nc7! and White resigned since Black mates in two moves with ...Na6, 0-1.

Suresnes (1908): Another match (ten games) between David Janowski and Marshall. Janowski won comfortably (5 wins, 3 draws, 2 losses).

Yet, did he really win in the overall scheme of things?

It turned out that after he lost their second match in 1905, Janowski's ego was nuked and, as a result, he immediately made a challenge for another match. One insane condition created by Janowski was: "I also offer you the advantage of four points: that is to say, my first four wins are not to count."

When this third match finally happened (in 1908) Janowski won by three games, but if he didn't count his first four wins that would mean Marshall got the money. I don't know if Janowski made changes after his misguided bravado, but the whole thing was crazy anyway.

The United States Champion

Marshall vs. José Raúl Capablanca, New York (1909)

This match was supposed to be for the U.S. Championship and Capa (who had never played in a strong European tournament) was relatively unknown, so everyone was sure Marshall would easily win. Marshall got eviscerated!

After the match, Marshall complained that Capablanca, a Cuban, wasn't an American citizen and therefore couldn't be the U.S. Champion (Cuba gained its independence from the United States on December 10, 1898).

Walter Penn Shipley, a strong chess player and lawyer, agreed and made it clear that Capa couldn't have the title. Shipley also said that Marshall didn't have the title either—since his opponent wasn't a U.S. citizen—and so the title was reverted to the old U.S. champion, Jackson Showalter. This led to a match between Showalter and Marshall a short time later, Marshall won decisively by crunching him (7-2) and Marshall finally was the official U.S. Champion. Marshall held the title for ages and didn't give it up until 1936.

The Marshall vs. Capablanca match was long—twenty-three games. But Marshall quickly realized that he was face-to-face with a monster. The final score was eight wins for Capablanca, one win for Marshall, and fourteen draws.

The "problems" that occurred (Marshall's loss and Capa's disqualification) could have made the two men enemies. However, Marshall wasn't a guy that kept grudges. In 1911 when the very strong San Sebastian (a seaside town in Spain) tournament was inviting the best of the best, Marshall insisted that Capablanca (still unknown in Europe) get into the event. Capablanca came in first, and a new chess god was born. Marshall came in fourth, ahead of Tarrasch, Schlechter, Nimzowitsch, Spielmann, Maróczy, Janowski, and others.

Here is Marshall's only win in the U.S. Championship match:

Frank Marshall vs. José Capablanca, New York (7) 1909

1.d4 d5 2.c4 e6 3.Nc3 Nf6 4.Bg5 Be7 5.e3 Ne4 6.Bxe7 Qxe7 7.Bd3 Nxc3 8.bxc3 Nd7 9.Nf3 0-0 10.cxd5 exd5 11.Qb3 Nf6 12.a4 c5 13.Qa3 b6?!

An error which let's White pressure the Black position.

14.a5!

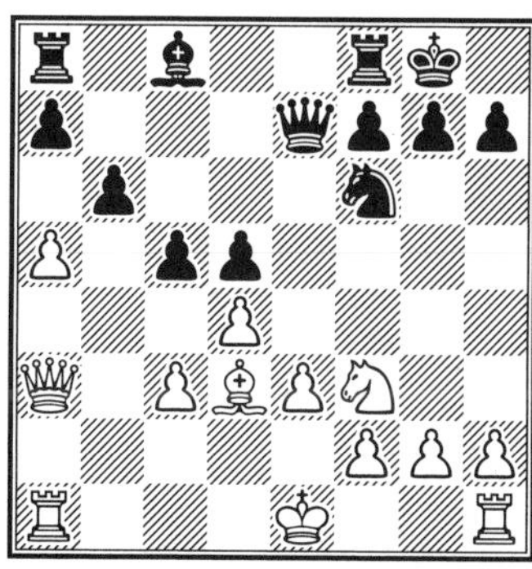

14...Bb7 15.0-0 Qc7 16.Rfb1 Nd7?! 17.Bf5

Marshall jumps on his opponent's 16...Nd7 error. Now White has an obvious advantage.

17...Rfc8?

White's straightforward play in this game has confused Capablanca. Now White wins material.

18.Bxd7 Qxd7

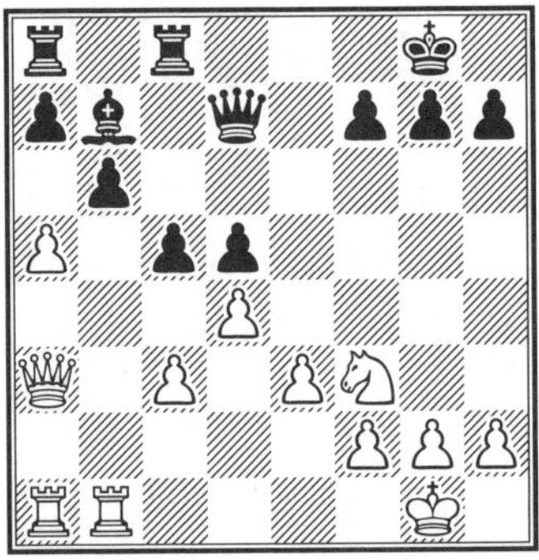

19.a6 Bc6 20.dxc5 bxc5 21.Qxc5 Rab8 22.Rxb8 Rxb8 23.Ne5 Qf5 24.f4 Rb6 25.Qxb6!, 1-0.

A very nice end! After 25...axb6 26.Nxc6 the a-pawn can't be stopped.

A really good game by Marshall (a mix of positional skill and tactics)! If he played like that throughout the match, he would have won several more games!

DSB-17 Kongress (1910): First Schlechter, second Duras, third Nimzowitsch, fourth Spielmann, and Teichmann and Marshall tied for fifth/sixth. There were seventeen players in this event, and players like Tartakower and Tarrasch failed to make the top six. But what stands out the most was a young Alekhine, who tied for seventh/eighth.

Marshall drew his game with Alekhine—but never beat him in all the years they played. Their life score for serious tournaments: 7 wins and 8 draws. Why was Alekhine so difficult for Marshall? That's simple: Marshall's main strength was attacking skills and tactics. Unfortunately for Marshall, Alekhine was the best in the world when it came to those two things.

Here's a very interesting (I should change "interesting" to "AWESOME") draw between these two men bashing it out in 1924. The end was full of fireworks!

Frank Marshall vs. Alexander Alekhine, New York 1924

1.d4 Nf6 2.Nf3 e6 3.c4 d5 4.Nc3 c6 5.cxd5 exd5 6.Bg5 Be7 7.e3 Bf5 8.Bd3 Bxd3 9.Qxd3 Nbd7 10.0-0 0-0 **11.Qf5**

Marshall wrote: "A very strong move and the key to the following play. White's activities on the queenside are clearly foreshadowed, indicating the necessity for counteraction by Black on the other wing. But, as will be seen, the presence of white's Queen at f5 is awkward for Black."

11...Ne4 12.Bxe7 Qxe7 13.Nxe4 dxe4 14.Nd2 Nf6 15.Rac1

Once again, we'll see what Marshall wrote: "Despite the equalizing tendency of the previous exchanges, the proactive chances are all on White's side. After this Rook goes to c5, Black will have to be on his guard against Re5 and also against the minority attack culminating in the advance of the b2-pawn to b5, with lasting pressure on Black's game."

15...Rfe8 16.Rc5 Nd5 17.Rfc1 Rad8 18.b4 a6

Marshall was hoping for 18...Nxb4, but Alekhine didn't bite since all he could get is a tiny inferiority and, with best play, a draw: Here's why: 19.Re5 Qc7 20.Rxe8+ Rxe8 21.Nxe4 Rd8 (21...Nxa2? 22.Ra1 Nb4 23.Rxa7 Na6 24.Ng5 g6 25.Qb1 Re7 26.Ne4 Kg7 [26...Qb8?? 27.Rxa6] 27.g4 h6 28.h3 and Black is under a lot of pressure.) 22.Nc5 b6 23.Nd3 Nxd3 24.Qxd3 Rd6 25.d5 h5 26.e4 Qd8, =.

19.a3 Rd6 20.g3

When I was playing in tournaments I would often think I'd have a small edge even if it was equal or, perhaps, a bit worse. Lots of chess professionals think highly about their position even if it's not reality. Marshall seems to have thought that way too!

[Marshall]: "A many-sided move which serves the following purposes: it opens up a loophole for the King; it prepares a retreat for the Queen (Qf5-h3-f1); in the event of ...Rh6 the continuation ...Qh4 is automatically prevents; in the event of ...g6 followed by ...f5 the advance ...f5-f4 is prevented." It's interesting to see Marshall's thought process!

20...h6 21.Nb1!

Let's have Marshall explain: "A simple but strong continuation. The idea is to exchange Knights with Nc3 after which the queenside attack (a2-a4 followed by b5) can be resumed. White hopes to give this plan decisive effect with a nice sacrifice of the exchange, but the whole idea is just barely parried by a really magnificent counter-combination by Alekhine, involving the sacrifice of a Rook and Knight!"

21...g6 22.Qh3 Qg5 23.Nc3 b6!!

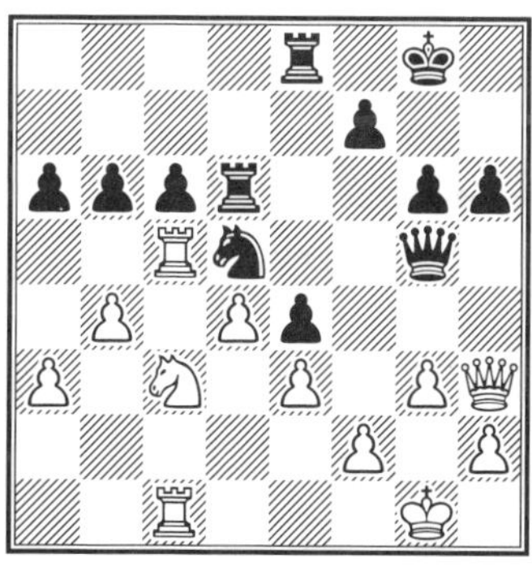

Believe it or not, this b6-pawn marches all the way down to f2!

24.Nxd5!

24.Rc4?? Nxe3 and Black wins.

24...bxc5 25.Nc7! cxd4!! 26.Nxe8 dxe3

26...Rd8? 27.Qg4 Rxe8 (27...Qxg4 28.Nf6+) 28.Qxg5 hxg5 29.exd4 and Black is in serious trouble.

27.Nxd6

27.f4 exf3 e.p. 28.Nxd6 f2+ 29.Kf1 e2+ 30.Kxf2 Qxc1 31.Kxe2 Qb2+ 32.Kd3 Qb3+ 33.Ke2 Qc2+, draw.

27...exf2+ 28.Kxf2 Qd2+ 29.Kg1 Qe3+!

And not 29...Qxc1+? 30.Qf1.

30.Kg2 Qf3+ 31.Kg1 Qe3+ 32.Kg2 Qf3+, ½-½.

An amazing game!

Rudolf Spielmann vs. Frank Marshall, DSB 17 Kongress (11) 1910

1.e4 e5 2.Nf3 Nf6 3.Nxe5 d6 4.Nf3 Nxe4 5.d4 d5 6.Bd3 Bd6 7.0-0 Bg4 8.c4 0-0 9.cxd5 f5 10.Nc3 Nd7 11.h3 Bh5 12.Nxe4 fxe4 13.Bxe4 Nf6 14.Bf5 Kh8 15.g4 Nxd5

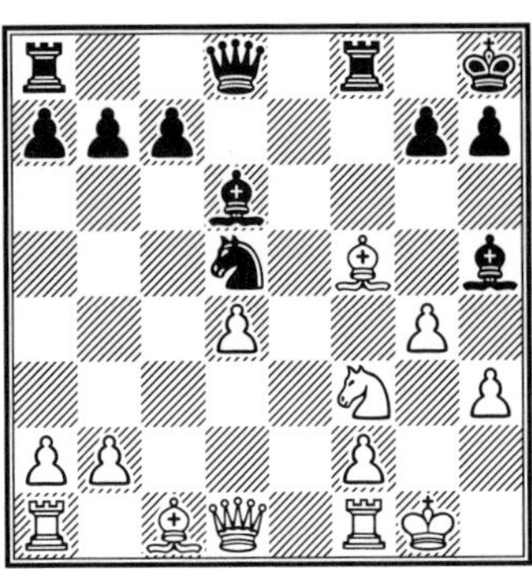

16.Qd3 Nb4 17.Qe4 Bf7 18.Bg5 Qe8 19.Ne5 Bd5 20.Qe2 Nc6 21.Qd3 Nxe5 22.dxe5 Qxe5 23.Qg3 Qxb2 24.Qh4 Rxf5 25.gxf5 Qe5 26.Qg3 Qxf5 27.Qg4 Qe5 28.Rfe1 Qh2+ 29.Kf1 Rf8 30.Ke2 Qxf2+ 31.Kd3 b5, 0-1.

Marshall: "He has had enough punishment. There is little he can do against the threat of ...Bc4+ followed by ...Rf3+." Here's a sample, courtesy of Marshall: 32.Bd2 Bc4+ 33.Kc2 Bb4 34.Red1 Rd8 35.Qf4 Rxd2+ 36.Rxd2 Qxf4 37.Rd8+ Bg8.

New York (1911): Marshall came in first (undefeated), Capablanca second. Capablanca lost to Roy Turnbull Black, who was a judge.

Capablanca, with an "I can beat this fish with any opening" mentality, played 1.e4 c5 2.b4. It didn't go well for the Cuban. Here's a quick and instructive look at the Capa vs. Black battle:

José Capablanca vs. Roy Turnbull Black, New York 1911

1.e4 c5 2.b4 cxb4 3.a3 bxa3 4.Bxa3 d6 5.Nf3 Nc6 6.d4 g6 7.h4 Bg4 8.c3 Bg7 9.Nbd2 Nf6 10.Qb3 Qb6 11.Qa2 Bxf3 12.gxf3 Nh5 13.Nc4 Qc7 14.Bc1 0-0 15.Rb1 Kh8 16.Bh3 b6 17.Bg4 Nf6 18.Ne3 h5 19.Bh3 Na5 20.Bd2 Bh6 21.Rc1 Kh7 22.c4 Nb7 23.Nf5 Ng8 24.Nxh6 Nxh6 25.Bxh6 Kxh6 26.Qd2+ Kh7 27.f4 e5!

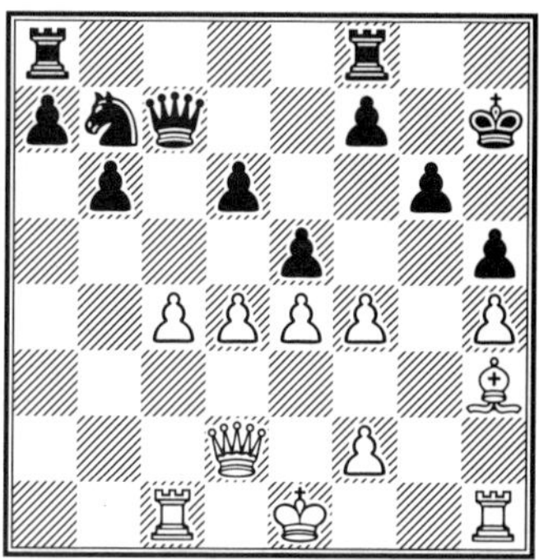

Black's Knight isn't happy on b7 so Mr. Black decides to create a very nice square for the horse.

28.fxe5 dxe5 29.d5 Nc5 and suddenly the Knight is a god.

Hamburg (1911): Frank Marshall vs. Paul Saladin Leonhardt: A seven game match. Marshall won (2 wins, 1 loss, 4 draws).

Karlsbad (1911): Twenty-six players. Teichmann first, Rubinstein and Schlechter tied for second and third, Rotlewi fourth, and Marshall and Nimzowitsch tied for fifth and sixth. The nineteen-year-old Alekhine tied for eighth/eleventh.

The following game is a humor piece. Nothing profound, just humor! When I was a child I read this and I enjoyed it so much that I never forgot it. All the notes for his game vs. Fedor Duz-Khotimirsky are by Marshall:

Frank Marshall vs. Fedor Duz-Khotimirsky, Karlsbad 1911

[Marshall]: "I felt rather nervous when I sat down to play the Russian master Duz-Khotimirsky in the last round; I knew that he had received considerable coaching in anticipation of his game with me. My excitable opponent also showed signs of great nervousness. This amusing little game was the result of our meeting.

1.d4 d5 2.c4 e6 3.Nf3 dxc4 4.e3 a6 5.Ne5

"Steering away from book lines.

5...Nd7 6.Nxd7

"A poor move with only develops Black's game. Simply 6.Nxc4 was in order.

6...Bxd7 7.Bxc4 Bc6 8.0-0 Bd6 9.Nc3 Qh4

"Black has developed with great rapidity.

10.f4 Nf6 11.Bd2 Ng4

"Already giving signs of suffering from a hallucination.

12.h3

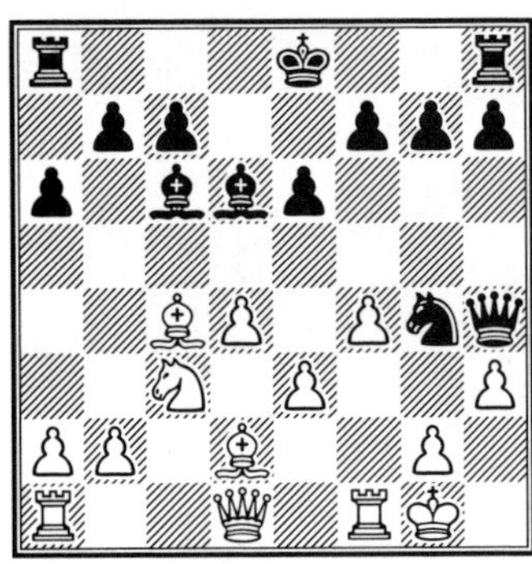

12...Qg3⁇

"My opponent made this move quickly, jumped up from his chair and went into the next room where most of the players were gathered. In his broken English he said, 'Poor Marshall dead!' The players ran in and clustered round the table. I looked at the position and saw that he threatened mate in two ways, either with ...Qxg2+ or ...Qh2+. Very threatening, but the solution was simple enough. I just played...

13.Qxg4, 1-0.

"My opponent returned to the board and looked at what I had done. He threw over the pieces and in a loud voice exclaimed, 'Oh, OH, Marshall not dead, I dead!'"

Marshall played in one tournament or match after another. The guy seemed to live for chess and he continued to compete all over Europe, Russia, and the United States. He couldn't fly in those days, so it would be a wild guess as to how much of his time was spent on ships and trains, and other means of transportation.

Personally, I would be exhausted—you traveled to where you had to be, you play in a tournament for a couple weeks, or a month, or even longer. Then, when the tournament is over, you do it all over again!

San Sebastian (1912): Marshall's first tournament of 1912 was the chess-friendly San Sebastian. He did okay, but I'm sure he wanted to do better: Akiba Rubinstein was first, Spielmann and Nimzowitsch tied for second/third, Tarrasch was fourth, Julius Perlis was fifth, and Marshall sixth. Other players were Duras, Teichmann, Schlechter, Leonhardt, and Forgács.

Bad Pistyan (1912): Marshall did better here, but the event was a triumph for Rubinstein who clobbered the rest of the field with twelve wins, four draws, and one loss. Spielmann came in second (2½ points) behind Rubinstein, and Marshall was third. Other players included: Schlechter, Duras, Teichmann, Alapin, Breyer.

Budapest (1912): Teleporting to a tournament in Budapest, Marshall and Schlechter tied for first/second, Duras and Maróczy tied for third/fourth, and Teichmann and Vidmar tied for fifth/sixth.

DSB Kongress, Breslau (1912): Marshall came in sixth out of eighteen players. This tournament is famous for Marshall's brilliant Queen sacrifice.

Marshall commented:

> Perhaps you have heard about this game, which so excited the spectators that they showered me with gold pieces! I have often been asked whether this really happened. The answer is yes, that is what happened, literally!

Stepan Levitsky vs. Frank Marshall, Breslau 1912

1.e4 e6 2.d4 d5 3.Nc3 c5 4.Nf3 Nc6 5.exd5 exd5 6.Be2 Nf6 7.0-0 Be7 8.Bg5 0-0 9.dxc5 Be6 10.Nd4 Bxc5 11.Nxe6 fxe6 12.Bg4 Qd6

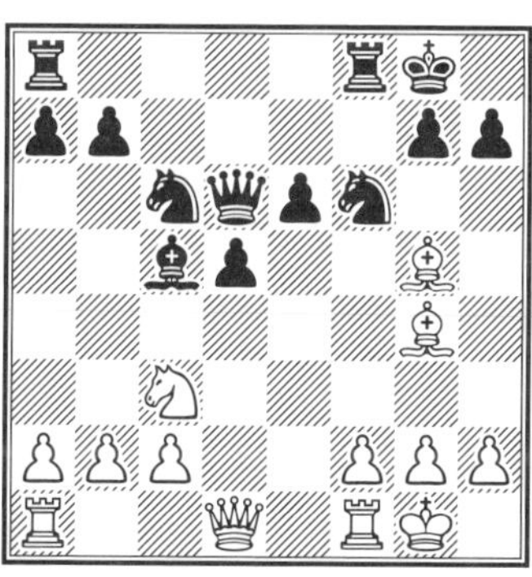

13.Bh3 Rad8 14.Qd2 Bb4 15.Bxf6 Rxf6 16.Rad1 Qc5 17.Qe2 Bxc3 18.bxc3 Qxc3 19.Rxd5 Nd4 20.Qh5 Ref8 21.Re5 Rh6 22.Qg5 Rxh3 23.Rc5 Qg3!, 0-1.

Gyula Breyer vs. Frank Marshall, Breslau 1912

1.e4 c5 2.d4 cxd4 3.Nf3 e6 4.Nxd4 Nf6 5.Nc3 Bb4 6.Bb5 Nxe4 7.0-0 Nxc3 8.bxc3 Bxc3 9.Rb1 a6 10.Ne2 Nf6 11.Bd3 0-0 12.Ng3 Nc6 13.f4 Bd4+ 14.Kh1 f5 15.Ba3 Rf6 16.c3 Ba7 17.Bd6 b5 18.c4 Rh6 19.h3 Bb7 20.Kh2 Nd4 21.a4

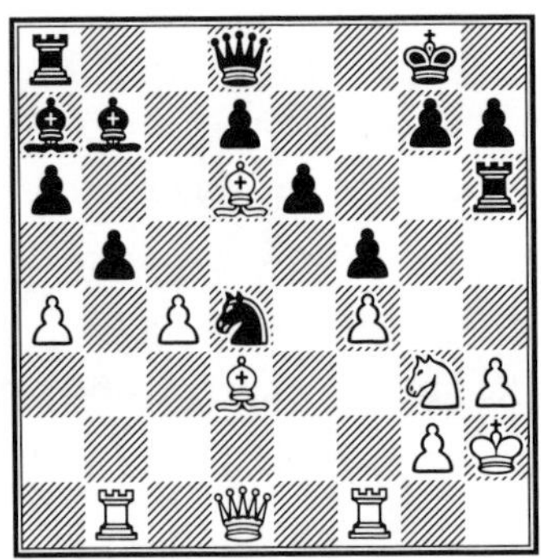

21...Qh4 22.c5 Rc8 23.axb5 axb5 24.Rb4 Bxg2 25.Kxg2

25.Rxd4 Qxh3+ 26.Kg1 Qxg3

25...Qxh3+ 26.Kf2 Qh2+ 27.Ke3 Qxg3+ 28.Kxd4 e5+ 29.fxe5 Rxd6+ 30.exd6

30.Kc3 Qxe5+ 31.Kb3 Qd5+

30...Rxc5 31.Qb3+ Rc4+ 32.Kd5 Rxb4 33.Qxb4 Qxd3+ 34.Ke5 Qe2+ (34...Bc5 is even better.), 0–1.

Biarritz (1912): Janowski vs. Marshall was a nine game match. Marshall slaughtered his eternal opponent (6 wins, 1 loss, 2 draws).

Marshall:

> I played still another match with Janowski. This took place in the pleasant atmosphere of Biarritz, and I had the satisfaction of trouncing my ancient rival in decisive fashion.

Here's the game Marshall was referring to:

David Janowski vs. Frank Marshall, Biarritz match (3) 1912

1.e4 e5 2.Nf3 Nf6

Lots of people think that the Petroff Defense is a drawish oppening. However, Marshall used it often with very good results.

3.Nxe5 d6 4.Nf3 Nxe4 5.d4 d5 6.Bd3 Bd6 7.c4 0-0 8.cxd5 Bb4+ 9.Kf1 Qxd5 10.Qc2 Re8 11.Nc3 Nxc3 12.bxc3 Qxf3! 13.cxb4

Of course, 13.gxf3?? is the End of Days after 13...Bh3+ 14.Kg1 Re1+ 15.Bf1 Rxf1 mate.

13...Nc6 14.Bb2?

This gets wiped off the board. Better was 14.Bxh7+ Kh8 15.h3 Qf6 16.Bd3 Nxd4 17.Qb1 Bf5 18.Bxf5 Nxf5 19.Bb2 Ng3+ 20.Kg1 Ne2+ 21.Kf1 (21.Kh2 Qf4+ 22.g3 Qxf2 mate.) 21...Qf4 Threatening to win material with ...Ng3+. White has no way to survive.

Another try is 13.Be3, though it dies a horrible death after 13...Bh3! 14.Rg1 Rxe3 and White should resign.

14...Nxb4

This wins (it's clear that Marshall couldn't resist sacrificing his Queen!), but better (though less exciting) was 14...Bh3! 15.Rg1 Nxb4 16.Qd1 Qxd3+ 17.Qxd3 Nxd3 18.gxh3 Nxb2 and Black is a piece up.

15.Bxh7+ Kh8 16.gxf3 Bh3+ 17.Kg1

White is, in effect, a Rook down since white's King can't move and the h1-Rook is also frozen.

17...Nxc2 18.Bxc2 Re2 19.Rc1 Rae8 20.Bc3

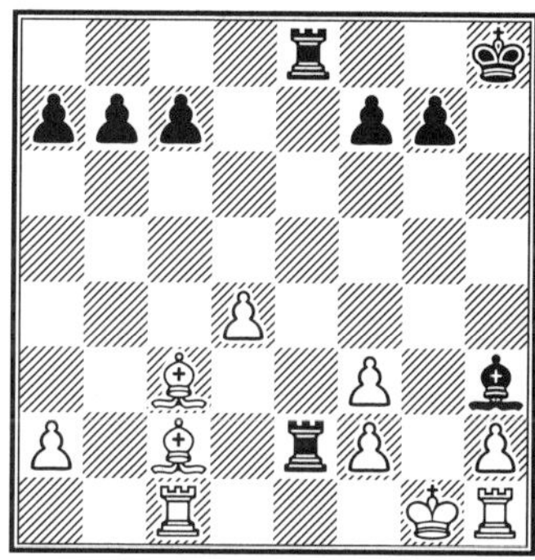

20...R8e3!

A fun, really cool move! Another, quicker way to end the game was 20...Rxc2! 21.Rxc3 Re6 and White gets mated by ...Rg6 mate.

21.Bb4

21.fxe3 (21.Be4 Rxc3) 21...Rg2+ 22.Kf1 Rxc2 23.Ke1 Rxc1+ and White will be a Rook down.

21...Rxf3 22.Bd1 Rf6!, 0-1.

23.Bc2 (To stop ...Rg6 mate) doesn't stop anything after 23...Rxc2 (23... Rexf2 is another killer) when mate is just a blink away.

American National (1913): With fourteen players, the big hitters were Capablanca, Marshall, and Janowski. Capablanca came in first (though he lost a game to Jaffe), and Marshall (who was the only undefeated player) was half-a-point behind.

Though Marshall continued to attack whenever possible (and sometimes he would attack when it wasn't possible!), Marshall had realized that, when you play a top guy you often can't bully him. Instead you need endgame skills (and Marshall was already very good in endgames), solid openings, and the ability to play solidly. In other words, he was becoming a well-balanced player who preferred sharp, attacking chess while accepting reality if the board told him to put on the brakes.

Havana (1913): Eight players (fourteen games each), the big three were, once again, Capablanca, Marshall, and Janowski. Marshall came in first, only losing one game to Janowski (Marshall won their other game.). Capablanca was second (he lost a game to Janowski and another loss to Marshall).

The following game shows that Marshall won due to patience and good defense. Yes, Capa was winning this game, but many "winning positions" have come a cropper thanks to solid defense.

José Capablanca vs. Frank Marshall, Havana (10) 1913

1.e4 e5 2.Nf3 Nf6 3.Nxe5 d6 4.Nf3 Nxe4 5.d4 d5 6.Bd3 Bg4 7.0-0 Nc6 8.c3 Be7 9.Nbd2 Nxd2 10.Bxd2 0-0 11.h3 Bh5 12.Re1 Qd7 13.Bb5 Bd6 14.Ne5 Bxe5 15.Qxh5 Bf6 16.Bf4 Rae8 17.Re3 Rxe3 18.fxe3 a6 19.Ba4 b5 20.Bc2 g6 21.Qf3 Bg7 22.Bb3 Ne7 23.e4 dxe4

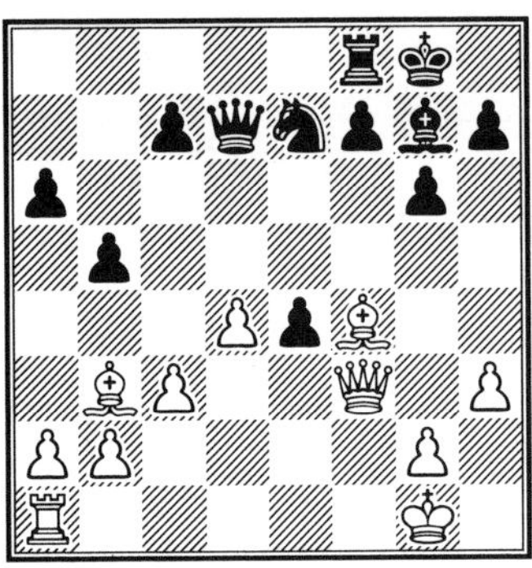

24.Qxe4 c6 25.Re1 Nd5 26.Bxd5 cxd5 27.Qe7 Qc8 28.Bd6 h6 29.Rf1 f6 30.Re1 Rd8 31.Bc5 Kh7 32.Qf7 Qf5 33.Be7 Qd7 34.Kf1 Rf8 35.Qe6 Qxe6 36.Rxe6 Re8 37.Re2 Kg8 38.b3 Kf7 39.Bc5 Rxe2 40.Kxe2 f5 41.Kd3 Ke6 42.c4 bxc4+ 43.bxc4 g5 44.g4 f4 45.Bb4 Bf6 46.Bf8 dxc4+ 47.Kxc4 f3 48.d5+ Ke5 49.Kd3 Kf4 50.Bd6+ Be5 51.Bc5 Kg3 52.Ke4 Bf4 53.d6 f2, 0-1.

New York (1913): Marshall vs. Oldřich Duras. Marshall won this match with a 3-0 score. A great victory as Duras was an exceptionally strong player.

Frank Marshall vs. Oldřich Duras, New York match (3) 1913

1.e4 e5 2.d4 exd4 3.c3 dxc3 4.Bc4 cxb2 5.Bxb2

Imagine a modern top ten player trying this stuff!

5...Nf6 6.e5 d5 7.exf6 dxc4?!

7...Bb4+ is better.

8.Qxd8+ Kxd8 9.fxg7 Bb4+ 10.Nc3 Re8+ 11.Nge2 Bf5

Though Marshall is a pawn down, he's better thanks to his extremely strong pawn on g7.

12.0-0-0+ Nd7 13.Nd5 Bd6 14.Bf6+?

This very tempting move wins the exchange but takes away a lot of the heat White was pouring on Black's position. Winning was 14.Nd4 followed by Rhe1 or 14.Rhe1 followed by Nd4.

14...Nxf6 15.Nxf6 Ke7

An interesting try is 15...Rxe2 since 16.g7-g8=Q Ke7 17.Nd5 Ke6 18.Qxa8?? (18.Nxc7+ Bxc7 19.Rd6! [white's King can now move to d1.] 19...Bxd6 20.Qxa8 Bf4+ 21.Kd1 Rd2+ 22.Ke1 Rc2, =. For example: 23.Qe8+ Kf6 24.Qh8+ Ke7 25.Qd4 Rc1+ 26.Ke2 Bg4+ 27.f3 Rc2+ 28.Kd1 Rc1+ 29.Ke2 Rc2+, draw.) 18...Ba3 mate. You'll find many fun tactical sequences after 15...Rxe2.

16.Nxe8 Rxe8 17.Rd4!

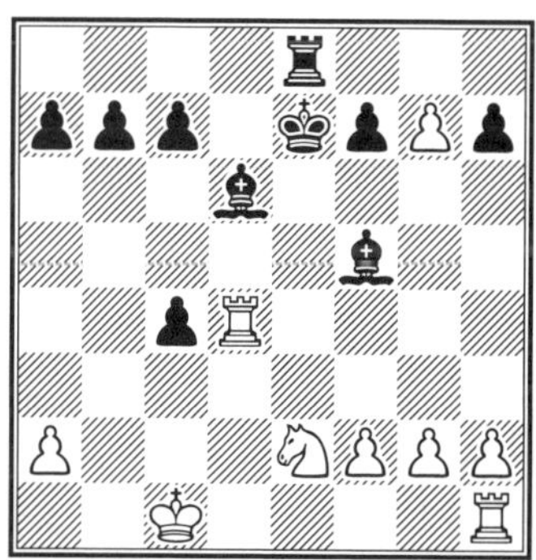

17...Kf6 18.Ng3 Ba3+?!

18...Bd3 was best. One possible line: 19.Nh5+ Kg6 20.Rg4+ Kxh5 21.g8=Q Rxg8 22.Rxg8 c3 23.Re1 Ba3+ 24.Kd1 c2+ 25.Kd2 Bg6, =.

19.Kd1 Bg6 20.f4

Suddenly Black finds himself in serious trouble!

20...Bd3 21.Nh5+ Kg6 22.Re1 Rg8 23.Rd5 h6 24.Re3 Bb2 25.g4 Bxg7 26.f5+ Kh7 27.Re7 Rf8 28.Rxc7 Bc3 29.Rxd3 Be5 30.Rxc4, 1-0.

New York Progressive (1913): Four players (twelve games): Frank Marshall, Oldřich Duras, Oscar Chajes, and Charles Jaffe. Marshall won with 5 wins, one loss.

Frank Marshall vs. Harry Kline, New York American National 1913

1.d4 d5 2.c4 e6 3.Nc3 Nf6 4.Nf3 Be7 5.Bg5 Nbd7 6.e3 0-0 7.Rc1 b6 8.cxd5 exd5 9.Qa4 Bb7 10.Ba6 Bxa6 11.Qxa6 c6 12.0-0 Ne4 13.Bxe7 Qxe7 14.Qb7! Rfc8

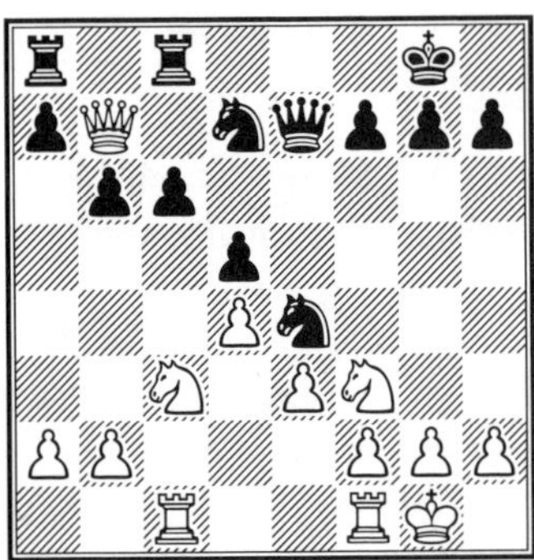

14...Qe6 15.Nxe4 dxe4 16.Ng5 Qd5 17.Nxe4.

15.Nxd5! Qd6 16.Rxc6!, 1-0.

St. Petersburg and the Gods of Chess – Preliminary (1914)

This was an extremely important tournament, and only the top five would make it to the final. Isidor Gunsberg and Joseph Blackburne didn't have a chance. That left Janowski, Ossip Bernstein, Marshall, Rubinstein, Capablanca, Tarrasch, Lasker, Nimzowitsch, and Alekhine. It wasn't a surprise when Janowski crashed and burned, and Ossip Bernstein did better than expected (he was tied for sixth and seventh with Rubinstein, which was nothing to be ashamed of, but he didn't reach the final.).

Nimzowitsch only reached eighth place (meaning he was out), and Rubinstein (thought to be a favorite) lost to Lasker and Alekhine, leaving him in sixth place and a "good but not good enough" trip back home.

Capablanca was on fire and came in 1½ points ahead of the second and third players, Lasker and Tarrasch. Alekhine was in fifth place, and Marshall surprised quite a few chess fans by coming in fourth (he only lost one game. Who was it? His nemesis Alekhine!).

A word about Lasker: he hadn't played in a tournament for five years (!) and it wasn't clear that the cobwebs would be able to vanish in time (or ever). Thus, equal second and third was perfectly okay.

Marshall's game against Ossip Bernstein was critical.

Frank Marshall vs. Ossip Bernstein, St. Petersburg Preliminary 1914

1.d4 d5 2.c4 c6 3.Nc3 Nf6 4.cxd5 cxd5 5.Nf3 e6 6.Bg5 Qb6 7.Qc2 Nc6 8.e3 Bd7 9.a3 Rc8 10.Bd3 Bb4 11.0-0 Bxc3 12.bxc3 Na5 13.Rab1 Qc6 14.Rfc1 Qa4

White is much better, but Black had confidence that his 14th move would take most of his problems away. Note that 14...Nc4 15.Bxc4 Qxc4 (15...dxc4 16.Ne5 Qc7 17.Rb4 b5 18.bxf6 gxf6 19.Nxd7 Qxd7 20.Rcb1 a6 21.a4 Rb8 22.axb5 axb5 23.Rxc4, winning) 16.Ne5 Qc7 17.Bf4 Qa5 18.Rxb7.

15.Qa2

White has a won game. Black's Queen is in trouble, White is ahead in development, and black's King is still in the middle.

15...Ne4?

Though bad, 15...b6 keeps the fight going.

16.Bxe4 dxe4 17.Ne5

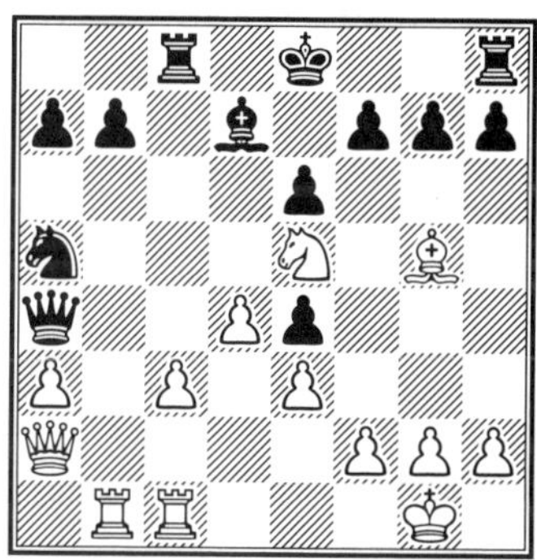

17...f6 18.Rb4

And there goes black's Queen! Marshall plays the rest of the game perfectly.

18...Rxc3 19.Qd2 Rxc1+ 20.Qxc1 0-0 21.Rxa4 Bxa4 22.Qc7 b6 23.Bf4 fxe5 24.Bxe5 Rf7 25.Qb8+ Rf8 26.Qxa7 Rf7 27.Qb8+ Rf8 28.Qc7 Rf7 29.Qc8+ Rf8 30.Qxe6+, 1-0.

St. Petersburg Final (1914)

It seemed that Capablanca would easily win since the results from the preliminary carried into the final. That means that, going into the final, Capablanca was 1½ points ahead of everyone else. However, Emanuel Lasker was now warmed up and he smashed the competition, scorching his rivals with a 7-1 finish (6 wins, 2 draws, no loses). Capablanca had 5 points, Alekhine had 4, and Tarrasch and Marshall had 2. When the preliminary points were added in, Lasker won the tournament by half a point over Capablanca.

British Empire Club Chess Tournament, 1927: [front row seated] Frank J. Marshall, William Winter, Efim Bogoljubov, Aron Nimzowitsch, William Fairhurst, Savielly Tartakower; [standing] William H. Watts, Maurice E. Goldstein, Hans Kmoch, Richard C. Griffith, Sir George A. Thomas, Ernest Busvine, Frederick D. Yates, Dr. Jacob Schumer, Edgard Colle, Victor Buerger, Richard Réti. (Photo: Courtesy of the Marshall Chess Club).

Savielly Tartakower and Edward Lasker, New York 1924.

According to Marshall, the Tsar of Russia "conferred on each of the five finalists the title 'Grandmaster of Chess.'"

Marshall wrote of his journey after St. Petersburg in *My Fifty Years of Chess:*[1]

> After visiting several places in Russia and Germany, giving exhibitions, I went to Mannheim. The tournament there was little more than half over when it ended abruptly by the outbreak of World War I. It was surprising how quickly the place became infested with soldiers. They seemed to spring up from nowhere. The one French representative, Janowski, and the three Russians, Alekhine, Flamberg and Bogoljubov, were promptly place under arrest. The German players, including Krüger, Carls, and John, at once joined the colors. Dr. Tarrasch saw two of his sons depart for the front. The remaining players were invited to make themselves scarce.
>
> I made for the Dutch border and arrived in Amsterdam after many adventures. Usually a seven-hour trip, it took me thirty-nine hours. Somewhere on the border I lost my baggage, containing all my belongings and the presents I had received in St. Petersburg and elsewhere. After a few days in Paris and London, I finally obtained 'special accommodations' on the S.S. Rochambeau and returned home.
>
> Five years later, much to my astonishment, my trunks arrived in New York, with their contents intact!

After St. Petersburg, it was clear that Lasker was still the world's best player with Capablanca a tad behind him. The third best player was a bit of a surprise: Alekhine! Indeed, these placements were shown to be 100% correct since in 1921 Capablanca finally took the world championship from an aging Lasker, and then it was Alekhine's turn—Capablanca lost the title to Alekhine in 1927.

However, let's not ignore Marshall, who (now in his prime) was not good enough to beat the three chess gods, but did well against just about everyone else. Marshall's excellent result in St. Petersburg proved that Marshall was (depending on his form, which came and went) between fourth and eighth in the world. This was proven in the very strong Mannheim event:

DSB-19 Kongress, Mannheim (1914): Alekhine dominated with 9½-1½. Vidmar and Spielmann tied for second/third, and Janowski, Marshall, Réti, and Breyer all tying for fourth/seventh. Other players included: Bogoljubov, Tarrasch, Duras, Tartakower, and Mieses.

1 Frank J. Marshall, *My Fifty Years of Chess*. New York: Chess Review, 1942. (Later published under the title *Marshall's Best Games of Chess*.)

Frank Marshall vs. Richard Réti, Mannheim 1914

1.d4 d5 2.c4 e6 3.Nc3 Nf6 4.Bg5 Be7 5.e3 0-0 6.Rc1 Ne4 7.Bxe7 Qxe7 8.cxd5 Nxc3 9.Rxc3 exd5 10.Qc2 c6 11.Nf3 Nd7 12.Bd3 Nf6 13.0-0 Bg4?

13...Ne4, equalized.

14.Ne5 Bh5 15.f4

White is better because his Knight is better than Black's, h7 is being eyed by white's Queen and Bishop, and black's h5-Bishop is in trouble due to h3 followed by g4 and f5.

15...Ne4

The idea is to block white's Bishop and also gets black's Bishop to safety by ...f7-f6 when the h5-Bishop can retreat along the e8-h5 diagonal.

16.Bxe4 dxe4

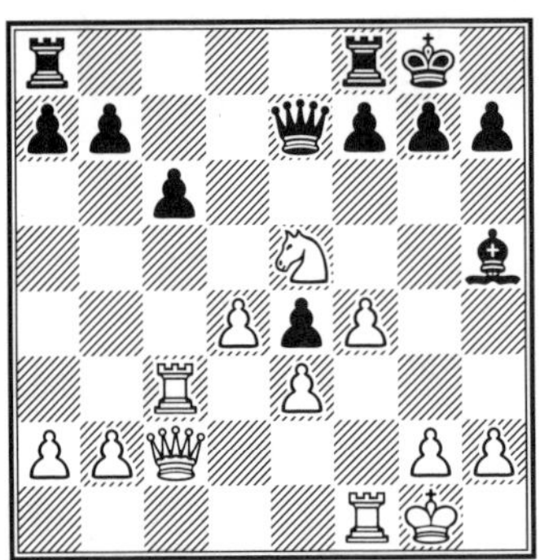

17.g4!

Not 17.Qxe4? f6 18.Qf5 Be2 19.Nd7 Rfd8 20.Re1 Rxd7 21.Rxe2 Rxd4 22.Qc2 Re8 23.h3 Re4 and Black has turned a poor position into a superior one.

17...Bg6

Réti didn't like 17...f6 18.Nxc6 bxc6 19.gxh5.

18.f5 f6 19.Nxg6

Also very good for White is 19.Nxc6 bxc6 20.fxg6 hxg6 21.Rxc6. However, 19.Nxg6 is even stronger.

19...hxg6 20.fxg6 f5 21.gxf5 Qg5+ 22.Qg2 Rxf5 23.Rxf5 Qxf5 24.Rc5 Qf6 25.Rh5 Re8 26.Qg4 Re6 27.Rg5 Rd6 28.h4 Re6 29.h5

29.Qh5 is another winner: 29...Qf3 30.Qh7+ Kf8 31.Qh8+ Ke7 32.Qxg7+ Kd6 33.Qf7 Rf6 34.Qxf6+! Qxf6 35.g7, and White wins.

29...Re8 30.Rf5 Qe6 31.Rf4 Qd5 32.Qf5, 1-0.

Perfect play by Marshall.

A Radical Change

Marshall played quite a bit in 1915, but mostly in the United States: the War made travel difficult and he opened the Marshall Chess Club in New York!

With new responsibilities and an inability to take the time to travel to Europe, it's logical that his chess would lose a bit of his strength. That wasn't the case. Marshall still had his attacking flare and was extremely hard to beat.

The New York National tournament was a great example. Capablanca took first and Marshall second (both were undefeated). The third and fourth places (Chajes and Kupchik) were five points behind Marshall! Capa and Marshall were so far ahead of the other players that the name of the event should have been changed to, "The Two Foxes in a Henhouse Tournament."

Here are two examples:

Einar Michelsen vs. Frank Marshall, New York National 1915

1.e4 e5 2.Nf3 Nf6

It's amazing how Marshall used this opening, which is usually thought of a drawing weapon, as a weapon of destruction.

3.Nxe5 d6 4.Nf3 Nxe4 5.d4 d5 6.Bd3 Bd6 7.0-0 Bg4 8.Qe2 f5 9.c4?

Marshall recommend 9.h3 Bh5 (Black is fine after 9...Bxf3! 10.Qxf3 [10. gxf3?! 0-0 11.fxe4 fxe4 12.Bb5 Rf3 would make Marshall very happy.] 10...0-0, =) 10.g4, which favors White.

9...Nc6! 10.cxd5

10.c5 Nxd4.

10...Nxd4 11.Qe3 Nxf3+

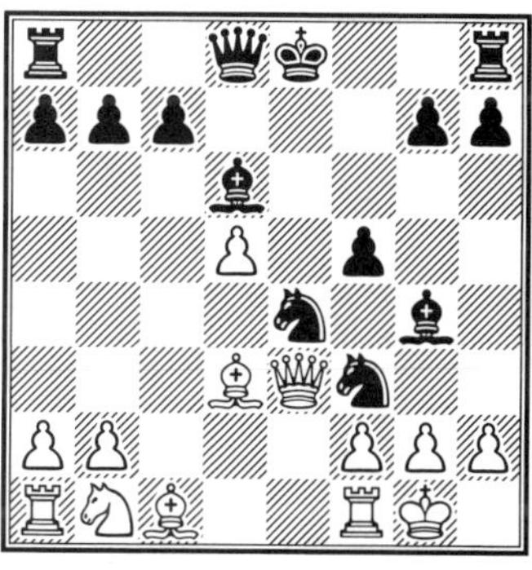

12.gxf3 Qh4 13.Re1 Qxh2+

One of many crushing moves: 13...0-0, 13...Bxh2+, 13...Qh3, etc.

14.Kf1 Bc5

Winning white's Queen and the game.

15.fxg4 Bxe3 16.Bxe3 Qh3+ 17.Ke2 Qxg4+ 18.Kf1 0-0 19.Nd2 Nxd2+ 20.Bxd2 Qh3+ 21.Ke2 Rae8+ 22.Be3 f4 23.Rh1 Rxe3+, 0-1.

Frank Marshall vs. Jacob Bernstein, New York National 1915

1.d4 d5 2.c4 e6 3.Nc3 Nf6 4.Bg5 Nbd7 5.e3 Be7 6.Nf3 0-0 7.Rc1 c6 8.a3 Ne4 9.Bf4 Qa5 10.Bd3 Nxc3 11.Rxc3 dxc4 12.Bxc4 Bxa3 13.0-0 Be7 14.e4 Qh5 15.Qc2 Qg4 16.Bc1 Qg6 17.Ne5 Nxe5 18.dxe5 Qh5 19.f4 f6 20.Rh3 Qg6 21.f5 Qe8 22.exf6 Bxf6 23.e5 Bxe5 24.Qe4 Bd6 25.Qh4 h5

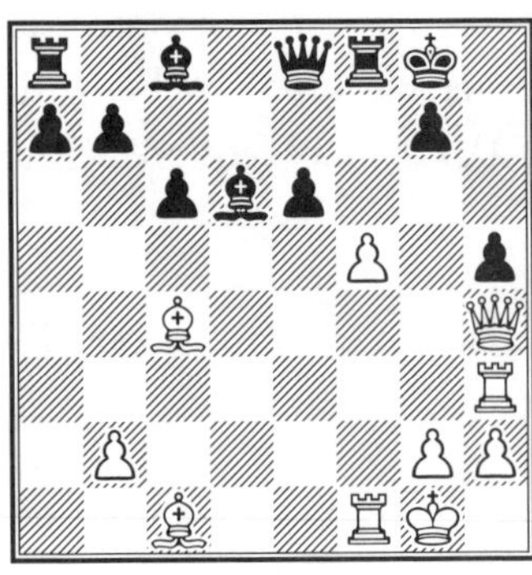

26.Qe4

26.f6! was even stronger.

26...Rb8 27.fxe6 Rxf1+ 28.Kxf1 b5 29.Bb3 c5 30.Bd5

30.Rxh5 Qxh5 31.e7+ was another way to execute his opponent.

30...Be7 31.Qf5, 1-0.

New York (1916-1917): This was a quiet time for Marshall and he rarely played. He did sneak in an eight game match against Janowski—he won decisively with a 5½-2½ score.

David Janowski vs. Frank Marshall, New York match (7) 1916

1.d4 d5 2.Bf4 c5 3.e3 Nc6 4.c3 e6 5.Nd2 Bd6 6.Bg3 f5 7.Ngf3 Nf6 8.Ne5 0-0 9.f4 Bxe5 10.fxe5 Ne4 11.Nxe4 fxe4 12.Qg4 cxd4

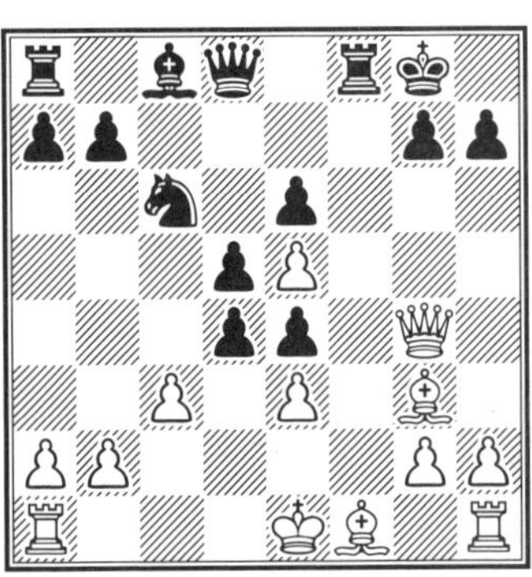

13.exd4 Nxd4! 14.cxd4 Qa5+ 15.Kd1

15.Ke2 Qb4 16.Rb1 Qxd4 17.Ke1 Qb4+ 18.Ke2 Bd7.

15...Bd7 16.Qe2 Ba4+ 17.Kc1

17.b3 Bxb3+ 18.axb3 Qxa1+.

17...Rac8+ 18.Kb1 Rxf1+ 19.Rxf1 Bb5 20.Qd1 Bd3+

Winning white's Queen and the game. The rest was:

21.Qxd3 exd3 22.a4 Rc2 23.Bf4 Qb4 24.Bc1 Rxg2 25.Ra3 d2, 0-1.

The Quiet Years (1919-1923)

These years went by with few tournaments played: 1919 wasn't even on the map, and 1920 offered one small tournament (Atlantic City, which he won) and a few games in the Metropolitan Chess League. Was he more or less retired from international play?

The view that Marshall was done continued through 1921 and 1922—he only sat down at the chessboard during a game at the Metropolitan Chess League.

The next year, 1923 was "do-it-or-die" time for Marshall. The Metropolitan Chess League games were dragging him down due to the poor competition, he was forty-five years of age and had owned the U.S. Championship for fourteen years, and Edward Lasker (age thirty-seven) wanted a match for the title. Arguments about the match for the U.S. Championship got heated, and Edward Lasker and Marshall became enemies. In the end they agreed to the match (animosity and all).

The match was played in New York, Chicago, Milwaukee, Cleveland, Detroit, Cincinnati, Baltimore, Washington, and Long Island. Marshall, no doubt out of form, lost the first two games, but after that his play improved and he managed to win the match, 9½-8½.

Zipping ahead a bit: In 1926 Edward Lasker and Marshall (still enemies) both played in the same tournament. Edward Lasker won a last-round game which enabled Marshall to win the tournament. Marshall gave the following speech:

> Ladies and gentlemen, I want to state publicly that I owe first place in this tournament to Edward Lasker. We had a misunderstanding during our match for the U.S. Championship and we have not been on speaking terms since then. I did not think he would try to defeat Torre and in that way make me come out first. He proved himself a true sportsman, and I want to express my gratitude.

Frank Marshall vs. Edward Lasker, U.S. Championship (4) 1923

1.d4 d5 2.Nf3 e6 3.c4 c5 4.cxd5 exd5 5.Nc3 Nc6 6.g3 Nf6 7.Bg2 Be6 8.0-0 Be7 9.dxc5 Bxc5 10.Bg5 d4 11.Bxf6 Qxf6 12.Ne4 Qe7 13.Nxc5 Qxc5 14.Rc1 Qb6 15.Ng5 Bf5 16.e4

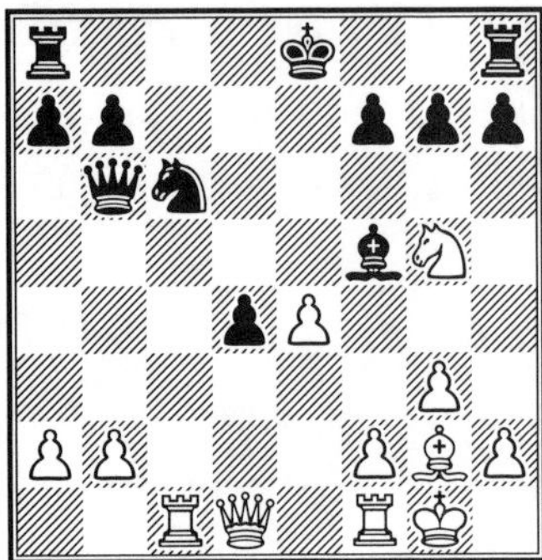

Taking advantage of black's King still being in the center.

16...dxe3??

Tempting but fatal. Black should have played 16...Bg6. One line: 17.h4! (17.f4 0-0 18.e5 d3+ 19.Kh1 h6 20.Ne4 Bxe4 21.Bxe4 Rad8, =) 17...h6 18.h5 hxg5 19.hxg6 and white's a bit better in a sharp position.

17.Rxc6! bxc6 18.Qd6 Bd7 19.Qe5+ Kf8 20.fxe3 f6 21.Rxf6+!

Marshall must have loved this, and it must have made him

feel that he was once again the "man," his opponent sprayed with his own blood. I wouldn't be surprised if, after 21.Rxf6+, he screamed, "I'm back!"

21...gxf6 22.Qxf6+ Ke8 23.Qxh8+ Ke7 24.Qe5+ Kd8 25.h4

25.Nf7+ was more accurate, but 25.h4 is also winning.

25...Kc8 26.Nf7 a5 27.Nd6+ Kb8 28.Nb5+ Kb7 29.Nd6+ Kb8

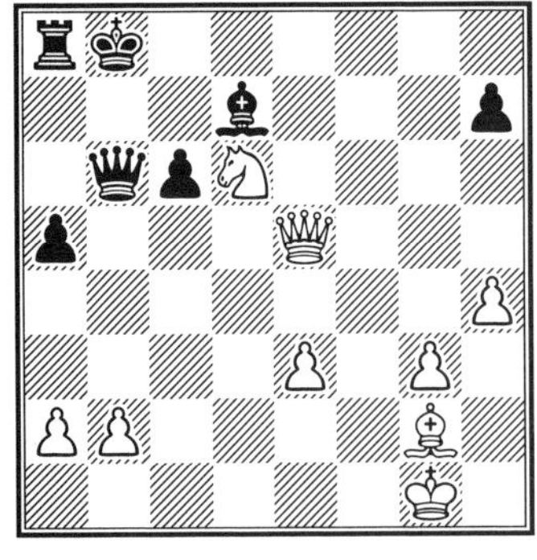

30.Qe7

Missing the flashy 30.Nc4+ Qc7 31.Nb6!

30...Qc7 31.Qf8+ Ka7 32.Nb5+ Kb6 33.Qxa8 Kxb5 34.Bf1+ Kb4 35.Qf8+ c5 36.Qg7 c4 37.Kh2 Qc6 38.Qc3+ Kb5 39.Qb3+, 1-0.

Lake Hopatcong (1923): Marshall (though he was undefeated) tied for first/second with Kupchik. Janowski was third.

Here's Marshall's favorite game from this event.

Abraham Kupchik vs. Frank Marshall, Lake Hopatcong 1923

1.d4 d5 2.Nf3 e6 3.c4 Nf6 4.Nc3 Bb4 5.Qb3 c5 6.cxd5 exd5 7.dxc5 Nc6 8.Bd2 Be6 9.Ng5 0-0 10.e3 Nd7 11.Nxe6 fxe6 12.Bb5 Nxc5 13.Qd1 d4!

White's opening was a disaster!

14.exd4 Nxd4 15.Bc4 Qh4 16.0-0 Rad8

A strong move, though even better was 16...Nf3+ 17.gxf3 Qxc4.

17.Be2 Bxc3 18.bxc3 Ne4! 19.cxd4 Rxd4

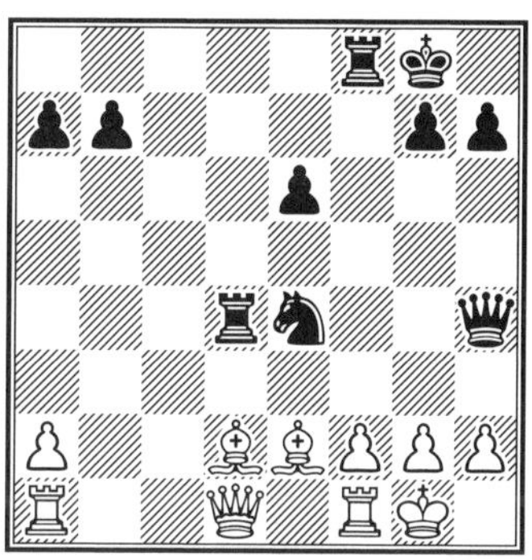

20.Qb3??

20.Bg5! was the only way to fight back: 20...Nxg5 21.Qb3 when after 21...Rd2 Black only has a small advantage.

20...Nxd2 21Qxe6+ Kh8 22.g3 Qe4 23.Qxe4 Rxe4

White loses material by force.

24.Bd3 Rd4 25.Bc2 Nxf1 26.Rxf1 b5 27 Kg2 Rd2 28.Bb3 a5 29.a4 Rb2 30.Bd1 Rb1 31.axb5 Rd8 32.Bg4 Rxf1 33.Kxf1 a4 34.b6 Rb8, 0-1.

New York (1924)

After his tournament and match victories in 1923, Marshall was getting closer and closer to his old form. The timing was perfect since the Manhattan Chess Club organized one of the greatest events ever: New York 1924.

The question for Marshall was: "Can I still hold my own with the big boys? Can I still play against the highest competition?"

The players: Capablanca, Emanuel Lasker, Alekhine, Bogoljubov, Maróczy, Réti, Tartakower, Janowski, Edward Lasker, Yates, and (of course) Marshall.

Marshall started off poorly; he drew his first two games (against Réti and Tartakower), lost to Bogoljubov, drew with Yates, and lost to Maróczy. Many play-

[top] U.S. team to the 1937 Olympiad: Fritz Brieger (who accompanied the team), Sammy Reshevsky, Isaac Kashdan, I. A. Horowitz, Reuben Fine, and Frank Marshall, the team won Gold; Frank Marshall. (Photos: Courtesy of the Marshall Chess Club.)

Marshall vs. Richard Réti (Photo: Courtesy of the Cleveland Public Library's John G. White Collection).

ers would psychologically collapse at this point, but Marshall always believed in himself and, suddenly, his skills came back and he was, once again, Marshall. He drew Alekhine (a very hard opponent for Marshall and his draw must have given him confidence); beat up Janowski; drew Emanuel Lasker (Lasker was on the ropes and only his famous defensive skill deprived Marshall of a glorious victory); drew Capablanca; and took down Edward Lasker.

The first half of the tournament was over and Marshall had turned a minus-two into an even score. Now he needed to show his stuff in the second round: he beat Janowski again; had a small setback by losing to Tartakower; showed his resilience by beating Réti (finally a plus score!); drew Capablanca again; drew Edward Lasker; got revenge by smashing Bogoljubov (plus two!); drew Maróczy; drew Alekhine again; beat Yates (plus 3); and ended with a thud when Emanuel Lasker outplayed him (back to plus 2 for Marshall).

The fifty-six-year-old Emanuel Lasker was clear first, 1½ points (with an amazing plus 12!) ahead of Capablanca, who was second. Alekhine came in third and, once again, Marshall showed that he was the real deal by coming in fourth. Réti was fifth, Maróczy sixth, Bogoljubov seventh, Tartakower eughth, Yates ninth, Edward Lasker tenth, and poor old Janowski last.

Richard Réti vs. Frank Marshall, New York 1924

1.Nf3 Nf6 2.c4 d5 3.cxd5 Nxd5 4.d4 Bf5 5.Nc3 e6 6.Qb3 Nc6 7.e4 Nxc3 8.exf5 Nd5

Marshall's opening is designed to take away Réti's positional skills while creating dynamics for his own pieces. It might not be fully sound, but Marshall dared his opponent to swim in the American's chaotic waters.

9.Bb5?!

9.Qxb7 (9.Bd2! seems to be the best bet to get an advantage.) 9...Bb4+ 10.Kd1 Nde7 11.fxe6 fxe6 12.Qb5 Rb8 13.Qc4 Qd7 14.Be3 0-0 with chances for both sides.

9...Bb4+ 10.Bd2 Bxd2+ 11.Nxd2 exf5 12.Bxc6+ bxc6 13.0-0 0-0 14.Qa4 Rb8 15.Nb3 Rb6 16.Qxa7 Qg5

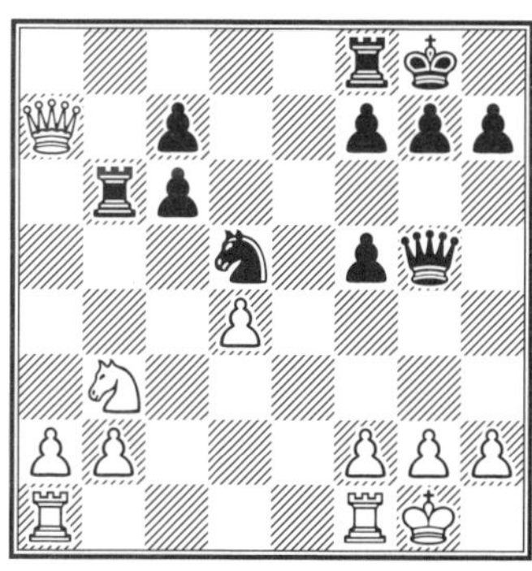

Marshall is in his element!

17.Qa5 c5 18.Qxc5 Nf4 19.g3 Rh6?!

Marshall should have played 19...Ne2+ which wins after 20.Kg2 Rh6.

20.Qxc7?

20.Qc2 was White's only chance to survive.

20...Ne2+

The rest is a slaughter.

21.Kg2 Qg4 22.Rh1 f4 23.f3 Qh3+ 24.Kf2 Rc8 25.Qa5 Nxg3 26.Rhg1 Qxh2+ 27.Rg2 Qh4 28.Rc1 Re8 29.Qb5 Ne4+ 30.Kf1 Qh1+, 0-1.

Frank Marshall vs. Efim Bogoljubov, New York 1924

1.d4 Nf6 2.Nf3 e6 3.Bg5 d5 4.e3 Nbd7 5.c4 c6 6.cxd5 exd5 7.Nc3 Qa5 8.Bd3 Ne4 9.Qc2 Nxg5 10.Nxg5 h6 11.Nf3 Be7 12.0-0 0-0 13.a3 Qd8 14.Rae1 a5 15.Qe2

Marshall was proud of this move, with the idea of 16.e4 when 16...dxe4 fails to 17.Qxe4 threatening both 18.Qh7 mate and 18.Qxe7. However, 15...Bd6 or 15...Re8 stops the threat and also White's f3-Knight to jump to e5.

I would have preferred 15.e4 dxe4 16.Nxe4 with an edge.

15...Nf6 16.Ne5 Bd6 17.f4

This setup is well-known, but it scared opponents in Marshall's day and it still freaks out players today. Note that, thanks to Black's ...h7-h6, Black can't eventually chase away the e5-Knight with ...f7-f6 since that would leave the g6-square (in fact, the whole b1-h7 diagonal) a great landing post for White's pieces.

17...c5 18.Bb1 Bd7 19.Qc2 Bc6

19...Be6 is better since 20.f5 isn't dangerous: The e5-square is weakened and the pawn on f5 also blocks the b1-h7 diagonal.

20.dxc5 Bxc5 21.Kh1

21.Ng4 looks very strong but Black survives after 21...Re8 22.Nxf6+ Qxf6 23.Qh7+ Kf8.

21...Re8

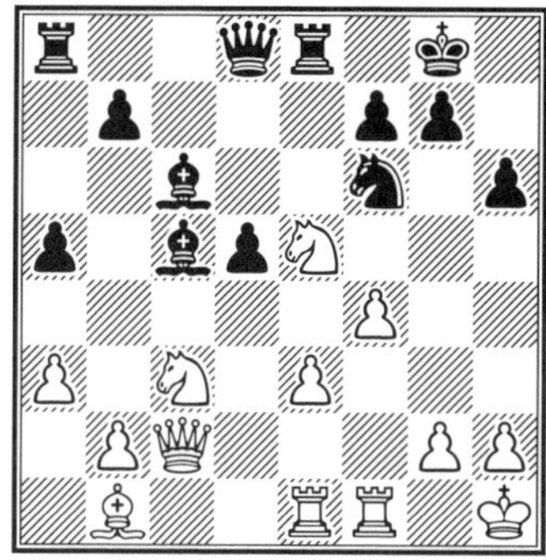

22.e4!

Excellent!

22...Bd4

If White played 22...dxe4 white's Bishop might, in some situations, move to a2 where it hits f7. However, the main line would have been 22...dxe4 23.Nxc6 bxc6 24.Nxe4 Nxe4 25.Rxe4 Rxe5 26.Qxe4 g6 27.f5 and Black is in trouble.

23.Nxc6 bxc6 24.e5 Ng4 25.Qh7+ Kf8 26.g3 Qb6 27.Bf5 Nf2+ 28.Rxf2 Bxf2 29.Qh8+ Ke7 30.Qxg7

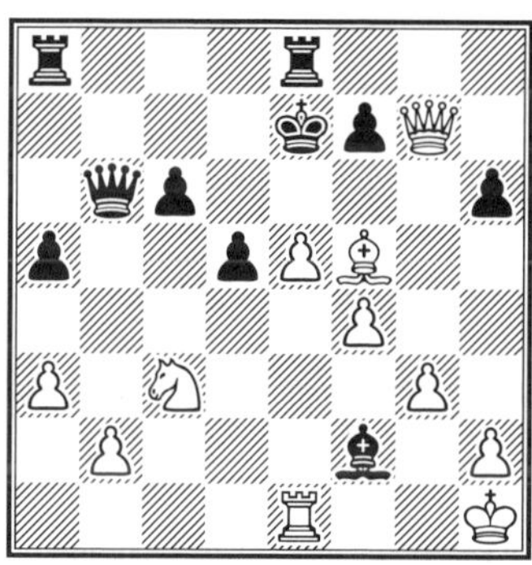

30...Kd8

30...Bxe1? 31.Qf6+ Kf8 32.Qxh6+ Kg8 (32...Ke7 33.Qd6 mate) 33.Bh7+ Kh8 34.Bg6+ Kg8 35.Qh7+ Kf8 36.Qxf7 mate.

31.Qf6+ Re7 32.e6

Another killer move was 32.Qxh6 (threatening Qf8+) 32...Bxe1 33.Nxd5!

32...Bd4 33.exf7 Bxf6 34.f8=Q+ Kc7 35.Rxe7+ Bxe7 36.Qxa8 Kd6 37.Qh8 Qd8 38.Qe5+ Kc5 39.Na4+ Kc4 40.Qc3+ Kb5 41.Bd3+ Kxa4 42.Qc2, 1-0.

New York 1924 rejuvenated his chess-lust. All of a sudden he was back and starving for strong events!

Baden-Baden (1925): A huge tournament, there were twenty-one players. Alekhine was first (1½ points ahead of the field), Rubinstein second, Sämisch third, Bogoljubov fourth, and Tartakower and Marshall fifth/sixth. Others included: Rabinovich, Grünfeld, Nimzowitsch, Torre, Réti, Spielmann, Tarrasch, Mieses.

Marshall once again showed he was hard to beat. His only loses were against Alekhine and Réti. His victims included Sämisch, Bogoljubov, and Tarrasch.

Frank Marshall vs. Ilya Rabinovich, Baden-Baden 1925

1.d4 d5 2.c4 c6 3.Nc3 Nf6 4.e3 e6 5.Qc2 Bd6 6.f4 0-0 7.Nf3 c5 8.Bd3 Nc6 9.a3 a6 10.b3 b6 11.0-0 dxc4 12.bxc4 cxd4 13.Ne4 Bc5 14.Kh1 h6 15.Nxf6+ Qxf6 16.Bb2

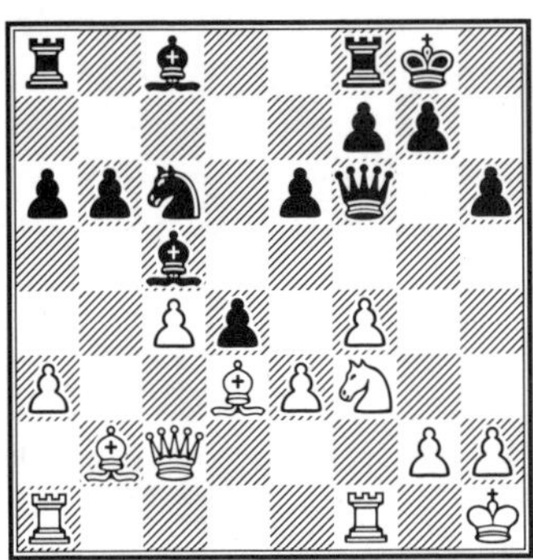

16...Bb7 17.Be4 d3 18.Bxd3 Qe7 19.Qc3 f6 20.Rae1 Rfd8 21.Bb1 Rd7 22.Qc2 f5 23.e4! Rf8 24.exf5 Rxf5 25.g4 Rxf4 26.Qh7+ Kf8 27.Bg6 Qf7

27...Qd6 28.Qh8+ Ke7 29.Qe8 mate.

28.Qh8+ Qg8 29.Rxe6, 1-0.

Marienbad (1925): Aron Nimzowitsch (Marshall beat him) and Akiba Rubinstein tied for first/second, with Marshall tying for third/fourth with Torre. I should add that Marshall was the only player who was undefeated! Others included: Tartakower, Réti, Spielmann, Grünfeld, Sämisch, and Janowski.

Having no fear, and wanting European blood, Marshall cracked open the Wing Gambit!

Frank Marshall vs. August Haida, Marienbad 1925

1.e4 c5 2.b4 cxb4 3.a3 e6 4.axb4 Bxb4 5.c3 Be7 6.d4 d6 7.f4 f5 8.Nd2 Nf6 9.Bd3 0-0 10.Ngf3 Nc6 11.0-0 a6 12.exf5 exf5 13.d5 Nxd5 14.Bc4 Qb6+ 15.Kh1 Be6 16.Rb1

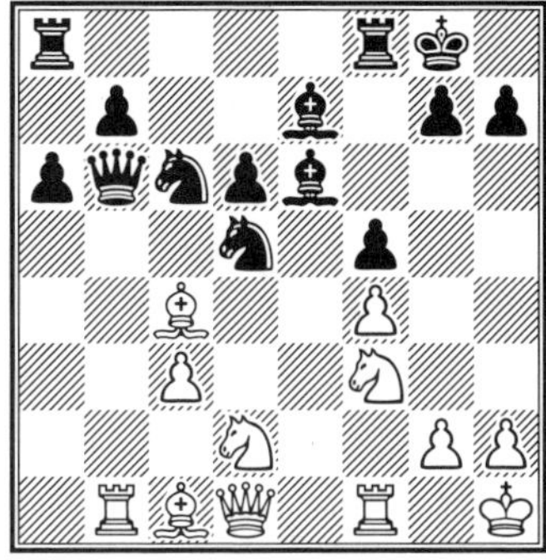

16...Qc7 17.Nb3 Nxf4 18.Bxe6+ Nxe6 19.Qd5 Ncd8 20.Nbd4 Rf6 21.Re1 Qc8 22.Nxe6 Nxe6 23.Nd4 Kf7 24.Rxb7 Qc5 25.Rxe7+ Kxe7 26.Qb7+ Kf8 27.Qxa8+ Kf7 28.Qb7+ Kg6 29.Nxe6 Rxe6 30.Rxe6+, 1-0.

Moscow (1925): A famous tournament (twenty-one players) and Bogoljubov's greatest victory. Efim Bogoljubov first, Emanuel Lasker second (at fifty-seven years old!), José Capablanca third, and Marshall fourth. Others included: Tartakower, Torre, Réti, Romanovsky, Grünfeld, Spielmann, and Rubinstein.

Fedor Duz-Khotimirsky vs. Frank Marshall, Moscow 1925

1.d4 d5 2.Nf3 Nf6 3.c4 e6 4.Nc3 Bb4 5.e3 0-0 6.Bd2 c5 7.Rc1 cxd4 8.Nxd4 e5 9.Nc2 Bxc3 10.Bxc3 Nc6 11.Nb4 Bg4 12.Qd3 12...d4 13.Nxc6 bxc6 14.exd4 exd4 15.Bxd4 Ne4! 16.a3

16.Qxe4 Re8 17.Be5 Qa5+.

16...Re8 17.Be3 Qf6

17...Qh4 also wins.

18.Be2

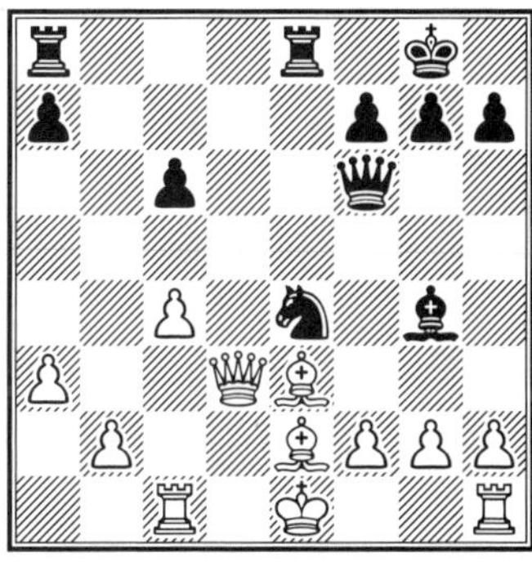

18...Nxf2! 19.Qc1 Nxh1 20.Qxf6 gxf6 21.Bxg4 Rxe3+ 22.Kf1 Rd8 23.Bf3 Rd2 24.Bxc6 Nf2 25.b4 Rxa3 26.c5 Nd3 27.Rb1 Nxb4 28.Be4 Rc3, 0-1.

Re-Living the Good Old Days

Hermann Hesse's fantastic novel, *Narcissus and Goldmund*, reminds me a bit of Marshall: In the novel (placed in the fourteenth century) Goldmund became a wanderer hoping to find who he really is. Marshall was also a wanderer. At the end of the book, an aged Goldmund decides to relive his adventures one more time, but things were not the same and Goldmund dies. Marshall, whose comeback in 1924 and 1925 was amazing, was luckier than Goldmund.

Sadly, nothing lasts. The forty-nine-year-old Marshall started his ups and downs in 1926 and, like every sportsman, you eventually becomes all used up and there are mainly only downs. It's up to every player to decide when that moment has arrived.

New York Dimock (1926): Four players, two games against each other, Marshall came in tied for first/second, but the competition wasn't very good.

Lake Hopatcong (1926): Five players, two games against each other, Marshall came in fourth, winning just one game and losing three.

Chicago (1926): Marshall was clear first, ahead of Torre, Maróczy, Kupchik, Jaffe, Kashdan, and others.

None of those 1926 tournaments were the "super events" that Marshall reveled in.

New York (1927): This was a super tournament (six players, all play each other four times), and Marshall, for the first time since he became a top player, came in last. Capablanca came in first, Alekhine second, Nimzowitsch third, Vidmar fourth, Spielmann fifth, and Marshall at the end. Out of twenty games, Marshall managed to win just one game (against Vidmar).

London British Empire Club (1927): Nimzowitsch and Tartakower tied for first/second, Marshall did well here, coming in third (once again he was the only player who didn't lose a game). Fourth was Vidmar, and Bogoljubov was fifth.

Bad Kissingen (1928): Twelve players, very good competition: Bogoljubov first, Capablanca second, Euwe third, Rubinstein fourth, Nimzowitsch fifth, Réti sixth, Tartakower seventh, Marshall eighth, Yates ninth, Spielmann tenth (Spielmann beat Capablanca), Tarrasch eleventh, and Mieses twelfth.

Brno (1928): Marshall came in fourth behind first place Sämisch, Réti second, and Kmoch third. Not a particularly strong tournament, the Marshall of 1924 and 1925 would probably have won it.

Budapest (1928): Capablanca first, Marshall second, Spielmann third, and the rest of the players were not in the same class.

Berlin (1928): Tageblatt, a very strong tournament, and another last place. Capablanca first, Nimzowitsch second, Spielmann third, Tartakower fourth, Rubinstein fifth, Réti sixth, and Marshall seventh.

Hastings (1928): A weak group, Colle, Marshall, and Takács all tied for first/third.

Bradley Beach (1929): Alekhine wiped out the others with eight wins, one draw, no losses. Marshall would have taken second place in his better days, but now he could only come in sixth. Second was Lajos Steiner, Kupchik third, Turover fourth, Fox fifth, Kevitz seventh, Herman Steiner eighth, Cintron ninth, and Bigelow tenth.

Karlsbad (1929): To me, this was the tournament that screamed, "Don't let Marshall play in top tournaments anymore!" Nimzowitsch first, Capablanca and Spielmann second/third (Spielmann beat Capablanca again), Rubinstein fourth, Becker, Vidmar, and Euwe fifth/seventh, Bogoljubov eighth, Grünfeld ninth, Canal and Matisons tenth/eleventh, Tartkower, Maróczy, Colle and Treybal twelfth/fifteenth, Sämisch and Yates sixteenth/seventeenth, Johner and Marshall eighteenth/nineteenth, Gilg twentieth, Thomas twenty-first, and Menchik twenty-second.

Liege (1930): Tartakower first, Sultan Khan second, Nimzowitsch, Ahues, and Colle third/fifth, Przepiórka sixth, Rubinstein, Soultanbeieff, and Weenink seventh/ninth, Thomas tenth, Marshall eleventh, and Pleci twelfth.

Although older players tend to crash, they also have moments when that old magic rears its head. This next game reminds us just how good Marshall was.

Frank Marshall vs. Aron Nimzowitsch, Liege 1930

1.d4 Nf6 2.Nf3 b6 3.e3 Bb7 4.Bd3 c5 5.0-0 e6 6.c4 Bxf3 7.Qxf3 Nc6 8.dxc5 Bxc5 9.Nc3 0-0 10.Rd1 Qc7 11.b3 Ne5 12.Qg3 Nh5 13.Nb5 Qb8 14.Qh4 g6 15.Be2 Ng7 16.Bb2 f5

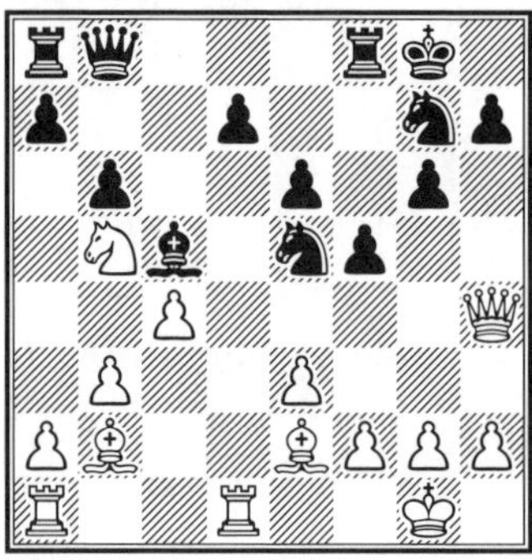

17.b4!

Forcing Black's dark-squared Bishop off of the g1-a7 diagonal for awhile.

17...Bxb4 18.f4 Nf7 19.Rxd7 g5 20.fxg5

Also good was 20.Qxg5.

20...Bc5 21.Nc7

21.Bxg7 and 21.g6 were also winning.

21...Bxe3+ 22.Kh1 e5

22...Qc8 23.Qh6! Nxh6 24.Rxg7+ Kh8 25.Rg6+ Bd4 26.Bxd4+ e5 27.Bxe5+ Rf6 28.Bxf6 mate.

23.Bc1!

Best, though many other moves would also get the job done.

23...Bxc1 24.Rxc1 Nh8 25.c5!, 1-0.

The threat of 26.Bc4+ is too much for Black to handle.

After Liege 1930, Marshall decided that the time was right to quit tournaments. However, he didn't completely step away from competitive chess! Instead, he still played in the Metropolitan Chess League and was a serious factor in four chess Olympiads:

Marshall was the only player on all four gold-medal winning U.S. teams of the 1930s (1931,1933,1935, 1937) who had a life time score of 67%. He won individual gold on board two in 1933. What is most impressive is Marshall did all this while in his fifties! He turned sixty during the 1937 Olympiad in Stockholm.

The U.S. was leading Czechoslovakia in the last round of the 1933 Olympiad held in Folkestone, England, by 2½ points but almost lost to their rival 4-0 in the last round. Around move eighteen Simonson and Kashdan had already lost and Fine was in trouble.

Marshall's position (against Karel Treybal, who in 1941 was arrested by the Gestapo and executed for illegal possession of firearms) was no better, but he saved the day by winning that very critical game.

In 1936, after holding the U.S. Championship title for twenty-seven years, he relinquished it to the winner of a championship tournament (Samuel Reshevsky). The first such tournament was sponsored by the National Chess Federation and held in New York. The Marshall Chess Club donated the trophy.

I'll end with a hilarious offhand game Marshall played in 1940:

Frank Marshall vs. Hyman Rogosin, New York 1940

1.e4 c5 2.b4 cxb4 3.a3 Nc6 4.axb4 Nf6 5.b5 Nd4 6.c3 Ne6 7.e5 Ndf4 8.c4 Ndf4 9.g3 Ng6 10.f4 Ngxf4 11.gxf4 Nxf4 12.d4 Ng6 13.h4 e6 14.h5

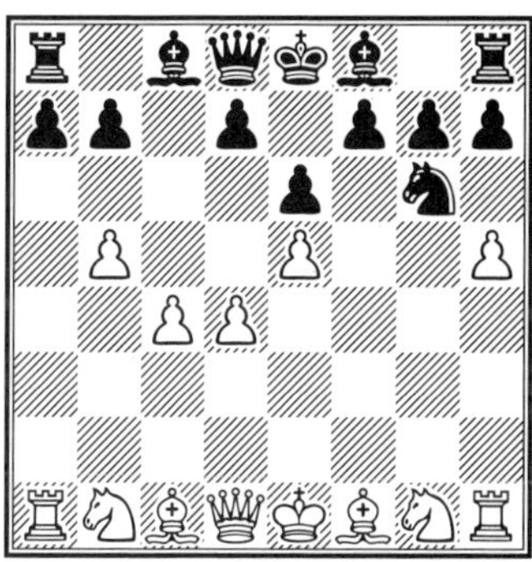

14...Bb4+

Fourteen moves have gone by and White has only moved pawns!

15.Bd2 Bxd2+ 16.Nxd2 Ne7 17.Ne4 Nf5 18.h6 g6 19.Nf6+ Kf8 20.Nf3 d6 21.Ng5 dxe5 22.dxe5 Qxd1+ 23.Rxd1 Ke7 24.Rh3 b6 25.Bg2 Rb8 26.Ngxh7 (26.Rhd3 is mate in 7), 1-0.

Marshall died in 1944 having lived as he wanted. He had traveled the globe and saw things and had experiences rare for a person of that time. He was loved by his fans, and although his death marked the end of an era, his chess games live on to this day, enjoyed by young and old alike as they marvel at Marshall's genius.

8

RUDOLF SPIELMANN

The Lethal Gentleman

Rudolf Spielmann was born in Vienna on May 5, 1883, and he learned how to play chess at a very young age. Richard Réti, in his classic book *Masters of the Chessboard*,[1] wrote:

> [Spielmann] learned to play while still a boy and was exhibited in public as a prodigy, but in spite of that he later became a great master.

Spielmann earned a degree in law, but never practiced it—he was addicted, body and soul, to chess, and he very much wanted to devote his life to the game.

1 Richard Réti, *Masters of the Chessboard*. Milford, CT: Russell Enterprises, Inc., 2011.

However, it wasn't just chess that attracted him, but rather *attacking* chess! His life-blood was gambits, vicious assaults against the enemy King, and shocking combinations that left the audience (and the defeated opponent) gasping in awe.

The first tournament Spielmann played in was the Berlin City Championship 1903/04. He did quite well (tied for second/third with Ossip Bernstein; Horatio Caro was first), and after that he played often. The fact that Spielmann learned how to play early in life explains why he was so strong in his very first events.

Here's are two game from that initial tournament:

Alfred Wagner vs. Rudolf Spielmann, Berlin City Championship 1903

1.d4 d5 2.c4 c6 3.Nf3 e6 4.Nc3 f5 5.Bf4 Nf6 6.e3 Bd6 7.Bxd6 Qxd6 8.c5 Qe7 9.Ne5 Nbd7 10.Nxd7 Bxd7 11.Bd3 e5

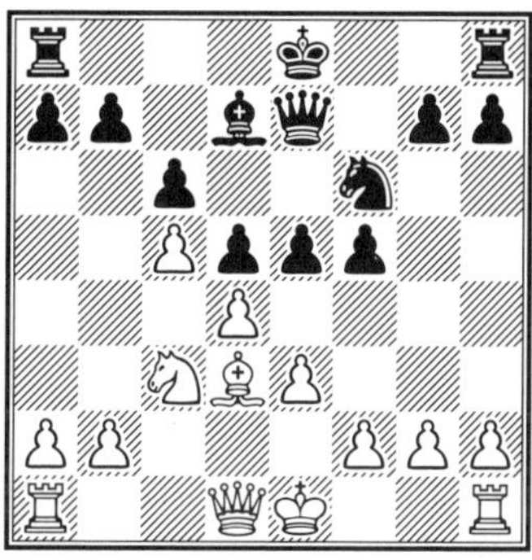

12.0-0 0-0 13.dxe5 Ng4 14.h3 Nxe5 15.Na4 f4 16.exf4 Rxf4 17.Re1 Re8 18.Re3 Qh4 19.g3 Qg5 20.Bf1 d4 21.Re2 d3 22.Re3 Rxf2 23.Kxf2 Rf8+ 24.Kg2 Qxe3 25.Qe1 Qd4 26.Nc3 Nf3, 0-1.

Rudolf Spielmann vs. Moisei Elyashiv, Munich 1903

1.e4 e5 2.f4 exf4 3.Nf3 g5 4.h4 g4 5.Ng5 h6 6.Nxf7 Kxf7 7.Bc4+ d5 8.Bxd5+ Kg7 9.d4 Qf6 10.e5 Qg6 11.h5 Qf5 12.Nc3 Bb4 13.0-0 f3 14.Ne4 Qxh5 15.Ng3 Qh4

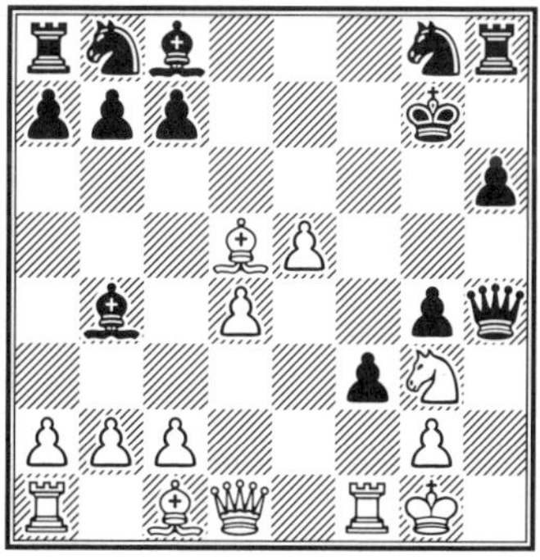

16.Rxf3!! gxf3 17.Qxf3 Nf6

There's no other defense: 17...Qxd4+ 18.Be3 and it's over.

18.exf6+ Kf8

18...Qxf6 19.Nh5

19.Bf4!!

The position after 18...Kf8 had been reached on a couple of occasions and was considered to be good for Black. In a game between Marco and Schlechter, White played 19.Be3 but after 19...Bd6 20.Nf5 Bh2+ 21.Kf1 Qxf6 Black easily won.

[Spielmann]: "Luckily, perhaps, for me, I did not know either game and therefore confidently and without hesitation, I played 19.Bf4 with the idea of 20.Qe4 and the double threat of 21.Bd6+ and 21.Qg6."

19... Na6

19...Qxf6 20.Bd6+ wins on the spot.

19...Bd6 20.Re1!! Qxf4 21.Qh5 Qxd4+ 22.Kh1 Qxf6 23.Qe8+ Kg7 24.Nh5+ Kh7 25.Nxf6+ Kg7 26.Qf7 mate.

19...Bg4 20.Qe4 Nd7 21.Bd2 Bd6 (21...Bxd2 22.Qe7 mate) 22.Qg6 and Black is dead.

20.Qe4 Qg4 21.Bxb7! Rb8

The actual game went: 21...Bxb7 22.Bxh6+ Rxh6 23.Qxg4 Rh7 24.Qg6 Rf7 25.c3 Bd6 26.Nf5 Be4 27.Qh6+ Kg8 28.Qg5+ Kf8 29.Nh6, 1-0.

21...Qe6 22.Bxa8 Qxe4 23.Nxe4 and White is three pawns ahead.

22.Bxc8!

22.Bxa6 Qe6 23.Bxc7 Qxe4 24.Nxe4 Ra8 25.Bc4 also wins, but 22.Bxc8 is even stronger.

22...Qxc8

22...Rxc8 23.Bxh6+ Rxh6 24.Qxg4.

23.Qg6 Qd7 24.Bxh6+ Rxh6 25.Qxh6+ Kg8 26.Rf1 Qf7 27.Rf4 and Black will be mated.

While Spielmann did exceptionally well in many tournaments, he bombed in others. Réti put it this way:

> With his nervous, and impressionable temperament, he obtains unequal results.

Unequal results indeed! In one event he would come in first or second and play like a world-beater, in the next he would end up in the middle of the field or even worse. Yet, though nobody could guess how he'd end up in any given tournament, they would be sure about one thing: his games would thrill the masses and stir the imagination.

Grandmaster Gideon Ståhlberg in his book, *Chess and Chessmasters*[1] had this to say about Spielmann:

> Ever a Knight *sans peur et sans reproche*," he seemed to love fighting and danger for their own sakes. Spielmann has made an impression that will go down in the annals as unique and of outstanding importance. It was no coincidence that, despite his extremely uneven results, he was one of the most popular of all masters. His intrepid and imaginative play contributed yet another attraction to great tournaments by making these events full of games of fighting interest and colorful content.

Réti, in *Masters of the Chessboard*[2] while discussing the "new romantic style" wrote:

> This appellation is misleading, because, even though it was no longer possible to win success in tournament play by mere technique, after the Steinitz principles were popularized and became common knowledge, the most modern players proceeded to develop the theory more widely and deeply where Steinitz left off. Spielmann, on the other hand, really merits the epithet of a new romantic. For he seeks the salvation of chess in a return to the style of the old masters, of course with the unavoidable retention of the Steinitz principles, which have become a necessary part of technique. His models are Anderssen and Chigorin. Spielmann is the last bard of the gambit game, and what he wanted to revive especially was the King's Gambit.

Here are a few games from his early years:

David Przepiórka vs. Rudolf Spielmann, Barmen Masters 1905

1.e4 e5 2.Nf3 Nc6 3.Bb5 f5 4.d3 fxe4 5.dxe4 Nf6 6.0-0 d6 7.Nc3 Be6 8.Qe2 h6 9.Be3 g5 10.Kh1 Bg7 11.Ng1 0-0 12.Bxc6 bxc6 13.f3 Qe8 14.b3 Qg6 15.g4 Rf7 16.Qg2 Raf8 17.Nge2

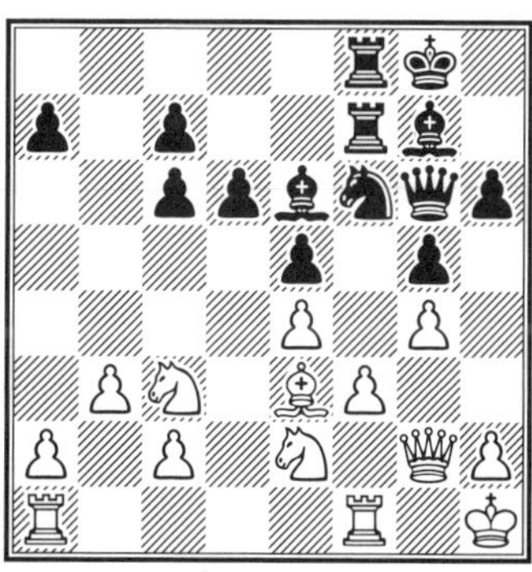

1 Gideon Ståhlberg , trans. Harry Golombek, *Chess and Chess Masters: The Greatest Players of the mid-20th Century*. Edinburgh: Hardinge Simpole, 2002.

2 Richard Réti, *Masters of the Chessboard*. Milford, CT: Russell Enterprises, Inc., 2011.

17...d5 18.Bc5 Rd8 19.Ng3 h5 20.h3 h4 21.Nf5 Bxf5 22.exf5 Qh6 23.Rae1 d4 24.Ne4 Nd5 25.Qd2 Nf4 26.Kh2 Bf8 27.Qa5 d3 28.Rd1 Rd5 29.c4 Bxc5 30.cxd5 Bb6 31.Qa6 cxd5 32.Nf2 Qd6 33.Kh1 e4 34.fxe4 Bxf2 35.Qxd6 cxd6 36.Rxf2 dxe4 37.Rfd2 Re7, 0-1.

Rudolf Spielmann vs. Oldřich Duras, Scheveningen 1905

1.e4 e6 2.d4 d5 3.Nc3 Bb4 4.Bd3 dxe4 5.Bxe4 Nf6 6.Bd3 c5 7.a3 Ba5 8.dxc5 Bxc3+ 9.bxc3 Qa5 10.Ne2 Bd7 11.0-0 Qxc5 12.a4 Bc6 13.Ba3 Qg5 14.f3 Nd5 15.Ng3 Qe3+ 16.Rf2 Nxc3 17.Qf1 Kd8 18.Bb2 Nd5 19.Rd1 Nd7 20.Be4 Qb6 21.Bd4 Qa5 22.c4 N5b6 23.Qd3 Kc8 24.Rb2 Ne5 25.Qe2

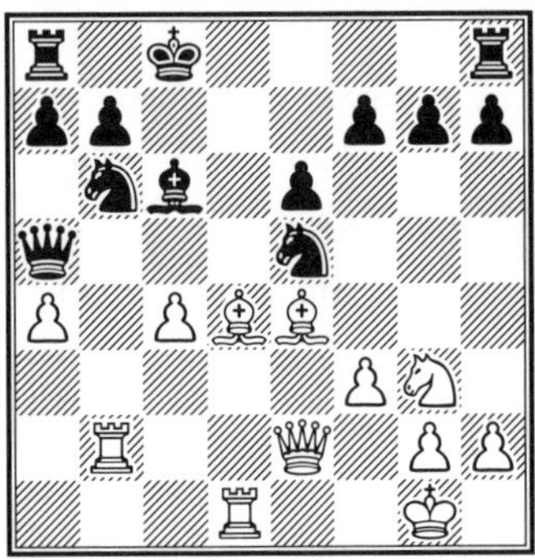

25...Nexc4 26.Rc2 Qb4 27.Rdc1 Na3 28.Rxc6+! bxc6 29.Rxc6+ Kd7 30.Bc5 Qc4 31.Qd2+ Nd5 32.Rd6+ Ke8 33.Bxa3 Rd8 34.Nf5! Qc7 35.Nxg7+ Kf8 36.Rxd8+ Kxg7 37.Qg5, 1-0.

Paul Leonhardt vs. Rudolf Spielmann, Nuremberg 1906

1.e4 e5 2.Nf3 Nc6 3.d4 exd4 4.c3 d5 5.exd5 Qxd5 6.cxd4 Bg4 7.Be2 Nf6 8.Nc3 Qh5 9.0-0 Bd6 10.h3 0-0-0 11.hxg4 Nxg4 12.g3

12.Re1! Nxd4 13.Qxd4 Bh2+ 14.Kf1 Rxd4 15.Nxd4, +=.

12...Qh3! 13.Ne4 Be7!

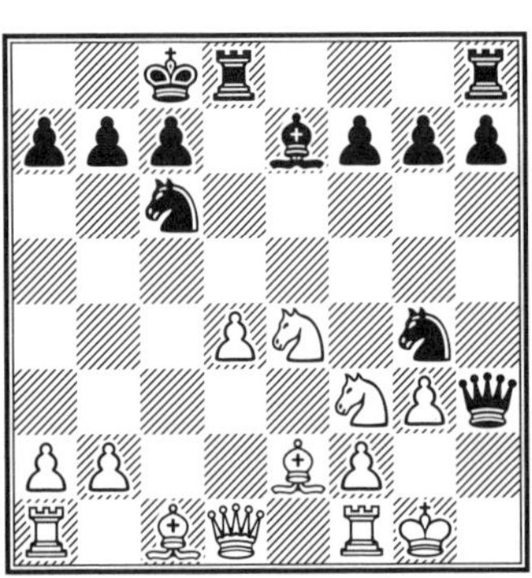

Avoiding 13... Bxg3?? 14.Neg5 Bh2+ 15.Kh1 Qh5 16.Kg2 h6 17.Nh3 Nh3 and Black doesn't have enough compensation.

14.Be3??

- 14.Bf4 loses to 14...Nxd4.
- 14.Re1! seems to draw: 14...Nxd4 15.Bc4 Nxf3+ 16.Qxf3 Qh2+ 17.Kf1 Qh5! 18.Kg2 (18. Ke2?? Rd4! is strong since 19. Bd3 runs into 19...Rxd3!) 18...Qh2+ 19.Kf1 Qh5 , =.

14...Rd5!

Most accurate. The threat of ...Rh5 is crushing. The actual game went 14...f5 15.Ned2 Nxe3 16.fxe3 Qxg3+ 17.Kh1 Rd6 18.Nh2 Rh6 19.Bh5 Bd6 20.Rf4 Bxf4 21.exf4 Qh4, 0-1.

15.Bg5 Nxd4! 16.Re1

16.Qxd4 Rxd4 17.Bxe7 Rxe4 is easy for Black.

16...Rxg5!

Other moves win, but this is by far the strongest and prettiest.

17.Nexg5 Nxf3+ 18.Nxf3 Bc5 19.Rf1 Qxg3+ 20.Kh1 Bxf2 and, after White is done giving away his Queen and other pieces (21.Qd7+), mate will follow.

Rudolf Spielmann vs. Savielly Tartakower, Munich 1909

1.e4 c6 2.d4 d5 3.Nc3 dxe4 4.Nxe4 Nf6 5.Ng3 e5 6.Nf3 exd4 7.Nxd4 Bc5 8.Be3 Qb6 9.Qe2 0-0 10.0-0-0 Nd5 11.Qh5 Nf6 12.Qh4 Bg4 13.Bd3 Bxd1 14.Rxd1 Nbd7 15.Ngf5 Ne5 16.Nxg7!

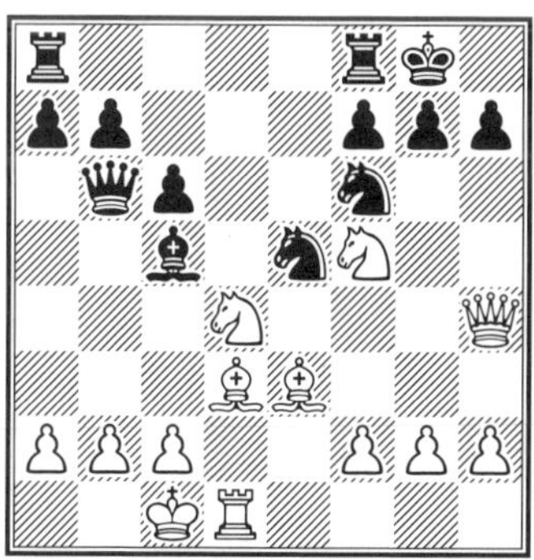

16...Qd8

16...Kxg7 17.Nf5+ Kg8 18.Qxf6 and mates.

17.Ngf5 Ng6 18.Qh6 Ne8 19.Nf3 Bxe3+ 20.fxe3 Qf6 21.Ng5 Qh8 22.Ne7+!, 1-0.

Rudolf Spielmann vs. Jacques Mieses, Regensburg match (8) 1910

1.d4 d5 2.c4 e6 3.Nc3 Nf6 4.Bg5 Nbd7 5.Nf3 c6 6.e3 Qa5 7.Nd2 Bb4 8.Qc2 dxc4 9.Bxf6 Nxf6 10.Nxc4 Qc7 11.Bd3 Bd7 12.a3 Bd6 13.e4 e5 14.f4 exd4 15.e5 Bf8 16.exf6 dxc3 17.Qe2+ Kd8 18.0-0-0 Qxf4+ 19.Kb1 Kc7 20.Rhf1 Qg5 21.h4

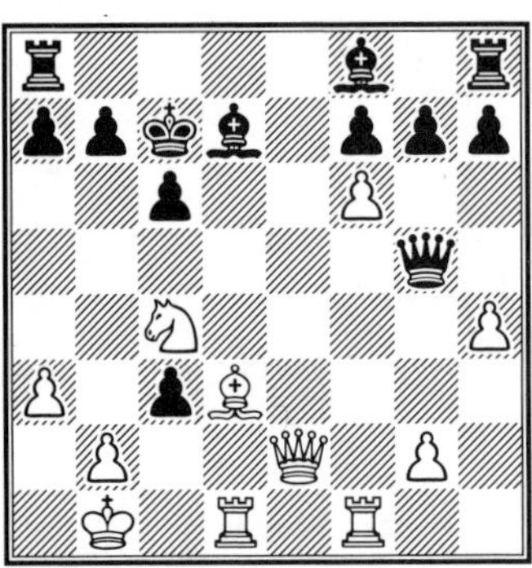

21...Qc5 22.fxg7 Bxg7 23.Rxf7 Bd4 24.Rxd7+ Kxd7 25.Qg4+ Kc7 26.Qf4+ Be5 27.Nxe5 Raf8 28.Qh2 Qf2 29.Bc2 Rhg8 30.Rd7+ Kb6 31.Nc4+ Ka6 32.Qc7 Qf1+ 33.Ka2 Qxc4+ 34.b3

34.Bb3?? Qb5.

34...Qb5 35.a4! Qb6 36.Bd3+ Ka5 37.Qe5+ c5 38.Rxb7!! Rxg2+ 39.Ka3 Rg4 40.Rxb6 axb6 41.Qc7 and mates in a couple moves, so Black resigned.

As pointed out earlier, Spielmann's results varied enormously. Following is a list of his tournaments from 1912 through 1914 that gives a great picture of this up and down madness:

Abbazia (1912): A gambit tournament. First place, ahead of Duras, E. Cohn, and Réti.

Breslau (1912): Seventh place behind Duras, Rubinstein, Teichmann, Schlechter, Tarrasch, and Marshall.

Pistyan (1912): Second place behind Rubinstein but ahead of Marshall, Duras, Schlechter, Teichmann.

Stockholm (1912): Fifth place behind Alekhine, E. Cohn, Marco, and Olland.

San Sebastian (1912): Shared second/third with Nimzowitsch, behind Rubinstein but ahead of Tarrasch, Perlis, Marshall, Duras, Schlechter, Teichmann, Leonhardt, and Forgács.

Budapest (1913): First place ahead of Tartakower, Fleischmann, Balla, Marco, Vidmar, and Réti.

Vienna (1913): First ahead of Tartakower, Réti, Schlechter, and Perlis.

Vienna (1913): In a match loss against Tartakower, Spielmann won 2, lost 5, and drew 4.

Baden (1914): A gambit tournament. First ahead of Tartakower, Schlechter, Breyer, Johner, and Réti.

Berlin (1914): Tied for first/second with E. Cohn, ahead of Teichmann and Mieses.

Mannheim (1914): Third behind Alekhine and Vidmar, ahead of Breyer, Marshall, Réti, Janowski, Bogoljubov, Tarrasch, Duras, John, and Tartakower.

Vienna (1914): Tied for third/fourth behind Schlechter and Kaufmann, ahead of Albin, and two other lesser players.

Leipzig (1914): Lost a match to Teichmann (Spielmann won 1, lost 5).

Akiba Rubinstein vs. Rudolf Spielmann, San Sebastian 1912

1.d4 e6 2.c4 f5 3.Nc3 Bb4 4.Bd2 Nf6 5.g3 0-0 6.Bg2 d6 7.a3 Bxc3 8.Bxc3 Nbd7 9.Qc2 c5 10.dxc5 Nxc5 11.Nf3 Nce4 12.0-0 Bd7 13.Rfd1 Rc8 14.Bxf6 Qxf6 15.Qb3 Rc7 16.Ne1 Nc5! 17.Qb4 f4! 18.Nd3 fxg3 19.fxg3 Nxd3 20.Rxd3 Qf2+ 21.Kh1 Bc6 22.e4 Rcf7 23.Re1 a5 24.Qc3 Qc5 25.b4

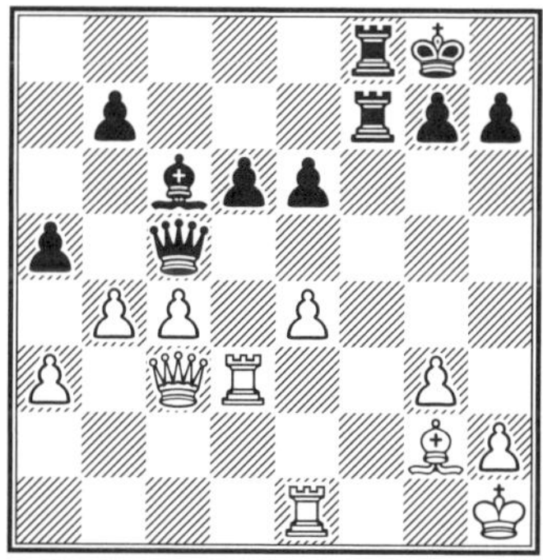

25...Bxe4!!

[Spielmann]: "The crowning point of this complicated sacrifice lies in the fact that through the sacrifice of a whole Rook the hostile King is forced into the open. It is therefore a King-hunt sacrifice. I could not calculate the combination more exactly, and I had to reply entirely on my conviction that favorable variations would occur as a matter of course. And events proved me to be right."

26.Rxe4?

The correct defense was 26.Bxe4! Rf1+ 27.Rxf1 Rxf1+ 28.Kg2 Rg1+ 29.Kf3 Qh5+ and now 30.Kf4! (30.Ke3? Qxh2 gives Black a crushing attack.) 30...g5+ (30...axb4 31.axb4 Rf1+ 32.Rf3 Rc1! 33.Qd3 [33. Qxc1 Qh6+ 34.Kg4 Qxc1] 33...Re1! 34.Qxd6 [34.Re3 g5 mate] 34...g5+ 35.Ke5 Qxf3 36.Qxe6+ Qf7 37.Qxf7+ Kxf7 38.c5 with a probable draw.) 31.Ke3 Qxh2 and now, thanks to 30.Kf4 g5+, the f6-square is now available to the white Queen: 32.Qf6 and white has various perpetual checks, while black has nothing better than 32...Re1+ 33.Kd4 Qb2+ 34 Rc3 Qd2+ 35.Rd3 (35.Bd3?? Qe3 mate) 35...Qb2+, draw.

26...Rf1+ 27.Bxf1 Rxf1+ 28.Kg2 Qf2+ 29.Kh3 Rh1!

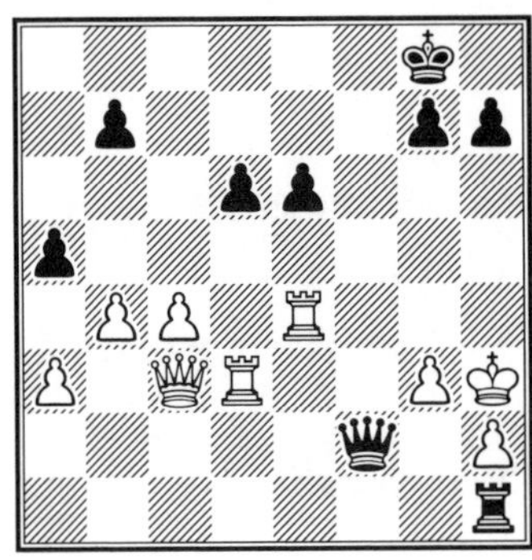

[Spielmann]: "This is as far as the combination was calculated. Black is a Rook down, but he drives the King up to the fourth rank. Such an attack must succeed!"

30.Rf3 Qxh2+ 31.Kg4 Qh5+ 32.Kf4 Qh6+ 33.Kg4 g5!

Threatens 34...Qh5 mate.

34.Rxe6 Qxe6+ 35.Rf5

35.Kxg5 h6+ 36.Kf4 Re1 gives Black a winning attack.

35...h6 36.Qd3 Kg7 37.Kf3 Rf1+ 38. Qxf1 Qxf5+ 39.Kg2 Qxf1+ 40.Kxf1 axb4 41.axb4 Kf6 42.Kf2 h5, 0-1.

His constant tournament activities stopped during World War I (he served in the Austrian army), but once the war ended Spielmann was back at the board (rusty but excited), doing what he loved most. And, as would be expected, the highs and lows continued:

Berlin (1919): Last place behind Bogolublow, Selezniev, and Réti.

Gothenburg (1919): Tied for first with Olson ahead of a fairly weak field.

Stockholm (1919): First ahead of Rubinstein, Bogoljubov, and Réti.

Stockholm (1919): Second, behind Bogoljubov and ahead of Réti.

Berlin (1920): Clear last behind Breyer, Bogoljubov, Tartakower, Réti, Maróczy, and other strong players.

Gothenburg (1920): Eleventh place behind Réti, Rubinstein, Bogoljubov and other very strong player, but oddly ahead of Nimzowitsch who bombed even worse than Spielmann did!

Triberg (1921): Tied for third/fourth place (with Sämisch) among five players. He was behind Rubinstein and Bogljubow and ahead of Selezniev.

Other matches (1921): Spielmann won 2-0 against Dyckhoff, split 1-1 with Maier, won 3, lost 2, and 1 draw against Tartakower, and wiped out the legendary Réti by 3 wins and 3 draws.

Innsbruck (1922): Tied for first (with Grünfeld), ahead of Carls, Müller, Kieninger, and Wolf.

The next tournament raised quite a few eyebrows.

Pistyan (1922): Tied for second/third with Alekhine, behind first place Bogoljubov, ahead of Grünfeld, Réti, Sämisch, Wolf, Tartakower, Tarrasch, Euwe, and many more.

After Pistyan the world thought Spielmann would follow his usual pattern and do badly in his next event—all the more so since he was almost forty years of age! Old dogs don't learn new tricks, do they? Yet, the chess world was in for a surprise.

Teplitz-Schoenau (1922): Tied first/second with Réti, ahead of Grünfeld, Tartakower, Rubinstein, Kostić, Teichmann, Maróczy, Treybal, Wolf, Mieses, Sämisch, Tarrasch, and Johner.

Had Spielmann somehow improved? Was he now in the top five? Sadly, our human yo-yo ended such speculation with his next event.

Vienna (1922): Tied for tenth/eleventh (with Vuković) behind Rubinstein, Tartakower, Wolf, Alekhine, Maróczy, Tarrasch, Grünfeld, Réti, and Bogoljubov.

Spielmann followed Vienna with a few bad results, but the worst was yet to come.

Karlsbad (1923): Tied for last place (with Chajes) behind Alekhine, Bogoljubov, Maróczy, Grünfeld, Réti, Nimzowitsch, Treybal, Yates, Teichmann, Tartakower, Tarrasch, Rubinstein, Jacob Bernstein, Wolf, Sämisch, and Thomas.

Maehrisch Ostrau (1923): Ninth place behind Emanuel Lasker, Réti, Grünfeld, Selezniev, Euwe, Tartakower, Bogoljubov, and Tarrasch.

Spielmann was now forty years old, and it seemed that the yo-yo was, perhaps, on his way down. But a trip to the fountain of youth (which evidently was filled with his favorite beverage, beer) showed that he wasn't done yet:

Scheveningen (1923): Tied first/second (with Johner) ahead of Maróczy Réti, Colle, Yates, and Mieses.

Vienna (1923): Third behind Tartakower and Réti, and ahead of Grünfeld, L. Steiner, Becker, Opočenský, and Takács.

Merano (1924): Second (behind Grünfeld) and ahead of Rubinstein, Przepiórka, Selezniev, Takás, Colle, Opočenský, and Tarrasch.

By now you know the drill. After all these good results, it's time for a bad one!

Baden-Baden (1925): Tied for eleventh/thirteenth (with Réti and Treybal) behind Alekhine, and the usual cast of characters.

He followed this with a seventh place finish (Marienbad 1925), a thirteenth place finish in a super tournament, as shown by the fact that first, second, and third were Bogoljubov, Lasker, and Capablanca! (Moscow 1925), and other typical scores (lots of events with very few successes).

Paul Leonhardt vs. Rudolf Spielmann, Berlin 1920

1.d4 d5 2.c4 e6 3.Nc3 Nf6 4.Bg5 Nbd7 5.e3 c6 6.Nf3 Qa5 7.Nd2 dxc4 8.Bxf6 Nxf6 9.Nxc4 Qc7 10.Rc1 Be7 11.g3 0-0 12.Bg2 Rd8 13.0-0 Bd7 14.Qe2 Be8 15.Rfd1 Nd7 16.e4 Nf8 17.a3 Rac8 18.Ne3 Qb6 19.Na4 Qb5 20.Qc2 b6 21.Nc3 Qa6 22.Qb3 b5 23.e5 Qb6 24.Ne2 Ng6 25.Rc3 c5 26.Rdc1 Bd7 27.dxc5 Bxc5 28.f4 b4 29.axb4 Bxe3+! 30.Rxe3

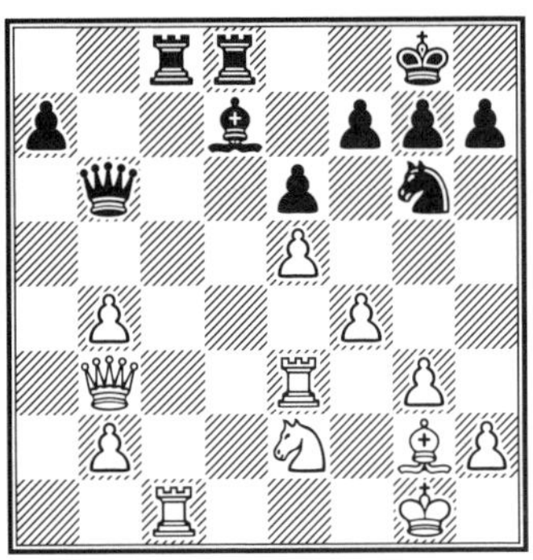

30...Ba4! 31.Qa3 Rxc1+ 32.Nxc1 Ne7!! 33.Be4 Bc6 34.Bxc6

34.Kg2 Bxe4+ 35.Rxe4 Qc6 wins.

34...Nf5 35.Kf2 Nxe3 36.Qxe3 Qxc6 with a winning position.

The following game is a true Spielmann creation. He sacrifices his Queen for insane complications and the initiative.

Rudolf Spielmann vs. Jörgen Möller, Gothenburg 1920

1.e4 e5 2.f4 exf4 3.Qf3 Nc6 4.c3 Nf6 5.d4 d5 6.e5 Ne4 7.Bb5 Qh4+ 8.Kf1 g5 9.Nd2 Bg4 10.Nxe4 Bxf3 11.Nxf3 Qh6 12.Nf6+ Kd8 13.h4

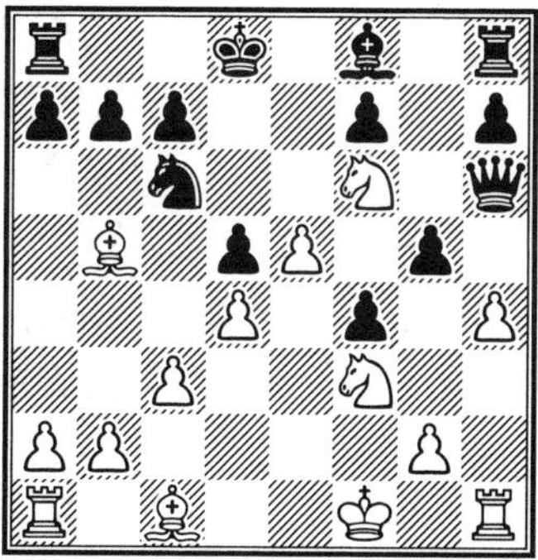

Computers think this Queen sacrifice is trash, and that may be right if you're playing a computer. But if you're playing a human (even a strong human), the sacrifice is fun and offers real chances to overwhelm your opponent.

Spielmann had this to say about the position after 13.h4:

"In such positions, analysis is impractical because of the ramification of possibilities: examination leads into too many byways. This enhances the attacker's prospects in over-the-board play, as he can always reckon with the probability that his adversary will not consistently hit on the strongest move."

13...Be7 14.Nxg5 Qg6 15.Nxd5 Bxg5 16.hxg5 Qc2?

16...Qxg5 was better, though White retains interesting compensation after 17.Nxf4 (Spielmann thinks white is for choice after 17.Nxf4).

17.Be2 Ne7 18.Nxf4 c5 19. Rh3! cxd4?

The Queen should run for her life with 19...Qf5.

20.Rd3!

Black's Queen is trapped and suddenly white is winning the game!

20...Kd7

20...Qa4 21.Rxd4+.

21.Bd1 and the loss of black's Queen left White with two Bishops and a pawn vs. a Rook. White won quickly.

Rudolf Spielmann vs. Jacques Mieses, Teplitz-Schoenau 1922

1.d4 f5 2.g3 b6 3.Bg2 Nc6 4.Nf3 e6 5.0-0 Bb7 6.c4 Bd6 7.Nc3 Nf6 8.a3 a5 9.Nb5 0-0 10.Qc2 Na7 11.Nxd6 cxd6 12.Bf4 Qc7 13.Rac1 Rac8

14.c5 bxc5 15.dxc5 e5 16.Be3 Ne4 17.Qb3+ d5 18.Nxe5 Qxe5 19.Qxb7 Nc6 20.Bf4 Qe6 21.Rfd1 g5 22.Bd6 Rfe8 23.Qb3 d4 24.Qxe6+ Rxe6 25.Bxe4 fxe4 26.Rc4 g4

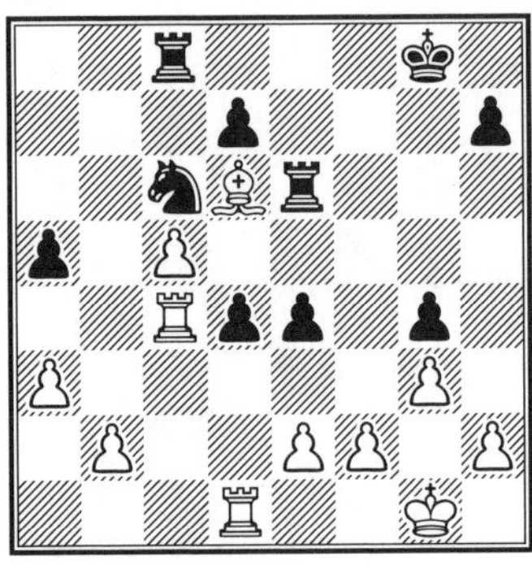

27.b4 Nxb4! 28.Rdxd4!

Better than 28.axb4 Rxd6 though White should still win after 29.bxa5.

28...Nc6 29.Rxe4 Rxe4 30.Rxe4 and White, who is now two pawns up, won easily.

In our next game it looks like White is in trouble, but Spielmann finds a way to stir the pot and create a Spielmann position!

Rudolf Spielmann vs. Savielly Tartakower, Marienbad 1925

1.e4 c5 2.Nf3 e6 3.d4 cxd4 4.Nxd4 a6 5.c4 Nf6 6.Nc3 Qc7 7.a3 Be7 8.Be2 0-0 9.0-0 d6 10.Be3 Nbd7 11.Rc1 b6 12.b4 Bb7 13.f3 Rac8 14.Qe1 Qb8 15.Qf2 Bd8 16.Na4 Ne5 17.Nb2 d5 18.exd5 exd5 19.Nf5 Nxc4 20.Nxc4 dxc4 21.Bxc4 Qe5 22.Bd3 Rxc1 23.Rxc1 Nd5 24.Bd4 Qf4 25.Re1 Bf6 26.Bxf6 gxf6 27.g3!

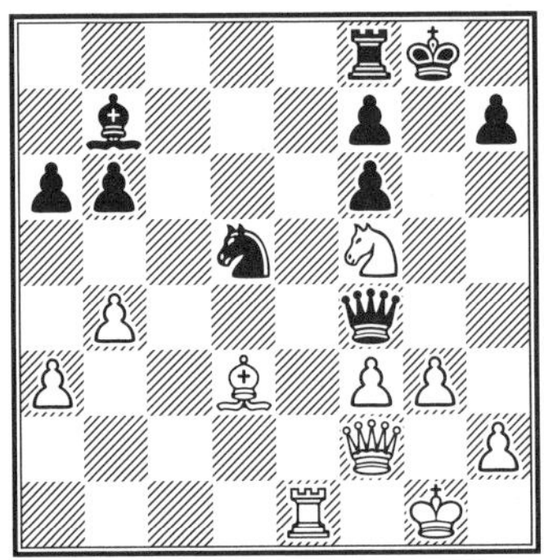

27...Qc7 28.Qd2 Qc3 29.Qh6 Qxe1+ 30.Bf1 Re8 31.Qg7, 1-0

The chess intelligentsia thought that (rightfully so!) he would yo-yo between good and bad results, and as age took its toll, his results would continue to get worse and worse. That was surely an easy bet to make, but Spielmann (who was aware of his flaws and wanted to enjoy at least a few more years of glory) made some changes. Gideon Ståhlberg wrote:

> Spielmann was not the most perfect attacking player that ever existed; but he was, to my way of thinking, the greatest type of combinational master. Combinations were for him the Alpha and Omega of the game and its very soul; indeed, for a long time he neglected the claims of positional play, as so many attacking players are easily inclined to do.
>
> Eventually, however, even such a great talent as Spielmann's was unable to bestow fresh life on variations that had been analyzed out ad nauseam, and it was all the more to his credit that he himself realized this in time. His fine victory at Semmering 1926, above Alekhine and Nimzowitsch, and his great success in the Carlsbad Tournament three years later, were due to a change in his style and opening repertoire.

I'll add that Semmering 1926 was a powerhouse event. Spielmann won it ahead of Alekhine, Vidmar, Nimzowitsch, Tartakower, Rubinstein, Tarrasch, Réti, Grünfeld, Janowski, and others.

Rejuvenated, Spielmann followed the fantastic victory at Semmering with another in Vienna:

Vienna (1926): Clear first ahead of Grünfeld and several other lesser foes.

He took a break from chess for a while, then returned to score yet another massive win in Magdeburg 1927—clear first ahead of Bogoljubov, Holzhausen, and various others.

Rudolf Spielmann vs. Rudolf L'Hermet, Magdeburg 1927

1.e4 e6 2.d4 d5 3.Nc3 dxe4 4.Nxe4 Nd7 5.Nf3 Ngf6 6.Nxf6+ Nxf6 7.Bd3 h6 8.Qe2 Bd6 9.Bd2 0-0 10.0-0-0 Bd7 11.Ne5 c5 12.dxc5 Bxe5 13.Qxe5 Bc6 14.Bf4 Qe7 15.Qd4 Rfd8 16.Bd6 Qe8 17.Rhg1 b6 18.Qh4 bxc5 19.Be5 Qe7 20.g4 c4 21.g5 Nd7

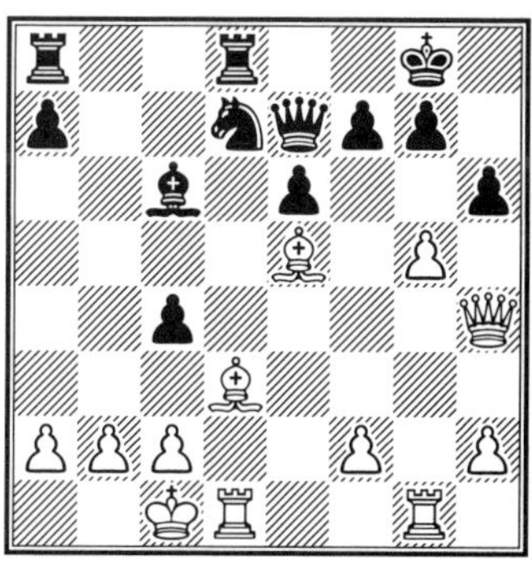

22.Qxh6

You can also take a bow if you played the very strong 22.Bxg7!

22...gxh6 23.gxh6+ Kf8 24.Rg8+!, 1-0.

Suddenly the fun-to-watch tactical genius that was always a bit behind the real greats was being viewed as a world championship candidate. The New York 1927 event was his big opportunity to make a statement and, if he did, perhaps get to play a match with Capablanca. Alas, he came in second to last, behind Capablanca, Alekhine, Nimzowitsch, and Vidmar. After this his results were increasingly poor, and 1928 clearly showed that his star was fading.

However, a yo-yo man will always have some ups along with a string of downs: Spielmann came in tenth in a twelve player tournament at Bad Kissingen (1928) however, his one win was against Capablanca. And in 1929 (forty-six years of age) he had a very fine result at Karlsbad, again beating Capa in their individual game as well as tying for second/third with him—Nimzowitsch's came in first, and Spielmann was ahead of Rubinstein, Becker, Euwe, Vidmar, Bogoljubov, Grünfeld and many other big names.

Very few players did well against Capablanca, but Spielmann's life score against the Cuban genius was 2 wins, 2 losses, 8 draws. Here are both of his wins:

José Capablanca vs. Rudolf Spielmann, Bad Kissingen 1928

1.d4 d5 2.c4 c6 3.Nc3 Nf6 4.Nf3 dxc4 5.e3 b5 6.a4 b4 7.Na2 e6 8.Bxc4 Be7 9.0-0 0-0 10.b3 c5 11.Bb2 Bb7 12.Nc1 Nc6 13.dxc5 Na5 14.Ne5 Nxc4 15.Nxc4 Bxc5 16.Nd3 Qd5 17.Nf4 Qg5 18.Bxf6 Qxf6 19.Rc1 Rfd8 20.Qh5

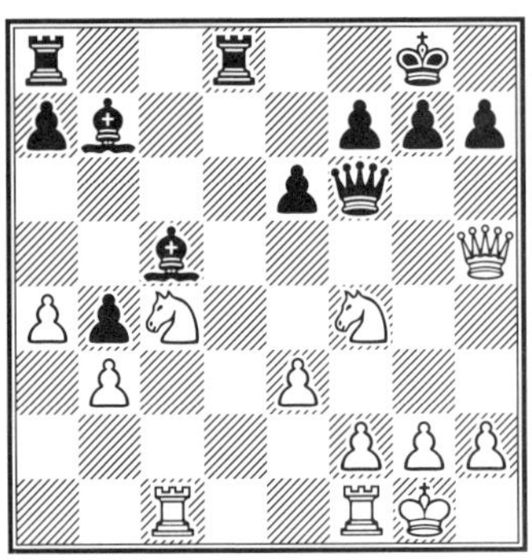

20...Rac8 21.Rfd1 g6 22.Rxd8+ Qxd8 23.Qe5 Be7 24.h3 Rc5 25.Qa1 Bf6 26.Rd1 Rd5 27.Rxd5 exd5 28.Ne5 Qd6 29.Nfd3 Ba6 30.Qe1 Bxe5 31.Nxe5 Qxe5 32.Qxb4 Bd3 33.Qc5 Qb8 34.b4 Qb7 35.b5 h5 36.Qc3 Bc4 37.e4 Qe7 38.exd5 Bxd5 39.a5 Qe4, 0-1.

Rudolf Spielmann vs. José Capablanca, Karlsbad 1929

1.d4 Nf6 2.c4 e6 3.Nc3 d5 4.Bg5 Nbd7 5.e3 c6 6.cxd5 exd5 7.Bd3 Bd6 8.Nge2 Nf8 9.Qc2 h6 10.Bh4 Qe7 11.a3 Bd7 12.e4 g5 13.Bg3 dxe4 14.Nxe4 Nxe4 15.Bxe4 Bxg3 16.hxg3 Qd6 17.0-0-0 Be6 18.Nc3 Qc7 19.Nb5 Qd7 20.d5!

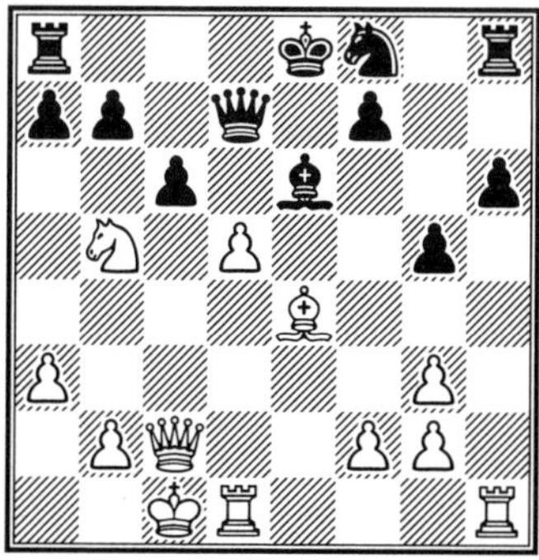

20...cxb5 21.dxe6 Qc8 22.exf7+ Kxf7 23.Rd6 Qxc2+ 24.Kxc2 Re8 25.Bxb7 Re2+ 26.Kd3 Rxf2 27.Re1 Rf6 28.Bd5+ Kg6 29.Rxf6+ Kxf6 30.Re8 h5 31.Ra8 h4 32.gxh4 gxh4 33.Rxa7 Ke5 34.Bc6 h3 35.gxh3 Rxh3+ 36.Kc2 b4 37.axb4 Ne6 38.Ba4 Nf4 39.Re7+ Kd6 40.Rd7+ Ke5 41.Bc6 Rh6 42.b5 Rd6 43.Re7+ Re6 44.Rc7 Kd6 45.Rc8 Re2+ 46.Kc3 Re3+ 47.Kc4 Re2 48.Rd8+ Kc7 49.Rd7+ Kc8 50.Kc5 Rxb2 51.Kb6 Re2 52.Rc7+ Kd8 53.Rd7+ Kc8 54.Rd4 Ne6 55.Bb7+ Kb8 56.Rc4, 1-0.

To Spielmann, life and chess were inseparable, and this highly liked grandmaster kept at it, and kept having his signature ups and downs: In 1932, at the age of 49, he beat Bogolubow in a ten game match (4 wins, 3 losses, 3 draws). He continued to win matches and tournaments into his 50s, and scored a very honorable fifth place at Moscow 1935 behind Botvinnik, Flohr, Lasker, and Capablanca, but ahead of a "who's who" of Russian legends: Kan, Levenfish, Lilienthal, Ragozin, Romanovsky, Alatortsev, Rabinovich, Ståhlberg, and many others. The fact that he was able to more than hold his own against a crop of young, modern players speaks volumes about this man's enormous chess strength.

The following game is a great example of Spielmann's chess philosophy.

Ernő Gereben vs. Rudolf Spielmann, Sopron 1934

1.d4 Nf6 2.c4 g6 3.Nc3 d5 4.e3 Bg7 5.Nf3 0-0 6.Bd2 c6 7.Qb3 b6 8.cxd5 cxd5 9.Rc1 Bb7 10.Ne5 Nfd7 11.Nxd7 Nxd7!

Sacrificing a pawn, which White refuses.

12.f4

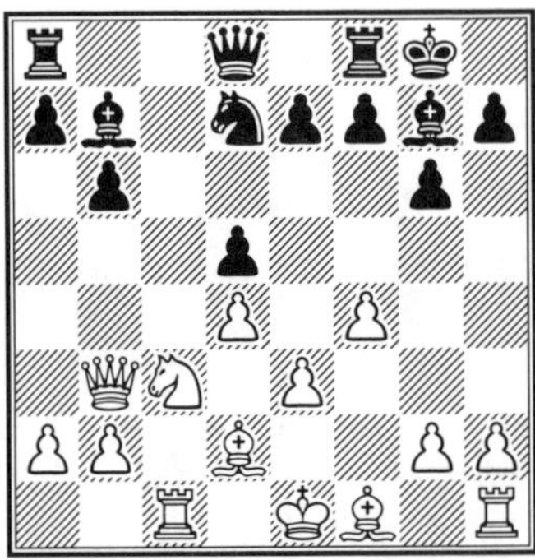

12.Nxd5 e5 ripping open the center and giving Black a huge lead in development. Wise men always tried their best to NOT give Spielmann a huge lead in development!

12...e5!!

Spielmann insists that the game will be a wild slugfest. A lesser (perhaps saner?) man would go for equality with 12...Nf6.

13.fxe5 Nxe5! 14.dxe5 d4!

[Spielmann]: "The opening up of lines must be carried out ruthlessly. In annotating this game for a chess periodical, I wrote the following comment at this stage: 'The sacrifice of the Knight cannot be vindicated by analysis, and it would possibly have been refuted in a correspondence game. But in a contest over the board and with a time limit of eighteen moves an hour, it would nearly always win through.'

"That is the practical standpoint frequently upheld in this book[1]. If each and every sacrifice had to be of that cast-iron soundness which can be verified by analysis, it would be necessary to banish from the game of chess that proud and indispensable prerogative of the fighter: enterprise. All real sacrifices would have to disappear; only the sham sacrifices, which are in effect not sacrifices at all, would be allowed to remain."

15.Nd1 Bxe5 16.e4 Bxe4 17.Nf2 Bd5 18.Qh3 Qe7 19.Be2 d3 20.Nxd3 Rfe8 21.Kf1 Bxb2 22.Re1 Qf6+ 23.Nf2 Bd4 24.Qg3

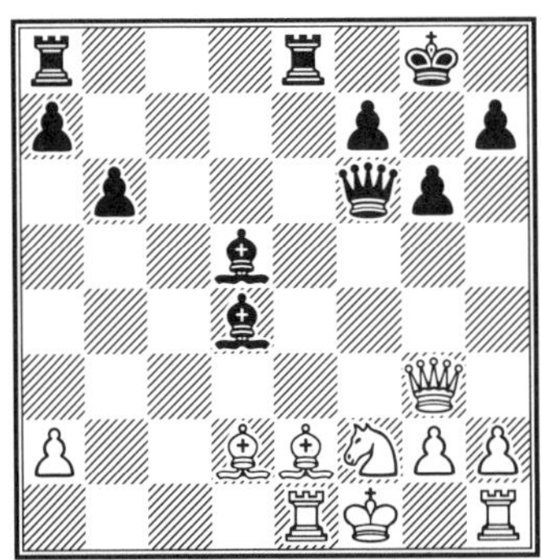

1 Rudolf Spielmann, *The Art of Sacrifice in Chess*. New York: McKay, 1951.

24...Re4??

A serious mistake. Both 24...Re5, intending ...Rf5, and 24...Rxe2! 25.Kxe2 (25.Rxe2 Bc4) 25...Bxf2 26.Qxf2 Bc4+ 27.Kd1 Qxf2 would have been winners.

25.h4? Rae8 26.Bb5 Rxe1+ 27.Bxe1 Re3! 28.Qg5 Rxe1+! 29.Kxe1 Qxf2+ 30.Kd1 Bxg2

The simple 30...Qxa2 also gets the job done, but Spielmann wanted to end with a bit of flash!

31.Re1 Bf3+ 32.Be2 Bc3! 33.Bxf3 Qxf3+ 34.Kc2

34.Re2 Qd3+ 35.Rd2 Qxd2+ leads to a three pawn up King and pawn endgame.

34...Bxe1, 0-1.

Nineteen-thirty-eight was a good year for the fifty-five year old Spielmann. He won a tournament and then came in second (undefeated!) behind Alekhine! In 1939 he tied for first with Flohr (at Gothenburg) with an undefeated score! He also won a small event that same year with a crushing 5½ out of 6 score. He won his final two tournaments (both in Sweden) in 1940 with a clean sweep 7-0, and in 1941 with a 4-0 score. His last event was a match vs. Karlin (also in 1941), which Spielmann won 2½-1½.

Rudolf Spielmann vs. Paul Schmidt, Noordwijk 1938

1.e4 e6 2.d4 d5 3.Nc3 Nf6 4.e5 Nfd7 5.Nce2 c5 6.c3 Nc6 7.f4 cxd4 8.cxd4 Bb4+ 9.Nc3 Nb6 10.Nf3 Bd7 11.Bd3 Ne7 12.0-0 Rc8 13.Nb5 Nc4 14.Nxa7 Ra8 15.b3 Nxe5 16.fxe5 Rxa7 17.a3 Nf5 18.g4 Nh4 19.Ng5 Rf8 20.Nxh7 Rh8 21.Ra2 Bc3 22.Bg5 Bxd4+ 23.Kh1 Qc7 24.Bxh4 Bxe5 25.Bg6!!

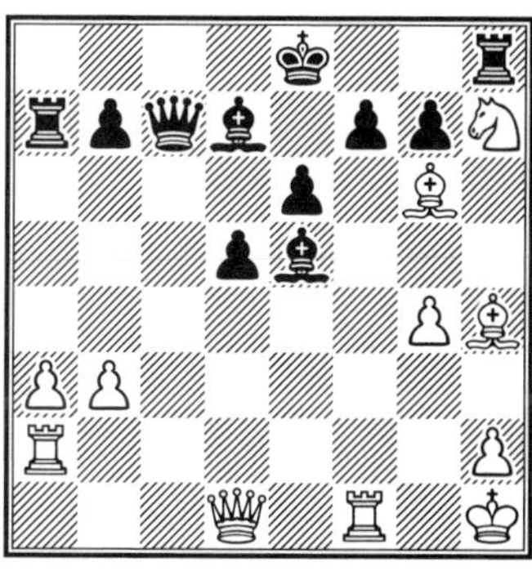

Black resigned after this move.

25...fxg6

25...Rxh7 26.Bxf7+! Kf8 27.Bg6+ Kg8 28.Raf2 Ra8 29.Be7! Qb8 and now the simplest way to win is 30.Rf8+ Qxf8 31.Bxh7+ Kxh7 32.Rxf8 Rxf8 33.Bxf8 and it's all over.

26.Qd3 Bc6 27.Qxg6+ Kd7 28.Rf7+ Kc8 29.Rxc7+ Kxc7 30.Bg3! Bxg3 31.Qxg7+, 1-0.

The lives of the chess greats don't always end well, and Spielmann's end was a tragic one. Fleeing the Nazis, he moved to Sweden where he lived for the last three years of his life. It was during these years that he had to watch as his loved ones suffered hell on earth: one sister died in a concentration camp, another sister was so traumatized by the war that she became mentally ill (she committed suicide in 1964), and his brother was picked up by the SS and also died in a concentration camp.

This kind and brilliant man's final moments were spent in abject poverty and, in 1942, he was found starved to death in his small, locked room.

Réti wrote:

> The past is dead, but, in the history of chess, Spielmann will have a place of honor as the last of the romantic tradition.

I'll let Gideon Ståhlberg end this portrait in a dignified manner:

> In contrast to the businesslike type of disciplined professional that has developed in recent years, Spielmann appears almost an adventurer, but in a better sense than one is generally accustomed to give to this word. The evanescent image of beauty rather than mere gain was his objective and in the course of this pursuit his games were one long series of cheerful adventures. It is true that his life was that of a solitary, a chess fanatic; but it was a noble life, well worth living.

9

ALEXANDER ALEKHINE

A Dance with Death

It's 1918 and you're one of the strongest chess players on Earth. You live in Odessa, during one of Russia's most chaotic periods. Trying to stay on top of the political upheaval, you take whatever side offers the best chance at survival. Unfortunately, being a captain in the Tsarist army turns out to be the wrong choice, and you find yourself tossed into prison and sentenced to death by firing squad by Trotsky himself.

Doomed and waiting for the axe to fall, four days pass in your cell when the door opens and several people enter. One of them is Trotsky. A guard tells you that Trotsky wants to play a game of chess with you, and a board is set up and you end up with the White pieces. It quickly becomes clear that the "people's commissioner" is no match for you, but when you can end the game and wipe him out with a few sharp moves you hesitate. What should you do? If you lose, will Trotsky be merciful and let you live? What will happen if you win? In fact, does it even matter? Most likely you'll be shot in either case. You agonize, play some weak moves so the game can continue, and continue wondering what the best course will be.

What would you do?

This is the dilemma Alexander Alekhine faced. He kept the game going for a while longer, then silently cursed to himself and began the mating sequence that would drag down the black King. And then—he waited. Trotsky resigned, quietly rose up from his chair and left the room. Alekhine was released the next day.[1]

Early Years

Born in 1892 into an aristocratic, very wealthy family, Alekhine learned how to play chess at six or seven years of age. When he was nine (in 1902) he watched a simultaneous blindfold exhibition given by Harry Nelson Pillsbury—seeing a foreign superstar give such an exhibition was a big deal for anyone, but it can easily be a turning point for a child. Now hooked on chess, he immersed himself in his brother's correspondence games and in 1905 he played in several correspondence tournaments himself. Like any beginner, his initial results were poor. However, he carefully analyzed each and every game (his and his brother's), got stronger and stronger, and eventually was actually winning some of those events!

Alekhine wrote about those early beginnings:

> I first heard about simultaneous blindfold games when I was nine. Moscow, my native town, was visited by Pillsbury who played twenty-two simultaneous games without looking at the chessboard. My brother Alexey took part in the event and drew. I viewed Pillsbury's performance as a miracle! At the age of twelve I started to play without looking at the chessboard myself.

This is significant because Alekhine eventually became one of the greatest blindfold players ever.

At the beginning of 1907, Alekhine joined the Moscow Chess Club—he had to lie about his age to get in! He played his first face-to-face tournament in the spring of that year (his result wasn't anything special), and he continued his chess education by participating in both tournaments and short matches. Unlike

---

1 This incident may be apocryphal as there are varying reports as to what transpired in Russia and as to whether or not Alekhine ever met Trotsky.

Capablanca, who seemed to have been born with a silver pawn in his mouth, and unlike modern chess geniuses who earn the grandmaster title by the age of twelve, Alekhine did things the old-fashioned way: he studied hard, used bad results as a learning tool, and by 1909 was quite a strong player (as shown by his clear first place finish in the All-Russian Amateur Tournament).

He followed this with an embarrassing drubbing (0-3) in a match vs. Nenarokov, a comeback wipeout (4 wins, 0 losses, 1 draw) against Blumenfeld, clear first in another correspondence tournament, and first place in two tournaments in Moscow (1909-1910). His big test occurred in Hamburg 1910 when he faced a gauntlet of old and upcoming legends. He ended up in seventh place (there were eighteen players) behind Schlechter, Duras, Nimzowitsch, Spielmann, Marshall, and Teichmann.

In 1911 he had another try at the chess elite, this time ending up in eighth place (twenty-six players) behind Teichmann, Rubinstein, Schlechter, Rotlewi, Marshall, Nimzowitsch, and Vidmar. He continued the "win some and lose some" template, carefully mending the flaws in his game. At this point he was clearly in the world's top twelve.

These sub-par results are the real story behind Alekhine's journey to the highest title. A tactical genius with a wonderful imagination, his downfall was positional chess and the endgame. By the age of twenty-one (1913) he realized that if he wanted to achieve his goal of world domination he would have to excel in every phase of the game—tactical genius alone wouldn't get the job done.

His hard work started paying off by 1914 he had put together a string of impressive results (equal first in Paris, equal first in the All-Russian Championship, and third behind Lasker and Capablanca in the legendary St. Petersburg event) that propelled him to the top five in the world.

However, he was honest enough to know that though he wasn't afraid of anyone, both Lasker and Capablanca were his superiors. Due to Lasker's age, Alekhine was positive that Capablanca would eventually be world champion, so he dedicated himself to increasing his skills in all the areas Capablanca excelled in. Alekhine knew this would take a long time to accomplish, but it was his life goal and nothing was going to prevent him from achieving it.

Nineteen-fourteen was his coming out party as an elite player, but it also acted as a stumbling block to his success. World War 1 fell on his head during the super-strong Mannheim tournament (he was dominating the event with 9 wins, 1 draw and 1 loss).

This led to eleven Russian players (including Alekhine) being interned in Germany. Some sources say he was released later and made his way back to Russia. Other sources offer a more romantic tale.

Anthony Guest, the chess correspondent of the *Morning Post*, wrote:

> [October 1914] — The brilliant Russian master, Alekhine, who was one of the tournament competitors stranded at Mannheim on the outbreak of war, paid a surprise visit to London on Friday (October 9), on his way back to St. Petrograd. Calling at the Chess Divan, 110 Strand, he gave an interesting account of his experiences. Alekhine was the only one of the French and Russian representatives to get away, nine of them still being detained at Baden-Baden, or at Mannheim, where Janowski remains. It is astonishing to hear that the German Chess Association, which has several influential members, left these players to shift for themselves. They were a fortnight in prison, where they were brutally treated by German soldiers who, from sheer savagery, assaulted them with the butt ends of their rifles. These competitors will have to remain in Germany till the end of the war, with the solitary exception of Alekhine, who escaped at the risk of his life. A friend gave him his own pass, and by means of this the young Russian got across the border, knowing that if the deception was discovered he would be shot at once.

The war years were hard on Alekhine, though when he managed to play (only in Russia) he always won (aside from his wartime tournament victories, he crushed Rabinovich in a four-game match via 3 wins and 1 draw, and Verlinsky by the lopsided scored of 6-0). His victory in early 1920 at the Moscow Championship (a clean sweep of 11-0), and his win at the first USSR Championship (9 wins, 6 draws, 0 losses) made his enormous strength clear to all. Nevertheless, he was still a distant third behind those two superhuman monsters, Lasker and Capablanca.

When Capablanca took the world title from an aging Lasker, Alekhine's ultimate goal was clear: continue to improve and take the world championship from the Cuban genius.

I would like to share an Alekhine loss (when he was fifteen years old) that showed his aggressive style. Fortunately for chess, one-dimensional aggression (no matter how creative it might be) doesn't always lead to victory! Pay special attention to the outrageous pawn structure that occurs!

Alexander Alekhine vs. Vladimir Nenarokov, Moscow 1907

1.d4 d5 2.Nf3 e6 3.e3 c6 4.Bd3 f5 5.Ne5 Qf6 6.Nd2 Nd7 7.f4 Nxe5 8.fxe5 Qf7 9.0-0 Qc7 10.c4 Nh6 11.b3 Bd7 12.a4 Be7 13.cxd5 cxd5 14.Ba3 Bxa3 15.Rxa3 0-0 16.Ra2 Rac8 17.Qe2 Qb6 18.Rc2 Rxc2 19.Bxc2 Rc8 20.Bd3 Qb4 21.h3 Nf7 22.Rb1 Rc3 23.Kh2 a6 24.Qf1 Qa3 25.Rd1 Qb2 26.Qe2 Nd8 27.Rb1 Qa3 28.Rf1 Qb4 29.Bb1 b5 30.g4

Rome is burning on the queenside, so Alekhine goes all-in on the opposite wing!

30...bxa4 31.gxf5??

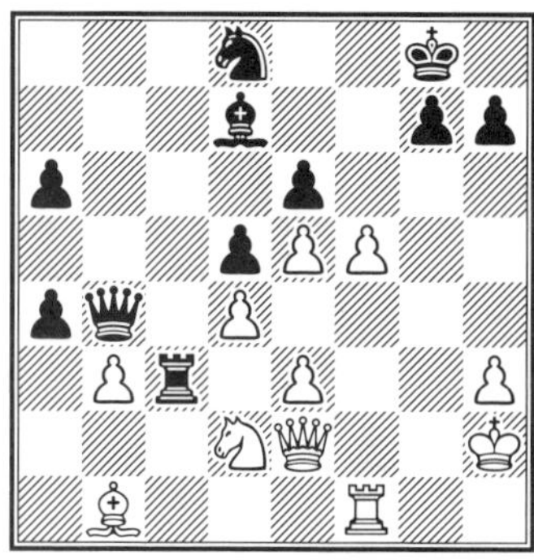

At that time Alekhine's credo was "No retreat, no surrender!" I might add, "No defense!" The older, more mature Alekhine would have realized the attack wouldn't work and played the sane 31.bxa4 Bxa4 32.Qe1! Bc2 (32...Bb5 33.Rg1) 33.gxf5 exf5 (33...Bxb1 34.Qxb1 Qxb1 35.Rxb1 [Threatening 36.Rb8] 35...Kf8 36.Nb3! Rxe3 37.Nc5 exf5 38.Ra1 Nc6 39.Ne6+! Kf7 40.Rxa6 Kxe6 41.Rxc6+ and White is okay) 34.Ba2! Qa5 35.Nb1! Bxb1 36.Bxb1! g6 37.Rg1 Ra3 38.Qh4 Ra1 39.Qe7 Rxb1 40.Rxb1 Qa2+ 41.Kg3 Qxb1 42.Qxd8+ =.

31...Bb5

Now Black is winning.

32.Nc4 Rxb3 33.fxe6

Do or die, all or nothing!

33...dxc4 34.Qf3 Rxb1 35.Rxb1 Qxb1 36.e7 Ne6 37.d5 Qg6 38.dxe6

Quadrupled pawns! Incredible and very rare.

38...Qe8

Oh well, that ends all the threats. White resigned in a few more moves. So much for the power of quads.

In the game that follows Alekhine was in serious trouble. But Black made a mistake and his tactical skills bailed him out. He commented about this game:

> It is possible that this game exerted a profound effect on my subsequent play and development. Certainly it stimulated my ambition and my desire to improve. On the other hand it endowed me with a curious psychological weakness which I had to work hard and long subsequently to eradicate—if I ever have eradicated it!—the impression that I could always, or nearly always, when in a bad position, conjure up some unexpected combination to extricate me from my difficulties. A dangerous delusion!

Alexander Alekhine vs. Vasily Ronsanov, Moscow 1907

1.e4 e5 2.Nf3 Nc6 3.d4 exd4 4.Nxd4 Nf6 5.Nxc6 bxc6 6.Bd3 d5 7.exd5 cxd5 8.0-0 Be7 9.Nc3 0-0 10.Bg5 c6 11.Qf3 Bg4 12.Qg3 Bh5 13.Qe5 Bg6 14.Bxg6 hxg6 15.Rad1 Bd6 16.Qd4 Qc7 17.Qh4 Nh7 18.Be3 f5 19.f4 Kf7 20.Bd4 Rh8 21.Rde1 Nf6 22.Qg5 Ng4

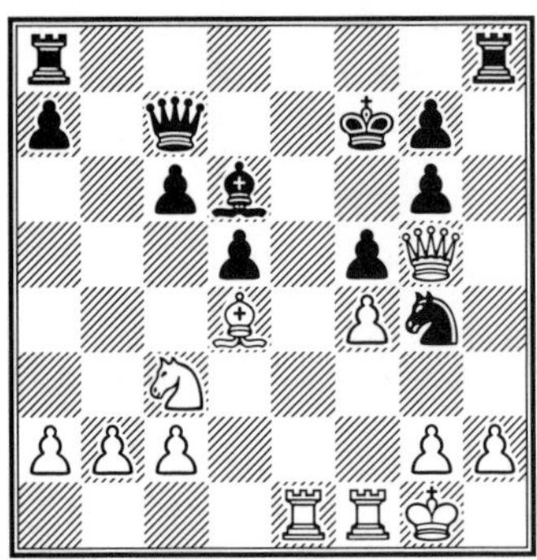

23.Re6!! Kxe6

23...Rh6 24. Rfe1 Nxh2 (24...Bxf4 25.Re7+ Kg8 26.Rxc7 Bxg5 27.Rxg7+ Kf8 28.Rb7 [threatening Bg7+] 28...Rxh2 [28…Bf6 is better, though after 29.Bxf6 Nxf6 30.Re6 Black is in a bad way.] 29.Re6 and Black is toast.) 25.Bxg7 Bc5+ 26.Kh1 Kxg7 27.Re7+ Bxe7 28.Rxe7+ Qxe7 29.Qxe7+ Kg8 30 Kg1 with excellent winning chances.

24.Qxg6+ Kd7 25.Qxf5+ Kd8 26.Qxg4 and White has turned a poor position into an advantageous one. He went on to win in forty-two moves.

Fedor Duz-Khotimirsky vs. Alexander Alekhine, Moscow consultation game 1907

1.d4 d5 2.c4 e6 3.Nc3 c5 4.e3 Nf6 5.Nf3 Nc6 6.a3 a6 7.dxc5 Bxc5 8.b4 Bd6 9.Bb2 dxc4 10.Bxc4 b5 11.Bd3 Bb7 12.0-0 0-0 13.Rc1 Ne5 14.Nxe5 Bxe5 15.f4 Bc7 16.Qe2 Bb6 17.Rfd1 Qe7 18.Kh1 Rac8 19.e4 Rfd8 20.Nb1 Rxc1 21.Rxc1

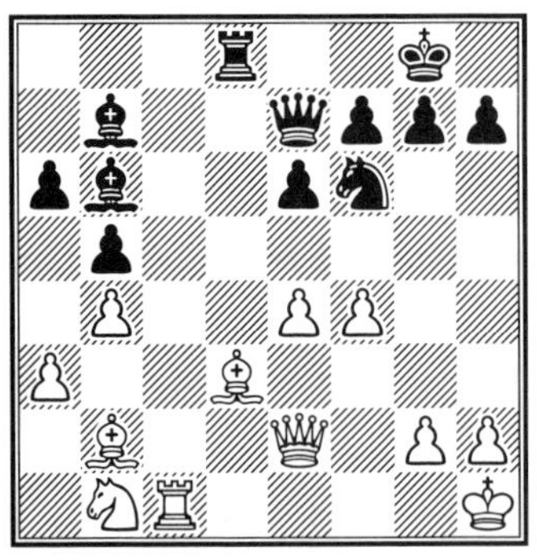

21...Rxd3!!

21...Qd6 hitting both d3 and f4 is also good.

22.Qxd3

22.Bxf6 Qd7! 23.Qg4 g6 24.Qe2 Bxe4!

22...Nxe4 23.Bd4 Qd6

Also good are 23...Qd8 and 23...Qd7.

24.Rd1 Qd5 25.Qe3 Bxd4

Not the only good move by any means. One sample is 25...e5! (Blocking the a1-h8 diagonal so that White's Qg3 won't threaten a mate on g7.) 26.fxe5 Nc3! 27.Qd2 Nxb1 28.Rxb1 Bxd4 29.Rd1 g6 and Black should win.

26.Rxd4 Ng3+! 27.Qxg3 Qxd4 28.Nc3 h5

It's a good idea to prevent a back rank mate, and ...h5-h4 is also a threat.

29.h4 Qd2 and the threat of ...Bxg2 gives Black an easily won game.

Alexander Alekhine vs. Friedrich Köhnlein, Düsseldorf 1908

1.d4 d5 2.Nf3 e6 3.e3 Nf6 4.Bd3 Nbd7 5.Nbd2 Bd6 6.e4 dxe4 7.Nxe4 Nxe4 8.Bxe4 0-0 9.Bg5 Qe8 10.0-0 f5 11.Bd3 e5 12.dxe5 Nxe5 13.Re1 Qh5 14.Nxe5 Qxg5 15.Bc4+ Kh8 16.Qxd6!

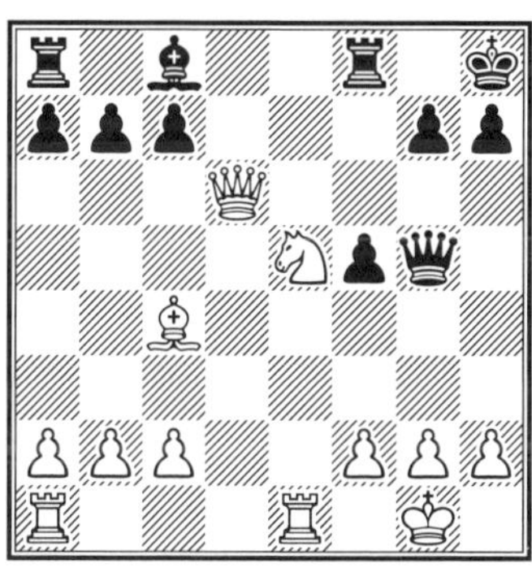

16.Nf7+ Rxf7 17.Bxf7 (17.Re8+ Rf8 18.Rxf8+ Bxf8 19.Qd5 Be6 20.Qxe6 Bd6) 17...Bd7 won't make Black happy, but 16.Qxd6 is simply game over.

16...cxd6 17.Nf7+ Kg8

17...Rxf7 18.Re8+ mates.

18.Nxg5+, 1-0.

Success and Despair

The year 1921 finds Alekhine living in Germany. At that time Russia (the Soviet Union was founded in 1922) wasn't the chess Mecca it eventually turned into, and he realized that if he wanted to be World Champion he needed to be closer to his competition.

The Plan

With the World Championship and nothing but the World Championship on his mind, Alekhine mapped out a clear plan: Play against the world's best and win every tournament, thus showing that he was the true challenger to the title. And, at first he would also avoid Capablanca until he felt he was closer to him in strength.

This strategy was already "on" as far back as 1914 when, before accepting a place in the Mannheim tournament (which he eventually won) he wired the organizers and asked, "Inform me, please, if Capablanca is going to play in the tournament."

The organizers, who thought that Alekhine wanted to compete against Capablanca, were embarrassed since the Cuban wasn't going to play. However, Peter Romanovsky, after joining Alekhine in Mannheim right before the event, asked him why he sent that wire. Alekhine replied:

> If Capablanca participated, I would not play. I must train for my match against Capablanca in the coming years to become the World Champion and there is a trick. I must come in first in every event. So far, I'm weaker than Capablanca and this means that if he took part I'd come in second. This does not fit my plans.

Note that as far back as 1914 Alekhine was sure that Capablanca would eventually take the title from the aging Lasker. Thus Capablanca was his ultimate target and he never took his eyes off of him.

On Top of the World

After dominating his final two Russian events (as mentioned above), he continued his collection of first prizes:

Budapest (1921): First with 6 wins, 5 draws, no losses, ahead of powerhouses like Grünfeld, Tartakower, Euwe, Bogoljubov.

The Hague (1921): First with 7 wins, two draws, no losses, ahead of Tartakower, Rubinstein, Maróczy, and Euwe.

Triberg (1921): First with 6 wins, 2 draws, no losses, ahead of Bogoljubov and Sämisch.

Hastings (1922): First with 6 wins, 3 draws, one loss, ahead of Rubinstein, Bogoljubov, and Tarrasch.

In these events Alekhine showed wonderful opening preparation, his usual tactical genius, an incredible imagination, solid positional skills, and surprising technical expertise. Here are a couple examples of his play in 1921.

The first example shows Alekhine's brand of active defense. In this position White, who intends to play for the central advance e2-e4-e5, appears to have the advantage since it's hard to find Black's counterplay. Alekhine refuses to play passively and instead sacrifices an exchange for a myriad of pluses:

Alexey Selezniev vs. Alexander Alekhine, Triberg 1921

1.d4 Nf6 2.Nf3 b6 3.g3 Bg7 4.Bg2 d6 5.0-0 Nbd7 6.Bf4 h6 7.Nc3 c5 8.d5 b5 9.Ne1 a6 10.a4 b4 11.Ne4 Nxe4 12.Bxe4 g6 13.c4 bxc3 14.bxc3 Bg7 15.Rb1 Rb8 16.c4 0-0 17.Qc2 a5 18.Nf3 Qc7 19.Bd2 Ba6 20.Bd3 Rb4!!

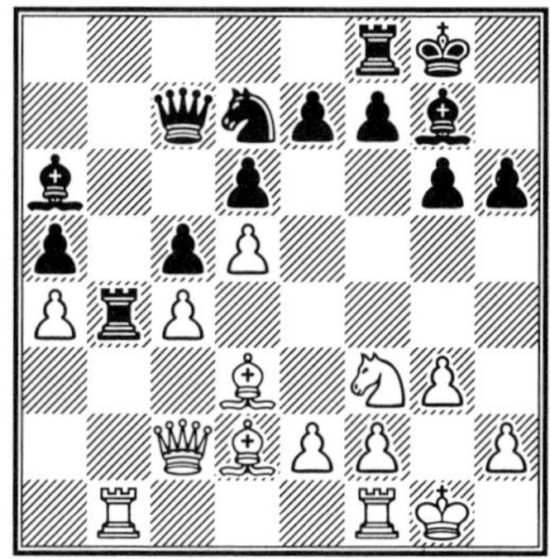

21.Bxb4 cxb4!

Opening the c-file so Black can pressure c4, and also giving black's Knight access to c5. Black now has an excellent position and, after many adventures, went on to win.

The next game demonstrates Alekhine's extremely original vision which allowed him to come up with ideas, even in the opening, that other players would never see:

Alexander Alekhine vs. Akiba Rubinstein, The Hague 1921

1.d4 d5 2.Nf3 e6 3.c4 a6 4.c5 Nc6 5.Bf4 Nge7 6.Nc3 Ng6 7.Be3 b6 8.cxb6 cxb6 9.h4 Bd6 10.h5!

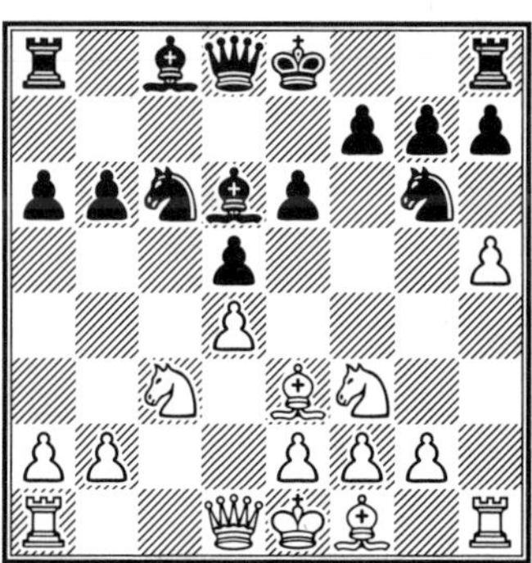

10...Nge7 11.h6 g6 12.Bg5 0-0 13.Bf6 b5 14.e3 Bd7 15.Bd3 Rc8 16.a4 b4 17.Ne2 Qb6 18.Nc1 Rc7 19.Nb3 Na5 20.Nc5 Nc4 21.Bxc4 dxc4 22.Ne5

And White had a clear advantage and went on to win.

And in the following game we see Alekhine as a dynamic monster—a human tidal wave that washes his famous opponent away:

Siegbert Tarrasch vs. Alexander Alekhine, Bad Pistyan 1922

1.d4 Nf6 2.c4 e6 3.Nf3 c5 4.d5 b5 5.dxe6 fxe6 6.cxb5 d5 7.e3 Bd6 8.Nc3 0-0 9.Be2 Bb7 10.b3 Nbd7 11.Bb2 Qe7 12.0-0 Rad8 13.Qc2 e5 14.Rfe1 e4 15.Nd2 Ne5 16.Nd1 Nfg4 17.Bxg4 Nxg4 18.Nf1 Qg5 19.h3 Nh6 20.Kh1 Nf5 21.Nh2 d4 22.Bc1 d3 23.Qc4+ Kh8 24.Bb2 Ng3+! 25.Kg1 Bd5 26.Qa4 Ne2+ 27.Kh1 Rf7 28.Qa6 h5 29.b6 Ng3+! 30.Kg1 axb6 31.Qxb6 d2 32.Rf1 Nxf1 33.Nxf1 Be6!! 34.Kh1

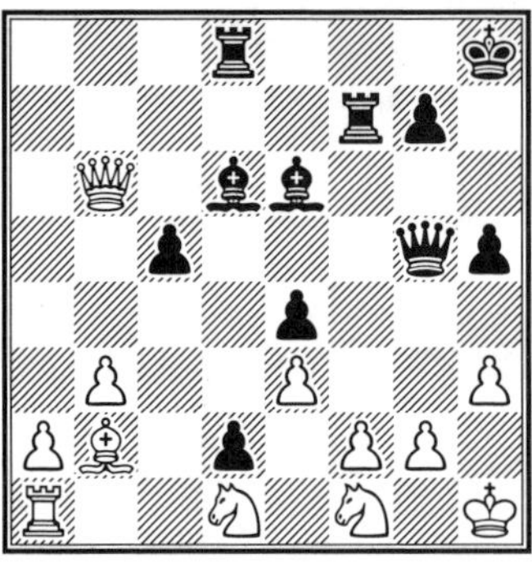

34...Bxh3! 35.gxh3 Rf3 36.Ng3 h4 37.Bf6 Qxf6 38.Nxe4 Rxh3+, 0-1.

Fall From Grace

This was an incredibly busy schedule and the stress of having to win "first and only first" must have been overwhelming. However, Alekhine's plan was working and everyone saw him as the only worthy challenger to Capablanca's title (the Cuban finally got, and won, a match with Lasker in 1921). When a super-strong tournament in London was organized, Alekhine decided to toss away his "no Capablanca" rule and duel with the World Champion face to face (other participants included: Vidmar, Rubinstein, Bogoljubov, Réti, Tartakower, Maróczy, Yates, and Euwe). When the smoke had cleared, Alekhine had the magnificent score of 11½ out of fifteen games (8 wins, 7 draws, no losses) but, alas, it was only good for clear second since Capablanca finished with an outrageous 13 points (11 wins, 4 draws, no losses).

Though it was clear that Alekhine was the second best player on Earth (barring Lasker, who wasn't interested in regaining the title), finding sponsors who would put up the money for a match had always been far from easy. Unfortunately, another occurrence at the London event made things even more difficult for Alekhine and anyone else that wanted to challenge Capablanca.

The London Protocol

During the event Capablanca got all the top players together and took them to one of London's top hotels. There he lavished them with expensive champagne and asked them to sign a document (called the London Protocol) approving Capablanca's proposed rules about future World Championship matches. Milan Vidmar, who wanted to challenge Capablanca, explained:

> I clearly remember the most important rules of the so-called London Protocol. The challenger must, first of all, raise $10,000 [$150,000 in 2021 dollars]. In addition, he must defray the travel and food expenses of both players. Another rule required that the winner receive $6000 and the loser $4000. There were several more clauses to protect the current World Champion.
>
> It was funny that, while signing the London Protocol, it did not occur to me that my youthful projects had been shattered and that my dream of winning the World Championship would never come true. It should have been clear to me that I did not have the slightest chance of raising $10,000 for my challenge.

Emotional Collapse

In my view Alekhine's disappointment of coming in second behind Capablanca mixed with the near impossible demands of the London Protocol proved severely debilitating to a man who was already under enormous stress.

When he failed to win his next event, Pistyan 1922 (he finished second with 12 wins, 5 draws, 1 loss, behind Bogoljubov), he must have gone into a deep depression. Thus it wasn't a surprise that the following tournament, in Vienna, was a total disaster: Alekhine, with 6 wins, 4 draws, and 3 defeats, tied for fourth/six with Maróczy and Tarrasch (Rubinstein was first, Tartakower second, Wolf third, Grünfeld seventh, followed by Réti, Bogoljubov, Spielmann, Vuković, Sämisch, Takács, König, and Kmoch).

Alekhine started the event well, but it quickly became clear that his nerves were shot. He rushed his play, he blundered, he botched one good position after another, the balanced style he created over the previous couple years had reverted to overt aggression and risk taking—put simply, he was a total mess.

A Fit of Despair

And now I come to a hotly contested tale. According to Alekhine's friend Edmond Lancel, Alekhine was frustrated and lonely after his last sub-par performance. And this led to an attempted suicide! Here's the tale:

> Alekhine rested for a few days at Aix-la-Chapelle (Aachen)—I also happened to be there. We had seen a good deal of each other since the beginning of the year and, while in Aix-la-Chapelle we spent time together at an evening party celebrating his birthday at the hotel Corneliusbad. He shared intimate details of his private life and pictures of his loved ones. We played, as we did from time to time, several training games in preparation for the great Vienna tournament. All of a sudden, in a fit of despair with no previous warning, Alekhine attempted suicide by stabbing himself in the belly!
>
> It was about 3AM and the main hotel lobby was deserted except for the two of us. Alekhine collapsed lifelessly at my feet. I summoned the hotel personnel: the manager, a physician, the ambulance, and the police and whoever else was needed. Things seemed grave, and Alekhine remained unconscious. However, thanks to prompt and efficient assistance he came to. A few days later he recovered.
>
> This event, just a few days before the Vienna tournament, was not without significance. I spared no effort to dissuade Alekhine from participating for I was convinced he would do badly. But there was no keeping him from competing, and he achieved one of the worst results of his career.

This story hasn't been proved or disproved. And, since chess historians tend to accept only what can be verified (understandably), most refused to believe it really happened. However, I feel that there is a very good chance that this did indeed happen. In fact, even one or two of the following points have led many people to end it all: depression, overwhelming stress, failure (in ones own eyes), loss of a life dream, loneliness (a common occurrence for an expat), facing a situation with no end in sight. A momentary impulse is all it takes.

Edmond Lancel wasn't some unknown person. A respected editor of *L'Echiquier* (a Belgium chess magazine), and publisher of chess books such as Marcel Duchamp and Vitaly Halberstadt's *L'Opposition et les cases conjuguées sont réconciliées* (*Opposition and Sister Squares are Reconciled*) he was known to be close friends with Alekhine, and a couple of his games against Alekhine had been published.

It would be hard to find a more credible witness. Lancel, out of respect for his friend, didn't publish this account of what occurred until after Alekhine's death (keeping this secret while Alekhine was alive is something a good friend would do). I see no reason why Edmond Lancel would make this up.

And so I'll leave Alekhine's bad situation for a moment and look at a few of his games from this period—after which I'll return to discuss how he threw off the chains of despair and did something most people felt was impossible.

First, I'll offer up one of Alekhine's greatest games:

Efim Bogoljubov vs. Alexander Alekhine, Hastings 1922

1.d4 f5 2.c4 Nf6 3.g3 e6 4.Bg2 Bb4+ 5.Bd2 Bxd2+ 6.Nxd2 Nc6 7.Ngf3 0-0 8.0-0 d6 9.Qb3 Kh8 10.Qc3 e5 11.e3 a5 12.b3 Qe8 13.a3 Qh5 14.h4 Ng4 15.Ng5 Bd7 16.f3 Nf6 17.f4 e4 18.Rfd1 h6 19.Nh3 d5 20.Nf1 Ne7 21.a4 Nc6 22.Rd2 Nb4 23.Bh1 Qe8 24.Rg2 dxc4 25.bxc4 Bxa4 26.Nf2 Bd7 27.Nd2 b5 28.Nd1

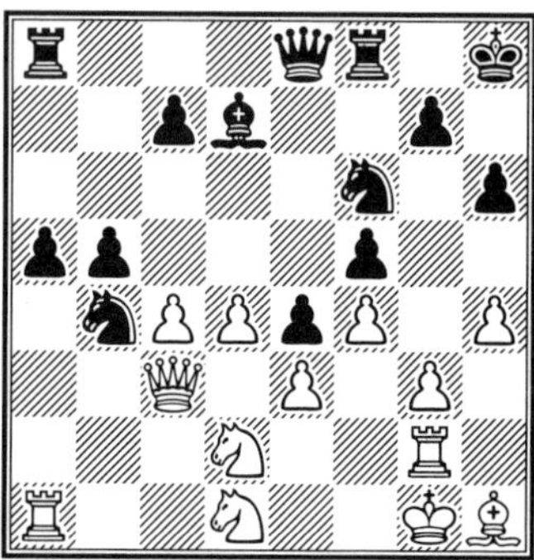

28...Nd3!

Sacrificing the a5-pawn.

29.Rxa5 b4 30.Rxa8

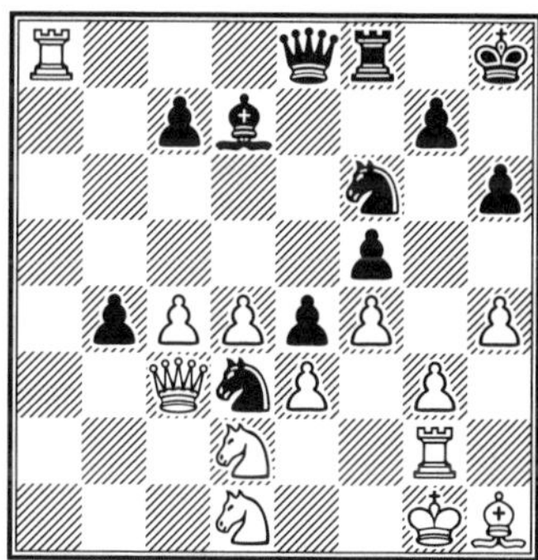

30...bxc3!!

30...Qxa8 would have won, but Alekhine saw something so beautiful that he ignored the "normal" win and went for high art.

31.Rxe8 c2! 32.Rxf8+ Kh7

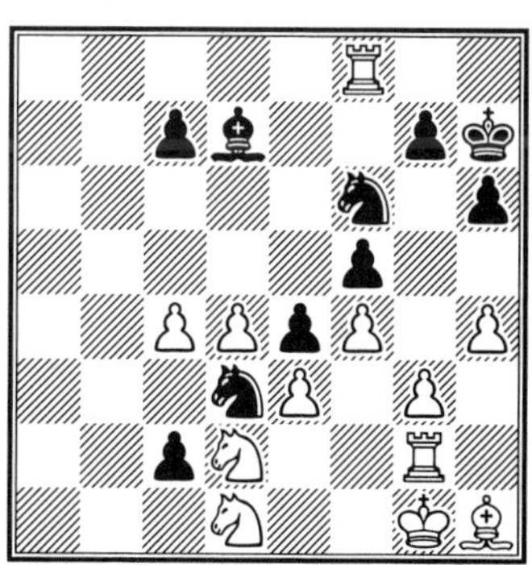

White's Rook has just eaten two black Rooks AND black's Queen, yet Black is winning. Incredible.

33.Nf2 c1=Q+ 34.Nf1 Ne1!

Threatening 34...Nf3 mate.

35.Rh2 Qxc4 36.Rb8 Bb5 37.Rxb5 Qxb5 38.g4 Nf3+ 39.Bxf3 exf3 40.gxf5 Qe2! 41.d5 Kg8 42.h5 Kh7 43.e4 Nxe4 44.Nxe4 Qxe4 45.d6 cxd6 46.f6 gxf6 47.Rd2 Qe2 48.Rxe2 fxe2 49.Kf2 exf1=Q+ 50.Kxf1 Kg7 51.Kf2 Kf7 52.Ke3 Ke6 53.Ke4 d5+, 0-1.

It's games like this that led one of the best player's in the world, Levon Aronian, to call Alekhine the greatest player who ever lived.

Alexander Alekhine vs. Zoltán Balla, Budapest 1921

1.d4 d5 2.Nf3 e6 3.Bf4 c5 4.e3 Nc6 5.c4 Nf6 6.Nc3 cxd4 7.exd4 Ne4 8.Bd3 Bb4 9.Rc1 Qa5 10.Qb3 dxc4 11.Bxc4 g5 12.Be3 g4 13.Ne5

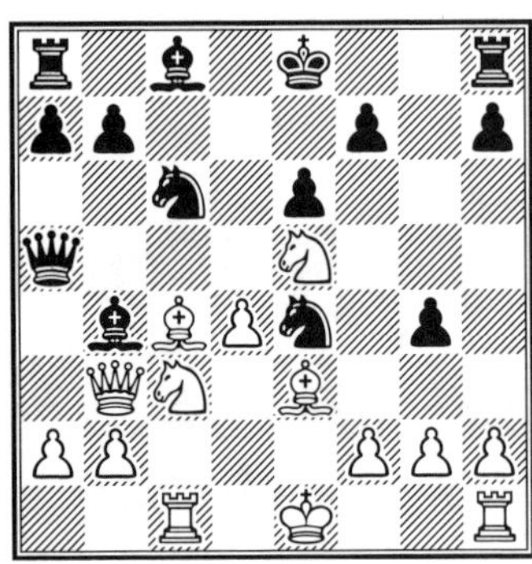

13...Nxe5 14.dxe5 Bxc3+ 15.bxc3 b6 16.0-0 Bd7 17.Rfd1

17.Bd3 Ba4 18.Qb1 Nxc3 19.Rxc3 Qxc3 20.Bb5+ Bxb5 21.Qxb5+ Kf8 22.Bh6+ Kg8 23.Qd7, 1-0.

17...Ba4 18.Qb1 Nxc3 19.Rxc3! Qxc3 20.Bb5+ Bxb5 21.Qxb5+ Kf8

21...Ke7 22.Rc1.

22.Bh6+

22.Rc1 was also very strong.

22...Kg8

22...Ke7 23.Rd1 gives White a winning attack.

23.Qd7, 1-0.

Alexander Alekhine vs. Károly Sterk, Budapest 1921

1.d4 d5 2.Nf3 e6 3.c4 Nf6 4.Nc3 Nbd7 5.e3 Bd6 6.Nb5 Be7 7.Qc2 c6 8.Nc3 0-0 9.Bd3 dxc4 10.Bxc4 c5 11.dxc5 Bxc5 12.0-0 b6 13.e4 Bb7 14.Bg5 Qc8 15.Qe2 Bb4 16.Bd3 Bxc3 17.Rfc1 Nxe4 18.Bxe4 Bxe4 19.Qxe4 Nc5 20.Qe2 Ba5 21.Rab1 Qa6 22.Rc4 Na4 23.Bf6!! Rfc8

This allows black's King to run to f8 in some key variations. 23...Rac8 24.Rg4! Qxe2 25.Rxg7+ Kh8 26.Rg6 mate.

24.Qe5!!

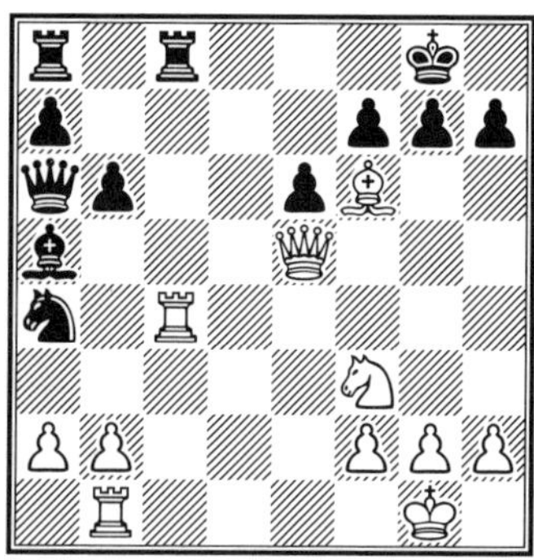

24...Rc5

- 24...Qxc4 25.Qg5 Kf8 (Better, but also hopeless, is 25...Qc1+ 26.Rxc1 Rxc1+ 27.Qxc1 gxf6 28.Qc6 Rd8 29.Qxa4) 26.Qxg7+ Ke8 27.Qg8+ Kd7 28.Ne5+ Kc7 29.Qxf7+ Kb8 (29...Kd6 30.Qd7+ Kc5 31.Be7 mate) 30.Nd7+ Kc7 31.Nc5+ Kc6 32.Qd7+ Kxc5 33.Be7 mate.
- 24...Rxc4 25.Qg5 Rg4 26.Qxg4 g6 27.Qxa4 –Alekhine.
- 24...gxf6 25.Rg4+ Kf8 26.Qd6+ Ke8 27.Rg8 mate.

25.Qg3

Also winning is 25.Rxc5 Qd3 (25...Nxc5 26.Qg5 Kf8 27.Qxg7+ Ke8 28.Ne5 and mates) 26.Rcc1 gxf6 27.Qxf6 with a material advantage and a strong kingside attack.

25...g6 26.Rxa4 Qd3 27.Rf1 Rac8 28.Rd4 Qf5 29.Qf4 Qc2 30.Qh6, 1-0.

Alexander Alekhine vs. Karel Hromádka, Pistyan 1922

1.d4 d5 2.Nf3 Nf6 3.c4 c6 4.Nc3 Qb6 5.e3 Bg4 6.cxd5 cxd5 7.Qa4+ Bd7 8.Bb5 a6 9.Bxd7+ Nbxd7 10.0-0 e6 11.Ne5 Qa7 12.Nxd7 Nxd7 13.e4!

If White wants to make use of the fact that black's King is still in the center, he needs to play with great energy and do his best to rip open as many lines as possible. Quite developing moves won't get the job done.

13...b5 14.Qc2 dxe4 15.d5! e5 16.a4 b4 17.Nxe4 Qb7 18.Rd1 Rc8 19.Qe2 Be7 20.Qg4

Other strong moves were 20.d6 and 20.Qf3 when 20...0-0 loses to 21.d6 Bd8 22.Nf6+ followed by 23.Qxb7.

20...g6 21.Bg5!

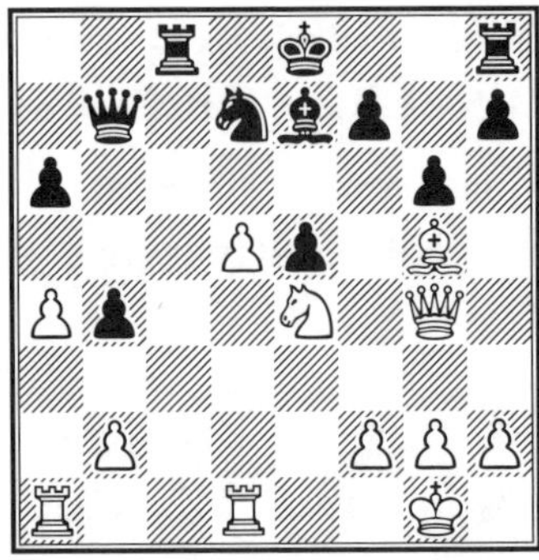

Keeping black's King in the middle since 21...Bxg5 loses immediately to 22.Nd6+.

21...h6 22.Bxe7 Kxe7 23.Qh4+ g5 24.Qg4 Rc4 25.Qf5 Rf8 26.b3 Rcc8 27.Nf6 Rc5 28.Nxd7 Qc8 29.d6+, 1-0.

Alexander Alekhine vs. Max Euwe, The Hague 1921

1.d4 d5 2.Nf3 c5 3.c4 e6 4.e3 Nc6 5.Nc3 Nf6 6.a3 Bd6 7.dxc5 Bxc5 8.b4 Bd6 9.Bb2 0-0 10.Rc1 Qe7 11.cxd5 exd5 12.Nxd5 Nxd5 13.Qxd5 a5 14.Bb5

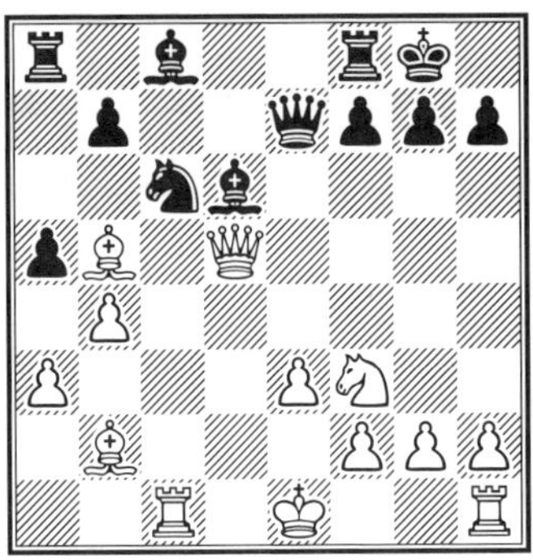

14...axb4 15.a4 Rd8 16.Qh5 g6 17.Qh6 Ne5 18.Ng5 f6 19.Bxe5 fxg5 20.Bc4+

Black resigned here.

20...Be6 21.Bxe6+ Qf7

The same make occurs after 21...Qxe6.

22.Qg7, 1-0.

Alexander Alekhine vs. Efim Bogoljubov, Triberg 1921

1.d4 Nf6 2.Nf3 e6 3.c4 b6 4.g3 Bb7 5.Bg2 c5 6.dxc5 Bxc5 7.0-0 0-0 8.Nc3 d5 9.Nd4 Bxd4 10.Qxd4 Nc6 11.Qh4 dxc4 12.Rd1 Qc8 13.Bg5 Nd5 14.Nxd5 exd5 15.Rxd5! Nb4

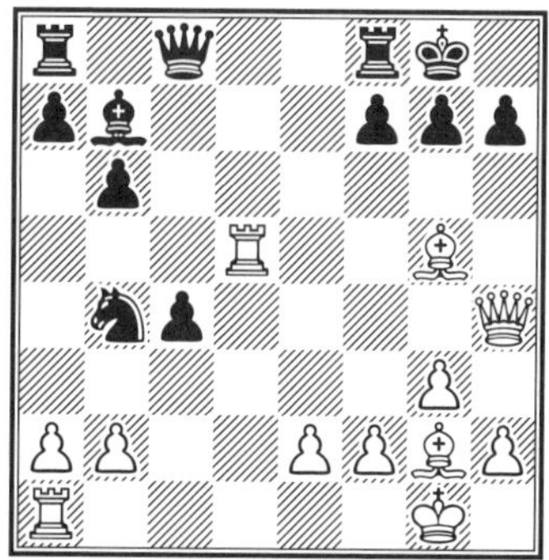

16.Be4!! f5

- 16…g6 17.Bf6! Nxd5 18.Bxd5 Qf5 19.Bxb7 and wins.
- 16…h6 17.Bxh6 f5 18.Rd6 (Alekhine's analysis was 18.Qg5 Qc7 19.Bxg7 Qxg7 20.Qxg7+ Kxg7 21.Rd7+ Rf7 22.Rxf7+ Kxf7 23.Bxb7 and wins) 18…fxe4 19.Bxg7 Qf5 20.Bd4 with a winning attack.

17.Bxf5 Rxf5 18.Rd8+ Qxd8 19.Bxd8 and Black resigned on move 30.

Alexander Alekhine vs. Frederick Yates, London 1922

1.d4 Nf6 2.c4 e6 3.Nf3 d5 4.Nc3 Be7 5.Bg5 0-0 6.e3 Nbd7 7.Rc1 c6 8.Qc2 Re8 9.Bd3 dxc4 10.Bxc4 Nd5 11.Ne4 f5 12.Bxe7 Qxe7 13.Ned2 b5

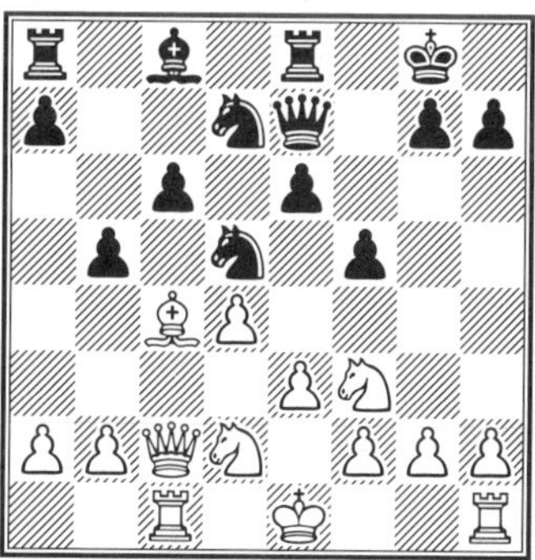

14.Bxd5!

White intends to exchange a pair of Knights, leaving him with a monster Knight vs. black's terrible Bishop.

14…cxd5 15.0-0 a5 16.Nb3 a4 17.Nc5 Nxc5 18.Qxc5 Qxc5 19.Rxc5 b4 20.Rfc1 Ba6 21.Ne5 and White has a strategically winning position.

Alexander Alekhine vs. Friedrich Sämisch, Vienna 1922

1.e4 c5 2.Nf3 Nc6 3.d4 cxd4 4.Nxd4 g6 5.c4 Bg7 6.Nb3 Nf6 7.Nc3 d6 8.Be2 Be6 9.0-0 h5 10.c5 dxc5 11.Nxc5 Bc8 12.Qxd8+ Kxd8 13.Rd1 Nd7 14.Bc4 Bxc3

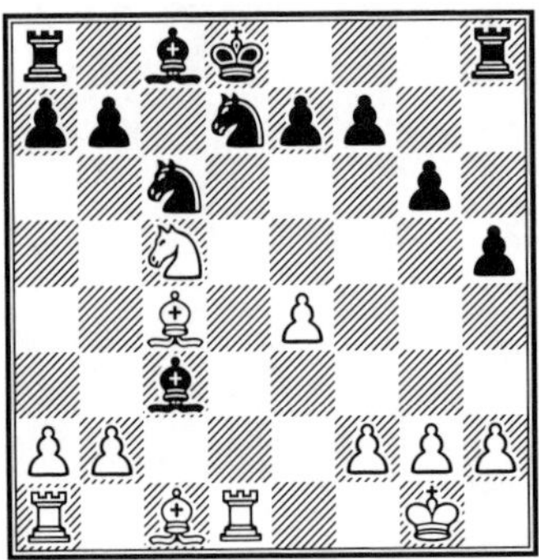

15.Bxf7! Kc7

15...Bf6 16.Ne6 mate.

16.Ne6+ Kb8 17.bxc3 Nde5 18.Bf4 Bxe6 19.Bxe6 Rf8 20.Bg3

Black resigned here. Play could have continued: 20...Rf6 21.Rd8+! Nxd8 Also hopeless is 21...Kc7 22.Rxa8 Rxe6 23.f4. 22.Bxe5, 1-0.

The Plan Fails

I previously described Alekhine's plan to force a match with Capablanca: "Play against the world's best and win every tournament, thus showing that he was the true challenger to the title. And, at first he would also avoid Capablanca until he felt he was closer to him in strength."

At first that plan was working, and he won tournament after tournament. However, winning every tournament is impossible (nobody has achieved this, including Capablanca, Fischer, and Kasparov.) so his plan was, ultimately, doomed to fail.

I left our hero in a bad state: his plan of winning every tournament was suddenly shattered, the stress of chess politics (i.e., getting a match with Capablanca) was dragging him down, and an attempted suicide (most chess scholars don't believe this happened, but the facts I listed in Part Two have convinced me that it did) added to his overall bleak situation.

The New Plan — Righting the Ship

Phase One

After his failure to win every tournament, his depression concerning his private life (or lack thereof), and the enormous wall created by the London Protocol , most people would accept "reality" and give up the near-impossible chase to gain a title bout. But chess was Alekhine's life, and if he was going to live, then his dream had to live too! Thus a new, more realistic two-part plan evolved. In phase one Alekhine participated in a few events (all in the first two thirds of 1923) to show he was still a top contender (the results renewed his confidence in his own chess powers):

Karlsbad (1923): Alekhine, Bogoljubov, and Maróczy tied for first with 11½ out of 17.

Margate (1923): Grünfeld first with 5½ from 7, Alekhine, Bogoljubov, Michell, and Muffang tied second/fifth with 4½.

Portsmouth (1923): Alekhine first with 10½ from 11. A great score, but the field was far weaker than Alekhine was.

Paris (1923): Two game Match vs. Muffang won by Alekhine with a 2-0 score.

Alexander Alekhine vs. Friedrich Sämisch, Berlin 1923

Both players were blindfolded.

1.e4 c5 2.Nf3 Nc6 3.Be2 e6 4.0-0 d6 5.d4 cxd4 6.Nxd4 Nf6 7.Bf3 Ne5 8.c4 Nxf3+ 9.Qxf3 Be7 10.Nc3 0-0 11.b3 Nd7 12.Bb2 Bf6 13.Rad1 a6 14.Qg3 Qc7 15.Kh1 Rd8 16.f4 b6 17.f5 Be5

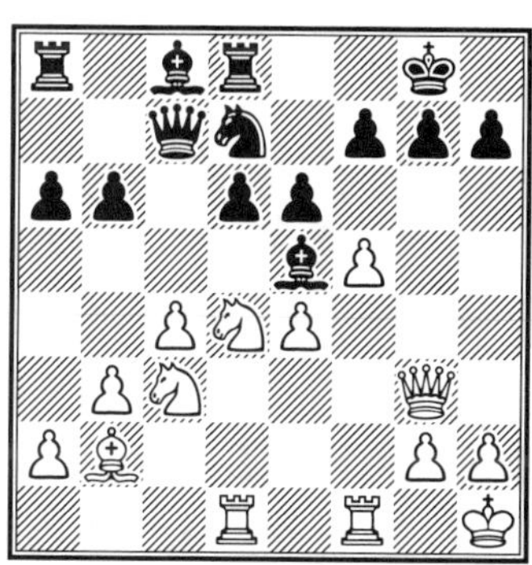

18.fxe6!! Bxg3 19.exf7+ Kh8 20.Nd5!

Sämisch resigned here, to the surprise of the confused audience!

20...Qb7

- 20...Qb8 21.Nc6 Qb7 22.Nxd8 Qb8 23.f8=Q+ mates.

- 20...Qa7 21.Nc6 Bh4 22.Nxa7 Rxa7 23.g3 Bg5 24.h4 Bh6 25.Nxb6 Nf8 26.Nxc8 Rxc8 27.Rxd6 (Threatening Rxh6) 27...Be3 28.Ba3 and Black doesn't have a good move: 28...a5 29.Rf3, 1-0.

21.Ne6 Rg8

21...Be5 22.Nxd8.

22.fxg8=Q+ Kxg8 23.Ne7+ Kh8 24.Bxg7, 1-0.

Alexander Alekhine vs. Philip Milner-Barry, Cheltenham 1923

Blindfold simultaneous exhibition.

1.d4 d5 2.c4 e6 3.Nc3 Nf6 4.Bg5 Nbd7 5.e3 Be7 6.Nf3 0-0 7.Rc1 c6 8.Bd3 h6 9.Bf4 Nh5 10.0-0 Nxf4 11.exf4 Nf6 12.Re1 dxc4 13.Bxc4 b6 14.Ne5 Bb7 15.Qf3 Qc7 16.Qh3 Rad8 17.f5 exf5 18.Qxf5 Bc8 19.Qf3 Bb7 20.Bb3 Rxd4

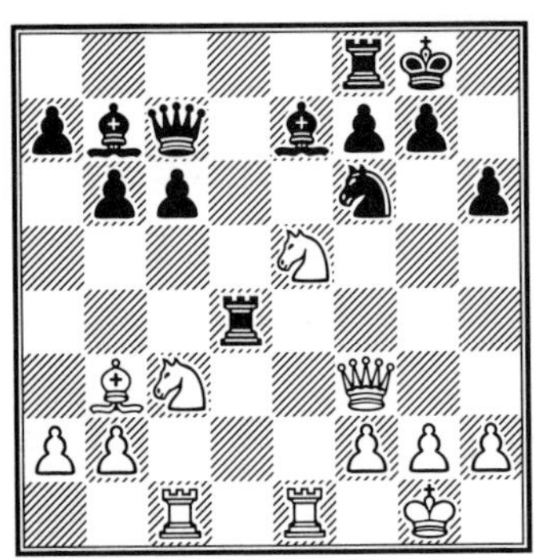

21.Nxf7!

Stronger than the immediate 21.Nb5.

21...Rxf7 22.Nb5 cxb5 23.Bxf7+ Kf8

23...Kxf7 24.Rxc7 Bxf3 25.Rexe7+

24.Rxc7 Bxf3 25.Rcxe7, and White won.

Alexander Alekhine vs. André Muffang, Margate 1923

1.d4 d5 2.c4 e6 3.Nf3 Nf6 4.Nc3 Be7 5.Bg5 Nbd7 6.e3 0-0 7.Rc1 c6 8.Qc2 dxc4 9.Bxc4 Nd5 10.Ne4 Qa5 11.Ke2 Re8 12.Rhd1 N7b6 13.Bb3 Qb5+ 14.Qd3 Qxd3+ 15.Rxd3 Bxg5 16.Nfxg5 Nf6 17.Nd6 Re7 18.e4 h6 19.Nf3 Rb8

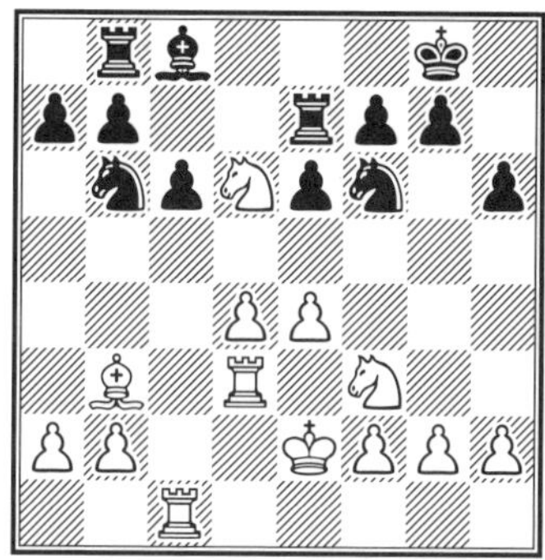

20.g4! Nxg4

20...Bd7 21.g5 hxg5 22.Nxg5 Nc8 23.Nc4 [Alekhine]: "with an overwhelming position for White."

21.Rg1 Nf6 22.Ne5! Nbd7 23.Nexf7! Nh5

23...Rxf7? 24.Bxe6.

24.Rf3 Kh7 25.e5! Nf8 26.Nxh6 b6 27.Nhf7 Kg8 28.Ke3 g6 29.Bc2 Kg7 30.Rg5!, 1-0.

Alexander Alekhine vs. Akiba Rubinstein, Karlsbad 1923

1.d4 d5 2.c4 e6 3.Nf3 Nf6 4.Nc3 Be7 5.Bg5 Nbd7 6.e3 0-0 7.Rc1 c6 8.Qc2 a6 9.a4 Re8 10.Bd3 dxc4 11.Bxc4 Nd5 12.Bf4 Nxf4 13.exf4 c5 14.dxc5 Qc7 15.0-0 Qxf4 16.Ne4 Nxc5 17.Nxc5 Bxc5 18.Bd3 b6 19.Bxh7+ Kh8 20.Be4 Ra7 21.b4 Bf8 22.Qc6 Rd7 23.g3 Qb8 24.Ng5!

Threatening 25.Nxf7+ Rxf7 26.Qxe8.

24...Red8 25.Bg6!!

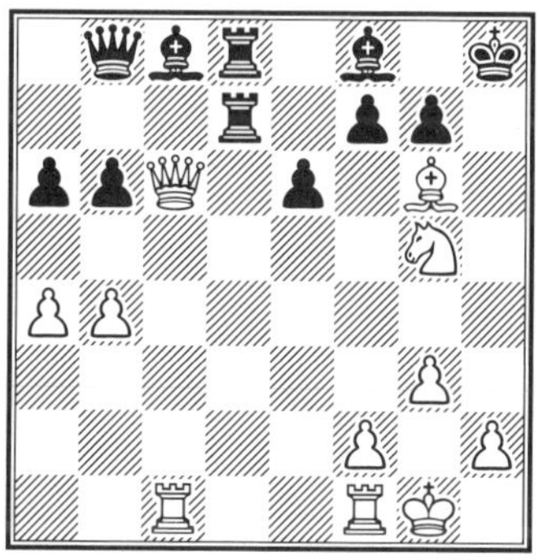

A famous move. It threatens to get white's Queen to the h-file (26.Qe4 followed by Qh4 mating, or 26.Qg2 and Qh3 mating), it threatens 26.Nxf7+, and it also stops ...g7-g6.

25...Qe5 26.Nxf7+ Rxf7 27.Bxf7 Qf5 28.Rfd1! Rxd1+ 29.Rxd1 Qxf7 30.Qxc8 Kh7 31.Qxa6 Qf3 32.Qd3+, 1-0.

Ernst Grünfeld vs. Alexander Alekhine, Karlsbad 1923

1.d4 Nf6 2.c4 e6 3.Nc3 d5 4.Bg5 Be7 5.Nf3 Nbd7 6.e3 0-0 7.Rc1 c6 8.Qc2 a6 9.a3 h6 10.Bh4 Re8 11.Bd3 dxc4 12.Bxc4 b5 13.Ba2 c5 14.Rd1 cxd4 15.Nxd4 Qb6 16.Bb1 Bb7 17.0-0 Rac8 18.Qd2 Ne5 19.Bxf6 Bxf6 20.Qc2 g6 21.Qe2 Nc4 22.Be4 Bg7 23.Bxb7 Qxb7 24.Rc1 e5 25.Nb3 e4 26.Nd4 Red8 27.Rfd1 Ne5 28.Na2 Nd3 29.Rxc8 Qxc8 30.f3 Rxd4!

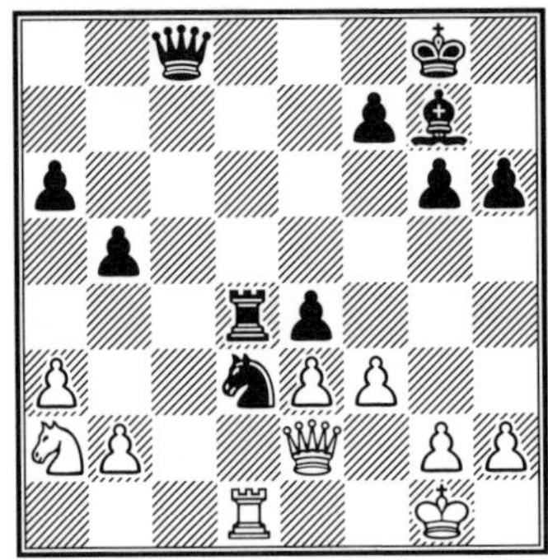

31.fxe4

31.exd4 Bxd4+ 32.Kf1 Nf4 33.Qd2 (33.Qxe4 Qc4+ 34.Ke1 Nxg2 35.Kd2 Be3+ wins) 33...Qc4+ 34.Ke1 e3! 35.Qxd4 Nxg2 mate.

31...Nf4!! 32.exf4 Qc4!

Threatening both 33...Qxe2 and 33...Qxa2.

33.Qxc4 Rxd1+ 34.Qf1 Bd4+, 0-1.

Alexander Alekhine vs. Géza Maróczy, Karlsbad 1923

1.d4 Nf6 2.c4 e6 3.Nf3 d5 4.Nc3 Be7 5.Bg5 0-0 6.e3 Ne4 7.Bxe7 Qxe7 8.Qb3 Nxc3 9.Qxc3 c6 10.Bd3 Nd7 11.0-0 f5 12.Rac1 g5 13.Nd2 Rf7 14.f3 e5 15.cxd5!

Opening up the center so White is better developed forces can penetrate.

15...cxd5 16.e4! fxe4 17.fxe4 Rxf1+ 18.Rxf1 exd4

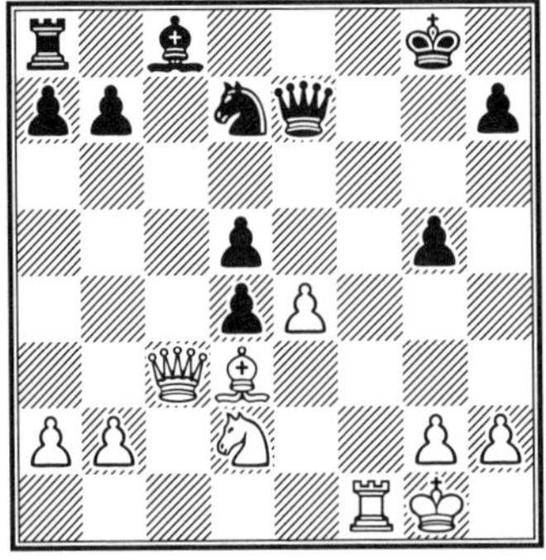

19.Qc7!

A dead winner since it freezes Black's whole army.

19...Kg7 20.Rf5 dxe4 21.Nxe4

21.Bc4 is also strong.

21...Qb4 22.Rxg5+

Black resigned here.

22...Kh6 23.Qg3! Stopping ...Qe1+ and threatening Qh4 mate. Black has to resign since there's no defense to the mate threat.

Phase Two—Chess Politician/Rock Star

Having come to terms with the fact that nobody could win every tournament, Alekhine decided that his best path would be to cut down on his playing schedule and instead go on a long tour (giving endless simultaneous exhibitions) that would make him a household name all over the world. By doing this he hoped to secure sponsors who would back his bid for a match vs. Capablanca. The Muffang match was his final event of 1923. He spent the rest of the year (from September on) traveling on his world simultaneous tour.

September and October were devoted to many exhibitions in Scotland and England. The most important part of his tour, though, was to be held in the "New World" where money was everywhere and potential backers would be eyeing his every move.

The Grand Canadian Tour

This was the first time Alekhine had left Europe. Here he did interviews, made friends in high places, constantly stayed in the public eye, gave six normal simultaneous exhibitions and one blindfold exhibition (where he played twenty-one games at once) for an overall score of 163 wins, 10 losses, and 17 draws.

The Great U.S. Tour and New York 1924

Alekhine hit U.S. soil on December 5. He went from one end of the country to the other, playing no less than twenty-four exhibitions from December 1923 to March of 1924 (three of them were blindfold simuls). His total score: 626 wins, 41 losses, 78 draws.

One would think he would be completely exhausted at this point, but not the case as the 1924 New York tournament was being held one week after his final exhibition!

Before the tournament the *Pittsburgh Post* reported Alekhine's prediction about everyone's chances:

> The international tournament, which will be held in New York beginning next Sunday, March 16, will, of course, have a great influence on U.S. chess. To my mind it will be the greatest tournament that has been played in the world since the Hastings tournament in 1895 since all the strongest exponents of the game living today will be represented. They are coming from every country where chess has become a favorite. England will have two, France two,

> Germany two, Russia and Hungary one, and, of course, the United States will present Marshall and Edward Lasker.
>
> Who will win? That is a hard question to answer, but I believe that Capablanca has the best chance, although there are others. Dr. Emanuel Lasker is still a very strong player to be reckoned with. Then there are Bogoljubov and Réti, who, while being the youngest [Alekhine was actually the youngest player in the tournament], are very strong indeed. It will be a wonderful event. How shall I do? The very best I can, you may be sure!

The legendary New York 1924 was dominated by three men: First was Emanuel Lasker with the insane score of 16-4, Capablanca was second with 14½-5½, and third Alekhine with 12-8.

Since Emanuel Lasker made it clear that he had no interest in the World Championship and didn't want to play another match with Capablanca, Alekhine was the obvious challenger for Capablanca's throne. However, it still seemed clear that Alekhine was a distant third behind Lasker and Capablanca (this meant that sponsors weren't lining up to pay for a Capablanca vs. Alekhine match). To make matters even worse, Réti was still in the conversation for a match, Nimzowitsch and Bogolubov were improving rapidly and had started scoring some very impressive victories of their own, and even Spielmann suddenly became a monster and joined in the now completely confusing "who is going to be the World Championship challenger" mess.

It's important to note that Alekhine wasn't happy about his third place finish in New York 1924! Nonetheless, it turned out that his first round game vs. Capablanca taught him something of enormous importance.

In his book *On the Road to the World Championship,* Alekhine wrote:[1]

> In spite of my failure in this tournament, I took home one valuable moral victory, and that was the lesson I leaned from my first game with Capablanca which had the effect of a revelation on me. Having outplayed me in the opening, having reached a won position in the middlegame and having carried over a large part of his advantage into a Rook ending, the Cuban then allowed me to neutralize his superiority in that ending and finally had to make do with a draw.
>
> That made me think, for Capablanca had been trying very hard in this game, so as to draw nearer to Dr. Lasker who was in the lead, and who had won against me the previous day. I was convinced that if I had been in Capablanca's position, I should certainly have won. Thus I had finally detected a slight weakness in my future opponent: increasing uncertainty when confronted with stubborn resistance! Of course I had already noticed Capablanca committing occasional slight inaccuracies, but I should not have thought that he would be unable to rid himself of this failing even when he tried his utmost. That was an exceedingly important lesson for the future!

1 Alexander Alekhine, *On the Road to the World Championship 1923-1927.* Oxford: Pergamon Press, 1984.

Alexander Alekhine vs. Richard Réti, New York 1924

1.d4 Nf6 2.c4 g6 3.g3 Bg7 4.Bg2 0-0 5.Nc3 d6 6.Nf3 Nc6 7.d5 Nb8 8.0-0 Bg4 9.h3 Bxf3 10.exf3 e6 11.f4 exd5 12.cxd4 c5 13.dxc6 Nxc6 14.Be3 Qd7 15.Qa4 Rac8 16.Rad1 b6 17.b3 Rfd8 18.Rd3 Ne7

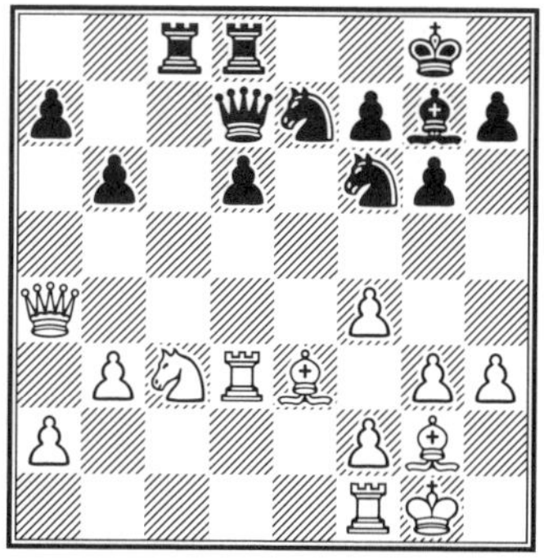

19.Nb5!

There's no good way to protect a7!

19...d5 20.Nxa7 Ra8 21.Bxb6 Qxa4 22.bxa4 Rd7 23.Nb5 Rxa4 24. Nc3 and White's extra pawn plus his two Bishops eventually led to victory.

Paris (1925): Alekhine dominated this small tournament (6½-1½) well ahead of Tartakower, Opočenský, Znosko-Borovsky, and Colle.

Hastings (1925): At year end, Alekhine tied for first with 8½ out of 9, an incredible score, but Vidmar was right with him all the way!

Alexander Alekhine vs. Rudolf Mikulka, Olomouc 1925 (simultaneous exhibition)

1.e4 e5 2.f4 exf4 3.Nf3 g5 4.d4 h6 5.Bc4 Bg7 6.Nc3 Nc6 7.Nd5 d6 8.c3 Nge7 9.0-0 Nxd5 10.Bxd5 Ne7 11.Bb3 Ng6 12.g3 fxg3 13.Nxg5 0-0 14.Qh5 gxh2+ 15.Kh1 hxg5 16.Qxg6 Qe8 17.Bxg5 Be6

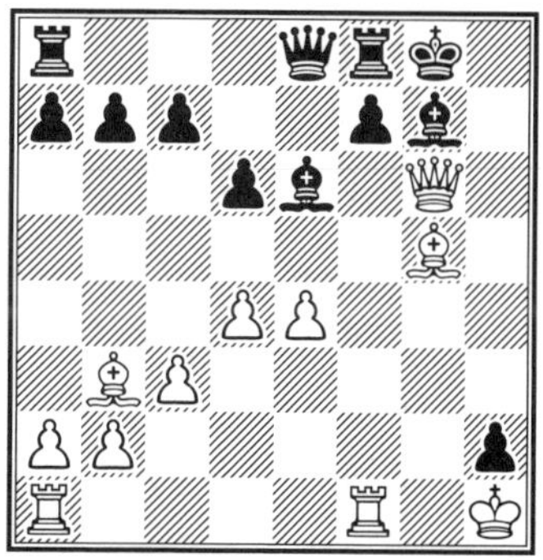

18.Rxf7!! Bxf7

18...Qxf7 19.Bxe6; 18...Rxf7 19.Bxe6 Kf8 20.Bd5 leaves Black in bad shape since it's hard to do anything. For example, 20...Rf2 21.Qh7 and Black has nothing better than 21...Rf7.

19.Bf6! and Black resigns.

Alexander Alekhine vs. Karel Opočenský, Paris 1925

1.d4 d5 2.c4 c6 3.Nc3 Nf6 4.e3 Bf5 5.cxd5 Nxd5 6.Bc4 e6 7.Nge2 Nd7 8.e4 Nxc3 9.Nxc3 Bg6 10.0-0 Qh4 11.d5 exd5 12.g3 Qf6 13.exd5 Bc5 14.Re1+ Kf8 15.Bf4 Nb6 16.Bb3 h5 17.h4 Kg8 18.Rc1 Bd4 19.dxc6 bxc6 20.Ne4 Bxe4 21.Rxe4 c5 22.Qe2 g6 23.Bg5 Qd6 24.Qf3 Qf8

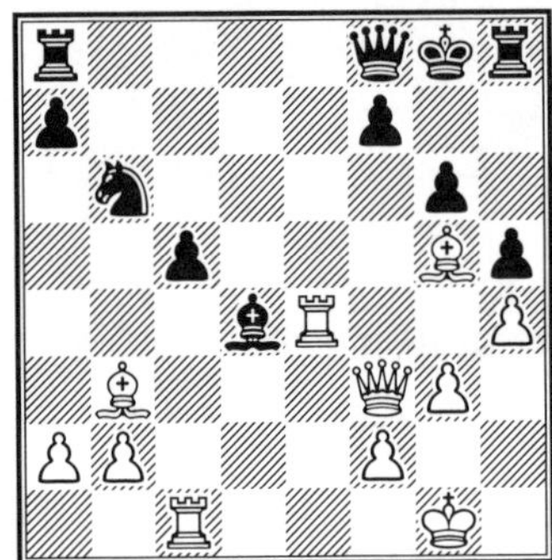

25.Rxd4! cxd4 26.Rc6

Threatening 27.Rxg6+.

26...Kh7

26...Qg7 27.Bf6 Qh6 28.Bxf7+ is crushing.

27.Bxf7 Rc8 28.Rxg6 and the threat of 29.Qxh5+ forces mate in a few moves, so Black resigned.

You can just stare in wonder at this next game between Réti and Alekhine—one of the finest combinations in the history of chess.

Richard Réti vs. Alexander Alekhine, Baden-Baden 1925

1.g3 e5 2.Nf3 e4 3.Nd4 d5 4.d3 exd3 5.Qxd3 Nf6 6.Bg2 Bb4+ 7.Bd2 Bxd2+ 8.Nxd2 0-0 9.c4 Na6 10.cxd5 Nb4 11.Qc4 Nbxd5 12.N2b3 c6 13.0-0 Re8 14.Rfd1 Bg4 15.Rd2 Qc8 16.Nc5 Bh3 17.Bf3 Bg4 18.Bg2 Bh3 19.Bf3 Bg4 20.Bh1 h5 21.b4 a6 22.Rc1 h4 23.a4 hxg3 24.hxg3 Qc7 25.b5 axb5 26.axb5

White has played very well and has a positional advantage. Many grandmasters would fall victim to this as Black, but Alekhine isn't anyone's victim. I'll keep the notes to a minimum so you can zip through the drama that occurs.

26...Re3!!

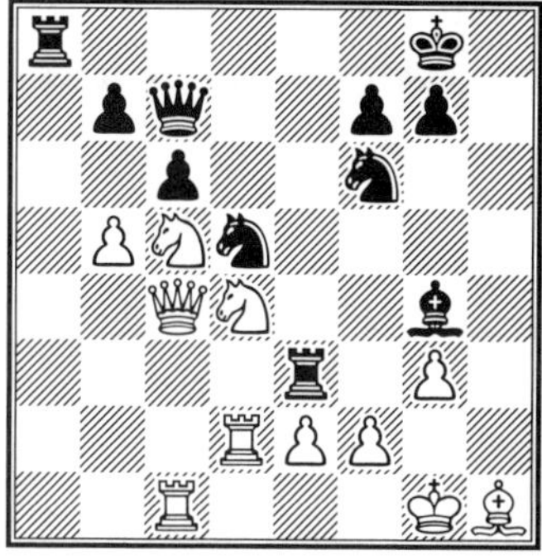

Suddenly white's King feels a bit loose.

27.Nf3?

[Kasparov]: "From now on Alekhine makes a series of moves that sweep White off the board."

27...cxb5! 28.Qxb5 Nc3 29.Qxb7 Qxb7 30.Nxb7 Nxe2+ 31.Kh2

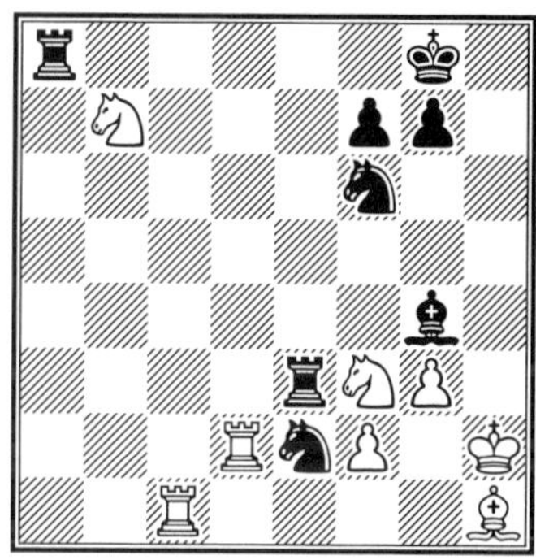

31...Ne4!! 32.Rc4 Nxf2 33.Bg2

[Kasparov]: "Black is clearly winning, but Alekhine's final combination makes this game a true masterpiece."

33...Be6! 34.Rcc2 Ng4+ 35.Kh3 Ne5+ 36.Kh2 Rxf3! 37.Rxe2 Ng4+ 38.Kh3 Ne3+ 39.Kh2 Nxc2 40.Bxf3 Nd4 41.Rf2 Nxf3+ 42.Rxf3 Bd5

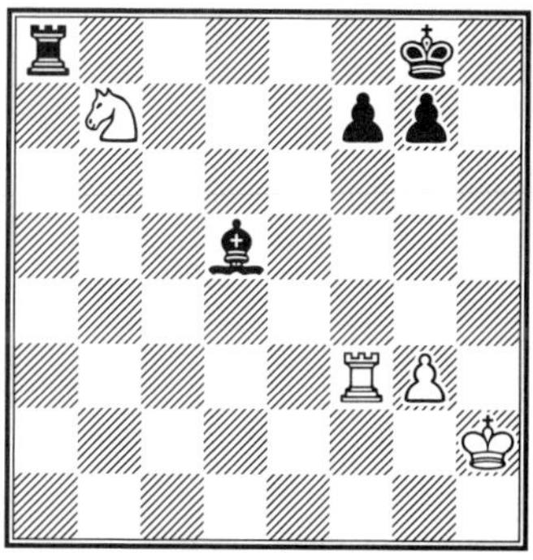

0-1. Alekhine calls this "the final point!"

[Kasparov]: "I think there is reason to nominate this game the most beautiful ever played in the history of chess."

Birmingham (1926): Alekhine first with 5-0 against a relatively weak field.

Dresden (1926): Nimzowitsch first with 8½ from 9, Alekhine second with 7-2. Both led Rubinstein, Tartakower, von Holzhausen, Johner, Sämisch, Yates, Blümich, and L. Steiner.

Scarborough (1926): Alekhine first with 5½ of 6 against a relatively weak field.

Semmering (1926): Spielmann first with 13-4, Alekhine second with 12½-4½ ahead of Vidmar, Nimzowitsch, Tartakower, Rubinstein, Tarrasch, Réti, Grünfeld, and others.

Buenos Aires (1926): Alekhine first with 10-0 against a relatively weak field.

Alekhine was viewed as Capablanca's most dangerous challenger, but the rest of the "who will play Capablanca" group—Nimzowitsch, Bogoljubov, Spielmann, and Réti—were neck and neck. Then, after Nimzowitsch dominated a couple more events, and Spielmann won another one, things were completely confused. All these players were worthy opponents, but in the end money talks (loudly!), and Alekhine was well aware that whoever came up with the London Protocol's demands would undoubtedly be chosen by Capablanca.

Striking Gold in South America

Alekhine failed to get the desperately needed financial backing for a World Championship challenge during his Canadian and American tour, however his South American tour (August-November 1926) struck gold! During his stay in Buenos Aires he was introduced to Argentina's president, various powerful government officials, and quite a few wealthy patrons of chess who gave him the financial guarantees he needed to meet the London Protocols outrageous stipulations. As a result, he was finally able to issue a challenge to Capablanca.

Alekhine gave thirty-one exhibitions in Argentina, with a total score of 202 wins, 18 losses, and 11 draws. He gave also three exhibitions in Uruguay and three in Brazil, with a total score of 69 wins, 3 losses, and 7 draws.

Match with Euwe

After returning to Europe, Alekhine played a ten game match with Euwe (Dec. 22, 1926 to Jan. 8, 1927). Alekhine was expected to wipe Euwe out, and Euwe himself felt the likely score would be 7½-2½ in favor of Alekhine. However, Alekhine played poorly (I can't image him not being completely burned out after his South American tour) and after nine games the score was even! Euwe would have been delighted to draw the final game and walk away with a

THE ILLUSTRATED LONDON NEWS, Dec. 10, 1927.—1064

How Dr. Alekhine Became the New Chess Champion.

AFTER the greatest struggle in the history of the game, the match for the Chess Championship of the World terminated in the victory of Dr. A. Alekhine, who wrested the honour from the holder, Señor Capablanca, with a score of six games to three, after twenty-three draws. The result was not altogether unexpected, although the difference between the characteristic styles of the combatants left no room for confidence either way. The following is a full score of the games that decided the result:—

FIRST GAME in the World's Championship Match, played at Buenos Ayres, between Señor J. R. Capablanca and Dr. A. Alekhine. Won by Dr. Alekhine. This was a reconnaissance in force by both sides; but Señor Capablanca out-generalled himself by over-refinement in his operations.

(French Defence.)

WHITE (Señor C.)	BLACK (Dr. A.)	WHITE (Señor C.)	BLACK (Dr. A.)
1. P to K 4th	P to K 3rd	23. B to B 3rd	R to Q 6th
2. P to Q 4th	P to Q 4th	24. B to K 5th	R to Q sq
3. Kt to Q B 3rd	B to Kt 5th	25. B takes B	R takes B
4. P takes P	P takes P	26. R to K 5th	Q to B 6th
5. B to Q 3rd	Kt to Q B 3rd	27. R takes R P	Q takes R
6. Kt to K 2nd	K Kt to K 2nd	28. R to K 8th (ch)	K to R 2nd
7. Castles	B to K B 4th	29. Q takes R (ch)	Q to Kt 3rd
8. B takes B	Kt takes B	30. Q to Q sq	R to K 3rd
9. Q to Q 3rd	Q to Q 2nd	31. R to Q R 8th	R to K 4th
10. Kt to Q sq	Castles (K R)	32. R takes P	P to Q B 4th
11. Kt to K 3rd	Kt takes Kt	33. R to Q 7th	Q to K 3rd
12. B takes Kt	K R to K sq	34. Q to Q 3rd (ch)	P to Kt 3rd
13. Kt to B 4th	B to Q 3rd	35. R to Q 8th	P to Q 5th
14. K R to K sq	Kt to Kt 5th	36. P to R 4th	R to K 8th (ch)
15. Q to Kt 3rd	Q to B 4th	37. K to Kt 2nd	Q to Q B 3rd (ch)
16. Q R to B sq	Kt takes B P	38. P to B 3rd	R to K 6th
17. R takes Kt	Q takes Kt	39. Q to Q sq	Q to K 3rd
18. P to Kt 3rd	Q to B 4th	40. P to K Kt 4th	R to K 7th (ch)
19. Q R to K 2nd	P to Q Kt 3rd	41. K to R 3rd	Q to K 6th
20. Q to Kt 5th	P to K R 4th	42. Q to K R sq	Q to B 5th
21. P to K R 4th	R to K 5th	43. P to K R 5th	R to K B 7th
22. B to Q 2nd	R takes Q P		

White resigns.

THE NEW CHESS CHAMPION OF THE WORLD: DR. A. ALEKHINE.

TWENTY-NINTH GAME. WON BY SEÑOR CAPABLANCA

A more typical illustration of Señor Capablanca's style [illegible] be given. Special attention should be paid to the manner in which he wards off Black's King in the closing stages of the game.

(Queen's Gambit Declined.)

WHITE (Señor C.)	BLACK (Dr. A.)	WHITE (Señor C.)	BLACK (Dr. A.)
1. P to Q 4th	P to Q 4th	36. R to R 6th	B to B sq
2. P to Q B 4th	P to K 3rd	37. R to B 6th	R to B 2nd
3. Kt to Q B 3rd	Kt to K B 3rd	38. R takes R	Q takes R
4. B to Kt 5th	Q Kt to Q 2nd	39. Kt to K 5th	B to Kt 2nd
5. P to K 3rd	P to B 3rd	40. Q to R 8th (ch)	K to R 2nd
6. Kt to B 3rd	Q to R 4th	41. Kt to B 3rd	B to B 3rd
7. Kt to Q 2nd	B to Kt 5th	42. Q to R 6th	K to Kt 2nd
8. Q to B 2nd	P takes P	43. Q to Q 3rd	Q to Kt 2nd
9. B takes Kt	Kt takes B	44. P to K 4th	Q to B 3rd
10. Kt takes P	Q to B 2nd	45. P to R 3rd	Q to B 2nd
11. P to Q R 3rd	B to K 2nd	46. P to Q 5th	P takes P
12. P to K Kt 3rd	Castles	47. P takes P	Q to B 6th
13. B to Kt 2nd	B to Q 2nd	48. Q takes Q	B takes Q
14. P to Q Kt 4th	P to Q Kt 3rd	49. K to B sq	K to B 3rd
15. Castles K R	P to Q R 4th	50. K to K 2nd	B to Kt 5th
16. Kt to K 5th	P takes P	51. Kt to Q 4th	B to B 4th
17. P takes P	R takes R	52. Kt to B 6th	K to B 4th
18. R takes R	R to B sq	53. K to B 3rd	K to B 3rd
19. Kt takes B	Q takes Kt	54. P to Kt 4th	P takes P (ch)
20. Kt to R 4th	Q to Q sq	55. P takes P	K to Kt 4th
21. Q to Kt 3rd	Kt to Q 4th	56. Kt to K 5th	B to Q 5th
22. P to Kt 5th	P takes P	57. Kt takes P (ch)	K to B 3rd
23. Q takes P	R to R sq	58. Kt to Q 8th	B to Kt 3rd
24. R to Q B sq	R to R 4th	59. Kt to B 6th	B to B 4th
25. Q to B 6th	B to R 6th	60. K to B 4th	B takes P
26. R to Kt sq	B to B sq	61. P to Kt 5 (ch)	K to B 2nd
27. B takes Kt	R takes B	62. Kt to K 5 (ch)	K to K 2nd
28. Kt takes P	R to Q 3rd	63. Kt takes P (ch)	K to Q 3rd
29. Q to Kt 7th	P to R 4th	64. K to K 4th	B to Kt 6th
30. Kt to B 4th	R to Q 2nd	65. Kt to B 4th	K to K 2nd
31. Q to K 4th	R to B 2nd	66. K to K 5th	B to K 8th
32. Kt to K 5th	Q to B sq	67. P to Q 6th (ch)	K to Q 2nd
33. K to Kt 2nd	B to Q 3rd	68. P to Kt 6th	B to Kt 5th
34. R to R sq	R to Kt 2nd	69. K to Q 5th	K to K sq
35. Kt to Q 3rd	P to Kt 3rd	70. P to Q 7th (ch)	Resigns.

London Illustrated News, December 10, 1927 (Courtesy of the Cleveland Public Library's John G. White Collection).

Alekhine giving a simultaneous exhibition at the Marshall Chess club, December 1927 (Photo: Courtesy of the Marshall Chess Club).

tied match, but Alekhine was about to challenge for the world title and couldn't afford such a result! Though he had the Black pieces, he put everything he had into the game and, after playing in dynamic but risky fashion, managed to grasp victory in both the game and match.

Having "survived" the Euwe match, and with his match against Capablanca around the corner, Alekhine still played in two more tournaments.

Here's the final game of the Euwe match:

Max Euwe vs. Alexander Alekhine, Amsterdam match (10) 1926

1.Nf3 e6 2.c4 f5 3.g3 Nc6 4.d4 Bb4+ 5.Bd2 Bxd2+ 6.Qxd2 d6 7.Nc3 Nf6 8.Bg2 0-0 9.Rd1 Ne7 10.0-0 Ng6 11.Qc2 c6 12.e4 Qa5 13.exf5 exf5 14.d5 cxd5 15.Nxd5 Bd7 16.Nd4 f4

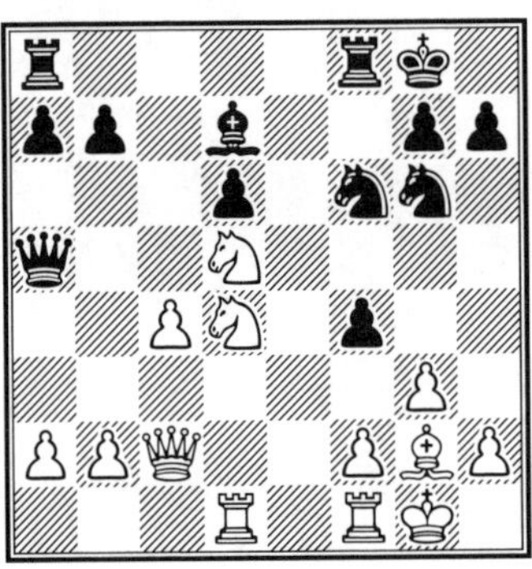

17.Rde1 Nxd5 18.Bxd5+ Kh8 19.Ne6 Rf6 20.Ng5 Raf8 21.Qb3 fxg3 22.Qxg3 Nf4 23.Re7 Rg6 24.Rf7 Rxf7 25.Nxf7+ Kg8 26.Ne5+ Qxd5 27.cxd5 Ne2+, 0-1.

New York 1927

This event allowed Alekhine to gauge his strength against an extremely formidable field: Capablanca, Nimzowitsch, Spielmann, Vidmar, and Marshall. Spielmann was a last-minute replacement for Bogoljubov whose financial demands didn't sit well with the organizers, and the telegram he sent to the tournament committee was the last straw:

> INSTEAD OF MEDIOCRE TOURNAMENT SUGGEST CONTEST CAPABLANCA VS. BOGOLJUBOV

Since Alekhine and Bogoljubov were friends, Norbert Lederer (one of the organizers) wrote the following letter to Alekhine that opened with the amusing first sentence of:

> I want to mention that friend Bogoljubov apparently no longer is entirely in his right mind...

Everyone had to play four games against everyone else. Capablanca ruled the roost with an undefeated 14-6, but the battle for the coveted second spot was tightly contested between Alekhine and Nimzowitsch. When the smoke cleared, Alekhine took second with 11½. He had a loss and 3 draws vs. Capablanca and a loss, win, and 2 draws vs. Nimzowitsch, who took third with 10½. Though it looked like Capablanca was invincible, it was also clear that Alekhine was indeed the correct challenger.

Kecskemet 1927

Everyone was shocked that Alekhine accepted the invitation to play in this tournament (held June 25 to July 12) with his match against Capablanca due to start in September—not to mention, in those days the ocean voyage from Europe to Buenos Aires would take a considerable long time!

Alekhine spoke of this in *On the Road to the World Championship*:

> It goes without saying that I was not satisfied either with my play against Dr. Euwe or with the way I performed in New York. Meanwhile my match with Capablanca had been settled and was soon to start. Had the labor of perfecting my play over the years been successful? Had I definitely remedied the faults in my style, retained the lessons of experience and fully understood what I had learned? I felt impelled to see if I had remembered everything that I had gradually been mastering, and so I was glad to accept the invitation to Kecskemet, despite the fact that it was only six weeks before my departure for the match in Buenos Aires.

Kecskemet had two groups with the top four in each playing a final event. The scores of both would be blended together and the guy with the most points would be the ultimate winner. Alekhine finished first (with 8 points) ahead of Asztalos, Kmoch, and Gilg (who also qualified for the final), while group two had Lajos Steiner scoring 8 ahead of Nimzowitsch with 6½, Ahues, and Vajda. Alekhine played it safe in the final scoring 1 win, no losses, and 7 draws (ending in first with a total of 12). Nimzowitsch caught fire and won 4 games but lost one and tied for second/third with Steiner with totals of 11½.

Alekhine had this to say about the second half of this tournament:

> I had convinced myself in the best possible way that I was playing logically and soundly and with the same facility as in Baden-Baden. The chess interest of the event was over for me by the end of the first half of the tournament. It was then just a matter of competing well enough to maintain a sufficient lead through until the finish.

Alexander Alekhine vs. Savielly Tartakower, Kecskemet 1927

1.e4 c6 2.d4 d5 3.Nc3 dxe4 4.Nxe4 Nf6 5.Ng3 e5 6.Nf3 exd4 7.Nxd4 Bc5 8.Qe2+ Be7 9.Be3 c5 10.Ndf5 0-0 11.Qc4 Re8 12.Bd3 b6 13.0-0-0

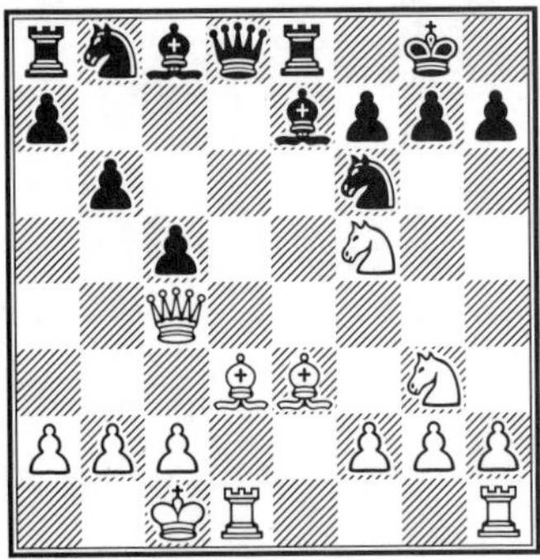

Ba6 14.Nh6+! gxh6 15.Bxh7+ Nxh7 16.Qg4+ Kh8 17.Rxd8 Rxd8 18.Qe4

Hitting two pieces at the same time and thus gaining a decisive edge in material.

18...Nc6 19.Qxc6 and White easily won.

The Fourth World Chess Champion

Going into the match, Alekhine had never won a game from Capablanca (their score was 5 wins for Capablanca, and 7 draws). Since the winner would be the first to win six games, and since Capablanca rarely lost even one game over a several year period, Alekhine's chances seemed to be zero. No wonder that the world was shocked by the result.

The match itself was a long, extremely tiring affair that covered thirty-four games before Alekhine achieved the necessary six wins (6-3 with 25 draws).

How did Alekhine take down his powerful foe?

There are several reasons:

- Alekhine had gotten better—he was yet to reach his prime!
- Capablanca wasn't aware of Alekhine's leap in strength, and was overconfident.
- Alekhine changed his style (just for this match), tossing out romantic leaps of fancy for a sturdier chess stance. Suddenly Capablanca was facing someone he had never played before—a guy who was positionally as solid as a rock, tactically supreme, and technically not too far from Capablanca himself.
- Alekhine was in fantastic physical shape, while Capablanca wasn't.

- Alekhine had discovered small weaknesses in his opponent's games and was determined to make maximum use of that knowledge, while Capablanca made no such preparations since he expected an easy match victory.
- Alekhine was completely focused on the match, while Capablanca explored the city every night, partied, and enjoyed the company of adoring female fans.

Personally, I think Capablanca was a slightly superior player in 1927, but the many factors above confused and ultimately overwhelmed the Cuban genius.

After the match Alekhine continued to improve, and by 1930 he was, without any doubt whatsoever, the strongest player on Earth. In a way, Alekhine's match victory was a form of "taking out the old and bringing in the new" since he created the blueprint that all modern chess pros follow today: Deep opening preparation, world class skills in every phase of the game, psychological preparation, physical preparation, and a deep study of the strengths and weaknesses of each of his opponents.

Alekhine's Prime Years

After winning the title in late 1927, Alekhine didn't play again (with the exception of blitz events and exhibitions) until June of 1929 at Bradley Beach in the United States. He easily won the event with 8 wins, 1 draw, no losses (Lajos Steiner came in second, a ½ point behind. Marshall came in sixth).

Alexander Alekhine vs. Herman Steiner, Bradley Beach 1929

1.d4 Nf6 2.Nf3 d5 3.c4 dxc4 4.e3 e6 5.Bxc4 c5 6.0-0 a6 7.Qe2 Nbd7 8.Nc3 Qc7 9.d5 exd5 10.Bxd5 Bd6 11.e4 0-0 12.Bg5 Ng4 13.h3 Nge5 14.Nh4 Nb6 15.f4

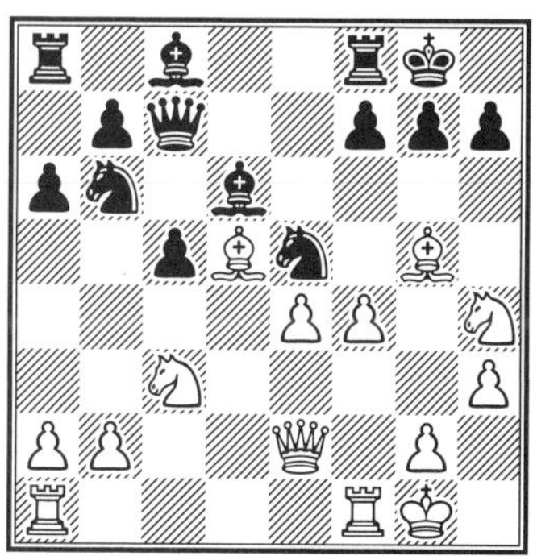

15...Nc6 16.f5 Ne5 17.Qh5 Re8 18.Rf4 Be7 19.f6 Bf8 20.fxg7 Bxg7 21.Raf1 Be6 22.Nf5 Bxd5 23.Nxg7 Ng6 24.Nxe8 Rxe8 25.Nd5, 1-0.

In September of 1929 Alekhine defended his title, in a twenty-five game match for the World Championship, against his old foe Bogoljubov, winning decisively (11 wins, 5 losses, 9 draws). Alekhine uncharacteristically turned several winning positions into draws, so the score could have been far worse for the challenger.

I'll take a moment out to share a story about these two players. I don't recall where or when it took place, but it's extremely funny and thus well worth sharing.

Both men (who were sometimes friends and sometimes not) played in the same tournament, and during the awards ceremony Alekhine found himself on the podium. Instead of doing the usual "thank you" routine, he said the following:

> Last night I had a dream. I had died and found myself at the Pearly Gates, but when I tried to enter I was told by Saint Peter that chess players were not allowed into Heaven! I wandered along the endless fence, hoping to find some other entry point, but it was hopeless. Then, suddenly I saw Bogoljubov on the other side, having a great time! I rushed back to Saint Peter and said, 'You told me that chess players weren't allowed in Heaven. But if that is so, why was Bogoljubov allowed in?'
>
> Saint Peter replied, 'Oh, he only thought he was a chess player!'

This shows that Alekhine had quite a sense of humor. Here's another example of his biting wit:

> When asked, "How is it that you pick better moves than your opponents?" I responded: "I'm very glad you asked that, because, as it happens, there is a very simple answer. I think up my own moves, and I make my opponent think up his."

Alexander Alekhine vs. Efim Bogoljubov, World Championship (1) 1929

1.d4 d5 2.c4 c6 3.Nf3 Nf6 4.Nc3 dxc4 5.a4 e6 6.e4 Bb4 7.e5 Nd5 8.Bd2 Bxc3 9.bxc3 b5 10.Ng5 f6 11.exf6 Nxf6 12.Be2 a6

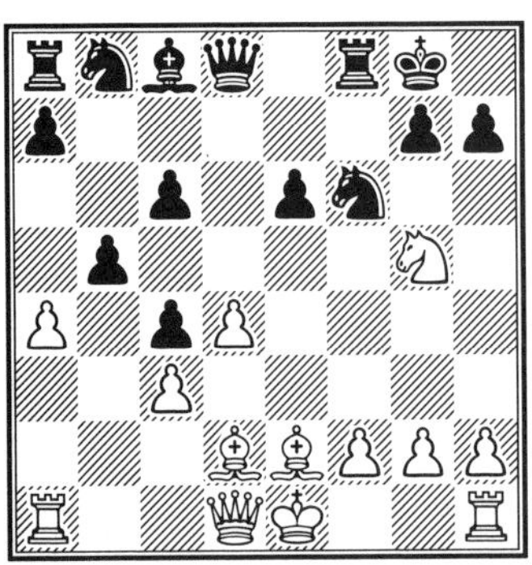

13.Bf3! h6 14.Bh5+ Nxh5 15.Qxh5+ Kd7 16.Nf7 Qe8 17.Qg6 Rg8 18.Bf4 Bb7 19.Bg3 Ke7 20.Bd6+ Kd7 21.0-0 c5 22.dxc5 Bd5 23.axb5 axb5 24.Rxa8 Bxa8 25.Ra1 Nc6 26.Ne5+! and Black resigned.

The years 1930 and 1931 showed Alekhine in his prime. An attacking/combinative genius, he was the world's greatest opening theorist, had magnificent positional skills, and was extremely strong in the endgame. In other words, he could do everything at the highest level, had no weaknesses, and was clearly superior to every other player on earth (including Capablanca).

After winning his match against Bogoljubov, his next two events left the chess world (and his opponents!) in awe.

San Remo 1930: Alekhine took first (13 wins, 2 draws, no losses). Nimzowitsch was second, 3½ points behind Alekhine! Others included: Rubinstein, Bogoljubov, Yates, Ahues, Spielmann, Vidmar, Maróczy, Tartakower, Colle, and Kmoch.

Some thought Alekhine would never improve on such a dominating performance, but he did just that in his very next event!

Alexander Alekhine vs. Aron Nimzowitsch, San Remo 1930

1.e4 e6 2.d4 d5 3.Nc3 Bb4 4.e5 c5 5.Bd2 Ne7 6.Nb5 Bxd2+ 7.Qxd2 0-0 8.c3 b6 9.f4 Ba6 10.Nf3 Qd7 11.a4 Nbc6 12.b4 cxb4 13.cxb4 Bb7 14.Nd6 f5 15.a5 Nc8 16.Nxb7 Qxb7 17.a6

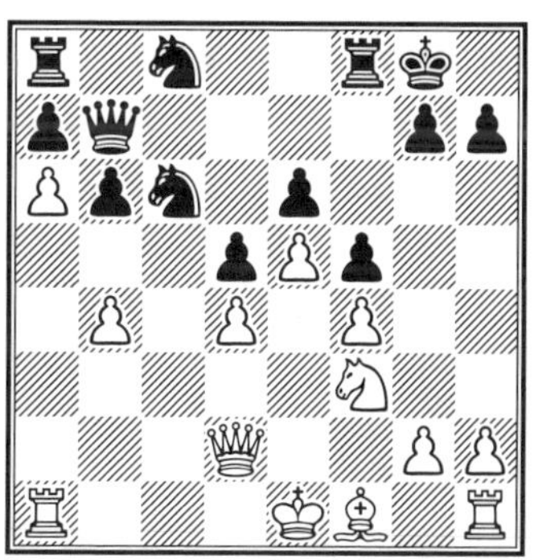

17...Qf7 18.Bb5 N8e7 19.0-0 h6 20.Rfc1 Rfc8 21.Rc2 Qe8 22.Rac1 Rab8 23.Qe3 Rc7 24.Rc3!!

With this move, Alekhine (for the first time) begins to set up a formation that was eventually named Alekhine's Gun.

24...Qd7 25.R1c2! Kf8 26.Qc1!

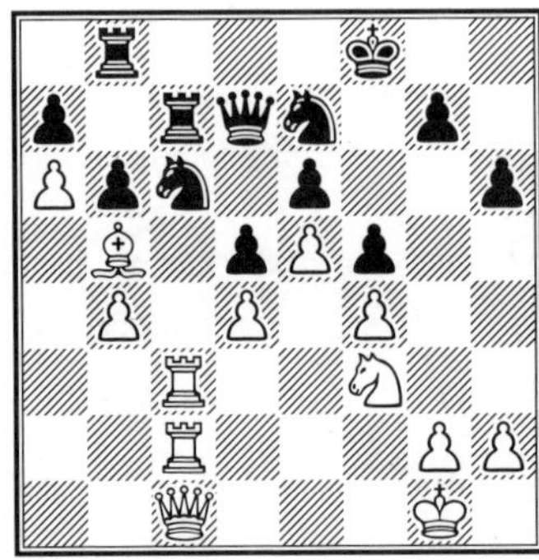

And the "Gun" is created (two Rooks in front with the Queen behind). Note the incredible pressure it creates down the c-file.

26...Rbc8 27.Ba4!

Threatening to win a piece with 28.b5.

27...b5 28.Bxb5 Ke8 29.Ba4!

Again threatening 30.b5.

29...Kd8

Defending the c7-Rook but dooming Black's whole army to total inertia.

30.h4!!

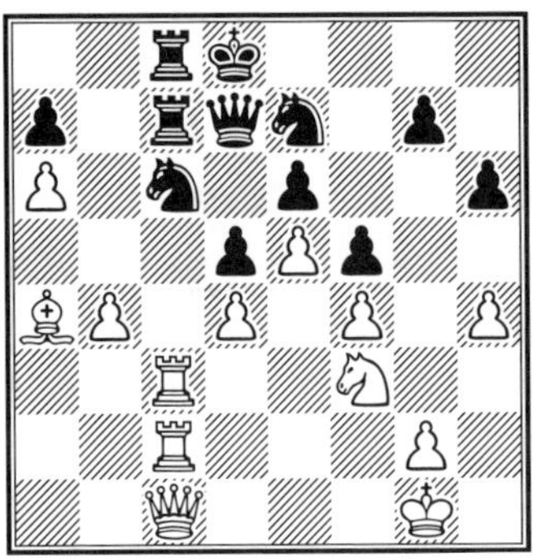

There are many other ways to win, but this is by far the most creative. 30.h4 creates a rare zugzwang. After Black runs out of pawn moves (which won't take long!) he'll be forced to move one of his pieces which will either leave c6 or c7 inadequately protected, resulting in a loss of a piece and the game. Though it's not clear if Black resigned here or after 30...Qe8 31.b5, I'll give a sample of what could occur:

30...g6

30...g5 31.hxg5 hxg5 32.Nxg5 and massive amounts of wood will vanish from the Black side.

31.Kh2

31.Kh1 or many other "passes" will also do.

31...h5 32.Kh1

"Passing" demonstrates the zugzwang, but 32.Ng5 is also crushing.

32...Ke8

32...Rb8 33.Bxc6; 32...Qe8 33.Ng5 Kd7 34.b5 is either tragic or funny, depending on your perspective.

33.b5 and Black's stuff starts to fall off the board.

Alexander Alekhine vs. Savielly Tartakower, San Remo 1930

1.d4 e6 2.c4 f5 3.g3 Nf6 4.Bg2 Bb4+ 5.Nd2 Ne4 6.a3 Nxd2 7.Bxd2 Bxd2+ 8.Qxd2 0-0 9.Nh3 d5 10.cxd5 exd5 11.Nf4 c6 12.0-0 Qe7 13.b4 a6 14.f3 Nd7 15.e4 fxe4 16.fxe4 dxe4 17.Qa2+ Kh8 18.Ne6 Rxf1+ 19.Rxf1 Nf6 20.Ng5 h6 21.Qf7 Qxf7 22.Nxf7 Kh7 23.Nd6 Be6 24.Nxb7 Bd5 25.Re1 Ra7 26.Nc5 a5 27.bxa5 Rxa5 28.a4 Ra8 29.Ra1 Ra5 30.Ra3 Kg6 31.h3 Kf5 32.Kf2 Ne8

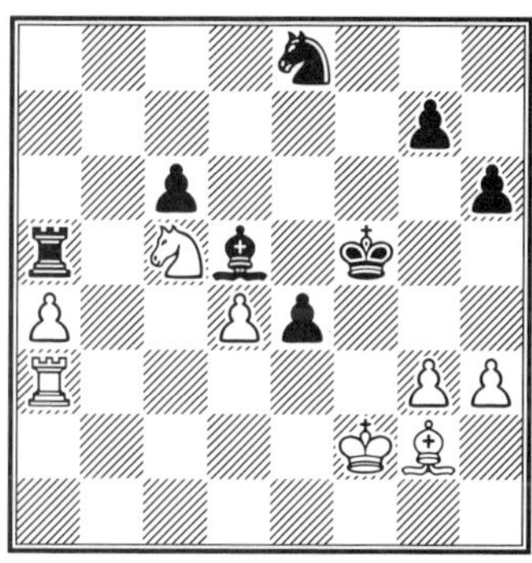

33.Bxe4+!

33.g4+ is also strong since 33...Kf4 34.Bxe4 amounts to the same thing as the game.

33...Bxe4 34.g4+ Kf6

34...Kf4?? 35.Ne6 mate.

35.Nxe4+ Ke6 36.Ke3 Nd6 37.Kd3 Nxe4 38.Kxe4 h5 39.g5 Rxg5 40.a5 Rb5 41.a6 Rb8 42.a7 and White went on to win.

Bled (1931): Alekhine took first (15 wins, 11 draws, no losses), Bogoljubov second, 5½ points behind Alekhine! Others included: Nimzowitsch, Flohr, Kashdan, Stoltz, Vidmar, Tartakower, Kostić, Spielmann, Maróczy, Colle, Asztalos, and Pirc.

It's important to understand that Nimzowitsch was the third best player on Earth (Alekhine and Capablanca being the top two) during the years 1927-1931. So imagine the impact it made on the world when the following game was played:

Alexander Alekhine vs. Aron Nimzowitsch, Bled 1931

1.e4 e6 2.d4 d5 3.Nc3 Bb4 4.Nge2 dxe4 5.a3 Bxc3+ 6.Nxc3 f5 7.f3 exf3 8.Qxf3 Qxd4 9.Qg3! Nf6 10.Qxg7 Qe5+ 11.Be2 Rg8 12.Qh6 Rg6 13.Qh4 Bd7 14.Bg5 Bc6 15.0-0-0

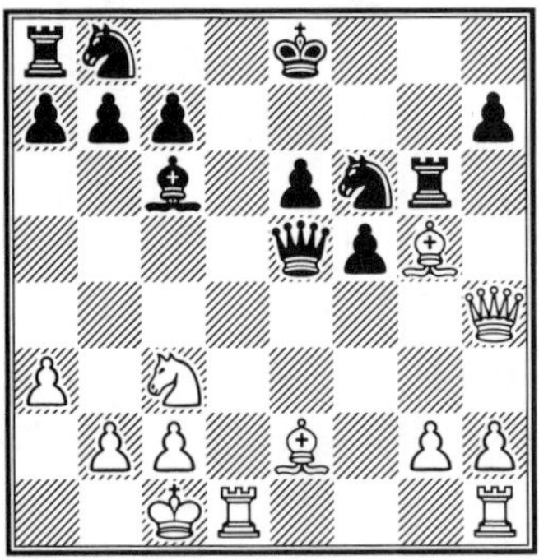

15...Bxg2 16.Rhe1 Be4 17.Bh5 Nxh5 18.Rd8+ Kf7 19.Qxh5, 1-0.

A nineteen move rout against the great Nimzowitsch? How is this possible? After this game Nimzowitsch commented: "He deals with us like inexperienced fledglings."

Vasja Pirc vs. Alexander Alekhine, Bled 1931

1.d4 d5 2.c4 e6 3.Nc3 c5 4.cxd5 cxd4 5.Qa4+ Bd7 6.Qxd4 exd5 7.Qxd5 Nc6 8.Bg5 Nf6 9.Qd2 h6 10.Bxf6 Qxf6 11.e3 0-0-0 12.0-0-0 Bg4! 13.Nd5 Rxd5! 14.Qxd5 Ba3!!

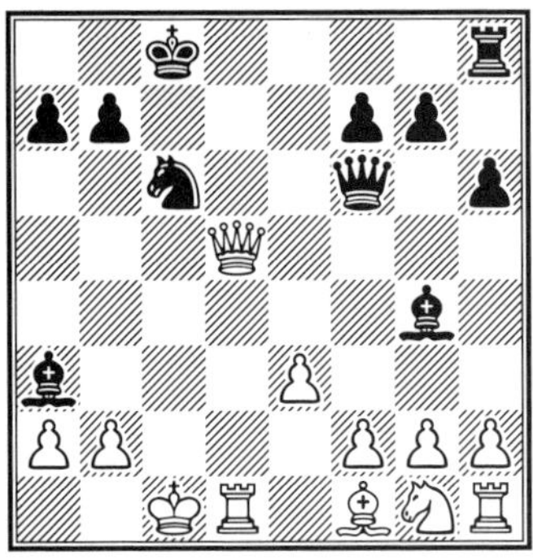

15.Qb3

15.bxa3 Qa1+ 16.Kc2 Bxd1+ 17.Qxd1 Qxa2+ 18.Kc3 Qxa3+ 19.Qb3 Qc1+ 20.Qc2 Qxf1 with an easy win for Black.

15...Bxd1 16.Qxa3

16.Kxd1 Qxf2 17.Nf3 Rd8+ 18.Kc1 Bxb2+! 19.Kb1 (19.Qxb2 Rd1+ 20.Kxd1 Qxb2) 19...Bf6 20.Kc1 Kb8 and White is doomed.

16...Qxf2 17.Qd3 Bg4 18.Nf3

18.Be2 Bf5.

18...Bxf3 19.Qf5+ Kb8 20.Qxf3 Qe1+ 21.Kc2

Better was 21.Qd1 Qxe3+ 22.Qd2 Qe5 though Black should win without much difficulty.

21...Rc8 22.Qg3+ Ne5+ 23.Kb3 Qd1+ 24.Ka3 Rc5 and White finally gave up.

It's clear that in this period, Alekhine was head and shoulders above everyone else. He simply overwhelmed anyone that dared sit across from him!

Garry Kasparov wrote:

> In the whole history of chess there has been no other player who decided so many games by brilliant tactical blows as did Alexander Alekhine...
>
> Alexander Alekhine is the first luminary among the others who are still having the greatest influence on me. I like his universality, his approach to the game, his chess ideas. I am sure that the future belongs to Alekhine chess.

Another admirer, Levon Aronian, currently, one of the strongest players in the world, considers Alekhine to be the greatest player of all time

It's easy to understand why Kasparov (one of the most dynamic players in history) loved Alekhine's style, but Fischer, who was more of a technician and sought clarity whenever possible, didn't care for Alekhine's chaos. Nevertheless, you don't have to love it to respect it. Bobby Fischer wrote:

> Alekhine has never been a hero of mine, and I've never cared for his style of play. There's nothing light or breezy about it; it worked for him, but it could scarcely work for anyone else. He played gigantic conceptions, full of outrageous and unprecedented ideas. He had great imagination; he could see more deeply into a situation than any other player in chess history. It was in the most complicated positions that Alekhine found his grandest concepts.

Alas, flesh and blood humans don't live in fairyland, at least not permanently, and by 1932 his gifts slowly started to deteriorate—he was almost forty and, more importantly, poor health started to whittle away his greatness. The decline was slow at first (he was still incredibly strong!), but the occasional loss found its way into his results as he embraced Bacchus more and more (according to Hans Kmoch, Alekhine was drinking at Bled in 1931, and drank heavily during his 1934 match with Bogoljubov).

Alekhine and Capablanca

I'm going to make one last effort to help the "Alekhine was afraid of Capablanca" people grasp a handful of reality. After you read this, feel free to misquote me (and other sources), hide from facts, and rave all you want. Here are the facts:

- First, Alekhine did lose more games in his career than Capablanca. No doubt about it. That's to be expected due to style. Alekhine played risky, wild, imaginative chess, while Capablanca always stayed in a comfort zone... little risk, playing for complete control of the position. Due to their different styles (and I love both), Alekhine lost more games but created some of the richest masterpieces ever seen.
- Alekhine did avoid Capablanca until 1922. Capablanca wasn't bothered by this at all since Alekhine wasn't in his class then. Alekhine avoided Capablanca so he could hone his skills, make a name for himself, and finally be in a position to challenge the Cuban. His early strategy makes sense and had nothing to do with fear. It had everything to do with reality. When they finally did meet in 1922, Alekhine's skills had improved to such a degree that he was now just slightly weaker than Capablanca.
- From 1922 to 1927 they played in three tournaments together (seven games total). The result was six draws, one win for Capablanca. Hardly the total domination everyone is yelling about.
- A word about Capablanca not taking his match with Alekhine seriously. That's true. BUT, you have to understand that Capablanca didn't take any tournament or match seriously! He was born with scary-amazing talent, but was also lazy and didn't care much for hard work. In my lifetime, I've seen many talented players fail to reach the top levels due to an inability to work. In general, you need both talent and a great work ethic to make it to the highest levels of the game—Capablanca was an exception since he ruled chess in his prime years on talent alone. But when he faced Alekhine in their match, the challenger had prepared to the max and was ready to wage war.

Capablanca was Capablanca—parties, women, fun, and expecting the match victory to happen by itself. This usually worked for him—it worked against an old Lasker. It worked in most of his tournaments, but it didn't work against a guy that was just a tad below him in strength but was physically and emotionally superior—a guy that had a talent Capablanca didn't have: the ability to improve himself by enormous effort and sacrifice. The greater natural talent lost the World Championship match, but the better man won it.

The *only* person who was happy about the London Rules (which forced a challenger to come up with 10,000 gold dollars) was Capablanca. It made it almost impossible for anyone to challenge him. Alekhine had to swim through rivers of man-eating piranha to make that match happen. When Alekhine was champion, he was very willing to have a rematch, as long as Capablanca abided by the same rules Capablanca himself insisted everyone else follow. Capablanca refused and walked away. In this case, Capablanca avoided Alekhine, not the other way round.

One gentleman complained that, "Alekhine initially offered a rematch in which he would take more than half the money even if he lost." But if he'd read Capablanca's London Rules, he'd realize that Alekhine was merely throwing Capablanca's demands back in his face. Capablanca's rules stipulated: The challenger had to come up with $10,000 and pay all travel expenses for both players; the champion would receive 20% of the "put up" money as a fee, and of the remaining 80% the winner would receive 60% and the loser 40%.

Thus, according to Capablanca's London Rules, Capablanca was guaranteed more than half the money even if he lost.

But running away like a little spoiled boy that didn't get his way wasn't enough. Capablanca also insulted Alekhine in interviews right after the match, continued to bad mouth him afterwards, and was so insulting that Alekhine wanted nothing to do with him. If you don't believe me, perhaps you'll believe Max Euwe (in an interview with Hans Bouwmeester):

> Euwe: [Capablanca] gave interviews in which he said a lot of nice things about himself but nothing much about his opponent, which offended Alekhine. Capablanca took it for granted that Alekhine would play a return match. He wrote to Alekhine in an arrogant tone which, the latter replied, was not the tone in which you should write to a champion of the world. Alekhine wanted to be paid in gold dollars (at that time worth twice ordinary dollars) and on this basis Capablanca could not or would not pay. He just stopped negotiating.
>
> Bouwmeester: If he had raised the gold dollars, would Alekhine have played?
>
> Euwe: Certainly, he was not afraid of Capablanca.

I doubt you could find many strong players (modern or from the past) who would deny that the Alekhine of 1930 and 1931 (his ultimate prime years) was, by far, the strongest player on Earth. This doesn't mean that the ultimate prime Capablanca (1918 to 1924) was better or worse than the ultimate prime Alekhine—fans can have fun arguing this for eternity.

Singing the Middle-aged Blues

After his magnificent victories at San Remo 1930 and Bled 1931, fans reacted as all fans do—they think their hero is invincible, forgetting that he's human, with human flaws, human worries, and a human body that, in time, breaks down. At forty years of age, Alekhine was still the world's best player, but he was also a "high-functioning alcoholic." He drank heavily, he kicked everyone's ass, and then he drank some more. Chess was the love of his life, but alcohol was the mistress that people in the know were aware of, while the public was not.

And so, tournaments came and went, and victories piled up with only an occasional blip to show that he wasn't quite (close, but not quite!) the same unstoppable monster who devoured everyone in his path in 1930 and 1931.

Bern (1932): Alekhine finished first with 11 wins, 3 draws, 1 loss. Euwe and Flohr were a point behind.

Alexander Alekhine vs. Sultan Khan, Bern 1932

1.e4 c6 2.d4 d5 3.exd5 cxd5 4.c4 Nf6 5.Nc3 Nc6 6.Nf3 Bg4 7.cxd5 Nxd5 8.Bb5 a6 9.Bxc6+ bxc6 10.Qa4 Nxc3 11.Qxc6+ Bd7 12.Qxc3

White is a pawn ahead, but Black has two Bishops and pressure against b3 as compensation. How did Alekhine solve his problems and claim a clear advantage?

12...Rc8 13.Qe3 Bb5 14.a4 Bc4 15.b3 Bd5 16.0-0 Qb6 17.Bd2 e6 18.Rfc1 Rb8 19.Ne5! f6

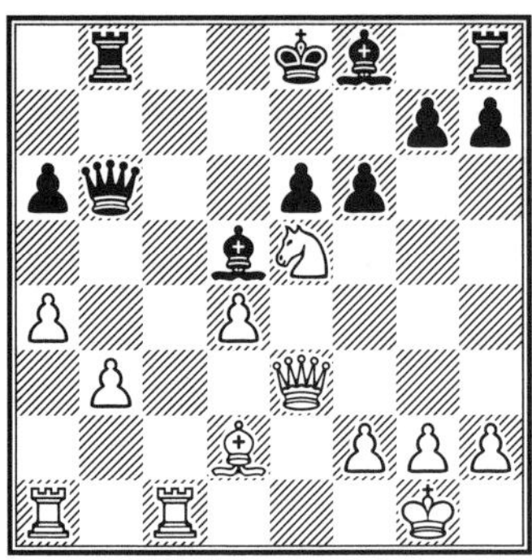

19...Qxb3 20.Qxb3 Rxb3 21.Rc8+ Ke7 22.Rac1 is winning for White; 19...Bxb3 20.Rab1 and the pin wins; 19...Be7 20.Qg3 0-0 21.Bh6 Bf6 22.Nd7 with a very funny mass-fork of both Rooks, the Queen, and the f6-Bishop!

20.Nc6! Ra8

20...Rc8 21.Nb4! Bb7 22.Rxc8+ Bxc8 23.Nd5 Qb7 24.Nf4.

21.Na5 when **b3** is safe and White's advantage (extra pawn and ownership of the c-file) is now clear. Note how Alekhine uses tactics for positional gains and even for defense. Yet another reminder that all phases of the game are connected, with tactics and positional play benefiting each other.

Alexander Alekhine vs. Salo Flohr, Bern 1932

1.d4 d5 2.Nf3 Nf6 3.e3 e6 4.Bd3 c5 5.c3 Nc6 6.Nbd2 Be7 7.0-0 Qc7 8.Qe2 0-0 9.e4 dxe4 10.Nxe4 cxd4 11.Nxd4 Nxd4 12.cxd4 Nxe4 13.Bxe4 f5 14.Bf3 Bf6 15.Rd1 Rd8 16.Be3 f4 17.Rac1 Qd6 18.Bd2 Bxd4 19.Ba5

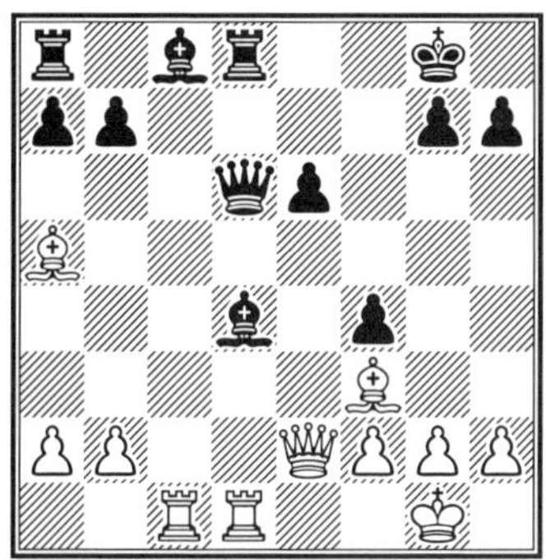

19...Rd7 20.Rxd4 Qxd4 21.Qxe6+ Rf7 22.Rxc8+ Rxc8 23.Qxc8+ Rf8 24.Qxb7 Re8 25.h3 Qc5 26.Bc3 Qe7 27.Bd5+ Kh8 28.Qxe7, 1-0.

London (1932): Alekhine first with 7 wins, 4 draws, 0 losses. Flohr second, a point behind.

Alexander Alekhine vs. Savielly Tartakower, London 1932

1.d4 Nf6 2.c4 e5 3.dxe5 Ne4 4.Nd2 Nc5 5.Ngf3 Nc6 6.g3 Qe7 7.Bg2 g6 8.Nb1 Nxe5 9.0-0 Nxf3+ 10.exf3 Bg7 11.Re1 Ne6 12.Nc3 0-0 13.Nd5 Qd8 14.f4 c6 15.Nc3 d6 16.Be3 Qc7 17.Rc1 Bd7 18.Qd2 Rad8 19.Red1 Bc8 20.Ne4 Nc5 21.Nxd6 Na4 22.c5 Nxb2 23.Re1 b5?

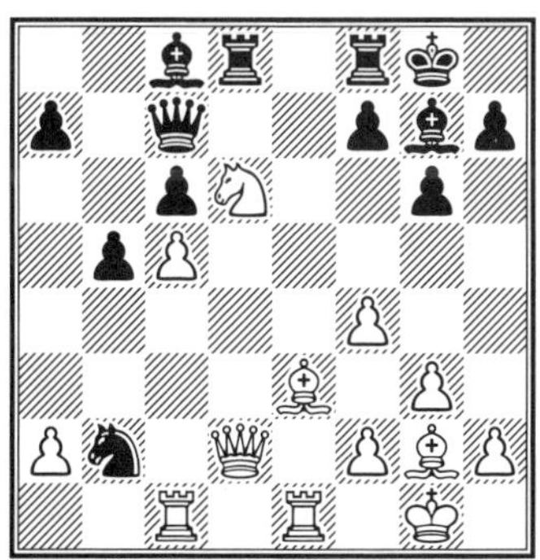

24.cxb6!! Qxd6

24...axb6 25.Rxc6.

25.Qxd6 Rxd6 26.bxa7 Bb7 27.Bc5 Rdd8 28.Bxf8 Kxf8 29.Bxc6 Bxc6 30.Rxc6 Ra8 31.Rb6 Rxa7 32.Rb8, 1-0.

Mexico City (1932): Alekhine and Kashdan tied for first, winning all their games (8 wins) and drawing each other.

Pasadena (1932): Alekhine first with 7 wins, 3 draws, 1 loss, ahead of Kashdan second, Dake third (the only player Alekhine lost to), Reshevsky, Fine, and others.

Reuben Fine on Alekhine:[1]

> When I first met [Alekhine] at Pasadena in 1932, I began to understand the secret of his genius. He was showing a game with Euwe played at Bern a few months earlier, and his eyes and bearing had a strange intensity which I had never seen before. The man loved chess, it was the breath of life to him. At the bridge table he would suddenly start talking about an obscure variation in the Scotch; on the train to Mexico he assiduously devoted four hours a day to the analysis of new lines; any game, played by anybody anywhere, was good enough to sit him down and evolve new ideas for hours on end; on off days and periods he amused himself by playing rapid transit. He lived for chess, and chess alone.

Paris (1933): Alekhine finished first with 7 wins, 2 draws, 0 losses an ahead of Tartakower, Lilienthal, Znosko-Borovsky, and others.

Alexander Alekhine vs. Josef Cukierman, Paris 1933

1.d4 d5 2.c4 e6 3.Nc3 Nf6 4.Bg5 Be7 5.e3 Nbd7 6.Nf3 0-0 7.Rc1 b6 8.cxd5 exd5 9.Bb5 Bb7 10.0-0 a6 11.Ba4 c5 12.Bxd7 Nxd7 13.Bxe7 Qxe7 14.dxc5 Qxc5 15.Nd4 Rac8 16.Nf5 Kh8 17.Ne2 Qb4 18.Qd4 Qxd4 19.Nexd4 Rxc1 20.Rxc1 Nc5 21.Nd6 Ba8 22.b4 Nd3 23.Rc7

23.Nxf7+ Kg8.

23...Kg8

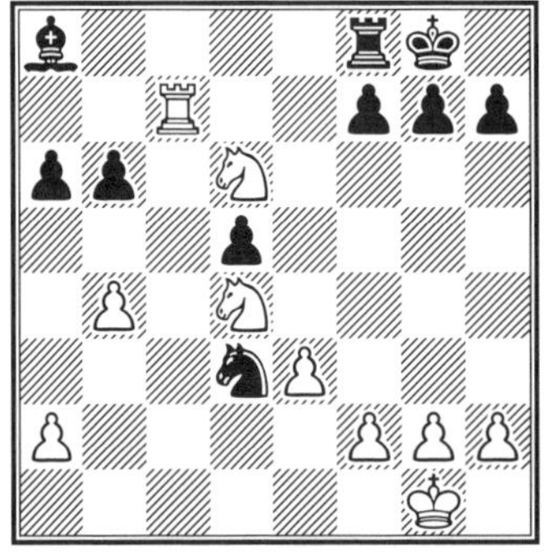

1 Reuben Fine, *Chess Marches On*. New York: Chess Review, 1945.

24.Nc8!

[Alekhine]: "With the text move, White starts an attack against the unfortunate Bishop which is obviously unable to escape from its fate."

24...Nxb4 25.Nxb6

Threatening Ra7.

25...Rb8 26.Nd7!

Not 26.Ra7 Bc6.

26...Rd8 27.a3 Nd3 28.Ra7

Finally rounding up the hapless Bishop!

28...Rc8 29.Kf1!, 1-0.

Hastings (1933/34): Flohr first, Alekhine and Lilienthal tied second/third (half-a-point behind).

Zurich (1934): Alekhine first with 12 wins, 2 draws, 1 loss. Euwe and Flohr tied for second/third a point behind. Others included: Bogoljubov, Emanuel Lasker, Bernstein, Nimzowitsch, and Ståhlberg.

Alexander Alekhine vs. Emanuel Lasker, Zurich 1934

1.d4 d5 2.c4 e6 3.Nc3 Nf6 4.Nf3 Be7 5.Bg5 Nbd7 6.e3 0-0 7.Rc1 c6 8.Bd3 dxc4 9.Bxc4 Nd5 10.Bxe7 Qxe7 11.Ne4 N5f6 12.Ng3 e5 13.0-0 exd4 14.Nf5 Qd8 15.N3xd4 Ne5 16.Bb3 Bxf5 17.Nxf5 Qb6

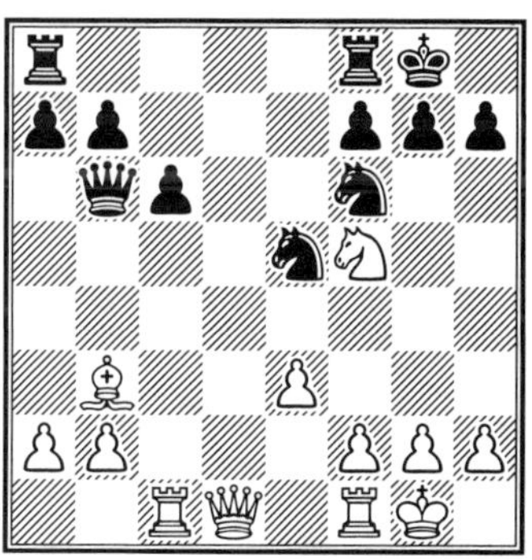

18.Qd6 Ned7 19.Rfd1 Rad8 20.Qg3 g6 21.Qg5 Kh8 22.Nd6 Kg7 23.e4 Ng8 24.Rd3 f6 25.Rd3 f6 25.Nf5+ Kh8 26.Qxg6!!, 1-0.

World Championship Match 1934

Then came a second match with Bogoljubov. Although Alekhine wasn't quite what he once was, neither was Bogoljubov, so it evened out and the result was the same—another dominating performance by the champion.

Bogoljubov should have won the first game: In a winning endgame for Bohim, Alekhine claimed a draw by three time repetition and, for reasons I don't fully grasp, Bogoljubov went along with it even though it wasn't a three-time repetition at all! After that, Alekhine won the second, fourth, ninth, and eleventh games, losing only once. A three-game lead after only eleven games was a bit much, but it got even worse when Alekhine won games sixteen and seventeen. The match was pretty much over by then, but it continued for another nine games, although Bogoljubov wasn't able to mount any kind of comeback and after twenty-six gamed it was Alekhine 15½, Bogoljubov 10½.

Keep in mind, Hans Kmoch claimed that Alekhine was "drinking heavily" during this match. If that's true, then Alekhine's impressive defense of his title suddenly becomes astounding!

Alexander Alekhine vs. Efim Bogoljubov, World Championship (2) 1934

1.d4 Nf6 2.c4 c6 3.Nf3 d5 4.e3 e6 5.Bd3 Nbd7 6.Nc3 dxc4 7.Bxc4 b5 8.Bd3 a6 9.0-0 c5 10.a4 b4 11.Ne4 Bb7 12.Ned2 Be7 13.a5 0-0 14.Nc4 Qc7 15.Qe2 Ng4 16.e4 cxd4 17.h3 Nge5 18.Nfxe5 Nxe5 19.Bf4 Bd6 20.Bxe5 Bxe5 21.Nb6 Ra7 22.Rac1 Qd6 23.Rc4 f5 24.exf5 exf5 25.Re1 Qg6 26.f3 Re8 27.f4 Qg3 28.fxe5 Rxe5

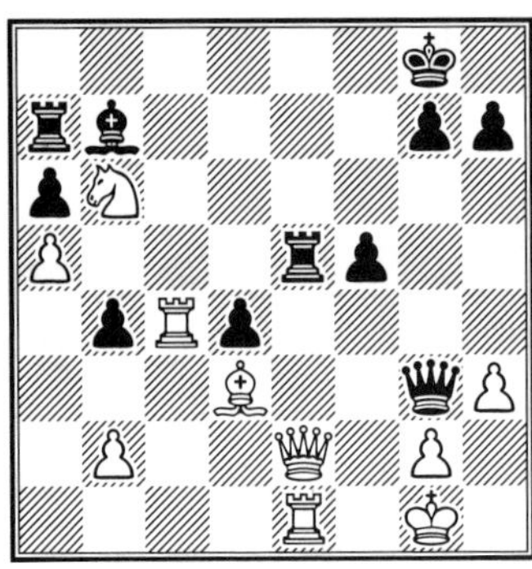

29.Rc8+

The only good move, and it turns out to be a killer! 29.Qxe5?? Qxg2 mate.

29...Kf7

29...Bxc8 30.Qxe5 Qxd3 31.Qe8 mate.

30.Qh5+!

By far the best. However, 30.Rc7+ and some other moves also won.

30...g6

30...Ke7 31.Re8+ Kd6 32.Rd8+ forces mate in a few moves; 30...Kf6 31.Rf8+ Ke7 32.Qf7+ Kd6 33.Qd7+ Kc5 34.Na4 mate.

31.Qxh7+

31.Bc4+ and 31.Rc7+ are also stone cold winners.

31...Kf6 32.Rf8+ Kg5

32...Ke6 33.Qd7 mate.

33.h4+ Kf4 34.Qh6+ g5 35.Rxf5+! Rxf5 36.Qd6+ Kg4 37.Bxf5+, 1-0.

Orebro (1935): Alekhine first ahead of Lundin, Ståhlberg, and Stoltz.

Alexander Alekhine vs. Erik Lundin, Orebro 1935

1.d4 d5 2.c4 e6 3.Nc3 Nf6 4.Bg5 Nbd7 5.Nf3 c6 6.e4 dxe4 7.Nxe4 Be7 8.Nc3 0-0 9.Qc2 e5 10.0-0-0 exd4 11.Nxd4 Qa5 12.h4 Nc5 13.Kb1 Rd8 14.Be2 Qc7 15.Bf3 a5 16.Rhe1 g6 17.g4 Ne6 18.Nxe6 Bxe6 19.h5 Rxd1+ 20.Nxd1 Ne8 21.Bh6 Bf6 22.hxg6 hxg6 23.Nc3 Bc4 24.Ne4 Qe5

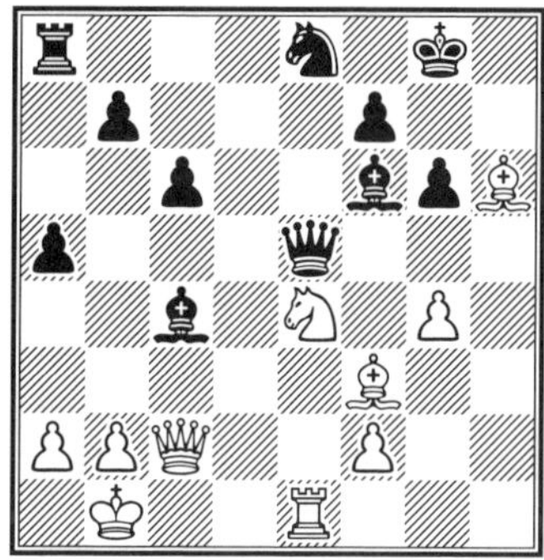

25.g5! Qb5

The poor Bishop can't move: 25...Bg7 26.Nf6+ winning black's Queen.

26.Nxf6+ Nxf6 27.Qc3 Re8

27...Nh5 28.Bxh5; 27...Ne8 28.Rxe8+.

28.Rc1 Qf5+ 29.Ka1 Kh7 30.Qxc4, 1-0.

His Worst "Combination" — Age + Booze

Alekhine reached his ultimate prime between 1930 and 1931. For a few years after that, he was still clearly the world's best player, but the march of time and the wrath of alcohol took more and more out of him, even though everyone still viewed him as unbeatable. Then came the first match against Euwe, and the chess world suffered a reality check.

World Championship Match 1935

The 1935 match was the real beginning of Alekhine's fall. Facing Max Euwe, a young, hungry, and very strong player, Alekhine entered the match full of confidence. Indeed, after nine games, Alekhine was three games ahead. That lead, which would have been decisive if Alekhine was still in his glory days, vanished in the next five games. Alekhine drew two, with three losses. He went up again by two after two wins and two draws in the next four games. But after that, he was only able to win one more game (while losing four), leaving Euwe with a one point lead and the title (Euwe 15½, Alekhine 14½ in thirty games).

I have to say that the quality of the games was outstanding, and every game was fought tooth and nail (not a good thing for the older player). It's easy to say that a prime Alekhine would have won, but that Alekhine no longer existed, and Euwe's level in this match was very high indeed.

Stories have appeared in various sources of Alekhine not showing up for a game. When the officials went looking for him, they found Alekhine drunk and unconscious in a field. I don't know whether that's true or not, but his results after this match clearly show that the Alekhine of 1935, while still one of the top three or four players in the World, was no longer number one. A forty-three-year-old lion falling victim to talented youth is an unavoidable fact of life. Indeed, a whole new generation of players had appeared (Flohr, Keres, Botvinnik, Reshevsky, and Fine, among others), and the newcomers were getting better with each passing year, while Alekhine's trajectory was going in the opposite direction.

Jan Hein Donner, who was always happy to voice his opinions, wrote about Alekhine in his epic book (one of my all time favorites), *The King: Chess Pieces:*[1]

> Euwe defeated this giant, but it was immediately clear that the chess world simply wasn't having it. General opinion internationally held it that Alekhine had once again been having a drop too much.

Alekhine had great respect for Euwe. At a pre-match party, Alekhine proclaimed:

> I am proud and happy that the world of chess has a champion who is a gentleman. I am proud and happy that this gentleman is honorable. I take this opportunity to officially challenge my opponent. And I am happy, without hypocrisy, that if I am not the champion, a Dutchman is the champion.

Alexander Alekhine vs. Max Euwe, Netherlands, World Championship (1) 1935

1.d4 d5 2.c4 c6 3.Nf3 Nf6 4.Nc3 dxc4 5.a4 Bf5 6.Ne5 Nbd7 7.Nxc4 Qc7 8.g3 e5 9.dxe5 Nxe5 10.Bf4 Nfd7 11.Bg2 Be6 12.Nxe5 Nxe5 13.0-0 Be7 14.Qc2

Threatening moves like 15.Nb5 or 15.Nd5, gaining the two bishops.

14...Rd8

14...Qa5 15.Nb5!

15.Rfd1

1 Jan Hein Donner, *The King: Chess Pieces*. Alkmaar: New In Chess, 2006.

Once again giving White the option of Nd5.

15...0-0 16.Nb5

Alekhine goes for the more tactical and flashy continuation. This ensures an edge since Black would be compelled to give up one of his bishops.

16...Rxd1+ 17.Rxd1 Qa5 18.Nd4 Bc8

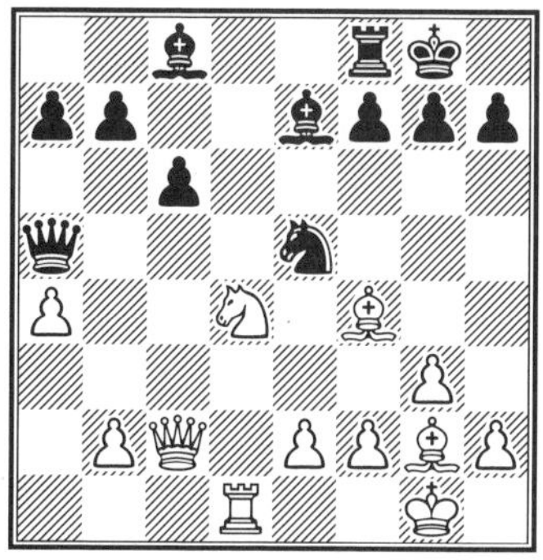

19.b4!! Qc7

19...Bxb4 20.Nb3 Qc7 21.Qe4 Bc3 22.Rc1 Bb2 23.Rc2 f5 24.Qb4! (analysis by Alekhine) and black's dark-squared Bishop is finding itself all alone, far, far from home.

20.b5 c5 21.Nf5 f6 22.Ne3 Be6 23.Bd5! Bxd5 24.Rxd5

24.Nxd5 was also strong.

24...Qa5 25.Nf5 Qe1+ 26.Kg2 Bd8 27.Bxe5 fxe5 28.Rd7! Bf6 29.Nh6+! Kh8 30.Qxc5, 1-0.

Max Euwe vs. Alexander Alekhine, Netherlands, World Championship (4) 1935

1.d4 Nf6 2.c4 g6 3.Nc3 d5 4.Qb3 dxc4 5.Qxc4 Bg7 6.Bf4 c6 7.Rd1 Qa5 8.Bd2 b5 9.Qb3 b4 10.Na4 Na6 11.e3 Be6 12.Qc2 0-0 13.b3 Rab8

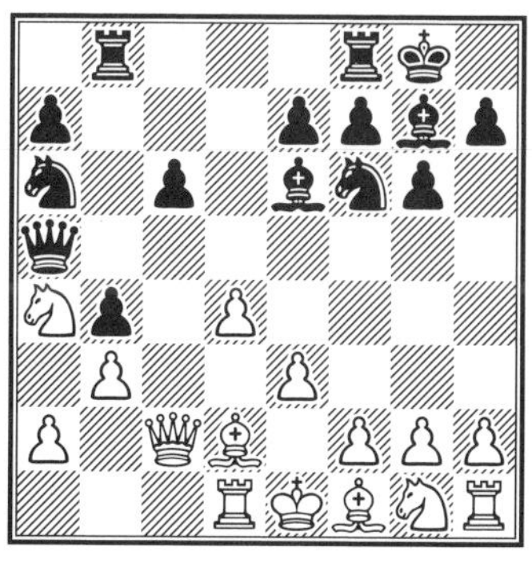

14.Bd3 Rfc8 15.Ne2 c5 16.Bxa6 Qxa6 17.Nxc5 Qb5 18.Nf4?

18.e4!! is best.

18…Bg4! 19.f3 e5 20.Nfd3

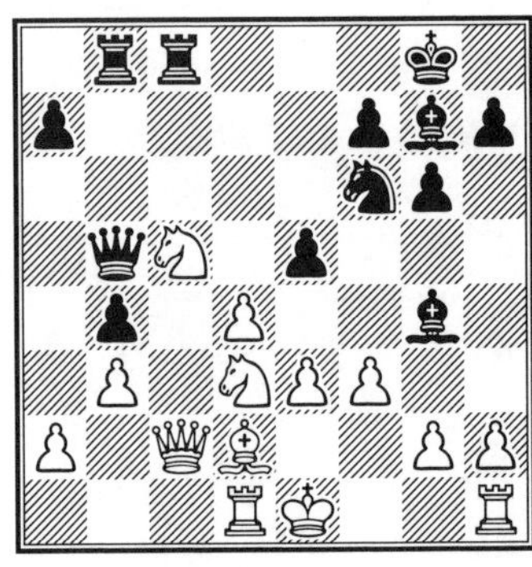

20… exd4!!

Now the open file is more important than material. The white King is still in the center.

21.fxg4 dxe3 22.Bxe3 Nxg4 23.Bf4

23.Bg1 Re8+ 24.Kf1 Rb6! [Alekhine] gives Black a decisive attack.

23…Bc3+ 24.Rd2 Rxc5

When Alekhine dragged his opponent down to defeat on move 44.

Amsterdam (1936): Euwe and Fine tied for first/second, Alekhine third.

Bad Nauheim (1936): Alekhine and Keres tied for first/second.

Carl Ahues vs. Alexander Alekhine, Bad Nauheim 1936

1.d4 d5 2.c4 dxc4 3.Nf3 a6 4.a4 Nf6 5.e3 Bg4 6.Bxc4 e6 7.Nc3 Nc6 8.Be2 Bb4 9.0-0 0-0 10.Nd2 Bxe2 11.Nxe2 e5 12.Nf3 Re8 13.Bd2 Bd6 14.Ng3 e4 15.Ne1 Bxg3 16.hxg3 Ne7 17.b4 Qd7 18.Nc2 Ned5 19.Na3 b5 20.axb5 axb5 21.Qe2 c6 22.Nc2 Qf5 23.Rfc1 h6 24.Ra5 Rac8 25.Na1 Ng4

Threatening 26…Qh5.

26.Kf1

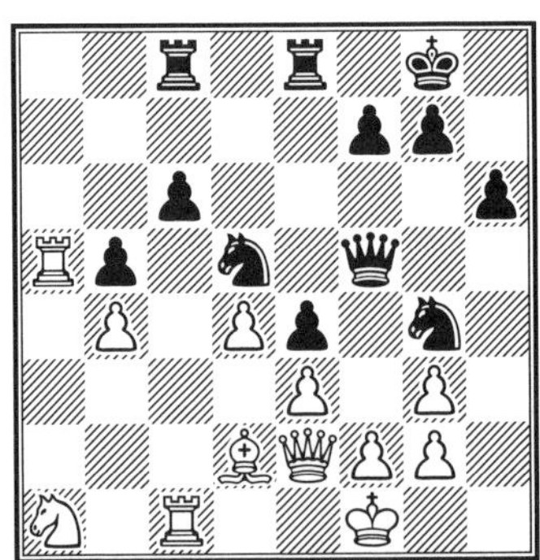

Running for the hills!

26...Re6! 27.Rxb5 Rf6

27...cxb5 28.Rxc8+.

28.Rbc5

28.Rxd5 cxd5 29.f4 exf3 30.Rxc8+ Qxc8 31.gxf3 Rxf3+ 32.Qxf3 Nh2+.

28...Nxf2 29.Ke1

29.Nc2 Nh3+! 30.Ke1 Ng1 31.g4 Qg5 32.Qa6 Qh4+ 33.Kd1 Qxg4+ 34.Ke1 Qxg2 35.Qxc8+ Kh7 36.Qa6 (To stop ...Qe2 mate.) 36...Nf3+ 37.Kd1 Qxd2 mate.

29...Nd3+ 30.Kd1 Qf1+ 31.Be1

31.Qxf1 Rxf1+ 32.Ke2 Rf2+ 33.Kd1 Rxg2 34.b5 Rg1+ 35.Ke2 Rxc1 36.Bxc1 Nxc5 37.dxc5 cxb5 and Black wins.

31...Rf2 32.Qxf1 Nxe3, 0-1.

Dresden (1936): Alekhine first, ahead of Keres, Bogoljubov, Sämisch, and others.

Black, in a lost position, has just played 39...Rd6-f6 hoping White would fall for 40.Rxa6 when 40...Bxd4 wins a piece. What did Alekhine do?

Alexander Alekhine vs. Efim Bogoljubov, Dresden 1936

1.e4 e5 2.Nf3 Nc6 3.Nc3 g6 4.d4 exd4 5.Nd5 Bg7 6.Bg5 Nce7 7.e5 h6 8.Bxe7 Nxe7 9.Qxd4 Nxd5 10.Qxd5 c6 11.Qd6 Bf8 12.Qd4 Qb6 13.0-0-0 Qxd4 14.Nxd4 d5 15.exd6 Bxd6 16.Bc4 0-0 17.Rhe1 Bg4 18.f3 Bc8 19.g3 Bc5 20.Nb3 Bb6 21.Nd2 Bh3 22.Ne4 Ba5 23.c3 Rad8 24.Nd6 b5 25.Bb3 Rd7 26.Ne8 Rxd1+ 27.Kxd1 Bg2 28.Nf6+ Kg7 29.Ne8+ Kh8 30.Kc2 Bxf3 31.Nd6 Bd5 32.Bxd5 cxd5 33.Nxb5 Bb6 34.Kd3 Kg7 35.b4 Rd8 36.a4 a6 37.Nd4 Rd6 38.Re8 h5 39.Ra8 Rf6

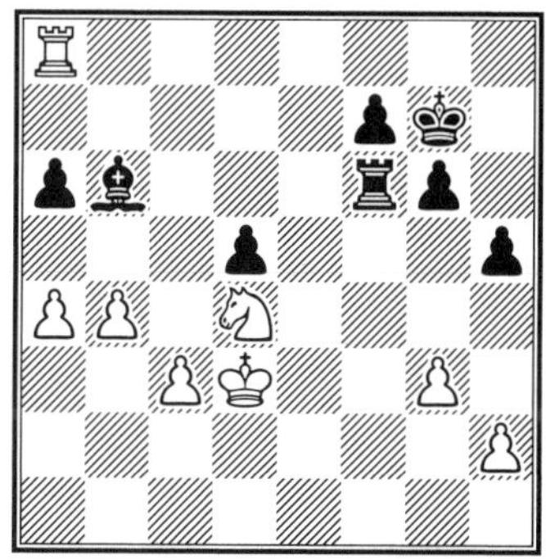

40.Rxa6!

[Alekhine]: "White walks into the trap and proves that this is the quickest way to win."

40...Bxd4 41.Rxf6 Bxf6 42.a5 Be5 43.b5 h4 44.a6, 1-0.

Nottingham (1936): Botvinnik and Capablanca tied for first/second, Euwe, Fine, and Reshevsky tied third/fourth/fifth, Alekhine finished sixth (a disaster!)

In his great book *100 Selected Games*[1] (a "bible" of mine from my early teens of which I have gone over every game and word numerous times) Botvinnik wrote of playing Alekhine at Nottingham:

Alexander Alekhine vs. Mikhail Botvinnik, Nottingham 1936

[Botvinnik]: "At the board Alekhine was so direct that, as he thought out some combination, he was unable to restrain his feelings. When the position was complex, after making his move he would get up and start circling round and round like a kite.

"During the Nottingham Tournament of 1936 I myself had to endure some difficult moments in a game against Alekhine. This game reveals how thoroughly he prepared for playing in tournaments.

1.e4 c5 2.Nf3 d6 3.d4 cxd4 4.Nxd4 Nf6 5.Nc3 g6 6.Be2 Bg7 7.Be3 Nc6 8.Nb3 Be6 9.f4 0-0 10.g4 d5 11.f5 Bc8 12.exd5 Nb4

"It was general knowledge that I had played this variation of the Sicilian Defense against Levenfish three months before the Nottingham tournament, and it was regarded as being favorable to Black. So at first I could not understand why Alekhine was playing this opening. But when the position as shown arose, I guessed from his expression that he had something up his sleeve, that he was preparing some combination. And I was right. He had prepared the maneuver 13.d6!

"Not every master would spot this move, for the pawn sacrifice is completely unexpected; its idea is to weaken Black's f6-square. I managed to 'wriggle out' of this unpleasant position, though not without suffering some nasty moments. At the critical point in my search for escape, I had to spend some twenty minutes in thought, and all that time Alekhine circled round and round our table. Summoning all my will power, I managed to free myself of this strong "psychological" pressure and find a way out of the trap.

13.d6 Qxd6

"The only move. If 13...exd6 then 14.a3 Nc6 15.g5 and 16.f6."

Opening theory always marches on, and this is no exception. Vladimir Vuković (author of the classic *Art of Attack in Chess*) pointed out that 13...exd6! is the best move: 14.a3 Nc6 15.g5 Re8! 16.gxf6 Rxe3 17.fxg7 Qh4+ 18.Kd2 (18.Kf1 Bxf5 wins for Black) and now instead of Vuković's 18...Qh6, 18...Qg5! is most accurate when 19.Ke1 (19.Qe1 is the subject of two 19...Bxf5 followed by ...Rae8 gives Black a winning attack.

1 Mikhail Botvinnik, *One Hundres Selected Games*. New York: Dover Publications, 1960.

14.Bc5

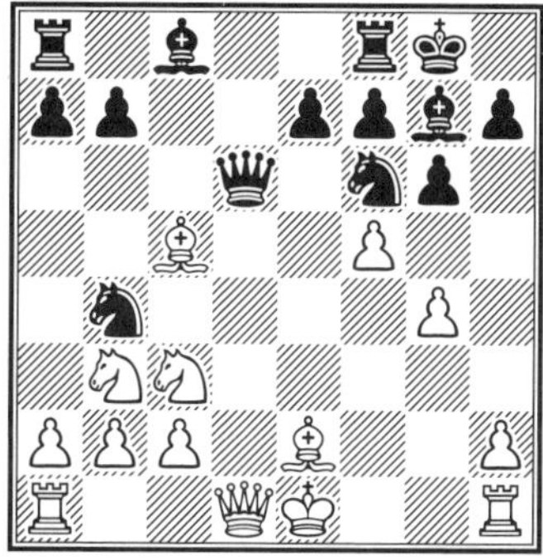

14.Qxd6? exd6 15.g5 Nfd5 is very much in Black's favor.

14...Qf4!

Better than 14...Qxd1+ 15.Rxd1 Nc6 (15...Nxc2+? 15.Kd2) 16.g5 Nd7 17.f6 exf6! (17...Bh8 18.Nd5 is better for White) 18.Bxf8 Nxf8 19.gxf6 Bxf6 and Black has sufficient compensation for the sacrificed exchange.

15.Rf1 Qxh2 16.Bxb4 Nxg4

Botvinnik thought that 16...Qg3+ was inferior due to 17.Rf2 Nxg4 18.Ne4, but this actually wins for Black: 18...Qh4 19.Bxg4 Qh1+, etc. Instead of 18.Ne4, just 18.Bxg4 Qg1+ 19.Rf1 Qg3+ is a draw

17.Bxg4 Qg3+ 18.Rf2

18.Kd2?? Bh6+!

18...Qg1+ 19.Rf1 Qg3+ 20.Rf2 Qg1+, ½-½.

[Botvinnik]: "During his first and second periods, Alekhine always sought for the truth in the game; but in his last period (1934-46) his play was characterized by a new, and one might say a Lasker-manner of approach to chess. During these years he did not so much attempt to penetrate into the secret of a position as to seek a convenient moment when, without blundering, he could shatter his opponent with the combinative weapon, even in positions where the prerequisites were lacking.

Summing up Alekhine's characteristic features as a chess player, one must specify first and foremost his exceptional fighting qualities, his profound psychological insight into the essence of the chess art, and his phenomenal combinative vision, which was a reflection of the specific features of the Soviet school of chess. At the same time I must again emphasize that during the last period of his career his imaginative powers declined."

Podebrady (1936): Flohr first, Alekhine second.

Alexander Alekhine vs. Erich Eliskases, Podebrady 1936

1.e4 e5 2.Nf3 Nc6 3.Bb5 a6 4.Ba4 Nf6 5.0-0 Be7 6.Re1 b5 7.Bb3 d6 8.c3 Na5 9.Bc2 c5 10.d3 Nc6 11.Nbd2 0-0 12.Nf1 Re8 13.Ne3 d5 14.exd5 Nxd5 15.Nxd5 Qxd5 16.d4 exd4 17.Be4 Qd7 18.cxd4 Bf6 19.Bg5 Rxe4 20.Rxe4 Bxd4 21.Nxd4 Nxd4 22.Qh5 Bb7 23.Rh4

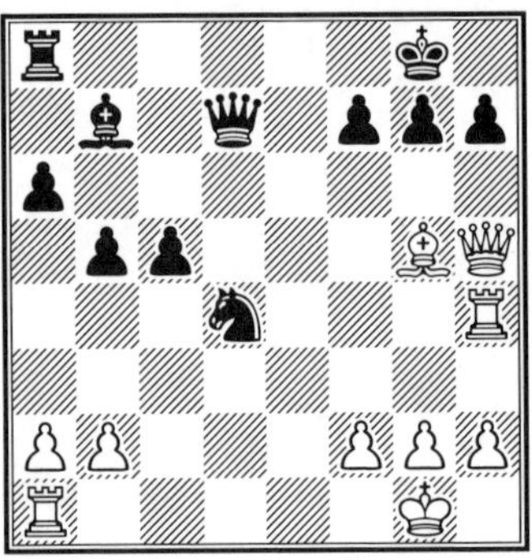

23...Qf5

23...h6 24.Bxh6 Nf5 25.Bxg7! f6 26.Qh7+ gives White an overwhelming attack.

24.Be3 Rd8 25.Rxd4!, 1-0.

Hastings (1937): Alekhine first, Fine second.

Alexander Alekhine vs. Reuben Fine, Hastings 1936

1.e4 e5 2.Nf3 Nc6 3.Bb5 a6 4.Ba4 Nf6 5.0-0 Be7 6.Re1 b5 7.Bb3 d6 8.c3 Na5 9.Nc2 c5 10.d4 Qc7 11.Nbd2 0-0 12.Nf1 Bg4 13.Ne3 Bxf3 14.Qxf3 cxd4 15.Nf5 dxc3 16.Qxc3 Rfc8 17.Qg3 Bf8 18.Bd3 Nc6 19.Bg5 Ne8 20.Rac1 Qb7 21.a3 g6 22.Nh6+ Bxh6 23.Bxh6 Nd4 24.Rcd1 b4 25.f4 exf4 26.Qxf4 bxa3 27.bxa3 Rc3 28.Qf2 Ne6 29.a4 Rac8 30.Rf1 R3c7 31.Rb1 Qc6

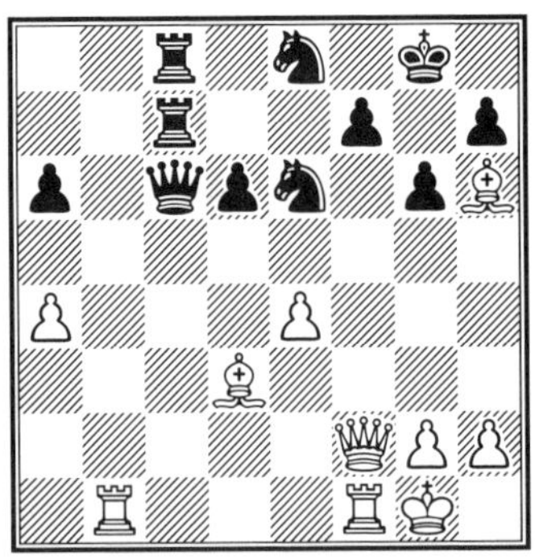

32.a5 Nc5 33.Bc4 Qd7 34.Qa2! Nxe4 35.Rxf7 Qxf7 36.Bxf7+ Rxf7 37.Qe6, 1-0.

Kemeri (1937): Flohr, Petrovs, Reshevsky tied for first/second/third, Alekhine and Keres tied for fourth/fifth

Alexander Alekhine vs. Reuben Fine, Kemeri 1937

1.d4 d5 2.c4 dxc4 3.Nf3 Nf6 4.Qa4+ Qd7 5.Qxc4 Qc6 6.Na3 Qxc4 7.Nxc4 e6 8.a3 c5 9.Bf4 Nc6 10.dxc5 Bxc5 11.b4 Be7 12.b5 Nb8 13.Nd6+ Bxd6 14.Bxd6 Ne4 15.Bc7 Nd7 16.Nd4 Nb6 17.f3 Nd5 18.Ba5 Nef6 19.Nc2 Bd7 20.e4 Rc8 21.Kd2 Nb6 22.Ne3 0-0 23.a4 Rfd8 24.Bd3 e5 25.Rhc1 Be6 26.Rxc8 Rxc8 27.Bb4 Ne8 28.a5 Nd7 29.Nd5 Bxd5 30.exd5 Nc5

White enjoys a huge positional advantage (space and two bishops). How did he push his opponent off the board?

31.Bf5

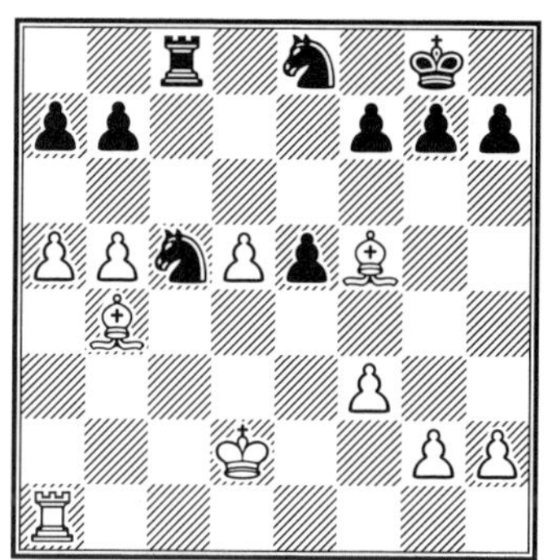

31...Rd8

31...Nb3+ 32.Kd3 Rd8 33.Re1 Rxd5+ (33...f6 34.Be6+ Kh8 35.Be7) 34.Kc4 and Black drops a piece.

32.Kc3 b6

32...Rxd5 33.Kc4 Rd4+ 34.Kxc5 b6+ 35.axb6 axb6+ 36.Kxb6 Rxb4 37.Ra8; 32...Nd7 33.Be7 Rc8+ 34.Kb4 Nc7 35.Rd1 Re8 36.Bd6.

33.axb6 axb6 34.Bxc5

Creating a powerful passed pawn.

34...bxc5 35.b6 Nd6 36.Bd7

The threat of Bc6 followed by b7 ends the game, so Black decided to allow a mate.

36...Rxd7 37.Ra8+ Ne8 38.Rxe8, 1-0.

A great example of using tactics to push home powerful positional concepts.

Margate (1937): Fine and Keres tied for first/second, Alekhine third.

World Championship Match 1937

The story goes that before his rematch with Euwe, Alekhine (taking the contest very seriously) quit drinking (unlike his overconfidence and alcohol guzzling in the first match). He knew this was his last chance to regain the title, and he put everything he had into achieving his goal. The spark of battle ignited, and though he wasn't the Alekhine of 1930 and 1931, he was close enough to it to shock the world. This wasn't just for the title, it was for his dignity, and when all was said and done, Alekhine could hold his head high.

The twenty-five game battle was hard fought, but Alekhine was two up with five games to go. Such a lead is pretty much decisive, and Euwe collapsed losing four games and drawing one. The final six game difference makes the match seem one-sided, but nothing could be further from the truth.

Alekhine: 15½ (once again World Champion!)

Euwe: 9½

After losing his title, Euwe (always a gentleman) wrote:

> Alekhine's perfect technique and combinative talent are so well known that it is unnecessary to talk about them. His conduct of the endgame was shining. Even so, I admire most how he finished the adjourned games. I had to analyze them too, so I know them well. When I think of how my opponent created ingenious ideas and how he finished them in unexpected ways, I have only the greatest admiration for Alekhine's playing style.

Alekhine maintained a lifetime winning score over Euwe (28 wins, 20 losses, and 38 draws).

Alexander Alekhine vs. Max Euwe, Netherlands, World Championship (6) 1937

1.d4 d5 2.c4 c6 3.Nc3 dxc4 4.e4 e5 5.Bxc4 exd4 6.Nf3 b5 7.Nxb5 Ba6

7...cxb5 8.Bd5

8.Qb3 Qe7

8...Bxb5? 9.Bxf7+ Kd7 10.Nxd4! with a raging attack. Here's a sample: 10...Kc8 11.Nxb5 cxb5 12.Be6+ Nd7 13.Qd5 Rb8 14.Bg5 Nf6 15.Rc1+.

9.0-0

An important move that many amateurs don't appreciate. Before continuing with the attack, White makes sure his King is safe and also brings the kingside Rook into play.

9...Bxb5 10.Bxb5 Nf6

10...cxb5? 11.Qd5.

11.Bc4

11.e5 is also very interesting.

11...Nbd7 12.Nxd4

12.e5 was also crushing.

12...Rb8 13.Qc2 Qc5 14.Nf5

14.Nxc6? Rc8 only helps Black.

14...Ne5 15.Bf4 Nh5

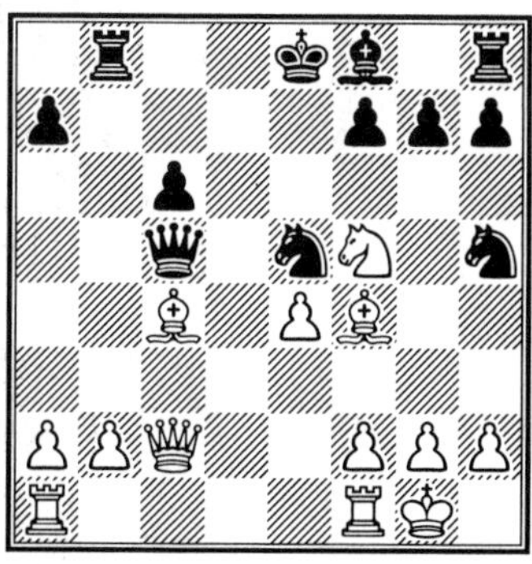

16.Bxf7+!

Exchanging pieces so White can reach an easily winning endgame. If you have an opponent face down in the grave, keep things as simple as possible.

16...Kxf7 17.Qxc5 Bxc5 18.Bxe5 and Black, who is two pawns down, resigned in a few more moves.

Alexander Alekhine vs. Max Euwe, Netherlands, World Championship (8) 1937

1.d4 Nf6 2.c4 e6 3.Nc3 Bb4 4.Qc2 d5 5.cxd5 Qxd5 6.e3 c5 7.a3 Bxc3+ 8.bxc3 Nbd7 9.f3 cxd4 10.cxd4 Nb6 11.Ne2 Bd7 12.Nf4 Qd6 13.Bd2 Rc8 14.Qb2 Nfd5 15.Nxd5 exd5 16.Bb4 Qe6 17.Kf2 Na4 18.Qd2 b6 19.Ba6 Rb8 20.e4 b5

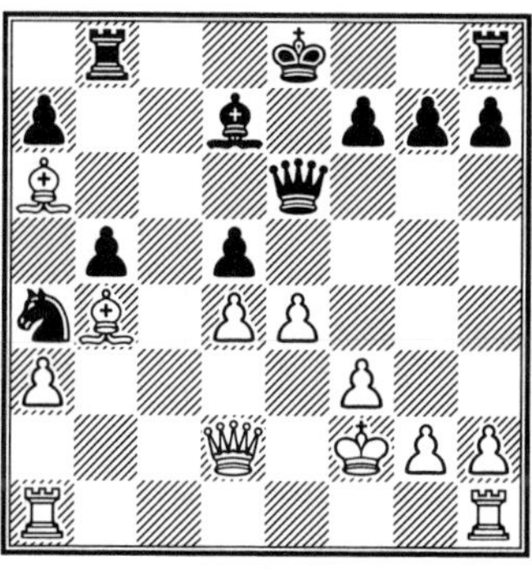

White's a6 Bishop seems to have wandered too far, and now it's trapped behind enemy lines and, apparently, doomed. What can White do?

21.Qf4!

Another way was 21.exd5! Qxa6 22.Rhe1+ Kd8 23.Rac1 Re8 24.Ba5+ Nb6 25.Qg5+ f6 26.Qxg7 and Black will fall victim to a mating attack.

21...Rb6 22.exd5 Qxd5 23.Rhe1+ Be6 24.Rac1 f6 25.Rc7 Kd8 26.Rxa7, 1-0.

The Dark Years

After shocking the world (and Euwe, who was sure he would finish Alekhine off once and for all) with his epic performance in capturing back the World Championship, Alekhine continued to show that, at forty-six he was still a force to be reckoned with! There were the occasional failures, but for the most part he played extremely well.

Montevideo (1938): Alekhine came in first ahead of a weak field.

Alexander Alekhine vs. Adhemar da Silva Rocha, Montevideo 1938

1.e4 c5 2.Nf3 Nc6 3.d4 cxd4 4.Nxd4 Nf6 5.Nc3 d6 6.Bg5 Bd7 7.Be2 a6 8. 0-0 e6 9.Nb3 b5 10.a3 Na5 11.Nxa5 Qxa5 12.Qd4 Be7 13.Rfd1 Qc7 14.a4 b4 15.Bxf6 gxf6 16.Qxb4 Qc5 17.Qd4 Rb8 18.Qxc5 dxc5 19.Bxa6 Rxb2 20.Bb5 Bxb5 21.Nxb5 0-0

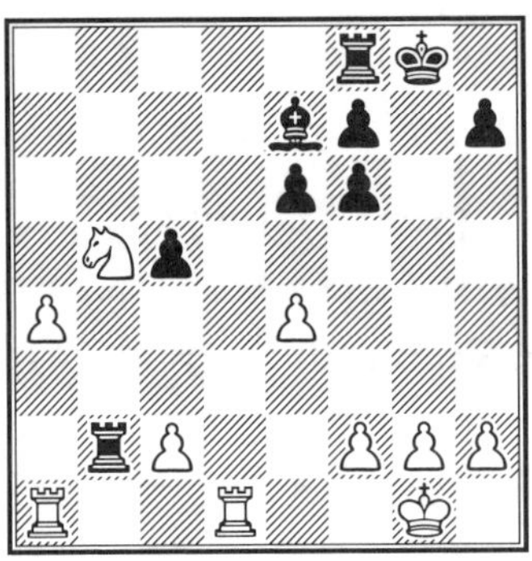

White is winning, but it's up to you to demonstrate your endgame technique.

22.c4 Ra8 23.a5

This whole endgame is all about breaking Black's blockade of the a-pawn.

23...Ra6 24.g3

Stopping a back rank mate once the white Rooks start penetrating into the enemy position.

24...Rb4 25.Rd7 Bf8 26.Ra7! Rxa7 27.Nxa7 Rb8 28.a6 Ra8 29.Nb5 Be7 30.a7

Threatening Nc7.

30...Bd8 31.Rd1 Bb6 32.Rd7 Kg7 33.Rb7, 1-0.

Julio Cesar Balparda vs. Alexander Alekhine, Montevideo 1938

1.d4 Nf6 2.Nf3 b6 3.g3 Bb7 4.Bg2 c5 5.c3 e6 6.0-0 Be7 7.b3 0-0 8.Bb2 cxd4 9.cxd4 b5 10.Nbd2 Qb6 11.e3 a5 12.a3 Nc6 13.Ne5 d6 14.Nxc6 Bxc6 15.Bxc6 Qxc6 16.Rc1 Qb7 17.Qf3 d5 18.Rc2 Bd6 19.Rfc1 Qe7 20.Qe2 Rfb8 21.Nb1

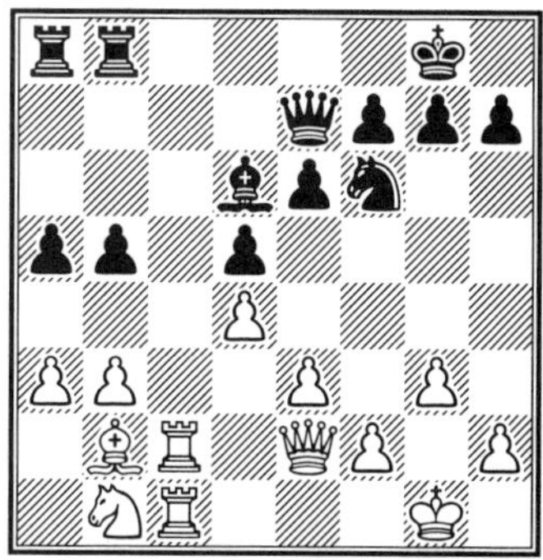

21...h5 22.Rc6 h4 23.g4 Ne4 24.f3 Ng5 25.Kg2 b4 26.a4 e5 27.Nd2 Re8 28.Qb5 e4 29.f4 h3+ 30.Kg3 Rad8 31.Rf1 g6 32.Qb6 Kg7 33.Bc1 Ne6 34.Rg1 Rh8 35.Kf2 Nxf4! 36.Ke1 Nd3+ 37.Kd1 Bxh2 38.Rf1 Bd6, 0-1.

Margate (1938): Alekhine first, Spielmann second, Petrovs third.

Alexander Alekhine vs. Eero Böök, Margate (6) 1938

1.d4 d5 2.c4 dxc4 3.Nf3 Bf6 4.e3 e6 5.Bxc4 c5 6.0-0 Nc6 7.Qe2 a6 8.Nc3 b5 9.Bb3 b4 10.d5 Na5 11.Ba4+ Bd7 12.dxe6 fxe6

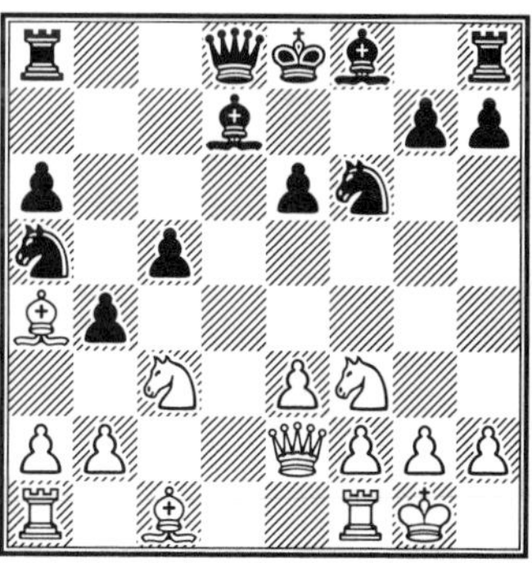

13.Rd1 bxc3 14.Rxd7! Nxd7 15.Ne5 Ra7 16.bxc3!!

An extraordinarily brave move that leaves Black a Rook up.

16.e4 makes a lot of sense, while 16.Qh5+ seems to be a forced draw: 16... g6 17.Nxg6 hxg6 18.Qxg6+ Ke7 19.e4 Bh6 (19...Nf6?? gets wiped off the board: 20.Bg5 Qd4 21.Bxf6+ Qxf6 22.Qe8+ Kd6 23.Qb8+ Rc7 24.Rd1+ Qd4 25.Qd8+ and blood is flowing off the board!) 20.Bxh6 Qg8 21.Bg5+ Kf8 22.Bh6+ Ke7 23.Bg5.

16...Ke7?

16... Qb8! is the best defense, but after 17.Nxd7 Rxd7 18.Qxa6 Qd6 19.Qb5! White has a very dangerous attack. Perhaps Black can survive it, perhaps not. Here's a sample of what could occur: 19...Ke7 20.Ba3 Nb7 21.Rb1 Rc7 22.Qe8+ Kf6 23.c4 e5 24.f4 Qe7 25.Qh5 g6 26.Qf3 Nd8 27.Bb2 Nf7 28.fxe5+ Kg7 29.e6+ and the end of the world has arrived.

17.e4 Nf6 18.Bg5 Qc7 19.Bf4 Qb6 20.Rd1 g6 21.Bg5 Bg7

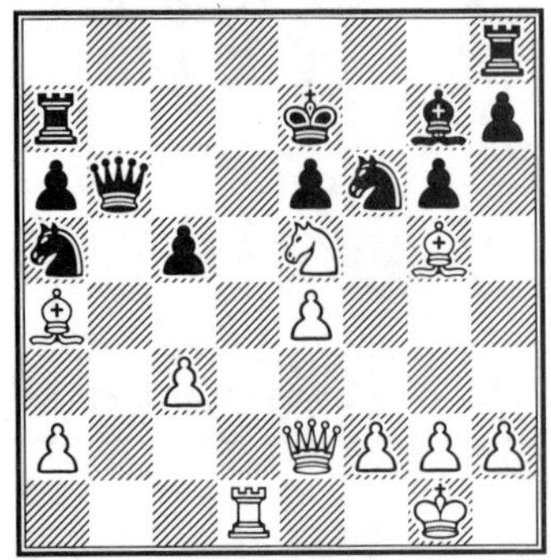

22.Nd7 Rxd7 23.Rxd7+ Kf8 24.Bxf6 Bxf6 25.e5, 1-0.

Alexander Alekhine vs. Harry Golombek, Margate (3) 1938

1.d4 Nf6 2.c4 e6 3.Nc3 Bb4 4.g3 d5 5.Bg2 0-0 6.Nf3 c5 7.cxd5 Nxd5 8.Bd2 Nc6 9.a3 Nxc3 10.bxc3 Ba5 11.0-0 cxd4 12.cxd4 Bxd2 13.Qxd2 Qe7 14.Qb2 Rd8 15.Rfc1 Qd6 16.e3!

Protecting d4, which allows white's Knight to roam.

16...Rb8 17.Ng5! Bd7 18.Qc2 f5

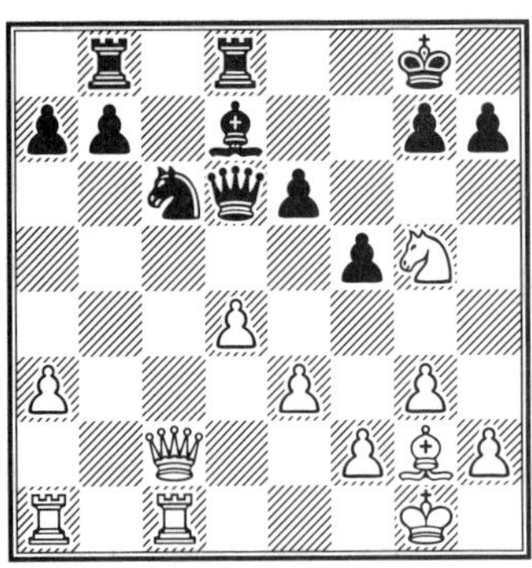

19.d5!! Ne7 20.dxe6 Bxe6 21.Rd1 Qe5 22.Bxb7! h6

22...Rxd1+ 23.Rxd1 Rxb7 24.Rd8 mate.

23.Nxe6 Qxe6 24.Qc7 Rxd1+ 25.Rxd1 Re8 26.Bf3 a6 27.Rd6 Qe5 28.Qc4+ Kh7 29.Rxa6 Rc8 30.Qf7 Rc1+ 31.Kg2, 1-0.

Plymouth (1938): Alekhine and George Thomas tied for first/second ahead of a weak field.

Alexander Alekhine vs. Rowena Bruce, Plymouth 1938

1.e4 c6 2.Nc3 d5 3.Nf3 dxe4 4.Nxe4 Bf5 5.Ng3

This is known to be inferior for Black, and the reply

5...Bg6

5...Bg4 should be tried.

6.h4 h6

Falls head first into a famous trap.

7.Ne5! Bh7

7...Qd6 had to be tried.

8.Qh5!

The trap springs shut!

8...g6

Now Black's light-squared Bishop is entombed on h7.

9.Bc4! e6

9...gxh5 10.Bxf7 mate.

10.Qe2 Nf6??

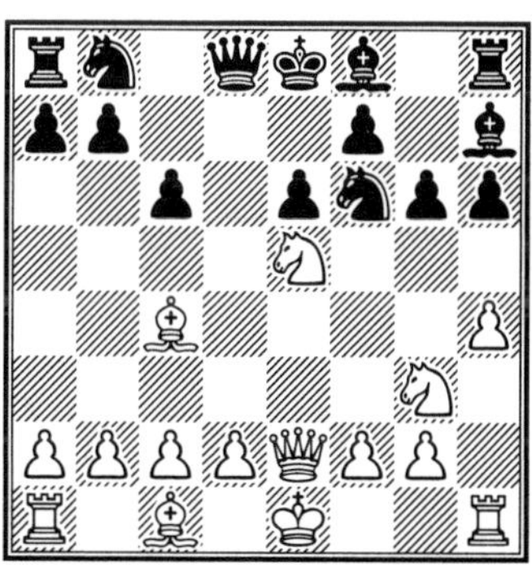

Black's game was horrid, but this loses on the spot.

11.Nxf7! Kxf7 12.Qxe6+, 1-0.

AVRO[1] (1938): Keres and Fine first/second, Botvinnik third, Alekhine, Euwe, Reshevsky fourth/sixth, Capablanca seventh, Flohr eighth.

1 ARVO was a tournament held in the Netherlands organized by the Dutch broadcating company, *Allgemeese Vereningun Radio-Omroep*.

Keres was undefeated at the AVRO tournament, while Fine lost three games. However, Fine's 2-0 score vs. Alekhine propelled him into a tie for first place (though Keres won on tiebreaks). Alekhine had an even score (3 wins and 3 losses) but his victory over Capablanca was a nice consolation prize. Though Alekhine showed that he was still an elite player, the younger generation was clearly on his heels. It should be mentioned that AVRO's venue changed every few days (it was moved from one Dutch city to another), and the constant traveling exhausted the older players (the youngsters took the first three spots).

Alexander Alekhine vs. Max Euwe, Netherlands, AVRO (3) 1938

1.d4 d5 2.c4 c6 3.Nf3 Nf6 4.cxd5 cxd5 5.Nc3 Nc6 6.Bf4 Bf5 7.e3 a6 8.Ne5 Rc8 9.g4 Bd7 10.Bg2 e6 11.0-0 h6 12.Bg3 h5 13.Nxd7 Nxd7 14.gxh5 Nf6 15.Bf3 Bb4 16.Rc1 Kf8 17.a3 Bxc3 18.Rxc3 Ne7 19.Qb3 Rxc3 20.bxc3 Qd7 21.Qb6 Nc8 22.Qc5+ Kg8 23.Rb1 b5

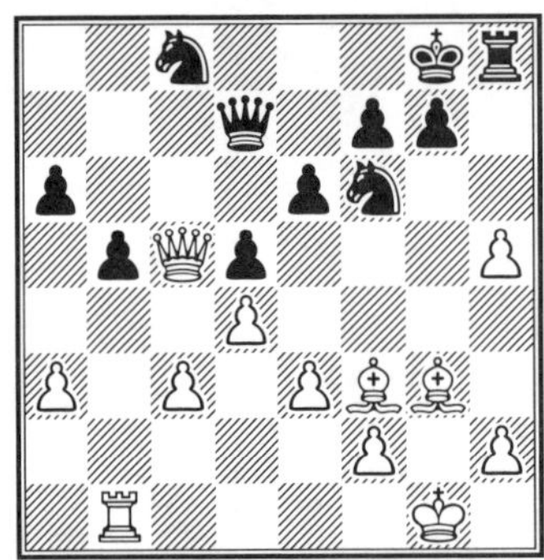

24.h6 gxh6 25.Be5 Kg7 26.a4 bxa4 27.c4 Ne7 28.cxd5! Nexd5

28...Rc8 is better, but after 29.dxe6 Qxe6 30.Qd6 White has a winning advantage thanks to better pawn structure and two bishops vs. two Knights.

29.Kh1

Preparing Rg1+.

29...Rc8 30.Rg1+ Kh7 31.Qa3 Rg8 32.e4

Winning a Knight.

32...Rxg1+ 33.Kxg1 Qb5 34.exd5 Qb1+ 35.Kg2 Qg6+ 36.Bg3 with an extra piece for White.

Alexander Alekhine vs. José Capablanca, AVRO (9) 1938

1.e4 e6 2.d4 d5 3.Nd2 Nf6 4.e5 Nfd7 5.Bd3 c5 6.c3 Nc6 7.Ne2 Qb6 8.Nf3 cxd4 9.cxd4 Bb4+ 10.Kf1 Be7 11.a3 Nf8 12.b4 Bd7 13.Be3 Nd8 14.Nc3 a5 15.Na4 Qa7 16.b5 b6 17.g3 f5 18.Kg2 Nf7 19.Qd2 h6

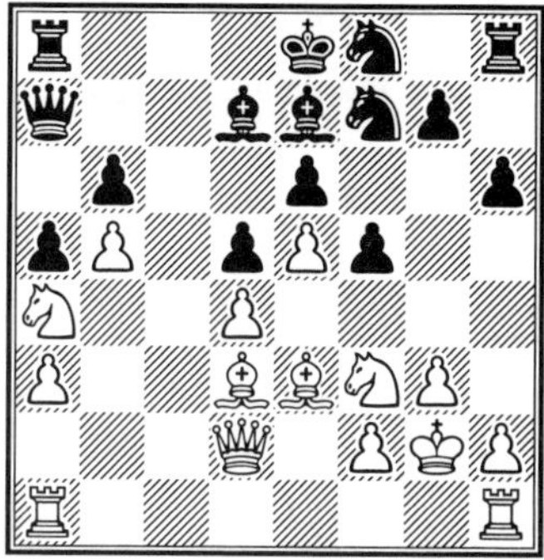

20.h4 Nh7 21.h5 Nfg5 22.Nh4 Ne4 23.Qb2 Kf7 24.f3 Neg5 25.g4 fxg4 26.Bg6+!

Also good was 26.f4 Ne4 27.Bxe4 dxe4 28.d5 exd5 29.Nxb6 Rad8 30.Nxd5.

26...Kg8 27.f4 Nf3

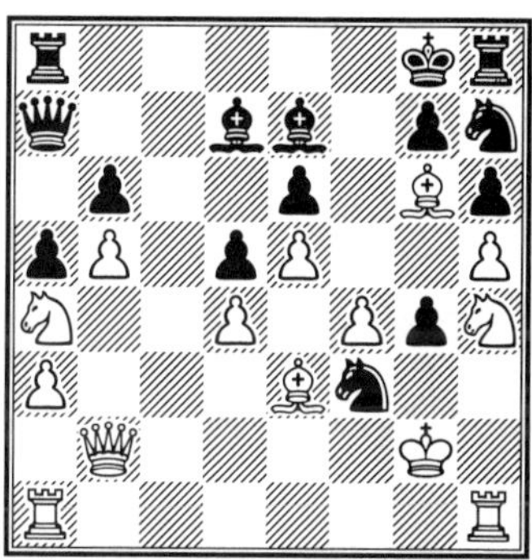

28.Bxh7+! Rxh7

28...Kxh7 29.Qb1+ Kg8 30.Ng6 is also easy for White.

29.Ng6

Black's position is hopeless since all of his pieces are passive and the f3-Knight is actually trapped behind enemy lines.

29... Bd8 30.Rac1 Be8 31.Kg3! Qf7 32.Kxg4

The f3-Knight is trapped!

32...Nh4 33.Nxh4 Qxh5+ 34.Kg3 Qf7 35.Nf3, 1-0.

Caracas (1939): Alekhine had a perfect (10-0) score, but the field was very weak.

Montevideo (1939): Alekhine first with 7-0, Golombek second, Vero Menchik third (the rest of the field was weak)

Alekhine was one of the greatest attacking players of all time (and perhaps the greatest tactician ever), but you need positional skills, too, if you hope to be a top player. In the next game we see those skills on display.

Alexander Alekhine vs. Harry Golombek, Montevideo 1939

1.e4 c5 2.Nf3 d6 3.d4 cxd4 4.Nxd4 Nf6 5.Nc3 g6 6.Be2 Bg7 7.Bb3 Nc6 8.0-0 0-0 9.Kh1 a5 10.a4 Be6 11.f4 Qc8 12.Be3 Bg4 13.Bg1 Rd8 14.Nd5 Bxe2 15.Qxe2 Nxd5 16.exd5 Nb4 17.c4 Qc7 18.Nd4

Black will soon find that his position has some serious flaws: the e7-pawn is a permanent target and White's queenside space advantage leaves Black passively placed. White intends to do the following: improve the position of his Knight by moving it to b5, defend a4 and c4 by b2-b3, add to the pressure along the e-file by Rae1 (which also gets the Rook off the a1-h8 diagonal), and then create kingside pressure with f4-f5.

18...Rdc8 19.b3 Na6 20.Rae1 Re8 21.f5 Nc5 22.Qf3

Defending b3 and putting some heat down the f-file. Black's position is now hopelessly lost.

22...Rf8 23.Nb5 Qd7

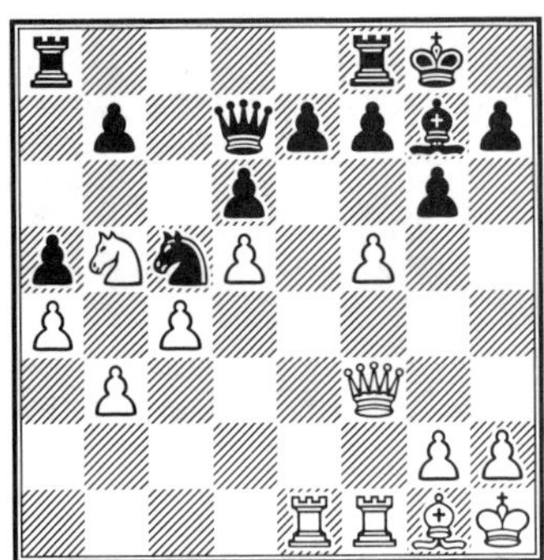

24.Bxc5!

An important move. This allows White to make use of a possible d5-d6 push, it rids the board of black's Knight (which tied White down to the protection of b3], and by forcing Black's d-pawn from d6 to c5 it deprives the black Bishop of the use of the e5-square.

24...dxc5 25.Qe3

Winning material by force, which will lead to a safe and easy win. The younger Alekhine would probably have chosen 25.d6! exd6 26.f6 Bh8 27.Re7 which wins in a more dynamic manner.

25...Rfe8 26.Qxc5

26.fxg6 hxg6 27.Qxc5 was also good.

26...gxf5 27.Qc7!

A nice move that carries a big punch!

27...Rad8 28.Qxa5 e5

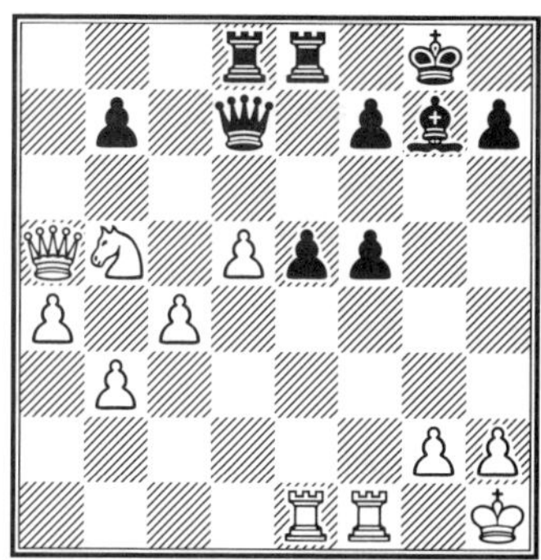

29.Qc7!

Back for seconds!

29...Qxc7 30.Nxc7 Re7 31.Nb5 e4

31...f4 32.Rxf4!

32.Rxf5 and Black resigned in a couple moves.

Alekhine's visit to Lisbon in 1940 as described by Francisco Lupi:[1]

In January of 1940, when the tiny Portuguese chess circle had never yet in its history had a visit from a World Champion, we were told that Alexander Alekhine and his wife Grace were on their way to Lisbon. We were tremendously excited. A reception program was outlined such as a Crown Prince on a pleasure-trip would not have disdained. The best suite of rooms was immediately reserved in Estoril's luxury hotel, and a magnificent eight-cylinder car was produced for our guest's exclusive use.

On a misty February morning, if my recollections are accurate, we all went to the dock to meet the ship in which he came from Buenos Aires, where he had led the French team during the "Match of the Nations." Even before the ship was moored, we had spotted on the upper deck a very blond, smiling man, carrying two kittens in his arms.

Later we grew used to seeing him, at his evening simultaneous matches, always wearing his dinner jacket of good English cloth, always using slightly theatrical gestures. He was perhaps a little too fat, his complexion was florid, and after three or four hours' concentration at the boards he would show evident signs of exhaustion.

After about every other passage round the 'ring' he would drink a cup of coffee. Once he drank more than twenty cups in seven hours. Meanwhile his wife would be sitting in one corner of the room, imperturbably knitting, while

1 Pablo Moran, *A. Alekhine: Agony of a Chess Genius.* Jefferson, NC: McFarland, 2010.

> the kittens played with the wool. "Be careful," she would murmur every time he passed. 'You are drinking too much coffee.'
>
> Alekhine delighted the Portuguese chess enthusiasts with his brilliance, his kindliness, his constant readiness to help young players, and his work for charity. But there was a war on, and the Russian-born was by adoption and inclination a Frenchman. In a fortnight, he was gone. Some weeks later I received a letter from him saying he was a Lieutenant-Interpreter in the French Army.

This account of Alekhine's first visit to Lisbon shows him in a light that many readers might not be aware of. Yes, he had his enemies (all famous people do), but he was also extremely kind to many people and had close friendships and a vast number of fans all over the world.

It's important to note that Mr. and Mrs. Alekhine didn't need to return to war-torn Europe. They were in South America and could have stayed there or made their way to the United States. However, Alekhine wanted to help France, and he returned so he could fight the Nazis side by side with his fellow Frenchmen.

After his return, things went badly, and France fell to the Nazis who arrived in the now helpless city of Paris on June 14, 1940. Seeing that things were grim, Alekhine returned to Portugal so he could arrange a rematch with Capablanca in America. His wife, a wealthy American (who was famous for being one of the first woman scenic artists), insisted on staying in France to defend their home and belongings (though eventually, the Nazis took over (and looted)their château). Alekhine's plan was to arrange the match, and then book passage for him and his wife to Rio de Janeiro or New York. Unfortunately, his plans failed due to Capablanca's lack of interest and in his inability to get the necessary visas.

Francisco Lupi continues:

> On the afternoon in which we reached the conclusion that the negotiations for this match were stillborn, Alekhine and I wandered disconsolately down the busy Rua Aurea. I should emphasize that ever since his 1935 match with Euwe, Alekhine had stopped drinking. The first time he arrived in Lisbon, he did not even smoke. On this second trip to Portugal, I immediately noticed he was smoking again. That afternoon, as we passed a café, he told me, without looking me straight in the eyes: 'I must buy some cigarettes. I see I have no more left.' And he asked me to wait for him while he went into the café to buy them. I waited; but as he took much time, I decided to go in after him. And then I saw that he had asked for a bottle of wine, and, glass by glass, was emptying it.

At this point in the story, it's important to briefly mention there has been a long-running controversy over Alekhine's activities during World War II, specifically as to whether or not he was a Nazi sympathizer. I have my own personal view on this subject, and feel that Alekhine was vilified, and this may have been what ultimately destroyed him. However, unbiased opinions on this subject are hard to come by and therefore to those readers interested, I recommend looking at Pablo Moran's excellent book *A. Alekhine: Agony of a Genius* and draw your own conclusions.

Krakow/Warsaw (1941): Alekhine and Paul Schmidt finished first/second, Bogoljubov third, Junge fourth.

Madrid (1941): Alekhine first with 5-0 ahead of a weak field.

Munich (1941): Stoltz first, Alekhine and Lundin tied for second/third, and Bogoljubov fourth.

Krakow/Warsaw (1942): Alekhine first, Junge second, Bogoljubov third, Keller and Sämisch tied for fourth/fifth.

Alexander Alekhine vs. Klaus Junge, Krakow 1942

1.e4 e5 2.Nf3 Nc6 3.Bb5 a6 4.Ba4 Nf6 5.0-0 Be7 6.Qe2 b5 7.Bb3 0-0 8.c3 d5 9.d3 dxe4 10.dxe4 Bg4 11.h3 Bh5 12.Bg5 Ne8 13.Bxe7 Bxf3 14.Qxf3 Nxe7 15.Rd1 Nd6 16.Nd2 c6 17.Nf1 Qc7 18.a4 Rad8 19.Ng3 Nec8 20.axb5 axb5 21.Nf5 Nb6 22.Qe3 Nxf5 23.exf5 c5 24.f6! gxf6 25.Qh6

Threatening Bc2.

25...f5

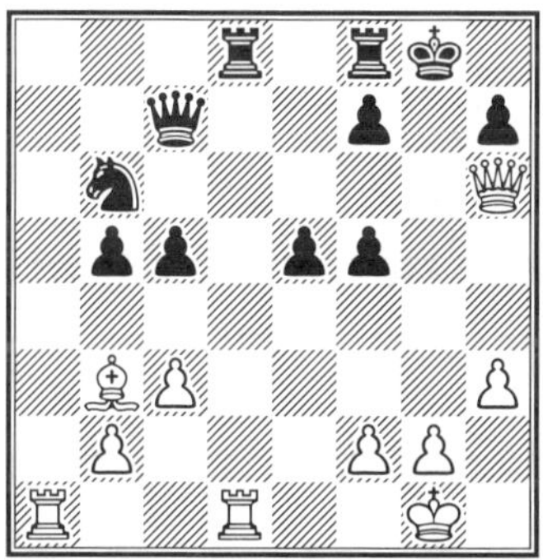

26.Bxf7+!!

Another winning line is 26.Qg5+ Kh8 27.Qf6+ Kg8 28.Rxd8 Rxd8 29.Bxf7+ Kf8 30.Bc4+ Ke8 31.Bxb5+ Nd7 32.Ra6 and mate.

26...Qxf7

26...Rxf7 27.Qg5+ Rg7 28.Rxd8+ is game over, while 26...Kxf7 27.Qxh7+ picks up the black Queen.

27.Rxd8! Na4

Blocking the a-file.

27...Rxd8 allows a triple-jump checker move: 28.Qg5+ Kh8 29.Qxd8+ Kg7 30.Qxb6.

28.b3!

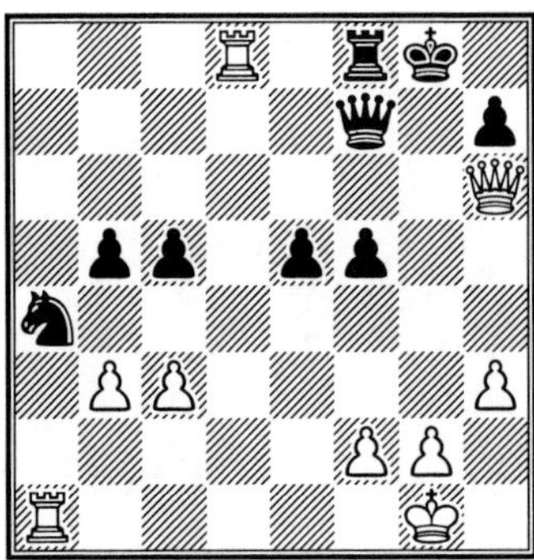

The most sadistic move.

28...Rxd8

28...Qxb3 29.Qxf8 mate.

29.Qg5+ Qg7 30.Qxd8+ wins the Knight and leaves White a whole Rook ahead.

Munich (1942): Alekhine first (he beat Keres in their individual game), Keres second, Bogoljubov, Richter, and Foltys tied third/fifth, and Barcza sixth.

Here's Alekhine's win over Keres, which features a mix of positional domination and tactical acumen:

Alexander Alekhine vs. Paul Keres, Munich 1942

1.d4 Nf6 2.Nf3 b6 3.c4 Bb7 4.g3 e6 5.Bg2 Be7 6.0-0 0-0 7.b3 d5 8.Ne5 c6 9.Bb2 Nbd7 10.Nd2 c5 11.e3 Rc8 12.Rc1 Rc7 13.Qe2 Qa8 14.cxd5 Nxd5 15.e4 N5f6 16.b4! Rfc8 17.dxc5 bxc5 18.b5 a6 19.a4 axb5 20.axb5 Qa7

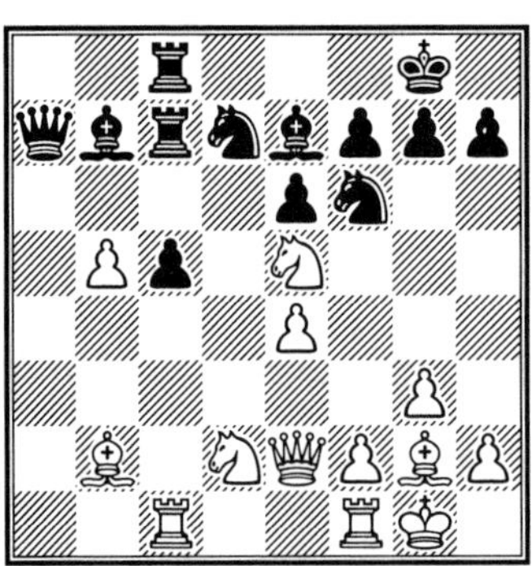

21.Nec4!

Black has a wretched position. The c5-pawn blocks both of black's Rooks, the d7-Knight, and the e7-Bishop! In the meantime the b5-pawn is very strong and can advance at any moment, and White's pieces are far more active than Black's.

21...Qa8 22.Bxf6! gxf6

22...Bxf6 23.b6 Rc6 24.e5 Be7 25.Ra1 Qb8 26.Rfb1 when Black is totally helpless, and White can win material whenever he wishes.

22...Nxf6 23.Nb6.

23.b6 Rc6 24.e5 Rxb6

24...Nxe5 25.Nxe5 fxe5 26.Nc4 Bf6 27.Rfd1 Rf8 28.Rd7.

25.Nxb6 Nxb6 26.Bxb7 Qxb7 27.exf6 Bxf6 28.Ne4 Be7 29.Qg4+ Kh8 30.Qf4 Bf8 31.Nxc5 Qc7

31...Rxc5 32.Rxc5 Bxc5 33.Qe5+ picks up the Bishop.

32.Nxe6! Qxf4 33.Nxf4 and White wins.

Prague (1942): Alekhine and Junge tied first/second, Foltys third, Opočenský and Zita tied fourth/fifth.

Salzburg (1942): Alekhine first, Keres second, Junge and Schmidt third/fourth, Bogoljubov fifth, Stoltz sixth.

The Salzburg event was a six-player double round robin event. The highlight was Alekhine's 2-0 score over Keres, but the World Champion also lost two games (splitting with Junge and Bogoljubov). In fact, out of the 10 games played, Alekhine only drew 1!

Paul Keres vs. Alexander Alekhine, Salzburg 1942

1.e4 e5 2.f4 exf4 3.Nf3 Nf6 4.e5 Nh5 5.Qe2 Be7 6.d4 0-0 7.g4 fxg3 8.Nc3 d5 9.Bd2 Nc6 10.0-0-0 Bg4 11.Be3 f6 12.h3 Be6 13.Ng5 fxg5 14.Qxh5 g6 15.Qe2 g4 16.hxg4 Bg5 17.Kb1 Bxe3 18.Qxe3 Bxg4 19.Qh6 Rf7 20.Bg2 Ne7 21.Rdf1 Rg7 22.Qf4 Be6 23.Ne2 Nf5 24.Bh3 Qd7 25.Rfg1 Rf8 26.Qd2

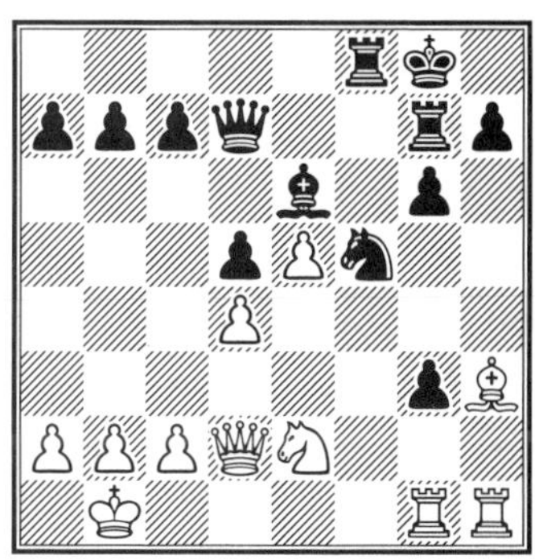

26...Nxd4! 27.Qxd4

27.Bxe6+ Nxe6.

27...Bxh3 28.Rxg3 Bf5 29.Qxa7 b6 30.Qa3 c5 31.Qb3 Be4 32.Rd1 Qf5

Taking aim at c2.

33.Nc3 c4 34.Qa4

34.Qxb6 Bxc2+.

34...Qxe5 and won without difficulties.

For a fifty year-old-man, Alekhine's results were extremely impressive. But he outdid himself in his next event!

Prague (1943): Alekhine finished first with an incredible undefeated score of 15 wins and only 4 draws!, Keres was second 2½ points behind Alekhine.

Salzburg (1943): Alekhine and Keres tied first/second.

Madrid 1943

In 1943 the Spanish Chess Federation organized a strong tournament in Madrid, and Alekhine and Keres were supposed to be the two biggest names. The Nazis sent Alekhine to Madrid as their chess representative, but didn't allow his wife to go with him (the Gestapo wouldn't give her an exit visa, thus using her to keep Alekhine on a "chain"). Alekhine arrived at the tournament late and he wasn't allowed to play (Keres won). Though Alekhine had promised to return to Germany after the event, he refused to do so, remaining in Spain.

When asked by a Spanish journalist about his future plans, Alekhine said:

> Plans? What plans can I have? The best part of my life has passed away between two world wars that have led Europe to waste. Both wars ruined me, with this difference: at the end of the first war I was twenty-six years of age, with an unbounded enthusiasm I no longer have.

Once the war ended, due to pro-Nazi accusations that were hurled against him, Alekhine was banned from playing in tournaments outside of the Iberian Peninsula. He found himself stuck in Spain and Portugal, while his wife decided to remain in Paris She had turned sixty-seven (much older than Alekhine), in poor health, and had decided that enough was enough—she died there in 1956.

Forced by circumstances to play in silly little events against weak players, and to giving endless exhibitions in order to survive, Alekhine became more and more depressed. He drank incessantly. The "Alekhine hatred," which he felt was unwarranted, dragged him deeper and deeper into a dark psychological pit. Not surprisingly, he got sicker and sicker (mentally and physically), and his chess became weaker and weaker.

Gijon (1944): Alekhine first, winning 7 and drawing 1.

Zaragoza (1944): A four-game match was arranged vs. Rey Ardid, Alekhine won 1 and drew 3.

Alekhine with his cat Chess.

At this point in his life Alekhine's chess skills were almost completely gone, he lived in abject poverty, and was a physical wreck. He was examined by Dr. Casimiro Rugarcia in July, 1945, was told that he had a fatal cirrhosis of the liver, but if he quit drinking and lived a pure life, he might last a few more years.

As told by Pablo Moran in *Agony of a Chess Genius*:

> Alekhine looked at the physician with obvious compassion, put on his jacket, turned away—and as he left, said, "Then it is not worthwhile to quit drinking."

Almeria (1945): Alekhine and Nunez Lopez tied for first.

Caceres (1945): Lupi first, Alekhine second followed by a weak field.

Gijon (1945): Rico Gonzalez first, Antonio Medina Garcia and Alekhine tied for second/third, Pomar was fourth.

Madrid (1945): Alekhine first.

Melilla (1945): Alekhine first.

Sabadell (1945): Alekhine first.

Alekhine's final months were pure agony. One of the biggest blows came after his invitation to London 1946: Alekhine was excited at the prospect of once again playing topflight chess, but a group of players demanded that his invitation be revoked due to his Nazi affiliations. The witch-hunt succeeded and Alekhine was once again denied access to a proper tournament and vilified by the post war state of mind.

Realizing that Alekhine was ripe to be beaten (by just about anyone!), Soviet-powers-that-be contacted Alekhine and offered him a sizable sum to play a match for the World Championship against Botvinnik. Delighted at this new chance in life, Alekhine was in the midst of preparing for the match when on March 24, 1946 he was found dead in his hotel room in Estoril, Portugal. The autopsy ruled out heart failure, and the cause of death was given as asphyxia due to a piece of meat (three inches long and unchewed) lodged in the larynx. However, many believe he was murdered (cramming an unchewed three inch long piece of meat down a person's throat would indeed do the job!). Alekhine is the only World Chess Champion to die holding the title.

Alexander Alekhine survived imprisonment by the Germans (in Mannheim) in 1914, he survived imprisonment (and a death sentence) in 1918 Russia, he survived two world wars, and he survived the Nazis. Oddly, in the end he was destroyed by his fellow chess players (many of whom had been friends).

Originally buried in the Estoril cemetery, in 1956 his remains were moved (by the French and Russian chess federations) to Montparnasse Cemetery in Paris. Alekhine's wife, Grace, who died in 1956, was buried next to him. Forced apart by the Nazis, they were finally able to be together in the city they loved.

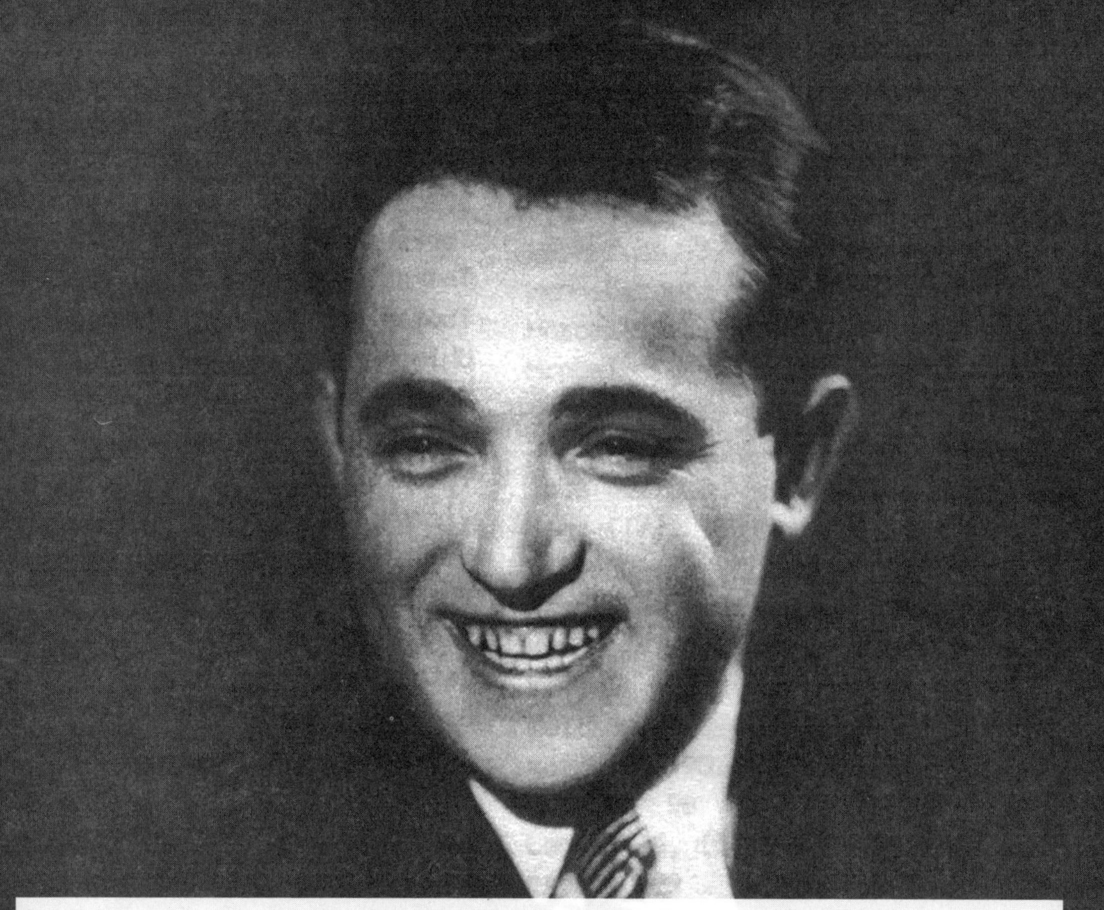

10

SALO FLOHR

The Fickle Winds of Fate

Salo (short for Salomon) Flohr was born 1908 in Horodenka, in the Austro-Hungarian Empire. Alas, 1908 was in close proximity to the start of World War I (1914), and when his parents were butchered during the war, Salo and his brother, suddenly orphans, successfully made their way to Czechoslovakia (1916). The brothers were accepted as war refugees, and the kindness of the Czechoslovakians allowed them to build a new life. Not everyone recovered from a trauma of that magnitude, and that might explain why he had trouble with school and problems finding a "normal" profession.

Fortunately his true calling found him, and when he discovered chess it became yet another example of the love affair between man and chess pieces.

Eventually he moved to Prague, where many cafés were filled with chess players. These cafés turned into his chess school and his job, as he quickly realized that he had an amazing talent for blitz chess. Years passed, he became the monster of the cafés, he made a living from blitz bets, and he learned more and more about the game as time ticked by.

This bohemian lifestyle might have gone on forever if a Czech journalist hadn't asked Flohr to come with him to a big international tournament (Kissingen) as an assistant. He accepted and found himself fascinated by the tournament atmosphere, but he did his job and pretty much stayed to himself. However, when the players would fill a local café to look at their games, he couldn't resist pointing out new ideas or improvements. Coming across an unknown who had such a deep understanding of chess is almost unheard of, and a buzz was created in the chess community.

The great Max Euwe wrote about Flohr's "outing" after the Kissingen event:

> A few weeks later a big tournament was held at Berlin; again Flohr was present as an assistant journalist, but this time he was no longer unknown. In the Café Konig, where the tournament was held, there was another room in which chess players regularly assembled. Every day after lunch, a busy chess life developed which only petered out after strenuous struggles with the waiters, at about 3AM. Mainly skittles were played, for money stakes. Here was something just to Flohr's taste! He came, he saw, he conquered; and within a few days everybody in the place, not excepting three or four of the competing masters, was in his debt. He was well known to all the masters by now, but another year elapsed before the international public got to know of him.

Flohr's first tournaments didn't have the nuclear bang that a Hollywood movie would create, but his initial results were nothing to be ashamed of.

Kautsky Memorial (1927/28): Flohr third, 9 wins, 3 losses, and no draws.

Prague (1928): Third again in a nine-man event.

Prague Championship (1928): This was a pretty strong tournament. Flohr came in fourth with 8 wins, 3 losses, and 4 draws.

Maehrisch-Schoenberg (1928): Flohr second, 5 wins, 1 loss, and 1 draw.

Flohr was quickly getting used to tournament chess, and after taking a couple months off to figure out what he was doing right, and what was wrong, he finally achieved the desired results:

Fifth Kautsky Memorial (1928/29): First with 10 wins, (plus another win by way of forfeit for a total of 11 wins), 1 loss, and 1 draw.

Czechoslovakia (1929) First with 4 wins, no losses, and 2 draws.

Prague (1929): Flohr tied second/fourth, 6 wins, 2 losses, and 3 draws.

Salo Flohr vs. F. Lustig, Kautsky Memorial 1928

1.e4 e5 2.Nf3 Nc6 3.Bb5 a6 4.Ba4 Nf6 5.Qe2 Be7 6.c3 b5 7.Bb3 d6 8.h3 Nh5 9.Bc2 c5 10.d4 Qc7 11.0-0 0-0 12.d5 c4 13.Be3 Bd7 14.Ne1 Nb7 15.Nd2 Rfe8 16.g4 g6 17.f4 exf4 18.Rxf4 Rf8 19.Rf2 Ne8 20.Nef3 Nd8 21.Raf1 f6 22.Bh6 Ng7 23.e5! dxe5 24.Ne4 Nf7! 25.Bxg7 Kxg7 26.Nh4! Nd6

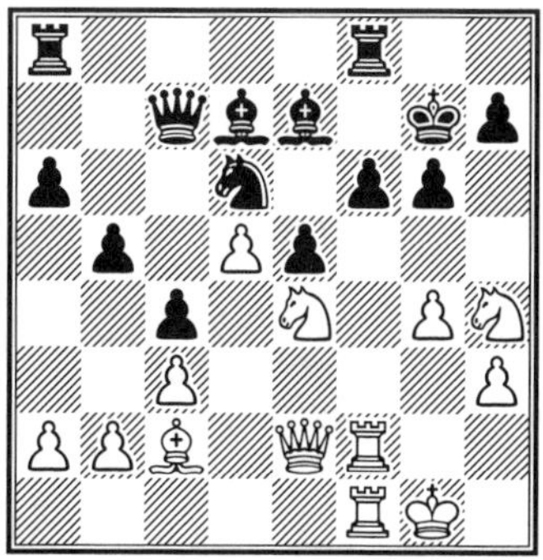

27.Nxf6! Bxf6 28.g5 Ne8 29.Nxg6 hxg6 30.Bxg6 Kxg6 31.Qe4+ Kg7 32.Qh4! Kg8 33.gxf6 Nxf6 34.Qg5+ Kh8 35.Rxf6 Qc5+ 36.Kh2, 1-0.

By this point he was no longer just a player with talent but zero experience, he was a player with talent and *some* experience. And that small amount of experience, and the confidence he gained by winning two events, came together when he was invited to play in the very strong Rogaska Slatina tournament (1929)and finished a clear second behind the great Rubinstein, and ahead of Maróczy, Pirc, Takás, Prezepiórka, Canal, Grünfeld, and others.

Salo Flohr vs. Friedrich Sämisch, Rogaska Slatina 1929

1.d4 Nf6 2.c4 e6 3.a3 d5 4.Nc3 Be7 5.Bg5 0-0 6.e3 b6 7.cxd5 exd5 8.Bd3 Nbd7 9.Nge2 Bb7 10.Ng3 Ne8 11.h4 g6 12.Bh6 Ng7 13.h5 f5 14.hxg6 hxg6

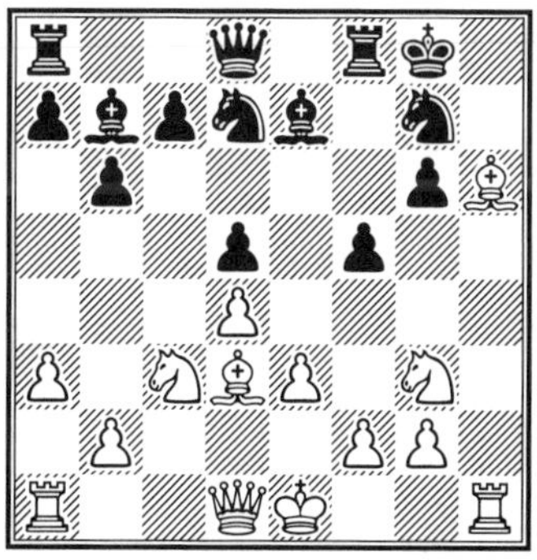

15.Qf3! c6 16.0-0-0 Bd6 17.Nce2 Qf6 18.Rh3 Kf7 19.Nxg7 Qxg7 20.Bxf5!

Both 20.Rdh1 and 20.Nf4 were also strong. Flohr goes for the prettier solution.

20...Nf6

20...gxf5 21.Nxf5 Qf6 22.Rh6.

21.Nf4

21.Rdh1 is also winning.

21...Bxf4 22.Qxf4 Rae8 23.Rdh1

23.Bxg6+ Qxg6 24.Rh6 is another way to victory.

23...Kg8 24.Rh8+ Black resigned here. 24.Rh6 and 24.Bxg6 were also dead winners. However, chess players are only allowed to play one move at a time!

The year 1930 saw a mix of first, second, and third places. In 1928 he had been a nobody, but by the beginning of 1931 (after a bit more than two years in tournaments) he was in the top ten in the world. His results kept improving as he ironed out his openings, fine-tuned his pure positional style, and honed his endgame ability to perfection. And along with this he gained more and more experience.

Hastings (1930/31): First ahead of Rellstab, Koltanowski, Noteboom, and Alexander.

Seventh Kautsky Memorial (1930/31): First ahead of players such as Opočenský and Richter.

Bled (1931): Flohr tied with Kashdan, Stoltz, Vidmar for fourth/seventh behind first place Alekhine (in one of his greatest victories), Bogoljubov second, Nimzowitsch third, and ahead of Tartakower, Kostić, Spielmann, Maróczy, Colle, Asztalos, and Pirc.

This was a very impressive result and showed he belonged among the world's elite. He followed it with:

Brno (1931): First ahead of H. Steiner, Mikenas, Noteboom.

Gothenburg (1931): First ahead of Lundin, Stoltz, Ståhlberg.

Prague (1931): Third behind Stoltz and Pirc.

Prague (1931): Flohr lost an eight game match to Stoltz by 1 point.

Prague (1931): Flohr avenged the loss to Stoltz in another eight game match by a 3-point stomp.

Hastings (1931/32): First ahead of Kashdan, Euwe, Sultan Khan, Vera Menchik, and others.

All great players can attack, combine, play brilliant positional games, and smoke the opponent in the endgame. Though Flohr was known as a positional god, he could also mix it up, as the following game demonstrates!

Salo Flohr vs. Ludwig Rellstab, Hastings 1930/31

1.c4 c5 2.Nc3 Nf6 3.g3 d5 4.cxd5 Nxd5 5.Bg2 Nc7 6.b3 e5 7.Bb2 Be7 8.Rc1 0-0 9.Na4 Nd7 10.Nf3 f6 11.Qc2 Ne6 12.Nh4! Nb6 13.Nf5 Nxa4 14.bxa4 Rb8 15.f4 exf4 16.gxf4

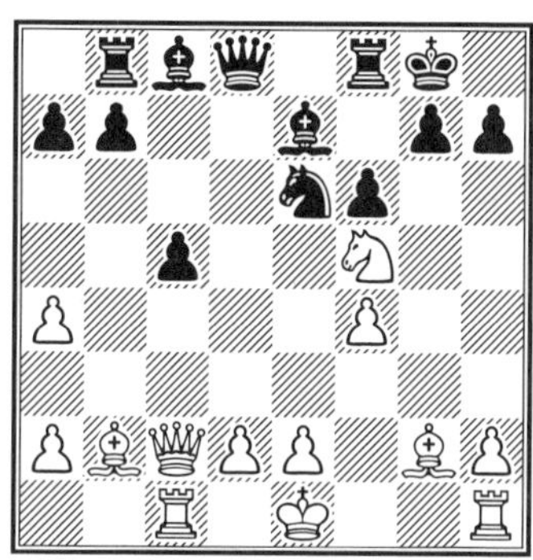

16...Re8

16...Nxf4 17.Qc4+ Ne6 18.Bd5 Qd7 19.Bxe6+ Qxe6 20.Nxe7+! (20. Qxe6+ Bxe6 21.Nxe7+ Kf7 22.Rxc5 Kxe7) 20...Kf7 21.Qxc5! (Most accurate, though 21.Nxc8 also wins.) 21...Qxe7 (21...b6 22.Qh5+ Kxe7 23.Ba3+) 22.Qxe7+ Kxe7 23.Ba3+ Ke8 24.Bd6! (Accuracy counts! White milks every drop from the position.)

24...Ra8 25.Bxf8 Kxf8 26.Rc7 and Black should resign.

17.Rg1 Bf8 18.Bc6! Nd4 19.Nh6+ Kh8 20.Nf7+ Kg8 21.Nh6+ Kh8 22.Nf7+ Kg8 23.Qc4 Rxe2+ 24.Qxe2! Nxe2 25.Nxd8 Nxg1 26.Bd5+ Kh8 27.Nf7+ Kg8 28.Kf2 Nh3+ 29.Kg3 b5 30.axb5 Bb7 31.Bc4 a6 32.a4 axb5 33.axb5 Nxf4 34.Kxf4 h5 35.Rg1 Kh7 36.Bxf6!, 1-0.

The next game shows the perfect blend between tactics and positional mastery. Each one supports the other.

Salo Flohr vs. Frederick Yates, Hamburg Olympiad 1930

1.d4 Nf6 2.c4 e6 3.Nc3 d5 4.Bg5 Be7 5.e3 Nbd7 6.cxd5 exd5 7.Bd3 0-0 8.Qc2 c6 9.Nf3 Re8 10.0-0 Nf8 11.a3 Ne4 12.Bxe7 Qxe7 13.Bxe4 dxe4 14.Nd2 Bf5 15.f3 Qg5 16.f4 Qe7 17.Ne2 Nd7 18.Ng3 Qf6 19.Nc4 Nb6 20.Ne5 Nd5 21.Rae1 Qe6 22.h3 Rad8

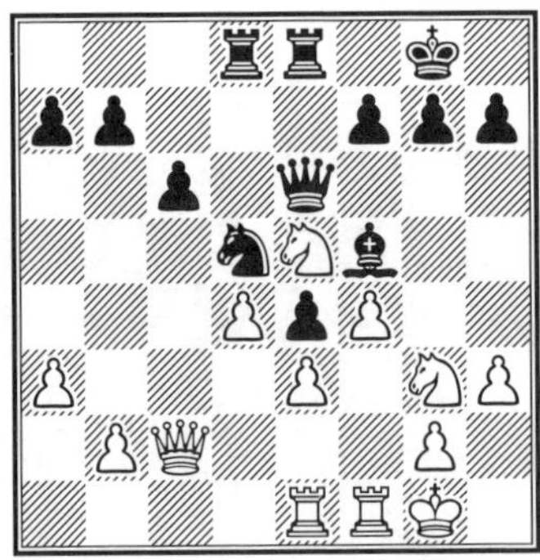

23.Nh1!

Starting a deep plan to tie Black's piece down to the defense of e4.

23...f6 24.Nc4 Bg6 25.g4 Bf7 26.f5 Qe7 27.Nd2

Two pieces are attacking e4.

27...Nb6 28.Ng3

Now three pieces are attacking e4.

28...Bd5 29.Rf4

Now it's four pieces!

29...Qc7 30.Kf2!

White sees that Black's pieces are passively posted when they have to babysit the e4-pawn. But if White takes that pawn too early, it would give Black some unearned activity.

30...Re7 31.h4 Rde8 32.g5

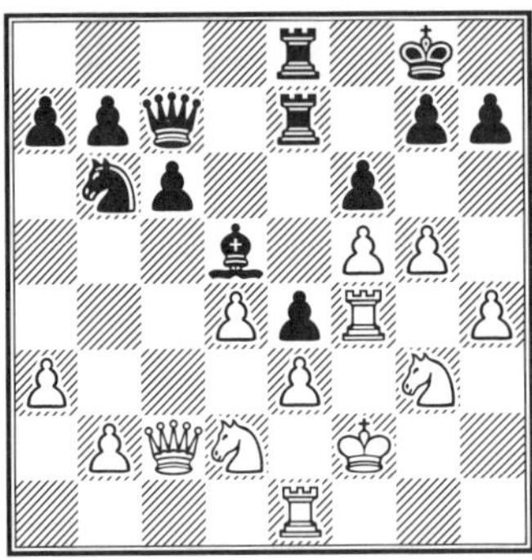

No more Mr. Nice Guy!

Black's e-pawn is a traitor that is killing the activity of his pieces. In the meantime, White builds a strong kingside attack.

32...Nd7 33.Rg1 Qc8 34.Ngxe4

From positional chess to the pain game! White finally chops the e4-pawn, and Black is game. But he only does so since the Knight on e4 is a tower of strength and directly aids the kingside attack.

34...fxg5 35.hxg5 Qb8 36.Rg3 Rf8 37.Nc3 Nb6 38.f6 Ref7 39.Qf5 Qe8 40.Rh4 Rxf6 41.gxf6, 1-0.

Salo Flohr vs. Josef Dobias, Kautsky Memorial 1930

1.d4 Nf6 2.c4 e6 3.Nc3 d5 4.Bg5 Nbd7 5.cxd5 exd5 6.e3 Be7 7.Bd3 c6 8.Qc2 Nh5 9.Bxe7 Qxe7 10.Nge2 g6 11.0-0-0 f5 12.h3 Ndf6 13.Rde1 Bd7 14.Nf4 Ng7 15.g4 Qd6 16.f3 b6 17.Kb1 0-0 18.Reg1 Nfe8 19.h4! Nc7 20.h5 g5

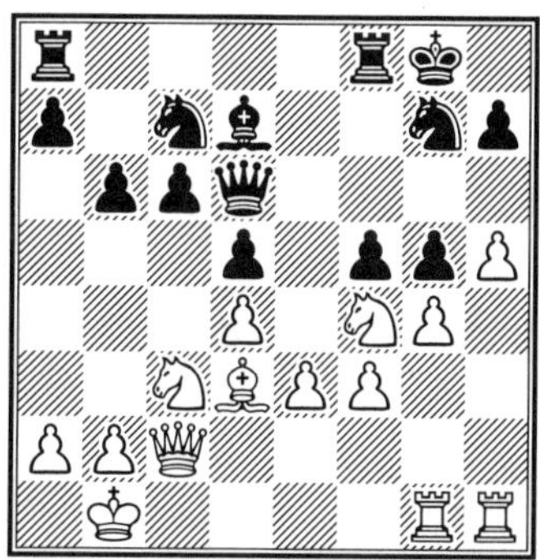

21.h6! gxf4 22.gxf5! Rf6 23.Rxg7+ Kh8 24.Qg2

Threatening Rxh7+ followed by Qg7 mate.

24...Rxh6 25.f6 Rxh1+ 26.Qxh1, 1-0 since mate is unavoidable.

Salo Flohr vs. Paul Johner, Bern 1932

1.c4 c5 2.Nc3 Nc6 3.Nf3 g6 4.d4 cxd4 5.Nxd4 Bg7 6.Nc2 d6 7.Qd2 Nf6 8.e4 a6 9.Be2 Rb8 10.0-0 0-0 11.Re1 Bd7 12.Rb1 Qc8 13.b3 b5 14.cxb5 axb5 15.Bxb5 Nxe4 16.Rxe4 Bxc3 17.Qxc3 Rxb5 18.Rc4

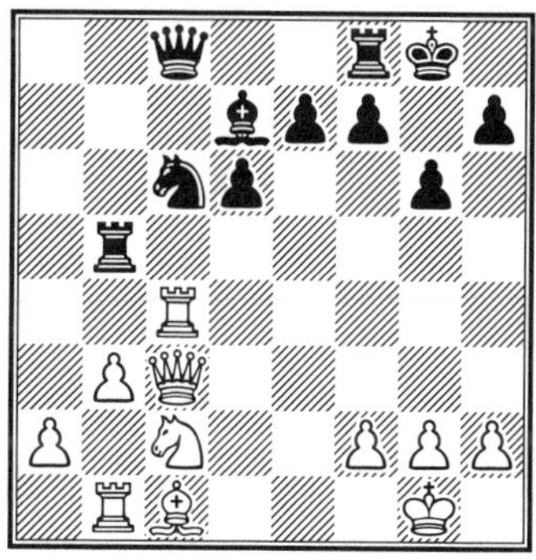

18...Rd8⁈

The tactics are too much for Black and he cracks. Instead, 18...d5! keeps the game alive: 19.Bh6 f6 20.Nd4 dxc4 21.Nxb5! (21.Qxc4+ Kh8 22.Nxb5 looks good but after 22...Ne5 it's not clear if White has anything at all.)

21...Rd8 22.Nd6! Qa6 23.Re1 and White is a bit better in a complicated position.

19.Bh6 f6 20.Nd4 Rb6 21.Rc1 Nxd4 22.Rxc8 Ne2+ 23.Kf1 Rxc8

23...Nxc3 24.Rxd8+.

24.Qxc8+ Bxc8 25.Rxc8+ Kf7 26.Be3, 1-0.

Max Euwe vs. Salo Flohr, Amsterdam match (6) 1932

1.d4 d5 2.c4 c6 3.Nf3 Nf6 4.Nc3 g6 5.Bf4 dxc4 6.a4 Nd5 7.Bd2 Nb4 8.Rc1 Bg7 9.Nb1 a5 10.Na3 c5 11.Nxc4 cxd4 12.Nb6 Qxb6 13.Rxc8+ Kd7 14.Rc4 Rd8 15.e3 Ke8 16.Nxd4 N8c6 17.Nxc6 bxc6 18.Qb1 Bxb2! 19.Rxb4

19.Qxb2 Nd3+.

19...axb4 20.Qxb2 Rxa4 21.Bc4 b3! 22.Bxb3 Rb8 23.0-0 Qxb3 24.Qh8+ Kd7 25.Qxh7

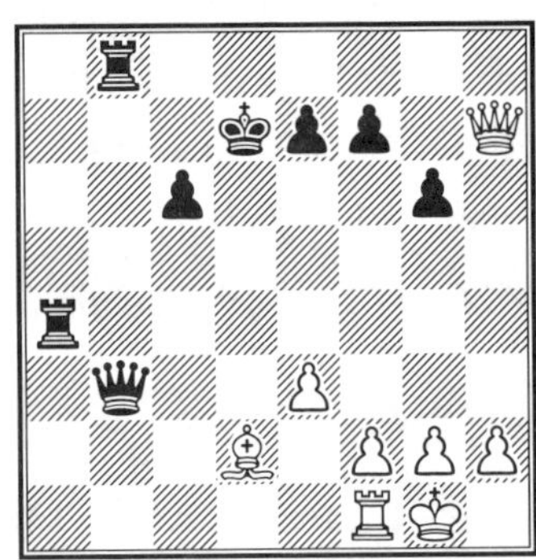

25...Ra1!

25...Qc2 and 25...Qd3 were also very strong.

26.Be1 Qc4 27.Qh3+ f5 28 g3 Rbb1 and the game is over (White actually played 29.f3 and resigned after 29...Qe2).

And on and on it went, mixing mostly good results with a few sub-par moments. Highlights:

Bad Sliac (1932): Tied for first/second with Vidmar ahead of Pirc, Canal, Maróczy, Spielmann, Bogoljubov.

Bern (1932): Tied for second/third with Euwe, behind first place Alekhine and ahead of Sultan Khan, Bernstein, Bogoljubov and others.

London (1932): Second behind first place Alekhine, and ahead of Kashdan, Sultan Khan, Maróczy, Tartakower.

Amsterdam (1932): Tied a four game match with Euwe.

Match (1932): Tied another four game match with Euwe.

Match (1932): Beat Sultan Khan in a six game match by a point.

Hastings (1932/33): First ahead of L. Steiner, Pirc, Sultan Khan.

Scheveningen (1933): First ahead of Maróczy, Bogoljubov, and others.

In 1933 Flohr won several matches against solid opposition, but the real test was a twelve game match against Botvinnik! The score was tied 6-6.

The following game is a very instructive position from the Flohr vs. Botvinnik match. It's always been a personal favorite of mine:

The position seems to be good for White since black's Knight is dead and Black's c-pawn is under pressure while his queenside pawn majority seems frozen. If Black ever plays ...c6-c5 then, after White replies with b5, the d5-square will be a magnificent home for the bishop. What can Black do?

Mikhail Botvinnik vs. Salo Flohr, Moscow match (5) 1933

1.c4 e5 2.Nc3 Nf6 3.Nf3 Nc6 4.d4 e4 5.Nd2 Nxd4 6.Ndxe4 Ne6 7.g3 Nxe4 8.Nxe4 Bb4+ 9.Bd2 Bxd2+ 10.Qxd2 0-0 11.Bg2 d6 12.0-0 Bd7 13.Nc3 Bc6 14.Nd5 a5 15.e4 Nc5 16.Rfe1 Re8 17.Rad1 a4 18.Re3 Bd7 19.Nc3 Be6 20.Qd4 f6 21.Bf1 Qe7 22.Nd5 Qf7 23.Rde1 c6 24.Nf4 Qc7 25.Nd3 b6 26.Nb4 Bf7 27.Qc3 Rad8 28.Nc2 Re7 29.Nd4 Bg6 30.f3 Rde8 31.b4 axb3 32.axb3 Ne6 33.Nf5 Bxf5 34.exf5 Ng5 35.Bg2 Rxe3 36.Rxe3 Rxe3 37.Qxe3 Kf8 38.f4 Nf7 39.b4

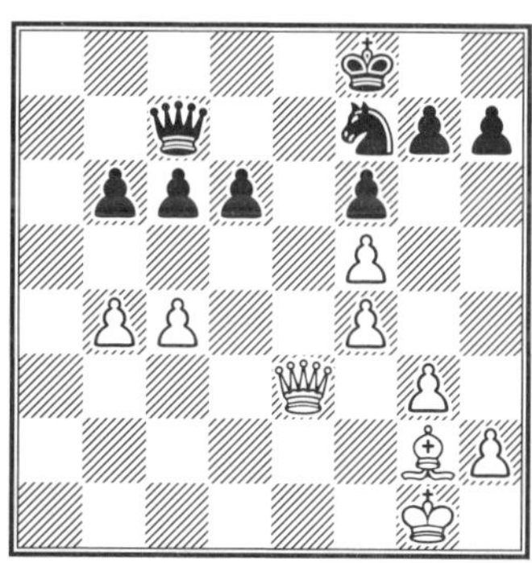

39...d5!! 40.cxd5 c5! 41.bxc5 bxc5 42.Qa3 Nd6

What has Black gained by his pawn sacrifice? Quite a few things! Black's "frozen" queenside majority is now a powerful (and mobile!) passed pawn. Black's "dead" Knight is now ideally placed on d6 and is suddenly superior to white's Bishop. White's once-powerful Bishop is blocked and bad. And White's passed d-pawn isn't going anywhere. The game was drawn after

43.Bf1 Kf7 44.Bd3 c4 45.Bc2 c3 46.Qb4 Nc4 47.Qxc3 Qc5+ 48.Kh1 Qxd5+, ½-½.

Flohr was at the top of his game at this point, and he was clearly in the top five in the world. Then something huge occurred: At Hastings (1933/34) Flohr finished clear first at ahead of Alekhine (!!). This marked the first time Alekhine had failed to come in first since he won the World Championship title in 1927.

Flohr followed this with:

Zurich (1934): Tied with Euwe for second/third behind Alekhine, ahead of Bogoljubov, Emanuel Lasker, Bernstein, Nimzowitsch, and others.

Hastings (1934/35): Tied for first/third with Sir George Thomas and Euwe, ahead of Capablanca and Botvinnik!

Moscow (1935): Tied for first/second with Botvinnik, ahead of Emanuel Lasker, Capablanca (again!), Spielmann, and many other legends.

Margate (1936): First ahead of Capablanca, Ståhlberg, etc.

Podebrady (1936): First ahead of Alekhine, Foltys, Pirc, Ståhlberg, and many more.

And now Flohr came to a sharp STOP!

Why didn't this man get to play a match for the World Championship? What happened to deprive him of his place in history as an all-time great? He was loved in Czechoslovakia, he was dominating the world chess scene, he was young, talented, and he was clearly very, very strong.

When one considers that Flohr had drawn matches with two of Alekhine's main rivals (Euwe and Botvinnik), and come ahead of both Alekhine and Capablanca in tournaments, the mystery appears to be even stranger.

The answer certainly couldn't be found in his personal life at that time—things were going very well for Flohr. He had just gotten married, and he was a "rock star" in Czechoslovakia! His name was on everyone's lips and, like businesses today, if a name is big, a wise company *must* use it to advertise their product(s)! And so Flohr paraphernalia appeared: Salo Flohr perfumes and scents, Salo Flohr cigarettes (he didn't smoke!), Salo Flohr collars, and even Salo Flohr slippers were hot products.

So, what could possibly cause Flohr, the golden boy, to fail? The answer comes in two parts:

Remember I said that after Flohr's parents were murdered in World War I, "not everyone would recover from a trauma of that magnitude." Now this man, a refugee during the first world war, witnessed Nazi Germany rumbling about taking territory from the nation (Czechoslovakia) that years before had taken him in, and this picked up steam in 1935 and 1936. Flohr, a Jew, was more than likely "freaking out" as the new war was brewing (Fascist Italy invaded and conquered Ethiopia in 1935 and Germany and Italy signed a treaty of cooperation in 1936).

It was no surprise, when in 1937 FIDE nominated Flohr as the official candidate to play Alekhine in a match for the World Championship. Unfortunately, Flohr wasn't the only person who saw war clouds on the horizon. It turned out that investors were impossible to find, and so all thoughts of the match were tossed away.

From this point on, Flohr's results became less and less consistent:

Nottingham (1936): Tied seventh/eighth with Lasker, behind Botvinnik, Capablanca, Euwe, Fine, Reshevsky, and Alekhine.

Oslo (1936): Second behind Fine, ahead of inferior players.

Kemeri-Riga (1937): Tied first/second with Petrovs and Reshevsky, ahead of Alekhine, Keres, E. Steiner, Tartakower, Fine. (Flohr drew the first ten players behind him, and beat the weakest seven players).

Parnu (1937): Tied for second/third/fourth with Ståhlberg and Keres behind first place Schmidt, and ahead of Tartakower, Opočenský.

Semmering-Baden (1937): Fifth place behind Keres, Fine, Capablanca, and Reshevsky.

Hastings (1937/38): Tied with Fine for fourth/fifth behind Reshevsky, Alexander, and Keres.

Efim Bogoljubov vs. Salo Flohr, Nottingham 1936

1.e4 e6 2.d4 d5 3.Nc3 Bb4 4.e5 c5 5.a3 Bxc3+ 6.bxc3 Ne7 7.Qg4 Nf5 8.Bd3 h5 9.Qf4 cxd4 10.cxd4 Qh4 11.Nf3 Qxf4 12.Bxf4 Nc6 13.c3 Bd7 14.h3 Rc8 15.Ke2 Na5 16.g4 Ne7 17.Bd2 Nc4 18.Rhg1 Nb2 19.Rgb1 Nxd3 20.Rxb7 Bc6

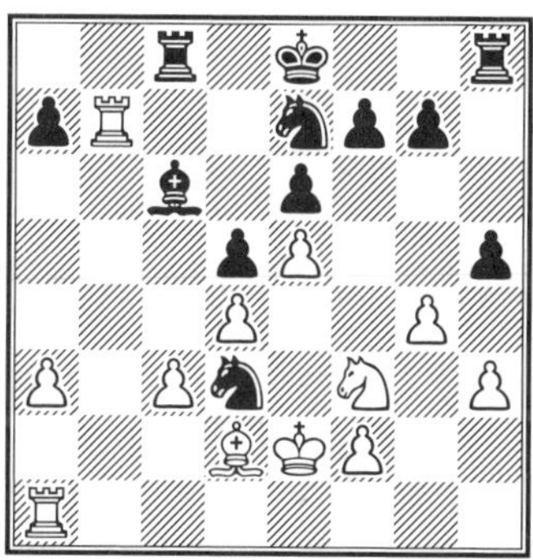

21.Rbb1 hxg4 22.hxg4 Rh3 23.Ng5 Rh2 24.Kxd3 Rxf2 25.Ke3 Rh2 26.Rh1 Rxh1 27.Rxh1 Ng6 28.Rb1 Ke7 29.Rf1 f6 30.exf6+ gxf6 31.Nh7 Rh8 32.Rxf6 Be8 33.Rxg6 Bxg6 34.Ng5 Rh4 35.Nf3 Rxg4 36.Ne5 Rg2

37.c4 dxc4 38.Nxc4 Be8 39.Bb4+ Kf6 40.Nd6 Bc6 41.Kd3 Bd5 42.Ke3 Kg5 43.Nb5 Kg4! 44.Nc7?? Bc4

Forces mate!

45.d5 e5!, 0-1 since White can't stop 46...Re2 mate.

Could Flohr have beaten Alekhine who was no longer near his peak? Probably not, due to something most people aren't aware of.

In *Meet the Masters* Euwe wrote:[1]

> ...we must also recall that he [Flohr] has never scored great successes against his fellow grandmasters. His specialty is beating masters who are not quite in the very top rank, and in this he is supreme. Even when scoring his greatest successes his record has been, almost monotonously, a series of wins against lower players but draws against fellow grandmasters.

Is that true? Let's take a look:

Podebrady (1936): First ahead of Alekhine, Foltys, Pirc, Ståhlberg, and many more. Flohr drew Alekhine and Foltys, beat Pirc, lost to Eliskases, and beat the vast majority of the tail-enders.

Kemeri-Riga (1937): Tied first/second with Petrovs and Reshevsky, ahead of Alekhine, Keres, Steiner, Tartakower, and Fine. Flohr drew the first ten players behind him, and beat the weakest seven players.

Then came the famous AVRO Tournament, one of the strongest events of all time. In this tournament there were no weak players, and when you add in the fact that Europe was on the verge of war (meaning Flohr was in full tilt!), his beyond bad result was understandable:

AVRO (1938): One of the strongest tournaments of all time. Flohr took last place (!!!) behind Keres, Fine, Botvinnik, Euwe, Reshevsky, Alekhine, and Capablanca.

Euwe's view seems vindicated—Flohr did win quite a few games against the world's best, just not as many as one would expect from a world championship candidate.

Fearing that he was going to die at the hands of the Nazis, he and his family eventually made their way to the safety of Moscow (with help from Botvinnik!). Now he was a refugee again, and his style became more cautious than ever. And, unfortunately, he gave up all aspirations for the World Championship. However, his play improved and he had some good results:

1 Max Euwe, *Meet the Masters: The Modern Chess Champions and Their Most Characteristic Games*. New York: David McKay Company, 1940.

Margate (1939): Tied with Capablana for second/third, behind first place Keres, and ahead of Najdorf, Golombek.

Moscow-Leningrad (1939): First ahead of Reshevsky, Levenfish, Lilienthal, Keres, Smyslov, Tolush, Bondarevsky, and a host of young Russian masters.

Baku (1943): First ahead of Makogonov, Bronstein, Abramian, and Ebralidze.

Kiev (1944): Tied for first/second with Sokolsky, ahead of Boleslavsky, Tolush, Bronstein, Makogonov.

Not bad at all, but returning to Euwe's idea that Flohr drew the good players and beat the bad ones, we can see more support of it here:

Baku (1943): First ahead of Makogonov, Bronstein, Abramian, and Ebralidze Two games vs. everyone. Flohr lost and drew against Makogonov, drew both games against Bronstein, beat Abramian both games, and won and drew vs. Ebralidze.

Kiev (1944): Tied for first with Sokolsky, ahead of Boleslavsky, Tolush, Bronstein, Makogonov. He drew all these guys, and beat all the other guys at the bottom.

Flohr's "beat the weak players and draw the strong ones" mentality wouldn't bode well in a match against a dynamo like Alekhine. To make a prime Flohr's chances against Alekhine even dimmer is the fact that he was never able to win a game off of Alekhine (5 wins for Alekhine, none for Flohr, and 7 draws). True, Alekhine had never won a game off of Capablanca until the match where he took the title from the Cuban genius. But I don't see Flohr doing the same thing to Alekhine—different personalities, different styles. Nevertheless, Flohr deserved a chance to try, and it was taken from him by the fickle winds of fate.

Unlike the unfortunate Zukertort and Spielmann, whose lives ended badly, Flohr continued to play the into the late 1960s (less and less frequently as the years went by) as chess journalism took precedence over chess combat. He died peacefully in Moscow in 1983.

I'll end this portrait with Flohr vs. Petrosian, Moscow 1949:

Salo Flohr vs. Tigran Petrosian, Moscow 1949

1.d4 Nf6 2.c4 d6 3.Nc3 e5 4.Nf3 Nbd7 5.Bg5 Be7 6.e3 0-0 7.Qc2 exd4 8.Nxd4 Ne5 9.Be2 Ng6 10.h4 c6 11.Nf5

This gives more space.

11...Bxf5 12.Qxf5 Qc7 13.0-0-0 Rfe8 14.h5 Nf8 15.Rh3!

15.Rh3! allows White to enjoy his space which allows room to create attacks.

15...d5 16.Rg3 g6 17.hxg6 fxg6 18.Bf4 Qc8 19.Qc2 Bb4 20.Bh6 Qe6 21.Qb3 Bxc3 22.Qxc3 Re7 23.Qd4 b5 24.Rf3 N8d7 25.Bg5 Rf7 26.cxd5 Nxd5 27.Rxf7 Qxf7 28.Bf3 N5b6

29.Bh6

After 29.Bh6 make sure that whites pieces are better than Black.

29...Re8 30.Kb1 Ne5 31.Be2 g5 32.Ka1 Qg6 33.Rh1 Qf6 34.Rh5 Qxf2 35.Rxg5+ Kf7

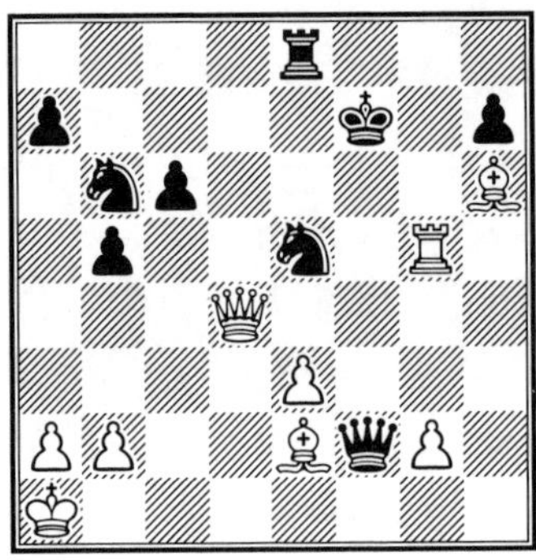

36.Rg7+ Ke6 37.Bg4+ Nxg4 38.Qxg4+ Kd5 39.Qd4+ Ke6 40.Qe4+ Kf6 41.Qd4+ Ke6 42.Qe4+ Kf6 43.Qxc6, 1-0.

11

EFIM GELLER

Killer on the Chessboard

Several years ago I was at a coffee shop in Pasadena California and started a conversation with a few young (mid-twenties) Taiwanese. After we chatted about Taiwan our talk took a turn into various kinds of pop music. I made it clear that most pop instantly sparks my gag reflex. Then I started raving about the wonders of ZZ Top, The Rolling Stones, The Doors, Pink Floyd, and Led Zeppelin. They all were looking at me with glassy eyes and one finally said, "Never heard of any of them."

Pal Benko and Efim Geller analyzing a game, early 1960s.

Lately I've experienced the same thing when I talk to young (ten to twenty years old) chess players: Have you read Eugene Znosko-Borovsky's books?—"What is a Borovsky?" Have you studied the games of Leonid Stein?—"Who?" How about Isaac Boleslavsky?—"A bowl of what?"

In my mind, if you don't know all the greats from the past, then you're missing the heart and soul of what chess is about. So many wonderful games. So many stories; some funny, some crazy, some very, very sad.

I want to discuss one forgotten player that did a lot for chess. This "oldie but goody" is Efim Geller (1925-1998). This "meat and potato" Soviet powerhouse, with a cigarette almost always hanging from his lips, was feared by everyone. You might say, "What does that mean? Surely the top players like Botvinnik, Smyslov, and others would have kicked him to the curb."

Well, not so fast! The fact is that he held his own against Mikhail Tal (6 wins, 6 losses, 23 draws) and Paul Keres (7 wins for Geller, 8 losses, 21 draws), and had plus scores against Mikhail Botvinnik (4 wins for Geller, 1 loss, 7 draws), David Bronstein (5 wins for Geller, 5 losses, 15 draws), Robert Fischer (5 wins for Geller, 3 losses, 2 draws), Lajos Portisch (4 wins for Geller, 2 losses, 12 draws), Vasily Smyslov (11 wins for Geller, 8 losses, 37 draws), and Tigran Petrosian (5 wins for Geller, 3 losses, 12 draws).

One might ask why such an obviously super strong master of attack was never World Champion. Bad luck perhaps, since in two Candidates cycles he had to face Boris Spassky, who was in his prime. He lost a match to Spassky in the 1965 Candidates by 5½-2½, and again in the 1968 cycle by the same score. Fate can be a very annoying protagonist.

Geller's Style

Geller was one of the first players to recognize the dynamic potential of the King's Indian Defense [KID]. Kotov, a well known attacking player, gets blown off the board.

Alexander Kotov vs. Efim Geller, Moscow 1949

1.d4 Nf6 2.c4 g6 3.Nc3 Bg7 4.g3 0-0 5.Bg2 d6 6.Nf3 Nbd7 7.0-0 e5 8.e4 exd4 9.Nxd4 Nc5 10.f3 Nfd7 11.Be3 c6 12.Qd2 a5 13.Rad1 Ne5 14.b3

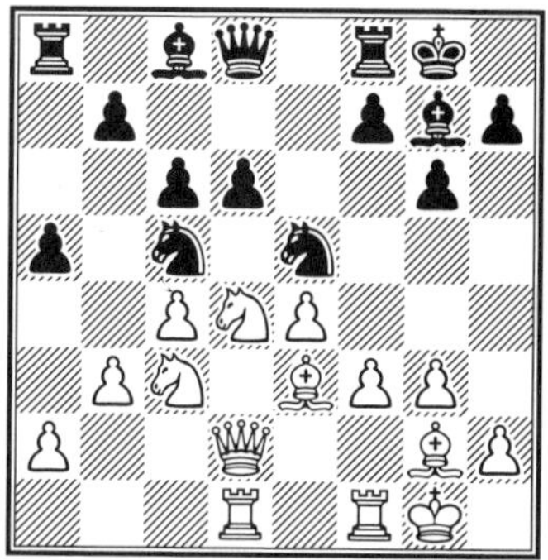

14...a4 15.Nde2

15.f4 Ned3 16.Nxa4! Bg4 (I would prefer 16...Nxa4 17.bxa4 Nc5 18.Nxc6! bxc6 19.Bxc5 Bg4 20.Bxd6 Bxd1 21.Qxd1 Qb6+ 22.Kh1 Rfc8 and White is much better, but Black has chances to fight back.) 17.Nxc5 Nxc5 18.Rde1 Re8 19.Bf2 and White is up a pawn.

15...axb3 16.Bxc5 Nxc4 17.Qc1 bxa2 18.Nxa2 Qa5 19.Qxc4 Be6 20.Qc1 dxc5 21.Nac3 b5

The more complications, the more fun. The philosophy is simple: create extreme complications, then hit him and hit him and hit him and eventually the opponent will crack.

22.Nb1

22.e5! Bxe5 23.f4 Bg7 24.Bxc6 Rab8 with chances for both sides.

22...b4

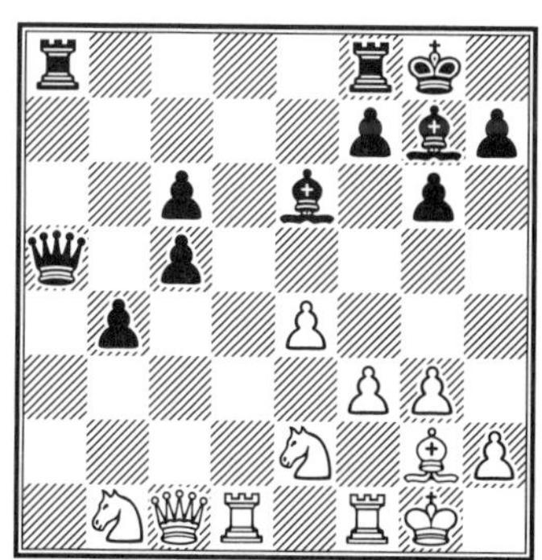

23.Nf4?

23.f4 had to be played, though Black is already better.

23...Bb3 24.Rd6 c4

24...Rfd8 is also possible.

25.Rxc6 c3 26.Nd5 Bxd5 27.exd5 Qxd5 28.f4 Qd4+ 29.Kh1 Ra2 30.Bf3 Rb2 31.f5 Be5 32.Qe1 Rd8 33.Be4 Kg7 34.f6+ Kg8 35.Ra6 h5 36.Ra5 h4 37.Bxg6 Rxh2+ 38.Kxh2 Bxg3+ 39.Qxg3 hxg3+ 40.Kh3 fxg6, 0-1.

The same two players went at it again in 1951 with Geller winning another KID. A third KID between these players occurred in 1952, which ended in a draw, and then later in 1952 a forth KID once again led to an execution with White giving up in twenty-three moves.

Alexander Kotov vs. Efim Geller, Voronovo 1952

1.d4 Nf6 2.c4 g6 3.g3 Bg7 4.Bg2 0-0 5.Nf3 d6 6.0-0 Nbd7 7.Nc3 e5 8.d5 a5 9.Ne1 Nc5 10.Nd3 Nxd3 11.exd3 Nd7 12.Be3 f5 13.Qd2 f4

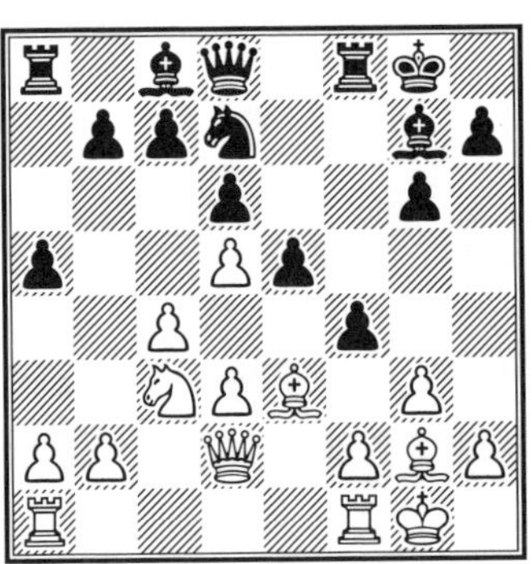

14.gxf4 Qh4 15.f3 exf4 16.Bf2 Qh5 17.Qe2 Nf6 18.Nb5 Rf7 19.Nd4 Bf5 20.Rfe1 Nd7 21.Ne6 Ne5 22.Nxg7 Rxg7 23.Rad1 g5, 0-1.

Fearing Geller's Fist

This wonderful game started out with a popular (at that time) anti-Grünfeld attacking line. By move twenty Geller had already built up a winning position, and then the fireworks hit the board!

Efim Geller vs. Vassily Smyslov, Moscow 1965

1.d4 Nf6 2.c4 g6 3.Nc3 d5 4.cxd5 Nxd5 5.e4 Nxc3 6.bxc3 Bg7 7.Bc4 c5 8.Ne2 0-0 9.0-0 Nc6 10.Be3 Qc7 11.Rc1 Rd8 12.f4 e6 13.Kh1 b6 14.f5 Na5 15.Bd3 exf5 16.exf5 Bb7 17.Qd2 Re8 18.Ng3 Qc6 19.Rf2 Rad8 20.Bh6

It looks like Black has central pressure, a smooth development, and domination along the h1-a8 diagonal. But looks don't mean anything in chess. The truth is that Black, though he's still twitching, is nothing more than a dead man walking.

20…Bh8 21.Qf4

White has the f5-pawn, both bishops, the Knight, the f2-rook, and the Queen all taking aim at black's King.

21…Rd7 22.Ne4! c4

22…Rxe4 23.Bxe4 Qxe4 24.Qb8+ leads to a quick mate.

23.Bc2 Rde7 24.Rcf1

Now ALL of white's pieces (except the white King) are working together to kill black's King.

24…Rxe4

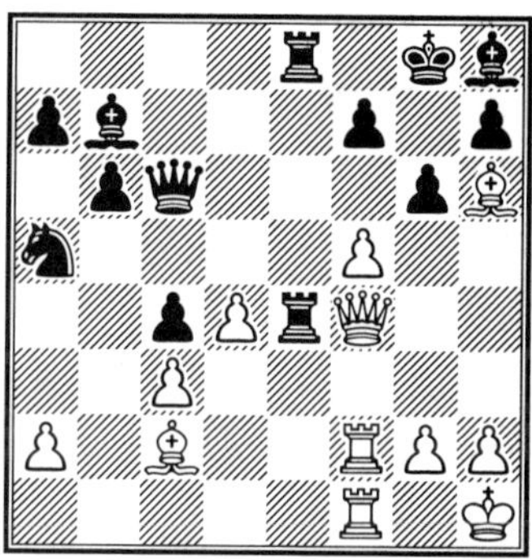

25.fxg6!

White offers his queen.

25…f6

25…Rxf4 26.gxh57 mate!

26.Qg5!

He offers his Queen again!

26…Qd7

26…fxg5 27.Rf8+ Rxf8 28.Rxf8 mate.

27.Kg1

One of many winning moves.

27…Bg7

27…Rg4 28.gxh7+ Kf7 29.Rxf6+ does the trick.

28.Rxf6 Rg4 29.gxh7+ Kh8 30.Bxg7+ Qxg7 31.Qxg4!, 1-0. Yet another Queen sacrifice!

Okay, lets to look at the following games.

Efim Geller vs. Vladimir Antoshin, Moscow 1970

1.e4 e5 2.Nf3 Nc6 3.Bb5 a6 4.Ba4 Nf6 5.0-0 Be7 6.Re1 b5 7.Bb3 d6 8.c3 0-0 9.h3 Na5 10.Bc2 c5 11.d4 cxd4 12.cxd4 Bb7 13.Nbd2 Nc6 14.d5 Nb4 15.Bb1 a5 16.Nf1 Qc7 17.Ng3 g6 18.a3 Na6 19.Bd3 b4 20.Be3 Nc5 21.Rc1 Nfd7 22.Bb5 Qb8 23.Nd2 Rd8 24.Qe2 Kg7 25.Rc2 Ba6 26.Bxa6 Nxa6 27.Rc6!

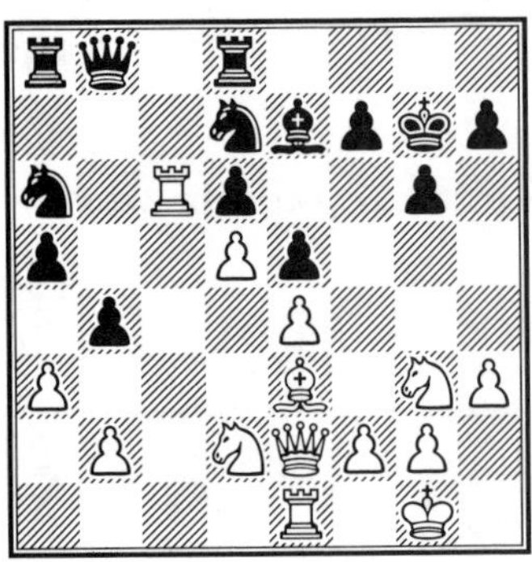

This move (a kind of plug) is very strong. Yes, it might end up trapped on c6, but while Black tries to do that, he will not be able to trade the Rooks via ...Rc8. In other words, Black has no queenside counterplay, which allows White to calmly build up on the kingside. Also notice the pressure on d6, which will be clearly shown when white's d2-Knight eventually lands on c4.

27...Ndc5

Has white's Knight gone too far into enemy territory?

28.Qg4 Kh8 29.Bh6 Rg8 30.Nc4 Qd8 31.Re3

Reinforcements. Though 31.Re3 is a good move, 31.f4 f6 32.Rf1 was better.

31...f6 32.f4 Nb8 33.Rxc5!

33.Rb6 is equal.

33...dxc5 34.fxe5 f5 35.exf5 gxf5 36.Qxf5

Other good moves are 36.Qf3 and 36.Qd1 and 36.Qf4 and 36.Qh5.

36...Qxd5 37.Nd6 Rg6 38.Rd3

38.Qc8+ was another winner: 38...Rg8 39.Qb7 Qxb7 40.Nf7 mate.

38...Qe6 39.Qf3 Ra7 40.Nf7+ Kg8 41.Nd8 whereupon Black resigned.

Bruno Parma vs. Efim Geller, Havana 1965

1.e4 e5 2.Nf3 Nc6 3.Bb5 a6 4.Ba4 Nf6 5.0-0 Be7 6.Re1 b5 7.Bb3 0-0 8.c3 d6 9.h3 h6 10.d4 Re8 11.Nbd2 Bf8 12.Nf1 Bd7 13.Ng3 Na5 14.Bc2 Nc4 15.a4 c5 16.axb5 axb5 17.Rxa8 Qxa8 18.dxc5 dxc5 19.Nh5 Nxh5 20.Qxd7 Nd6 21.Qg4 Nf6 22.Qh4 Re6 23.Nd2 c4 24.Nf1

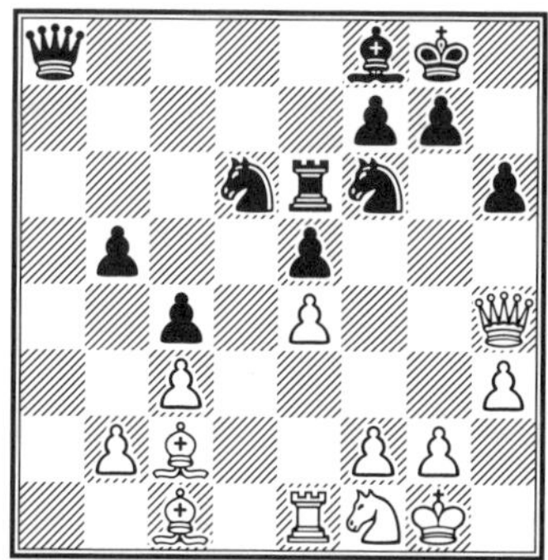

Who stands better? Or is it equal? Finally, what is White trying to do, and what is Black trying to do?

24...b4!

Threatening ..b3 pushing the light-squared Bbshop to b1.

25.cxb4

Black now takes aim at the hole on d4.

25...Nb5

Positional dynamics!

26.Bd2 Qa2 27.Qg3 Qxb2 28.Ba4 Nd4

28...Bxb4!

29.Qc3 Qa2 30.Qa1 Qxa1 31.Rxa1 Ra6 32.b5 Nxb5 33.Ng3 c3 34.Bc1 c2 35.Bb2 Nd4 36.Bxc2 Rxa1+ 37.Bxa1 Nxc2 38.Bxe5 Nd7, 0-1.

Efim Geller vs. Lajos Portisch, Moscow 1967

1.e4 e5 2.Nf3 Nc6 3.Bb5 a6 4.Ba4 Nf6 5.0-0 Be7 6.Re1 b5 7.Bb3 d6 8.c3 0-0 9.h3 h6 10.d4 Re8 11.Nbd2 Bf8 12.Nf1 Bb7 13.Ng3 Qd7

How would you play his position?

14.dxe5! dxe5

14...Nxe5 15.Nxe5 dxe5 (15..Rxe5 16.f3) 16.Qf3 with good kingside chances.

15.Nh5! Qe7

Or 15...Qxd1 16.Nxf6+, and white has a small advantage.

16.Nh4!

The threat is not only 17.Nf5, but also 17.Ng6.

16...Nxh5 17.Qxh5 Na5

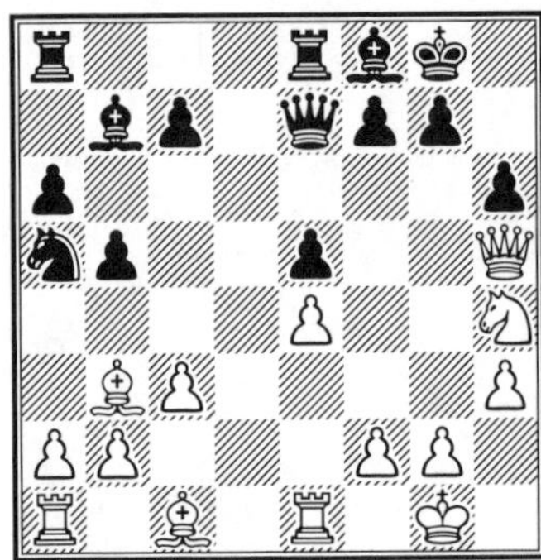

Hoping to chase away White's light-squared bishop from the a2-g8 diagonal.

18.Bg5! Qd7

18...hxg5 19.Ng6 mates.

19.Rad1 Bd6 20.Bxh6! gxh6

20...Nxb3 21.Bxg7 Kxg7 22.Nf5+

21.Qg6+ Kf8

21...Kh8 22.Qxh6+ Kg8 23.Ng6 and White will mate by Qh8 mate.

22.Qf6

Threatening 23.Ng6+ followed by 24.Qh8 mate.

22...Kg8 23.Re3, 1-0.

Efim Geller vs. Svetozar Gligorić, Belgrade 1970

1.e4 e5 2.Nf3 Nc6 3.Bb5 a6 4.Ba4 Nf6 5.0-0 Be7 6.Re1 b5 7.Bb3 b5 8.c3 0-0 9.h3 h6 10.d4 Re8 11.Nbd2 Bf8 12.Nf1 Bb7 13.Ng3 Na5 14.Bc2 Nc4 15.b3 Nb6 16.Bb2 Nbd7 17.Qd2 c5 18.Rad1 Qa5 19.dxc5 dxc5 20.c4 b4 21.a4 Qc7 22.Nf5 Nb8

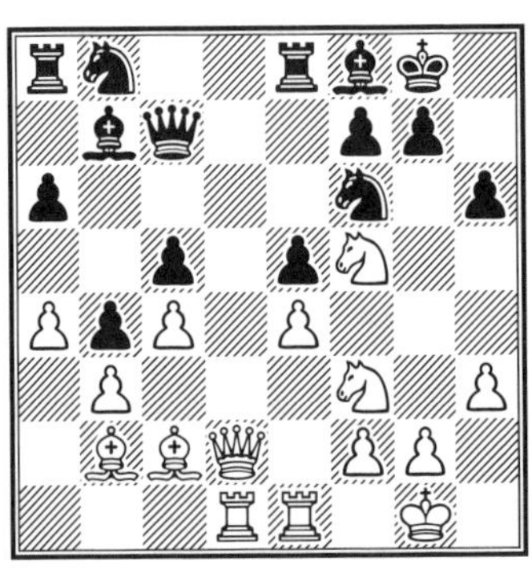

White is better, but it seems like Black is solid. How can White improve his position?

23.Nxe5! Rxe5 24.Bxe5 Qxe5 25.f4 Qe6

25...Qc3 26.Qf2.

26.e5 Ne8

26...Ne4 27.Bxe4 Bxe4 28.Nd6 Bxd6 (28...Bh7 29.g4) 29.Qxd6 Qxd6 30.Rxd6 followed by Rd8+.

27.Nh4! Nc6

27...g6 28.f5.

28.Qd3 g6 29.f5 gxf5 30.Nxf5 Qg6 31.Qe2 Qg5?

White was winning anyway.

32.h4

Black's Queen is lost!.

32...Qf4 33.g3 Qxe5 34.Qg4+ Qg7 35.Nxg7 and Black resigned in a couple move moves.

Efim Geller vs. Lev Polugaevsky, Moscow 1961

1.e4 c5 2.Nf3 d6 3.d4 cxd4 4.Nxd4 Nf6 5.Nc3 a6 6.Be2 e5 7.Nb3 Be7 8.0-0 0-0 9.Be3 Qc7 10.Qd2 Be6 11.f4 exf4 12.Rxf4 Nbd7 13.Nd4 Ne5 14.Nf5 Rac8 15.Raf1 Rfe8 16.Bd4 Bf8 17.Bd3 Nfd7 18.Rh4 Ng6 19.Rh3 Nde5 20.Qd1 b5 21.Qh5 h6 22.Rg3 Kh7 23.Nd5 Bxd5 24.exd5 Nxd3 25.cxd3 Qb7 26.Kh1 Rc2

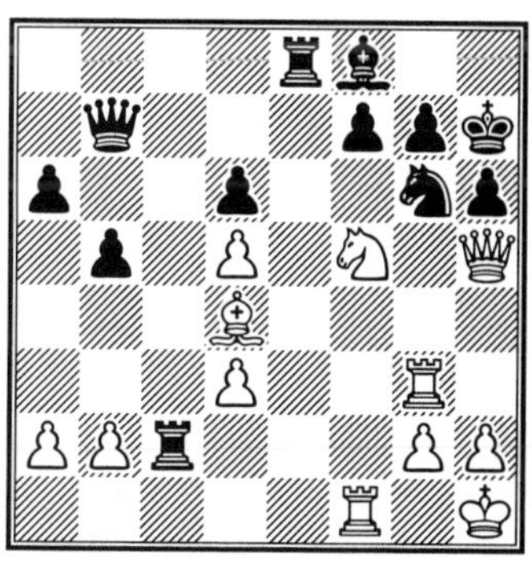

White has a very nice attacking position. How should White continue?

27.Ne3!

Geller: "By no means the signal to retreat. The Knight switches with gain of tempo to the important square g4, from where it attacks not only h6, but also f6. At the same time the file is opened for the Rook at f1."

27...Rd2 28.Ng4 Qd7

28...Rde2 29.Be3 Rxb2 30.Bxh6 gxh6 31.Nf6+ Kh8 32.Nxe8.

29.h4

Geller: "The tempting 29.Qxh6+ will not run away. Now this threat is even stronger: 30.Qxh6+ gxh6 31.Nf6+ Kh8 32.Nxd7 Bg7 33.Bxg7+ Kxg7 34.h5 Black loses a piece."

29...Qe7 30.Re3 Qd7 31.Qxh6+ Kg8

Geller: "The Queen cannot be taken: 31...gxh6 32.Nf6+ Kh8 33.Nxd7+ Ne5 34.Bc3 Rc2 35.d4."

32.Rxe8, 1-0.

Viktor Kupreichik vs. Efim Geller, Moscow 1969

1.e4 e5 2.Nf3 Nc6 3.Bb5 a6 4.Ba4 Nf6 5.Qe2 Be7 6.c3 b5 7.Bb3 0-0 8.d4 d6 9.dxe5 Nxe5 10.Nxe5 dxe5 11.a4 Bb7 12.f3 Nd7 13.Be3 Nc5 14.Bc2 Bc6 15.a5

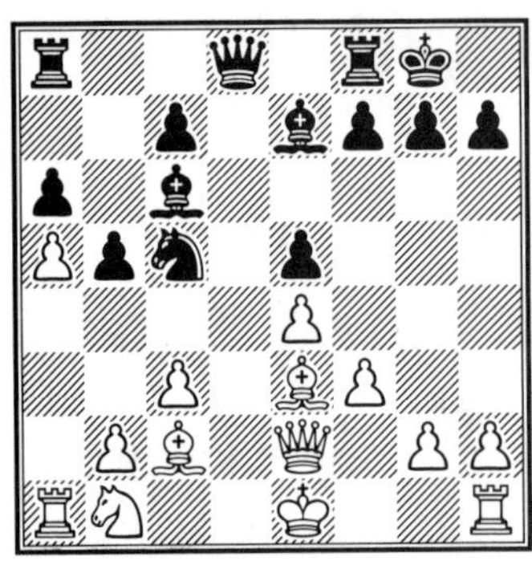

An interesting middle game. How would you play the Black side?

15...b4!

A very strong move. If you tried the nice maneuver 15...Bd7 followed by ...Be6, then you deserve applause. Why is that so good? Because the bishop, once it gets to e6, will be working with the Knight to put pressure on White's weak squares on the a2-g8 diagonal. Note that after Black gets his bishop to e6, if White plays b2-b4 the Knight will go back to d7 and then Black will disrupt White's pawn structure by ...c7-c5.

If, after 15...Bd7, White tries to stop Black's plan (Bishop on e6) by 16.Qf2, Black will play 16...Ne6 followed by ...c7-c5.

However, 15...b4 is clearly the best.

16.0-0

16.cxb4 Ne6 17.Nc3 (17.Qd2 Nd4 18.0-0 Rb8; 17.0-0) 17...Nd4 18.Qf2 Rb8.

16...Rb8 17.Rd1 Qc8 18.Nd2 bxc3 19.bxc3 Rb2 and Black had an edge and won.

Ernő Gereben vs. Efim Geller, Budapest 1952

1.e4 c5 2.Nf3 d6 3.d4 cxd4 4.Nxd4 Nf6 5.Nc3 a6 6.h3 Nc6 7.g4 Nxd4 8.Qxd4 e5 9.Qd3 Be7 10.Bg2 Be6 11.b3 0-0 12.Bb2 b5 13.0-0-0 b4 14.Ne2 a5 15.f4

White has just played f2-f4. What's going on for both sides, and what's the best reply for 15.f4?

I would have been happy if you played 15…a4 since you're ignoring White's stuff and going all out to kill white's King. However, there is an even better way to do this. See if you can find it.

15…Nd7! 16.f5 Nc5 17.Qf3

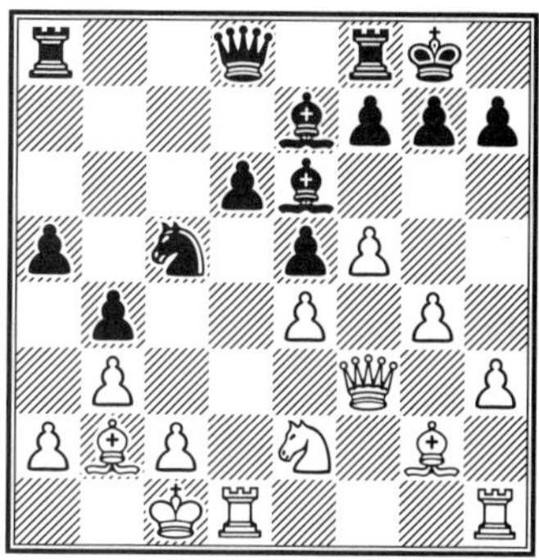

17…a4!

17…Bd7 is also strong, but 17…a4 is just as good and also makes a massive blow to the opponent's psychological state.

18.h4

18.fxe6 fxe6 19.Qg3 Bh4 20.Qh2 axb3 21.axb3 Bg5+ 22.Rd2 (22.Kb1 Qa5 23.Nc1 Bxc1 24.Kxc1 Nxb3 25.cxb3 Qc5+ 26.Kd2 [26.Kb1 Rf2 mates] 26…Rf2+ 27.Kd3 Qc2+ 28.Ke3 Qe2 mate) 22…Ra2 and White is getting destroyed.

18…axb3 19.axb3 Ra2!

And White is doomed.

20.fxe6 fxe6 21.Qe3 Qa5 22.c4 Rxb2 23.Kxb2 Qa3+ 24.Kb1 Ra8 25.Nc1 Qa1+ 26.Kc2 Ra2+ 27.Nxa2 Qxa2+ 28.Kc1 Nxb3+ 29.Qxb3 Qxb3 30.Rd2 Qc3+ 31.Rc2 Qe3+ 32.Kb2 Qa3+ 33.Kb1 b3 34.Rb2 Qb4 35.g5 Bd8 36.Rc1 Bb6 37.Bh3 Kf7 38.h5 Bd4 39.g6+ hxg6 40.hxg6 Ke7, 0-1.

I've already discussed Geller's pioneering work with the King's Indian Defense (Mikhail Botvinnik said, "Before Geller we did not understand the King's Indian Defense."). I discussed how he held his own against the best of the best, and

Geller had a plus record against the six World Champions he crossed swords with (Botvinnik, Fischer, Petrosian, Smyslov, Tal, and Spassky, who was the only World Champion that had a plus score against him).

Geller was a fantastic opening theoretician and, as a result, he was a master of many openings, with the Sicilian (on both sides!) being his main money-earner.

In his book *Application of Chess Theory*[1] Geller wrote:

> From time to time, like many other players, I glance through my own games of earlier years and return to positions and variations which have gone out of practice. I attempt to restore them, to find new ideas and plans. In this search much has to be deemed exhausted, but much remains and is worked out more precisely and in more detail. In a well-known scheme nuances are found, and fast intuition is reinforced by knowledge.

I also want to share what Geller said about this variation:

> **1.e4 c5 2.Nf3 d6 3.d4 cxd4 4.Nxd4 Nf6 5.Nc3 a6 6.Be2 e5 7.Nb3 Be6 8.0-0 Nbd7 9.f4 Qc7 10.f5**
>
> Today, instead of 10.f5 I would possibly choose 10.Kh1, not revealing my cards and maintaining the tension in the center, and would also wonder whether or not to advance the pawn to f4 a move earlier, before castling. After all, in the game Black could have answered 9.f4 not only with 9...Qc7, but also more flexibly—9...Rc8, avoiding determining immediately the position of the queen. Is all this of any significance? I think it is, since by no means always does it reduce to a simply transposition of moves.

Geller played a zillion Sicilians from both sides of the board. So, instead of overwhelming you with hundreds of pages on the subject, I'll show how he-played the Sicilian by giving his decisive games against Fischer.

Efim Geller vs. Robert Fischer, Curacao, Candidates (2) 1962

1.e4 c5 2.Nf3 d6 3.d4 cxd4 4.Nxd4 Nf6 5.Nc3 a6 6.Be2 e5 7.Nb3 Be7 8.0-0 0-0 9.Be3 Qc7 10.a4 Be6 11.a5 Nbd7 12.Nd5 Nxd5

13.exd5 Bf5 14.c4 Bg6 15.Rc1 Nc5?

15...Rad8!? stops White's c4-c5: 16.c5? dxc5 17.Nxc5 Nxc5 18.b4 Be4 and the d5-pawn falls.

16.Nxc5 dxc5 17.b4! Rac8

17...cxb4 18.Bb6 Qd7 19.Qb3 Be4 20.Rfd1 with c4-c5 to follow.

18.Qb3 Bd6 19.Rfd1 Qe7 20.bxc5 Bxc5 21.Bxc5 Rxc5 22.Ra1! Rd8 23.Ra4! Bf5 24.Rb4 Bc8 25.Rb6 Rd6

1 Efim Geller, translated by Ken Neat, *Application of Chess Theory*. London: Everyman, 1984.

25...Rxa5 26.d6 Qd7 27.Qe3! (Stops the a5-rook from going back to c5.) 27...Qf5 28.Bf3 and Black is positionally busted.

26.Qb4 Qc7 27.Rxd6 Qxd6 28.Rb1 Qc7 29.Qa4!

Threatening 30.Rb6 (not to mention 30.Qe8 mate).

29...Bd7 30.Qa3 Rxa5

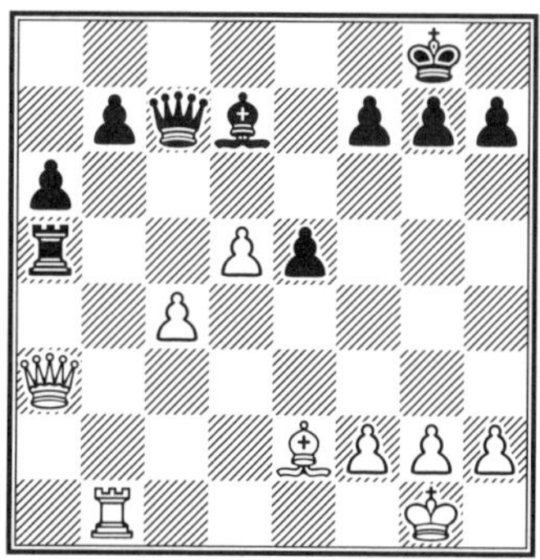

31.Rxb7!

Strong, but even stronger is 31.Qe7! when it's hard for Black to find a move.

31...Qxb7?!

Black had to try 31...Rxa3 32.Rxc7 Ra1+ 33.Bf1 Bf5 when White has to play very accurately to win: 34.f3! h5 35.Kf2 Ra2+ 36.Be2 g5! (36... Bd3 37.Rc8+ Kh7 38.Ke3 Bxe2 39.d6 wins) 37.d6 Kf8 38.c5 Bd3 39.Ke1 Rxe2+ 40.Kd1 Bb5 41.Rc8+ Kg7 42.Rb8 Kf6 43.Rxb5, etc.

32.Qxa5 g6 33.h3 Qb1+ 34.Kh2??

I suspect that both players are very low on time. 34.Bf1! is a dead winner: 34...Bf5 35.d6 and, since 35...Bd3 is met by 36.d7, Black should resign.

34...Bf5?

34...Qc2! draws: 35.Qd8+ Kg7 36.Qxd7 Qxe2 37.Qc7 Qe4 (Threatening perpetual check.) 38.g3 Qd4 39.Kg1 e4 40.Qe7 Qd1+ 41.Kh2 Qf3 42.Qc5 e3 and the game's drawn since 43.Qxe3 loses to 43...Qxe3 44.fxe3 Kf6 and while black's King can stop white's c- and d-pawns, White can't stop Black's a pawn.

35.Qc3 Qe4 36.Bf3 Qd4 37.Qxd4 exd4 38.g4 Bc8 39.c5 a5 40.c6 Kf8 41.d6, 1-0.

After beating Fischer with the White pieces in the Najdorf Sicilian, Geller (in their next game) beat Fischer on the Black side of the same opening!

Robert Fischer vs. Efim Geller, Curacao, Candidates (9) 1962

1.e4 c5 2.Nf3 d6 3.d4 cxd4 4.Nxd4 Nf6 5.Nc3 Nc6 6.Bc4 e6 7.Bb3 Be7 8.f4 0-0 9.Be3 Nxd4 10.Bxd4 b5 11.e5 dxe5 12.fxe5 Nd7 13.0-0

13.Nxb5? Qa5+ 14.Nc3 Nxe5 is very much in Black's favor.

13...Bc5! 14.Bxc5 Nxc5 15.Qxd8 Rxd8 16.Nxb5 Ba6 17.Bc4

17.Nc7 Bxf1 18.Nxa8 Bb5 19.Nc7 Bc6 20.Bc4 Rd2 with an edge for Black.

17...Rab8 18.a4

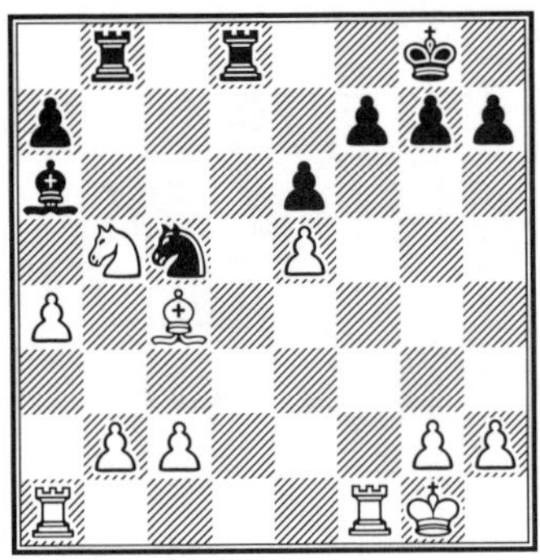

18...Nxa4! 19.Nd6?

19.Rxa4 Bxb5 20.Bxb5 Rxb5 21.Rxa7 Rxb2 22.Rfxf7 Rd1+ 23.Kf2 (23.Rf1 Rxf1+ 24.Kxf1 Rxc2, =) 23...Rxc2+ 24.Kg3 Rd3+ 25.Rf3, = (an not 25.Kf4? Rxg2).

19...Bxc4 20.Nxc4 Nxb2 21.Nd6 Rd7 22.Rfb1 Rc7 23.h3?

23.c4 is much better.

23...Rb6 24.c4 h6 25.Nb5 Rc5

25...Rxc4?? 26.Rxb2 a6 27.Nd6.

26.Rxb2 a6 27.Rf2 axb5 28.Ra7 Rxe5 29.Rfxf7 Rg5 30.Rfb7 Rxb7 31.Rxb7 bxc4 32.Rc7 Rf5 33.Rxc4 Kf7 34.g4 Rf3 35.Kg2 Rd3 36.Rc7+ Kf6 37.h4 Ra3 38.Rb7 Rc3 39.g5+ hxg5 40.hxg5+ Kg6 41.Re7 Re3 42.Kf2 Re5 43.Kf3 Rf5+ 44.Ke3 e5 45.Ke4 Rxg5 46.Re8 Rg1 47.Kf3 Rf1+ 48.Kg3 Rf5 49.Rb8 Kg5 50.Re8 Kf6 51.Rf8+ Ke6 52.Re8+ Kf6 53.Rf8+ Ke6 54.Re8+ Kd5 55.Ra8 Rf7 56.Kg4 Re7 57.Ra5+ Ke6 58.Ra6+ Kf7 59.Kf3 Re6 60.Ra8 e4+ 61.Ke3 g5 62.Ra1 Kg6 63.Rb1 Re5 64.Kd4 Kf6 65.Re1 Ra5 66.Rxe4 Kf5 67.Re8 Kg4 68.Ke3 Kg3, 0-1.

Robert Fischer vs. Efim Geller, Skopje 1967

1.e4 c5 2.Nf3 d6 3.d4 cxd4 4.Nxd4 Nf6 5.Nc3 Nc6 6.Bc4 e6 7.Be3 Be7 8.Bb3 0-0 9.Qe2 Qa5 10.0-0-0 Nxd4 11.Bxd4 Bd7 12.Kb1 Bc6 13.f4 Rad8 14.Rhf1

Okay, though it seems a little too soft. Instead, 14.f5 gives White a clear advantage: 14...exf5 (14...e5 15.Bf2 with the idea of Bh4xf6 and then Nd5 when White has all the chances.) 15.exf5 Rfe8 16.Qd3.

14...b5 15.f5

15.a3!?

15...b4?

15...e5 was better when 16.Be3 b4 17.Nd5 Nxd5 18.Bxd5 Bb5 19.Bc4 Bxc4 20.Qxc4 Rc8 leaves Black with a playable position.

16.fxe6!

Fischer's going for the kill!

16...bxc3 17.exf7+

Fischer had two promising ways to play this attack. The most straight forward (and best) is 17.Rxf6! gxf6 (17...Bxf6 18.Bxf6 gxf6 19.e7 Qe5 20.exd8=Q Rxd8 21.Qc4 Be8 22.Qxc3 when Fischer, with his fantastic technique, would most likely win the game.) 18.exf7+ Kh8 (18...Rxf7 19.Bxf7+ Kxf7 20.Qc4+ is winning for White) 19.Qg4! Rb8 (19... Bd7 20. Qh4 Kg7 21. Rd3 Rxf7 22.Rg3+ Kf8 23. Qxh7!) 20.Bxc3 Qd8 21.Be6 Bb5 22.Qh4 (The threat is Rxd6!) 22...Rb6 23.Rd5 intending Rh5. However, White still has a powerful attack, though now the right way to play it is far harder than 17.Rxf6.

17...Kh8 18.Rf5! Qb4 19.Qf1!

A high-class move.

19...Nxe4

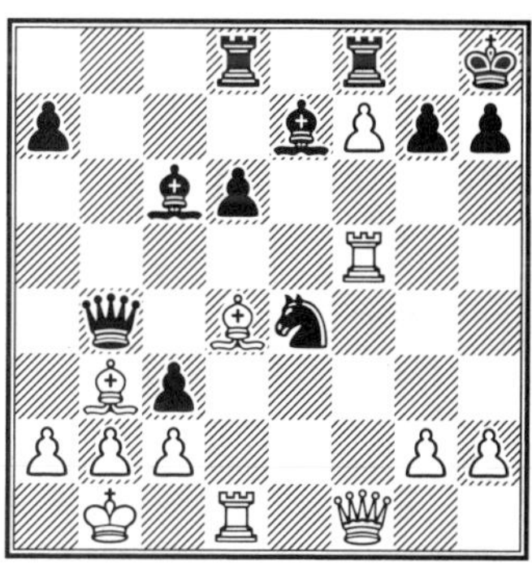

20.a3?

And just when he could go for the gold, he hesitates with 20.a3. Fischer could have won with 20.Qf4! d5 (20...cxb2 21.Rh5 Nf6 22.Rh6! Ne4 23.Qf5 Ng5 24.h4 Be4 25.Qg4 and Black is dead.) 21.Qe5 Nf6 22.Rxf6 Bxf6 23.Qxf6!

20...Qb7

Black's only move.

21.Qf4⁈

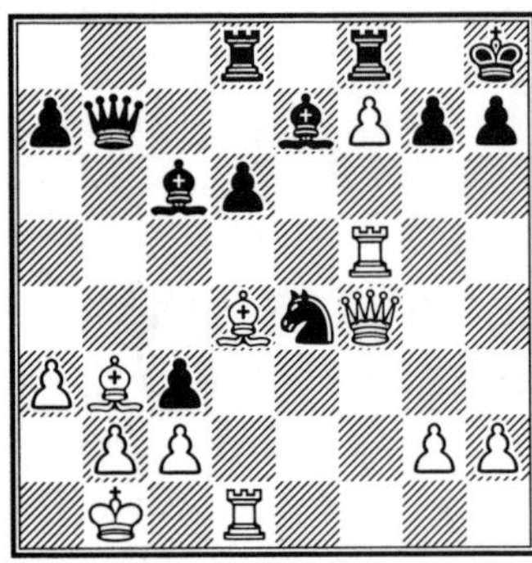

Total collapse! 21.Rh5! would have kept the battle going.

21...Ba4!

Suddenly White is dead lost

22.Qg4 Bf6 23.Rxf6 Bxb3!, 0-1.

When it came to positions with massive tactical chaos, Geller's nerves were better than Fischer's. In chess, there is always someone whose style drives you crazy. Players like Geller and Tal were those kinds of players.

Here's another such game. Fischer won the Monte Carlo tournament. Smyslov was second and Geller third. Fischer's only loss was to... yep, you guessed it. Geller!

Robert Fischer vs. Efim Geller, Monte Carlo 1967

1.e4 c5 2.Nf3 d6 3.d4 cxd4 4.Nxd4 Nf6 5.Nc3 a6 6.Bg5 e6 7.f4 Qb6 8.Qd2 Qxb2 9.Rb1 Qa3 10.f5 Nc6 11.fxe6 fxe6 12.Nxc6 bxc6 13.e5 Nd5 14.Nxd5 cxd5 15.Be2 dxe5 16.0-0 Bc5+ 17.Kh1 Rf8 18.c4 Rxf1+ 19.Rxf1 Bb7 20.Bg4 dxc4 21.Bxe6

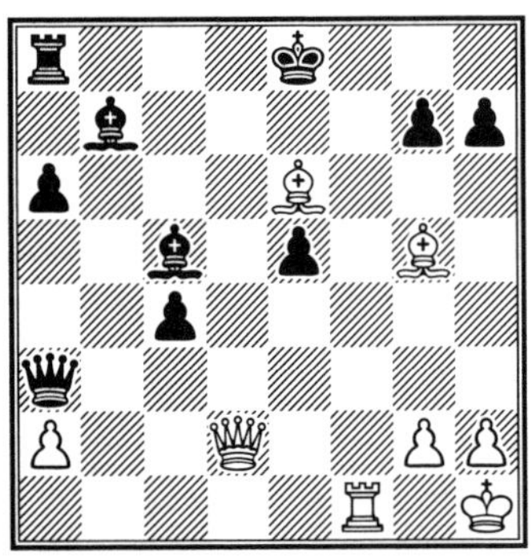

Qd3 22.Qe1 Be4 23.Bg4 Rb8 24.Bd1 Kd7 25.Rf7+ Ke6, 0-1.

For the Fischer fans, here is his only win against Geller in the Sicilian Defense:

Robert Fischer vs. Efim Geller, Curacao, Candidates (23) 1962

1.e4 c5 2.Nf3 d6 3.d4 cxd4 4.Nxd4 Nf6 5.Nc3 Nc6 6.Bc4 e6 7.Bb3 Be7 8.0-0 Nxd4 9.Qxd4 0-0 10.f4 b6 11.Kh1 Ba6 12.Rf3 d5 13.exd5 Bc5 14.Qa4 Bb7 15.Be3 exd5 16.Bd4 Re8 17.Rd1 Ng4 18.h3 Qh4 19.Rdf1 Bxd4 20.Qxd4 Rad8 21.Nxd5 Bxd5 22.Bxd5 Nf6 23.c4 Rd7 24.Re3 Red8 25.Qe5 h6 26.Bf3 Rd2 27.b4 Rf2 28.Ree1 Rxf3 29.Rxf3 Re8 30.Qxe8+ Nxe8 31.Rxe8+ Kh7

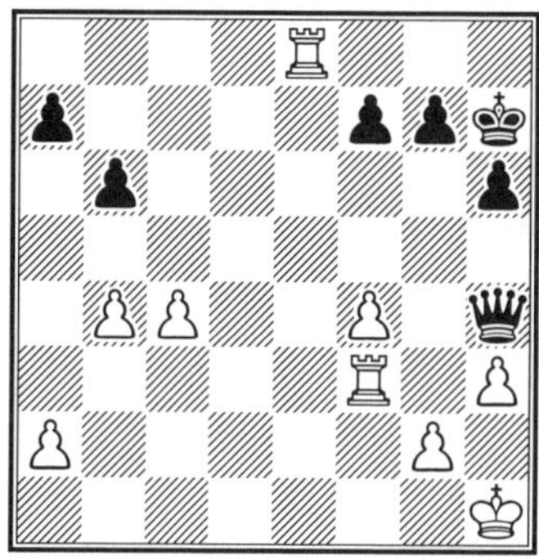

32.c5 Qf6 33.Re1 bxc5 34.bxc5 Qb2 35.Rff1 Qxa2 36.c6 Qa5 37.Rc1 Qc7 38.Rfd1 g5 39.fxg5 Kg6 40.gxh6 Kxh6 41.Rd6+ Kg7 42.Rd4 Kg6 43.Ra4, 1-0.

Efim Geller vs. Lev Polugaevsky, Moscow 1961

1.e4 c5 2.Nf3 d6 3.d4 cxd4 4.Nxd4 Nf6 5.Nc3 a6 6.Be2 e5 7.Nb3 Be7 8.0-0 0-0 9.Be3 Qc7 10.Qd2 Be6 11.f4 exf4 12.Rxf4 Nbd7 13.Nd4 Ne5 14.Nf5 Rac8 15.Raf1 Rfe8 16.Bd4 Bf8 17.Bd3 Nfd7 18.Rh4 Ng6 19.Rh3 Nde5 20.Qd1 b5 21.Qh5 h6 22.Rg3 Kh7 23.Nd5 Bxd5 24.exd5 Nxd3 25.cxd3 Qb7 26.Kh1 Rc2 27.Ne3!

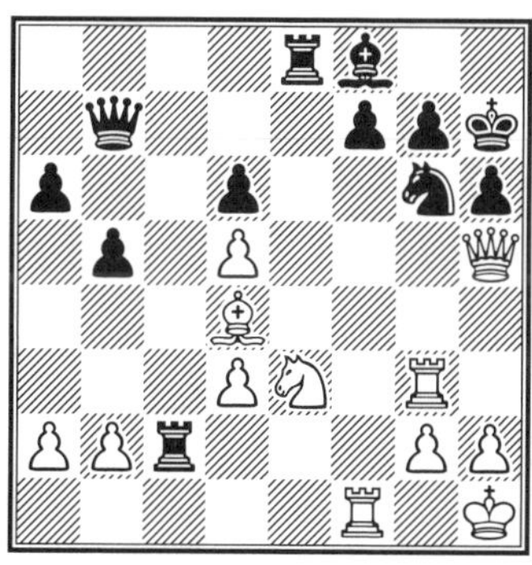

Teenager Joel Benjamin vs Efim Geller (Jay Whitehead is on Geller's right), Lone Pine 1980 (Photo: Stella Monday, courtesy of Mechanics' Institute, San Francisco).

[Geller]: "By no means the signal to retreat. The Knight switches with gain of tempo to the important square g4, from where it attacks not only h6, but also f6. At the same time the file is opened for the Rook at f1."

I should add that by moving the Knight off of f5, in some lines the Queen can move to f5 pinning the black Knight and threatening h2-h4-h5.

27...Rd2 28.Ng4

28.Qf5 is stronger, though it's hard to criticize.

28.Ng4

28.Qf5 is stronger though it's hard to criticize 28.Ng4 when you see the crushing finish.

28...Qd7 29.h4 Qe7 30.Re3 Qd7 31.Qxh6+! Kg8 32.Rxe8, 1-0.

In my mind Geller was as good as the best in the world (for example, he blasted Fischer over and over). He played in twenty-three USSR Chess Championships (a record Geller shared Taimanov). In 1963 Geller was ranked as the second best player in the world. In fact, by 1951 he had been considered among the best ten players in the world for twenty years!

Geller kept his personal life private.

Geller died of cancer November 17, 1998, in Moscow, at the aged of seventy-three.

PART
THREE

Portraits and Stories

1

CHESS, CRIMINALS AND THE GAMES THEY PLAY

Recently I read an excellent book, *Shady Side: The Life and Crimes of Norman Tweed Whitaker, Chess Master*, about a chess master who happened to be a criminal. I first heard of Whitaker a long time ago, and though I've encountered players who cheated during play, or got into fist fights, or even stole chess clocks when people weren't watching, I wondered how rare dangerous chess playing criminals were.

Over the years I've received dozens and dozens of letters from incarcerated chess lovers—from those who have committed white collar crimes to murderers. Chess seems to sooth them and give them something to grasp onto. The criminals I've chosen to write about here are killers who were tournament chess players before they started living a life of crime—or went bonkers.

Alexander Pichushkin

The Russian Alexander Pichushkin (b. 1974), also known as the "Chessboard Killer," was a pretty good chess player and one of the world's most "successful" serial killers. Like all good chess players, he needed an opponent, and this led him to try and kill more people than another serial killer—Andrei Chikatilo who had killed fifty-three. Thus Pichushkin's goal was sixty-four kills, which not only would put him ahead of Chikatilo, but also take him back to his love of chess since the chessboard has sixty-four squares.

I was left wondering what a chess criminal's games would look like. Do chess killers attack? Do they grab space and try and grab the whole board? Or do they quietly build up their position, leaving their opponent clueless as to the criminals true intentions? Unfortunately I wasn't able to find any of Pichushkin's games. So, we'll move on!

Claude Frizzel Bloodgood

If you're going to be a killer, the name "Bloodgood" is an excellent choice. It makes me think of a super villain (other crazed villain names are Doctor Doom, Darkseid, Dr. Death, Clayface, Red Skull, Scarecrow, Captain Nazi, Rag Doll, Mad Hatter, Solomon Grundy, Vandal Savage, Crime Doctor, Headshot, Killer Moth, Captain Cold, Gorilla Grodd, Molten Man-Thing, General Zod, Shadow Thief, Sinestro, Fin Fang Foom, Mole Man, Chronos, Destroyer, Gargoyle, The Skrulls, Baron Mordo, The Blob, Baron Zemo, The Vulture, Red Ghost, Executioner, Green Goblin, Kang the Conqueror, Kraven the Hunter, etc. etc.). Bloodgood fits right in there! As for the name "Frizzel," it's clear why he had so much animosity towards his mother (it's as bad as naming a boy Sue).

Claude Frizzel Bloodgood (1937-2001) was active in the chess scene in the 1950s and was probably a class "A" player (1800 to 1999). However, he "cracked" in the 1960s and became a full-time criminal. Burglary (which put him in prison for a while), forgery (stealing from his parents and getting more time in prison), and finally, in 1969, murder (he killed his mother only nine days after he was released from prison). It's clear that he and his family had a "*very* loving relationship".

Though he was sentenced to death (which was commuted to life), the real chess story starts with his life in prison. He played one chess game after another with his fellow inmates, day after day, year after year, and he always sent in his results to the USCF (United States Chess Federation) so his games would be rated. Since he was playing in a "closed pool" (which means he played the same small group of people over and over), and since he won almost every game he played against them, his rating rose and rose until he was the second highest rated player in the United States, peaking at 2789.

Chess was his life! He published three books on the game: *The Tactical Grob,*[1] *Nimzovich* [sp.] *Attack: the Norfolk Gambits,*[2] and *The Blackburne-Hartlaub Gambit,: 1.d4 e5 2.dxe5 d6!? (Chess Openings for Hustlers).*[3]

After Bloodgood's death (from lung cancer), an obituary appeared in *The Week in Chess* written by French journalist Pierre Barthélémy:

> On a personal note, I knew Claude for close to a decade and became good friends with him. I found him to have a brilliant mind, a great sense of humor,

1 Claude F. Bloodgood, The Tactical Grob. : UK, Chess Ltd.

2 Claude F. Bloodgood, *Nimzovich Attack: the Norfolk Gambits*. Dallas: Chess Digest, 1997.

3 Claude F. Bloodgood , *The Blackburne-Hartlaub Gambit,: 1.d4 e5 2.dxe5 d6!? (Chess openings for hustlers)*. Dallas: Chess Digest, 1998.

to be a loyal friend, and to be kind and generous with others. Even though he had only limited finances, for example, he was always quick to share what little he had with other inmates, particularly when it came to promoting prison chess . . . The chess world will be less interesting without him. I will miss him very much.

Claude Bloodgood vs. B. Evans, Norfolk 1961

1.g4 d5 2.Bg2 c6 3.g5 e5 4.h4 Bd6 5.d3 Be6 6.e4 Ne7 7.Nd2 0-0 8.Bh3 Bxh3 9.Nxh3 f5 10.gxf6 Rxf6 11.exd5 Nxd5??

A positional blunder that hands the square to White. Correct was 11...cxd5.

12.Ne4 Rf7 13.Bg5 Be7 14.Qg4 Qa5+ 15.c3 Bxg5 16.Nhxg5 Rf8 17.Qe6+ Kh8 18.Nf7+ Kg8 19.Nh6+ Kh8 20.Qg8+ Rxg8 21.Nf7, 1-0.

Claude Bloodgood vs. Cetenski, Winston-Salem Ladder 1971

1.e4 c5 2.Nf3 d6 3.d4 cxd4 4.Nxd4 Nf6 5.Nc3 a6 6.Bg5 e6 7.f4 Qb6 8.Qd2 Qxb2 9.Rb1 Qa3 10.f5 Nc6 11.fxe6 fxe6 12.Nxc6 bxc6 13.e5 dxe5 14.Bxf6 gxf6 15.Ne4 f5 16.Be2 Be7

16...fxe4 17.Bh5+ Ke7 18.Rf1

17.Bh5+ Kf8 18.Qh6+ Kg8 19.Rb3, 1-0.

Claude Bloodgood vs. Barnsley,[1] correspondence game 1997

1.Nf3 d5 2.b3 c5 3.e4 dxe4 4.Ne5 Nd7

Bloodgood won many games when his opponents got greedy with 4...Qd8-d4 5.Bc1-b2 Qd4xb2 6.Nb1-c3 Qb2-a3 7.Bf1-b5+ Bc8-d7 8.Ne5-c4 Qa3-b4 9.Bb5xd7+ Nb8xd7 10.a2-a3, 1-0.

5.Bb5 a6 6.Bd7 Bd7 7.Bb2 Bf5 8.0-0 e6 9.f3 exf3 10.Qxf3 Qc7 11.Na3 f6 12.g4 Bg6 13.Rae1 0-0-0 14.Nec4 h5 15.g5 Bf5 16.gxf6 gxf6 17.Bc3 Qg7 18.Kh1 Rh6 19.Ba5 Rd4 20.Nb6+ Kb8 21.Nac4 Qc7 22.Nd5 Qc6 23.Bc7+ Ka7 24.Bb6+, ½-½.

In the following game White is dead lost, but once again he wins.

Claude Bloodgood vs. Sanderson, Virginia Penitentiary 1973

1.g4 e5 2.d3 Bc5 3.h4 d5 4.g5 Bg4 5.c4 Ne7 6.Bg2 Be6 7.Qb3 Bb6 8.Nc3 dxc4 9.Qb5+ Nbc6 10.dxc4 a6 11.Qa4 O-O 12.Bh3 Bxh3 13.Nxh3 f5 14.c5 Ba7 15.Qc4+ Kh8 16.h5 Nd4 17.Nd1 Qe8 18.h6 g6 19.f4 Rd8

1 Barnsley was the British Postal Champion at the time.

20.fxe5 Nec6 21.Nf4 Nb4 22.e6 Nbc2+ 23.Kf2 Nxa1 24.e3 Nc6 25.Qc3+ Nd4 26.exd4 Qe7 27.d5+ Kg8 28.Be3 b6 29.Nxg6 hxg6 30.h7+, 1-0.

Claude Bloodgood vs. George Trifler, VA Open 1958

1.g4 d5 2.Bg2 c6 3.g5 Bf5 4.d3 e5 5.h4 Qb6 6.e4 dxe4 7.dxe4 Be6 8.Nd2 Bc5 9.Qe2 Ne7 10.Ngf3 Bg4 11.Nc4 Qc7 12.Be3 Bxe3 13.Qxe3 O-O 14.O-O-O f5 15.Qb3 fxe4 16.Nfxe5 Bxd1 17.Nb6+ Nd5 18.Nxd5 cxd5 19.Qxd5+ Kh8 20.Rxd1 Nc6 21.Ng6+ hxg6 22.h5 Nb4 23.Qb3

White is completely busted, but that doesn't stop him from winning the game.

23...Nxc2 24.Kb1 Qh2 25.Bxe4 Rxf2 26.Qxb7 Re8 27.h6 Rg8 28.Rh1 Nd4 29.hxg7+ Rxg7 30.Rxh2+ Rxh2 31.Qb8+ Rg8 32.Qxh2+, 1-0.

Humphrey Bogart vs. Claude Bloodgood, Santa Monica 1955

1.d4 f5 2.Nf3 e6 3.e4 fxe4 4.Ng5 d5 5.f3 exf3 6.Qxf3 Nf6 7.Bd3 g6 8.Nxh7 Rxh7 9.Bxg6+ Rf7 10.O-O Bg7 11.Bg5 Nbd7 12.Nc3 Kf8 13.Bxf7 Kxf7 14.Rae1 c5 15.Nxd5 exd5 16.Qxd5+ Kg6

16...Kf8 17.Qd6+ Kg8 18.Re7 Ne8 19.Qe6+ Kh8 20.Rxg7, 1-0. Humphrey Bogart - NN, Santa Monica 1955

17.Bxf6 Bxf6 18.Re6 Qh8 19.Qf5+ Kf7 20.d5 Qh4 21.c3 Qg5 22.Qh7+ Qg7 23.Rfxf6+ Nxf6 24.Re7+ Kxe7 25.Qxg7+ Kd6 26.Qxf6+ Kxd5 27.Qd8+, 1-0.

As you can see, Bloodgood's games were frenetic. In life he attacked, and he did the same on the chessboard.

Norman Tweed Whitaker

Unlike Bloodgood, who clearly had problems with his family, Norman Tweed Whitaker (1890-1975) was blessed with very nice, supportive parents. His father was a mathematics teacher and his mother was a champion whist player. Norman had a good education, earning a Bachelor's degree in German literature (University of Pennsylvania) and a law degree from Georgetown University.

Whitaker's father taught him how to play chess when he was fourteen, and he spent a lot of time watching (and learning!) Harry Nelson Pillsbury play (in Philadelphia). After playing simultaneous exhibitions against some of the best players in the world, he entered (during his stint at the University of Pennsylvania) intercollegiate team competitions (successfully), and with both his education and chess going on the fast-track, a reader of a crystal ball would have predicted affluence in youth and adulthood. The sky, as they say, was the limit!

By 1913 he was master strength and did well in that year's New York National round-robin tournament. He dominated everyone but top notch players (such as Cabablanca, Marshall, Janowski, and Jaffe, though I have to say he gave both Cabablanca and Marshall a scare!). He continued to play in tournaments, getting stronger and stronger. In 1916 he was wiped off the map in a seven-game match with the former U.S. Champion Walter Showalter. However, Whitaker turned the tables when they played another match in 1918, winning 4 to 1 with 3 draws.

By 1916 Whitaker was also practicing law, and was working for the United States Patent and Trademark Office. And by 1921 he was international master strength, doing well in very strong tournaments and beating giants like Edward Lasker and Frank Marshall. It seems the crystal ball was right, and his future was going to be nothing less than glorious.

Then, his world started to combust. For reasons beyond my comprehension, he convinced his brother and two sisters to join him in an insurance fraud scheme. This led to Whitaker spending two years in Leavenworth. He was disbarred in 1924.

When he was released from prison in 1927 he jumped back into chess, representing the United States in several international events. It seemed that he was back on track, married in 1928, and doing well in his chess career. His friends were sure that the insurance fraud was nothing but a bizarre blip on his screen, and such madness would never happen to him again.

On March 1932, Charles Lindbergh's infant son was kidnapped (and eventually murdered). The country went mad, calling it the "Crime of the Century." H. L. Mencken (the brilliant satirist) called it, "the biggest story since the resurrection." Whitaker, who couldn't resist "easy money," jumped at the opportunity. He joined forces with Gaston Means (a crooked man who had been an agent for the Department of Justice) and they did their best to swindle a wealthy lady named Evelyn Walsh McLean by saying they were in touch with the kidnappers and, for a huge amount of money, would make sure the baby would be safely returned.

Chaos ensued, it all went to hell, and both were arrested and sent to prison. Gaston Means was sentenced to fifteen years (dying in prison), while our chess anti-hero only received a mere eighteen months. Upon release from prison Whitaker continued his life of crime, scamming everyone and anyone he could, going back to prison, doing more crime, and back to prison again. He even befriended Al Capone in Alcatraz!

Whitaker would play in various chess tournaments between incarcerations, and in 1965 was given the International Master title by FIDE.

Like Bloodgood, Whitaker played aggressive, tactical chess.

I begin with a Whitaker loss. If you're a tactician, you live by the sword, you die by the sword.

Norman Whitaker vs. David Przepiórka, The Hague 1928

1.e4 c6 2.d4 d5 3.exd5 cxd5 4.Bd3 Nc6 5.c3 Nf6 6.Nd2 Bg4 7.Qb3 Qc7 8.Nf1 e6 9.Bf4 Bd6

9...Qxf4 10.Qxb7

10.Bxd6 Qxd6 11.Qxb7?! Rb8 12.Qa6 0-0 13.Rb1 e5 14.dxe5 Qxe5+ 15.Ne3 d4 16.Qxc6

16.cxd4 Nxd4 17.Ne2 Bxe2 18.Bxe2 Rfd8 19.0-0 Rb6 20.Qc4 Rc6 21.Qd3 Nf3+ 22.gxf3 Rxd3

16...dxe3 17.Ne2 exf2+ 18.Kf1

18.Kxf2 Rfe8+

18...Rfe8 19.Qc4 Rbd8 20.Kxf2? Qe3+ 21.Kf1 Rxd3, 0-1.

Okay, White got smashed. However, everyone has an off day, and the following games will convince you that Whitaker was a very strong player!

Gustave Simonson vs. Norman Whitaker, Manhattan 1909

1.e4 e5 2.Nf3 Nc6 3.Bc4 Bc5 4.c3 Nf6 5.0-0 d6 6.d4 exd4 7.cxd4 Bb6 8.h3 0-0 9.d5 Ne7 10.Nc3 Ng6 11.Kh2 Re8 12.Bd3 Nh5 13.Ne2 Nh4 14.Ng3 Nf6 15.Nxh4 Ng4+ 16.hxg4 Qxh4+ 17.Kg1 Qxg3 18.Qf3 Qxg4 19.Qxg4 Bxg4 and Black, who has an extra pawn, went on to win the game.

José Capablanca vs. Norman Whitaker, Philadelphia (simultaneous exhibition) 1909

1.e4 e5 2.Nf3 Nc6 3.Bb5 a6 4.Ba4 Nf6 5.0-0 Be7 6.d3 d6 7.c3 0-0 8.Nbd2 Be6 9.Re1 Ne8 10.Nf1 f5 11.exf5 Bxf5 12.Ne3 Bg6 13.Qb3+ Kh8 14.Qxb7 Na5 15.Qb4 c5 16.Qg4 Nf6 17.Qh3 Bxd3 18.Ng5 Nh5 19.Ne6 Nf4 20.Nxf4 exf4 21.Nd5 Bf5 22.Qf3 Bg5 23.Bxf4 Rb8 24.b4 Bxf4 25.Qxf4 Bc2 26.Qg3 Bxa4 27.bxa5 Rf5 28.Re7 Qf8 29.Ne3 Rf6 30.Ra7 Rb2 31.Ng4 Qb8 32.Re7 Rb1+ 33.Re1 Rxa1 34.Rxa1 Qb2 35.Re1 Re6 36.f4 Qxa2 37.f5 Re2 38.h3 Bc6 39.Rxe2 Qxe2 40.Kh2 Qe4 41.Qf2 Kg8 42.f6 g6 43.f7+ Kf8 44.Nf6 Qf5 45.Nxh7+ Kxf7 46.Qd2 Qe5+ 47.Kg1 d5 48.Qf2+ Kg7 49.Qxc5 Be8 50.Qa7+ Bf7 51.Qf2 Qxc3 52.h4 Qc1+ 53.Kh2 Qc7+, 0-1.

Okay, that was a simultaneous exhibition. He would get wiped off the board in a real tournament game, right? Well, check out the following tournament game:

Norman Whitaker vs. José Capablanca, New York National 1913

1.d4 Nf6 2.Nf3 d6 3.Nc3 d5 4.Bf4 e6 5.e3 Bb4 6.Bd3 c5 7.0-0 c4

Casablanca thinks he's being tricky. However, it's not so easy as the legendary Cuban thought.

8.Be2

Another option was 8.Nb5! cxd3? (Black can equalize with 8...0-0 9.Nc7 Bd6 10.Bxd6 Qxd6 11.Nxa8 cxd3 12.cxd3 Nc6 1.Qb3 Qb8 14.Nb6 axb6 15.Qxb6, =) 9.Nc7+ Kf8 10.Nxa8 Na6 11.cxd3 Bd7 12.Nc7 Nxc7 13.Qb3 a5 14.a3 Be7 15.Qxb7 and White has a winning position.

8...Bxc3 9.bxc3 Ne4 10.Qe1 Qa5?!

Greedy.

11.Nd2! Nxc3?

11...Nf6 was better.

12.Bxc4 Nc6 13.Nb3

13.Bd3 is probably more accurate, but White gets a clear advantage with 13.Nb3 too. The rest of the game shows Casablanca fighting to equalize, and then slowly but surely outplaying the young Whitaker.

13...Qb4 14.Bd3 Na4 15.Qe2 0-0 16.Qh5 f5 17.g4 Qe7 18.gxf5 exf5 19. Kh1 Nb2 20. Be2 Nc4 21. Nc5 b6 22. Qf3 bxc5 23. Qxd5+ Be6 24. Qxc6 Rac8 25. Qg2 cxd4 26. exd4 Qd7 27. c3 Rf6 28. Rg1 Rg6 29. Qh3 Bd5+ 30. f3 Rg4 31. Rxg4 fxg4 32. Qg3 Qf5 33. Rg1 h5 34. h3 Rf8 35. Bxc4 Bxc4 36. Bd6 Rf6 37. Be5 Rg6 38. Kh2 Bd5 39. Qf4 Qc2+ 40.Rg2 Qd3 41. hxg4 Bxf3 42. Rd2 Qf1 43. g5 Qh1+ 44. Kg3 Bd5 45. Rf2 h4+ 46. Kg4 h3 47. Rb2 Be6+ 48. Kh5 Kh7 49. Re2 Qd1 50. Qd2 Qg1 51. Qf4 Bd5 52. Rd2 Bg2 53.Kh4 Kg8 54. Rb2 Kh7 55. c4 Qe1+ 56. Kg4 Qg1 57.d5 Bxd5+ 58. Qg3 Be6+ 59. Kf3 Qf1+ 60. Ke3 Qxc4 61. Bd4 Qc1+ 62.Rd2 Bf5 63. Qh4+ Kg8 64. Be5 Re6 65. Qd4 h2 66. Qd8+ Kh7, 0-1.

Capablanca must have been very happy when this game ended!

Norman Whitaker vs. Jackson Showalter, Western Open 1915

1.e4 e5 2.Nf3 Nc6 3.Bb5 a6 4.Ba4 Nf6 5.0-0 d6 6.Re1 b5 7.Bb3 Be7 8.a4 b4 9.a5 0-0 10.d3 Rb8 11.Bc4 Nd7 12.Be3 Bf6 13.Nbd2 Nd4 14.Nf1 Nc5 15.c3 Nde6 16.Ng3 g6 17.d4 Nd7 18.Qd2 exd4 19.cxd4 Qe7 20.Bh6 Rd8 21.Nf5 gxf5 22.exf5 Ne5 23.dxe5 dxe5 24.fxe6 Bxe6 25.Qe2 Bf5 26.Nxe5, 1-0.

Norman Whitaker vs. Samuel Reshevsky, Detroit 1924

1.e4 e5 2.Nf3 Nc6 3.c3 Nf6 4.d4 exd4 5.e5 Ne4 6.Qe2 d5 7.exd6 f5 8.dxc7 Qd5 9.cxd4 Bb4+ 10.Bd2 Bxd2+ 11.Nbxd2 0-0 12.Qc4 Be6 13.Qxd5 Bxd5 14.Bc4 Bxc4 15.Nxc4 Rac8 16.Rc1 Rxc7 17.0-0 Rfc8 18.Rcd1 Nxd4 19.Nxd4 Rxc4 20.Nxf5 Rf8 21.Ne7+ Kh8 22.Rd7 Rb8 23.Rfd1 h6 24.Nf5 Nf6 25.Rf7 Rbc8 26.h3 R4c7 27.Nxh6 Kh7 28.Rxc7 Rxc7 29.Ng4 Nxg4 30.hxg4 Rc2 31.Rb1 b5 32.g3 Kg8 33.a3 Kf7 34.Rd1 Ke6 35.Rd8 Rxb2 36.Ra8 b4 37.Rxa7 bxa3 38.Rxa3 Kf6 39.Ra5 Rb4 40.f4 Rb2 41.Ra6+ Kf7 42.g5 Rc2 43.Ra1 Kg6 44.g4 Rc3 45.Kg2 Rc2+ 46.Kg3 Kf7 47.Ra7+ Kf8 48.f5 Rc6 49.Kh4 Rc8 50.Kh5 Kg8 51.Kg6 Kh8 52.f6 Rg8 53.Rxg7 Rxg7+ 54.fxg7+ Kg8 55.Kh6, 1-0.

Norman Whitaker vs. Samuel Factor, National Chess Congress 1927

1.e4 e5 2.Nf3 Nc6 3.Bb5 a6 4.Ba4 Nf6 5.0-0 Be7 6.Re1 b5 7.Bb3 d6 8.c3 Na5 9.Bc2 c5 10.d4 Qc7 11.a4 Rb8 12.axb5 axb5 13.dxe5 dxe5 14.Nxe5 Qxe5 15.Rxa5 Ng4 16.f4 Qc7 17.Ra1 c4 18.h3 Qb6+, 0-1.

Isaac Kashdan vs. Norman Whitaker, Fort Worth 1951

1.d4 d5 2.c4 e6 3.Nc3 Nf6 4.Nf3 Nbd7 5.Bg5 Be7 6.e3 0-0 7.cxd5 exd5 8.Bd3 Re8 9.0-0 Nf8 10.Qc2 c6 11.Rfe1 Ne4 12.Bxe7 Qxe7 13.b4 Ng6 14.b5 Bd7 15.bxc6 Bxc6 16.Ne2 Rac8 17.Rac1 Bd7 18.Qb3 Bg4 19.Rxc8 Rxc8 20.Bxe4 dxe4 21.Nd2 Bxe2 22.Rxe2 Nh4 23.g3 Rc1+ 24.Nf1 Qd7, 0-1.

2

THE AMAZING ARGENTINIAN CHESS TRAGEDY

The Gothenburg Interzonal (Sweden) in 1955 was a twenty-one player round robin that was held from August 15 to September 21.

The top group was the Soviet players (in no particular order): David Bronstein, Efim Geller, Paul Keres, Tigran Petrosian, Boris Spassky, and Georgy Ilivitsky. Ilivitsky had come in third by tiebreaks in the Soviet championship earlier that year, half a point behind Smyslov and Geller (Geller beat Smyslov in the playoff), but ahead of Spassky, Petrosian, Botvinnik, Taimanov, and Keres.

The second strongest group was Argentina, which at that time was considered a chess powerhouse: Oscar Panno, Miguel Najdorf, Herman Pilnik, and Carlos Guimard.

The other players: Arthur Bisguier, Wolfgang Unzicker, Jan Hein Donner, Bogdan Śliwa, Miroslav Filip, Luděk Pachman, Braslav Rabar, László Szabó, Andrija Fuderer, Gideon Ståhlberg, and Antonio Medina Garcia.

In the first part of the tournament Keres beat Panno in a variation of the Najdorf Sicilian. Since all three players from Argentina intended to use that opening as Black, they had little time to find a new way to play.

Here's the Keres vs. Panno game.

Paul Keres vs. Oscar Panno, Gothenburg Interzonal 1955

1.e4 c5 2.Nf3 d6 3.d4 cxd4 4.Nxd4 Nf6 5.Nc3 a6

Keres wrote: "The variation in the Sicilian Defense chosen by Black here was very popular at Gothenburg and new methods of development were discovered, both for White and for Black. In the present game White employs a continuation that is nowadays very well known but was practically new territory at Gothenburg."

6.Bg5 e6 7.f4

In 1955 the popular move was 7.Qf3.

7...Qb6 8.Qd2 Nc6

8...Qxb2 is the critical move, but since the position after 8.Qd2 was first played in 1954 in the game Nezhmetdinov vs. Shcherbakov (it was drawn), the whole thing was pretty much unknown. Daring to chop by 8...Qxb2 against an attacker like Keres would probably feel like suicide to a positional player like Panno. Thus, Panno avoided it. I will add that a few rounds later Fuderer tried this same line against Keres and, instead of Panno's 8... Nc6, he braved 8...Qxb2. Unfortunately Black lost in eighteen moves!

9.0-0 Qxd4 10.Qxd4 Nxd4 11.Rxd4 Nd7 12.Be2 h6 13.Bh4 g5 14.fxg5 Ne5 15.Na4 Be7 16.Nb6 Rb8 17.Bg3 hxg5 18.Rhd1 f6 19.c4 0-0 20.R4d2 f5 21.c5 f4 22.cxd6 Bxd6 23.Rxd6 fxg3 24.hxg3 Rf7 25.Kb1 Rc7 26.Rd8+ Kg7 27.Rc1 Nc6 28.e5 Kg6 29.Bd3+ Kf7 30.Rh8 Ke7 31.Bg6, 1-0 since 32.Re8 mate was threatened.

To Live or Die!

After this blow, and after the Argentinians realized that the Russians would all play the new (and apparently very powerful) 7.f4 (it was also first played in 1954), they understood that they needed to come up with something themselves.

On their off day they desperately looked for another Najdorf line that would suit their tastes, and when they realized that Pilnik had tried (after 7.f4) 7...Be7 8.Qf3 h6 9.Bh4 g5 in an earlier game in 1955 against Friðrik Ólafsson (White won!), the Argentinian players decided that they could fix what went wrong in the Ólafsson game. After hours and hours of analysis they walked away in confidence, hoping that someone would walk into their opening trap.

What they didn't know was something extremely bizarre would occur, which was given the name: The Argentinian Tragedy!

The line that both sides would live or die on!

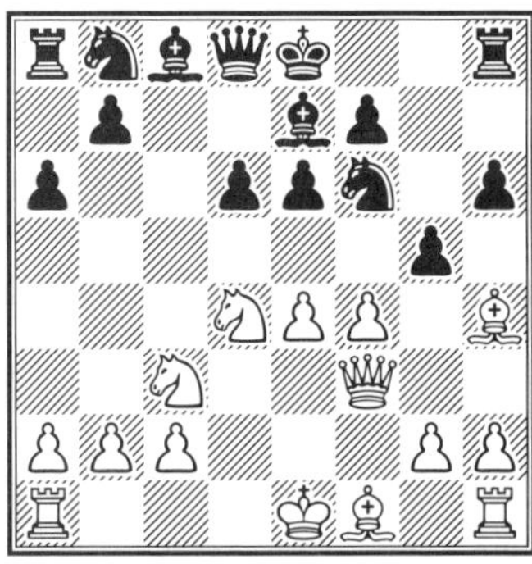

1.e4 c5 2.Nf3 d6 3.d4 cxd4 4.Nxd4 Nf6 5.Nc3 a6 6.Bg5 e6 7.f4 Be7 8.Qf3 h6 9.Bh4 g5

Geller wrote (in his wonderful book, *Application of Chess Theory*):[1]

> Several times in my career situations have occurred which are known by the name of 'twin games'. This was the case when in the nineteenth USSR Championship two games were played, between Geller vs. Flohr, and Petrosian vs. Smyslov, which up to a certain point were identical.
>
> In one of the rounds of the 1956 USSR vs. Yugoslavia match the games Geller vs. Karaklajić and Averbakh vs. Ivkov coincided, and at the international tournament in Budapest in 1973 the same happened in Geller vs. Karpov and Hort vs. Hecht.
>
> Finally, the present game had simultaneously two 'twin brothers': Keres vs. Najdorf and Spassky vs. Pilnik—a unique instance in the history of chess! Subsequently it received the name of the "Argentinian Tragedy."
>
> In twin games it is in principle more advantageous to occupy the second position, since it is possible to introduce corrections using the experience of one's neighbor. Unfortunately it has never worked out that way: it has always been me who has had to commit himself first. Sometimes this was provoked by an urge to solve the problems of the position myself, sometimes because I learned of the existence of the 'twins' later than my colleagues.
>
> At times I had to pay for the 'haste' (against Flohr and Karaklajić), whereas my neighbors, Petrosian and Averbakh, achieved more. In the present game, on the other hand, priority was rewarded by a quicker win than in the other games.

One of the "twins" that Geller referred to was a later round in the Gothenburg tournament when Keres was White against Najdorf, Spassky was White against Pilnik, and Geller was White against Panno. The Argentinian players were delighted since they were sure that at least one of the Soviet players would walk into their analysis. As it turned out, ALL three Soviet players entered the opening trap!

So what occurred? The position after **9...g5** appeared on all three boards at the same time, and as all three players reached the position after **10...Nfd7**, Spassky and Keres pondered whether or not to sacrifice on move eleven, while Geller did it quite quickly.

And from that moment on, Spassky and Keres simply watched Geller's board and copied everything he did!

Efim Geller vs. Oscar Panno, Gothenburg Interzonal 1955

1.e4 c5 2.Nf3 d6 3.d4 cxd4 4.Nxd4 Nf6 5.Nc3 a6 6.Bg5 e6 7.f4 Be7 8.Qf3 h6 9.Bh4 g5

[Geller]: "This advance is the idea of the defense worked out by the Argentinian players. They wanted, by exchanging the f4-pawn, to obtain the

1 Efim Geller, trans. by Ken Neat, *Application of Chess Theory*. London: Everyman, 1984.

eternal square e5 for a Knight, which in their opinion, should compensate for White's superior development."

10.fxg5 Nfd7 11.Nxe6 fxe6 12.Qh5+ Kf8

[Geller]: "And here something unexpected occurred. The point was that at this moment Spassky and Keres were still deliberating over whether to sacrifice the Knight on e6, and their opponents Pilnik and Najdorf were observing our game and animatedly discussing something. Then Najdorf came up to me and very brusquely, interrupting my thoughts, declared: 'Your game is lost; all this has been analyzed by us!'"

13.Bb5!!

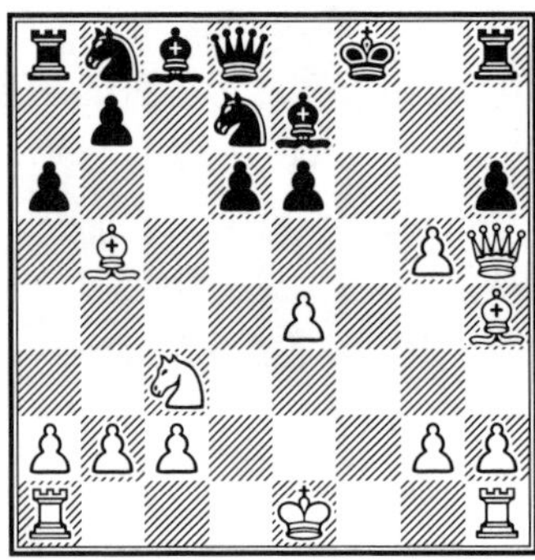

[Geller]: "Aimed indirectly against the future black Knight at e5, on which Black's entire system of defense is based. The quiet 12.Be2 or 12.Bd3 would have allowed him after 13...Ne5 14.0-0+ Kg7 15.Bg3 to support the Knight at e5 with his other Knight via 15...Nbc6. But now White will take on c6, then on e5, and will give mate!"

13...Ne5 14.Bg3!

Let's have Geller tell us why 14.Bg3 was so strong

[Geller]: "In their preparations the Argentinians had assumed that after 14.0-0+ Kg8! 15.Bg3 hxg5 White's attack would misfire. They overlooked that, after the move order employed in the game, 14...Kg8 fails to 15.Bxe5 and 16.Qg6+, while 14...Kg7 could have been met by 15.Bxe5+ dxe5 16.0-0 Qg8 17.Be8, etc.

"Incidentally, Najdorf and Pilnik awaited the development of events in our game, saw that things were bad for Black, and diverged from their prepared analysis by playing 13...Kg7. This merely enabled them to prolong their resistance."

14...Bxg5 15.0-0 Ke7 16.Bxe5 Qb6+ 17.Kh1 dxe5 18.Qxf7+ Kd6 19.Rad1+ Qd4 20.Rxd4+ exd4 21.e5+ Kc5 22.Qc7+ Nc6 23.Bxc6, 1-0.

A possible continuation: 23...bxc6 (23...dxc3 24.b4+ [24.Bxb7+ and 24.Be8+ also mate in 4] 24...Kc4 25.Bb5+ Kxb4 26.Rb1+ Ka3 37.Qa5 mate) 24.Qa5+ Kc4 25.b3 mate.

Here's what happened to Keres:

Paul Keres vs. Miguel Najdorf, Gothenburg Interzonal 1955

1.e4 c5 2.Nf3 d6 3.d4 cxd4 4.Nxd4 Nf6 5.Nc3 a6 6.Bg5 e6 7.f4 Be7 8.Qf3 h6 9.Bh4 g5 10.fxg5 Nfd7 11.Nxe6 fxe6 12.Qh5+ Kf8 13.Bb5!! Kg7 14.0-0 Ne5 15.Bg3! Ng6 16.gxh6+ Rxh6 17.Rf7+ Kxf7 18.Qxh6 axb5 19.Rf1+ Ke8 20.Qxg6+ Kd7 21.Rf7 Nc6 22.Nd5! Rxa2

Keres: "It is interesting to observe that, up to now, the game was gone exactly as in the Spassky vs. Pilnik encounter. Here Spassky played 23.h3, rekindling the threat of 24.Nxe7 followed by 25.Bh4, but there is of course no noticeable difference between the two pawn moves. Black was still faced by the same difficulties wwwthat were present on the previous move."

23.h4 Qh8 24.Nxe7 Nxe7 25.Qg5, 1-0.

The same continuation (with White's pawn on h3 instead of h4) in the Spassky game could still have occurred, but Najdorf had enough and resigned.

And here's Spassky's game:

Boris Spassky vs. Herman Pilnik, Gothenburg Interzonal 1955

1.e4 c5 2.Nf3 d6 3.d4 cxd4 4.Nxd4 Nf6 5.Nc3 a6 6.Bg5 e6 7.f4 Be7 8.Qf3 h6 9.Bh4 g5 10.fxg5 Nfd7 11.Nxe6 fxe6 12.Qh5+ Kf8 13.Bb5!! Kg7 14.0-0 Ne5 15.Bg3! Ng6 16.gxh6+ Rxh6 17.Rf7+ Kxf7 18.Qxh6 axb5 19.Rf1+ Ke8 20.Qxg6+ Kd7 21.Rf7 Nc6 22.Nd5! Rxa2

22...exd5 23.Qxd6+ Ke8 24.Qg6 dxe4 (24...Kd7 25.exd5 Na5 [25... Rxa2 26.dxc6+ bxc6 27.Bd6] 26.d6 among other moves.) 25.Rg7+ Kd7 26.Qd6+ Ke8 27.Rg8+ Kf7 (27...Bf8 28.Rxf8 mate) 28.Qg6 mate.

23.h3

In his game, Keres played 23.h4, which led to the same basic position.

23...Qh8 24.Nxe7 Nxe7 25.Qg5 and here Najdorf resigned to Keres.

Pilnik decided to continue the game:

25...Ra1+ 26.Kh2 Qd8 27.Qxb5+ Kc7 28.Qc5+ Kb8 29.Bxd6+ Ka8 30.Bxe7 Ra5 31.Qb4, 1-0.

After this the variation was named the Gothenburg Variation.

Fischer Finds a Draw

This line seemed to have been refuted and everyone avoided it. However, in 1958 the great Svetozar Gligorić was shocked when a fifteen-year-old Bobby Fischer walked right into the "refuted" line!

As it turned out, Fischer had analyzed the Geller game to death and decided that 13...Rh7 would, with best play, lead to a forced draw. Here's the game:

Svetozar Gligorić vs. Robert Fischer, Portoroz Interzonal 1958

1.e4 c5 2.Nf3 d6 3.d4 cxd4 4.Nxd4 Nf6 5.Nc3 a6 6.Bg5 e6 7.f4 Be7 8.Qf3 h6 9.Bh4 g5 10.fxg5 Nfd7 11.Nxe6 fxe6 12.Qh5+ Kf8 13.Bb5!! Rh7! 14.Qg6

14.0-0+ Kg8 15.g6 Rg7 16.Rf7 (16.Qxh6 Ne5 17.Bxe7Qxe7 favors Black, who has conquered the e5-square for the Knight.) 16...Bxh4 17.Qxh6 Rxf7 18.gxf7+ Kxf7 19.Qh7+ Ke8 20.Qh5+ Kf8 21.Rf1+ Bf6 22.Qh6+ Ke7 23.Qh7+ Kf8 24.Qh6+ Kf7 25.Qh7+ Ke8 26.Qg8+ Ke7 27.Qh7+ with a draw by perpetual check.

14...Rf7 15.Qxh6+ Kg8 16.Qg6+ Rg7 17.Qxe6+ Kh8 18.Bxd7 Nxd7 19.0-0-0 Ne5 20.Qd5 Bg4 21.Rdf1 Bxg5+ 22.Bxg5 Qxg5+ 23.Kb1 Qe7 24.Qd2 Be6 25.g3 Rd8 26.Rf4 Qg5 27.Qf2 Kg8 28.Rd1 Rf7 29.b3 Qe7 30.Qd4 Ng6 31.Rxf7 Qxf7 32.Qe3, ½-½.

And here's a modern grandmaster game that proves, once and for all, that 13...Rh7 does indeed lead to an exciting draw:

Sergei Zhigalko vs. Eltaj Safarli, Nakhchivan 2012

1.e4 c5 2.Nf3 d6 3.d4 cxd4 4.Nxd4 Nf6 5.Nc3 a6 6.Bg5 e6 7.f4 Be7 8.Qf3 h6 9.Bh4 g5 10.fxg5 Nfd7 11.Nxe6 fxe6 12.Qh5+ Kf8 13.Bb5!! Rh7! 14.0-0+ Kg8 15.g6 Rg7 16.Rf7 Bxh4 17.Qxh6 Rxf7 18.gxf7+ Kxf7 19.Rf1+ Bf6 20.Qh7+ Ke8 21.Qg6+ Kf8 22.e5 dxe5 23.Ne4 Qb6+ 24.Kh1 axb5 25.Nxf6 Ke7 26.Qh7+ Kd8 27.Qg8+ Kc7 28.Ne8+ Kd8

28...Kc6?? 29.Qxe6+ Kc5 30.Qe7+ Kc4 31.Rd1! Qc5 32.Qh4+ Qd4 33.Rxd4+ exd4 34.Qg5 Kb4 35.Nd6 and Black gets mated in a few moves.

29.Nd6+ Kc7 30.Ne8+ Kd8 31.Ng7+, ½-½.

Returning to the 1955 Gothenburg Interzonal Tournament, Bronstein (15 points) was undefeated with 10 wins and 10 draws. Keres was second (13½ points), and Panno was third (13 points). fourth was Petrosian (12½). Geller and Szabó tied for fifth/sixth (12), and Filip, Pilnik, and Spassky tied for seventh/ninth (11 points). Pachman and Ilivitsky tied for tenth/eleventh (10½). Guimard and Najdorf took twelfth/thirteenth (9½ points). Rabar and Fuderer tied for fourteenth/fifteenth (9 points). Unzicker was sixteenth (8½). Ståhlberg and Bisguier shared seventeenth/eighteenth (8 points). And Garcia, Śliwa, and Donner all tied for nineteenth/twenty-first (5½ points).

3

IN MEMORIAM TO SOME FRIENDS

A Legendary Chess Zen Master

When I was nineteen and living in San Francisco, a friend and I would travel across the bay to Berkeley and visit the Hare Krishna temple. Were we into the Hare Krishna? No, not at all. But every evening they offered free (very tasty!) food, and when you are broke and starving, you are willing to listen to any blather if there's food at the end of the rainbow.

The friend that came with me was Steve Brandwein, who, after we left the building would always say, "I came, I ate, and I left."

Returning to the Haight, we would play dozens of blitz games and analyze openings. Then Steve would rush home and do what he loved the most—read. Steve was the most passionate reader I've ever seen. He often knew more about things he wasn't interested in than people who studied that particular subject in great depth. His forte, though, was world history.

Going to the library, he borrowed books on chess history, Russian history, Chinese history, the history of the Vikings—he was the go-to guy if you had questions on just about anything. After reading a stack, he returned the books to the library and immediately took out more! Visiting whatever hovel he happened to be staying at, I was struck by how little he cared about money or possessions. He had a small mattress (surrounded by several piles of library books), a few old clothes (but always crisp and clean), and that's about it.

Steve Brandwein (1942-2015) was a remarkably strong player who understood chess better than many grandmasters I knew (he was an amazing analyst with a deep understanding of every facet of chess, and his comments when we looked at games made me far stronger than I would have been without him), a world-class blitz chess player (he would dominate everyone but a few super grandmasters at five-minute chess, and even then he drew lots of blood), a master at Scrabble, and (as I mentioned before) he blazed through endless books on just about every possible subject.

One might say, "He's your friend, so you're pouring on the praise! Get real and tell us the truth."

Okay, here are a couple other voices that had the pleasure of meeting and playing Steve.

National Master Andy Sacks wrote:

> In the late 1960s and early '70s, several apartments, duplexes, and rented houses in Berkeley were home to strong chess players, and their residences often served as meeting places and "crash pads" for their fellow competitors. Speed chess was the order of the day, and quite often all night.
>
> On a trip to the Bay Area in one of those early '70s years—you must forgive my temporal uncertainty here and naturally it is completely unrelated to any illegal drug consumption during that most conservative of periods and places—I found myself with my dear and recently deceased friend Alan Pollard "vacationing" at one of those chess dens. Dennis Fritzinger was present, and, I believe, one of the hosts. In and out, day and night, were the likes of Alan Benson, Frank Thornally, Dennis Waterman, Frank Street, and other young experts and masters of our generation.
>
> One mid-afternoon the totally unexpected occurred: one of the players brought over Steve Brandwein (whom many of us had always referred to as "Brandywine" for some reason). He was in California somehow (perhaps on chess business, perhaps not) and, with very little persuasion necessary, was ready to join in the play. We took turns playing him and eagerly spectating. No stakes were involved.
>
> If you have any previous familiarity with the legendary Brandwein, you already know the result. Our group was composed of players whose ratings and actual speed chess strengths ranged from about 2225 to 2375. We were out of our league. No one was able to nick him for even a draw. However, much more interesting than the sporting result, I thought, was the playing demeanor and style of our distinguished visitor.
>
> His bearing was remarkably matter-of-fact while playing, and his moves were made extremely rapidly and with an air of nonchalance, even unconcern. It was rather eerie. Often it seemed as if he had seen all these positions before

> and was reacting mechanically, from a type of memory that today we associate with chess-playing computer programs. He was always significantly ahead on time after fifteen to twenty moves.

Andy has hit the nail on the head, and done so beautifully. Steve would seem bored when he played, and at some point in every game he would stand up (with his clock ticking) and calmly step around and sit on the other side of his chair. We eventually came to call this the "Brandwein shuffle."

Bored or not, he would reach out and quietly (seemingly slowly!) make one move after another, and then your flag would fall or your position would simply melt into a losing blob.

Grandmaster Larry Kaufman (interviewed by Jim Eade[1]) admitted that Brandwein played an important role in his game:

Eade: Who were your biggest influences?

Kaufman: Fischer was my biggest influence in my teens, although the book that influenced me the most was Reshevsky's (*How Chess Games are Won*). On a personal level I would say Steve Brandwein.

Eade: How so?

Kaufman: When I was a college student at MIT, Steve lived nearby and we became friends. I was very impressed with his intellect, knowledge, and memory; he was (and presumably still is) a very brilliant man. At the time I was a high expert while Steve was already retired from regular tournament play with a 2300 rating, which was pretty good back in the mid 1960s. At blitz chess he was much better still, certainly way beyond my level. He taught me a lot about chess (and other things too), but the biggest impact was a twenty game match we played. Due to the rating disparity we agreed to a 2-1 time handicap; I think Steve took thirty minutes to my hour. I thought this would make for a fair match, but I was soon to realize how wrong this was. After nineteen games I was still seeking my first win; the score was 10 wins for Steve and 9 draws. Finally by some miracle I won the final game. Just a few weeks later, I was the American Open champion! This shows both how much I learned from this match and how strong Steve must have been to score so well against me giving me time odds; my own rating soon hit 2300.

I played many other training matches over the years with various masters, but this was the only one I lost. My match victims in these matches included Bill Hook, Mark Diesen, Larry Gilden, and Arnold Denker. There was also a drawn match in my very early days with Frank Street, who soon became the nation's second Black chess master.

---

1 Interview for U.S. Chess Trust, 2008.

> Keep in mind that 2300 in the early '60s would be 2500 now.
>
> Brandwein is mentioned in the Stefan Fatsis book, *Word Freak*, and was referenced in a *USA Today* review of that book as follows:
>
> Midway through his quest to master Scrabble, author Stefan Fatsis meets "game-room legend" Steve Brandwein, a well-read bookie and expert at Scrabble and chess who refuses to play in tournaments. He's the epitome, Fatsis writes, "of the game-playing mind and character: brilliant, unconventional, and unapologetic."
>
> Looking at some chess.com forums (which happened to mention Brandwein), I noted that some ignorant folk viewed Steve as a hustler. This is completely false. A hustler pretends he's not very good in the hope of fleecing you of your money. Steve only played if you approached him and insisted on a game, and if you were lucky enough to get a 'yes' from him you would know beforehand that you had absolutely no chance to win. In effect, you were paying him for a lesson.

Born in Boston, Brandwein made his way to New York in the mid-1960s and eventually found himself (more or less permanently) in San Francisco. San Francisco was the perfect place for a Zen-like chess god, and as his legend grew, people sought him out in the hope of playing one single game with him or getting lessons. I remember one young man that kept following him around begging for chess lessons.

Steve said "no" and the guy would ask again, day after day, week after week, month after month. Finally Steve said yes and the young man sat down with his chess hero. Steve cleared the chessboard and said, "If you want to truly understand chess, you have to create a relationship with the board. Once you understand the board, moving the pieces to their best squares will be easy. I want you to look at the board for one hour and then we'll take it from there."

The young man did as he was told, putting his heart and soul into glaring at the board, demanding it to share its secrets. Then, after the hour was up, he looked for his teacher, but Steve had left the building a few minutes after the lesson started.

In one way, Steve was the ultimate Jewish intellectual—a man that lived, ate, and breathed knowledge. He was a man that didn't care for wealth or fame or detailed relationships or anything to do with ego. He simply glided in and out of the Haight or the Mechanics' Institute (the oldest chess club in the United States), and then vanished (in most cases rushing back to his beloved books).

In my early Haight years, a man named Jim Buff (a friend of Fischer's, now deceased) was renting a San Francisco flat in the Avenues—521 Third, to be precise. A whole book could be written about 521 Third and the comings and goings of famous players and the eye-popping super fun insanity that was the

[left] Steve Brandwein at thirteen, 1955; [above] handling the wall board for Torre vs. Tal.

norm rather than the exception. A lot of people (many with very high ratings) moved in and out (I also lived there for a time), and in 1981 the highest rated of all stayed for a short while—Bobby Fischer!

During Fischer's stay, Brandwein was also living at Buff's and he and Fischer played dozens of blitz games. Fischer won 80% of the games, but the 20% he didn't kept Bobby interested. Note, that Brandwein's performance was much better than many of the grandmasters who played blitz with Fischer.

Longtime *Boston Globe* columnist Harold Dondis wrote of Brandwein in his column of October 11, 1964:

> Stephen Brandwein, winner of the James Burgess trophy, is the highest placed Massachusetts player in the U.S. Open. He has favored us with a game annotated by him from that event. Brandwein is a unique figure in chess circles. He plays with airy unconcern, being apparently more taken with getting the game over with than winning. He plays at amazing speed and will upon the vaguest pretense of equilibrium, either offer or accept a draw. He has not lost a game for longer than we can remember.
>
> Against John Collins in the U.S. Open, Brandwein accepted a draw with a superior position and with almost an hour ahead on his clock! He has an enormous knowledge of the openings, gained not so much from study but from genuine interest in other peoples' games. Either there is method in his casualness or Brandwein is one of the more gifted players in the United States.
>
> In the game below Brandwein makes a succession of three bad moves out of five, leaves a pawn *en prise*, saddles himself with a backward pawn but of course wins the game.

Before showing the game, allow me to add something. Only three or four Brandwein games exist (hopefully some of his opponents from the early '60s will share some with us). My guess is that he simply tore up the scoresheet after the game ended—in what would have been a typical Brandwein act.

What makes the following game particularly interesting is that he actually wrote a few comments. All of these comments were negative: "Crushes me" and "I didn't see the pawn was *en prise*."

Glancing at the written score, I saw Steve's comments and was quite sad. Why is he annotating a bad game? It was only after I looked at the game that I realized that Steve was doing what Steve always did; he was putting himself down and thus minimizing his complete domination over his hapless foe. Remember: Steve didn't like praise, and he didn't like people fawning over him. He was, in many ways, a man without an ego. In the following game I've included Steve's comments in my analysis.

Neil McKelvie vs. Steve Brandwein, U.S. Open 1964

1.d4 Nf6 2.c4 g6 3.Nc3 Bg7 4.e4 d6 5.Be2 O-O 6.f4 c5 7.Nf3 cxd4 8.Nxd4 Nbd7 9.Be3 a6 10.O-O e5!

[Brandwein]: "Probably bad."

Actually, it's one of Black's best choices. It's funny how Steve immediately insults his own move, knowing that it's actually quite good!

11.Nc2 exf4

[Brandwein]: "Afraid of f5, g4 etc."

12.Bxf4 Ne5

The most natural move in the world. 12...Re8 is probably best, with complete equality. However, the game gets a bit dull after that. Steve probably wanted to complicate matters.

13.Qd2

13.c5 Be6 14.cxd6 Ne8 15.Nd4 Qxd6 16.Nxe6 Qxe6, =.

13...Be6 14.b3 b5!

[Brandwein]: "Very bad."

Once again Steve insists that everything he does is wrong. The reality (which he was well aware of) is that 14...b5 is the best move.

15.c5!?

[Brandwein]: "Crushes me."

Steve once again announces that he's doomed, though I'm sure he expected the move and thought it led to active play for Black. The alternative is 15.cxb5 axb5 16.Bxb5 when Black has several good moves, like 16...Qb6+, 16...Nxe4, and even 16...Neg4!? 17.h3 Qb6+ 18.Kh1 Nh5 19.hxg4 Nxf4

20.Rxf4 Bxc3 21.Qxc3 Qxb5 with equal chances since 22.Nd4 Qe5 23.Qd2 Bxg4 24.Rxg4?? Qh5+ picks up the Rook.

15...b4!!

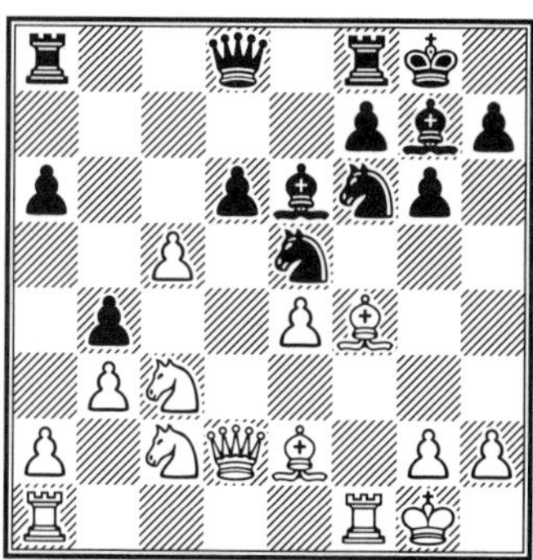

[Brandwein]: "I didn't see the pawn was *en prise* when I pushed it (whoever heard of a Knight on c2?), but it seems to be the best chance."

LOL!!! He didn't see it was hanging. Yeah, sure. The fact is that 15...b4 is simply a brilliant move. Black could have played the simple 15...Rc8 16.cxd6 Qb6+ 17.Kh1 Qc5 with a very nice position, but his 15... b4 is even better.

16.Nxb4 Qa5

Natural and perfectly playable, though 16... dxc5 was probably best since 17.Qxd8 Rfxd8 18. Nxa6 Nd3 (18...Nh5 is better) is extremely comfortable for Black thanks to his very active pieces.

17.Bxe5

White has so many possible continuations that it's a bit overwhelming. White's capture on e5 is probably best since it blocks the g7-bishop's long diagonal. Other moves:

17.Qxd6 (17.cxd6 Qxb4 18.Bxe5 Nxe4 19.Nxe4 Qxd2 20.Nxd2 Bxe5 is easy for Black.) 17...Qxb4 18.Bxe5 Ne8 19.Nd5 Nxd6 (Interesting is 19...Qd4+!? 20.Bxd4 Bxd4 21.Kh1 Nxd6 22.cxd6 Bxa1 23.Ne7+ Kg7 24.Rxa1 Rad8 25.Rd1 Rd7 26.Kg1 [26.Bxa6 Rfd8 27.e5?? Rxe7; 26.e5 f6] 26...f6 27.Nc6 Rc8 and Black is okay.) 20.Nxb4 Bxe5 21.cxd6 Bd4+! (Chasing White's King to the side of the board. 21...Bxd6 is also playable.) 22.Kh1 Bxa1 23.Rxa1 Rfc8 24.Nxa6 Rc6 25.Rd1 Rcxa6 26.Bxa6 Rxa6 27.d7 Bxd7 28.Rxd7 Rxa2 29.Kg1 Re2 and the game should be drawn.

17...dxe5 18.Nd3 Rfd8 19.Qb2

19.Rac1 Rd4 followed by 20...Rad8 with mutual chances in a complicated game.

19...Rd4 20.b4 Qc7

20...Qd8 is also good.

21.a3

21.b5 looks imposing since taking on b5 allows a Knight fork by Nxb5. However, 21...Qa5 (21...Bc4!? might be even better.) 22.b6 Rb8! when threats like 23...Nd7 hitting c5 and 23...Nxe4 assure Black good chances.

21...Rb8 22.Rad1

22.Nf2 Qxc5!

22...Nxe4 23.Nxe4 Rxe4 24.Nf2 Re3!

Threatening both 25...e4 and 25...Rb3.

25. Bxa6

White is a pawn up and he has three connected passed queenside pawns, but he's dead lost!

25...e4 26.Qc1 Rc3! 27.Qg5 h6 28.Qh4 Rxa3 29.b5

Loses a piece, but there wasn't a defense: 29.Be2 Re3! is even better than 29...Rxb4 30.Rd2 g5 leaves White material behind and paralyzed.

29.Rd6 fails to 29...Rxb4 30.Qd8+ Qxd8 31.Rxd8+ Kh7 32.Be2 Ra2 33.Bg4 f5 34.Bh3 Bd4 and White can resign.

29...e3 30.Ne4

White now finds himself with catastrophic material loss. The rest was easy.

30...e2!

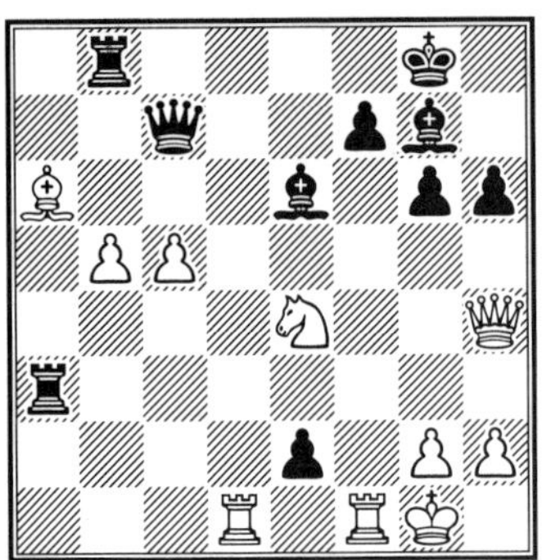

31.b6 exf1=Q+ 32.Bxf1 Qc8 33.Bb5 Bf5 34.c6 Qe6, 0-1.

A fantastic game by Black, and a very instructive illustration of the power of active pieces working together.

Most of Steve's games have vanished, but here's one that remains which I'll give for history's sake:

Denis Strenzwilk vs. Steve Brandwein, U.S. Open 1964

1.e4 Nf6 2.Qe2 e5 3.Nf3 Nc6 4.g3 Bc5 5.Bg2 d6 6.c3 Bg4 7.d3 h6 8.Be3 Qd7 9.h3 Bxf3 10.Bxf3 Bxe3 11.Qxe3 0-0 12.Nd2 d5 13.exd5 Nxd5 14.Qc5 Nde7 15.Be2 Rad8 16.Qc4 Kh8 17.Qe4 f5 18.Qg2 e4 19.d4 Nd5 20.0-0 Rde8 21.Bc4 f4 22.Rfe1 f3 23.Qh1 e3 24.Nxf3 Qf5 25.Be2 exf2+ 26.Kxf2 Ne3 27.Rac1 Nc2 28.Red1 Qe4 29.Rd2 Qe3+ 30.Kg2 Rxf3 31.Qd1 Rf2+ 32.Kh1 Qxg3, 0-1.

Over the years, Steve and I hung out a lot and we probably played several hundred blitz games. I remember asking him why he didn't play in tournaments anymore (he had regularly played in tournament between 1961 and 1965, and then he quit), and why he hadn't become a history professor (his favorite subject aside from chess). He looked at me with absolutely no emotion and quietly said, "I'm a bum, I've always been a bum, and I'll always be a bum."

Steve died on December 12, 2015. He was one of a kind, gentle, unbelievably well educated, a master of many games, deeply philosophical, and incredibly intelligent. Such men are extremely rare, and I'll certainly miss him.

Dave (aka Bandog)

To me, dying in battle is eminently preferable to a helpless demise in a hospital bed, hooked up to tubes and waiting for the inevitable. Ancient warriors relished a noble death with a sword in one hand and a song (or battle cry) on one's lips. And in old Japan, a conscious death was of great importance, which led many to create a "death poem" and recite it as one's final moments ticked away.

A great example of the death poem was seen when Ota Dokan (1432-1486), a scholar of military arts and a poet, was fatally stabbed while bathing. Most modern day men would scream piteously and perish in a state of fear and hysteria. Dokan-san reacted differently. He stood up, clutched the murder weapon while it was still sheathed in his body, and quietly said:

"Had I not known
that I was dead already
I would have mourned
my loss of life."

And then he died.

I've always entertained the romantic notion that chess players are also warriors. We wage war on a battlefield of sixty-four squares and (especially if we lose!) suffer serious physical and emotional trauma. Wouldn't it be appropriate then, that chessboard warriors also meet their end while in chess combat?

There are many instances of this happening. I remember (at thirty years of age) playing a tournament in Seattle and looking at a gentleman of seventy that appeared to be in far better physical condition than I was. I thought, "I wish I was in shape like that guy is."

Imagine my surprise when, two hours later, I spotted this poor man on the floor surrounded by paramedics. He had suffered a massive heart attack while in the middle of a tournament game.

The most stirring story of a chess player dying with his boots on concerned world-class postal player and renowned chess teacher Cecil Purdy. He was playing in an over-the-board event and was up an exchange in his game. It was clear that he was eventually going to win, but his well-wishers' smiles soon turned to horror when he fell off his chair and collapsed in a heap on the ground. His brother (who was also playing at the event) rushed to his side and Cecil whispered something into his ear. Then he died. His final words were not what one might imagine: such as, "Tell my wife I love her," or, "The gold is hidden under the bedroom floorboards." No, this is a chess player and so his last thoughts were about chess. His dying words were: "I have a win, but it will take time!"

My friend Dave and I often talked about death, but he wasn't enthused with the notion at all. In fact, he was, at fifty-five years of age, a bit of a hypochondriac. On the morning of August 3, 2007 Dave went to his doctor for a checkup and was told that his health was excellent. He called his wife and told her that all was well, and she told him she would be back from work a bit later than usual.

That evening, Dave did what he often did to unwind: he logged onto the ICC (his handle was Bandog) and played chess. This is his game:

Bandog vs. Vague1 ICC August 3, 2007

Time Control: 3-minutes each and 12-second increment per move.

1.d4 g6 2.e4 Bg7 3.Nc3 d6 4.f4 c6 5.Nf3 h6 6.Bc4 Nf6 7.0–0 Qb6 8.Kh1 Ng4 9.h3 h5 10.f5 gxf5 11.exf5 Bxf5 12.Bxf7+ Kxf7 13.Ng5+ Kg6 14.Rxf5

Dave is easily winning.

14...Kxf5

This leads to a quick death.

15.Qf1+

15.Qf3+ mates one move sooner.

15...Kg6 and here Black waited for the axe to fall.

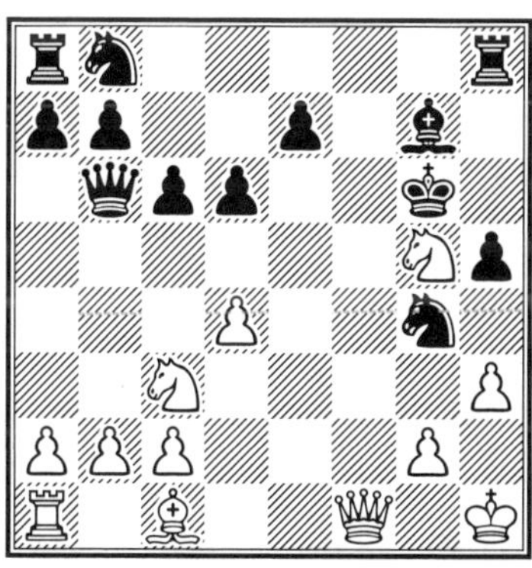

It doesn't take a genius to see 16.Qf7+ Kh6 17.Ne6+ followed by 18.Qxg7 mate. White had 1 minute and 33 seconds left on his clock (ample time to wipe his opponent out) but he never moved again and—I'm sure to Black's considerable surprise—White's time ran out and he forfeited the game.

Two hours later Dave's wife got home and found him dead on the floor, the diagrammed position on his computer screen. Evidently, he passed away before his hand could reach out and make the final mating sequence. His opponent couldn't have imagined what was transpiring as he waited for White's move. Dave's time, metaphorically and literally, ran out. Dying with his boots on, Dave, like Purdy, had a win, but he didn't have anymore time.

John Grefe — Talent Isn't Enough

My relationship with International Master John Grefe was complex, with many ups and downs. I met him two days after I arrived in San Francisco. At that time I was a penniless nineteen-year-old chess professional who was sleeping on Dennis Waterman's floor.

To my surprise, Dennis told me that the new U.S. Champion, John Grefe, was going to be sharing the floor space with me! When he appeared, fresh from his U.S. Championship triumph, we shook hands and, in true "ignorant youth" fashion, I asked, "Can I show you one of my games?"

His answer, the first words he ever spoke to me, taught me a quick lesson about chess etiquette: "Where's your money?"

After Grefe's well deserved slap-down (he was 100% right) we got along just fine. He showed me some of his games from the Championship, we hung out, and (a couple months later) we ended up facing off for first place in my first ever Berkeley tournament:

Silman vs. John Grefe, Berkeley 1974

1.e4 c5 2.Nf3 d6 3.d4 cxd4 4.Nxd4 Nf6 5.Nc3 a6 6.Bg5 e6 7.f4 Be7 8.Qf3 Qc7 9.0-0-0 Nbd7 10.Bd3 h6 11.Qh3 Rg8 12.Bxf6 Nxf6 13.Nf3 e5 14.f5 Bd7 15.g4 b5 16.Qg2 Qb7 17.g5 b4 18.Nd5 Nxd5 19.exd5 hxg5 20.Be4 Rc8 21.Nxe5 dxe5 22.d6 Qb6 23.dxe7 Kxe7 24.Qxg5+ f6 25.Qg3 Bc6 26.Bxc6 Qxc6 27.Qb3 Qc4 28.Rhg1 Qxb3 29.axb3 Rcd8 30.Rxd8 Kxd8 31.Kd2 Ke7 32.Ke3 Kf7 33.Rd1 Ke7 34.Rg1, ½-½.

A great result for me since Grefe was much, much stronger than I was. How strong was he? Here's a list of some of his better-known victims:

Arthur Bisguier, Edmar Mednis, William Martz, Walter Browne, Donald Byrne, Pal Benko, Norman Weinstein, Kim Commons, Lawrence Gilden, Tibor Weinberger, Sal Matera, Andrew Soltis, William Lombardy, Jack Peters, Jorge Szmetan, Eugenio Torre, Miguel Quinteros, Arhur Dake, Miguel Najdorf, Ron Henley, Lawrence Day, Samuel Reshevsky, Bernard Zuckerman, Dumitru Ghizdavu, Jim Tarjan, John Fedorowicz, Milan Vukcevich, Arnold Denker, Kamran Shirazi, Nick de Firmian, Yehuda Grünfeld, Utut Adianto, Lubomir Ftacnik, and the "hit list" goes on and on.

John's style was based on cutting edge opening play, powerful attacking mojo, and a magnificent tactical vision. He backed these things up with solid positional skills and good technique. So, how could such an obviously talented player fail to get the grandmaster title?

The fact is, that after winning the 1973 U.S. Championship (tied with Kavalek), he slowly but surely lost interest in the game. Gone was the deep preparation. Gone was the inner-fire that's needed to reach the highest heights. Though he continued to play, and remained a threat to anyone at any time, his results diminished as happens to any player once he stops treating the game seriously.

Over the years we had many adventures together, and butted heads more than once. We shared living space many times, many wonderful highs, and some difficult lows. As I age, I find the lows to be far more interesting than the highs (of course, at the time you experience it, this view is reversed!). We hadn't seen each other for quite a few years and I had hoped to get to San Francisco and, over an expensive meal that we never could have afforded in our glory/poverty days, have a long talk about our mutual experiences, lost friends, and lost opportunities. Sadly, that's not going to happen now. John Grefe died on Sunday, December 22, 2013.

The following game, where he wipes out Grandmaster Arnold Denker (Arnold was U.S. Champion in 1944 and 1946), shows just how hard it was to deal with Grefe's aggressive, and at times overwhelming, style.

John Grefe vs. Arnold Denker, Lone Pine 1979

1.e4 c6 2.d3 d5 3.Nd2 Qc7 4.f4

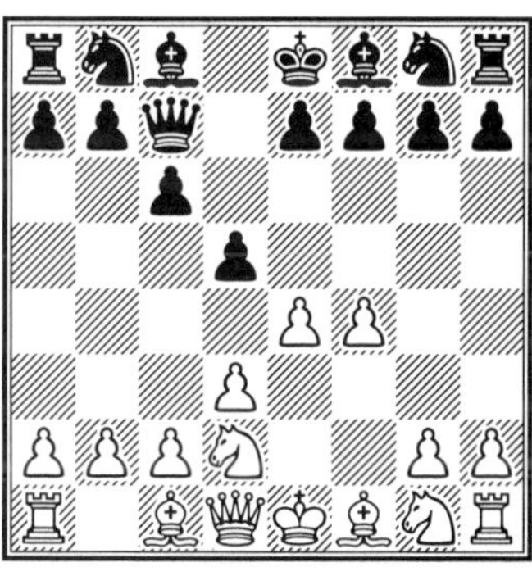

4...Qxf4 5.Ngf3 Nf6 6.Nb3 Qc7 7.e5 Ng4 8.d4 Bf5 9.Nh4 Bd7 10.Be2 Nh6 11.Bxh6 gxh6 12.0-0 Na6 13.Bxa6 bxa6 14.Nc5 e6 15.Qh5 Bc8 16.Rf6 Bxc5 17.dxc5 Rb8 18.Raf1 Rf8 19.Qxh6 Qxe5 20.Qxh7 Rxb2 21.Rxf7 Rxf7 22.Qg8+, 1-0.

In the following game Grefe outplayed the great Reshevsky in the opening and early middlegame, and then finished up with a series of perfect moves that simply swept his opponent off the board.

Samuel Reshevsky vs. John Grefe, U.S. Championship 1977

1.d4 Nf6 2.Nf3 e6 3.c4 b6 4.Nc3 Bb7 5.Bg5 h6 6.Bh4 g5 7.Bg3 Nh5 8.e3 Nxg3 9.hxg3 Bg7 10.Bd3 Nc6 11.g4 Qe7 12.a3 0-0-0 13.Qc2 h5 14.hxg5 g4 15.Nd2 f5 16.Ne2 Qg5 17.0-0-0 Rxh5 18.d5 Ne5 19.Nf4

John Grefe at Lone Pine. (Photo: Stella Monday, Courtesy of the Mechanics' Institute Chess Club Archives.)

Nxd3+ 20.Qxd3 Qf6 21.Qc2 Rxh1 22.Rxh1 Bh6 23.dxe6 dxe6 24.Rh2 Bxf4! 25.exf4 g3!

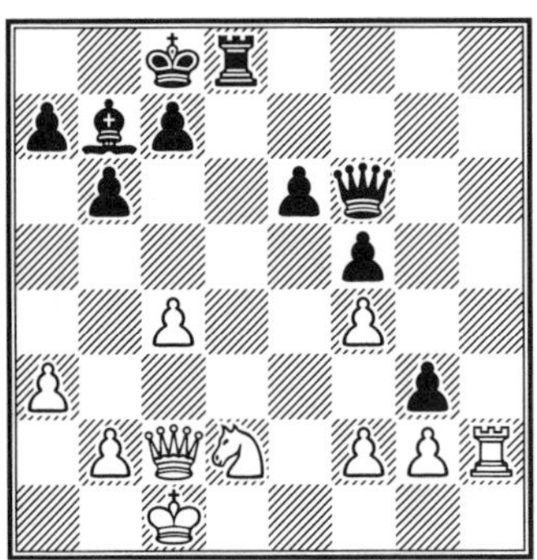

26.fxg3 Qd4! 27.Rh1 Bxg2 28.Re1 Qf2! 29.Qd1

29.Rxe6 Be4! 30.Qd1 (30.Nxe4 Qe1+) 30…Rxd2! 31.Qxd2 (31.Re8+ Kd7 32.Qxd2 Qxd2+ 33.Kxd2 Kxe8) 31…Qf1+ 32.Qd1 Qxc4+ 33.Kd2 Qxe6 and White should resign. The best defense is 29.Rd1 but after 29… Qxg3 30.Qc3 Qxf4 White's position is hopeless.

29…Bf3! 30.Rf1

30.Nxf3 Rxd1+; 30.Qxf3 Qxd2+ 31.Kb1 Qxe1+.

30…Rxd2!, 0-1.

Grandmaster Arthur Bisguier (1929-2017) was a feared attacking player for many decades but he struggled this entire game.

Arthur Bisguier vs. John Grefe, U.S. Championship 1973

1.c4 g6 2.e4 Bg7 3.d4 d6 4.Nc3 e5 5.Nf3 Nd7 6.g3 Ngf6 7.Bg2 0-0 8.0-0 c6 9.b3 Re8 10.Bb2 exd4 11.Nxd4 Nc5 12.Qc2 a5 13.Rad1 Qb6 14.Nde2

John Grefe

John Grefe was joint chess champion of the United States in 1973. He recently shared first place in the Australian Championships in Brisbane. For his performances in recent championships, John has been awarded the official title *International Master.*

a4 15.Nxa4 Nxa4 16.bxa4 Qb4 17.a3 Qxa4 18.Qc1 Qb3 19.Nf4 Ra4 20.Qa1 Nh5 21.Bxg7 Nxg7 22.Rxd6 Rxa3 23.Rd3 Rxa1 24.Rxb3 Ra4 25.Rc1 Rd8 26.Bf1 Kf8 27.f3 Ke7 28.Rd3 Rxd3 29.Nxd3 Ne6 30.Bh3 Ra3 31.Ne1 Nd4 32.Rd1

- 32.Bf1 Nxf3+ 33.Nxf3 Bxh3 wins.
- 32.Bxc8 Ne2+ 33.Kf1 Nxc1 when 34.Bxb7 Kd7 traps the Bishop!

32...Ne2+ 33.Kg2

33.Kf1 Nc3.

33...Ra2!

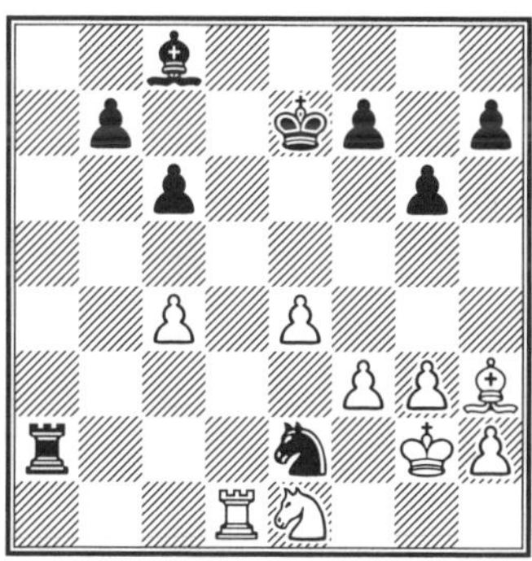

34.Bxc8 Nc3+ 35.Kg1 Nxd1 36.Bxb7 Kd7!, 0-1.

The Bishop is lost after ...Kc7.

Julius Loftsson (1941-2009) was a gentle, extremely nice man who had amazing positional skills, and he could outplay anyone if the game remained in calm, strategic waters. However, he was vulnerable (as Grefe demonstrates) if you managed to mix things up.

Julius Loftsson vs. John Grefe, Lone Pine 1971

1.d4 Nf6 2.c4 c5 3.d5 e5 4.Nc3 d6 5.e4 Be7 6.Nf3 0-0 7.Be2 Ne8 8.0-0 g6 9.a3 f5 10.exf5 gxf5 11.Ne1 Kh8 12.b4 b6 13.Bb2 Bf6 14.Qxd2 Rg8 15.f4 a6 16.bxc5 bxc5 17.fxe5 dxe5 18.Nd3 Qe7 19.Na4 Nd7 20.Qe3 Qg7 21.Rf2 Rb8 22.Bf1 Nd6 23.Nc1 Rxb2 24.Nxb2 e4 25.Rb1 Bd4 26.Qf4 Ne5 27.Nb3 Nf3+ 28.Kh1 Bxf2 29.Qxd6 Bg1!

Other strong moves are 29...Qg5 and 29...f4

30.gxf3?

30.h3 f4 31.Qxf4 Bxh3! 32.gxf3 Bxf1 33.Qg4 Qh6+

30...Bf2! 31.Bh3 Qg1+, 0-1.

32.Rxg1 Rxg1 mate.

Andrew Karklins is a very strong player. Two of his most famous victims are Grandmaster Peter Svidler at the 1995 World Open and Grandmaster Jaan Ehlvest at the 2009 Western States Open. Andrew is a fine attacking player, but he didn't fare well against Grefe.

John Grefe vs. Andrew Karklins, Lone Pine 1971

1.g3 Nf6 2.Bg2 e5 3.c4 d6 4.Nc3 Be7 5.Nf3 c6 6.0-0 0-0 7.c5 dxc5 8.Nxe5 Bd6 9.Nc4 Bc7 10.b3 Ng4 11.Bb2 f5 12.f4 h5 13.e4 h4 14.Ne3 hxg3 15.hxg3 Nh6 16.exf5 Nxd5 17.Ne4 Na6 18.Ng5 Nxg3 19.Qc2 Ne2+ 20.Kh1 Ng3+ 21.Kh2 Nf5 22.Qc4+!

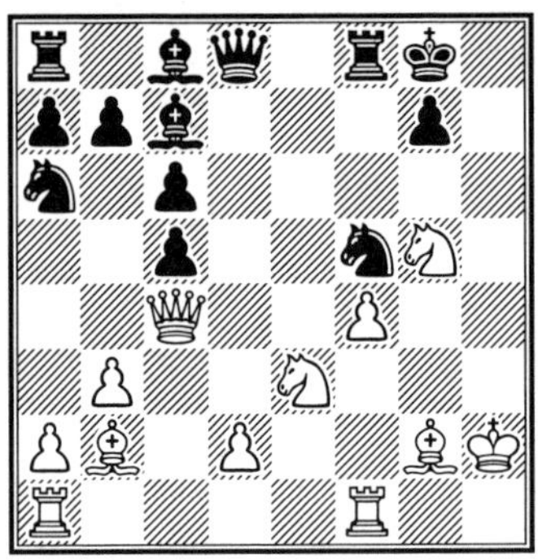

22...Kh8 23.Rh1! Qxg5

The actual game went: 23...Nh6 24.Kg1 Qd6 25.Nf7+, 1-0.

24.Nxf5 Qxf4+

24...Bxf5 25.Kg1+ Bh7 26.fxg5.

25.Kh1+ Qh2+

25...Qh6 26.Rxh6 mate.

John Grefe and Walter Browne, at Browne's home in Berkeley, California, circa 1975.

26.Rxh2+ Bxh2+

A rare instance of a pair of dueling checks!

27.Kxh2 Bxf5 28.Rh1! Rad8 29.Kg3+

29.Kg1+ is the same thing.

29...Bh7 30.Qe4

30.Be4 is equally good. After 30.Qe4, mates in a few moves.

Wolfgang Heidenfeld (1911-1981) had quite an interesting life—besides being an international master strength player (he earned the title but refused to accept it from FIDE!), he was also a writer, journalist, crossword puzzle designer, and he helped decode Nazi messages for the Allies during World War II. Some of his most prestigious victims included World Champion Max Euwe, and Grandmasters Miguel Najdorf, and Luděk Pachman.

John Grefe vs. Wolfgang Heidenfeld, London 1973

1.e4 e6 2.d3 c5 3.Nf3 Nc6 4.Nbd2 d5 5.g3 Nf6 6.Bg2 Be7 7.0-0 0-0 8.Re1 Qc7 9.e5 Nd7 10.Qe2 b5 11.Nf1 Bb7 12.Bf4 Rac8 13.h4 Rfd8 14.N1h2 Nf8 15.h5 Qb6 16.Ng4 c4 17.h6 g6 18.Be3 Qc7 19.d4 b4 20.c3 Nd7 21.Bg5 Nb6 22.Bxe7 Nxe7 23.Nf6+ Kh8 24.Ng5 Ng8 25.Qf3 Qe7 26.Ngxh7 Nxh6 27.Qf4 Kg7 28.g4 Rh8 29.Re3!

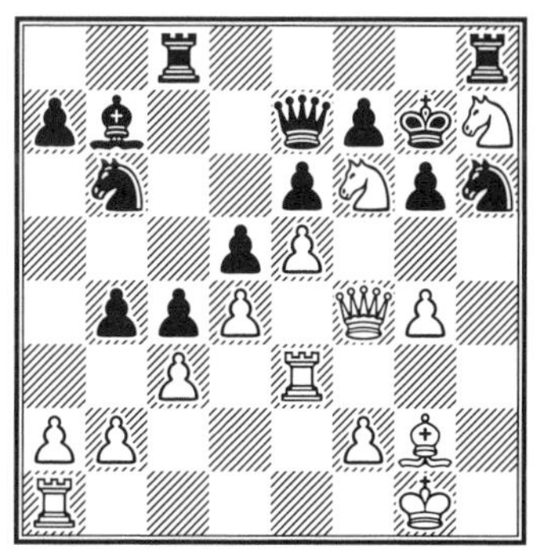

29...Rxh7 30.Nxh7 Kxh7 30.Rh3 g5 32.Qh2 Qf8 33.f4 Qg7 34.Rh5 Rh8 35.fxg5 Kg6 36.gxh6 Rxh6 37.Rf1 Nd7 38.Bxd5 Bxd5 39.Qc2+, 1-0.

Grandmaster Walter Browne (1949-2015) won the U.S. Championship six times in the 1970s and early '80s! And for more than a decade (after Bobby Fischer's retirement) Browne (along with Lubos Kavalek) was considered the best American player.

The following is a famous (and key) game in Grefe's acquisition of the U.S. Championship:

John Grefe vs. Walter Browne, U.S. Championship 1973

1.e4 c5 2.Nf3 d6 3.d4 cxd4 4.Nxd4 Nf6 5.Nc3 a6 6.Bg5 e6 7.f4 h6 8.Bh4 Be7 9.Qf3 Nbd7 10.0-0-0 Qc7 11.Be2 Rb8 12.Qg3 Rg8 13.Rhf1 g5 14.fxg5 Ne5 15.Nf3 b5 16.Nxe5!

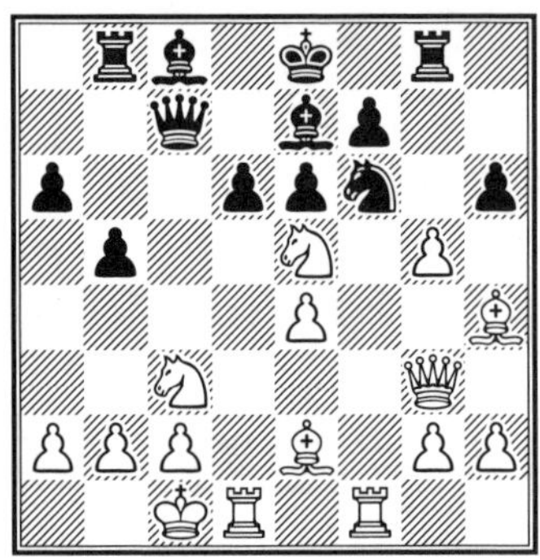

16...b4

16...dxe5 17.gxf6 Rxg3 18.fxe7 Rg5 19.Bxg5 hxg5 20.Bh5 Qxe7 21.Bxf7+ Kf8 22.Bxe6+ Ke8 (22...Kg7 23.Rf7+ Qxf7 24.Bxf7 Kxf7 25.Rd8 is an easy win for White) 23.Bf7+ (23.Nd5 is also strong) 23...Kf8 24.Bd5+ Ke8 25.Bc6+ Bd7 26.Rxd7 Qxd7 27.Bxd7+ and it's all over.

17.Nxf7!

17.gxf6 is also strong.

17...bxc3 18.gxf6! Rxg3 19.fxe7 Rg5 20.Bxg5

20.Nxd6+ Kxe7 21.Rf7+ Kd8 22.Bxg5+ hxg5 23.Nb7+ Ke8 24.Rxc7.

20...hxg5 21.Nxd6+, 1-0.

Rest in peace, old friend.

Silman and Jerry Hanken at a tournament in Los Angeles circa 1988.

Parting With the Lady

Today we'll enjoy a lighthearted (with a tad of "morbid" tossed in) look at the time-honored Queen sacrifice. I'm calling it "Parting With the Lady" in honor of the late Jerry Hanken, who wrote a number of excellent articles with that title.

At some point, Grandmaster Joel Benjamin—who put out the fantastic chess humor magazine *Chess Chow*—wrote a very funny article titled "Parting With the Gentleman."

I suppose I could follow this up with games where people mate themselves, but I'm not sure if that would be very well received. Worse yet, perhaps people would emulate it, and we'd see a spate of self-mates in tournaments all over the globe! Hmmm—lemming chess—it just might catch on!

I often do trips down memory lane, so when Hanken's ghost came to visit me I was reminded of an internet announcement of his death in 2008.

However, he didn't die in 2008. Turns out some idiot made it up, and Jerry Hanken himself had to set the record straight:

> I have always wanted to be able to quote my favorite humorist Mark Twain who said "reports of my death have been greatly exaggerated."
>
> Anyway, I will resist the temptation to write my own obit. I simply can't go now as I must wait at least until I play in my fiftieth U.S. Open in 2017 and then I will have to put it off until I play in my sixtieth consecutive American Open in 2024. After that, I'll think of something.
>
> "Down you mongrel death, back into your kennel, I have stolen breath from a reed of fennel..." (Edna St. Vincent Millay).

Sadly, he really did die a year later, in 2009. I visited him in the hospital and, as fate would have it, was the last chess player to see him alive.

Jerry Hanken's great loves were chess and Shakespeare, and it's clear that his Parting With The Lady is a play on words from *Romeo and Juliet* ("...parting is such sweet sorrow..."). Perhaps Hanken is the only person in history to seamlessly merge both chess and Shakespeare into a homogeneous whole.

So Jerry, I'm going to mix your Shakespearian-bred title with my *Rocky Horror Picture Show* brain. Ready? Okay, "let's do the time warp again!"

4

WHEN MEN WERE MEN

During the romantic era of chess, the 1850s through 1870s, MEN WERE MEN! They played gambits. They went for mate. They drank whiskey while pondering their next attacking move. If someone made a material sacrifice (which loses if the opponent simply refuses the "gift"), a *real* man would take it and dare his opponent to beat him. And if some attractive women were watching the games, the players didn't notice since they only had eyes for the enemy King!

Steinitz wrote the following account of his physical battle with the hard-drinking Joseph Henry Blackburne (who was also known as the Black Death):

> After a few words Blackburne pounced upon me and hammered at my face and eyes with fullest force about a dozen blows...but at last I had the good fortune to release myself from his drunken grip, and I broke the window pane with his head, which sobered him down a little.

It's clear that watching these guys go at it was far more fun in those days than watching games today!

"No mercy!" was the romantic battle cry. If one of these chess gods played someone in a simultaneous exhibition, he would do his best to rend his opponent limb from limb. If someone who was ill said that his biggest dream was to play one game against a Blackburne or Adolf Anderssen, one of the two grandmasters would go to the hospital, wipe out the sick player as quickly and brutally as possible, and then leave (his bloodlust satisfied for that moment).

Men!

The next game is Blackburne playing in a simultaneous exhibition. He was blindfolded while his opponent was able to clearly see how his King was hunted from one side of the board to the other. See if you can find Blackburne's brutal continuation.

When Men Were Men—The Sixteen Leading Chess Players of the World (1886).
[Standing] Captain George MacKenzie (United States), Baron Ignatz von Kolisch (Austria-Hungary), Szymon Winawer (Germany), Henry Edward Bird (England), Jules Arnous de Riviére (France), Samuel Rosenthal (France), James Mason (United States), William Norwood Potter (England), Reverend George Alcock MacDonnell (England), Emil Schallopp (Germany):
[Seated} Joseph Henry Blackburne (England), William Steinitz (United States), Johannes Zukertort (England), Bertold Englisch (Austria-Hungry).

Joseph Henry Blackburne vs. NN, (blindfold simultaneous exhibition) 1863

1.e4 e5 2.d4 exd4 3.c3 dxc3 4.Bc4 d6 5.Nxc3 Nc6 6.Nf3 Ne5 7.Nxe5 dxe5 8.Bxf7+ Ke7 9.Bg5+ Nf6 10.Qh5 c6 11.Rd1 Qa5 12.f4 Qc5 13.fxe5 Qxe5 14.0-0 h6 15.Be8!

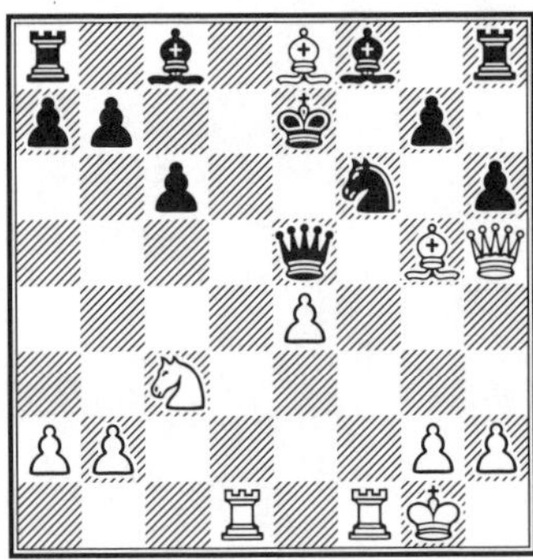

15.Bb3 was also crushing.

15...Be6 16.Rxf6! gxf6

16...hxg5 17.Rd7+! Bxd7 18.Qf7+ Kd8 19.Qxd7 mate.

17.Rd7+ Bxd7 18.Qf7+ Kd6 19.Qxd7+ Kc5 20.Be3+ Kb4 21.Qxb7+ Ka5

Blackburne announced mate in three!

22.b4+!

22.Bb6+ also wins, but it allows the game to continue after 22...axb6 23.Qxa8+ Kb4. The idea of 22.b4+ is to take the b4-square away from black's King.

22...Bxb4 23.Bb6+ axb6 24.Qxa8, 1-0.

Amazing! Blackburne did all this in a simultaneous without sight of the board!!

One of the greatest attackers of all time was Adolf Anderssen, whose two most famous games are called the "Immortal Game" and the "Evergreen Game."

Here is a great example of both players going for a kingside mate at the same time. Can you find what Anderssen found?

White, who is a Rook down, threatens both Rd8 doubled discovered checkmate and the simple Qxc1. White seems to be doing fine, but he missed one move.

Fritz Riemann vs. Adolf Anderssen, Breslau match 1876

1.e4 e5 2.Nf3 Nc6 3.Nc3 Nf6 4.Bb5 Bb4 5.0-0 Bxc3 6.bxc3 0-0 7.d4 Nxe4 8.Qd3 d5 9.Nxe5 Nxe5 10.dxe5 c6 11.Ba4 b5 12.Bb3 a5 13.a4 Bxa4 14.Bxa4 Ba6 15.Qd4 c5 16.Qe3 Bxf1 17.Kxf1 f5 18.f4 Ra6 19.Ba3 Rh6 20.h3 Qb6 21.Rd1 Rb8 22.Rxd5 Qa6+ 23.Kg1 Rb1+ 24.Bc1 Qb6 25.Bb3 Rxc1+ 26.Kh2 c4!!

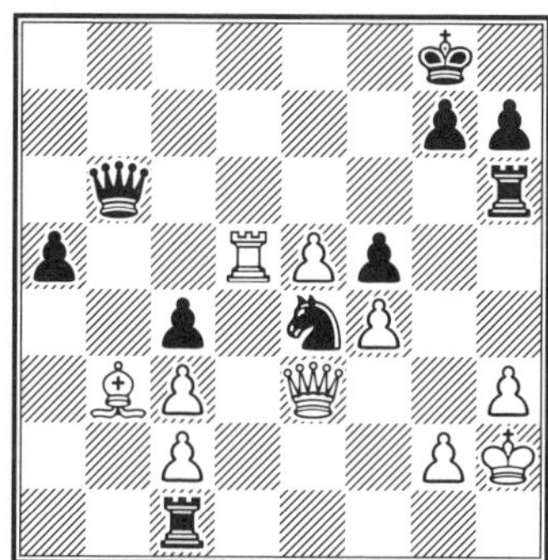

The only winning move.

27.Bxc4 Kf8 28.Qxc1 Rxh3+!, 0-1.

Impressive! The problem is that when these romantic players defined chess as a human version of a cockfight—though their attacking skills were off the chart—other areas of the game were, at times, pathetic.

Though a one-trick-pony attacker will create some amazing works of art, the many games he lost when his attack fell on its face are often ignored. In the following game Anderssen throws everything (including the kitchen sink) at his opponent. And when there was nothing left to throw, he resigned.

Adolf Anderssen vs. Fritz Riemann, Breslau match 1876

1.e4 e5 2.Nf3 Nc6 3.Bc4 Bc5 4.b4 Bxb4 5.c3 Ba5 6.d4 exd4 7.0-0 dxc3 8.Qb3 Qf6 9.e5 Qg6 10.Nxc3 Nge7 11.Ba3 Rb8 12.Nb5 a6 13.Nd6+ cxd6 14.exd6 b5

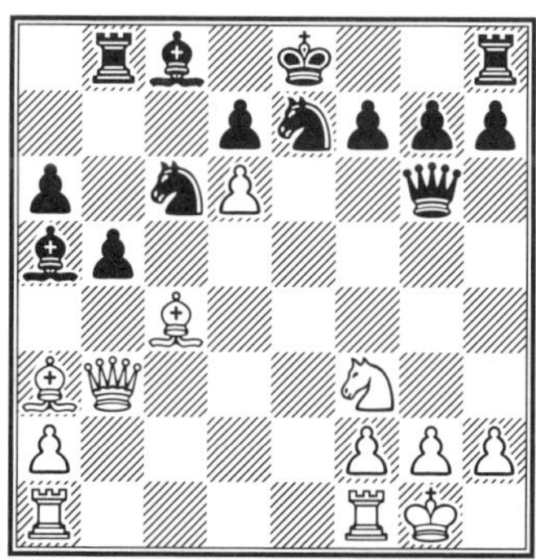

15.Bd3 Qe6 16.dxe7 Qxb3 17.axb3 Bc3 18.Rad1 b4 19.Bc1 Nxe7 20.Be3 0-0 21.Bc5 Re8 22.Rfe1 Bxe1 23.Rxe1 d6 24.Bxd6 Rb7 25.Be4 Rb6 26.Bxe7 Rxe7 27.Bxh7+ Kf8 28.Ne5 Rbe6 29.f4 g6 30.Rc1 Bb7 31.Nd3 Kg7 32.f5 Re2 33.fxg6 Rxg2+ 34.Kf1 Rxh2 35.Nf4 Rh1+ 36.Kf2 Rxc1 37.Nh5+ Kh6, 0-1.

Okay, I've been playing with you (just a bit). Though the monsters of the romantic era attacked at (almost) every opportunity, many were savvy enough to realize when these kinds of attacks were simply not going to work. When that happened they would (gasp!) switch into positional mode and, in many cases, it turned out that they were quite proficient!

Joseph Henry Blackburne vs. Wilhelm Steinitz, England 1875

1.e4 e5 2.Nf3 Nc6 3.d4 exd4 4.Nxd4 Nf6 5.Nxc6 bxc6 6.Bd3 d5 7.Qe2 Be7 8.0-0 0-0 9.Bf4 Rb8 10.Nd2 Re8 11.e5 Bf8 12.Nb3 Nd7 13.Bg3 c5 14.c4 d4 15.f4 Rb6 16.Rae1 Nb8 17.Qc2 g6 18.Nd2 f5 19.exf6 Rxe1 20.Bxe1 Qxf6 21.Ne4 Qe7 22.Ng3 Nc6 23.a3 Bg7 24.Bd2 Bd7

One would think that a ferocious player like Blackburne would go after black's King with an eventual f4-f5. However, that advance gives black's Knight the e5-square and, as Blackburne realized, trying for anything on the kingside isn't going to lead to anything good. So, White tosses away silly hopes of tactical battles and a King hunt and instead seeks to make positional inroads on the queenside.

25.Re1

25.f5? Ne5.

25...Qf8 26.b4!

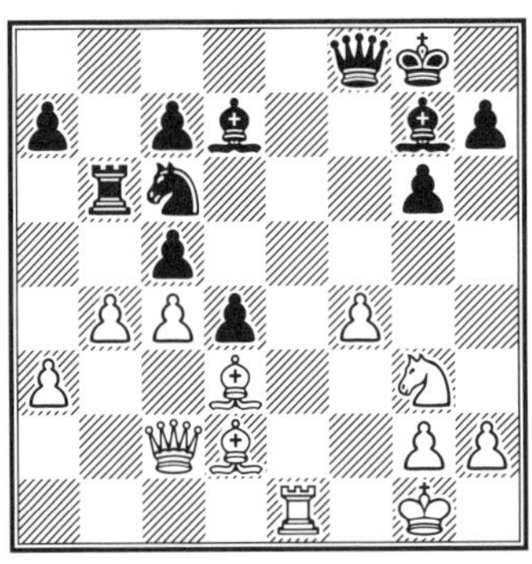

26...cxb4

26...Rb8 27.b5 Ne7 28.Ne4 gives White a serious advantage, thanks to the weakness of c5.

27.c5 Rb8

27...b3 28.Qc4+.

28.axb4 Re8 29.Rxe8 Bxe8 30.b5 Nd8 31.Qa2+ Kh8 32.Qxa7 Ne6 33.b6 Time for Black to resign. **33...Qxc5 34.Qa8 Qxb6 35.Qxe8+ Nf8 36.Qf7**, 1-0.

Burn was a master of defense, but once he tied you up and left you in a helpless state, he would turn into a carnivore and demonstrate his attacking/tactical skills.

Amos Burn vs. William Hunter, Glasgow 1875

1.e4 e5 2.Nf3 d6 3.d4 exd4 4.Qxd4 Nc6 5.Bb5 Bd7 6.Bxc6 Bxc6 7.0-0 Nf6 8.Nc3 Be7 9.Be3 0-0 10.Rad1 Ne8 11.Qc4 Qc8 12.Nd4 Bd7 13.f4 Be6 14.Qd3 f5 15.Nd5 Bxd5

15...Bd8 16.Nxe6 Qxe6 17.Qb3 Rf7 18.exf5 Qxf5 19.Qxb7.

16.exd5

Now White owns the e6-square.

16...Rf6 17.Ne6 c5 18.Bd2 Nc7 19.Bc3 Rf7

19...Rg6 20.Nxc7 Qxc7 21.Qxf5.

20.Rfe1 Bf6 21.Re3 Bxc3 22.Qxc3 Rf6 23.Nxg7!

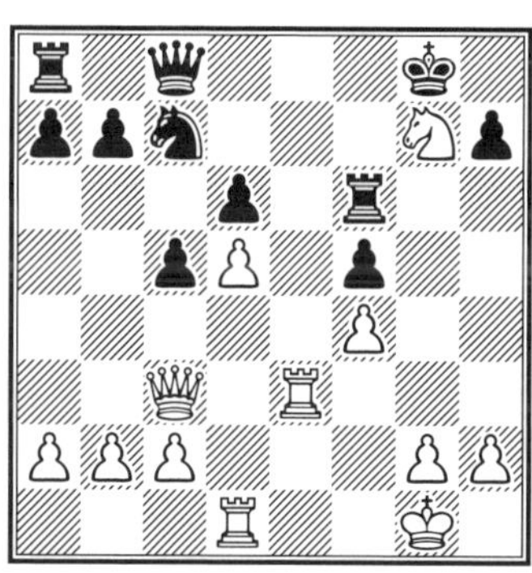

First total positional domination, and then a tactical thrust to the enemy's heart!

23...Kf7

23...Kg7 24.Re7+ Kg6 25.Qg3+ Kh6 26.Qg5 mate.

24.Nh5 Rg6 25.Rde1 Nxd5 26.Qc4 Qc6 27.Rd1 Re6 28.Rxe6 Kxe6 29.Rxd5 Rf8

29...Qd5 30.Ng7+ picks up black's Queen.

30.Rxc5+, 1-0.

In modern times, we still have masters of attack. But all of them (Tal, Kasparov, Shirov, etc.) understood that in the majority of cases, brute force won't get the job done.

Most top-flight games are won or lost by strategic acumen and excellent endgame technique. In a nutshell: if you don't have the whole package of balanced skills, then don't expect to reach the heights you might be dreaming of.

PART
FOUR

Musings, Theory, Instruction, and FAQs

1

MY FAVORITE CLASSIC GAMES

As a young teen I was affected by a number of games in a profound manner. In general, they were positional games—for a kid that grew up on attacking chess and combinations, strategic considerations were left behind and, as a result, were alien.

When discussing great games, many chess fans always think of slashing attacks and outrageous combinations. While every world-class player tossed out more than a few epic combinations at some point in his career, positional masterpieces are far harder to find.

This is strange in a way, because I was a very aggressive player in my youth. But perhaps it's not so strange after all, since I could understand combinations and tactics (in other words, they weren't that special), but the subtle positional magic the greats were capable of always left me dumbfounded.

Thus, when I was finished studying games by Anderssen, Morphy, Spielmann, Marshall, Alekhine, and Tal, I decided to check out less extreme players and broaden my chess horizons.

The games I've selected to share might or might not be masterpieces; my criterion for this selecting these games was based on whether they taught me important lesson(s) that made me well rounded and thus much stronger. I'm hoping that these games will teach you the same lessons, thereby improving your positional understanding and helping you become a better player.

I'll start by taking a close look at a Rubinstein masterpiece.

Georg Rotlewi vs. Akiba Rubinstein, Lodz 1907

1.d4 d5 2.Nf3 e6 3.e3 c5 4.c4 Nc6 5.Nc3 Nf6 6.dxc5 Bxc5 7.a3 a6 8.b4 Bd6 9.Bb2 0-0 10.Qd2 Qe7! 11.Bd3 dxc4 12.Bxc4 b5 13.Bd3 Rd8 14.Qe2 Bb7 15.0-0 Ne5 16.Nxe5 Bxe5 17.f4 Bc7 18.e4 Rac8 19.e5 Bb6+ 20.Kh1 Ng4!

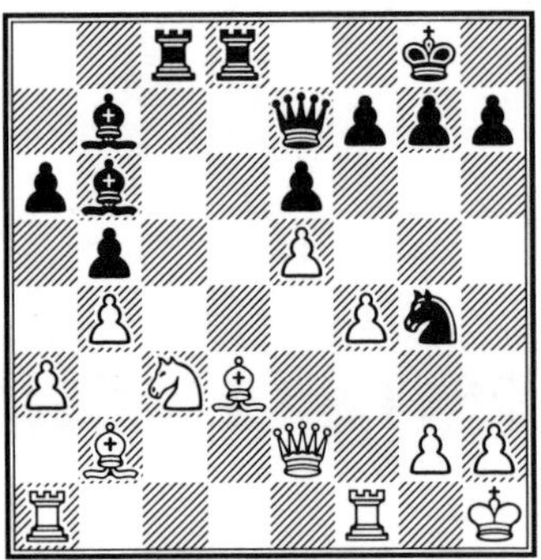

21.Be4

White desperately tries to put out the fire along the a8-h1 diagonal. Other moves were also hopeless: 21.Qxg4 Rxd3 threatening ...Rxc3. 22.Ne2 (22. Rac1 Rd2 threatening both 23...Bxg2+ and 23...Rxb2. A fun line is 23.Ba1 Qh4! 24.Qg3 Qxg3 25.hxg3 Bxg2+ 26.Kh2 Bxf1+ 27.Kh1 Bg2+ 28.Kh2 Bf3+ 29.Kh3 h5 and mates.) 22...Rc2 23.Bc1 h5 24.Qxh5 Bxg2+ 25.Kxg2 Qb7+ and it's all over; 21.Ne4 Qh4 22.h3 Rxd3 23.Qxd3 (23.Qxg4 Qxg4 24.hxg4 Bxe4 leaves Black with an extra piece and a nasty threat of ...Rh3 mate!) 23...Bxe4 24.Qxe4 Qg3 25.hxg4 Qh4 mate.

21...Qh4

21...Nxh2 was also a winner.

22.g3

22.h3 Rxc3! 23.Qxg4 (23.Bxc3 Bxe4 24.Qxg4 [24.Qxe4 Qg3 25.hxg4 Qh4 mate] 24…Qxg4 25.hxg4 Rd3 threatening ...Rh3 mate. 26.Kh2 Rxc3 and White should resign; 23.Bxb7 Rxh3+ mates.) 23…Rxh3+! wins: 24.Qxh3 (24.gxh3 Bxe4+ 25.Kh2 Rd2+) 24…Qxh3+ 25.gxh Bxe4+ 26.Kh2 Rd2 27.Kg3 Rg2+ 28.Kh4 Bd8+ 29.Kh5 Bg6 mate.

22...Rxc3!

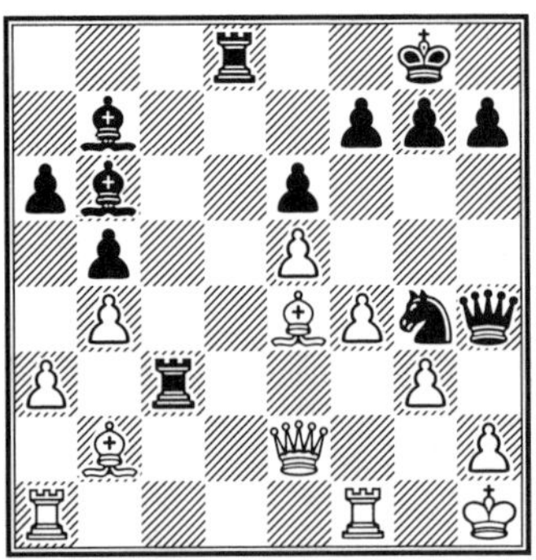

23.gxh4

- 23.Bxb7 Rxg3 24.Rf3 (24.Bf3 Nxh2 25.Qxh2 Rh3) 24...Rxf3 25.Bxf3 Nf2+ 26.Kg2 (26.Kg1 Ne4+ 27.Kf1 Nd2+ 28.Kg2 Nxf3 29.Kxf3 (29.Qxf3 Rd2+) 29...Qh5+ picks up white's Queen and also mates in a few moves.) 26...Qh3+ 27.Kg1 Ne4+ 28.Kh1 Ng3 mate. Very pretty!
- 23.Bxc3 Bxe4+ 24.Qg2 Qxh2 mate.

23...Rd2!

A satisfying move that pulls white's Queen away from the defense of the e4-Bishop.

24.Qxd2

24.Qxg4 Bxe4+ 25.Rf3 Rxf3.

24...Bxe4+ 25.Qg2 Rh3!!, 0-1.

A GREAT way to end the game. The threat of ...Rh2 mate can't be dealt with.

Okay, that was fun. I admit it! It's a true evergreen game. But profound? No. Exciting and flashy and brilliant, YES!

And so we finally get to this section's main game. It taught me a lot in my early teens, and improved my positional understanding by leaps and bounds.

Heinrich Wolf vs. Akiba Rubinstein, Teplitz-Schoenau 1922

1.e4 e5 2.Nf3 Nc6 3.Nc3 Nf6 4.Bb5 Bb4 5.0-0 0-0 6.d3 d6 7.Bg5 Bxc3 8.bxc3 Qe7

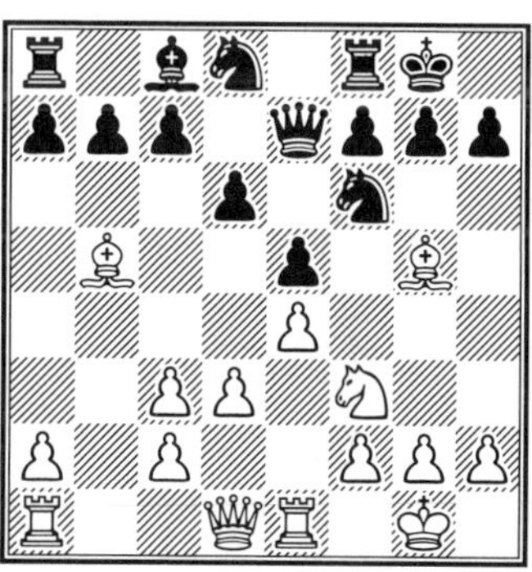

This Queen move, with the followup 9...Nd8, is known as the Metger Unpin (the idea is to break the g5-Bishop's pin by ...Nc6-d8-e6 when if the Bishop moves back to h4 Black can continue with ...Nf4-g6, ...Rd8 followed by ...Nf8-g6, or simply go for an eventual ...h6 followed by ...g5).

Once upon a time, the thirteen-year-old Silman was relaxing between rounds in a skittles room, looking at this position in a chess book hoping the basic moves would be easy to memorize. I wasn't aware of the Metger Unpin, but all the moves made sense. A very strong player came by (I have no idea who he was), noticed me (he was most likely bored) and asked:

Player: "What do all those moves mean? What do they do?"

Me: [Quickly labeling him an idiot] "Uhhh, they develop pieces and get castled, which all the books tell you to do." [Quite proud of this answer.

Player: "Yes, but other than development, what else are they actually trying to accomplish? And what is 8...Qe7 all about?"

Me: [I remember thinking, This guy is a complete moron.] "I have no idea what you're talking about. I'm developing. What more am I supposed to be doing?" [He then shocked me with a mini-lecture]

Player: "Both sides are indeed developing and castling, and they are also fighting for control of all the key central squares. Also, at any moment the structure can change if one side decides to chop on c3 or c6 and double the enemy pawns. However, if one side does that, he's also giving the side with doubled pawns more control over the d4 or d5 square. So that's a trade-off—weakening the enemy pawn structure but giving him more central control. The line you played on the board has Black chopping on c3, but now White has two Bishops and control over d4. As for 8...Qe7, Black wants to get out of that pin by the g5-Bishop. By moving the Queen to e7, he vacates d8 and prepares to play the maneuver ...Nc6-d8-e6, hitting the Bishop. If it retreats to h4 and continues the pin, then ...Rd8 followed by ...Nf8-g6 ends the pin once and for all. Got it? Okay, I have to go!"

I sat there stunned. Oddly, I no longer had any problem remembering those particular moves since they suddenly meant something to me; they made sense! I even remembered the Knight maneuver from c6-d8-e6-f8-g6 since it made a huge emotional impression on me. The moral is: brute force memorization is useless if you can't make sense of what it all means. However, if you learn the meaning/goals behind something first, the actual steps are easy to remember and often easy to recreate.

9.Re1 Nd8 10.d4 Bg4

A reasonable move, though 10...Ne6 is by far the most popular option.

11.h3 Bh5 12.g4 Bg6 13.Nh4 h6 14.Nxg6

I would prefer 14.Nf5 Bxf5 15.Bxf6 Qxf6 16.exf5 when black's Knight isn't ideally placed and White has a bit of pressure in the center.

14...fxg6 15.Bc4+ Kh7 16.Bh4 g5 17.Bg3 Nf7 18.Qf3 Rae8 19.Qe3 b6

An interesting position. We have a battle between two Bishops and two Knights. One might give the nod to the Bishops, but they don't really have any weak points to snip at, while the f7-Knight will find a nice home on f4 by ...Nf7-h8-g6-f4.

20.Bb5 Rd8 21.a4

White wants to play a5, getting rid of his isolated a-pawns and opening a file for his a1-Rook.

21...Nh8!!

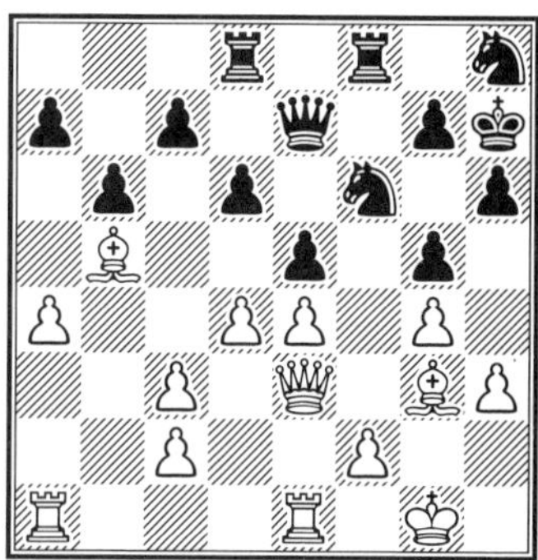

Why would I give this move one exclamation mark, let alone two? The reason is that 21...Nh8 is the start of a very deep plan based on the queenside pawn structure. Of course, the "normal" move would be 21...a5, preventing White's a4-a5, but Black's idea actually welcomes it!

22.a5 Ng6 23.f3 Nf4

It's time to address an important question: why didn't Black stop a4-a5, and why isn't White chopping on b6 and opening the a-file for his Rook? The answer is that Black wants White to capture on b6 since he would answer 24.axb6 with 24...cxb6! opening the c-file, which will allow Black to place his Rooks there, putting serious heat against c3. Another point is that after 24...cxb6 Black suddenly has a passed a-pawn.

24.Bf1 Kh8!

Intending ...Nh7 followed by ...Rf6, and ...Nh7-f8-g6.

25.Bxf4

Chopping before ...Nf6-h7 occurs when the capture on f4 would be answered by ...Rxf4.

25...gxf4 26.Qf2 g5 27.d5??

An awful move. White not only devalues his own Bishop by blocking the a2-g8 diagonal, it also hands the c5-square to black's Knight. For lower rated players this is a VERY instructive mistake.

27...h5 28.Bg2?

An overreaction to Black's kingside pawn push. The Bishop is now clearly inferior to black's Knight.

28...Kg7 29.Qe2 Rh8 30.Kf2 Ra8 31.Reb1 Nd7 32.Qb5

32.gxh5 Nc5 33.Rg1 Rxh5 favors Black.

32...hxg4 33.hxg4 Nc5

If anyone doubted which minor piece was superior, those doubts should fall away after 33...Nc5.

34.Rh1 Rh4!?

A deep and creative move, though 34...a6 35.Qb4 bxa5 36.Qxa5 Qd7 is an excellent alternative. Black is, in effect (due to the doubled c-pawns) a pawn up.

35.Rxh4 gxh4

Black's plan is based on creating a passed a-pawn, but he's adding an extra bow to his quiver by creating a passed h-pawn too! But there's more to his 34...Rh4 idea than this. He intends to eventually move his King to g5 and, after ...h4-h3, the black King will penetrate into White's position by ...Kg5-h4.

36.Bh3

36.axb6 cxb6.

36...bxa5! 37.Qxa5 Qd8 38.Rb1 Rb8 39.Rb4 a6 40.Ke2 Rb6

Black is showing his cards on the queenside, and in doing so is tying White's army down.

41.Qa1 Kg6 42.Kd2 Kg5

Notice how Black is calmly optimizing the placement of all his pieces. He will only begin the final push when everything is ready, willing, and able.

43.Rb1 Qb8 44.Rh1

Dreaming of Qe1 followed by Bg2 and Qxh4+. Dreams are nice, while (at least for White) reality is a sad, painful place.

44...a5!!

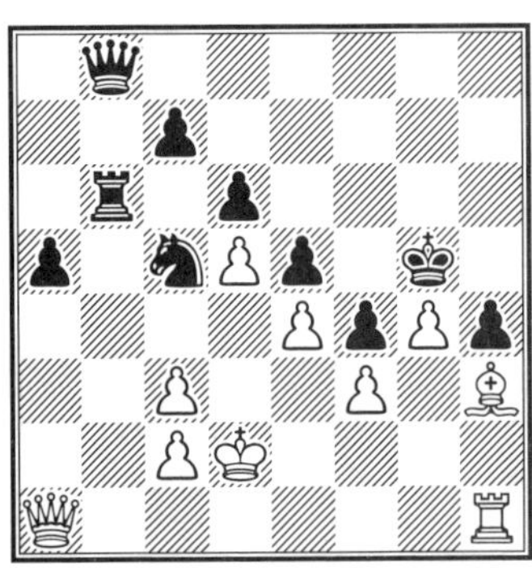

Ignoring White's fantasies and kicking his a-pawn into gear!

45.Bg2

The pawn is poison: 45.Qxa5 Rb2 46.Qa3 Nb3+ and it's all over.

45...a4

Even better is 45...Rb2 when the game ends quickly. Here's a sample: 46.Qe1 Nb3+ 47.Ke2 Qb5+ 48.Kf2 Rxc2+ 49.Kg1 Rc1.

46.Qe1

Since his position is so bad, making this obvious threat must have given White a tiny bit of pleasure.

46...Qh8

Alas, White's pleasure was fleeting.

47.Qc1 Ra6

47...a3 48.Qxa3 Qb8 was another way to win, but Black went for the "safe but sure" option.

48.Bf1 Ra8 49.Bc4 a3

The passed a- and h-pawns are more than White can handle.

50.Ba2 Qh7 51.Rh3 Nd7 52.Qf1 Qh8 53.Rh1 Nc5 54.Qc1 Rb8!

A nice way to finish. By sacrificing the pawn white's Bishop and Queen end up cowering on the queenside, which allows Black to burst decisively into the kingside.

55.Qxa3 Ra8 56.Qb2 h3 57.Bc4 Qh4 58.Be2 Qf2 59.Rxh3 Qe3+ 60.Ke1 Na4, 0-1.

White gets mated after 61.Qb5 Nxc3 62.Rh5+ Kg6 63.Qd3 Ra1+.

Lessons I Picked Up From This Game

- At times it's possible to play on both sides of the board, "stretching" the opponent's defensive needs to the limit.
- When the opponent is helpless, take your time and optimize the placement of all your pieces.
- The battle of Bishop versus Knight is seen all the time, and it's very important to master!
- This means that you need to learn how to maximize the powers of both these pieces –- in one game you'll be singing songs about the wonders of the speedy Bishop, and in another game you'll whisper (as if it was a secret) that your true love has a horse's head.
- The manipulation of pawn structure is one of the great keys to chess mastery. You will change the nature of the pawn structure to suit whichever minor piece you own, you'll do your best to avoid structural

weaknesses, and (as in the game we just looked at) you'll create whole strategies around a potential passed pawn or some other anomaly that you created. Note the word "created." These things just don't happen by luck, you have to create them, nurture them, and eventually unleash them!

- Memorizing moves is useless if you don't understand what those moves do.

Everyone knows that Black's fianchettoed dark-squared Bishop is a powerhouse, and everyone also knows that if you let the opponent swap dark-squared Bishops Black's kingside dark-squares can become weak, and his King can become vulnerable.

A Typical Kingside Fianchetto

1.e4 c5 2.Nf3 Nc6 3.d4 cxd4 4.Nxd4 g6 5.c4 Bg7

Though we all know this rule, it doesn't mean that we have to obey it!

Indeed, there are times when trading your fianchettoed "must-keep" dark-squared Bishop is exactly what the position calls for!

As a teenager, I gave this a lot of thought after picking up an issue of *Chess Digest* magazine (Vol. 2, 1969) and reading a book review on Mikhail Yudovich's *King's Indian Defense*. Who wrote the review? None other than Bobby Fischer himself. It was a real eye-opener! Bobby wrote:

> A great disappointment. Perhaps because I had been eagerly awaiting this book when it finally came into my hands in 1968. Most of the references are from the late fifties and early sixties. None from the Havana Olympiad, practically none from *Shakmatny Bulletin* or minor Soviet tournaments. There was very little I didn't already know. 229 pages of nothing. I did learn one important thing of value:
>
> **1.d4 Nf6 2.c4 g6 3.g3 Bg7 4.Bg2 0-0 5.Nf3 d6 6.0-0 Nc6 7.Nc3 Bg4 8.h3 Bxf3 9.Bxf3 Nd7 10.Bg2 Nxd4 11.Bxb7 Rb8 12.Bg2 Rb4 13.e3 Ne6 14.Qe2.**

A Key Position

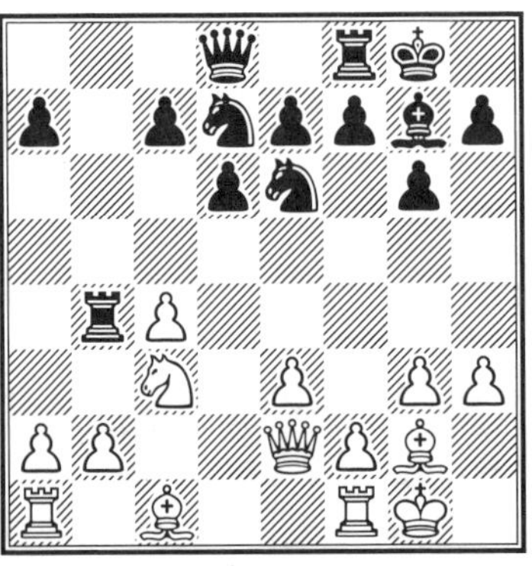

Now Yudovich gives **14...Bxc3!** I didn't know this move, but judging from the quality of his book, I assume it was copied from another source. Black gets the better of it by destroying White's pawn formation; White's attacking chances are not real. Yudovich does not continue his analysis after 14...Bxc3! but after 15.bxc3 Ra4! is clearly right.

Would you give up your mighty bishop here? This actually occurred a couple years later in the game S. Cvetković vs. D. Velimirović, Yugoslavia 1971:

14...Bxc3! 15.bxc3 Ra4 16.Rb1 Nec5 17.e4 Qc8 18.Bh6 Re8 19.e5 Qa6 20.Rb5 Rxa2

Black was much better but later blundered and allowed a draw.

Okay, that actually makes sense, since Black is rupturing White's pawn structure in exchange for the bishop.

My Favorite Larsen Game

The game that really put me over the top when it came to tossing away your fianchettoed dark-squared Bishop was the following masterpiece by Bent Larsen, which I first saw in his book, *Larsen's Selected Game of Chess, 1948-1969.*[1] Larsen was an exceptional writer and several years before his death in 2010, I tried my best to get Bent to collaborate on an instructional book based on his games. Alas, his health was bad and our plans never came to fruition.

Eleazar Jiménez vs. Bent Larsen, Palma de Mallorca 1967

1.e4 Nf6 2.e5 Nd5 3.Nf3 d6 4.d4 dxe5 5.Nxe5 g6 6.Bc4 Be6 7.Bb3 Bg7 8.0-0 0-0 9.Qe2 a5

An annoying move. If White stops the pawn by 10.a4 then a later c2-c4 would create a huge hole on b4.

10.Nc3 c6 11.Nxd5?

I'll quote Larsen: "I do not understand such moves! Black gets a fine center and his Knight the c6-square."

11...cxd5 12.a4 Nc6 13.c3 Qb6 14.Ba2

Black has a very comfortable position, but it's hard to see how he'll continue.

14...Bxe5!!

1 *Larsen's Selected Games of Chess* was reprinted and expanded as *Bent Larsen's Best Games: Fighting Chess with the Great Dane*. Alkmaar: New In Chess, 2014.

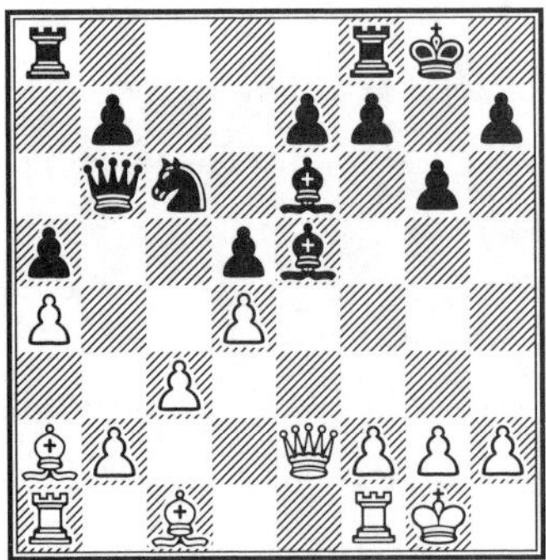

A magnificent move! Black sees that his weakened dark-squares won't have any significance since Black will follow with 15...d4 and create immediate central action (keep in mind that central play usually trumps wing play). On top of that, the e5-pawn will prove to be vulnerable to attack.

15.dxe5 d4! 16.Bh6 Rfd8 17.Bxe6 fxe6

A lot of players might be thinking, "Hey, Black's pawns are doubled and his kingside dark-squares are weak—just look at white's Bishop on h6 staring at black's King!" The problem with this logic is that white's Queen can't get to black's King. In the meantime, serious stuff is going on in the middle of the board.

18.Rfe1 Rd5

The e5-pawn is starting to quiver in fear.

19.Bf4

So much for White's kingside attack.

19...Rf8 20.g3 Rf5

Beautiful. White is suddenly under serious pressure: e5 is weak, a4 might become a target if Black plays ...Qb3, the b2-pawn needs constant attention, and the pawn advance ...d4-d3 is always something to worry about.

21.Rad1 Qb3!

Winning material.

22.h4 Qxa4 23.Qe4 Qb3 24.cxd4 Qxb2 25.Rb1 Qxd4! 26.Rxb7

White was counting on this position. After the exchange of Queens he thought he would have serious chances to hold a draw. And he was right, with one small glitch, which Black had prepared on move 23.

26...Rdxe5!!

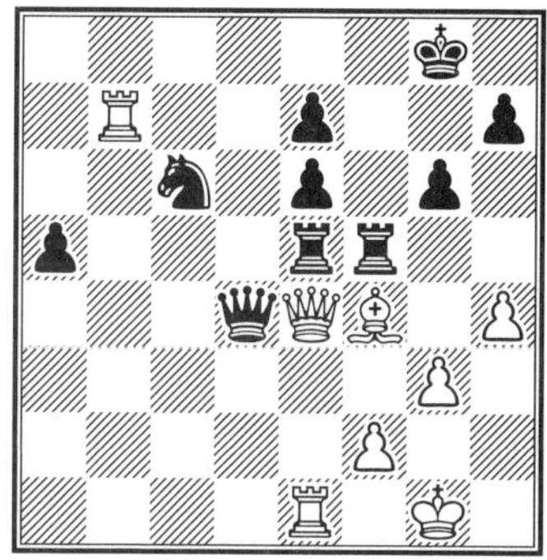

27.Qb1

Black wins easily after 27.Bxe5 Qxf2+ 28.Kh1 Rxe5 29.Rb8+ Kg7 30.Qxe5+ Nxe5 31.Rxe5 Qxg3 32.Reb5 Qxh4+ (32...a4 is also a winner.).

27...Rxe1+ 28.Qxe1 Qd5

Centralizing all his pieces! Other centralizing moves like 18...Rd5 and 18...Rf5 made a big impression on me.

29.Qc1 Nd4 30.Rb8+ Rf8!

Not 30...Kf7 31.Qc8.

31.Rxf8+ Kxf8 32.Bh6+ Ke8!

As before, 32...Kf7? gave White too much counterplay with 33.Qc8.

33.Qc8+ Qd8 34.Qc4 Nf5 35.Bf4 Kf7

I'll quote Larsen again: "The King is now completely safe. The winning method consists of a combination of threats against the white King and advancing the a-pawn."

36.Be5 Qd1+ 37.Kh2 Qd2 38.Qc5 a4 39.Bc3 Qc2 40.Kg1 Qd1+ 41.Kh2 Qd5 42.Qb4 Qf3 43.Kg1 a3, 0-1.

White resigned since 44.Qxa3 Nd4 45.Bb2 (45.Qb2 Ne2+ 46.Kf1 Nxc3) 45...Ne2+ 46.Kf1 Nxg3+ 47.Kg1 (47.Ke1 Qe2 mate) 47...Qh1 mate.

A Saidy Classic

One last thing on the fianchettoed Bishop: My dear friend International Master Tony Saidy who has played many of chess legends, always dreamed of doing battle with Victor Korchnoi. Hearing that the Russian great was going to play in the National Open in 1993, Saidy entered the event hoping against hope that he would be paired with him.

Sure enough, as if in a Hollywood movie, Saidy was indeed paired with Korchnoi. In that game, a Maróczy Bind, he gave up his fianchettoed Bishop for a superior pawn structure and—won! Here's his game, which once again demonstrates the dark squares vs. pawn structure battle.

Victor Korchnoi vs. Anthony Saidy, National Open 1993

1.c4 c5 2.Nf3 Nf6 3.Nc3 g6 4.d4 cxd4 5.Nxd4 Nc6 6.Nb3 Bg7 7.e4 d6 8.Be2 Nd7 9.Be3 Bxc3+

Going for it!

10.bxc3 b6!

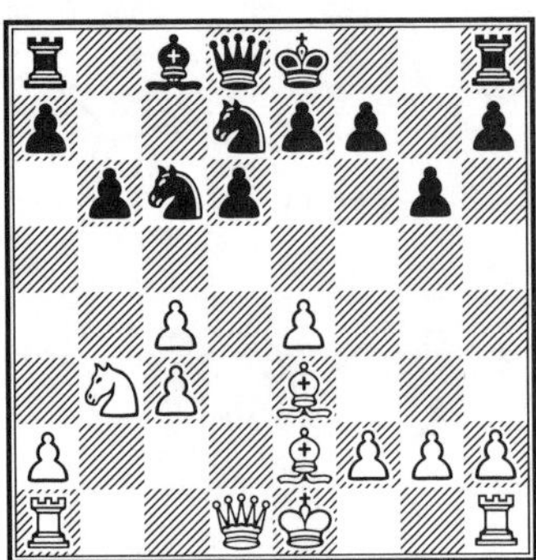

Freezing the weak c4-pawn by preventing a possible c4-c5 advance.

11.Bh6 Bb7 12.h4 Qc7 13.Rh3 0-0-0 14.Nd4 Nc5 15.Bg4+ e6 16.Bg5 Rd7 17.Bf6 Re8 18.Nb5 Qb8

White's pieces are "here and there," while Black's pieces are working together.

19.Re3 a6 20.Na3 Ne5 21.Qe2 Nxg4 22.Qxg4 h5 23.Qg5 Nxe4

Saidy has completely outplayed Korchnoi.

24.Rxe4 Bxe4 25.f3 Bc6 26.Rb1 Rb7 27.Nc2 Qc7 28.Ne3 Ba4 29.Rb4 Bd7 30.Qh6 Qc5

Saidy is playing beautifully, while Korchnoi doesn't know what to do.

31.g4 Bc6 32.Kf2 Qa5 33.Rb2 Rd7 34.Bd4 e5 35.Bxb6 Qa3

Korchnoi should have given it up, but he tries to see if Saidy makes a mistake.

36.Rd2 Qxc3 37.Rc2 Qb4 38.c5 d5 39.a3 Qf4 40.Qxf4 exf4

Now it's painful to watch.

41.Ng2 d4 42.gxh5 gxh5 43.Nxf4 Re3

At this point, Saidy is having fun.

44.Nxh5 Rxf3+ 45.Ke1 d3 46.Rh2 Rd5, 0-1.

Big Pawn Centers

Chess players hear a lot about big pawn centers and how strong they are. But those centers can also be viewed as a target to attack.

At times the big center gets kicked into bits, leaving weak, ruptured pawns behind, waiting for their eventual demise. But at other times the center remains intact—solid but filled with holes. This is the kind of center I'll address here.

My first eye-opening experience (I was fourteen) in this kind of center was a game of Nimzowitsch's. For me, the big moment occurred on move 8 (!) with the rest of the game adding to the overall effect.

Aron Nimzowitsch vs. Stefano Rosselli, Baden-Baden 1925

1.Nf3 d5 2.b3 c5 3.e3 Nc6 4.Bb2 Bg4 5.h3 Bxf3 6.Qxf3 e5 7.Bb5 Qd6

Black has built a big pawn center that controls the b4-, c4-, d4-, e4-, and f4-squares. But White's next move completely changes the complexion of the game.

8.e4!

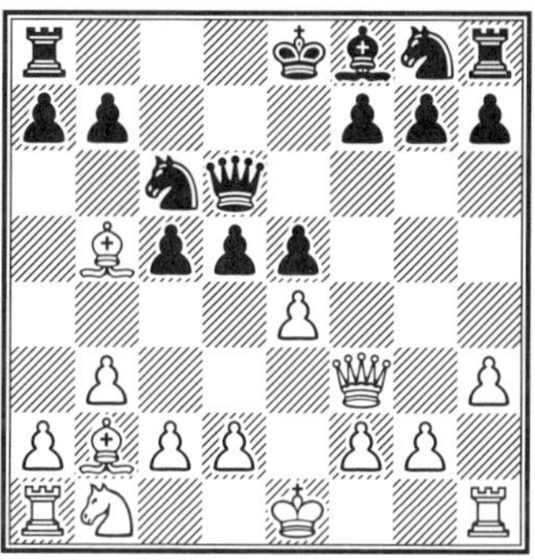

Keep in mind that I had only learned how to play when I was twelve, so at fourteen (with just one-and-a years of experience) Black's center was, in my view, extremely formidable. The idea of 8.e4 is simple, but to me it was like a lightening bolt hit the board! By getting rid of the d5-pawn, or by making it move forward, White will suddenly have gained a square on c4.

8...d4 9.Na3

This move also affected me. White is going right after that c4-square.

9...f6

9...a6 fails to 10.Nc4 Qc7 11.Bxc6+ bxc6 when c4 is permanently in White's hands. (11...Qxc6? 12.Nxe5).

10.Nc4 Qd7 11.Qh5+ g6 12.Qf3 Qc7

Black's Knight can't move due to Qxf6, while 12...a6 loses to 13.Nb6 forking black's Queen and Rook.

13.Qg4 Kf7 14.f4

Striving to open the f-file and start an attack against the black King. I couldn't believe my eyes: a few moves ago Black had a powerful center, and now all hell had broken loose!

14...h5 15.Qf3 exf4 16.Bxc6 bxc6

Better was 16...Qxc6 17.Qxf4 Bh6 18.Qf3 Re8 19.0-0-0 and White has an edge.

17.0-0 g5 18.c3

Another punch to Black's center, which strives to open up the a1-h8 diagonal so white's Bishop can join in the attack.

18...Rd8 19.Rae1 Ne7 20.e5 Nf5 21.cxd4 Nxd4 22.Qe4

Even stronger was 22.Bxd4 Rxd4 23.exf6 Kxf6 24.Re8.

22...Be7

Black had to try 22...f5 when White would continue with 23.Qb1 (or 23.Qd3) 23...Kg6 24.Bxd4 (24.Ne3! is very interesting.) 24...cxd4 25.h4 and Black's kingside pawn structure is pretty much destroyed.

23.h4 Qd7 24.exf6 Bxf6 25.hxg5, 1-0.

A year later (I had improved a lot during that year!) I happened upon a game of Smyslov's which took the idea of turning a big pawn center into a complex of holes to a whole new level.

Svetozar Gligorić vs. Vassily Smyslov, Kiev 1959

1.d4 Nf6 2.c4 g6 3.Nc3 d5 4.cxd5 Nxd5 5.e4 Nxc3 6.bxc3 Bg7 7.Bc4 c5 8.Ne2 0-0 9.0-0 Nc6 10.Be3 Qc7 11.Rc1 Rd8

A very important position. Is White's space gaining center strong or weak? This position exudes a wonderful sense of balance and teamwork. White has a huge pawn center, but Black is taking aim at it with everything he can muster. Note that he's not just attacking randomly, he's doing his best to beat down d4. This is being carried out by Black's dark-squared Bishop, his c-pawn, his Knight, and his d8-Rook—many pieces, one goal! On the other hand, White wants to make his center indestructible. If he can do that, then he can squeeze his opponent and eventually turn Black's helplessness into an attack on the wing, or a breakthrough down the middle. Thus, he is meeting Black's aggression against d4 with his own tightening of that pawn—his c-pawn, dark-squared Bishop, Knight, and Queen are all holding life and limb together.

12.h3

The immediate 12.f4 can be met by 12...Bg4, undermining d4. 12.h3 prepares f2-f4 by preventing ...Bg4.

12...b6 13.f4 e6 14.Qe1 Bb7 15.Qf2?!

White is worse after this, so the natural 15.f5 needed to be played. However, Black would have a problem-free game after 15...Na5 16.Bd3 exf5 17.exf5 Re8.

15...Na5 16.Bd3 f5!

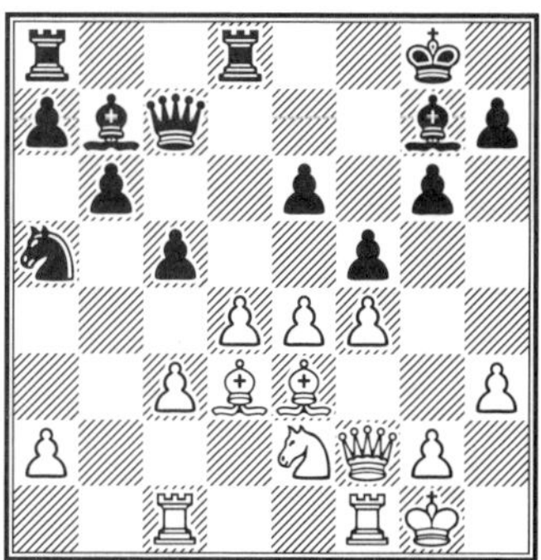

An enormously important move that does many useful things for example:

- It continues the attack against White's center.
- It blocks the f4-pawn (White's whole attack was based on the f4-f5 advance), which in turn blocks White's dark-squared Bishop, Knight, Queen, and f1-Rook. 3) It forces open the h1-a8 diagonal, thereby increasing the activity of the b7-Bishop.

17.e5

17.Ng3 Qd7.

17...c4 18.Bc2 Nc6

Black is better. White's kingside attack has been stifled and his zombie pieces are knocking against their own pawns on c3, d4, and f4 (the c2-Bishop is snuffed by the c4- and f5-pawns). Black, on the other hand, has a mobile queenside pawn majority, a light-squared Bishop that seems more laser beam than chess piece, and a Knight that can set up shop on d5.

19.g4

This loosens up the h1-a8 diagonal and thus puts his own King in jeopardy. However, it was either this attempt at kingside counterplay or passively waiting around to die.

19...Ne7

A good place for the Knight—it keeps an eye on his kingside pawn structure while threatening to leap to d5.

20.Kh2 Qc6

This move speaks for itself—the problem White faces along the h1-a8 diagonal takes on a concrete form.

21.Ng3 b5 22.a4

Note that Black isn't worried about 22.gxf5 exf5, though this leaves White with two connected passed center pawns. Why wouldn't White be delighted with such a turn of events? The answer is that passed pawns aren't very useful if they can't be pushed, and in this position the d-pawn will be liquefied if it ever dares move to d5.

22...a6 23.Rb1 Rab8 24.Bd2 bxa4?!

Black opens lines on the queenside, thinking that he is the one that can profit from it. However, White's pieces also gain a bit of activity and, in general, one should not allow the opponent anything if he's bound and helpless. Instead, he should have put this move off for a moment in favor of 24...Ba8! This strange looking retreat actually has a clear-cut point: by getting the Bishop out of the b8-Rook's way, Black threatens 25...bxa4 when, depending on White's 25th move, he has ideas like ...Rb2 (if white's Rook moved off of the b-file) or the exchange sacrifice with ...Rb3 (as occurred in the actual game). These ideas more or less force 25.axb5 (or 25.gxf5 exf5 26.axb5) when 25...axb5 gives Black two new aims: he can play for an eventual ...b5-b4 push by ...Nd5 (the ...b4 push turns the c4-pawn into a passer and also undermines d4), and/or he can get the Bishop off of a8, follow with ...Ra8, and play for penetration down the a-file.

25.Ra1 Ba8 26.Bxa4 Qc7 27.Ra2 Rb6 28.gxf5 exf5 29.Bc1 Nd5 30.Ne2 a5 31.Bc2 Rb3!

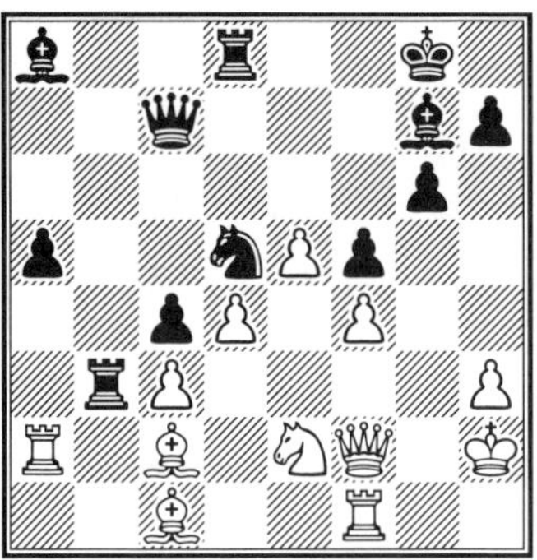

32.Bxb3 cxb3 33.Ra4 Bf8 34.Bb2 Ne3!

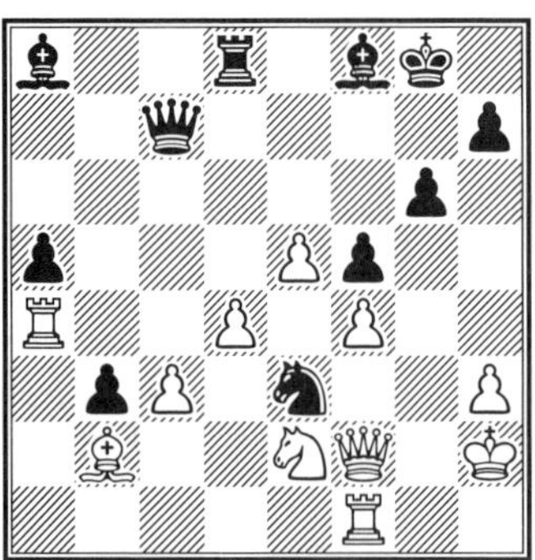

35.Rfa1

35.Qxe3 Qc6 (threatening both 36...Qxa4 and 36...Qg2 mate) 36.d5 Rxd5! (36...Qxa4 37.d6 keeps White in the game.) 37.Raa1 Rd2 threatening ...Qg2 mate. 38.Rf2 Rxb2 and Black wins.

35...Nc4 36.Ng3 Be7 37.Nf1 Qc6 38.Rxc4 Qh1+ 39.Kg3 h5, 0-1.

The threat is 40...h4 mate, and any move of white's Queen gives up the key g1- or f3-square, allowing a quick mate.

After this game showed how to handle Black's position, everyone jumped on the bandwagon and White eventually gave up on 12.h3 altogether (it's still seen from time to time, but it's no longer viewed as a serious way to strive for an opening advantage). Nowadays, 12.Bf4 and 12.Qd2 are White's most popular replies to 11...Rd8.

Passed Pawns

The following game is something I first saw in my mid-teens. I have to admit that going over this game was like a slap in the face and it completely changed the way I looked at passed pawns. It not only taught me about blocking an enemy passed pawn, and it not only taught me how to retain that blockade, but it also taught me what the side with the passed pawn should try to do.

Here are the first moves:

Max Euwe vs. Herman Pilnik, Amsterdam 1950

1.d4 Nf6 2.c4 g6 3.g3 Bg7 4.Bg2 d5 5.cxd5 Nxd5 6.e4 Nb6 7.Ne2 c5 8.d5 0-0 9.0-0 e6 10.Nbc3 Na6 11.Nf4 e5 12.Nfe2

So, what is this position all about? The answer is that it's all about the d6-square (if you can control that square then White's pawn can't advance), AND the e5-square (that's right! You'll see why the e5-square is so important later on). In fact, controlling the d6-square is a matter of life and death!

12...Nc4

The Knight is heading for the lovely blockade square on d6.

13.b3

I very much like the idea of 13.Nb5 trying to deny a blockading Knight on d6. However, it doesn't work due to ...Bd7 and ...Nc7. But in other situations, something like that might be very important and effective!

13...Nd6 14.Be3 b6 15.Qd2 Re8

This might seem odd since e5 is already defended by the Bishop on g7. However, White will eventually try and break down the e5-point so Black gives the e5-pawn extra protection AND he also envisions certain tactical opportunities down the e-file and h8-a1 diagonal. You'll see this in the note to White's 18th move.

16.f4

There was no reason to rush this move. However, White wants to break that blockade and this move is the most obvious way to do that. Unfortunately for Euwe, it doesn't work.

16...Nc7 17.Rf2?!

This leaves the a1-Rook without protection. The punishment is positional gain for Black via a small tactic.

17...exf4 18.Bxf4

White would love to take on f4 with his g-pawn when e4-e5 would break the d6-blockade and wipe Black off the board. Sadly for Euwe, he suddenly realized that he can't do it due to 18.gxf4 Nxe4! 19.Bxe4 Rxe4! 20.Nxe4 Bxa1. With this in mind you can see why Black played 15...Re8.

18...Ba6

Black can't chop on e4 anymore:

18...Nxe4?? 19.Nxe4 Bxa1 20.Bg5 Qd7 21.Bf6 Re5 (21...Rxe4 22.Bxa1) 22.d6 Bb7 23.N2c3 and Black is dead lost.

19.Re1 Qe7 20.g4

In a perfect world White would like to play 21.Kh1 with the idea of Ne2-g1-f3 followed by e4-e5. However, Black won't allow that to happen: 20.Kh1 Ncb5! (20...Bxe2 21.Rfxe2 Be5 with a comfortable position.) 21.a4 (21.Nxb5? Nxe4!) 21...Nxc3 22.Nxc3 Be5 and Black has stopped White's e4-e5 dreams. After 20.g4 both sides solidify their respective armies..

20...Be5 21.Bxe5 Qxe5 22.Ng3? Re7 23.Bf1 Bc8 24.Be2 Bd7 25.Ref1 Rf8 26.Qc1 Nce8 27.Kh1 f6 28.Rg1 Ng7 29.Bf3

Black is better due to the completely blocked d5-pawn (his blockade has been a great success!) and the juicy square on e5. However, Black now seems to go berserk. Or did he?

29...Qg5!?

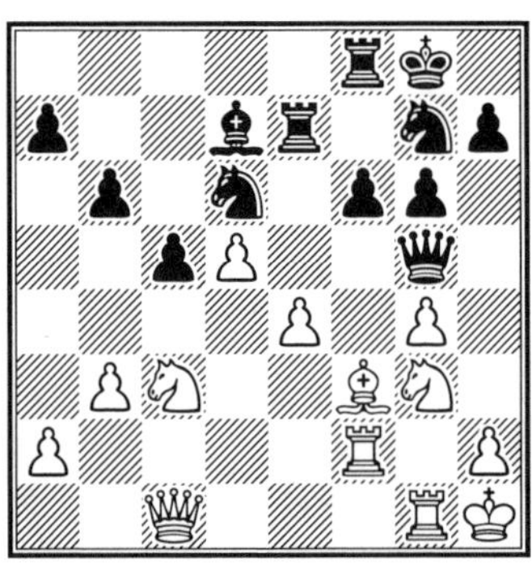

A remarkable move that lets White double Black's pawns, leaving White with two connected passed pawns! Has Black gone crazy??? When I first saw this move many decades ago, I couldn't believe my eyes. To this day I still look at 29...Qg5 and smile. Nevertheless, the best move was probably 29...Rc8 preparing to push his queenside pawns: 30.Nd1. This Knight is heading for d3 when it will kick Black's pieces off of e5. Black won't allow this to happen!

30...Nge8 31.Nb2 Bb5! Stopping White from destroying Black's control of the e5-square. 32.Rc2 Rec7 33.Be2 Bxe2 34.Rxe2 c4 and Black is better.

Though 29...Rc8 might be best, I have to admit that I absolutely love 29...Qg5!

30.Qxg5 fxg5 31.Rgf1 Nge8

Black starts to move this Knight to the e5-square.

32.Be2 Rxf2 33.Rxf2 Kg7 34.h3 Nf6 35.Bf3 Be8 36.Re2

White is on the verge of victory since e4-e5, destroying the two blockades on d6 and e5, would end the game in White's favor on the spot. Fortunately, it's Black's move and not White's.

36...Nd7 37.Rd2 Ne5

Ahhhh! To me, this double blockade is as beautiful as the finest van Gogh. I've been seen staring at this position for an hour or so while I shovel the finest chocolate cake into my mouth.

38.Be2 b5!

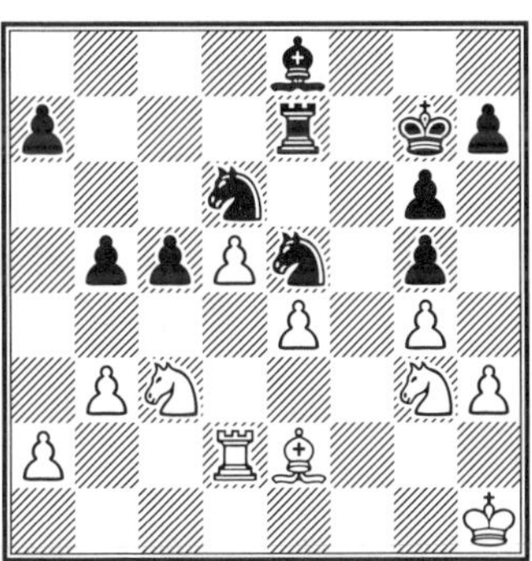

White can't do anything, so (thanks to his magnificent blockades) Black decides to create his own passed pawn courtesy of his queenside pawn majority.

39.Rc2 Rc7 40.Nd1 c4 41.bxc4 bxc4 42.Nc3 Kf6 43.Nb1 Rb7 44.Nd2

Believe it or not, Black will now sacrifice his passed c-pawn! You might think I'm kidding, but just watch!

44...Ba4 45.Rc1 Rb2 46.Nxc4 Nexc4 47.Bxc4 Bc2! 48.Bb3

Okay, now you might think that Black will play 48...Bxb3 49.axb3 Rxb3. But no, he trades Rooks instead!

48...Rb1!

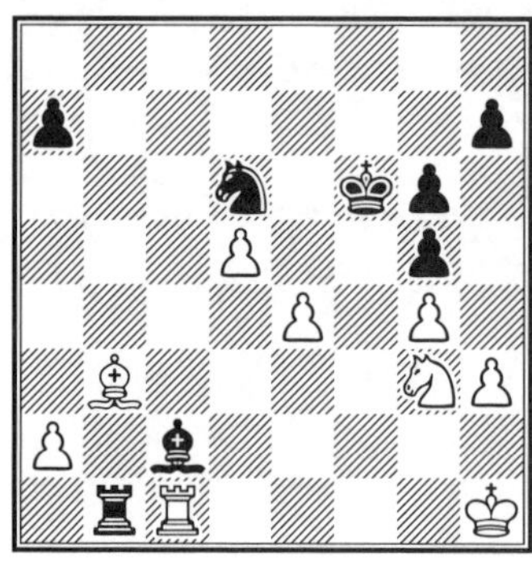

49.Rxb1 Bxb1

Now we see Black's strategy. He will bring his King to e5 (a great blockade square for black's King!) and then gobble up White's e4 and d5 pawns. The extra pawn and the far superior King position leads to a winning endgame.

50.Ne2 Bxe4+ 51.Kh2 Ke5 52.Nc3 Bd3 53.Kg3 Ne4+ 54.Nxe4 Bxe4 55.d6 Kxd6 56.Bg8 h6 57.Bf7 Bd5 58.Bxg6 Bxa2 59.h4 a5 60.hxg5 hxg5 61.Kf3 a4 62.Ke3 Be6 63.Kd4 Bxg4 64.Kc3 Bd1 65.Bf5 Ke5 66.Bd7 Kf4 67.Kb4 Bc2

Not falling for 67...g4?? 68.Bxg4! Kxg4 69.Ka3 with a basic draw.

68.Kc3 Bb3 69.Kb4 Bf7 70.Kxa4 Bg6 71.Kb4 Bf5 72.Bc6 g4 73.Kc5 Be4 74.Bd7 g3 75.Bh3 Ke3 76.Kd6 Bf5 77.Bg2 Kf2, 0-1.

78.Bc6 Bg4 followed by 79...Bf3 ends the game.

The Battle of Mutual Imbalances

The following game was a revelation when I first saw it, and it still blows my mind when I play over it today. It's not particularly complex, and it's not full of tactical candy.

Instead, it's incredibly instructive, demonstrating the battle of mutual imbalances (in this case each side has a pawn majority), how to maximize one's Knight, and how to create an artificial support point.

I'll show how Nimzowitsch successfully carried out his plan due to strong play and a lack of understanding from the White side. Then I'll demonstrate how White, if he used a logical plan based on his own pawn majority, might have been successful against many opponents. And finally, I'll show how proper play for both sides leads to an interesting position with more or less equal chances.

Here are the initial moves that take us to the key position.

Norwegian Amateurs vs. Aron Nimzowitsch, Oslo 1921

1.e4 e6 2.d4 d5 3.Nc3 Bb4 4.exd5 exd5 5.Nf3 Bg4 6.Be2 Ne7 7.0-0 Nbc6 8.Bf4 Bd6 9.Ne5 Bxe2 10.Nxe2 Bxe5 11.Bxe5 Nxe5 12.dxe5

The uneducated eye would see a boring position, but the position is actually filled with tension and interesting ideas.

The basics are clear: White has a kingside pawn majority and Black has a queenside pawn majority. White's Knight would love to live on the d4-square, and black's Knight fully intends to make the f5-square a home for his Knight.

This stuff, as simplistic as it might seem, is the map that drives both sides' future plans.

If you're not able to read that map, then you'll also be unable to play the position properly.

12...Qd7

12...0-0 is playable, but Nimzowitsch decides to castle queenside so he can make use of his h-pawn in the battle for the f5-square. For some readers, this might sound too advanced or even unintelligible, but it will all make sense in a few moves.

13.f4

The logic of this move is that White is trying to make use of his own pawn majority. It's hard for me to criticize anyone that strives to kick his positive imbalances into gear! However, the move has some collateral damage: it deprives the white Knight of the f4-square and it creates a hole on e3. Whether or not these things will affect the game is another matter, but it's always important to be aware of the good and bad side of every move you play. In any case, all our future exploration will be based on the position after 13.f4.

13...0-0-0 14.c3 Kb8 15.Qb3?

An awful move that has absolutely nothing to do with the position. We'll look at White's proper plan after we finish with this game.

15...c5

We have a classic battle: An e5/f4 pawn majority vs. a c5/d5 pawn majority. Now the silliness of 15.Qb3 sticks out like a sore thumb since white's Queen isn't helping its pawn majority in any way. Note that Black's c5/d5 pawns are controlling all the squares in front of them (b4, c4, d4, and e4), while White's pawn majority has a hole in it—namely the f5-square.

16.Rae1 h5!

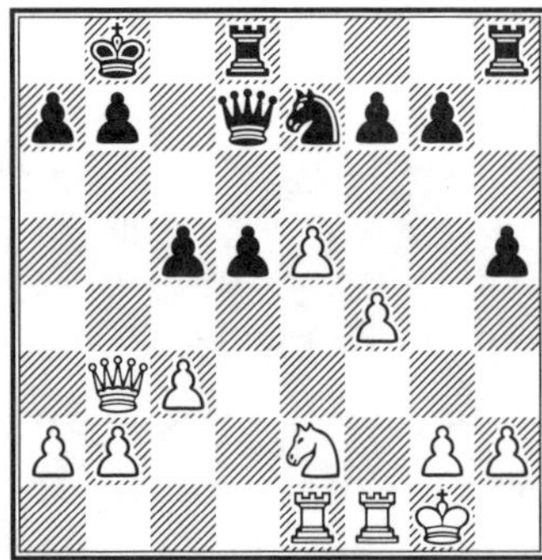

This move has a couple of points: the pawn can continue forward via ...h5-h4-h3, and the pawn solidifies Black's control of the critically important f5-square since g2-g4 is no longer possible. If Black had castled kingside, this advance wouldn't have been playable.

17.Kh1 Nf5

Black is clearly better. His pawn majority is mobile, while White's is frozen, and black's Knight is beautifully placed on f5 while white's Knight is rather sad to look at.

18.Ng1

White would have loved to exchange his passive Knight for Black's dynamic one, but 18.Ng3 loses to 18...Nxg3+ 19.hxg3 h4.

18...h4 19.Nh3

Stopping the h4-pawn's advance and avoiding a ...Ng3+ tactic:

19.Nf3?? Ng3+! 20.hxg3 hxg3+ 21.Kg1 Rh5 22.Re3 Rdh8 and White is toast.)

19...d4

Not only turning his majority into a passed pawn, but also creating a support point on e3 for the f5-Knight.

20.cxd4 cxd4 21.Qd3 Ne3

It doesn't take a genius to figure out who won the battle of the Knights!

22.Rf2 Qd5!

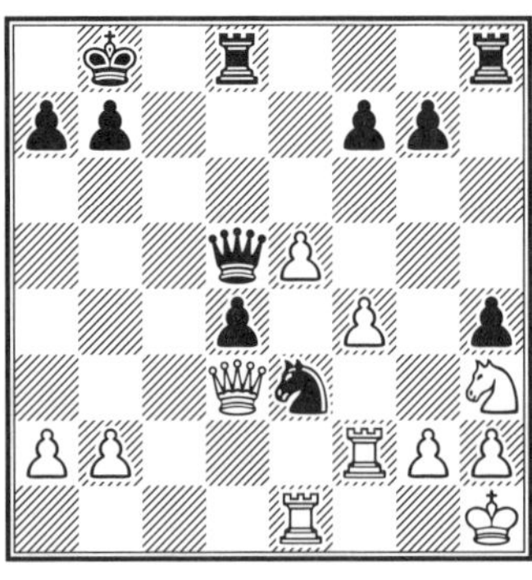

A beautiful move, and a great example of the power of centralization. Black's Queen not only attacks a2, but also eyes g2 while shooting sparks of energy in all directions.

23.a3 f6!

A killer. By exchanging White's important central pawn for Black's wing pawn, the g5-square is no longer accessible to white's Knight, and both the e- and g-files are ripped open and ready for the h8-Rook to make use of them.

24.exf6 gxf6 25.f5!

Bravo! White fights back! This advance gives white's Knight—which is a nonentity on h3—access to the f4-square.

25...Rhe8!

Nimzowitsch's improvement over the move he actually played. Here's how the real game continued: 25...Rhg8 26.Nf4 Qc6 27.Ng6 Rde8? (27...h3 was crushing.) 28.Nxh4 Rg4 29.Nf3 Qd5 30.Rd2 Rge4 31.Nxd4 Nxg2 32.Rxe4 Rxe4 33.Nc6+ bxc6 34.Qxd5 cxd5 35.Kxg2 Re5 36.Rf2 Kc7 37.Kg3 Kd6 38.Kg4 Re4+ 39.Kh5 d4 40.Kg6 Ke5 41.b4 Rg4+ 42.Kf7 Rf4 43.Rxf4 Kxf4 44.Kxf6 d3 45.Kg6 d2 46.f6 d1=Q, 0-1.

So why is 25...Rhe8 so strong? Aside from the fact that it creates a fantastic photo of centralization, it also creates some very specific tactical threats down the e-file.

26.Rfe2

26.Rg1 Re4 More centralization! 27.Nf4 Qe5 and now 28.Ng6 dies to 28... Ng4 threatening both 29...Qxh2 mate and 29...Nxf2 mate. 29.Nxe5 Nxf2 mate.

26.Nf4 gets wiped off the map by 26...Ng4 threatening f2 and e1.

26...Nxg2! 27.Rxe8 Nf4+ 28.Qe4 Rxe8 and White has to give up.

This is a game you need to look at over and over until you have a firm grasp of Nimzowitsch's strategic and tactical nuances. Then it's time to move on to the next example!

Let's return to the position after 14...Kb8.

1.e4 e6 2.d4 d5 3.Nc3 Bb4 4.exd5 exd5 5.Nf3 Bg4 6.Be2 Ne7 7.0-0 Nbc6 8.Bf4 Bd6 9.Ne5 Bxe2 10.Nxe2 Bxe5 11.Bxe5 Nxe5 12.dxe5 Qd7 13.f4 0-0-0 14.c3 Kb8

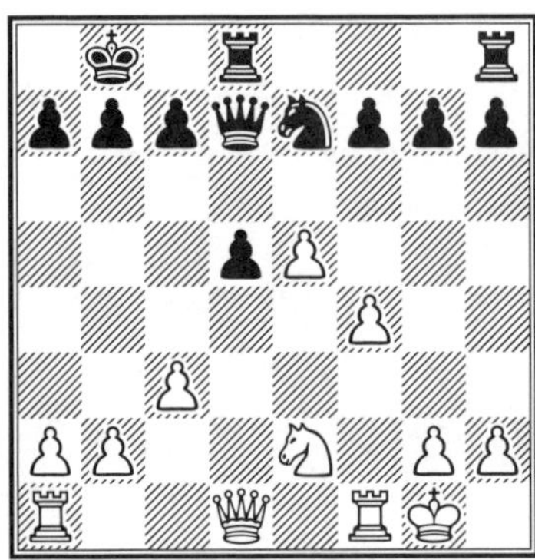

After looking at Nimzowitsch's game, you should understand that f5 is a very important square. So, if you chose 15.Qd3 you should be proud of yourself.

Another thought is this: why is black's Knight getting all the fun? Why can't White find a home for his horse too? If you decided that Ng3 was the bomb, then you need some fine-tuning since the only reason your Knight is on g3 is to make a swap after Black plays ...Nf5. However, 15.Ng3 also walks into 15...h5 when taking that pawn is very risky.

Hopefully, most of you are looking at d4 as the Knight's best home—it eyes f5 and also spreads its tendrils all over the board. The immediate 15.Nd4 is met by 15...c5, so you need to find a way to prepare Nd4.

That "way" is 15.b4, stopping ...c5 and turning d4 into a support point.

15.b4 Nf5

One of many possibilities. 15...h5 16.Nd4 h4!? 17.f5 h3 18.g3 lets White win the battle of the pawn majorities (not to mention that white's Knight is now superior to Black's). White is better, but there is still a lot of play in that position (a move like 18...g6 muddies the waters).

16.Qd3 h5 17.Nd4 Nxd4 18.cxd4

18.Qxd4 h4 19.h3 Qf5, =.

18...h4 19.h3 followed by f4-f5 with the kind of position White wanted—Black's pawn majority is frozen while White's is in full bloom.

In our first example, Black was allowed to make all his dreams come true: powerful pawn majority vs. frozen enemy majority, killer Knight vs. a neutered one, and chances for central expansion by ...d5-d4 and kingside play with ...h5-h4-h3.

In our second example White was on to Black's tricks and immediately stopped ...c7-c5 in its tracks, then fought for control of the key f5-square. Once that square fell, White was able to push his pawn to f5 when it was his pawn majority that was active, not Black's.

Now it's time to see both sides fight tooth and nail for their own individual visions. Nobody will bow to the other, and nobody will allow the opponent to grab the goodies that he so desperately wants to grab.

15.b4 d4!

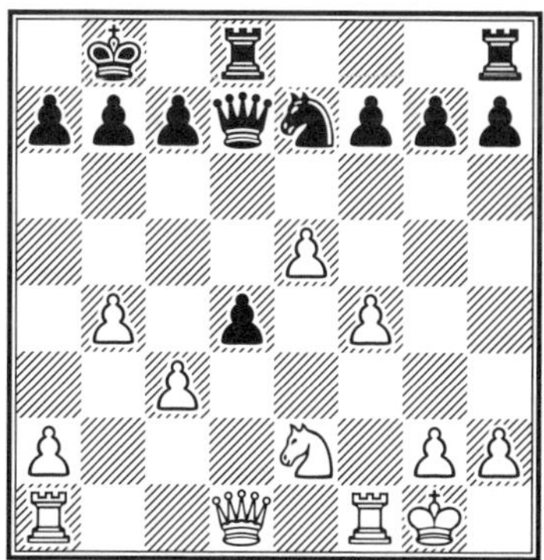

15...c5!? 16.bxc5 Rc8 17.Qe1 (17.Rb1 Rxc5 18.f5 Nc6 and Black is better.) 17...Rxc5 18.f5 Qc7 19.e6 f6 20.h3 (20.Qh4 Rc4) 20...Rc4, +=.

15...d4! is shocking, but is it okay!? Black cracks the center and demands active play before White can finish his development.

Before 15...d4!, let's try a more placid idea: 15...Nf5 16.Qd3 h5 17.Nd4 g6! 18.Nxf5 (This doesn't seem to give White much, so 18.b5! seems best, when it's not easy for Black to create active play.) 18...Qxf5 (18...gxf5!?) 19.Qxf5 gxf5 20.Rad1 c6 21.Rd2 Kc7 22.Rc1 Rhe8 with the idea of 23.a4 f6! 24.exf6 Re4! 25.Rd3 Kd6 26.Rh3 Rh8 and Black is fine.

16.Qxd4

16.Nxd4 Nd5 17.Qd3 Nxc3 is nothing for White.

16.cxd4 Nf5.

16...Qc6! 17.Qe3!?

Black often wants to play ...Nd5 in this line, so White tries to redirect the Knight to f5. 17.Qf2 Rd2 gives Black serious compensation for the sacrificed pawn.

17.Qc5 Qxc5+ 18.bxc5 Rd5! 19.Rad1 Rhd8 20.Rxd5 Rxd5 21.e6 f5 8.c4 Rd3 9.Kf2 Kc8 10.Rc1 Nc6, =.

17...Nf5 18.Qf2

18.Qh3 g6 19.Rfd1 (19.Rad1 Qb6+ 20.Kh1 Ne3 favors Black.) 19...Qb6+ 20.Kh1 Qf2 21.Qf3 Qxf3 22.gxf3 Ne3 23.Rxd8+ (23.Rd4 Nc2 24.Rxd8+ Rxd8 and black's Rook will penetrate down the d-file.) 23...Rxd8 24.Nd4 Kc8 25.a4 Nd5 26.Ne2 Ne3 with a draw.

18...Rd2 19.Rfd1 Qd5

Not 19... Rhd8?? 20.Nd4!

20.Rxd2 Qxd2 21.Qe1 Qe3+ 22.Kh1 Rd8 23.Rd1 Rxd1 24.Qxd1 a6 and, thanks to Black's activity, White has absolutely nothing.

Lessons I Learned from These Games

- We saw Nimzowitsch dominate the game by centralizing all his pieces. In our last example, Black (by sacrificing a pawn) solved his problems by shifting the battle to the center instead of the wings. It should be obvious that centralization, an idea attributed to Nimzowitsch, is something you really need to think about.
- In situations with mutual pawn majorities, it's important to not allow the opponent to freeze your majority, while you do your best to stop his majority in its tracks.
- Creating holes in the enemy position is always something you need to look for!
- Whatever battle might be raging, always do your best to make your minor pieces superior to the enemy minor pieces.

2

A WORD ABOUT OPENINGS

The Black Knights' Tango (or The Mexican Defense)

A favorite opening of mine is the Black Knights' Tango (also know as the Mexican Defense). I have played this opening for Black many times, and have even helped with the creation of some of its theory:

1.d4 Nf6 2.c4 Nc6

The main American heroes of this system are International Master Georgi Orlov and Grandmaster Joel Benjamin, though quite a few other creative players—like Grandmaster Larry Christiansen—have also made good use of it over the years. It's certainly an interesting opening, but you can't really force the main lines if White simply avoids it by 1.d4 Nf6 2.Nf3 and now 2...Nc6 3.d5 isn't exactly what Black was looking for. On the other hand, after 2.Nf3 you can enter some other opening where White has made a concession (placing the Knight on f3). This means that after 1.d4 Nf6 2.Nf3 g6 White can't play a Sämisch Variation against the KID, and if you choose 2...e6 after 2.Nf3, White might have preferred a Nimzo-Indian with the king-Knight back on g1.

Also, after 1.d4 Nf6 2.c4 Nc6 3.Nf3 e6 4.Nc3 Black might as well play 4...Bb4, entering a Nimzo-Indian, while 4.g3 Bb4+ takes Black into a Bogo-Indian.

Zhu Chen vs. Larry Christiansen, U.S. vs. China Summit, Seattle 2001

1.d4 Nf6 2.c4 Nc6 3.Nc3 e5 4.d5 Ne7 5.g3 Ng6 6.Bg2 Bc5 7.e3 0-0 8.Nge2 a6 9.0-0 d6 10.Bd2 Bd7 11.Rb1 b5 12.b4 Bb6 13.a4 bxc4 14.a5 Ba7 15.b5 axb5 16.Nxb5 Bf5 17.Ra1 Bc5 18.Nec3 Bd3 19.e4 Qd7!

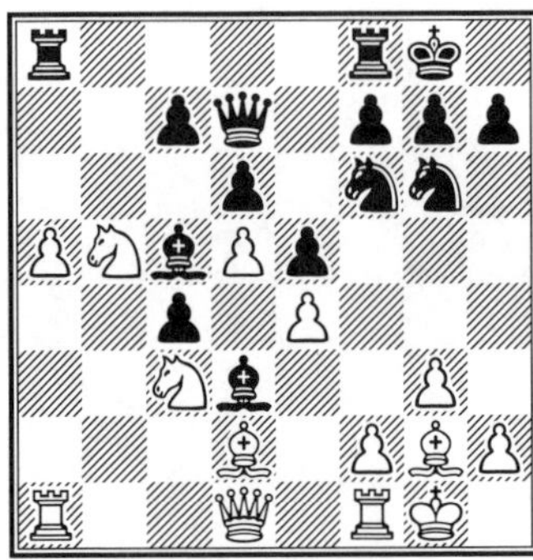

Ignoring the offered exchange and instead playing for a direct attack against white's King. 19...Bxf1 was possible, but Christiansen (who is a legendary attacker) decides to go for the King.

20.Re1 Rfb8 21.Qa4 Ng4 22.Be3 Nxe3 23.fxe3 h5!

Intending to loose up White's kingside pawn structure with ...h5-h4.

24.Bf1 h4 25.Bxd3 cxd3 26.Kg2 hxg3 27.hxg3 d2 28.Re2 Qg4 29.Rh1 Nf4+! 30.exf4 exf4

Black's Bishop, f4-pawn, and Queen will prove to be too much for white's King.

31.Rxd2 Qxg3+ 32.Kf1 Qf3+ 33.Ke1 Qxh1+, 0-1.

Stephen Brudno vs. Joel Benjamin , U.S. Open 2001

1.d4 Nf6 2.c4 Nc6 3.Nc3 e5 4.d5 Ne7 5.e4 Ng6 6.Be3 Bb4 7.f3 Bxc3+

Not falling for 7...d6?? 8.Qa4+.

8.bxc3 d6 9.c5 0-0 10.Bd3 Nd7 11.cxd6 cxd6 12.Ne2 Qa5 13.0-0 Nc5

Black, who owns the c5-square and will pressure c3 down the c-file, is already much better.

14.Bc4 Bd7 15.Bb3 Rac8 16.g3 f5

Owning the queenside wasn't enough. Black decides to mate his opponent too.

17.Bc2 fxe4 18.fxe4 Rxf1+ 19.Kxf1 Bh3+ 20.Kg1 Rf8 21.Qd2 Qxa2!

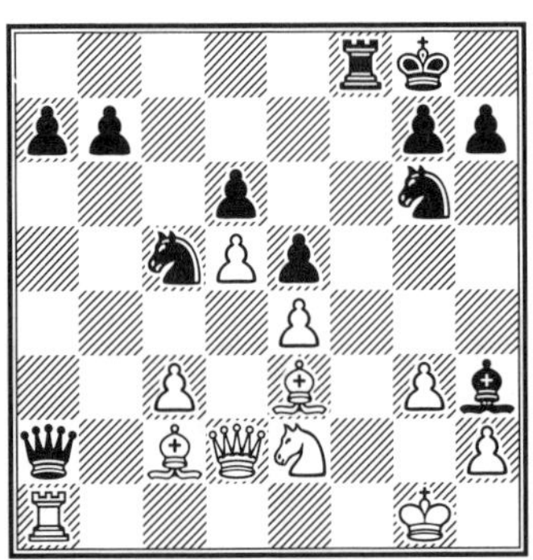

A satisfying move to play.

22.Re1 Qc4 23.Bf2 a5 24.Nc1 Rf3 25.Ne2 a4 26.Qg5 Nxe4, 0-1.

Okay, Christiansen and Benjamin make the Tango look like a mating machine. In the next game I was satisfied to win in less dramatic fashion against a very strong opponent.

Dao Thien Hai vs. Silman, Budapest 1994

1.d4 Nf6 2.c4 Nc6 3.Nc3

The key line is (after 1.d4 Nf6 2.c4 Nc6) 3.d5 Ne5 4.e4 e6 (4...Nxe4?? 5.Qd4! wins a piece) 5.f4 Ng6 6.Bd3 (6.e5 Ne4 7.Qf3 Bb4+ 8.Kd1 f5 9.Bd3 0-0 10.Bxe4 fxe4 11.Qxe4 d6 12.Nf3 Ba5! left Black with lots of development and a safe King in R.Potter vs. Benjamin, World Open 2003. White got just what he deserved after 13.Nc3 dxe5 14.fxe5 exd5 15.cxd5 Bf5 16.Qd4 c5 17.Qxc5 Rc8 18.Qd4 Bxc3 19.bxc3 Qa5 20.Bd2 Qb5 21.d6 Rc4 22.Qxa7 Nxe5 23.Nxe5 Qxe5 24.Qa3 Qd5 25.Re1 Rfc8 26.Kc1 h6 27.Re7 Qd3 28.Qb3 Kh7 29.Rc7 R8xc7 30.dxc7 Rxc7 31.a4 Bg6 32.Ra2 Rf7 33.Rc2 Rf1+ 34.Kb2 Rf2 35.Kc1 Rxg2 36.h4 Rh2 37.a5 h5 38.Qa4 Rxd2 39.Kb2 Rxc2+ 40.Qxc2 Qxc2+, 0-1.) 6...exd5 7.e5 Ne4 8.cxd5 Qh4+ 9.g3 Bb4! 10.Bd2? (10.Nc3) 10...Nxg3! 11.Nf3 Nxf4! 12.Bf1! (and not 12.Nxh4 Nxd3 mate!) 12...Bxd2+! 13.Nbxd2 Qh3!! 14.Ng5 (14.Bxh3? Nd3 mate) 14...Qg2!! and Black is winning—analysis by Orlov.

3...e5 4.d5 Ne7 5.e4 Ng6 6.Be3 Bb4 7.f3 Bxc3+ 8.bxc3 d6 9.Bd3 0-0 10.Ne2

I would have answered 10.c5 with 10...Nd7 11.cxd6 cxd6 when the open c-file will allow me to create easy pressure against White's c-pawn.

10...Nd7 11.Qd2 b6 12.Bg5 f6 13.Be3 Nc5 14.Bxc5 bxc5 15.h4 f5 16.h5

White didn't like the look of 16.exf5 Nxh4.

16...Nf4!

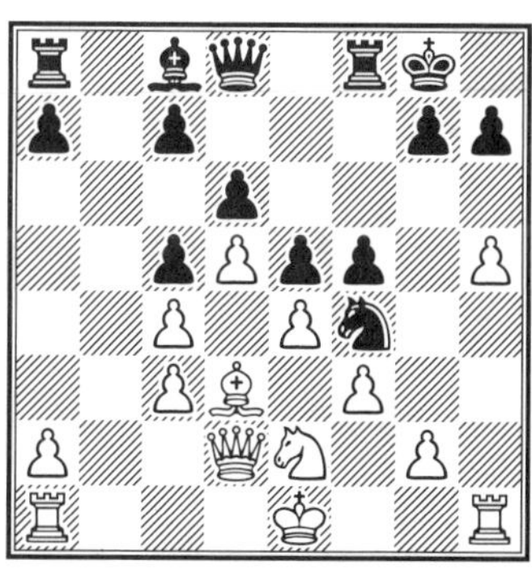

This puts the initiative firmly in Black's hands.

17.Nxf4 exf4 18.Qc2

18.Qxf4? fxe4 19.Qxe4 Re8 loses on the spot while 18.exf5 Bxf5 19.Bxf5 Rxf5 favors Black due to the weakness of White's c-, g- and h-pawns.

18...Qg5 19.0-0-0 fxe4 20.Bxe4 Bf5 21.Rde1

The position is far from pleasant for White. For example, 21.Bxf5 Rxf5 22.Rde1 Re5 leaves Black with all the chances.

21...Bxe4 22.Rxe4 Rae8 23.Rhe1!?

White decides to sacrifice a pawn in the hope of getting a bit of counterplay. The position after 23.Re2 Re3 couldn't have been to his taste.

23...Rxe4 24.Qxe4 Qxh5

It's important that my Queen be in a position to rush back for defense. One way to implode would be 24...Qxg2? 25.Qe6+ Kh8?? (25...Rf7) 26.Qf7! Rg8 27.Re8 when Black must resign.

25.a4 a5 26.Qe7 Qf7

It's a technical win, but a high degree of technique is required to reel in the full point. At this point in my life I found such endgames to be "relaxing puzzles" that I enjoyed solving.

27.Re4 h6 28.Qxf7+ Rxf7 29.Re8+ Kh7 30.Kd2

Black's h-pawn turns out to be far stronger than White's a-pawn after 30.Ra8 Re7 31.Kd2 (worse is 31.Rxa5 Re2) 31...Re5 32.Rxa5 Rg5.

30...Rf5!

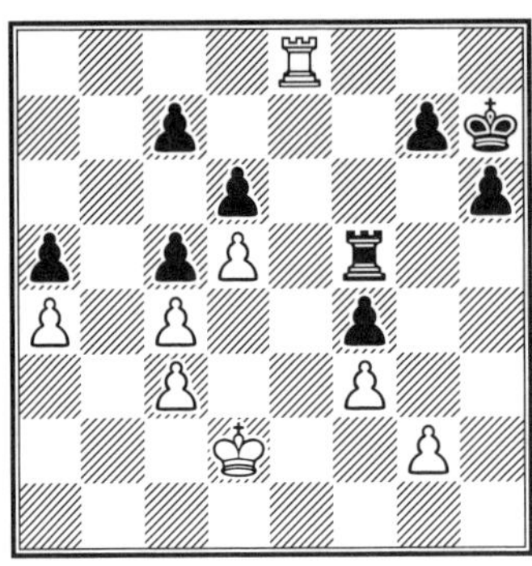

This Rook lift to g5 makes the win possible.

31.Kd3

31.Re7 Rg5.

31...Rg5 32.Re2

32.Re7 Rxg2 33.Rxc7 h5! wins by force. One example: 34.Rf7 Rf2 35.Rxf4 g5! 36.Rf6 g4.

32...Kg6 33.Rb2 Kf5 34.Rb7 Rxg2 35.Rxc7 Rg6 36.Rf7+ Ke5 37.Re7+ Kf6 38.Ra7 h5 39.Rxa5 h4 40.Rb5 Rg2 41.Rb8 Rf2 42.a5

Better resistance can be had by 42.Ke4, though Black would still ultimately prevail after 42...Kg5 43.a5 Re2+ 44.Kd3 Ra2. It's still very complicated, and thus well worth analyzing for the reader interested in improving his endgame skills.

42...Rxf3+ 43.Kc2 Rf1 44.Kb2 Re1 45.Rd8 Kg5 46.a6 Re7 47.Rxd6 f3 48.Re6 Rf7 49.Re1 f2 50.Rf1 Kg4 51.a7 Rxa7 52.Rxf2 h3 53.Rd2 g5 54.d6 Rd7 55.Kc2 Kg3 56.Rd5

No better is 56.Rd3+ Kh4 followed by ...g5-g4.

56...g4, 0-1.

No doubt about it, the Black Knights' Tango is a pretty cool opening!

Overextending Your Pawns with Black e5

I want to mention something to be aware of when Black opens ...c5: **1.e4 c5 2.e5?!**

Your reaction 2...d5 3.d4 e6 is perfectly playable (3...Nc6 is more challenging, when 4.c3 Bf5 is very comfortable for Black.), though you have inadvertently transposed into the French Defense (1.e4 e6 2.d4 d5 3.e5). White's 4.Bb5+ isn't very good (4.c3 is correct, giving support to d4) since after 4...Bd7 White will either have to trade off his "good" Bishop for Black's "bad" one with 5.Bxd7+, or run away, thereby losing time for no reason whatsoever.

1.e4 c5 2.e5?! d5 3.d4 e6 is perfectly playable, though it's important to notice that you're now in a French Defense (1.e4 e6 2.d4 d5 3.e5 c5). More challenging is 3...Nc6 when 4.c3 Bf5 is very comfortable for Black.

4.Bb5+ isn't very good (4.c3 is correct, giving support to d4) since after **4...Bd7** White will either have to trade off his "good" Bishop for Black's "bad" one with 5.Bxd7+, or run away, thereby losing time for no reason whatsoever.

Nevertheless, I would be much happier if a student noticed the weakness of e5 and tried to capitalize on it by moves like 2...Nc6 (developing and hitting e5) or 2...d6 (freeing the c8-Bishop and once again hitting e5). This doesn't mean that 2...d5 is worse, just that you decided to take advantage of a move that's clearly sub-par.

Here's an example of what might occur if you tried either of those ("hit the e5-pawn!") moves:

Punishing 2.e5

1.e4 c5 2.e5?! Nc6

Developing a piece and hitting e5. 2...d6 is also logical: 3.Nf3 (3.exd6 Qxd6 when White has moved his e-pawn twice so it could trade itself for a pawn that only moved once. The result: Black has more central space thanks to the c5-pawn. Black also has a piece developed while White has no pieces developed. Not a very good opening for White!) 3...Nc6 4.Bb5 (White has other moves, of course, but Black is doing well against all of them.) 4...Bd7 5.exd6 e6 6.d4 Bxd6 and Black has no problems whatsoever.

3.Nf3 Qc7

Again, Black has other good responses. I like 3...Qc7 since, if White doesn't want to sacrifice his e5-pawn, he has to play his Queen to e2 which blocks the f1-bishop.

4.Qe2

Yech!

4...f6!

Okay, this continues our e5-bloodlust. A wild choice is:

4...g5!? Which not only threatens to win the e5-pawn with ...g5-g4, but also intending ...Bg7 hitting e5 again. Hopefully this will teach you that once you see a target, hit it again and again until it crumbles. If you don't like to make "crazy" moves, then the conservative 4...e6 followed by ...a6 gives Black a nice Sicilian position.

5.exf6 Nxf6 with a dream opening for Black (lead in development, more central space, and more central pawns).

In a nutshell, sometimes an advanced pawn can be overextended, or an annoying knife in the enemy position (many battles are about this difference of opinion). However, rushing the pawn forward for no reason like **1.e4 c5 2.e5** is nothing more than a misguided overextension. It's up to you to view it as such and then, if possible, find a way to milk as much from your opponent's dubious choice as you can. In this case hitting it with 2...Nc6 followed by ...Qc7 is a logical and strong reaction.

Two Years of Opening Preparation

The story goes that the Grandmaster Frank Marshall (a legendary attacking player) had come up with a promising gambit against the Ruy Lopez and wanted to use it against Capablanca. Most renditions of this tale claim that Marshall kept this line a secret for several years before he was able to unleash it against the Cuban god.

However, though a long, long wait makes the legend red hot, Capablanca himself set the record straight in a note after 7...0-0: "I now felt that Marshall had prepared something... and had kept it for two years, awaiting the opportunity of playing it in a tournament against me."

So much for "several years." But preparing a line against a certain foe for two years is still epic in my book, so the whole "let's prepare a monster gambit so that next time I face off against Capablanca I'll wipe him off the board" is more than worthy of its legendary status.

But, as is well known for those that studied chess history, the story gets even better since Capablanca not only walked into the "trap" but defended like the genius he was and won the game!

José Raúl Capablanca vs. Frank Marshall, New York 1918

1.e4 e5 2.Nf3 Nc6 3.Bb5 a6 4.Ba4 Nf6 5.0-0 Be7 6.Re1 b5 7.Bb3 0-0 8.c3 d5 9.exd5 Nxd5 10.Nxe5 Nxe5 11.Rxe5 Nf6 12.Re1 Bd6 13.h3 Ng4 14.Qf3 Qh4 15.d4!

Capablanca doesn't fall for the following nightmare: 15.hxg4 Bh2+ 16.Kf1 Bxg4 17.Qe4 Bf4! 18.g3 Qh2 19.Re3 (19.Bxf7+ Kxf7 20.Qd5+ Kg6 21.Re6+ Bxe6 22.Qxe6+ Kh5 23.Qd5+ Bg5 24.Qg2 Rxf2+ 25.Qxf2 Qh1+ 26.Ke2 Re8+, analysis by Tal.) 19...Rae8 20.Qd5 Bxg3! 21.Rxg3 (21.Qxf7+ Kh8) 21...Be2+ 22.Ke1 Bf3+ 23.Kf1 Qh1+ 24.Rg1 Qh3+ 25.Rg2 Qxg2 mate.

15...Nxf2

Capablanca wrote: "Very likely a mistake and overlooking the reply. 15...h5 was perhaps the best way to keep up the pressure."

16.Re2!

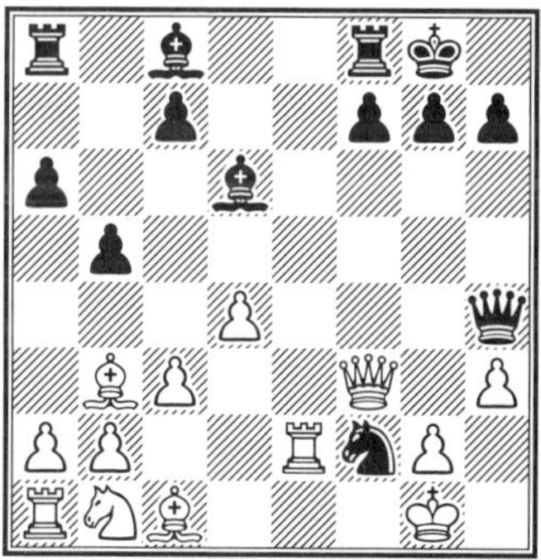

The great Cuban defends in a remarkably cool manner. Playable is 16.Qxf2 (16.Bd2 is more highly thought of.) 16...Bh2+ 17.Kf1 Bg3 18.Qd2! Bxh3 19.gxh3 Qxh3+ 20.Qg2 Qxg2+ 21.Kxg2 Bxe1 and though Black has a Rook and two pawns for White's two minor pieces, White's position is preferable.

16...Bg4

Marshall continues playing with confidence and energy, but that doesn't make the position viable for Black!

17.hxg4

Perfect play by Capa. 17.Qxf2?? Bg3 18.Qf1 Bxe2 19.Qxe2 Rae8 is winning for Black.

17...Bh2+ 18.Kf1 Bg3 19.Rxf2 Qh1+ 20.Ke2 Bxf2 21.Bd2 Bh4 22.Qh3 Rae8+ 23.Kd3 Qf1+ 24.Kc2 Bf2 25.Qf3

Black has run out of ammunition and the rest is technique.

25...Qg1 26.Bd5 c5 27.dxc5 Bxc5 28.b4 Bd6 29.a4 a5 30.axb5 axb4 31.Ra6 bxc3 32.Nxc3 Bb4 33.b6 Bxc3 34.Bxc3 h6 35.b7 Re3 36.Bxf7+, 1-0.

The game might have concluded in the following manner: 36...Rxf7 (36...Kh7 37.Qf5+ Kh8 38.Rxh6 mate) 37.b8=Q+ Kh7 38.Rxh6+ Kxh6 (38...gxh6 39.Qxf7 mate) 39.Qh8+ Kg6 40.Qh5 mate.

Capablanca wasn't called a "chess machine" for nothing! The way he effortlessly refuted Marshall's attack deserves to be the stuff of legend!

What's interesting is that Marshall not only claimed to have created the line (8...d5, which is now called the Marshall Gambit), but he also claimed that he was the first player to castle on move 7 (1.e4 e5 2.Nf3 Nc6 3.Bb5 a6 4.Ba4 Nf6 5.0-0 Be7 6.Re1 b5 7.Bb3 0-0—usually Black played 7...d6 first).

Of course, without databases it's impossible to ascertain who was first. Indeed, even a database can't give you a 100% guarantee, since many unpublished games might have been "first" in countless lines. Due to this, what's far more important is who popularized the line and who did the really deep research that made it viable at the highest levels.

It turns out that a game in 1893 not only was the first known game with 7...0-0, but also the first known game with 8...d5! Oddly, it occurred in Capablanca's birth nation, Cuba! The game was between the very strong (2550 rating according to Edo Chess) Carl Walbrodt vs. four opponents in consultation.

Carl August Walbrodt vs. Conill/Ostolaza/Lopez/Herrera, Havana consultation 1893

1.e4 e5 2.Nf3 Nc6 3.Bb5 a6 4.Ba4 Nf6 5.0-0 Be7 6.Re1 b5 7.Bb3 0-0 8.c3 d5 9.exd5 e4 10.dxc6 exf3 11.g3 Bg4 12.d4 h5 13.Bg5 Re8 14.Nd2 Nh7 15.Bxe7 Rxe7 16.h3 Bxh3 17.Nxf3 Rxe1+ 18.Qxe1 Qf6 19.Qe3 Bg4 20.Ne5 Ng5 21.f4 Ne6 22.Nxg4 hxg4 23.Bxe6 fxe6 24.Re1 Re8 25.d5 Kf7 26.Qe4 Re7 27.dxe6+ Qxe6 28.Qxe6+ Rxe6 29.Rxe6 Kxe6 30.Kf2 a5 31.Ke3 g6 32.Ke4 a4 33.Kd4 Kf5 34.Kd5 Kf6 35.b4 axb3 36.axb3 Kf5 37.b4 Kf6 38.c4 bxc4 39.Kxc4 Ke6 40.Kc5 Ke7 41.b5 Kd8 42.b6 cxb6+ 43.Kxb6 Kc8 44.c7, 1-0.

I highly doubt that Marshall was aware of this game. But if one wants to call the line with 8...d5 the Conill/Ostolaza/Lopez/Herrera Gambit, then go for it.

What Marshall clearly did invent was 9.exd5 Nxd5 10.Nxe5 Nxe5 11.Rxe5 Nf6, since before that the only two "Marshall Gambit" games known featured 9...e4. The second game that used the gambit was played by Marshall himself in 1917, a year before he played Capablanca!

Walter Frere vs. Frank Marshall, New York Training 1917

1.e4 e5 2.Nf3 Nc6 3.Bb5 a6 4.Ba4 Nf6 5.0-0 Be7 6.Re1 b5 7.Bb3 0-0 8.c3 d5 9.exd5 e4 10.dxc6 exf3 11.d4 fxg2 12.Bf4 Bg4 13.Qd3 Nh5 14.Bxc7 Qxc7 15.Qe4 Nf4 16.Qxe7 Qxe7 17.Rxe7 Bf3, 0-1.

NOTE that it wasn't played in a tournament, it was a training game. This reminds us of Pillsbury going over his new move again and again with William Napier. Analyzing with friends and even playing training games to get ready for the "real thing" is common and actually helps to verify that Marshall was indeed keeping this line ready for a shot at Capablanca, but only after he ironed things out.

This explains why Marshall played 9...e4 against Frere, but most likely rejected it after further analysis and uncorked 9.exd5 Nxd5 10.Nxe5 Nxe5 11.Rxe5 Nf6 for the first time in history.

This leaves us with one more petite mystery to solve. Who came up with 11...c6!

In Marshall's super-enjoyable book, *My Fifty Years of Chess*,[1] there's an opening theory section at the end of the book which offers up original analysis that Marshall and his friend, Tom Emery, worked on together. Naturally, the pair took a look at the Marshall Gambit.

Marshall analysis and comments::

> I have made some changes in my variation of the Ruy Lopez which tend to strengthen it. The opening moves of this line are as follows:
>
> **1.e4 e5 2.Nf3 Nc6 3.Bb5 a6 4.Ba4 Nf6 5.0-0 Be7 6.Re1 b5 7.Bb3 0-0 8.c3 d5 9.exd5 Nxd5 10.Nxe5 Nxe5 11.Rxe5**
>
> Here our analysis deviates from previous play. In this position,11...Nf6 or 11...Bb7 have hitherto been played. We now recommend the following:
>
> **11...c6! 12.d4 Bd6 13.Re1 Qh4 14.g3 Qh3 15.Bxd5 cxd5 16.Qf3 Bf5 17.Qxd5**
>
> As ...Be4 was threatened.
>
> **17...Rae8 18.Rxe8 Rxe8 19.Bd2 Be4**, and Black wins.

1 Frank J. Marshall, *My Fifty Years of Chess*. New York: Chess Review, 1942. (Later published under the title *Marshall's Best Games of Chess*.)

Okay, the analysis is pretty bad, but what's important is that Marshall called this line "...my variation of the Ruy Lopez," which clearly shows that he felt he was its creator.

Note: Marshall's book first appeared in 1942 but I have no idea when Marshall and Emery cranked out their analysis although Marshall made it clear that they had been analyzing together for "many years".

I bring all this up because the first known game where 11...c6 appeared was Alberto Dulanto vs. Conel Alexander, Buenos Aires Olympiad 1939.

It doesn't really matter if Marshall and Emery analyzed 11...c6 in 1936 or 1940, it's clear that:

- Marshall honestly thought that he was the first to ever play 8...d5 (turns out he was the second player to have played it).
- Marshall clearly WAS the first to ever play 11...Nf6.
- Marshall really did keep the line under wraps so he could use it against Capablanca, though he only waited two years instead of "several."
- Marshall was the first player to deeply analyze the position after 8...d5.
- Marshall's use of 8...d5 put it on the map, and the name "Marshall Gambit" is fully deserved.

I'll add that after Marshall lost to Capablanca, he played the gambit again (in the same tournament!) and won:

John Morrison vs. Frank Marshall, New York 1918

1.e4 e5 2.Nf3 Nc6 3.Bb5 a6 4.Ba4 Nf6 5.0-0 Be7 6.Re1 b5 7.Bb3 0-08. c3 d5 9.exd5 Nxd5 10.d4 exd4 11.cxd4 Bb4 12.Bd2 Bg4 13.Nc3 Nf6

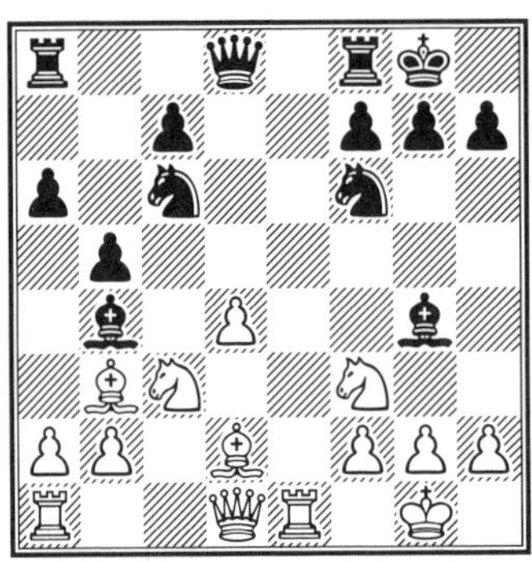

14.Be3 Bxf3 15.gxf3 Qd7 16.d5 Ne7 17.Bg5 Qh3 18.Bxf6 gxf6 19.Qd4 Bd6 20.Qg4+ Qxg4+ 21.fxg4 Ng6 22.Ne4 Be5 23.Rab1 Nf4 24.g5 fxg5 25.Nxg5 Rae8 26.Re3 h6 27.Rbe1 hxg5 28.Rxe5 Rxe5 29.Rxe5 Kg7 30.Rxg5+ Kf6 31.Rg4 Ke5 32.h4 a5 33.a3 Rh8 34.f3 f5 35.Rg7 Kd6

36.Kf2 Re8 37.Rf7 Re2+ 38.Kg3 Nh5+ 39.Kh3 Nf4+ 40.Kg3 Nh5+ 41.Kh3 Rxb2 42.Bd1 Nf4+ 43.Kg3 Nh5+ 44.Kh3 Ke5 45.Re7+ Kd6 46.Rf7 Nf4+ 47.Kg3 Nxd5 48.h5 f4+ 49.Kh3 Rb1 50.Be2 Rh1+ 51.Kg4 Ke6 52.Rf8 Rg1+ 53.Kh3 Rh1+ 54.Kg4 Nf6+ 55.Kxf4 Rxh5 56.Ke3 Nd5+ 57.Kd4 Ke7 58.f4 Rh2 59.Rc8 Rxe2 60.Kxd5 Rc2 61.Rb8 c6+ 62.Ke5 Rc5+ 63.Ke4 Rc3 64.a4 bxa4 65.Ra8 Rc5 66.Rh8 a3 67.Rh7+ Kd6 68.Rh6+ Kc7 69.Rh7+ Kb6 70.Rh2 Rb5 71.Ra2 Rb4+ 72.Ke5 Rb3 73.f5 Kb5 74.f6 Rf3 75.Ke6 Ka4 76.f7 Kb3 77.Rg2 a2 78.Rg3 Rxg3 79.f8=Q Re3+ 80.Kd7 Rd3+ 81.Kxc6 a1=Q 82.Qf7+ Ka3 83.Qf8+ Ka4 84.Qf4+ Qd4, 0-1. Whew! Exhausting!

3

PSYCHOLOGY AT THE BOARD

When I use the term "chess psychology" I'm referring to the "state of mind" that plays a crucial part in a players results: self-confidence (or the lack thereof), fear of threats (real or imagined), fear of losing, to name a few. These psychological "illnesses" often manifest via extremely powerful internal phrases that drag you on paths that you never should walk on. Thus, when that internal voice says, "He can't!" or "I can't!" or "I have too!" you obey, and fall victim to this unconscious demand—all chess players are susceptible to this.

Mikhail Tal wrote:

> [There is] a subjective or perhaps psychological element in chess which one cannot and, indeed, should not attempt to escape. I believe most definitely that one must not only grapple with the problems of the board; one must also make every effort to combat the thoughts and will of the opponent.

Amateurs bathe in the waters of unconscious demands usually not aware that they are doing so—if they are aware of this invisible battleground, they are clueless as to how to navigate through it! Even grandmasters get snookered by those gremlin voices from time to time.

Deadly Mindsets — He Can't/I Can't

Unlike memorizing an opening or remembering various tactical or positional patterns, a state of mind is not something you can always control.

So, what is "He can't/I can't?"

"He can't" appears when you look at a possible move/plan for the opponent and you say to yourself (consciously or unconsciously), "He won't be able to pull that off!" or "I don't think he'll play that move!"

"I can't" is similar: "I shouldn't make that move!"

You would be amazed at how often "He can't/I can't" appears in amateur chess.

And though it's a constant there, it also rears its ugly head in grandmaster chess too, though it's not nearly as common.

One of the many advantages that masters have over amateurs is that they have awareness of "I can't"/"He can't." When a master sees the move he wants to play, and then notices "I can't do that because of blah, blah..." trying to kick his brain into submission, he smiles and fights "I can't" tooth and nail.

Here's a typical example:

Silman vs. Hodges, Santa Barbara 1987

1.d4 Nf6 2.c4 e6 3.Nf3 c5 4.d5 exd5 5.cxd5 d6 6.Nc3 g6 7.Nd2 Nbd7 8.e4 Bg7 9.Be2 0-0 10.0-0 a6 11.a4 Re8 12.Qc2 Nh5 13.Bxh5 gxh5 14.Nd1 Rb8 15.a5 b5 16.a4-b6 Nb6 17.Ne3 Bd7 18.Rd1 Bd4 19.Nf3 Qf6 20.Ra3 h4 21.h3!!

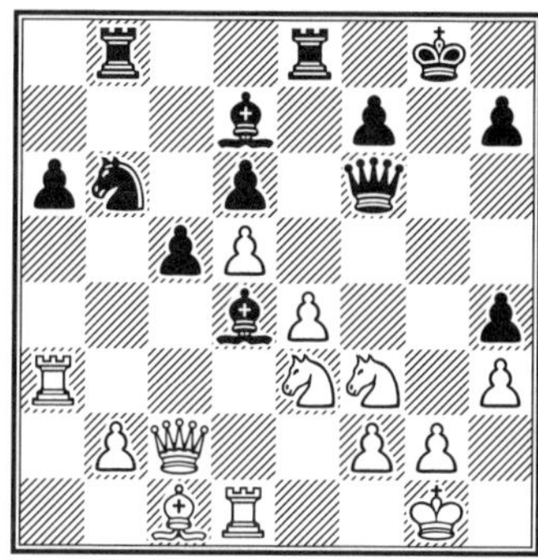

Black had just played 20...h4, hoping to disrupt White's kingside pawn cover by ...h4-h3. Ideally, White would like to stop this by 21.h3 (retaining the integrity of his kingside pawns and also freezing the h4-pawn, which could easily turn out to be a target) but then 21...Bxh3 follows. Many players would lament, "I want to play 21.h3 but I can't due to 21...Bxh3."

But is that so? If you want to play h3 but fear 21...Bxh3, don't give up on your h2-h3 move. Instead, look at the position after 21...Bxh3 with clear eyes and see what that position offers.

Before you say, "I can't" you need to prove it in a court of law. In this case the initial thought was, "I want" to play h3. He can reply with ...Bxh3 but just how good is that for Black?" You won't find the truth unless you seek it!

21...Bxh3 22.gxh3!?

I had calculated a long tactical line that I deemed really good for White. However, modern computers show that Black is equal with best defense. Thus 22.e5! is correct when 22...dxe5 (22...Qg7 23.Nxd4 cxd4 24.Rxd4 is extremely strong for White due to the hanging h4-pawn, the weakness of black's King, the weakness of Black's kingside dark-squares, and the fact that both white Rooks can easily leap to the kingside—the d4-Rook along the 4th rank and the a3-Rook along the 3rd rank.) 23.gxh3 Qxf3 24.Ng4 and since black's Queen is trapped, he has nothing better than 24…Bxf2 25.Nxf2 and White is a piece up.

22...Qxf3 23.Rxd4!

This was my big idea. I felt that the Knight and dark-squared Bishop would overrun black's King on the dark-squares.

23...cxd4 24.Ng4 Rec8 25.Qd2 d3 26.Qg5+ Kh8

On 26…Kf8 White retains a winning attack with 27.Bf4 Nc4 28.Nh6.

27.Be3

This was the position I saw when I played 21.h3. At the time I thought that White had a decisive attack, however Houdini makes it clear that I was badly mistaken.

27...Nd7

Possible was 27…Rc4 though White wins out after 28.Rxd3 f6 29.Nxf6 Ra4 30.Ra3! Rxa3 31.bxa3 Nc4 32.Qh6 Rb1+ 33.Bc1 Rxc1+ 34.Qxc1 Qxf6 35.Qxc4 Qa1+ 36.Kg2 Qxa3 37.e5! and White's central advanced passed pawn will reel in the win.

28.Bd4+ f6 29.Nxf6 Ne5⁈

My opponent and I somehow overlooked 29...Rc1+ 30.Qxc1 Nxf6 31.Kh2 Rg8 32.Bxf6+ Qxf6 33.Qc3 and Black should draw.

30.Ng4 Rb7

30…Rg8 31.Bxe5+ dxe5 32.Qxe5+ Rg7 33.Qxb8+ and Black has to resign.

31.Nxe5 Rg7 32.Nxf3, 1-0.

This game was extremely interesting. But it was only possible due to my challenge to "I can't" and the negativity that comes with it.

I'll finish with a typical amateur "I can't" moment:

Black is a pawn down and it looks like White threatens Bxe7 removing the f5-Bishop's protection. Sighing sadly, Black said to himself, "I have to trade on d3."

When you realize that your mind is saying, "I can't", ignore it and look for the move you feel the position really wants. Then put all your energy into making that ideal move work.

If, after a deep study, you decide that you really can't play it, then fair enough. However, once you embrace this kind of thought you'll find that many of the "I can't" moves are actually "I can!"

Chess Psychology 101

To quote Alekhine:

> I consider the three following factors essential for success. First, a realization of your strong and weak points; second, an accurate knowledge of your opponent's strong and weak points; third, a higher objective than momentary satisfaction. I see this objective to be scientific and artistic achievements which place chess on a level with the other arts.

How can we rid ourselves of this chess scourge? The first step is to acknowledge that there's a problem. After that take note when you feel you've fallen victim to these landmines (a qualified chess teacher can be a big help assessing this). Once you've identified when demons sneak up on you, try to root it out by replacing negative ideas such as:

- Fear of giving up or taking material.
- Bowing to panic.
- The curse of "I can't."
- Making lazy/soft moves.
- Lack of patience.

With positive ideas:

- Step beyond the fear.
- It's my party and I'll move what i want to.
- The art of insistence.
- Push your own agenda.

It's important to understand that, though you might try hard to avoid those nasty internal voices, it is often very hard to notice during a tough game. I've had (and have) students that proudly show me a game where they insist they avoided all the psychological pitfalls we were discussing here, only to discover (during the lesson) that they were still far off the mark.

In the following game, Black has a very comfortable position, and he has decided that he wants to trade his undeveloped dark-squared Bishop for White's active f4-Bishop. Okay, nothing wrong with that. However, he first played 5...a6, proudly explaining how it's keeping his opponent's pieces at bay.

I was not too happy with this. It's playable of course, but (since ...Bd6 is what Black wants to do) why not just DO it? However, instead of "just do it," Black bowed to a common will-o-the-wisp (something that is impossible to get or achieve/something unattainable).

Mitchell Jayson vs. Bertram Buggs, Los Angeles Chess Club 2015

1.d4 d5 2.Nc3 Nf6 3.Bf4 Bf5 4.e3 e6 5.h3 Bd6

5...a6 was played in the actual game, which (though playable) turned out to be a complete waste of time. Black's 5...a6 takes him back to his old habit of **fearing things** that shouldn't be feared.

6.Bxd6

More fear. Correct was 6.Bd3 Bxf4 7.exf4 0-0 8.Nf3 Qd6, =.

6...Qxd6

Nothing wrong with 6...cxd6 covering a bunch of important squares and also opening up the c-file for his Rooks.

7.Nb5

The only thing that might have spooked Black. Of course, 7.Bb5+ is more than useless: 7...Nbd7 (7...c6 is another way to laugh at White's check.) 8.Nf3 0-0 and one has to wonder what white's Bishop is doing on b5.

7...Qb4+

Safer is 7...Qe7 and now if White plays 8.c4 then simply 8...dxc4 is strong since 9.Bxc4?? Qb4+ wins for Black.

Also good is 7...Qb6!? when Black can chase white's Knight back with ...a6 WITH TEMPO if he wants to bother chasing the enemy Knight at all.

8.c3 Qe7!

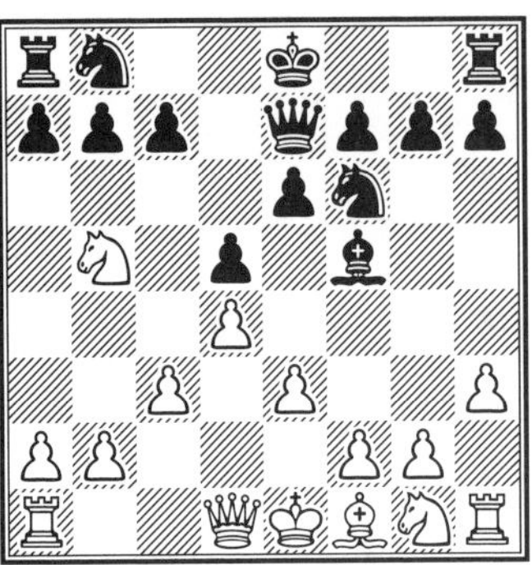

Now the Knight can't move back to c3 and 9.c4 dxc4 transposes into the other line that favors Black. 8...Qxb2 9.Nxc7+ Kd7 10.Nxa8 Qxc3+ 11.Ke2 Qb2+ 12.Kf3 Ne4 will probably end in a draw: 13.Ne2 Nd2+ 14.Kg3 Ne4+ 15.Kf3 Nd2+, etc.

9.Nf3 a6

With tempo.

10.Na3

A bad square for the Knight.

10...0-09 with a comfortable position for Black.

This same kind of fear ("Maybe he'll do that move, so I have to stop it!") affects much higher-rated players too. Here's a game where a master plays solid moves that simply aren't up to snuff in the greater scheme of things:

Conrado Diaz vs. Bertram Buggs, Los Angeles Chess Club 2015

1.d4 Nf6 2.c4 e5 3.dxe5 Ng4 4.e4 Nxe5 5.f4 Ng6

Not the best. Instead, 5...Nec6 6.Nc3 Bc5 and Black is doing very well.

6.Be3 Bb4+ 7.Nd2

7.Nd2 stops Black from destroying White's queenside pawn structure. On the other hand, 7.Nc3 Bxc3+ 8.bxc3 is quite happy allowing it: 8...d6 9.Ne2 Nd7 10.Ng3 (10.h4 h5 11.Ng3 Nc5, =) 10...Nf6 (10...0-0 is also okay) 11.Be2 0-0 12.c5 Re8 with chances for both sides.

7...Nc6?!

Black doesn't understand the opening. The main ideas are 7...d6 8.a3 (8.g3 is better) 8...Bc5 9.Bxc5 dxc5 10.Qf3 Nc6 and Black's doubled pawns on ...c7 and ...c5 are useful since the hole on d4 will eventually be a plus.

The other way is 7...Qe7 which cuts to the chase by striving to "win" the dark squares on c5 and/or d4: 8.a3 Bc5 9.Bxc5 Qxc5 10.Qf3 a5.

8.Ngf3 Qe7

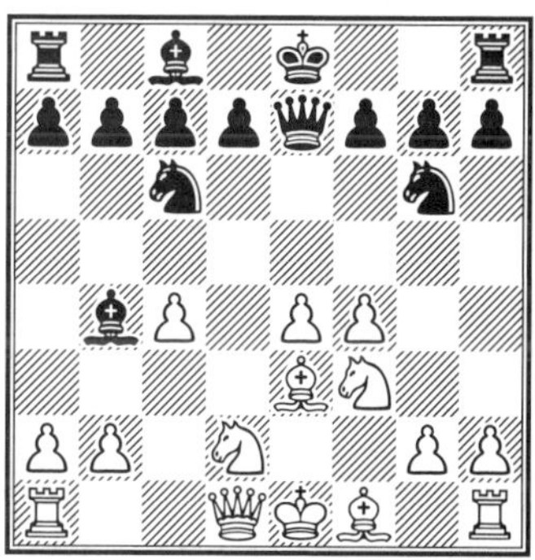

9.a3

9.Bd3 Qd6! wins a pawn due to the double attack against both d3 and f4. Better choices were 9.Qe2, 9.Qb3, or 9.Qc2 but Black will still get his share of the play thanks to his dark-square strategy.

9...Bc5 10.Qe2 d6 and Black is more than okay.

Liora Ginzburg vs. Bertram Buggs, Los Angeles Chess Club 2019

1.Nf3 Nf6 2.d4 g6 3.e3 Bg7 4.Be2 O-O 5.Nbd2 d6 6.O-O c5 7.b3 Nc6 8.Bb2 a6 9.a4 cxd4 10.exd4 d5

So far Black is playing very well!

11.c4 Bf5 12.Bc3 Rc8 13.c5 Re8

Okay, but better was 13...Ne4 14.Qc1 Nxc3 15.Qxc3 Qa5 and White in trouble.

14.b4 Ne4 15.Nxe4 dxe4 16.Ne5 Nxe5 17.dxe5 Qc7?!

Best is 17...a5! 18.Qb3 Qc7 19.Bc4 e6 20.Bxb4 exf2+.

18.f3 Bxe5 19.Bxe5 Qxe5 20.fxe4 Bxe4

Now White is in trouble again. However, it can't be helped.

21.Bf3 Rcd8 22.Qe1 Qd4+ 23.Kh1 Bxf3 24.Rxf3 e6

24...e6 is good, but 24...e5 is even better.

25.Rf1 Qc4?!

25...e5! was better (in fact, Black is winning)

26.Rb1 Rd3 27.Qe2 Red8 28.Qf2 f5!

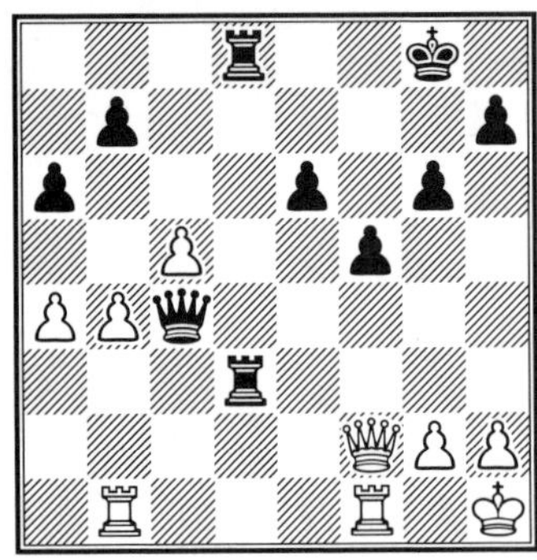

29.Qe1 Qd5

Beautiful!

30.Rc1 Rd2 31.Rg1 e5 32.h3 e4

Now Black owns everything.

33.Qe3 Qa2 34.Ra1 Qb2 35.Rab1 Qd4 36.Qb3+ Kf8 37.Rge1 Qf2 38.Rg1 R8d3 39.Qxd3 Rxd3 and Black easily won.

All in all, chess is a game of mental and creative domination. You create a certain agenda (one that embraces the imbalances) and you do your best to force your opponent to drink your Kool-Aid (i.e., to accept your vision of what's going on, thereby making your opponent follow your lead even though he is probably not aware of doing so).

There *will* be many moments where you can cave in to your opponent's demands or threats or his overall vision. Your mission, if you choose to accept it, is to kick all of that to the curb and win the battle of wills.

Here's a great example by Capablanca.

José Capablanca vs. Rudolf Spielmann, New York 1927

1.d4 d5 2.Nf3 e6 3.c4 Nd7 4.Nc3 Ngf6 5.Bg5 Bb4 6.cxd5 exd5 7.Qa4 Bxc3+ 8.bxc3 0-0 9.e3 c5 10.Bd3 c4

Black creates a 3 vs. 2 pawn majority on the queenside but Spielmann is paying a huge cost by doing so: he is taking the pressure off of d4, and White can make use of his central pawn majority via a well-timed e3-e4 advance.

11.Bc2 Qe7 12.0-0 a6 13.Rfe1 Qe6 14.Nd2

Continuing to prepare his e3-e4 strategy.

14...b5

Black hopes that his queenside majority will counter White's central e3-e4 advance.

15.Qa5

White is better since Black's queenside pawns are immobile while White's central pawns are ready to roll (by an immediate e3-e4 or, more commonly, via f2-f3 followed by e3-e4.

15...Ne4 16.Nxe4 dxe4

Black has stopped White's e3-e4 push, but he's created other problems.

17.a4

An important moment. White has positionally outplayed his opponent, and now Black has a few paths to choose from (all of which White had to be prepared for). Positional reactions would leave Capablanca in the driver's seat with a huge (and safe!) strategic advantage. However, Black can also try to make use of the undefended state of White's g5-Bishop by 17...Qd5, and where other moves for Black created positional domination for White, 17...Qd5 calls for a tactical answer. Due to this, some players might have held back on 17.a4 and instead played the safer 17.Bf4 or 17.Qc7. But 17.a4 is the thematic move and Capablanca (a player that never gave in to doubt and fear), making sure that 17...Qd5 wasn't a problem, went for the move he thought was best.

17...Qd5

17...Rb8 18.Bf4 Rb6 19.Bc7 Rb7 20.Reb1 would have left Black under serious pressure.

Black's move (17...Qd5) makes an announcement: you HAVE TO move or protect your Bishop! How did Capablanca react?

Now it's up to you to play like the Cuban Machine.

18.axb5!!

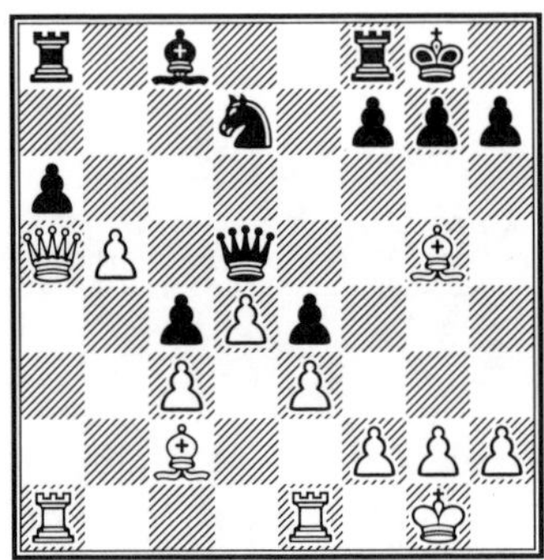

Qxg5 19.Bxe4 Rb8

19...Ra7 20.b6 Qxa5 (20...Qe7 21.Bxh7+ Kxh7 22.bxa7 Bb7 23.Qc7 Ba8 24.Qxc4) 21.bxa7! and the threats of 22.Rxa5 and 22.a8=Q forces Black to resign.

20.bxa6 Rb5

20...Qxa5 21.Rxa5 and there's no answer to a6-a7: 21...Rb3 22.a7 Nb6 23.Rc1! Be6 24.a8=Q and White, after Black captures on a8, ends up with two extra pawns.

21.Qc7 Nb6 22.a7 Bh3 23.Reb1 Rxb1+ 24.Rxb1 f5 25.Bf3

One of many winning moves.

25...f4 26.exf4, 1-0.

In this game Spielmann was comprehensively outplayed. Capablanca outplayed him in the opening, and when the middlegame appeared, Capablanca refused to bow to the fear of various scary complications. Instead, he pushed his agenda and (after his intuition and calculation both assured him that all was well) was ready to face whatever positional and tactical landmines his opponent would use.

Fear of a higher-rated player, trusting a player's move instead of challenging it, or falling victim to the ubiquitous (and deadly) "I can't" and "I have to" are things will rip your rating to shreds.

The simple fact is that a courageous player often has better results than another player who is timid. Mr. Timid might be somewhat superior in every area of the game, but the brave player will be more successful.

Here's a game by the legendary Giulio Cesare Polerio (1550-1610), which not only shows that Polerio was a very poor player, but also shows how doubt and fear lead to one bad decision after another.

Giulio Cesare Polerio vs. Lorenzo, Sora 1575

1.e4 e5 2.Nf3 Nc6 3.Bc4 Bc5 4.c3 Qe7 5.O-O d6 6.d4 Bb6 7.Bg5 Nf6 8.a4 a6 9.Bd5?!

White announces that he will double Black's pawns with Bxc6. Unfortunately, Black bought into this nonsense ("I have to stop it!") by playing:

9...Nb8?

With 9...Nb8 Black has already bowed to his opponent and that mindset will eventually lead to his downfall. Just 9...0-0 10.Bxc6 bxc6 11.dxe5 dxe5 when Black's pawns are messed up, but White has light-square weaknesses (on d3 and along the e6-a2 diagonal) due to the loss of his light-Bishop. Both sides have chances.

10.Nbd2 c6 11.Ba2 Bg4 12.Qb3

Black is in serious trouble.

12...Ba7 13.Qd1??

Incomprehensible! Simply 13.Nc4 would have taken the fight to Black: 13...0-0 (13...Bxf3 14.Nxd6+ Qxd6 15.Qxf7+ Kd8 16.Qxg7, 1-0.) 14.Nxd6! Qxd6 (14...Bxf3 15.Nf5 Qc7 16.Bxf6 gxf6 17.gxf3) 15.dxe5 Qc7 16.exf6 Bxf3 17.fxg7 Kxg7 18.gxf3 and Black is lost.

So, why did White play 13.Qd1? There is no way to know, but I think he feared ...Bxf3 if the d2-Knight moved, and ...Be6. Only fear (clearly not based on concrete analysis) could make a player choose 13.Qd1 over all the other tasty opportunities. 13.dxe5 dxe5 14.Nxe5 was also strong: 14...Be6 15.Nec4 b5 16.e5 bxc4 17.Nxc4 0-0 18.exf6 gxf6 19.Bf4.

13...g6??

And Black replies to White's incomprehensible 13.Qd1?? with his own incomprehensible 13...g6. In fact, I'm at a loss as to why this atrocity against all that's holy was played. Instead, simply 13...Nbd7 gave Black a playable position.

14.dxe5 dxe5 15.Bxf7+??

Good grief! Yes, it was the 1500s, but I expected the top players of that day to be better than this!

15...Kd8??

Arrrgghhh!!! A move like this is more or less a resignation (A pawn down and a feeble King equals no hope at all.). The obvious (and best) move was 15...Kxf7 posing the question: "What do you have? Show me!" 16.Nxe5+ (Better is 16.Bh6 but Black easily consolidates with 16...Re8 17.Ng5+ Kg8 18.Qb3+ Be6 19.Nxe6 Qxe6 20.Qxb7 Nbd7) 16...Qxe5 17.Bxf6 Qe6! and White should resign.

15... Qxf7 is also in Black's favor: 16.Nxe5 Bxd1 17.Nxf7 Kxf7 18.Raxd1 Nbd7 leaves White with two pawns for a piece.

16.Nxe5??

White decides to have some fun and sacrifice his Queen. This allows Black to get back in the game. There were several winners, with the main crusher being 16.Nc4+! Kc7 (16...Nbd7 17.Ncxe5 not the only winning move, but the simplest: 17...Bxf3 18.Nxf3 Qxf7 19.Ne5 [19.e5 also won.] 19...Qe6 20.Nxd7 and the sky falls on Black's head.) 17.Ncxe5 Bxf3 18.Qxf3 and it's over.

16...Qxe5?!

More fear. Black doesn't have much going for him, so he might as well eat white's Queen and dare him to demonstrate sufficient compensation. After 16...Bxd1 17.Raxd1 Kc8 (not the only move) leads to a very interesting position. Black should be okay. One crazy possibility: 18.Ndc4 b5 19.Rd6 bxc4 20.Re6 Qc7 21.Bxf6 Nd7 22.Bxh8 Nxe5 23.Be8 Ng4 24.Rxc6 Kb7 25.Rxc7+ Kxc7 26.Bd4 Bxd4 27.cxd4 Rxe8.

17.Bxf6+?!

17.Nc4+ was game over.

17...Kc8

It seems clear that both players were completely drunk. Black can live to fight on with 17...Qxf6 18.Qxg4 Qxf7.

18.Qxg4+ and White mated his opponent on move 32.

The moral is:

- Don't drink several bottles of alcohol before and during a game or;
- Don't allow doubt and fear to scramble your brains.

Let's give Polerio another chance:

Giulio Cesare Polerio vs. Busnardo, Rome1590

1.e4 e5 2.f4 exf4 3.Bc4 Qh4+ 4.Kf1 g5 5.Nf3 Qh5 6.d4 d6 7.h4 g4 8.Ng5 Nh6 9.Bxf4 f6

How should White continue?

10.Kg1!

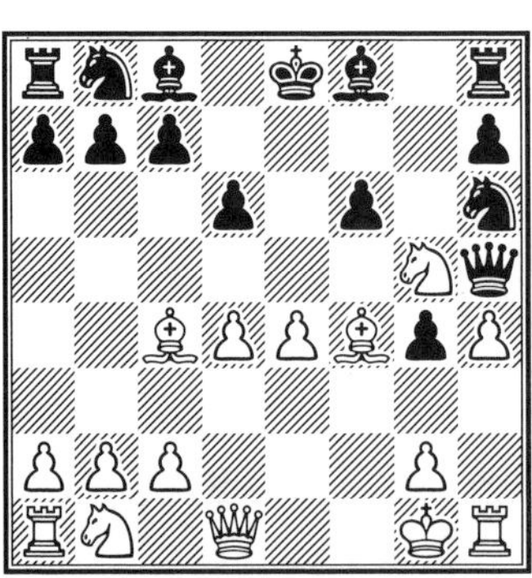

Move the g5-Knight? No way! I'll only move it when I have to move it, not when you want me to move it! In the actual game White obeyed his opponent's dictate to move his Knight 10.Ne6 Bxe6 11.Bxe6 and the score ended here pointing out that White won. Things would have been interesting after 11...Qb5+ 12.Qd3 Qxb2 13.Qc3 Qxc3 14.Nxc3 Nc6 15.Nb5 Kd8 16.d5 Ne5 17.Nd4 when White is a pawn down but he has a lovely bind on the e6- and f5-squares.

10...Qg6

10...fxg5 11.hxg5 The point of 10.Kg1. The King defends the h1-rook, making these moves possible. 11...Qg6 12.gxh6.

11.h5 Qg7 12.Ne6

Now the Knight has to move, but Black won't be able to pick up that extra pawn which we saw could have happened in the reply 10.Ne6 Bxe6 11.Bxe6 Qb4+.

12...Bxe6 13.Bxe6 and now, with material equality, far more active pieces, and more space, White enjoys a winning position.

Of course, nowadays grandmasters don't run screaming from every little threat ("I have to defend") or every little self-destructive dictate ("I can't"). They know what needs to be done and they insist that they find a way to do it.

Here's a case in point:

Maxime Vachier-Lagrave vs. Anish Giri, London Classic 2015

1.e4 e5 2.Nf3 Nc6 3.Bb5 Nf6 4.0-0 Nxe4 5.d4 Nd6 6.Bxc6 dxc6 7.dxe5 Nf5 8.Qxd8+ Kxd8 9.h3 Ke8 10.Nc3 h5 11.Ne2 b6 12.Rd1 Be7 13.Bg5 Bb7 14.Bxe7 Kxe7 15.Ned4 Nxd4 16.Nxd4

How would you play Black's position? What does Black want to play?

16...c5!

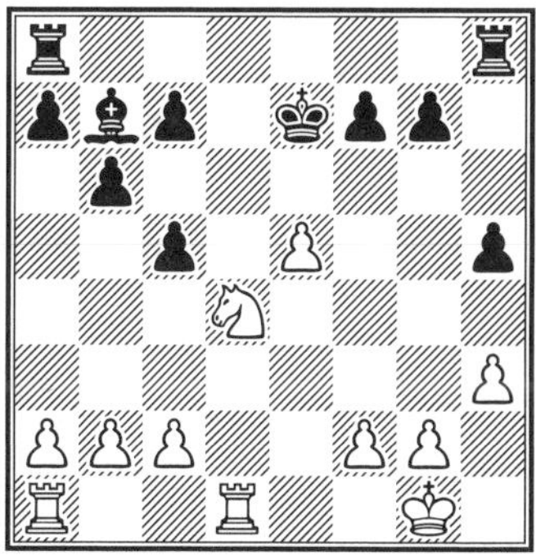

Well done! This is the move Black wants to play (chases the Knight and activates the Bishop), but many players would be spooked by White's "threat"of Nf5+ and play 16...g6, which is really just a waste of time.

17.Nb5

17.Nf5+? Ke6! 18.Nxg7+? White should accept humiliation and retreat to e3. 18...Kxe5! 19.Rd7 Kf6 20.Rxc7 Be4 and White loses his Knight and the game. Once again, Black wanted to play 16...c5 and refused to accept that 16...g6 was a "must" defensive move. By not bowing to fear ("I have to"), he looked at the position in a concrete manner and realized that the "threat" (Nf5+) wasn't a threat at all.

17...Rhc8 18.f4 Bc6 19.Nc3 Ke6 20.Kf2 h4

And Black had an excellent position (superior Bishop vs. inferior Knight, a lovely home for black's King on f5 when the f4-pawn comes under attack, and an eventual ...f7-f6 break) and went on to win the game.

These decisions are regularly made in positional and tactical situations. The following game is all about tactics.

Kelson vs. Silman, Reno 1993

1.e4 c5 2.Nf3 Nc6 3.d4 cxd4 4.Nxd4 g6 5.Nc3 Bg7 6.Be3 Nf6 7.Nxc6 bxc6 8.e5 Ng8 9.f4 Nh6 10.Qf3 0-0 **11.**0-0-0 **d6! 12.Qxc6 Bd7 13.Qd5 Ng4 14.Qf3 Nxe3 15.Qxe3 Be6 16.Nd5 Rc8 17.Ba6 Rc5!**

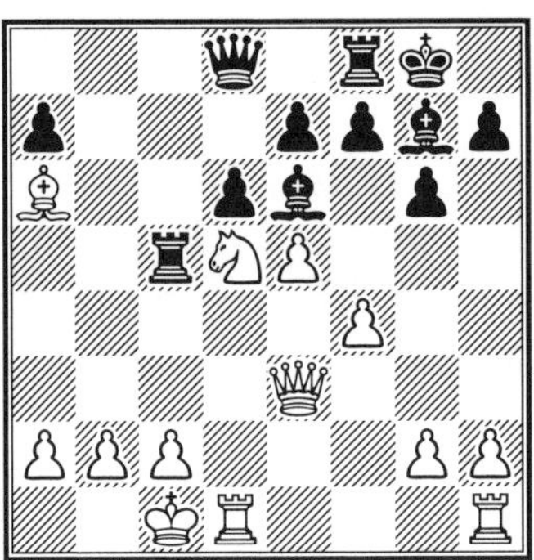

18.c4 Bxd5 19.Rxd5 Rxd5 20.cxd5 Qa5 21.Bc4 Rc8 22.b3 Qxa2 23.Re1 dxe5 24.fxe5 Bh6! 25.Qxh6 Qxb3 26.Re4 Rxc4+ 27.Rxc4 Qxc4+ 28.Kb1 Qe4+ 29.Kc1 Qxd5 30.Qe3 Qxg2 31.Qxa7 Qh1+, 0-1.

During the game I had to prepare myself for 18.Nxe7+ Qxe7 19.exd6, which looks scary since both the black Queen and the c5-Rook are hanging. In fact, it would be easy to reject 17...Rc5 and try something else. However, instead of freaking out, you need to stand by your convictions, only doing an about face if you have convinced yourself (after an honest assessment) that 18.Nxe7+ is simply too strong.

An End to Nerves

Another question that arises when the student starts to play in tournaments: "I can't seem to avoid getting very nervous before and during my games, which sometimes causes me to blunder. Can you make suggestions on how to stay calm and focus on the game?"

Frayed nerves in over-the-board play is very common. I clearly remember being freaked out during my initial tournaments. I would literally be shaking from the mix of stark terror and competitive hormones coursing through my body that demanded I club my opponent to death with any weapon I could reach!

At that time I lived in San Diego but occasionally played in Los Angeles, where I didn't know one player from another. Thus when I was paired, I made a point of not looking at my opponent's rating. The first time I tried this was a turning point in my chess psychology: I clearly remember winning a game and thinking, "Well, nothing to be proud of since this guy is clearly rated 1400 or 1500." Then I looked at his rating and was stunned to see that he was rated 2150! After that, my nerves started to fade away, and my fear of higher rated players eventually vanished.

After several tournaments I finally calmed down, and from that point on, I no longer had any problem with nerves—even in big game finals where a win would give me a tournament victory. I consider myself somewhat lucky (if luck has anything to do with it) as I know some seasoned veterans that still feel the attack of the butterflies at the start of each and every event!

Being nervous at a tournament won't cure itself overnight, but there are some things that might help.

- Do you drink fifty cups of coffee before starting your over-the-board battles? Try to cut down to twenty cups.
- Is your mind a seething mass of chaos and, as a result, completely out of control? Heavy meds might be the answer, or (a far more healthy alternative) give meditation a try. If you view meditation as being some strange, anti-American thing, change the name! Call it "freedom thinking."
- Do you eat lots of sugar before or during play? If so, stop.
- On the other hand you may start out playing well, but at a certain point you find that you are unable to focus anymore at the board (this usually happened after four hours) tired and weak and evincing muddied/slow/unclear thinking, and you end up making simple blunders as a result.

  I'm not a doctor ("I'm a chess player, not a doctor!"—a gift to *Star Trek* fans), but I would guess (note that I said, "guess.") the diagnoses to be low blood-sugar). Symptoms include feeling tired and weak and evincing muddied/slow/unclear thinking.

We've all been there and nerves are a natural part of the process— players (from amateurs to grandmasters) have experienced this during play. Grandmaster Walter Browne went so far as to say that he would happily buy his opponent a huge steak dinner before the game since, ultimately, it would wreak havoc on his opponent's blood-sugar making it impossible for him to think clearly. For more on this subject See: Things That Go Down Your Throat at a Chess Tournament (see 9. FAQ).

People may be screaming that a tidal wave is coming—Who cares? All that matters is the position. Godzilla is heading your way? It's just a lizard, so ignore that and figure out what's happening on the board!

4

MASKED GRANDMASTER
(The Greatest Amateur Game of All Time)

I first told this tale more than three decades ago (originally in *Chess Life* magazine[1]) but it never seems to get old. Here is my current version.

Aside from being highly instructive and extremely entertaining, R. Catig vs. Michael Mills offers hope to the millions of amateur players who hold onto a dream that someday, somehow, they too will play an "eternal" game that will be enjoyed, talked about, and revered until chess is no longer played or the human race vanishes from the face of the Earth.

Before continuing, here are some highlights of the upcoming game that will allow you to test yourself and see if you can find what Black, a 1500 player, found! I suspect that even masters will have trouble keeping up! Keep in mind that there's nothing to be ashamed of if you fail to solve most of these; it is, after all, the greatest amateur game of all time!

The game illustrates the proper mentality that's needed when faced with a central enemy King. Here are some of the instructive "how to attack" lessons you should pay attention to:

- If you are castled and your opponent's King is still in the middle, get excited and see if there's any way to punish it! Keep in mind that he will likely castle soon, so if you want to take advantage of the situation, you need to act fast and play with enormous energy.
- Note how Black strives to crack open the center so he can reach his royal target. In this game, Black will offers pawns and even Rooks to create roads to the enemy King!
- Note how Black makes use of a "mating net"—this is an important attacking device.
- Note how Black lowers the boom by making use of overworked enemy pieces.

1 *Chess Life*, April 1980.

- Finally, note how Black (incredibly!) never calculated more than three moves ahead! Understanding and using the above attacking concepts alone enabled him to create a work of art.

This remarkable story is about Micky Mills, a class "C" player (1500) who had a very poor grasp of attacking fundamentals. Way back in 1974, when I was his teacher, seeing this flaw I recommended that he read *The Art of Attack in Chess*[1] a classic book by Vuković. He evidently took this recommendation to heart!

Some months after he read *The Art of Attack*, Mills was playing in an open tournament (players of every rating were mixed together) that happened to have a brilliancy prize. There were quite a few strong players, including the U.S. Champion John Grefe and many time U.S. Champion Walter Browne, so everyone expected one of the "big guns" to pick up the cash bonus.

Mills (rated 1503) was not doing particularly well in the event, and was paired with another "C" player (rated 1618). Nobody paid much attention to the game, but after the game (with Mills, two Senior Masters, and John Grefe in tow) Micky squealed, "Look at my game! Look at my game! I've played a brilliancy!"

I'm not proud of this, but I have to admit that we all burst into laughter. "Okay," we said in our most sarcastic tone, "show it to us!"

R. Catig vs. Michael Mills, San Francisco, Carroll Capps Memorial 1974

1.e4 c5 2.Nf3 Nc6 3.d4 cxd4 4.Nxd4 g6 5.Nc3 Bg7 6.Be3 Nf6 7.Be2 0–0 8.Qd2 d5!

So far we were all silent. Black has played the opening well and has no problems.

9.Nxc6

The continuation 9.exd5 Nxd5 10.Nxd5 Nxd4! is very nice for Black: 11.Nxe7+? (11.Bc4 keeps black's edge to a minimum, while 11.Bxd4? Qxd5 12.Bxg7 Qxg2! has led to many Black victories) 11...Qxe7 12.Bxd4 Bxd4 13.Qxd4 Re8 and white's King is trapped in the center.

Attacking Concept Alert!

This is our first example of a King being trapped in the center!

White's best is to offer a Queen trade by 14.Qe3, but Black (who is after the enemy King) won't accept it: 14...Qb4+ 15.c3 Qa4 16.Qd2 (better is 16.Qd4, though 16...Qa6 17.c4 Bf5 is also miserable for White) 16...Bg4 17.f3 Rad8 and White's position is horrible. A possible continuation: 18.Qg5 Bf5! 19.0-0 h6 20.Qf6 Rd2 21.Bd1 Qf4 22.Bb3 (22.Kh1 Re6 traps white's Queen) 22...Rxg2+! 23.Kxg2 Bh3+ 24.Kxh3 Qxf6 and Black wins.

1 Vladimir Vuković, *The Art of Attack in Chess*. London: Pergamom Press, 1965.

Attacking Concept Alert!

When attacking, you usually want to retain the Queens since they are the "fist" of the attack!

9...bxc6 10.e5 Ng4

A good response. Also possible is 10...Nd7 11.f4 e6 when the following trap has claimed many victims: 12.Na4? (placing the Knight on an undefended square) 12...Nxe5! 13.fxe5 Qh4+ 14.Bf2 Qxa4. I've actually reached this position (as Black of course) in a couple of tournament games!

Attacking Concept Alert!

Undefended pieces often lead to tactical punishment!

11.Bxg4 Bxg4 12.h3

Black is also doing well after 12.f4 f6 13.h3 Bc8 14.exf6 Bxf6 15.0–0–0 Qd6.

12...Bf5 13.g4?

Desperate to find something to criticize, we all became hysterical. "You fool!" we howled, "Why did you allow him to attack your Bishop with gain of time?"

"Well," Michael replied coolly, "I was trying to egg him on." This was too much for us. We fell on the floor and laughed uncontrollably. Undaunted, Michael ploughed ahead and simply ignored us.

Imbalances

The e5-pawn is weak and if that pawn vanishes, then the g7-Bishop will rule the a1-h8 diagonal. However, the other problem is the reason this example is being presented here: white's King is still in the center!

13...Be6

We were too busy making fun of Michael to notice 13...Bxe5! 14.Bh6 (14. gxf5 d4) 14...d4! 15.Qe2 (15.Bxf8 dxc3 is grim for White, but 15.Na4 keeps the game going) 15...Bf6 16.Bxf8 dxc3 17.b3 Qd2+ 18.Qxd2 cxd2+ 19.Kxd2 Kxf8 20.gxf5 Rd8+ 21.Ke2 Bxa1 22.Rxa1 gxf5 and Black is a pawn up in the endgame.

14.Qd4?

The idea of this move (other than the fact that it defends e5) is to post the Queen on c5—not a bad concept, but it walks into various tactical problems. Far better was 14.f4.

14...f6

A good move that tries to rip open the center and get at the uncastled King, but interesting alternatives existed. For example, 14...Qb8 creates a double attack against b2 and e5.

Attacking Concept Alert!

Ripping open the center so you can reach the vulnerable enemy King

15.f4?

Very poor. White should play 15.exf6 when 15...Bxf6 leaves Black better, but it's still a fight.

15...Qc7

We ribbed Mills for not playing 15...fxe5 16.fxe5 Qc7, which nets a free pawn since 17.Bf4 c5 is crushing. However, the text move also leaves White in a bad way, and might even prove stronger than 15...fxe5.

16.exf6 Bxf6 17.Qc5 Bh4+

More straightforward is 17...d4 18.Bxd4 Qxf4 19.Bxf6 Rxf6 with a winning attack. The path Mills chose is far deeper and far more elegant.

18.Ke2

Other moves:

- 18.Kd1 d4! 19.Nb5 Qa5 20.Qxc6 dxe3 21.Qxe6+ Kg7 22.Nc3 Rxf4 wins for Black.
- 18.Bf2 Bxf2+ 19.Qxf2 Rxf4 20.Qe3 Bf7 21.0-0-0 e5 has to be winning for Black.
- 18.Kd2 d4 wins on the spot (for example, 19.Bxd4 Qxf4+ 20.Be3 Rad8+ 21.Kc1 Qf1+ and mates).

18...Bc8!!

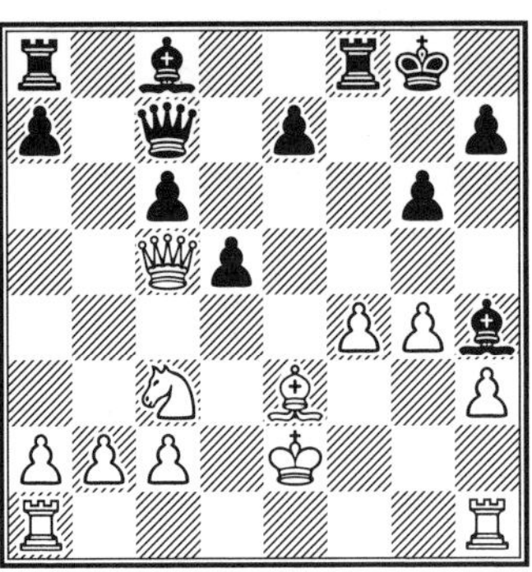

This super-grandmaster level move, which was beyond the powers of the first crop of computers for many years [now chess engines get it in several seconds. Depressing!], sets up ...Ba6+ possibilities and also frees the e-pawn, which can now advance to e5 and nuke the center (going after that central enemy King). Michael's earlier moves had not made much of an impression on us, but when we saw this move our pompous smiles began to fade.

19.Nxd5

Very tempting and very greedy, but there really isn't a fully acceptable defense. Other tries:

- 19.Kd2 Ba6 (intending both ...d4 and ...Rxf4) 20.Rad1 (20.Kc1!?) and now 20...Rxf4 leads to fascinating tactics, but 20...e5 is simple and probably best: 21.fxe5 d4 22.Bxd4 Rfd8 23.Kc1 Be7 and Black wins a piece.
- 19.b4 e5 20.fxe5 Qxe5 looks grim.
- 19.Rag1 Ba6+ 20.Kd1 e5 and all I can say is that I wouldn't want to be White.
- 19.Kf3 and now both 19...Bb7 (20.Nxd5 Qe5 21.Nc3 Rxf4+) and 19...Ba6 are strong.

19...Ba6+ 20.c4

Black has many possibilities after 20.Kf3, the simplest of which is 20...Qe5 when White has to jettison a piece by 21.Nxe7+ (21.Qxc6 Rac8 is game over) 21...Qxe7 22.Qxe7 Bxe7.

20...Qb7! 21.Nb4 e5!

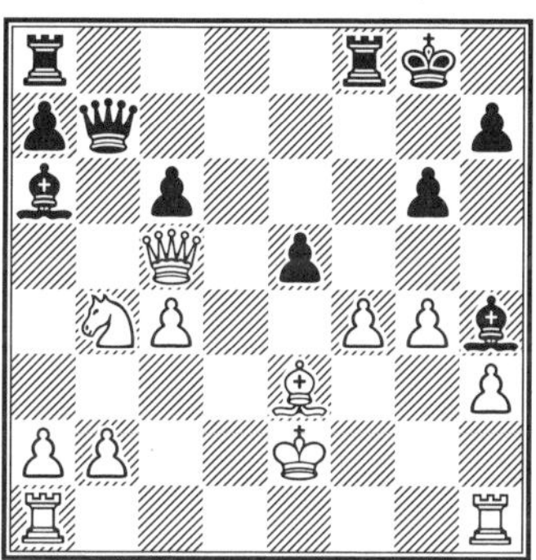

White is holding on as best he can, but Mills (who appears to be channeling Alekhine) won't stop playing great moves!

At this point we were no longer saying anything. Instead we silently watched the game unfold as Mills made comments like, "His King in the center and I have to get it!" and "I'm busting open the center so that my pieces can penetrate!"

Attacking Concept Alert!

Pay close attention to the two Mills' comments above!

22.Nxa6

Other moves were a bit better but still depressing from White's point of view. For example, 22.f5 Be7 23.Qxc6 Bxb4 is an extra piece for Black, 22.a3 exf4 is fun for only one side, and 22.fxe5 Be7 23.Qxc6 Qxb4 gives Black an extra piece and an attack.

22...exf4?

Black learned that he's supposed to open lines in this kind of position and he's making sure he does it! Unfortunately, more direct measures were called for: 22...Qxb2+ 23.Bd2 (23.Kf3 e4+ is horrific) 23...Rxf4! and White is dead lost.

23.Bd4

Worse is 23.Bd2 f3+ 24.Kd1 Qxb2 25.Rc1 Rad8.

23...Rae8+?

The most natural move in the world, but it turns out to be inaccurate. Instead, 23...f3+ is quite strong: 24.Kd3 Rad8 25.Nb4 Be7 (the immediate 25...Rxd4+ is also good) 26.Qe5 Rxd4+ 27.Qxd4 Qxb4 28.Qc3 Qc5 29.Kc2 Rf4 30.b4 Qf2+ 31.Kb3 Bf6 32.Raf1 Qe2 33.Qc2 Qe3+ 34.Ka4 f2 gives Black a winning advantage.

24.Kf3??

Kindly allowing a stunning finish. White had to play 24.Kd3 when 24... Qxa6 25.Qxa7 Qxa7 26.Bxa7 f3 27.Bc5 Rf7 28.Rad1 Rd7+ 29.Kc2 Re2+ still leaves White in serious trouble due to the power of the passed f-pawn and the vulnerability of the white King.

After this final mistake by White, Mills really does turn into Alekhine!

24...Re3+!!

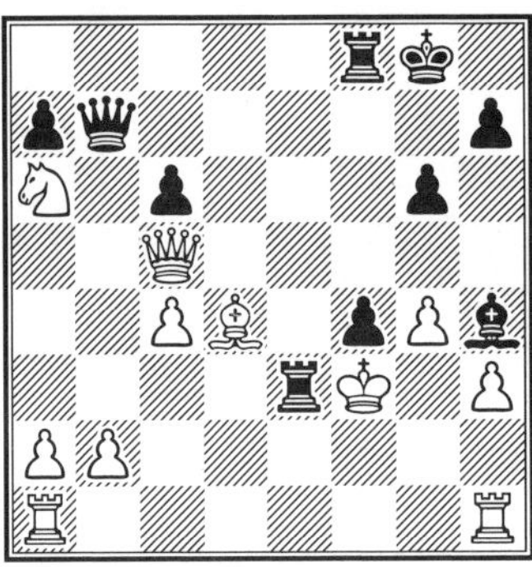

Still clearing lines like a maniac! At this point all of us were exhibiting signs of shock, jaws hanging to the floor.

Attacking Concept Alert!

A line clearing sacrifice so that black's army can stream into the enemy position.

25.Kg2

After 25.Bxe3 fxe3+ 26.Ke4, Black would be able to choose from a multitude of winning ideas, with 26...Re8+ 27.Kd3 Rd8+ 28.Ke4 Qxb2 being my personal favorite.

25...f3+ 26.Kf1

26.Kg1 Rfe8 27.Bc3 (27.Nb4 Re1+ mates) 27...Rxc3 28.bxc3 (28.Rh2 lasts longer, but the result isn't in doubt after 28...Rce3) 28...Qb2 mates.

26...Rfe8!!

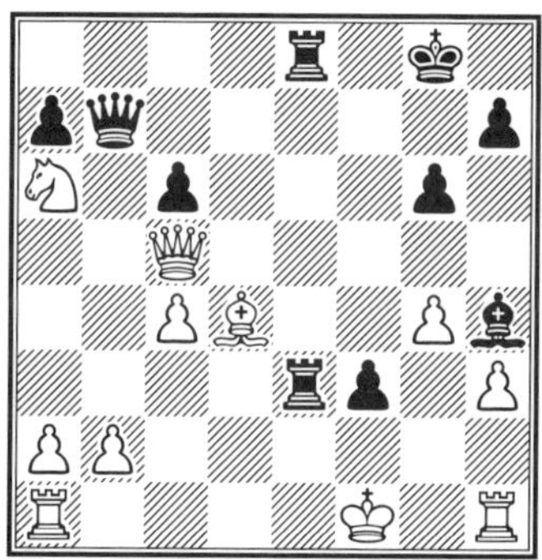

Black now threatens to mate with ...Re1+. Of course, White cannot play 27.Bxe3 due to ...Qxb2.

27.Kg1 Bg3!

Tightening the net around white's King. The Rook is still immune to capture—an incredible situation. Of course, 27...Re1+ also won easily.

Attacking Concept Alert!

Note how Black took a moment to build a mating net. Now the white King has nowhere to run.

28.Rf1 Re1 29.Bc3

29.Be5 Qxb2! creates a geometric oddity

Attacking Concept Alert!

Now Mills makes use of the overworked piece theme—the c3-Bishop defends both e1 and b2 and Black takes devastating advantage of that fact.

29...Qxb2!!

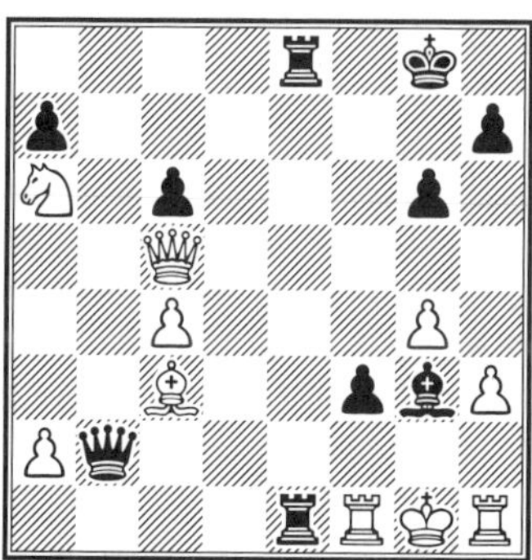

Now, since **30.Bxb2 Rxf1+ 31.Kxf1 Re1** is mate, White resigned.

"Who was that masked grandmaster?" Larry Christiansen asked when I showed him the game some months later.

What is of particular interest to me is that Mills didn't offer any variations at all as he was playing through the game (nor was he able to defend his moves with actual variations). Instead, he explained everything he did by naming a pattern that he learned from the aforementioned Vuković book. Thus we were pelted by verbal nutshells of wisdom like, "Central King, kill it!" and "Ripping open the center!" and "Maximizing the activity of my pieces!" and "Sacrificing to open lines to his King!" and "It's a double attack!" and "I'm building a mating net!"

Mills won the brilliancy prize, and none of us could do anything but applaud him. Few players (of any rating) ever create an evergreen such as this, so he can consider himself blessed. It's truly a fantastic creative effort and, perhaps, the greatest game by a non-master of all time!

After my original *Chess Life* article appeared, this game had a couple of curious ramifications. The first "oddity" occurred when Mills was accused of purposely losing games (to qualify for large class prizes at bigger events) in his chess club's one game a week tournaments. The club officials said he was clearly of master strength, and their proof was a certain article in *Chess Life* titled "Masked Grandmaster!"

When these fools asked me to testify at their monkey trial, I pointed out that Mills was barely "B" strength and that he lost all those evening games because he had narcolepsy, a disease that causes a person to suddenly fall asleep. It also made Mills the perfect chess student: he would demand a five-hour "intensive" chess lesson. I would lecture for thirty minutes and he would fall into a deep sleep. I would wake him up two hours later and he'd say, "Okay, tell me that again." I would repeat the same information, he would fall asleep, and round and round we'd go until the five hours was up.

In the end, the club morons (who ignored everything I said since it didn't fit in with their false/insane/misinformed view of reality) banned him for a significant period of time.

The second oddity hit me in the face when I was in Eastern Europe acting as head coach of the American junior team. These events always featured Russians selling books outside for next to nothing, and this led to me buying (for $2) a very nice 441 page book by Belov, Shakarov, Tsaturian, and Vilensky (with a foreword by Kasparov) called *Ant[h]ology of Chess Beauty* (Yes, they misspelled the word anthology, but such things are common when hasty translations of Russian to English are made). This is a fine anthology of 1,640 games (All with notes!) that have won official brilliancy prizes from 1876 to 1995. Looking through it, I saw games by one chess legend after another. And then I happened upon a certain game by M. Mills! That's right, the Mills masterpiece, now immortalized, proudly stood side by side with history's greatest chess names!

5

BRUTAL TACTICS AND POSITIONAL TACTICS

The year was 1969, I was fifteen years old and had just made the trip from San Diego to beautiful Santa Monica to participate in the American Open (at that time, held at the luxurious Miramar Hotel). I arrived early, checked out the playing room, and noticed a guy a couple years my senior named Roy Ervin looking at some openings. Being young, it didn't occur to me that he might want to be left alone, and I sat across from him and began commenting on the lines he was exploring. He took it in stride, a conversation began, and we quickly stepped into other chess spheres like chess history and, of course, our favorite players. Tal was mentioned, I said, "My favorite Tal game was against Gurgenidze."

Ervin looked at me and replied, "You mean the one from Moscow 1957?"

Surprised that he was so well versed in chess culture, I nodded yes, set up the pieces, and played **1.d4**, which was the first move of the Bukhuti Gurgenidze vs. Tal, Moscow 1957 game. He quickly replied with **1...Nf6**, I continued with **2.c4**, he played **2...c5** and it became clear that we had both memorized this game! After **3.d5 e6** we discussed the Benoni, which I was using at that time. Then a rapid string of moves followed:

Bukhuti Gurgenidze vs. Mikhail Tal, Moscow 1957

4.Nc3 exd5 5.cxd5 d6 6.Nf3 g6 7.e4 Bg7 8.Be2 0-0 9.0-0 Re8 10.Nd2 Na6 11.Re1 Nc7 12.a4 b6 13.Qc2

After making the Qc2 move I looked up and smiled, and he responded by gently sliding the f6-Knight to g4—it was obvious that he now viewed himself as Tal while my role was that of the victim. Fair enough! Even the loser can appreciate a work of art!

13...Ng4 14.h3?!

Daring Black to pull the trigger. It actually hurt to play this move since I knew that I was about to be splattered over the board. Clearly, I was about to feel Gurgenidze's pain!

14...Nxf2!!

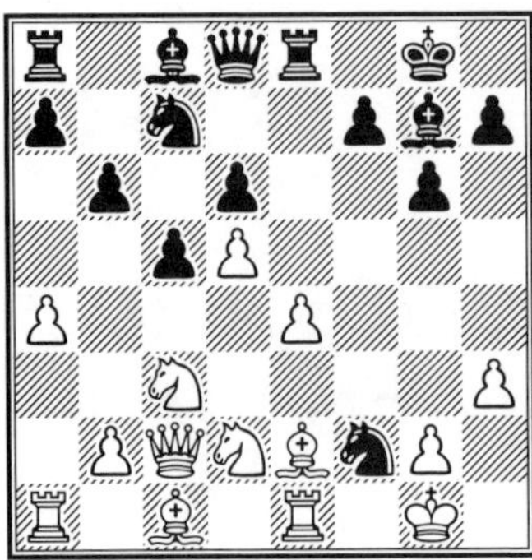

I expected Roy to do this in a violent manner, but he played it slowly, ecstatically, and with great reverence.

15.Kxf2 Qh4+ 16.Kf1

Since Roy was getting so much pleasure from the game, I decided to fully embrace the role of human-piñata. I took 16.Kf1 back, said, "Well, 16.Kg1 Qxe1+ isn't what White wants, but what about 16.Ke3?"

He tossed out 16...Bxc3! (even better than 16...Qxe1) 17.bxc3 Nxd5+ 18.Kd3 (18.Kf3 Qf4 mate) 18...Nf4+ 19.Ke3 (we had a good laugh over 19.Kc4 Be6+ 20.Kb5 a6+ 21.Kxb6 Qd8+ 22.Kb7 Rb8+ 23.Kxa6 Qb6 mate) 19...Nxg2+ 20.Kd3 Nxe1+ 21.Ke3 Nxc2+ and we stopped. It's not a surprise that there's a forced mate: 22.Kd3 Ne1+ 23.Ke3 Qg3+ 24.Nf3 Rxe4+! 25.Kxe4 Bb7+ 26.Ke3 Re8+ 27.Kd2 Rxe2+ 28.Kxe2 Bxf3+ 29.Ke3 Bg4+ 30.Kd2 Qf2 mate. Good times! We went back to the game:

16...Bd4! 17.Nd1

Stopping ...Qf2 mate.

17...Qxh3!!

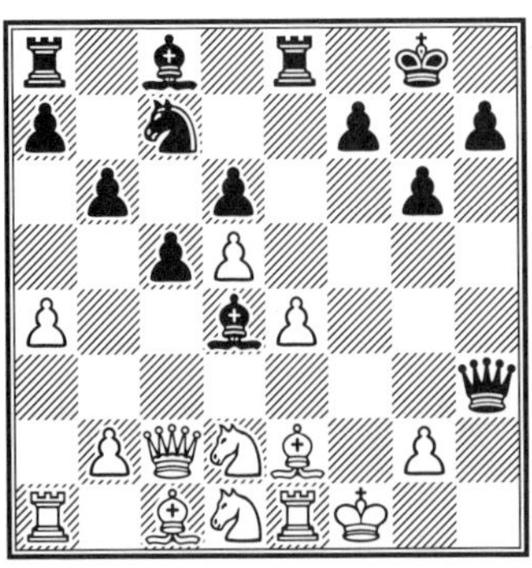

As sweet as sweet can be. Ervin was now in some sort of quasi-religious state of bliss.

18.Bf3

No bliss for me! 18.Nf2 Qe3 forces mate. Of course, 18.gxh3 allows 18... Bxh3 mate.

18...Qh2 19.Ne3 f5!

Ripping open the center.

An instructive move: Black wants to rip open the center so his pieces can pour into the enemy position along the e-file.

20.Ndc4 fxe4 21.Bxe4 Ba6

Total helplessness! I had always looked at this game from the Black side, and it was only after Roy played 21...Ba6 that I fully appreciated the sheer helplessness of White's position: White's King is in the firing line, his Knights are frozen in place, and all of Black's pieces (except for the a8-Rook and c7-Knight) are in full assault mode.

22.Bf3 Re5!

There are other good moves too, but this is very strong, very instructive, and very human: Black prepares to get his "forgotten" a8-Rook into the game by doubling on the e-file.

23.Ra3 Rae8 24.Bd2 Nxd5!!

A true team effort! Now ALL of Black's pieces (except his King) are taking part in a brutal beat-down of the enemy position.

It turned out that both Roy and myself had first seen this game in P. H. Clarke's classic book, *Mikhail Tal's Best Games of Chess*. Clarke's comment: "Such a mighty clash of pieces is a rare sight. It gives us a wonderful opportunity to study the comparative strengths of aggressive and defensive pieces. Although all White's are in play, they are absolutely helpless."

25.Bxd5+

25.Rd3 Nxe3+ 26.Rdxe3 Rxe3 27.Bxe3 Bxe3 28.Rxe3 Rxe3 and, thanks to the pin along the a6-f1 diagonal, the game is over.

25...Rxd5 26.Ke2 Bxe3 27.Rxe3 Bxc4+, 0-1.

A good time to resign since 28.Qxc4 falls on its face to 28...Qxg2+ 29.Kd1 Qxd2 mate, while 28.Kd1 Rxe3 29.Rxe3 Qg1+ 30.Re1 Qf2 (threatening 31...Bb3) 31.Kc1 Bb3 32.Qxb3 (32.Re8+ Kf7) 32...Qxd2+ 33.Kb1 Qxe1+ leaves Black with an extra Rook and three pawns!

After this tournament we occasionally ran into each other at chess events, and we even played on several occasions (he had three wins to my one, with a couple draws). He was a very sweet man and an extremely strong player (solid international master strength). Unfortunately he suffered from some severe psychological problems which led to multiple attempts at suicide, and when the *Los Angeles Times* reported his death, I wasn't surprised (sad, but not surprised). Oddly, I got my international master title at the Roy Ervin Memorial (1987) in San Francisco, only to discover that he was still alive!

Recently I read (on chess.com!) that he eventually did pass away in 2001, though I wouldn't be surprised to see him again at some chessboard, alive and passionately moving pieces about. If so, perhaps we'll look at this game one last time.

The Tal game is an illustration of how the study of master games can deeply enrich your understanding of chess. That one example taught us that one always has to be aware of a potential sacrificial Knight explosion on f2 or f7, that it's important to (if possible) bring all your pieces into an attack, and that opening the center (even if it calls for a sacrifice) allows the more active army to enter the enemy position with, quite often, decisive effect.

Roy Ervin and I enjoyed sharing Tal's tactical magic, and though my one win against Roy was based on tactics, it was a far cry from the kind of tactics most people are familiar with. Instead, we both used sacrifices and tactics to gain positional perks:

Roy Ervin vs. Silman, Berkeley 1976

1.Nf3 c5 2.g3 Nc6 3.Bg2 g6 4.d4 cxd4 5.Nxd4 Bg7 6.Nb3 Nf6 7.Nc3 d6 8.0-0 0-0 9.h3 Bd7 10.e4 Ne5 11.a4 Rc8 12.Nd4 a6 13.Nc3 e2 Bc6 14.f4 Nd7 15.Nxc6 bxc6 16.Be3 Rb8 17.b3 c5 18.Rb1 Qc7 19.c4

What can Black do?

I hadn't played the opening particularly well and now was facing slow suffocation due to my lack of counterplay (it's almost impossible to attack b3 in any meaningful way), White's two Bishops, White's superiority in space, and White's long-term chances against my King. Realizing that the situation was critical, I thought for an hour and came up with a interesting plan.

19...Rfc8!!

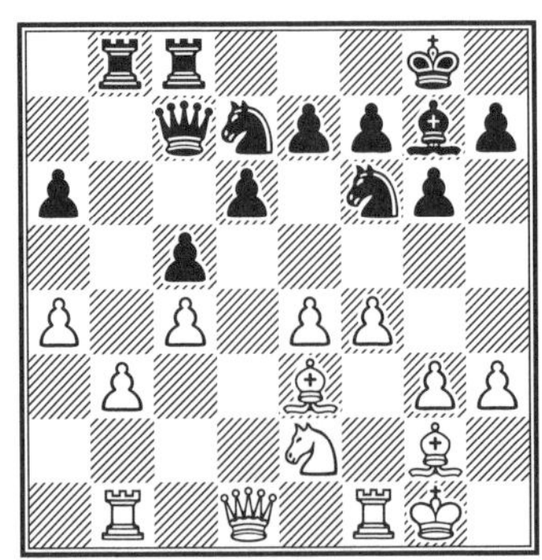

Setting up a strategic pawn sacrifice.

20.Qd2 Nf8 21.g4 Ne6 22.g5 Nd7

It was only now that White realized what my intensions were!

23.Kh1

His intended 23.f5 would be met by 23...Nd4 24.Nxd4 cxd4 25.Bxd4 Bxd4+ 26.Qxd4 Qc5 27.Qxc5 Nxc5 with a good position since b3 is very weak and white's Bishop is clearly inferior to black's Knight.

Black now demonstrates the point.

23...Nd4

Now the point of 19...Rfc8 can be seen: by making the f8-square accessible to my Knight, I was able to maneuver this piece to d4 where it can take part in an assault against b3. If White chops on d4 and wins a pawn, the newly opened queenside lines and my remaining Knight's access to c5 gives Black tremendous compensation and active play.

24.Nxd4 cxd4 25.Bxd4 Bxd4 26.Qxd4

Now 23.Kh1 makes sense! The purpose of White's "odd" 23.Kh1 is now clear, since Black could force the trade of Queens by 26...Qc5 if the white King still stood on g1. Why would Black want to exchange Queens when he's down a pawn? Because Black is doing very well on the queenside, while White's main hope is a counterattack against the black King. A kingside attack wouldn't be possible if the Queens were no longer on the board.

26...Rb4 27.Qd1 Rcb8

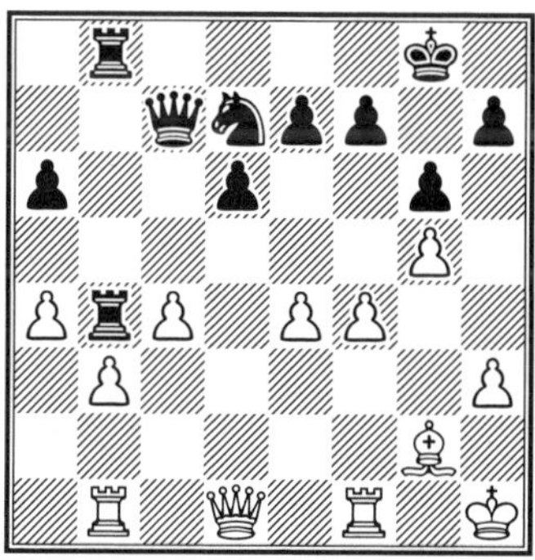

Though a pawn down, Black has an excellent position. White can play the mundane 28.Rf3, but Ervin decided on a more artistic approach. Can you spot it?

Embrace a moment of art.

28.e5!

A lovely move! White gives the pawn back to activate his Bishop. This also clogs up the e5-square in anticipation of an f4-f5 advance, or opens up the f-file if White decides to meet 28...dxe5 with 29.fxe5. The immediate f4-f5 would let black's Knight leap to e5, and would also doom the white Bishop to permanent passivity. 28.e5 loosens up the e5-square and also turns the tall-pawn on g2 into the mighty ruler of the h1-a8 diagonal. Black eventually won the game after mutual time pressure blunders, but that doesn't take away from Ervin's excellent move 28.e5.

As you can see, tactics are not all about brutal knockouts or traps. Tactics also help you make deep positional ideas feasible. If you want to be a good player, you need a good opening repertoire, you need to know basic endgames, you need to be able to attack, you need to be able to calculate, and you need an understanding of positional/strategic building blocks. All these things are important, all these things compliment and work with all the other things, and all of them mesh together to form a well rounded, powerful player.

For those that are curious about the Ervin vs. Silman game, here's the rest of it:

28.Rf3 is also reasonable, but lacks the instructive content of the pretty 28.e5. After 28.Rf3 Nc5 29.f5 White can try to get some kingside play and, by waiting, has deprived black's Knight of a quick jump to e5.

28...dxe5 29.f5

29.fxe5 Nxe5 30.Qc2 might be a better try.

29...gxf5!?

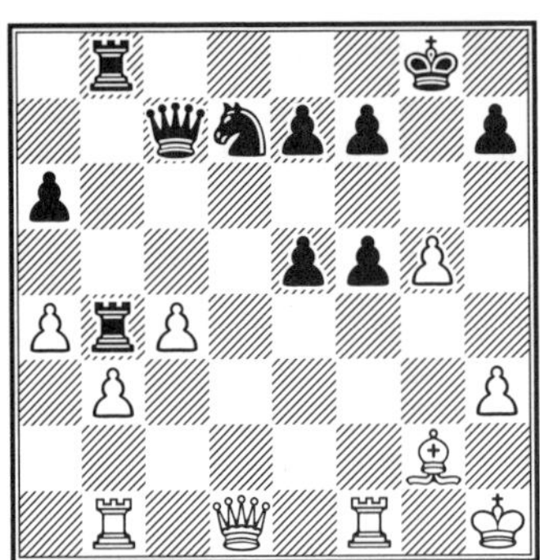

With the thrill of battle burning through my veins, I "forgot" about my usual "safety first" approach and decided to enter into a long tactical sequence that seemed so interesting that I simply couldn't resist it. 29...Nc5 was sensible.

30.Rxf5 e6 31.Rf1

31.Rf6 Nxf6 32.gxf6 Qxc4! 33.Qg1 Qd4.

31...Nc5 32.Qh5 Rxb3 33.Rbe1 Nd3??

This pushes the envelope a bit too far! Instead of the suicidal text, the obvious 33...Rb2 would have given Black a clear advantage. My move was based on a serious tactical miscalculation.

34. Be4 f5??

This looks like I'm going berserk, but it was based on a very faulty calculation. Instead 34…Nf4 was forced: 35.Qxh7+ Kf8 36.Qh8+ Ke7 37.Qf6+ Ke8, with a draw.

35.gxf6 Nf4 36.Rxf4??

This is what I had expected. For some reason I had completely missed the obvious 36.Qg5+ Kh8 37.f7 Rxh3+ 38.Kg1 when Black can resign. Fortunately my opponent shared my hallucination!

36...exf4 37.Rg1+ Rg3 38.Rxg3+ fxg3 39.Qg5+ Kh8 40.f7

This was the position I had envisioned when playing 33...Nd3. My opponent thought he was winning, (40...Qxf7 41.Qe5+ picks up black's Rook with check), but he completely underestimated my reply.

40...g2+!!, 0-1.

This nice move turns the tables, but his resignation was a bit premature. He should have played on (he had nothing to lose) by 41.Kg1 (41.Qxg2 Qxf7; 41.Bxg2 Rb1+) 41…Qb6+ 42.c5 Qb2 43.Qf4 Qd4+ 44.Kxg2 though after 44…Qg7+ followed by 45…Rf8 White's position is very unpleasant.

6

VERY OLD COMBINATIONS

White to Play and Win

We have all heard of the legendary Lucena (think Rook endgame), but few have actually seen any of his games. In the following game, Black was fine throughout, however Quintana went wrong, and is now a pawn down, though he must have thought that his seventh-rank Rook would quickly lead to material parity. He was wrong.

Luis Ramírez Lucena vs. Quintana, Huesca 1515

1.c3 Nc6 2.d4 e6 3.e4 d5 4.exd5 exd5 5.g3 Bd6 6.Bh3 Bxh3 7.Nxh3 Qd7 8.Nf4 Nf6 9.Qf3 Bxf4 10.Bxf4 0-0-0 11.0-0 Qh3 12.Bg5 Ng4 13.Qg2 Qxg2+ 14.Kxg2 f6 15.Bd2 Rhe8 16.Re1 Rxe1 17.Bxe1 Re8 18.Nd2 Nh6 19.Nf1 Nf5 20.Bd2 Nd6 21.h4 Ne4 22.Be3 g5 23.hxg5 fxg5 24.f3 Nd6 25.Bxg5 Re2+ 26.Kh3 Rxb2 27.Ne3 Nb5 28.Nxd5 Rc2 29.Re1!

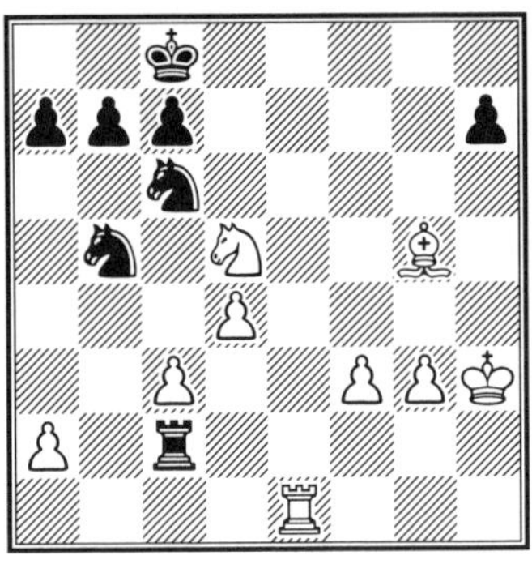

All three of White's pieces take aim at black's King.

29...Nxc3

29...Kd7 30.Nf6+ Kc8 (30...Kd6 31.Bf4+) 31.Re8+ Nd8 32.Nd5 and the d8-Knight falls.

29...Nd6 is the best defense, when 30.Bf4 is a technical win (with bits of tactics thrown in): 30...Rxa2 31.Re6 when ideas like Nc7 and Rh6xh7 will eventually win the game.

29...b6 30.Re6 Na5 (30...Kb7 31.Rxc6 Kxc6 32.Nb4+ Kd6 33.Nxc2) 31.f4 Nxc3 32.Nxc3 Rxc3 33.f5 Rf3 34.f6 Nb7 (34...Rf5 35.Kg4 Rf1 36.Bf4) 35.Bf4 Nd8 36.Re8 Kd7 37.Re7+ Kc6 38.Rxc7+ Kb5 39.f7 Nxf7 40.Rxf7 and Black should resign.

30.Re8+!

Even stronger than 30.Nxc3 Rxc3 31.d5 Nd8 (31...Nb4 32.Re8+ Kd7 33.Rd8 mate) 32.Re8 winning a piece and the game.

30...Kd7 31.Nf6+ Kd6 32.Bf4+ Ne5

A sad move to make, but it's forced.

33.Rxe5!

Of course every Knight-capture wins, but 33.Rxe5 doesn't just win the Knight, it wins the house!

33...Rxa2

33...Kc6 gets mated: 34.Rc5+ Kb6 35.Bc7+ (Fastest, but 35.Nd7+ Ka6 36.Nb8+ Kb6 37.Bxc7 mate has a beauty all its own) 35...Ka6 36.Ra5 mate.

34.Re3+ Kc6 35.Rxc3+, 1-0.

Polerio is another legendary name, and one of the best players of his day. I decided to give the following game because it offers several very instructive attacking themes (mentioned in the notes), and it also features the Fried Liver Attack, which is a fan favorite.

How Would You Continue White's Attack?

Giulio Cesare Polerio vs. Domenico D'Arminio, Rome 1610

1.e4 e5 2.Nf3 Nc6 3.Bc4 Nf6 4.Ng5 d5 5.exd5 Nxd5 6.Nxf7 Kxf7 7.Qf3+ Ke6 8.Nc3 Ne7 9.d4 c6 10.Bg5 h6 11.Bxd7

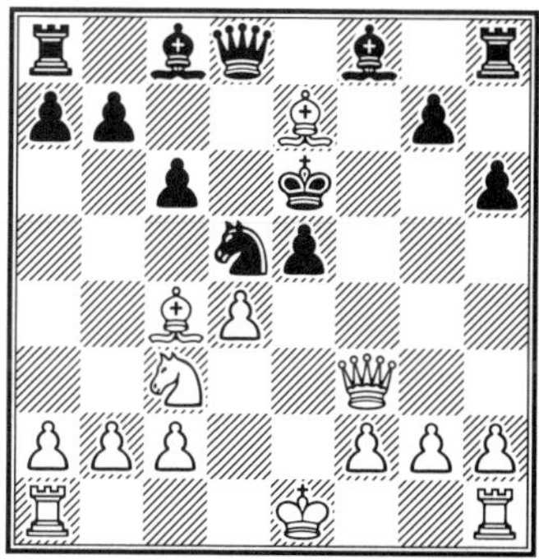

11... Bxe7 12.0-0-0 Rf8 13.Qe4 Rxf2 14.dxe5!

Most players try 14.Qxe5+? because ... well ... it's check! However, this "mighty" check allows Black to see the game: 14...Kf7 (14...Kd7?? 15.Nxd5 cxd5 16.Bb5 mate) 15.Nxd5 cxd5 16.Bxd5+ (Black is made in the shade after 16.Rhf1 dxc4! 17.Rxf2+ Kg8) 16...Kg6 (16...Ke8 is playable, but White has full compensation after 17.Rhe1) 17.Be4+ Kf7 18.Bd5+ with a draw by repetition. Think about the position before White played 14.dxe5. He is putting pressure on d5 three ways (Queen, Knight, and Bishop). 14.Qxe5+ doesn't add to that pressure, but 14.dxe5 gets the d1-Rook into the game by adding a fourth unit that can strike at d5. Also note that by moving the d-pawn to e5, that pawn becomes a powerful attacking piece in its own right.

14...Bg5+

14...Kd7 15.Nxd5 cxd5 16.Rxd5+ Kc7 17.Rxd8 Bf5 18.Qxf5 Rxf5 19.Rxa8 and White is a Rook up in the endgame.

15.Kb1 Rd2 16.h4!

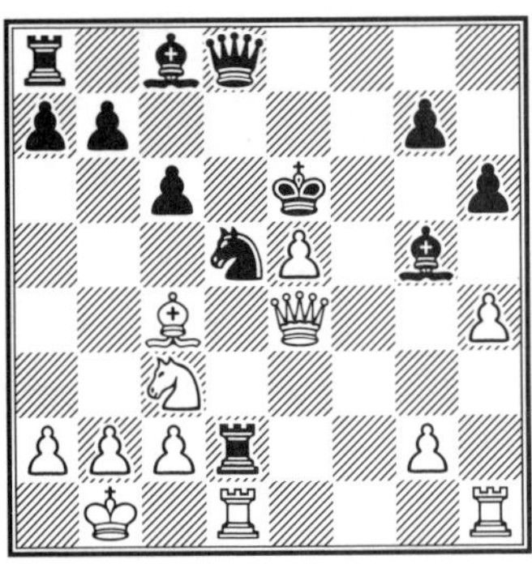

16...Rxd1+ 17.Rxd1 Bxh4 18.Nxd5 cxd5 19.Rxd5 Qg5 20.Rd6+ Ke7 21.Rg6! Qd2 22.Rxg7+ Kf8 23.Rg8+ Ke7 24.Qh7, 1-0.

Gioacchino Greco (1600-1634) was an extremely strong player who not only was a master of combinations but also had some serious positional skills, though he didn't get to demonstrate them too often since his opponents were not close to his level. Greco also discovered or created many of the opening traps we take for granted today.

Usually each generation of chess players is stronger than the next, but I have always believed that Greco would have spliced and diced Philidor, who was born ninety-two years after Greco's death. Of course, it's a matter of opinion, and I might well be the only person in the world who thinks this!

Mate Isn't the Only Way to Win a Game

Gioacchino Greco vs. NN, Europe 1620

1.e4 e5 2.f4 exf4 3.Bc4 Qh4+ 4.Kf1 Bc5 5.d4 Bb6 6.Nf3 Qh6 7.g3 Qh3+ 8.Kf2 fxg3+ 9.hxg3 Qg4 10.Bxf7+!

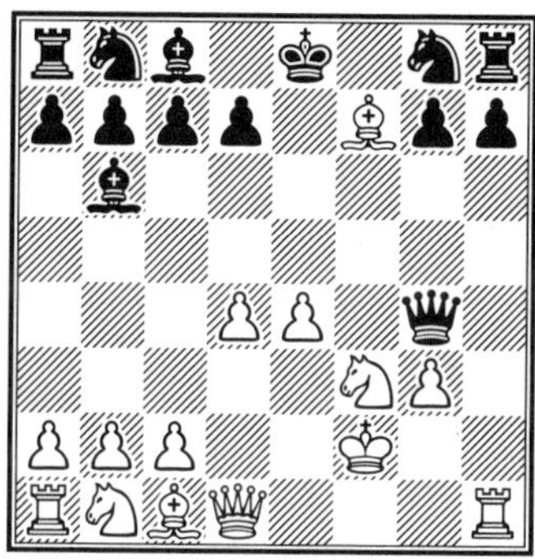

Even better than 10.Rh4 which is also strong.

10...Kf8

10...Kxf7 11.Ne5+ forking black's King and Queen.

11.Rh4, 1-0. Black's Queen is a goner.

Sharp and Precise

Gioacchino Greco vs. NN, Europe 1620

1.e4 e5 2.Nf3 d6 3.Bc4 Bg4 4.h3 Bh5 5.c3 Nf6 6.d3 Be7 7.Be3 0-0 8.g4 Bg6 9.Nh4 c6 10.Nxg6 hxg6 11.h4 b5 12.Bb3 a5 13.a4 b4 14.h5 gxh5 15.g5 Ng4 16.Rxh5 Nxe3 17.Rh8+

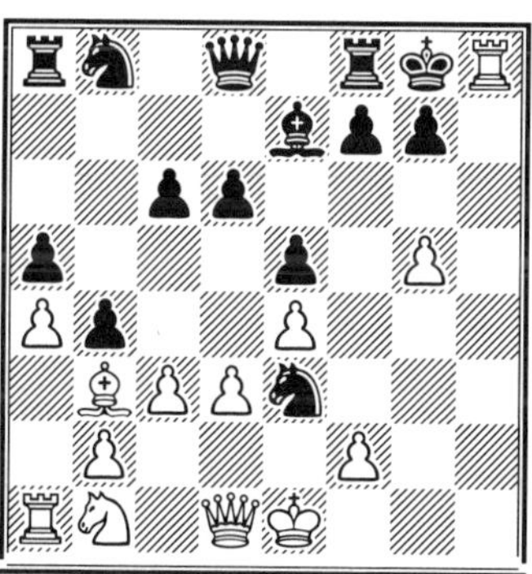

The point. 17.fxe3 g6 is fine for Black

17...Kxh8 18.Qh5+ Kh8 19.g6 Re8 20.Qh7+

Taking on f7 with the pawn or Bishop followed by Qh8 mate also works.

20...Kf8 21.Qh8,1-0.

Deep and Brilliant

Gioacchino Greco vs. NN, Europe 1620

1.e4 e5 2.Nf3 Nc6 3.Bc4 Bc5 4.c3 Qe7 5.0-0 d6 6.d4 Bb6 7.Bg5 f6 8.Bh4 g5 9.Nxg5!!

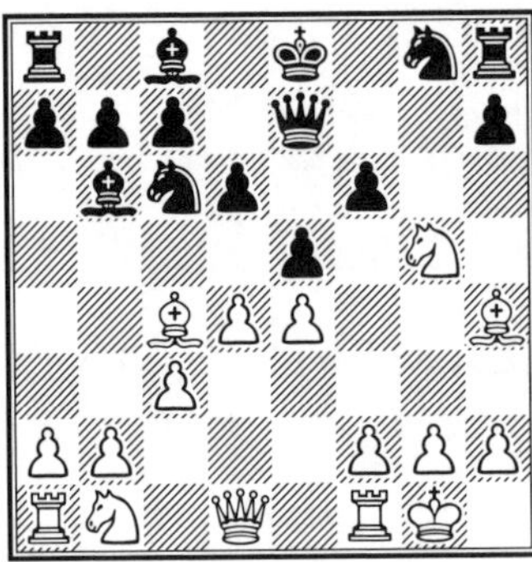

A brilliant sacrifice!

9...fxg5 10.Qh5+ Kf8?

✦ 10...Kd8? Also fails: 11.Bxg5 Nf6 12.Qh6 Rf8 13.f4 exd4 14.e5! dxc3+ 15.Kh1 cxb2 16.exf6 with a fascinating position that is, unfortunately for Black, completely winning for White. It turns out that another Greco game reached this position with the following finish: 16...bxa1=Q 17.fxe7+ Nxe7 18.Qxf8+ Kd7 19.bb5+ Nc6 20.Qe2 mate.

✦ 10...Kd7! is the best defensive try, but White can keep the flame alive by 11.Bxg5 Nf6 12.Qh4 Rf8 and now 13.f4! exd4 14.Kh1 with a raging attack.

11.f4!!

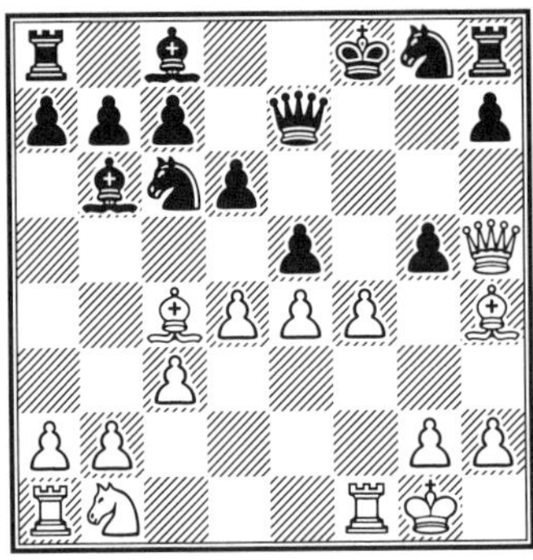

A lovely way to continue the attack. Unfortunately, Greco played the inferior 11.Bg5 (the most natural move in the world) 11...Qe8 12.Qf3+ Kg7 13.Bxg8 Rxg8?? 14.Qf6 mate.

11...Be6

11...exf4 12.Bxg5 lets the armies of hell pour through into Black's position.

12.fxe5+ Kg7 13.Rf6!

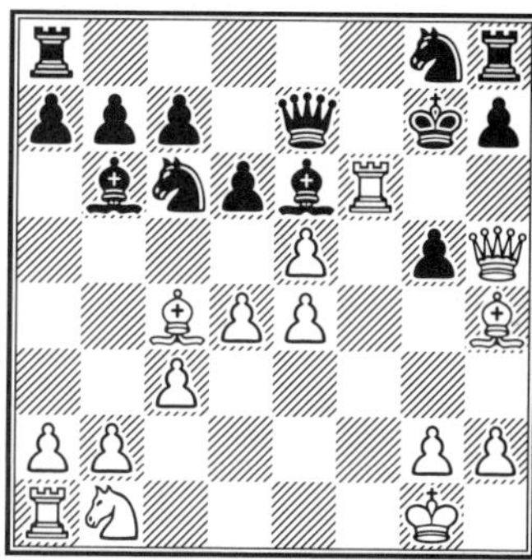

13.Bxg5 also wins: 13...Bxc4 14.Bxe7 Ngxe7 15.Rf2 Nxd4 and things look crazy for most humans, though a computer will yawn and tell Black to give up. I would go for 13.Rf6 because it keeps complete control over the game.

13...Nxf6 14.Qxg5+ Kf8 15.exf6 Qf7 16.Bxe6 Qg6 17.Qe3 Re8 18.Bd5 when White has a powerful attack, a minor piece and three pawns for black's Rook, and Black has zero counterplay. In other worlds, White should easily win the game.

Sometimes Only Mate Will Do

Gioacchino Greco vs. NN, Europe 1620

1.e4 e5 2.Bc4 Bc5 3.Qe2 Qe7 4.f4 exf4 5.Nf3 g5 6.h4 f6 7.hxg5 fxg5 8.Nc3 c6 9.d4 g4 10.Nh4

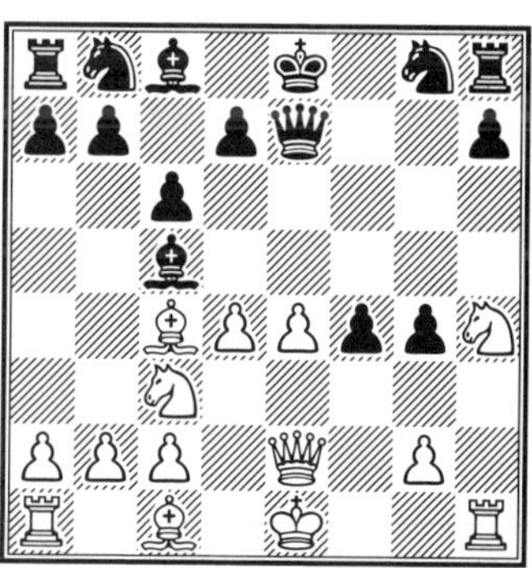

10...Bxd4 11.Nf5 Bxc3+ 12.bxc3 Qf6 13.Bxf4 Qxc3+ 14.Kf2 b5 15.Bb3 a5 16.Nd6+ Kd8 17.Qxg4

17.Be5 was also strong since it gets a winning material advantage: 17...Qc5+ 18.Qe3 Qxe3+ 19.Kxe3, etc. However, Greco wanted mate!

17...Ne7 18.Nf7+ Ke8 19.Qh5 Qd4+ 20.Kf3 Qc3+ 21.Ke2 Rf8 22.Nd6+ Kd8 23.Qe8+! Rxe8 24.Nf7, 1-0.

White Can Play Positions and Endgames Too

Gioacchino Greco vs. NN, Europe 1620

1.d4 d5 2.c4 c5 3.dxc5 Qa5+ 4.Qd2 Qxd2+ 5.Nxd2 dxc4 6.Nxc4 e6 7.Nd6+ Bxd6 8.cxd6 Nf6 9.f3 0-0 10.e4 e5 11.b3 Rd8 12.Ba3 Ne8 13.Rd1 Be6 14.Bc4 Bd7 15.g3 b5 16.Bd5 Bc6 17.Bc5 Bxd5 18.Rxd5

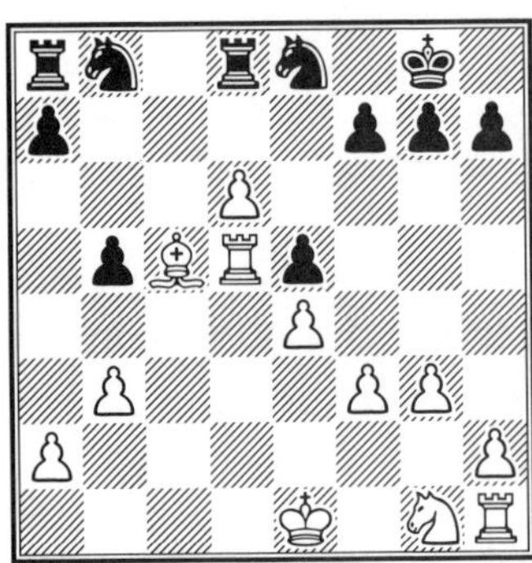

18...Nd7 19.b4 a5 20.a3 axb4 21.axb4 Ra1+ 22.Kf2 Rc1 23.Kg2 Nxc5 24.bxc5 b4 25.Ne2 Rc2 26.Kf2 b3 27.Rb1 b2 28.Ke1 f6 29.Kd1 Rc4 30.Rxb2 Kf7 31.Rb7+ Ke6 32.Re7, 1-0.

Positions Play!

NN vs. Gioacchino Greco, Europe 1620

1.e4 e6 2.d4 d5 3.e5 c5 4.c3 Nc6 5.Nf3 Bd7 6.Be3 c4 7.b3 b5 8.a4 a6 9.axb5 axb5 10.Rxa8 Qxa8 11.bxc4 dxc4

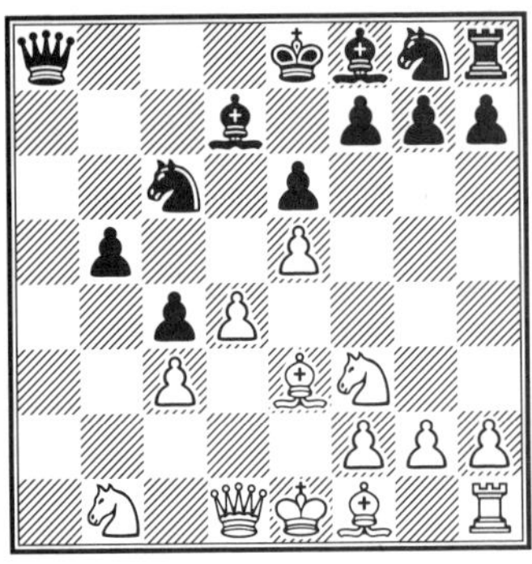

12.Be2 Nge7 13.0-0 Nd5 14.Bd2 Be7 15.Ng5 Bxg5 16.Bxg5 0-0 17.Bf3 Na5 18.Bxd5 Qxd5 19.f4 Bc6 20.Qd2 Nb3 21.Qc2 Nxd4 22.cxd4 Qxd4+ 23.Kh1 Be4 24.Qc3 Qc5 25.Nd2 Bd3 26.Rc1 Rc8 27.Nb3 cxb3 28.Qxc5 Rxc5 29.Rxc5 h6 30.Rc3 b2 31.Rb3 b1Q+ 32.Rxb1 Bxb1 33.Be7 Kh7 34.g4 Be4+ 35.Kg1 Bf3 36.h3 h5 37.g5 Kg6 38.Kf2 Bd5 39.Ke3 h4 40.Kf2 Kf5 41.Ke3 Bg2 42.Bf8 g6 43.Bb4 Bxh3 44.Be1 Kg4 45.Bd2 Bg2 46.Kf2 h3 47.Bc1 Bd5 48.Kg1 Kg3 49.Be3 h2+ 50.Kf1 h1Q+, 0-1.

After Philidor became the guru of chess from the mid-to-late 1700s, the game became a lot more boring as masses of players tried to use their pawns in strange plodding ways, leaving all those crazy attacking dudes to wonder what in the world happened. However, not everyone went "positional."

Testosterone-fueled males were still walking the Earth, and they kept the flame of insane attack flickering. After all, what was that pawn stuff really all about? No, no, to these anachronistic creatures, pawns and pieces were there to be sacrificed for attack. "Kill, kill!" was their motto, and those few singlehandedly kept the chessboard in flames.

The largely unknown D. Bowdler was one of those "Sac it all for the sheer joy of it" type of player. Following is the first part of the game to show you how little Bowdler thought of material.

D. Bowdler vs. M. Conway, London 1788

1.e4 e5 2.Bc4 Bc5 3.d3 c6 4.Qe2 d6 5.f4 exf4 6.Bxf4 Qb6 7.Qf3

I can image Bowdler thinking, "Defend my pawn and Rook? Why would I do that?"

7…Qxb2

White is busted, but Bowdler couldn't care less.

8.Bxf7+ Kd7

8…Kxf7?? 9.Be5+ pieces up black's Queen.

9.Ne2 Qxa1 10.Kd2 Bb4+ 11.Nbc3 Bxc3+ 12.Nxc3 Qxh1

Though White is dead lost, I have a feeling that he was quite pleased with his game. After all, who needs Rooks?

13.Qg4+ Kc7 14.Qxg7 Nd7 15.Qg3 b6 16.Nb5+

There's nothing like the smell of napalm in the morning!

16…cxb5??

Black would still be on top with 16...Kb8, but in those days manly men didn't run from such sacrifices! How did Bowdler finish off his opponent?

17.Bxd6+

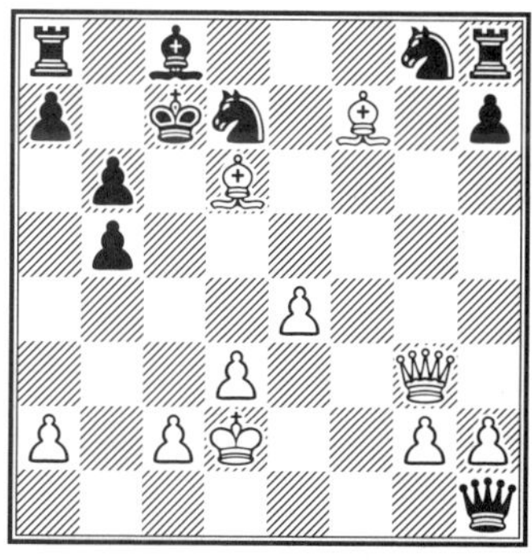

17...Kb7 18.Bd5+ Ka6 19.d4!

Threatening 20.Qa3 mate.

19...b4

19...Nc5 loses to the obvious and effective 20.dxc5.

20.Bxb4 Kb5 21.c4+ Kxb4 22.Qb3+ Ka5 23.Qb5, 1-0.

23.Qa3 mate is also instant death.

7

TRAIN YOUR BRAIN! TARGET CONSCIOUSNESS

What is Target Consciousness? I coined this phrase long ago, and I still consider it to be of enormous use, for students who appreciate high-level games and strive to play much stronger chess, . The concept is simple: you need to train your mind to spot targets on the chessboard (or, if there aren't any, play to create targets) and then to immediately focus on making use of whatever target you have.

The most basic targets are weak squares and weak pawns, so that's what I'll focus on here. When I teach, it's not unusual to discover that a student has no idea which side of the board to play on. Once I make him a Target Consciousness addict, though, he no longer has a problem concerning vicinity—suddenly the correct side of the board to play on is lit up with shockingly bright colors!

Of course, training the mind so it becomes a bloodhound that always seeks (and then destroys or uses) a target is far from easy. But you have to start somewhere, and once you embrace the concept completely and always do your best to look for the target (this will also teach you to not create targets in your own camp!), it will eventually become second nature—an unconscious use of (target) consciousness!

The first example is a very simple illustration of how you create a weakness and then devote yourself to its destruction.

Silman vs. Jose Marcal, San Francisco 1981

1.d4 f5 2.g3 g6 3.b3 Bg7 4.Bb2 Nf6 5.Bg2 0-0 6.Nd2 d6 7.Ngf3 c6 8.0-0 Qc7 9.Re1 Na6 10.a3 Bd7 11.e4 fxe4 12.Nxe4 Nxe4 13.Rxe4 Rae8 14.Ng5 e5 15.dxe5 dxe5 16.Re1 Nc5 17.Qe2 Kh8 18.Qc4 Ne6 19.Nxe6 Bxe6 20.Qc5 Bf5 21.Be4 Bxe4 22.Rxe4

This kind of position is easy. You see a target (e5), you block it (Rook on the e4-hole) so it can't move, and then you hit it with everything you've got. The "hitting weapons" are the Queen, both Rooks, the Bishop and the f2-pawn. A real team effort!

22...Rf5 23.Rae1 b6 24.Qe3 Ref8

Everything hits the target! The threat is 25.f4 when e5 is attacked by no less than FIVE White units!

25.Rxe5!

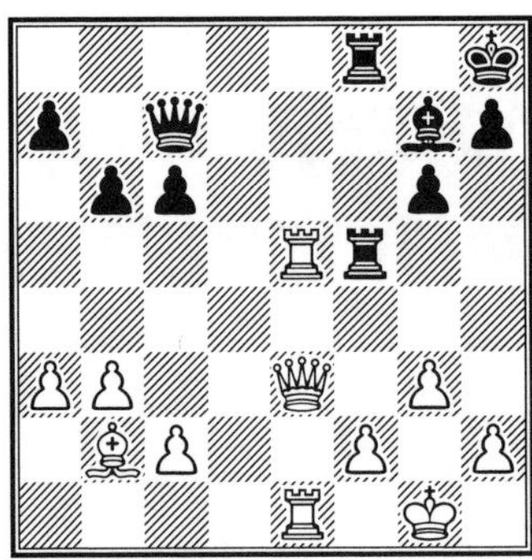

More accurate than 25. Bxe5 Bxe5 26. Rxe5 Rxf2 when Black can fight on for a while.

25...Rxe5 26.Bxe5 Qxe5 27.Qxe5 Bxe5 28.Rxe5 Rf7 29.Kf1 Kg7 30.Ke2 Kf6 31.f4 Rd7 32.b4 Rd8 33.a4 Rd4 34.c3 Rd6 35.a5 Rd8 36.g4 Rd6 37.h4 Rd8 38.h5 Rd7 39.h6 Rd8 40.a6 Kf7 41.Re4 Rd5 42.Rd4 Ke6 43.Rxd5 Kxd5 44.c4+ Ke6 45.Ke3 Kf6 46.Ke4 Ke6 47.g5 b5 48.c5 Kf7 49.Ke5 Ke7 50.f5 gxf5 51.g6, 1-0.

Another thing a student discovers when he embraces Target Consciousness is that his opponents often can't handle the heat and fall on their faces, losing without a fight.

Silman vs. Rasmussen, Grants Pass 1984

1.d4 Nf6 2.c4 e6 3.Nc3 d5 4.Nf3 c6 5.e3 dxc4 6.Bxc4 b5 7.Bd3 a6 8.0-0 Bb7 9.Qe2 Nbd7 10.e4 c5 11.d5 e5 12.b3 Be7

Black is not okay! Black seems to be doing okay—White's passed d-pawn isn't going anywhere (it's static), and Black's queenside majority is dynamic. The first thing White wants to do is create a target. Thus his next move speaks for itself.

13.a4!

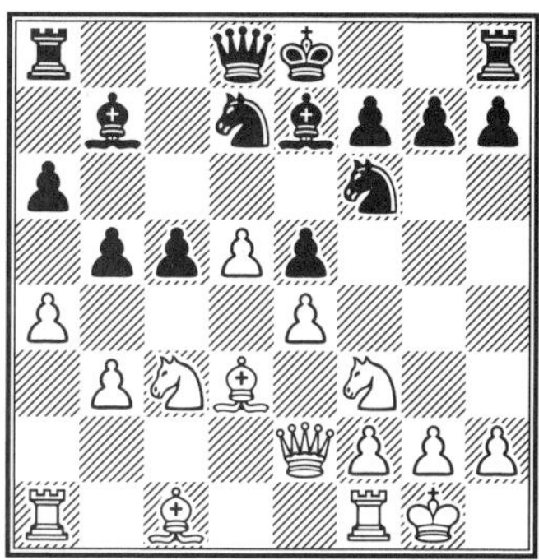

13...b4⁈

A positional cave-in. And Black immediately caves! In fact, he's strategically lost after this move. Instead, he had no choice but to sacrifice a pawn by 13...c4! 14.bxc4 b4 when, though Black is a pawn behind, he has a passed b-pawn and use of the very nice c5- and d6-squares (Black's dark-squared Bishop will end up on d6 while a black Knight will find that c5 is a fine post).

White is better after 13...c4, but at least Black would have some positive things to make use of, and he could put up a real fight.

After 13...b4 Black's queenside majority is no longer dynamic (it's frozen), and what is left is a weak pawn on c5 (the e5-pawn is also under pressure) and a weak square (a huge hole, in fact) on c4. Worse still, Black's position is suddenly passive and without prospect. In short, Black has no targets to make use of, while White has targets on c4, c5, and e5.

14.Nd1 0-0 15.Bb2

White has a huge advantage.

15...Re8

In the actual game Black played **15...Bxd5⁇** in despair and lost quickly.

16.Ne3 Bf8 17.a5!

Keeps the d7-Knight off of b6 and turns the a6-pawn into a frozen target.

17...Nh5 18.g3 g6 19.Nc4 and it's hard for Black to find a useful move.

Next is another example of weak squares as targets. The creation and use of the weak squares/targets in this game is clear and useful for players great and small, but the technique required is more advanced. However, the fact that the technical phase is also ruled by Black's creation of enemy targets creates a satisfying picture:

Alex Kuznecov vs. Silman, Oregon Open 1986

A famous opening trap.

1.e4 c5 2.Nf3 Nc6 3.d4 cxd4 4.Nxd4 g6 5.c4 Bg7 6.Be3 Nf6 7.Nc3 0-0 8.Be2 b6 9.0-0 Bb7 10.f3 Nh5 11.Nxc6

11.f4? Nxf4!! 12.Rxf4 (12.Bxf4 Bxd4+; 12.Nxc6 Nxe2+) 12...Nxd4 (12...e5?? 13.Nxc6) 13.Bxd4 e5 14.Bxe5 Bxe5 and White is in very bad shape due to the weakness (target) of e4, black's two Bishops, and the immense power of that dark-squared Bishop on e5.

11...dxc6 12.Qb3 Bd4!

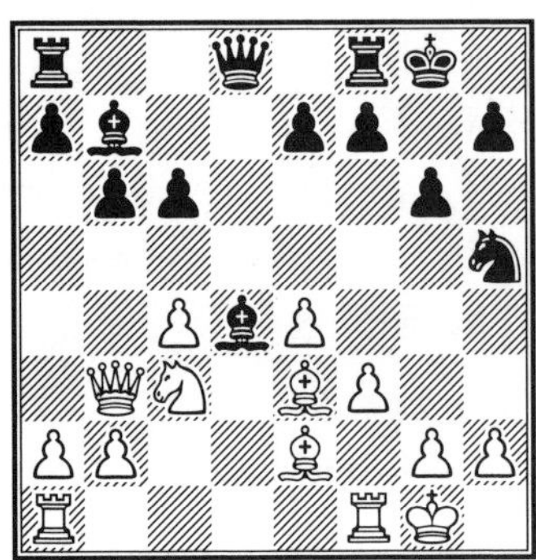

Target: d4

Black is already targeting the d4-square/hole for annexation. Since White's dark-squared bishop supported that square, Black makes a point of trading it off.

13.Bxd4 Qxd4+ 14.Kh1 Nf4 15.Rfd1 Qe5 16.Bf1 Rfd8 17.a4?! Ne6 18.Ne2 Nc5 19.Qc2 a5

Suddenly the c5-square has also fallen into Black's hands!

20.Rab1 Qc7 21.Nc3 Rxd1 22.Rxd1 Rd8 23.Rd2 e5

Targets - b4, c5, d4

Notice White's weak squares (which Black has targeted): b4, c5, and d4. (The importance of b4 is that White can't challenge c5 by b2-b4. Thus control over b4 also gives Black control over c5!). In comparison, Black's squares on b5, and d5 are firmly controlled by the c6-pawn.

24.Qd1 Rxd2 25.Qxd2 Ne6 26.Ne2 Qe7 27.Nc1 Kg7 28.Nb3 c5

You give something, you get something.

Black gives up b5 and d5 but sees that it turns white's Bishop into a tall pawn, and that white's Knight isn't able to reach the dream square/target on d5. Another point, though, is that it freezes White's queenside pawns so that they are stuck on light squares. This means that they are potentially vulnerable to the affections of black's Bishop for the rest of the game.

29.Nc1 Bc6 30.Qd1 Qd7 31.Qxd7 Bxd7 32.b3 Nd4

Targets - d4, b3

The b3-pawn is an obvious problem and white's Bishop is quite wretched.

33.Kg1 f5 34.Bd3 Bc6 35.exf5 gxf5 36.Kf2 Kf6 37.Ke3 Kg5 38.Bb1 h5 39.Bd3 h4 40.h3

Now White's kingside pawns are also trapped on light squares.

40...Be8 41.Be2 Bg6 42.Bd1 f4+ 43.Kf2 Bb1

Breaking on through to the other side. Black's Bishop is getting closer and closer to the tasty morsels on a4, b3, and c4.

44.Ne2

We'll end this game with a puzzle...demonstrate your technique!

44...e4!

There's no longer a defense. White is completely busted.

45.fxe4

45 .Nxd4 e3+.

45...Nxe2! 46.Bxe2 Bxe4

White is helpless since his King has to defend g2, his Bishop will be stuck defending b3 (if it moves to d1), and Black's plan of doing a King march via ...Kg5-f6-e5-d4-c3 can't be stopped.

47.Bg4

47.Bd1 Kf6 48.Kf1 Ke5 49.Kf2 Kd4 is also hopeless.

48...Bc2

48...Bxb3 also wins.

48.Kf3 Bd1, 0-1.

Silman vs. Elliott Winslow, U.S. Open 1981

1.Nf3 Nf6 2.g3 b6 3.Bg2 Bb7 4.0-0 g6 5.c4 c5 6.b3 Bg7 7.Bb2 0-0 8.Nc3 Na6 9.d4 cxd4 10.Qxd4 Ne4 11.Qe3 Nxc3 12.Bxc3 Bxc3 13.Qxc3 Nc5 14.Rfd1 Qc7 15.Qe3 Ne6 16.Rd2 d6 17.Nd4 Nxd4 18.Rxd4 Bxg2 19.Rh4

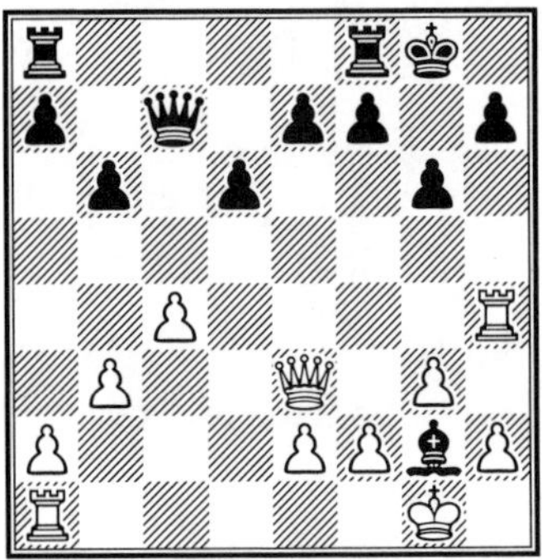

19...e5 20.Kxg2 Rad8 21.Rd1 f5 22.Rd5 Qe7

It's clear that d6 is the target. White's first order of business is to get his Rook on h4 back into the battle against d6. Note that some might think the Rook on h4 gives White chances of a kingside attack, but that's just a fantasy. Instead, it MUST help out the rest of White's army go after the position's target. Thus:

23.Rhd4!

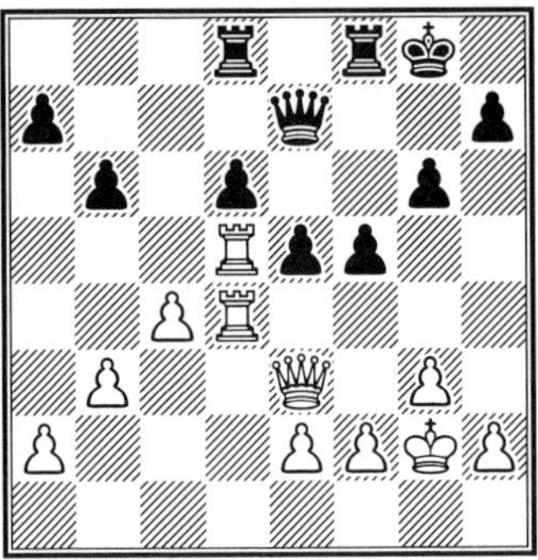

Thanks to the pin along the e-file, the Rook is able to return to its proper home in the center.

23...Rd7 24.Rd1 f4 25.Qe4

The targets are obvious: holes on d5 and e4, and huge pressure against d6.

25...Rf6 26.a4!

A very important move! One target is nice, but your position will have much more punch if you have two targets! The idea of 26.a4 is to create a new pawn weakness in Black's camp by a4-a5.

26...Rc7 27.a5! and, since (after axb6) White can attack two enemy targets while Black can only sit around and try and hold on, White enjoys a very comfortable advantage. White went on to win on move 50.

Silman vs. Ozdal Barken, U.S. Open 1981

1.d4 d5 2.c4 e6 3.Nc3 Nf6 4.Nf3 Nbd7 5.Bf4 c6 6.e3 Be7 7.h3 0-0 8.Rc1 a6 9.a3 Re8 10.c5 Nh5 11.Bh2 g6 12.Be2 f6 13.e4 Bf8 14.0-0 Bh6 15.Rc2 Kh8 16.Re1 Nf4 17.Bf1 Rg8 18.b4 Nf8 19.a4 g5 20.Bxf4 gxf4 21.Nh2 Ng6 22.Qh5 Bf8 23.exd5 cxd5 24.Bd3 f5

Target: the backward pawn on e6!

25.Nf3 Be7 26.Rce2

White puts maximum pressure on e6. The trick here is to realize that e6 is a massive target since it holds Black's whole position together, keeps white's Rooks from rushing down the e-file, defends d5, and defends f5.

26...Bf6 27.Rxe6!!

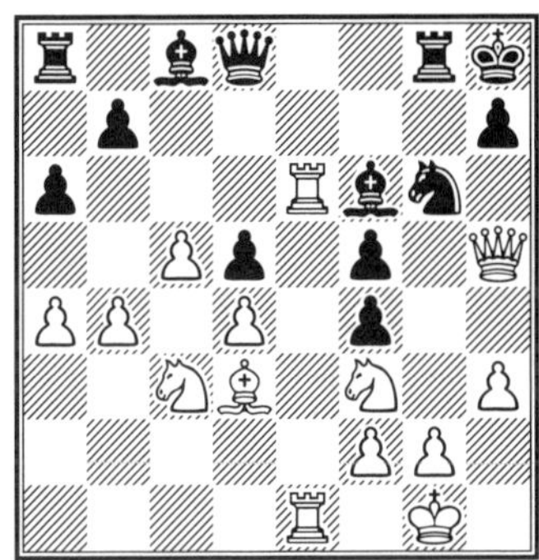

27...Bxe6 28.Rxe6

Black's game is already resignable, but of course he plays on.

28...Be7 29.Bxf5 Nf8 30.Ne5 Qe8 31.Nf7+ Kg7 32.Nxd5! Nxe6 33.Qh6+ Kxf7 34.Bxe6, 1-0.

The following game was a very important one for me—I had to win this final round game to tie for first!

Silman vs. Dennis Gogel, U.S. Open 1981

1.d4 Nf6 2.c4 g6 3.Nc3 Bg7 4.e4 d6 5.Be2 0-0 6.Bg5 c5 7.d5 e6 8.Qd2 exd5 9.exd5 Re8 10.Nf3 Bg4 11.0-0 Nbd7 12.h3 Bxf3 13.Bxf3 a6 14.a4 b6 15.Rae1 Rxe1 16.Rxe1 Qf8 17.Bd1 h6 18.Be3 Rb8 19.Be2 Ne8 20.f4 Nc7 21.Bd3 Re8 22.Bf2 f5 23.Rb1 a5 24.g4! Qf6

24...fxg4 25.Bxg6 Bxc3 26.bxc3 Qg7 27.Qd3 Rf8 28.Bg3! gxh3 29.Kh2 and White's two Bishops and the threat of Rg1 leaves Black in very bad shape. However, after 24…Qf6 Black quickly realizes that he's positionally busted.

25.gxf5 gxf5 26.Ne2!

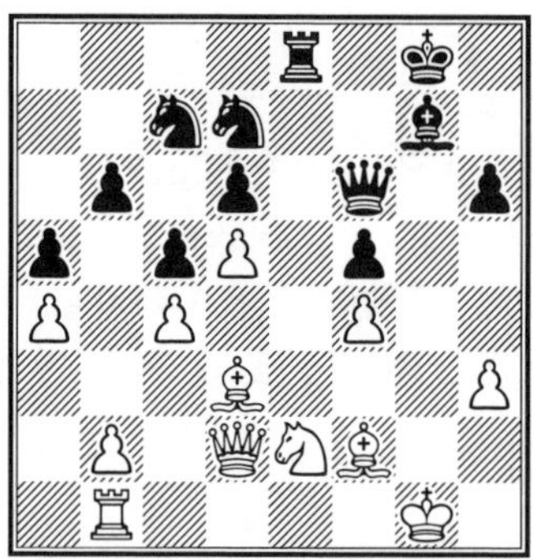

All I have to do is pile up against the target on f5 and it's game over.

26...Qg6+ 27.Ng3 Rf8 28.Kh2 Ne8 29.Rg1

29.Nxf5 Rxf5 30.Qc2 was also strong. I wanted to avoid complications and keep things very simple.

29...Qh7 30.Qc2, 1-0.

Erik Osbun vs. Silman, Berkeley 1981

1.d4 Nf6 2.c4 e6 3.Nc3 Bb4 4.e3 c5 5.Nge2 cxd4 6.exd4 d5 7.a3 Be7 8.c5 0-0 9.g3 b6 10.b4 a5 11.Bb2 axb4 12.axb4 Rxa1 13.Bxa1 bxc5 14.bxc5 Nc6

A smorgasbord of targets for Black

Here's the list: d4 is under pressure, the whole f1-a6 diagonal is weak (due to the upcoming ...Ba6), the c5-pawn might fall after an eventual ...e6-e5 which destroys its defender on d4, and finally, due to White's lack of development, the b-file can easily be claimed by a black Rook.

15.Bg2 Ba6 16.0-0 Qa5 17.Re1 Rb8 18.Bf3 Bc4

The Bishop claims the tasty hole/target on c4.

19.Qa4 Qxa4 20.Nxa4 Nd7!

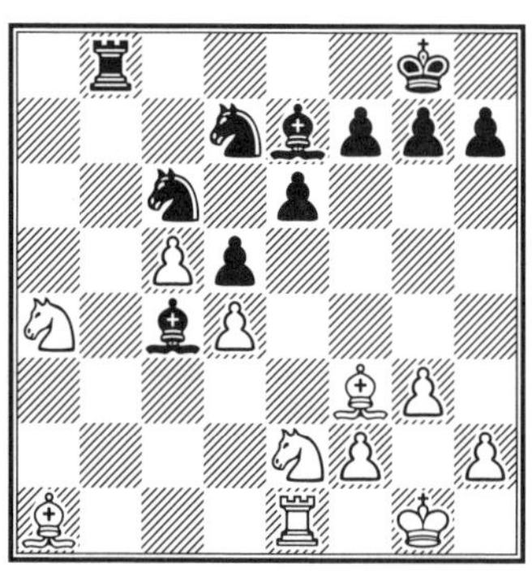

Prevents Nb6 and prepares to add some heat to d4 by ...Bf6.

21.Bc3 Bf6 22.Rd1 Bb3 23.Ra1 Ra8 24.Nb6 Rxa1+ 25.Bxa1 Nxc5! 26.Bc3 Na4 27.Nxa4 Bxa4, 0-1.

Since 28.Kg2 Bb5 allows Black to win a second pawn (at his leisure) by ... Bxe2 followed by ...Bxd4.

Silman vs. Craig Mar, San Jose 1983

1.d4 Nf6 2.c4 c5 3.d5 e6 4.Nc3 exd5 5.cxd5 d6 6.Nf3 g6 7.Bg5 Bg7 8.e3 h6 9.Bh4 0-0 10.Nd2

White's 10.Nd2 prevents 10...g5 11.Bg3 Nh5 (since the Queen now covers h5), while eyeing the c4-square which would be an ideal square for the Knight since it would place pressure on d6.

10...Nbd7 11.Be2 a6 12.a4 Re8 13.0-0 Rb8 14.h3

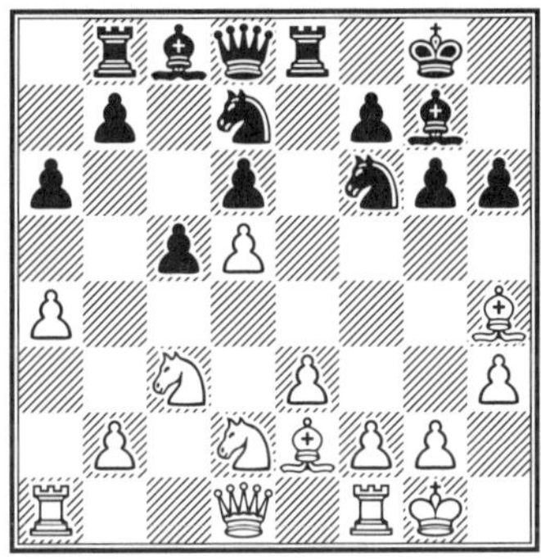

A small but useful improvement.

This move keeps Black's pieces out of g4 and also allows White's dark-squared Bishop to hide on h2 in some lines. It's surprisingly difficult for Black to create active play from this position.

14...g5 15.Bg3 Ne5 16.Qc2 Qe7 17.Rfe1 Bd7 18.a5 g4 19.hxg4 Nfxg4 20.Na4

The b6-square is calling

20...Qg5

Hoping to bail out of his predicament with tactics like ...Nxe3.

21.Nf1

Defending e3 and g3 and ending any tactical nonsense before it occurs.

21...Qg6 22.Qxg6!

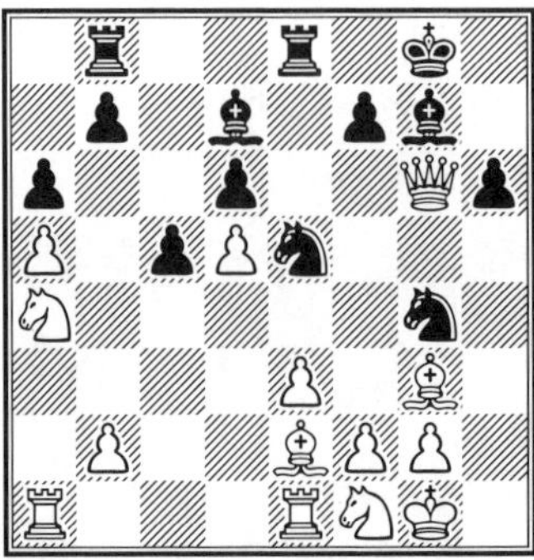

22...fxg6 23.Nb6

White seeks domination of both b6 and c4.

23...Bf5 24.f3 Nf6 25.e4 Bc8 26.Bxe5!

Winning the c4-square and blocking the g7-Bishop

26...dxe5

Black loses material after 26...Rxe5 27.Nc4. Now (after 26...dxe5) Black's dark-squared Bishop finds itself in a sad state since the a1-h8 diagonal is closed.

27.Ne3 Nd7 28.Nec4 Nxb6 29.Nxb6

The monster Knight rules both b6 and c4. This Knight can now leap effortlessly between b6 and c4. It's a very happy horse.

29...Bf8 30.Rec1

Targeting the whole c-file. The c5-pawn is obviously under fire but, ultimately, White wants the whole c-file since the b6-knight would prevent a black Rook from moving to c8 and challenging for the file. Black is hopelessly lost.

30...Kf7 31.Bd1!

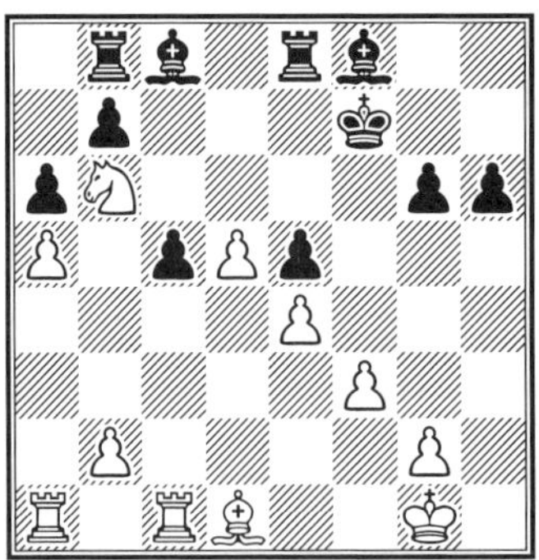

Making sure every piece reaches its optimal square. The Bishop wasn't doing anything on e2, but it will be a major player on a4!

31...h5 32.Ba4 Rd8 33.Kf2!

Just say NO to counterplay!

As usual, I always try to deny my opponent counterplay. This move prevents ...Bf8-h6-e3+ when that formerly bad piece would find a nice home on d4.

33...h4

Find the death blow!

34.b4!

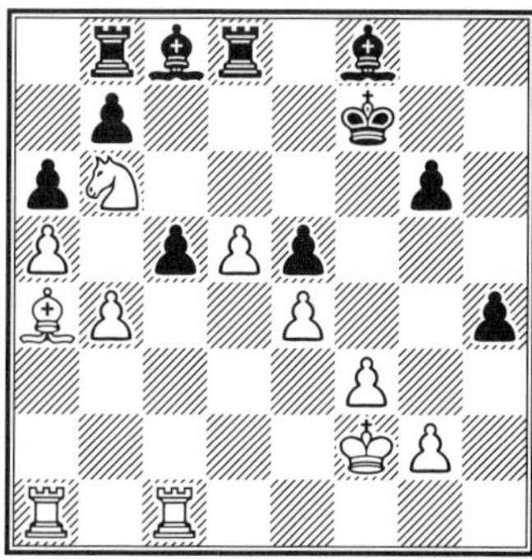

Breaking through and ending Black's resistance by "stealing" all the squares along the c-file.

34...Bh6

34...cxb4 35.Rc7+ followed by 36.Rac1 is more than the enemy position can handle.

35.Rxc5 Bf4 36.Rc7+ Kf6 37.Bd7!, 1-0.

A pleasing finish.

I hope I've convince you to train your brain in the wonders of Target Consciousness.

8

COMPUTERS

A Chess Engine is Not Your Friend!

Several years ago I was visiting a friend and he was online looking at live games in a team match event. One game was between a grandmaster (who had the Black pieces) and an international master. A zillion people were using a zillion chess engines and they were all raving about how the grandmaster was in trouble.

I found this funny since the computer only had White a tiny bit ahead. I also found it funny because I was well-acquainted with that kind of pawn structure, and understood that if anyone was going to win this game, it would be Black.

Under my friend's name (since I was logged in to his profile), I mentioned that Black was for choice, and it would either be a draw or a Black victory.

A zillion people, in perfect unison, wrote, "You're an idiot! You don't know anything! Can't you see that White is 0.21 ahead?"

At the time, this reminded me of a trip I took on a very hot summer day with my parents to the San Diego Zoo. I was twelve and was looking at a large ape, and my mother said, "Here's a banana, give it to him."

A sign said, "Danger! Don't feed the animals!"

I pointed this out, but my mother insisted, "Feed the poor thing!"

So, I took the banana and slowly reached closer and closer to the ape's hand, which was reaching out of the cage, apparently desperate for the meal I was about to give him.

Then, suddenly, the ape grabbed my wrist, screamed out crazed monkey-speak, and started pulling my hand towards his mouth, which was now wide open and filled with huge, sharp teeth.

I panicked and desperately pulled back and, fortunately, the heat from the sun on my arm caused the ape to lose his grasp on me. Later I learned that this same ape had bitten off someone's finger.

The zillion comments reminded me of that aggressive ape's scream, and I knew that anything I said would be met with violence via another chorus of nasty derision. I told my friend to move on to another game, but he implored me to set the record straight.

So I wrote a couple of instructive paragraphs on why Black had all the chances. Sure enough, the same zillion cut me to bits. After all, any fool could see that it was 0.21, right?

So, Black played the strategy I had given to the masses, and twenty moves later White resigned. All the viewers quickly left, went to another game, and again started to parrot their chess engines numbers.

The engine might be right or wrong, but it distracts from the whole point of whatever lesson is being taught. And this is a terrible shame since the lesson's concept will help you for the rest of your chess life, while an odd number (e.g. 0.21) will be quickly forgotten.

Here's an extremely instructive game by Fischer—it's not just instructive, It's also a work of art, a thing of beauty. For many years, Fischer's play in this game was considered to be perfect. Fischer annotated it and thought so, and many other grandmaster and writer also annotated it and considered it to be, from White's point of view, devoid of errors.

Though Fischer's moves were akin to the finest of musical compositions, he botched it at the end and allowed his opponent to draw.

However, Fischer himself never knew that Black had a way to draw, nor did the endless grandmaster annotators who studied this game. It took the engine Houdini to spot the brilliant save.

Robert Fischer vs. Samuel Reshevsky, Piatigorsky Cup 1966

1.e4 e5 2.Nf3 Nc6 3.Bb5 a6 4.Ba4 Nf6 5.0-0 Be7 6.Re1 b5 7.Bb3 0-0 8.c3 d6 9.h3 Nd7 10.d4 Nb6 11.Nbd2 exd4 12.cxd4 d5 13.Bc2 Be6 14.e5 Qd7 15.Nb3 Bf5 16.Bg5! Rfe8 17.Bxe7 Rxe7 18.Rc1 Nb4 19.Nc5 Bxc2 20.Qd2!

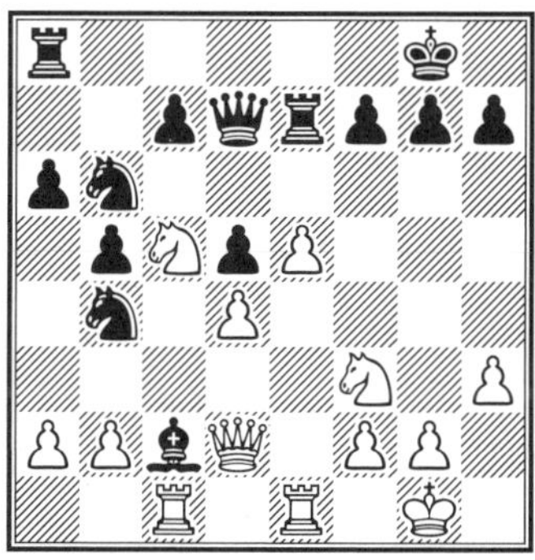

20...Qe8 21.Qxb4 a5 22.Qc3 Bg6 23.Nh4 Na4 24.Qb3 Nxc5 25.Rxc5 c6 26.Rec1 Re6 27.f4 f5 28.a4 bxa4 29.Qxa4 Rb8 30.Qa3 Qd8 31.Nxg6 hxg6 32.Rxc6 Rxc6 33.Rxc6 Qh4 34.Rxg6 Kh7 35.Rg5 Rb4?!

35...Qxf4! 36.Qe7 Rg8 (Not 36...Qe3+?? 37.Kh2 Qf4+ 38.Rg3 and White wins) 37.Rh5+ Kg6 38.Rh4 Qe3+ 39.Kh2 and now the wonderful point 39...Rh8!! When there's no way to win the game since taking on h8 leads to a perpetual check: 40.Rxh8 Qf4+ 41.Kg1 Qc1+, =.

36.Qf3 Kh6 37.g3! Qxh3 38.Qxd5, 1-0.

Does this make the game any less beautiful, any less artistic? No, not at all.

Have Computers Destroyed Chess?

The question arises,"Will chess be solved in the near future?" In other words, is it possible that computers will find all possible moves and positions?

In answer to this, check out these numbers first calculated by mathematician Claude Shannon:[1]

> The number of legal positions in chess is estimated to be between 10^43 and 10^50, with a game-tree complexity of approximately 10^123. The game-tree complexity of chess was first calculated as 10^120, a number known as the Shannon number. Typically an average position has thirty to forty possible moves, but there may be as few as zero (in the case of checkmate or stalemate) or as many as 218.

And from Chesmayne:[2]

> Chess is infinite: There are 400 different positions after each player makes one move apiece. There are 72,084 positions after two moves apiece. There are 9+ million positions after three moves apiece. There are 288+ billion different possible positions after four moves apiece. There are more forty-move games on Level-1 than the number of electrons in our universe. There are more game-trees of Chess than the number of galaxies (100+ billion), and more openings, defences, gambits, etc. than the number of quarks in our universe!

For fun, let's say a quantum computer does solve chess 100 years from now and says, "After 1.d4 White has a forced mate in 328 moves!" Who cares? The solution would be nonsensical to human minds (just as many computer moves today make absolutely no sense). So, even if chess is solved someday, it would have no impact on the enjoyment people have in playing the game.

As for chess variants (like adding an extra file, or filling each piece with absinthe and being forced to drink it whenever a capture is made), I have no interest in any of them. *Real* chess is still very very hard, and it's still as beautiful as ever.

---

1 www.chessmaniac.com, "Chess Mathematics and computers," December 22, 2006

2 www.chess-poker.com. "Did you know...?"

9
FAQ

Can Anyone Become a Grandmaster?

> Question: I am nineteen years and have been toying with the idea of making chess a career (either playing professionally or teaching chess). I only started to play recently and don't have an official rating as yet. Before I spend many hours of studying chess and many hundreds (and thousands) of dollars, I have several questions: First, how do I know if I'm really that good, that given enough time I can do well at chess? And if I am good, how long would you expect it to take for me to get my International Master and/or Grandmaster title? Ten years? Fifteen? And finally, has anyone actually started their chess career at my age, and achieved world class status?

First, I'll toss out a bit of reality. I hear this question often (in slight variations) from people who dream of being a chess professional and/or titled player. Fellow International Master Andrew Martin when he was writing a column for chess.com (and doing a great job) received a similar, though less, realistic question. If memory serves me right, the letter was from a guy twenty-one years old with a very low rating who wanted to know how long it would take him to become grandmaster—the tone of the letter was flippant and made it seem as if he thought getting a chess title was a "piece of cake" and simply a matter of a passage of time. Andrew was insulted. He had worked extremely hard for many years to get to where he was—an International Master and a highly regarded teacher and writer.

Andrew made it clear in his column that the gentleman would never get the grandmaster title. And when Andrew's answer posted, a zillion anonymous internet know-it-alls (or was it two zillion?) screamed that he had "crushed the man's dream". Apparently, those no-names don't like truth, so they (in effect) wanted Andrew to lie. As a result of the abuse from these ignorant trolls he stopped writing for chess.com and I inherited his column.

Ironically, when chess.com hired me to write the column the very first letter I received was, "...how long will it take for me to become a grandmaster?" LOL! I was horrified. I don't recall my exact answer, but I'll now respond to this question for the last time—in the future, I'll tell anyone that asks to read this book.

I imagine most people don't realize how much time and energy goes into attaining an international or grandmaster title, so I suppose the question is quite reasonable. However, the answer isn't what most people want to hear.

Earning an International Master or Grandmaster title demands endless effort. You study and you fail, you continue to study, you fail again, and again, for years and years. The pain of losing and failing is agony, and few can handle it as the time (as I said a moment ago, years and years) goes by. And money (for chess books, chess software, traveling to tournaments, chess teachers, etc.) must be dealt with to earn either title.

Nowadays, to have any chance to be a top-ten (or even fifty) player, you have to start playing chess very early—best is five or six years of age—and make grandmaster by your teens. Yes, there are always exceptions, but for the most part, that's the way it is. We now have an international master who is ten years old and grandmasters that are twelve, thirteen, and fourteen. Nakamura got the grandmaster title at the "old age" of fifteen.

In general, a player wanting to reach the level of international master or grandmaster needs to "go over" 100,000 or more master games—while the vast majority can be looked over very quickly, you should make serious study of others. Going over games allows you to see and subconsciously absorb the many structures and patterns that are "must knows" to reach a very high level.

In my own case, I learned to move the pieces at the old age of twelve and immediately became absorbed by chess and worked on it for at least eight hours a day, every day (during my junior high and high school years I rarely went to classes more than twice a week, preferring to stay at home and stare at a chessboard). I became a master strength player by sixteen, but since I lived in a bad chess area, I didn't obtain a master ranking until I left home and moved to San Francisco at eighteen. I eventually received the international master title, but only after getting sidetracked by various aspects of life in rip-roaring Haight Ashbury.

Being a chess pro might sound romantic (it certainly did to me when I was young), but the romance quickly melts away when you realize that you're broke, starving, and living in a hovel. If you live in America, you can forgot about health insurance—way, way too expensive. Other than the top ten or twenty grandmasters, most of the rest will never make a lot of money. As a result, grandmasters usually teach chess and write chess books to get by. It wasn't what they expected to do when they started out, but when reality hits you in the face, you have to bow to it. On the other hand, being an international master or grandmaster and teaching students and writing books isn't bad. But you would make far more money and have much more security if you attended a university and received a degree entered into an established career. Don't forget: very few people ever become international masters and grandmasters—there are 600 million to 800 million chess players in the world and only 1721 grandmasters among them (as listed by FIDE in 2020).

It's Not All Bad News!

To discuss this in a positive light, making expert (USCF 2000-2199) or master (USCF 2200-2399) is a realistic goal and I've known many low-rated chess players who have made a career of teaching and are absolutely excellent. Teaching is a skill, and even if you're rated 1500, you might be "just what the doctor ordered" for children or beginners of any age. Naturally, you have to know a great deal more about chess than you do at an unrated level, but that is quite doable.

However, you don't need to leap into teaching right way. Instead, why not try to see how good you can be? The question about whether or not you can be a grandmaster will fall into place as you get more experience with the game. Here are my recommendations:

- **Take a step-by-step approach**: Create a goal that can be reached in a reasonable time period! I was twelve when I started out and had a very low tournament rating (something like 1068). My first goal was to reach 1400 since 1400 players were wiping me out. After that, 1600 was my goal. Then 1800. As you can see, I pretty much went for 200-point gains. Expert followed, then master. Each time I reached a goal, I would sit down and honestly look at my strengths and weaknesses. I didn't have a regular coach, so I had to be quite brutal with myself. Self-delusion is common in chess, so you need to make sure you don't fall into that trap. Instead of mulling about world domination walk step by step to a doable goal, then ratchet up the effort for your next, more difficult goal.
- **Be honest with yourself:** Though your online rating may be in the 1400s, your tournament rating would be closer to 1100 or 1200. Online ratings are often higher than tournament ratings, and they may give you a false sense of where you stand. You need to be very honest about that. Note, that when playing online you should resist the temptation to use a computer to find you next move. This will NOT help you improve! As well, its considered cheating.

Be aware that in youth, many players are very good at tactics but as they age their tactical vision isn't what it once was. If you find that this applies to you and is becoming a problem, try to master positional play and endgames, and create an opening repertoire that really excites you and fits in with your strengths.

- **Try to reach your "fantasy" rating:** Figure out the things a player of your "fantasy" rating needs to know and study and learn that information from practice, books or computer programs. For example, in my book *Silman's Complete Endgame Course* I ask the 1400 student to only learn the endgames for players from beginner to 1400 (the material is listed by rating group). Then I ask him to put the endgame book down and make sure his openings, strategic understanding, and tactical acumen catches up to that same level. Once there, a new goal of 1600 would be right (which means you once again crack open the endgame book and study material for that level and the levels before it), and on and on it goes.
- **Figure out your weaknesses:** Look for articles and books that discuss those areas of the game. If the book is too advanced, put it away and look at it again when you've improved.

  Have a stronger player point out your weaknesses (you might think you know your weaknesses, but you probably can't see them all). A good coach can really help in these areas. However, as I always say, "If you don't feel a connection with the coach (no matter how nice or strong they may be) look elsewhere."
- **Lots of practice and study** will eventually lift your chess understanding to new heights. Take note of your improvement, and ask yourself, "Okay, I'm better than I was, but what is holding me back from being even stronger?" Once again, your coach will help you there.
- **Seek out opponents around** 100 points higher than you. Beating players much weaker than you might make your ego feel good, but it will ultimately stop your growth as a player.
- **Create a study program:** Set up (or have someone else set up) a serious study program for you that allows you to become proficient in all areas of the game. If you have the money, hire a chess teacher to help create that plan for you. The needs of the player are different from person to person, and you have to have the plan that's right for you.
- **Study books that are right for you and your level.** For example, let's say you are pretty good at tactics but has very little positional understanding. You also have an opening repertoire but don't really

understand it (you might think do, but really don't). And you may know a few basic endgame situations, but your endgame know-how is rather feeble. In this case you should buy a good middlegame book. Look for books that "speak" to you. Instead of just grabbing something, read ten pages at the bookstore and, if the author's writing style doesn't put a smile on your face, look for something else. The same goes for a good endgame book. There are tons of them, so seek authors that you trust and like.

Opening books are sometimes a bit dull, but if it contains great material it's often worth grabbing it! Not everyone writes well, but if they are fantastic teachers, or they are *the* expert in a certain line, you might want to pick their book up. The one issue to consider (and again you must be honest with yourself) is, "how good are you." I love super-detailed opening books by grandmasters, but I wouldn't recommend them to a beginner, or even a 1700 player (it will probably be over their heads). A beginner should look for a book that explains an opening's basics: pawn structures, typical tactics, patterns, and typical plans.

As time goes on, you'll begin to see where you stand. You might leap forward at warp speed, or you might see that chess is damned hard and improvement is harder than you thought it would be. Either way, you'll have a better grasp about what needs to be done.

In conclusion: As for being a chess pro, I would have to say starting out at a "late" age makes the international master/grandmaster dream almost impossible—it's always possible, there have been exceptions, but it's rare and requires an enormous commitment to the game. However, it is possible with time and hard work to make master.

That said, why put the "grandmaster or bust" monkey on your back? Keep your dreams, and do your best to make them happen, but be realistic and go one step at a time by the repetitive 200-point goal leap that I've mentioned above. But if you find long hours of study isn't for you, then just play chess and enjoy it. Even if you do study and train and play in tournaments yet find that you've only made meager improvements, you're still a winner. Hopefully, you had a good time, and continue to get enjoyment for as long as you play the game. It really is a win-win.

To me, the real reason to play chess is because it's a rush, as well as a creative outlet. When I was playing professionally winning a tournament was no big deal. However, winning a game that I deemed to be artistically pleasing was everything to me! A professional has to love chess, love its history, love looking at every facet of it—there's not much money in the sport, but that love makes everything worthwhile.

Do Titled Players Blunder?

> Question: Do international masters and grandmasters ever make beginner mistakes in tournaments? How often do they blunder? For example, one could have had too much to drink the night before a game and just give away a free piece (like a Knight or Bishop) simply because they didn't see something, and not because of a inspired tactic played by the opponent.

Titled players do make mistakes, and though some blunders may appear to be the same as ones beginners make, they're NOT! A large percentage of beginner's blunders happen because they don't understand basic positional ideas and/or basic tactics. Whereas titled players make horrific errors due to exhaustion, drunkenness, chess blindness (somehow the mind short circuits and you simply hang something), time pressure (which makes everyone look like a fool), emotional duress, or a momentary loss of concentration (caused by a tidal wave, a two-foot long insect's mandibles clamping onto your ankle, and other common scenarios of this sort).

For some reason, many players think that grandmasters would never make a double question mark move. However, they all do from time to time. Here's one where Anand tossed a key game in his World Championship match vs. Topalov:

Veselin Topalov vs. Viswanathan Anand, World Championship (8) 2010

1.d4 d5 2.c4 c6 3.Nf3 Nf6 4.Nc3 dxc4 5.a4 Bf5 6.Ne5 e6 7.f3 c5 8.e4 Bg6 9.Be3 cxd4 10.Qxd4 Qxd4 11.Bxd4 Nfd7 12.Nxd7 Nxd7 13.Bxc4 Rc8 14.Bb5 a6 15.Bxd7+ Kxd7 16.Ke2 f6 17.Rhd1 Ke8 18.a5 Be7 19.Bb6 Rf8 20.Rac1 f5 21.e5 Bg5 22.Be3 f4 23.Ne4 Rxc1 24.Nd6+ Kd7 25.Bxc1 Kc6 26.Bd2 Be7 27.Rc1+ Kd7 28.Bc3 Bxd6 29.Rd1 Bf5 30.h4 g6 31.Rxd6+ Kc8 32.Bd2 Rd8 33.Bxf4 Rxd6 34.exd6 Kd7 35.Ke3 Bc2 36.Kd4 Ke8 37.Ke5 Kf7 38.Be3 Ba4 39.Kf4 Bb5 40.Bc5 Kf6 41.Bd4+ Kf7 42.Kg5 Bc6 43.Kh6 Kg8 44.h5 Be8 45.Kg5 Kf7 46.Kh6 Kg8 47.Bc5 gxh5 48.Kg5 Kg7 49.Bd4+ Kf7 50.Be5 h4! 51.Kxh4 Kg6 52.Kg4 Bb5 53.Kf4 Kf7 54.Kg5

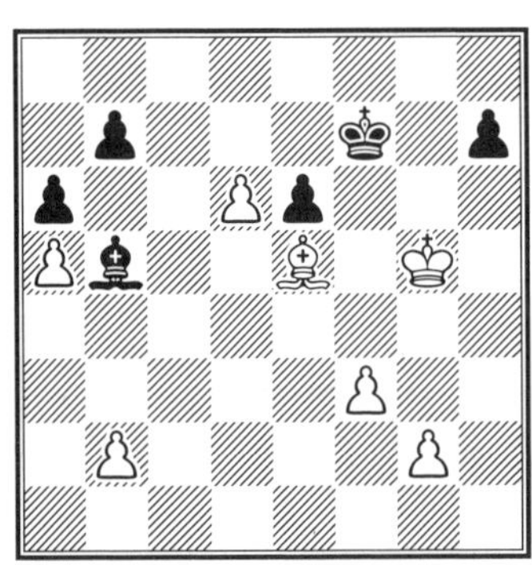

And here Anand "forgot" that he needed to be able to defend h7 with his Bishop (54...Bd3 drew) and literally tossed the game away with

54...Bc6?? 5.Kh6 Kg8 56.g4, 1-0.

Deep Fritz 10 vs. Vladimir Kramnik, Germany, Man vs. Machine match (2) 2006

1.d4 d5 2.c4 dxc4 3.e4 b5 4.a4 c6 5.Nc3 b4 6.Na2 Nf6 7.e5 Nd5 8.Bxc4 e6 9.Nf3 a5 10.Bg5 Qb6 11.Nc1 Ba6 12.Qe2 h6 13.Be3 Bxc4 14.Qxc4 Nd7 15.Nb3 Be7 16.Rc1 0-0 17.0-0 Rfc8 18.Qe2 c5 19.Nfd2 Qc6 20.Qh5 Qxa4 21.Nxc5 Nxc5 22.dxc5 Nxe3 23.fxe3 Bxc5 24.Qxf7+ Kh8 25.Qf3 Rf8 26.Qe4 Qd7 27.Nb3 Bb6 28.Rfd1 Qf7 29.Rf1 Qa7 30.Rxf8+ Rxf8 31.Nd4 a4 32.Nxe6 Bxe3+ 33.Kh1 Bxc1 34.Nxf8

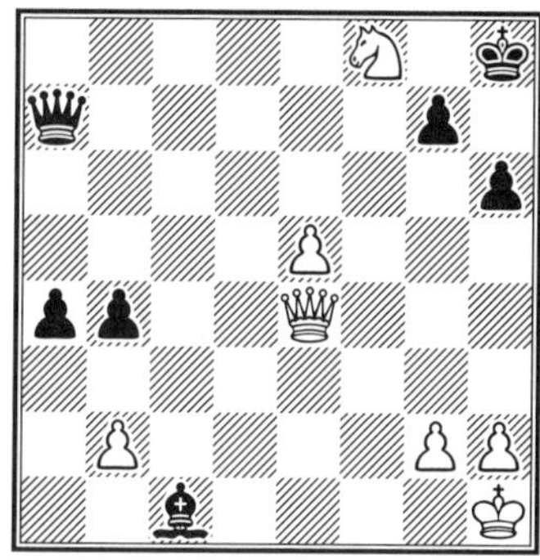

Now 34...Kg8 35.Ng6 Bxb2 36.Qd5+ Kh7 37.Nf8+ Kh8 38.Ng6+ is a forced draw. However Kramnik had been playing for this position for several moves and felt his queenside pawns should give him serious winning chances (since he can make a passer with ...a4-a3). When looking at this position several moves back, he had decided that 34...Qe3 was crushing since he would be threatening white's Queen and also a back rank mate. So he calmly played...

34...Qe3??

No doubt thinking he was going to win, one can only imagine his horror when...

35.Qh7 mate was the reply!

ChessBase.com reported that, "Fritz operator Mathias Feist kept glancing from the board to the screen and back, hardly able to believe that he had input the correct move. Fritz was displaying mate in one, and when Mathias executed it on the board Kramnik briefly grasped his forehead, took a seat to sign the score sheet and left for the press conference, which he dutifully attended."

A couple more examples of self-immolation:

Silman vs. Jim McCormick, Berkeley 1974

1.e4 c5 2.Nf3 d6 3.d4 cxd4 4.Nxd4 Nf6 5.Nc3 Nc6 6.Bg5 e6 7.Qd2 a6 8.0-0-0 Bd7 9.f4 h6 10.Bh4 Rc8 11.Nf3 Qa5 12.Bc4 b5 13.Bb3 b4 14.Bxf6 gxf6 15.Ne2 Qb6 16.f5 Na5 17.Nf4 Nxb3+ 18.axb3 h5 19.Kb1 a5 20.e5 fxe5 21.Nxe5 Bb5 22.Nxf7 Kxf7 23.fxe6+ Ke8 24.Nd5 Qc5 25.Qg5 Qxc2+

Now I reached for my King, thinking that he would resign after either of my two legal replies.

26.Ka2⁇

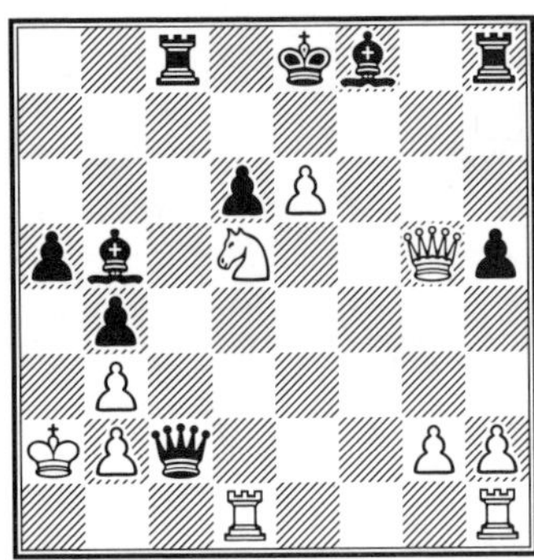

26.Ka1 would have forced resignation since after ...a4 a subsequent capture on b3 would not be with check, thus giving White an extra move.

26...a4, drawn since White can force perpetual check.

I'll finish with a game I played in Wijk aan Zee. It was a must win for me, and when my opponent arrived fifty-nine minutes late (one minute before being forfeited!), I thought it was going to be easy.

Silman vs. Tom De Jong, Wijk aan Zee 1989

1.d4 Nf6 2.c4 g6 3.Nc3 Bg7 4.e4 0-0 5.Be2 d6 6.Bg5 c5 7.d5 b5 8.cxb5 a6 9.a4 axb5 10.axb5 Rxa1 11.Qxa1 Nbd7 12.Nf3 Bb7 13.Nd2 Qc7 14.Qa2 Ra8 15.Qb3 Nb6 16.0-0 Bc8 17.Nc4 h6 18.Bf4 Nfd7 19.Ne3 Ne5 20.Bg3 Ra5 21.f4 Ned7 22.Kh1 Qa7 23.Be1 Bd4 24.Bd2 Nf6 25.Qd1 Bd7 26.Qb1 c4 27.Nxc4 Bxc3 28.Bxc3 Nxc4 29.Bxc4 Bxb5 30.Bxa5 Bxc4 31.Rc1 Ng4 32.Be1 Qd4 33.h3 Bd3 34.Rc8+ Kh7 35.Qd1 Ne3

I've been winning for most of the game, and now one way to ice the game was 36.Bf2 Qxe4 37.Bxe3 Qxe3 38.Rc3 Be2 39.Rxe3 Bxd1 40.Rxe7. However, something strange occurred. I had been moving fairly quickly (a stupid thing to do, which earns me full baboon status) since I felt the game was over. And here I zipped out one of the worst blunders of my life.

36.Bc3????

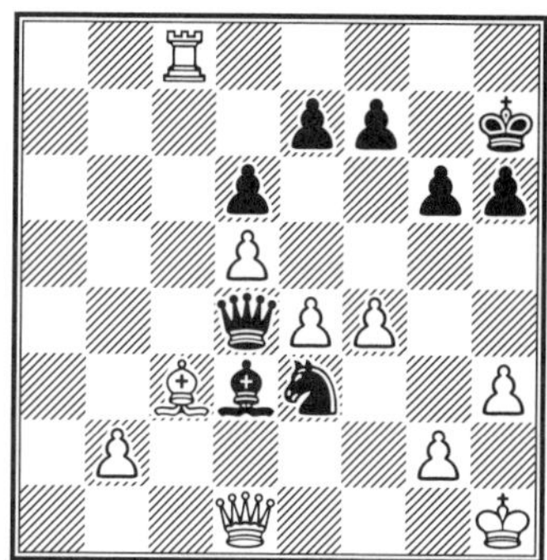

36...Qxc3 37.Rxc3 Nxd1 38.Rxd3 Nf2+

Suddenly reality hit me in the face. Hysterical, I resigned, stormed out of the hall and slammed the door behind me—on my foot! I broke a toe. Hobbling in the snow and cursing the gods of chess, I went to the pizza parlor and ordered a large one so as to drown my sorrows in food. However, I forgot about the European habit of putting olives on their pizzas with pits. I bit down on one and my tooth exploded! Rushing out of the restaurant in a fully lobotomized state, I slipped and fell face first into a puddle of "arctic" water. It was one of those days that you never forget.

Over the years I've noticed that whenever a grandmaster hangs his face, the masses online (with fake-names) go berserk and not only berate the unfortunate player but toss sick (and completely ignorant) accusations his way:

- "He lost on purpose! It's a fix!" (Apparently you forgot to take your meds.)
- "He has insulted the chess community and needs to apologize to all of us!" (No, you have insulted the chess community by making chess fans look like fools, and *you* need to apologize.
- "If he had studied the Russian school of chess, this wouldn't have happened. Real grandmasters, with real knowledge, are hard to find nowadays." (Polite people, who are smart enough to know when they don't understand something, are hard to find nowadays.)
- "His blunder is unforgivable!" (No, a blunder is no big deal. Your idiotic comment is unforgivable.)

So, what causes grandmasters blunder?

The easiest answer is that they are human, and humans make mistakes for a variety of reasons.

Here are a few:

- For one quick moment, they stop paying attention (and then it's too late).

- Being overly tired. An exhausted brain is capable of any bozo act.
- Your wife left you, your dog picked her over you, and your bank account was emptied right before the game started. How would YOU play in that situation?
- Depression. When a strong player has a bad tournament, usually his bad tournament gets worse and worse as it progresses.
- Your blood sugar crashes, turning you into a temporary zombie (sadly, this often happened to me).
- Stress! An important game can be extremely stressful. And, when you are overwhelmed with stress during a tough battle, you can (and often do) miss things that you would normally see in a blitz game.
- The brain does flip-flops and you hallucinate (takes us back to tiredness, depression, and a drop in blood sugar).

The fact is everyone blunders! Everyone!

Okay, that is some crazy stuff. But I am sure old legends like Petrosian and Bronstein wouldn't miss such elementary things. Right?

White to move and Black has been in bad shape for a long time, and it was quite clear that the legendary Bronstein was going to be another victim of Petrosian's slow death technique. In the present position Black is completely busted and I'm sure he entertained resignation. However, why not play on for a while? Who knows, maybe Petrosian will hang his Queen (Black is threatening ...Nxb4)? Anything is possible!

Tigran Petrosian vs. David Bronstein, Candidates Tournament 1956

1.c4 Nf6 2.Nc3 g6 3.g3 Bg7 4.Bg2 0-0 5.Nf3 c5 6.0-0 Nc6 7.d4 d6 8.dxc5 dxc5 9.Be3 Nd7 10.Qc1 Nd4? 11.Rd1 e5 12.Bh6 Qa5 13.Bxg7 Kxg7 14.Kh1 Rb8 15.Nd2 a6 16.e3 Ne6 17.a4 h5 18.h4 f5 19.Nd5 Kh7 20.b3 Rf7 21.Nf3 Qd8 22.Qc3 Qh8 23.e4! fxe4 24.Nd2 Qg7 25.Nxe4 Kh8 26.Rd2 Rf8 27.a5 Nd4 28.b4 cxb4 29.Qxb4 Nf5 30.Rad1 Nd4 31.Re1 Nc6 32.Qa3

Okay, no Queen hang. But Bronstein decided to keep playing so he could watch Petrosian do his thing.

32...Nd4

Bronstein has decided to move his Knight back and forth to c6 and d4 and, when Petrosian decides to finish him off, Bronstein will give up.

33.Rb2

Typical Petrosian. He's saying, "If you're having fun here, I'll let you suffer for a long, long time."

33...Nc6

Yeah, whatever.

34.Reb1 Nd4 35.Qd6 Nf5 36.Ng5??

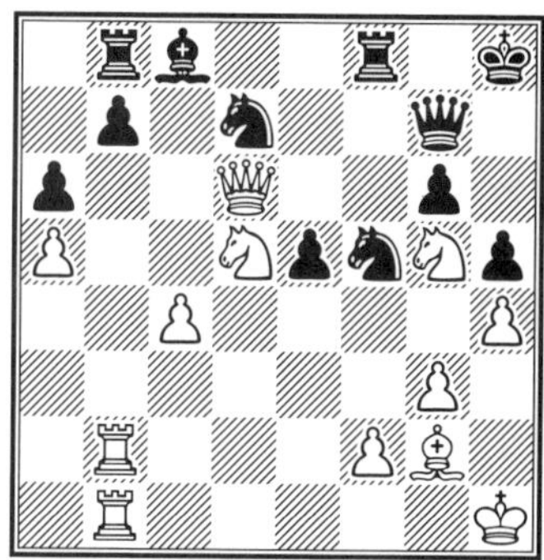

Petrosian, seeing that his opponent was only moving that one Knight back and forth, got hypnotized by the c6-d4-c6 rhythm. So, in his mind black's Knight had returned to c6. Reality hit him when Black played...

36...Nxd6, 0-1.

So much for the Soviet school of chess teaching people not to blunder.

Let's take a look at the mighty Anatoly Karpov in his prime, one of the most dominating world champions of all time!

Larry Christiansen vs. Anatoly Karpov, Wijk aan Zee 1993

1.d4 Nf6 2.c4 e6 3.Nf3 b6 4.a3 Ba6 5.Qc2 Bb7 6.Nc3 c5 7.e4 cxd4 8.Nxd4 Nc6 9.Nxc6 Bxc6 10.Bf4 Nh5

Normal stuff. Black kicks the f4-bishop off the h2-b8 diagonal so Black can claim that diagonal for his own.

11.Be3

Now 11...Qb8 gives Black an excellent position since he's covering the e5- and f4-squares. However, Karpov decided to control those dark-squares with his f8-Bishop when ...Qb8 could follow if the need arose.

11...Bd6??

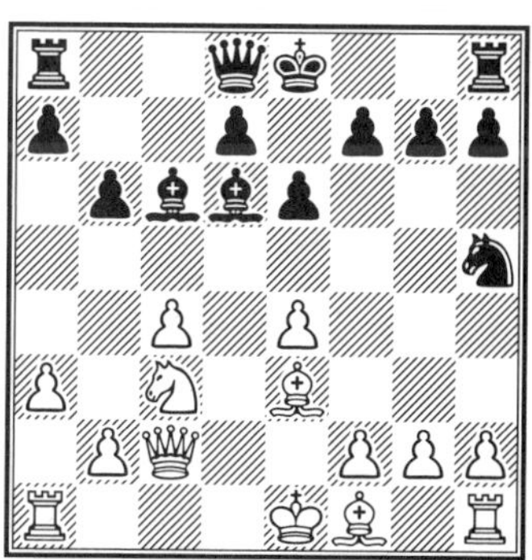

This move is oozing with strategic goodness. Unfortunately, he made the beginner mistake of leaving two pieces undefended at the same time.

12.Qd1!, 1-0.

DOH! White threatens both 13.Qxd6 and 13.Qxh5 and, since Black was going to be a piece down, he gave up.

There's a *lot* more hanging to see, and nobody is immune! There isn't a grandmaster in the history of the game that hasn't blundered (more than once!). In fact, I can't count how many pieces and pawns I've hung over the years. Here's one of my most painful moments.

Black has a good position. I was about to play 29...Rd6 with complete equality (sure that a quick draw would result) when a friend entered the room. I very much wanted to say hello, so, while looking at my friend, I grabbed my Rook and moved it to the d-file.

John Fedorowicz vs. Silman, American Open 1989

1.e4 c5 2.Nf3 Nc6 3.d4 cxd4 4.Nxd4 Nf6 5.Nc3 e5 6.Ndb5 d6 7.Bg5 a6 8.Bxf6 gxf6 9.Na3 b5 10.Nd5 Bg7 11.c3 Ne7 12.Nc2 Nxd5 13.Qxd5 Rb8 14.Ne3 Bh6 15.Qd3 Bxe3 16.Qxe3 Qb6 17.Qf3 Ke7 18.Bd3 Rg8 19.h3 Be6 20.0-0 Rg6 21.Kh2 Rbg8 22.Rg1 Qc6 23.Qe3 f5 24.g3 Rf6 25.exf5 Bxf5 26.Rad1 Bxd3 27.Rxd3 Qc5 28.Qxc5 dxc5 29.Kg2 Rd8??

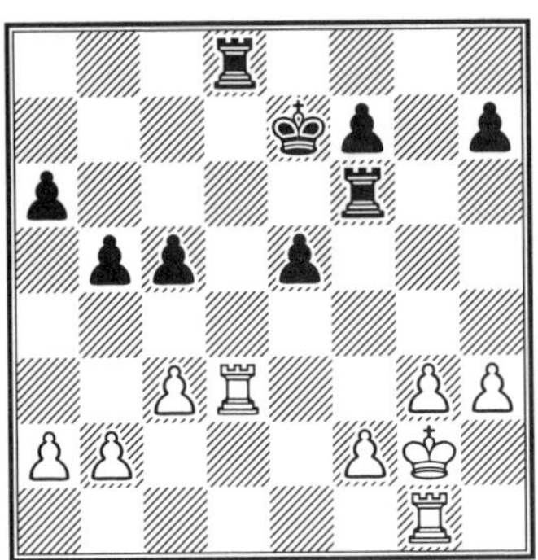

I grabbed the wrong Rook! The Fed looked me in the eye and said, "You have to pay attention!"

And after...

30.Rxd8 Kxd8 31.Rd1+ Kc7 32.Rd5 I lost a pawn and the game.

I think Fed's wise words say it all: "You have to pay attention!"

Unfortunately, no human on earth has the ability to always pay attention. Everyone gets tired from time to time, stress kills, and periodic brain-melt is pretty much impossible to prevent.

The Time Trouble Blues

Question: I get into time trouble in most of my games while my opponents always have plenty of time left on their clocks. How can I improve my time management? My tournament games are one hour and thirty minutes plus thirty seconds per move.

Time trouble plagues beginners, strong amateurs, masters, and grandmasters. There is no universal cure. Some players simply accept that it's a part of the "chess rush." Some, like Sammy Reshevsky (one of the best three or four players in the world during his prime), never did find a way to avoid time pressure, but he did something most can't do: With seconds left, he suddenly played even better!

The Grandmaster Walter Browne was famous for his time-pressure scenes, and when the final ticks on the clock filled his ears, he would often "share" his horror with the spectators by twitching, grabbing his ears, drooling, throwing the clock out of a window, and putting on quite a show. I played him many times, and, since I also suffered from time pressure, we would (on an occasion or two) simply accept a draw since the game was no longer chess. It was just a contest to see who could make more moves before their time ran out!

Why Do People Get into Time Trouble?

Strong players tend to get into time trouble if they find a position particularly interesting. They want to know the "truth" of the position, so they think and think, and in some instances, they even forget that there's a battle going on.

In other instances, an opponent might toss out a new move in the opening. Since playing the "usual" move just won't do, the chess pro goes into a long, deep think so that he can fully understand the opponent's intentions. A similar situation occurs when you realize that you don't like your position. Instead of just making reasonable-looking moves, the person who isn't overly happy with their game will take a very long think. They are basically trying (by dint of will) to find a way to equalize or a plan that gives them reasonable chances.

Very Little Pattern Recognition

Whenever I bring up pattern recognition, quite a few readers get upset because learning zillions of chessboard patterns means you need to put in a lot of work! Telling people that they need to work hard to be really good is, somehow, an insult to those that hope to wake up one day and find themselves a grandmaster. Dream on! Yet, if you think about it with a clear mind, it becomes obvious that knowing patterns not only helps you avoid time trouble, but it also makes you a far stronger player. The more patterns you master, the stronger you'll get. Following is an example of a game that has no patterns.

Silman vs. Jonathan Speelman, England 1978

1.e4 c5 2.Nf3 Nc6 3.Bb5 Qb6 4.Nc3 e6 5.0-0 Nd4 6.Bc4 Ne7 7.d3 a6 8.Nxd4 cxd4 9.Ne2 g6 10.Bg5 Bg7 11.Bb3 Qc5 12.f4 b6 13.f5 gxf5 14.Bxe7 Qxe7 15.exf5 Bb7 16.Ng3 Be5 17.Qh5 Bxg3 18.fxe6!

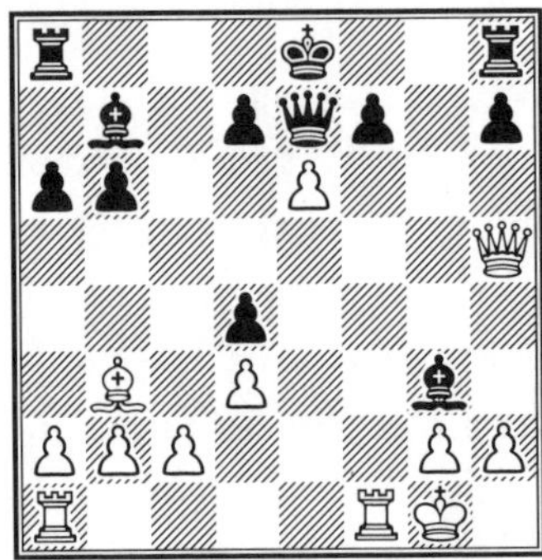

This was my point. Now 18...Bxh2+ 19.Kxh2 dxe6 20.Bxe6 favors white, as does 18...dxe6 19.hxg3. So Black is forced to sacrifice a pawn, but that also turns out to be nice for me.

18...0-0-0 19.exd7+ Rxd7 20.hxg3 Qe3+ 21.Kh2 Rd6

The threat of 22...Rh6 is dealt with by a nice triangulation maneuver by the white Queen.

22.Qg4+ Kb8

The alternative was 22....Kd8, but White would then have played 23.Qh4+ Kc8 (This is almost an identical position to that which occurred after 21... Rd6. However, there is an important difference: White's Queen now stands on h4 where it is protected.) 24.Rae1 Qd2 25.Qg4+ Kb8 26.Re2.

23.Qf4 Qxf4 24.Rxf4 Re8 25.Raf1 Re2 26.Rf6 Rxg2+ 27.Kh3

Black has managed to restore material equality, but this is only temporary ... his many pawn weaknesses leave him in a hopeless position.

27...Rg1 28.Rxd6 Rxf1 29.Rxb6 Kc7 30.Rb4 Bf3 31.g4 Kd6 32.Rxd4+ Ke5 33.Ra4 h5 34.gxh5 f5 35.Kh4 Bc6 36.Rc4 Bb5 37.Rb4 f4 38.Re4+ Kf6 39.Ba4 Kf5 40.Kh3 Bxa4 41.Rxa4 Rh1+ 42.Kg2 Rc1 43.Rc4 Kg4 44.h6 Rd1 45.h7 Rd2+ 46.Kg1 Rd1+ 47.Kf2 Rd2+ 48.Ke1 Rh2 49.Rc7 f3 50.d4 Kg3 51.Rg7+ Kf4 52.d5, 1-0.

Later I played Speelman again, and I had prepared this system a year before, thinking that all is good. After a bit I looked at it again (17.Bd3 g6 18.h4). Indeed, it looks dangerous for Black, but as I sat there wondering why my opponent exuded an air of confidence, I decided to take a deep look at the position for the first time (mindlessly memorizing a book and exploring a variation seriously are two very different things!). Sure enough, after pondering the situation for a long while, I realized that White didn't have anything at all!

As a result of seeing reality for the first time, I decided to put on the brakes. Here's the game:

Silman vs. Jonathan Speelman, England 1978

1.e4 c5 2.Nf3 d6 3.d4 cxd4 4.Nxd4 Nf6 5.Nc3 a6 6.Bg5 Nc6 7.Qd2 e6 8.0-0-0 Bd7 9.f4 b5 10.Nxc6 Bxc6 11.Qe3 Be7 12.Bxf6 Bxf6 13.e5 Be7 14.exd6 Bxd6 15.Ne4

This stops any problems for both sides.

15...Bxe4 16.Qxe4 0-0 17.Qd4

This forces an endgame pattern.

17...Bc7 18.Qxd8 Raxd8

18...Bxf4+?? 19.Qd2.

19.Rxd8 Rxd8 20.g3

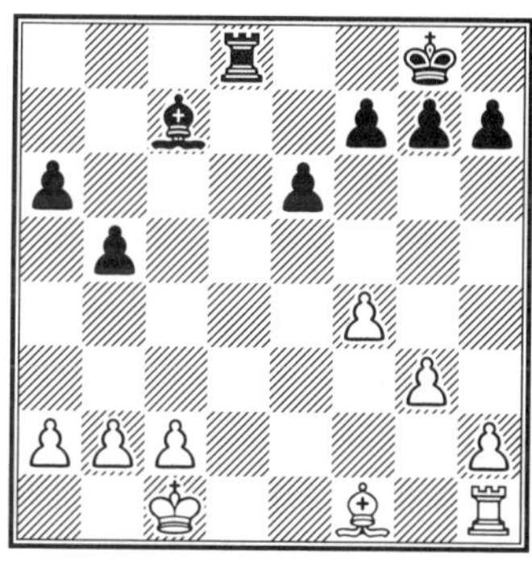

At this point I thought, "It's a dead draw. In fact, if I trade Rooks, and then I trade off my three queenside pawns for two of Black's queenside pawns, and if I also trade off all my kingside pawns for two of Black's (leaving Black pawns on f7 and e6) it would still be a draw, even though Black is two pawns ahead!" All this didn't need calculation since I realized that I could, at worst, create that endgame pattern I showed you earlier.

20...h5 21.Be2 h4 22.Rd1 Rxd1+ 23.Kxd1 g5 24.fxg5 hxg3 25.hxg3 Kg7 26.a4 bxa4 27.Bxa6 Kg6 28.Bb5 Kxg5 29.Bxa4 Bxg3 30.Ke2 f5 31.Kf3 Bd6 32.c3 e5 33.Bc2, ½-½.

As I mentioned, this is still a dead draw even if I lose my two queenside pawns. Though I used quite a bit of time on my clock on move 17, I wasn't worried since I already knew what to do and what positions could arise. That is all thanks to the wonders of patterns.

Lack of Opening Knowledge

It's tough trying to reinvent the wheel over and over again. However, amateurs often don't understand the most basic things in their openings, and this means that they will not only make huge mistakes (moves that have nothing to do with the position's needs), but they will also take lots of time on the clock to try and figure out what should be done.

Time disappears quickly! Using it all in the opening will rarely bring good results—to avoid time pressure, you *must* know and be able to quickly recognize a large number of opening patterns!

Patterns in the Ruy Lopez

The Ruy Lopez. White should know that there are various choices. White can close the center with 13.d5 gaining central space. If so, White might chip away at the queenside with a well-timed a2-a4, White might play b2-b4 (with or without a2-a4), White might go for the enemy King with g2-g4 followed by Nd2-f1-g3, or White might make use of all of these ideas in the same game! The black side often makes use of a particular piece placement, placing Knights on both g7 and f7.

Robert Fischer vs. Ratmir Kholmov, Capablanca Memorial 1965

1.e4 e5 2.Nf3 Nc6 3.Bb5 a6 4.Ba4 Nf6 5.0-0 Be7 6.Re1 b5 7.Bb3 0-0 8.c3 d6 9.h3 Na5 10.Bc2 c5 11.d4 Qc7 12.Nbd2 Nc6 13.dxc5 dxc5 14.Nf1 Be6 15.Ne3 Rad8 16.Qe2 c4 17.Ng5 h6 18.Nxe6 fxe6 19.b4 Nd4!

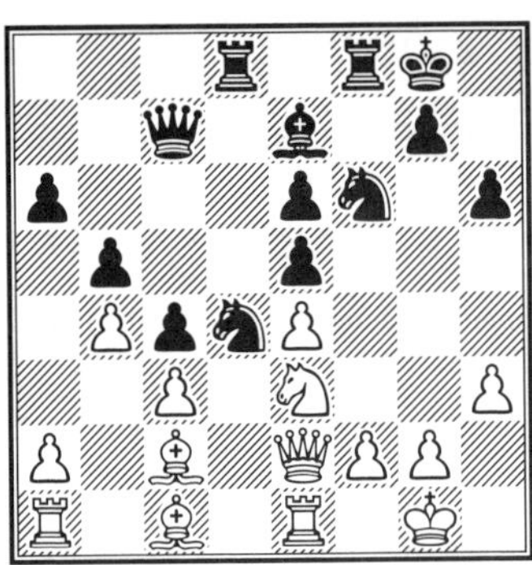

A massive blow to White's position!

20.cxd4 exd4 21.a3 d3 22.Bxd3 Rxd3 23.Ng4 Kh7 24.e5 Nxg4 25.Qe4+ g6 26.Qxg4 Rf5 27.Qe4 Qd7 28.Be3 Qd5 29.Qxd5 Rxd5 30.f4 g5 31.g3 gxf4 32.gxf4 Rf8 33.Kg2 Kg6 34.Rg1 Rd3 35.Kf3+ Kf5 36.Rg7 Bd8 37.Rb7 Rg8 38.Rb8 Rg7 39.a4 h5 40.axb5 axb5 41.Rxb5 Bh4 42.Ke2 Rg2+ 43.Kf1 Rh2 44.Kg1 Re2 45.Bb6 c3 46.Kf1 Rh2, 0-1.

After this game, everyone (Black and White) knew that this idea had to be avoided or only allowed if the sacrifice wasn't quite sound. To repeat: Did you notice that, though this section is about time pressure, I leaped into patterns. Why? Because everything in chess is interconnected. Not having pattern recognition means that you will make errors and get into time pressure. Lack of pattern recognition is a major cause of time pressure in the amateur ranks.

Going Over Your Analysis Again and Again

Yes, we're talking about the good old, "I go there, he goes there, I go there, and—hmmm—Let's look at that again. Seems good, but if I'm wrong, I'm toast. So I'll look again."

Repeating an exciting line, or a defensive series of moves, is something everyone does from time to time. Some do it all the time. However, it's a massive clock eater! Often the problem is a lack of confidence which makes you repeat calculations endlessly, leaving you short of time and emotionally frazzled.

This is a tough one; if you can't calculate, there is nothing you can do. The only cure is to improve your tactics, pick up some patterns (opening patterns and middlegame patterns), and improve your openings. This brings us right back to hard work!

Imbalances

> Question: I wonder if I should look for imbalances before I start calculating or does this not apply when you know there's a tactical shot in the position?

Imbalances (space, material, pawn structure, weak squares, superior/inferior minor pieces) offer a player a firm grasp of what's happening in any given position. Instead of looking at a position and not knowing what in the world is going on, you can train yourself to quickly recognize any and all imbalances for both sides. Then, any move you consider will have something to do with the positive features on the board.

Most players simply calculate. For example, when looking at their position (as the clock ticks) they internally say, "I go there and he goes there and I go there, etc." However, if I were to ask them at that exact moment to lecture me on the ins and outs of the position, they will usually be way off, or in many cases even clueless.

Having the ability to calculate deeply is a huge plus, but few can do it. In fact, though you can work on and improve your ability to calculate to some degree, possessing the ability to calculate deeply, quickly, and accurately (at a minimum 2400 level) is a god given gift, but don't mix this up with learning tactical patterns—it's relatively easy to vastly improve your tactical IQ by the study of each mating pattern, each basic tactical pattern (forks, pins, etc.), and going over all sorts of tactical positions.

I tend to place very high-level calculation under the umbrella of "talent," while positional skills are something everyone can learn and excel at. Oddly, few players hone their positional skills, preferring to muddle through with a good tactical IQ and poor calculation. Sadly, many players that do have serious calculation mojo rely on that skill set while ignoring all the others. I've known several internationals that have grandmaster level tactical ability but 2200 positional skills.

When looking over a "find the tactic" type problem, you can indeed just look for the tactical solution (since it's been announced that there is one). Be aware that almost all tactics are based on double attacks, undefended (or inadequately defended) pieces, and/or a vulnerable King—that will make it easier to find.

However, in actual play no voice of authority says, "Tom, there is a tactic here. Find the tactic Tom!" Thus (in a real game), it's important to do that imbalance rundown so you know exactly what's going on in every position you reach, while also asking (after you do the imbalance thing) if there are any double attacks and/or undefended/inadequately defended pieces, and if the enemy King appears vulnerable to a karate chop to the throat.

In some situations you'll find that there is a tactic, but it gives you less than the correct positional move. Here's a line in the Semi-Slav that used to be fairly popular:

1.d4 d5 2.c4 c6 3.Nc3 e6 4.e3 Nf6 5.Nf3 Nbd7 6.Bd3 Bd6 7.0-0 0-0 8.e4 dxe4 9.Nxe4 Nxe4 10.Bxe4 e5⁇

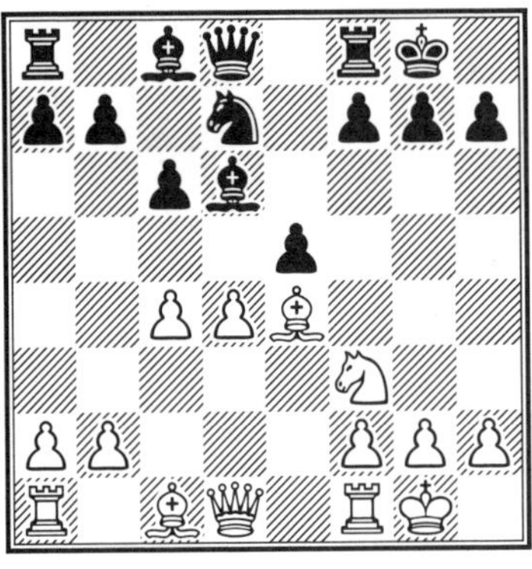

10...h6 intending 11...e5 is a better try.

11.dxe5 Nxe5 12.Nxe5 Bxe5.

Black has an undefended piece, so White finds a tactic based on that and a double attack.

13.Bxh7+ Kxh7 14.Qh5+ Kg8 15.Qxe5

Leaves White with a solid extra pawn and a huge plus.

An almost identical position was often reached by

1.d4 d5 2.c4 c6 3.Nc3 e6 4.e3 Nf6 5.Nf3 Nbd7 6.Bd3 Bb4 7.0-0 0-0 8.a3 Bd6

It seems that White got a2-a3 win for free ... why would Black allow this?

9.e4 dxe4 10.Nxe4 Nxe4 11.Bxe4 e5

Here, in the game Kasparov vs. Hübner, Brussels 1986, the great K played:

12.Bc2 Re8 13.Re1 exd4 14.Rxe8+ Qxe8 15.Qxd4 Be7 16.Bg5 Bxg5 17.Nxg5 Nf6 18.Rd1 Be6 19.Re1 Qd8 20.Nxe6 fxe6 21.Qe3 Kh8 22.h3 Qd7

23.Qxe6?? Re8 24.Qxd7 Rxe1+ wins for Black.

23.g4 Re8 24.Qe5 Qd8 25.Kg2 Qb6 26.Rd1 c5 27.Ba4 Rf8 28.Rd6 Qc7 29.Rxe6 Qf7 30.Qxc5 Nxg4 31.Qxf8+ Qxf8 32.hxg4, 1-0.

White regains the Queen with ...Re8 and ends up with an extra piece.

At this point, astute readers will be asking, "Wait a second! Did Kasparov really miss the same tactics from the previous example?" Let's see if it still works:

1.d4 d5 2.c4 c6 3.Nc3 e6 4.e3 Nf6 5.Nf3 Nbd7 6.Bd3 Bb4 7.0-0 0-0 8.a3 Bd6 9.e4 dxe4 10.Nxe4 Nxe4 11.Bxe4 e5

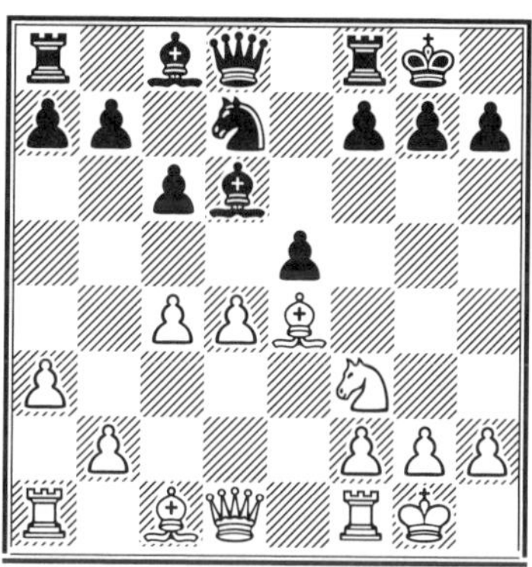

12.dxe5 Nxe5 13.Nxe5 Bxe5 14.Bxh7+ Kxh7 15.Qh5+ Kg8 16.Qxe5

With an extra pawn.

Of course, Kasparov saw that he could do this, but was also aware that this position (after 16.Qxe5), though a bit better for White, is basically drawn!!!

I can imagine that many of you are now shaking your head with pity. "Silman must have hit his head again! The poor fool doesn't realize it's the same position."

But is it really the same position? There's one "small" difference: White's a-pawn is on a3 in the Kasparov game, and on a2 in the earlier position with 6...Bd6. In fact, the player with Black often chose 6...Bb4 7.a3 Bd6 hoping to get this very same pawn down (drawn) position, while the pawn down position with the a-pawn on a2 is more or less lost.

This still sounds like gibberish (thereby strengthening the concussion theory), but here's the rub: All the tactical skill in the world won't give you the answer, but a positionally trained eye will tell you that, with a2-a3 in, the b3-square is weakened and, after 16...Qd3, White is forced to push his c-pawn (in the position with 6...Bd6 White would simply play 17.b3), thereby giving Black's light-squared Bishop access to d5 (that, combined with the Bishops of opposite colors, makes it more or less impossible for White to win). Many games were drawn from this position. Here's one example:

16...Qd3 17.c5 Be6 18.Bf4 Bd5 18.Rfe1 f6 20.Qh5 Bf7 21.Qg4 Rfe8 22.h3 Qc4

And Black drew without too much difficulty in Larsen vs. Bisguier, San Juan 1969.

You may see a number of tactics in various games, but is the pretty combination really the best way to play the position? If you don't have a grasp of the imbalances, you'll have no way to answer that question. Ultimately, high-level chess is a game that demands balance. Tactics without positional skills just won't hold up. While positional skills without tactics will also fall on its face.

What in the World is a Chess Style?

Question: You hear about "style" everywhere (from chess books and articles to the kibitz room to the man-on-the-street) with statements like, "You should choose your opening based on what suits your style" and "Steer games towards positions that are more suited to your style." You hear players categorized based on style: Positional (such as Kramnik, Karpov, Aronian, Carlsen) or Tactical (such as Kasparov, Shirov, Tal, Alekhine). How does one know what their style is? Is it something they choose based on what they like to play or is it something that is shown by their play?

I'll give my two cents, but I know that various players will scream the mandatory, "You're wrong!" For those know-it-alls, gnash your teeth and scream your discontent all you want since I like the sound of "squeals in the morning" (a loose take on *Apocalypse Now*: "I like the smell of napalm in the morning").

Since I began with an aggressive stance—no, I'm not angry, but I'm about to leap into boxing and I want to create an ambience of violence. I'll start with a boxing analogy because what could be more instructive than two people beating each other's faces in?

When people are learning the ins and outs of serious boxing, they don't talk about their boxing skills or their boxing style (hmmm, okay, maybe they do, but after a few lessons all that nonsense goes away). Instead, they learn how to throw a punch, how to stand, footwork, defense, and how to do all the basics. Once they pick all those things up, the hopeful boxer will discover that their cherished "style" might have nothing to do with their real strengths.

For example, your favorite boxer might be Manny Pacquiao, who has extremely fast hands. You want to be like him, but "fast hands" isn't something you can learn: it's something you either do or don't have.

You might find that you love the way Wilfred Benitez fought in his prime. This guy was a fantastic defensive fighter (Floyd Mayweather Jr. and Willie Pep were two other defensive geniuses). However, if your footwork isn't anything special, and if your feet just won't take up the slack, then you won't be a defensive fighter even if you really want to be.

I would guess that many would-be fighters want to be a knockout king. Alas, if your hands are made of feathers then you have to embrace reality and find skills that you can be good at.

In other words, your style isn't something you choose. Instead, your style chooses you.

Let's switch to chess. In my view players below master level often want to embrace a particular style but if they don't have the right skills to make that style work then they won't have that style at all. Instead, they have what could be called a "favorite" style and these are two different things completely. Once again, if you *don't* have fast hands, you *won't* ever have fast hands—there is nothing you can do about it. You may be able to calculate very well, but if don't have that extra ability to calculate extremely deeply, you'll never be an Alekhine, or Kasparov, or, Tal (that kind of calculation is a gift, not something you can learn).

I'm playing with semantics here, and this doesn't mean you are trapped into one mode or skill. If you want to call your "favorite style" your "style", then go for it. For example, a 1500 player might have 2000-level endgame skills and 1700 positional understanding, but he wants to attack (though his tactical level is 1500)! Thus, he sacrifices something every game (sound or not sound), chases enemy Kings, and has a great time. If someone asked what his style was, he would most likely say (with a lot of pride!), "I'm an attacking player!"

The truth though, is that if he reached master level he would probably find that his true style is positional (with good endgame skills attached). Attacking is his favorite style, but like men that dream of dating supermodels, it's just not going to happen in real life.

Actually, I wonder how many real chess styles there are. In boxing you have many: the swarmer, the defensive fighter (also called boxer and even out-boxer), slugger, counter puncher, and my favorite, the boxer-puncher. Again, these styles are created by the boxer's particular skill-set and talent.

In chess, though, we mostly view style as tactical or positional. I might add dynamic to this list: kind of like the boxer-puncher this would be a well-rounded, aggressive chess player who can do just about everything well (I would put Fischer in this category). Other style names are sometimes used ("calculating", and "intuitive", and even "practical"), but all they really do is point out a particular skill among all their other skills. In general, you would not say, "His style is a calculator!" Instead, you would point out that he's a great tactician/attacking/positional player with an incredible ability to calculate very deeply.

Books and articles that mention styles usually point out a titled player's style (not an amateur's). The titled player's style wasn't created by a wish, it was created by the skills that made him a strong player. Also understand that though a player might be labeled "positional", he can play in any style if the board demands it. Keep in mind that the titled player doesn't care what people say his "style" is. In fact, usually the player's style is given by someone else to explain that particular player's strengths.

Personally, I never talk to my students about what their style might be, it's just not important and pretty much useless in their development as a player. And why is it useless? Because in a game many different kinds of positions will occur, and (much of the time) you'll have to react in a specific manner that has nothing to do with the "style" you prefer.

Here's an example:

Style, Style, Who Has the Style?

You'te playing a game in which it's clear that Black is on top due to White's inferior pawn structure. To make matters worse, you view yourself as an attacker and here there is nothing to attack! Fortunately, just because you love going after the opponent's King doesn't mean you are ignorant about other parts of the game. White, thanks to his endgame studies, understands that passive defense here probably won't stave off the wolves. But if he can trade off the queenside pawns he will be able to make a draw. Thus:

White defends or dies

As you can see, being a good player is important, but coveting a style label of "attacker" is completely useless.

Over-the-Board Code of Conduct

Question: I'm considering the move from internet chess to a real over-the-board tournament. Are there rules of conduct or polite behavior that I should know about?

Yes, there are rules of conduct you should be aware of and the best place to find complete information is on the website of the USCF or FIDE. However, I'll supply the following anecdotes that demonstrate what NOT to do.

Even though a player isn't supposed to disturb their opponent, players still do so in ways that vary from personality quirks to overt illegal behavior. Over the years, I've seen players touch a piece, realize the intended move is bad, and move something else (denying that they ever touched it). I witnessed one well known chess personality write a note on a piece of paper and thrust it at the opponent under the table—it read, "If you win, I'll beat you to a pulp."

Come to think of it, I suddenly remember an opponent of mine sending me a note under the table too! I was losing badly to a strong player at the New York Open, and suddenly I felt something pressing into my thigh. I moved back, looked down, and there was his hand with a note in it! It read, "Silman, I love watching you drool in despair as I crush you like the bug you are. Suffer, you idiot! Suffer!" My first reaction was to leap across the table and grab the guy by the throat, but I managed to contain myself and I did the correct thing, I gave the note to the tournament director who warned my opponent—I had hoped for something a bit more Draconian.

A Gentleman's Game

> Question: I thought chess was supposed to be a gentleman's game, but at times my opponents act rudely during tournament play. What can I do about this?

During a tournament in Los Angeles, two players got into a fight while playing and began stabbing each other with their pens. This is probably not a good way to deal with a rude opponent. The only correct thing to do when an unruly imbecile is sitting opposite you is to find the tournament director and ask him to put an end to your opponent's deplorable behavior before it escalates into something like the aforementioned pen battle.

Rude and/or crazy behavior is a time-honored part of the game. The sixteenth century Spanish priest and chess player Ruy Lopez de Segura recommended that, when playing outside, you should always face your opponent toward the sun so he will be blinded during key moments of the game.

I've personally faced players that covered the whole spectrum of bizarre behavior: one guy would whistle a song (his tone would get more dominating if he felt he was doing well, and it would taper off into a beaten, pathetic drone if he was losing), another would mumble, I faced an old man who made disgusting gagging sounds from the first move to the last, another old man kept saying, "Go get the body! Go get the body!" over and over, and one guy that appeared to have a bird's nest on his head kept picking at it, popping whatever he had gotten from the nest into his mouth.

Here are a few more that I've faced, all of which are 100% true.

A well-known international master used to empty one of those huge plastic coke bottles and fill it with tequila. He'd keep it on the table, ready for use in case of an "emergency". His philosophy was, if something unpleasant happens on the board, take several deep glugs directly from the bottle and drink your worries away. He tried this on me once, emptied the bottle, and ended up with his face literally lying flat on the table. When it was his turn to move, his hand would rise up blindly, grope for a piece to move, and then (after pushing some piece somewhere) fall limply back to the ground. After he hung all his pieces, he quietly resigned and stumbled out of the hall.

I first experienced this one while playing a well-known chess politician. After I made a move that my esteemed opponent felt was annoying, he slowly took a sandwich out of his backpack, carefully unwrapped it, and then took huge, loud bites—chomping sickeningly as if he was a lion eating human flesh. Once the sandwich was consumed, he then made eye contact with me, smiled, calmly reached into his pocket, and took out some dental floss. Then he flossed away, bits of sandwich flying all over the board.

One famous American grandmaster always acted in a polite way—if things were going well. But as soon as his position soured, he'd try any trick in the book to break your concentration. We were playing in the last round for (potentially) first place in a major event (it turned out that it was only good for second since my competitor also won). As usual, he started out as a gentleman. However, after he'd made a mistake, he became belligerent and started kicking me under the table. I looked up, said, "Hey, what in the hell do you think you're doing? Stop it!" But he just kept on kicking. Fortunately, I was married to my first wife at that time and had learned how to tune out unpleasant things, so I went on to win the game.

Many decades ago, I was teaching a fourteen-year-old girl who was all the rage. She did TV interviews, was big with celebrities, and was considered to be the next big chess thing by many pundits. While watching her play a tournament game, she hung a piece and, shockingly, quickly wrote a letter and handed it to her opponent under the table. It said, "Please don't take my piece. My father will beat me if you do!"

Finally, when things have gone badly and it's time to resign, some players have a final bit of fun by making use of creative ways to give up. At Vienna in 1922, Alekhine lost and threw his King across the room. Nimzowitsch (Baden-Baden 1925), after losing, climbed on the table and shouted, "How can I lose to this idiot!?" While playing an event in London, an opponent of mine found a far calmer way to end the game—he simply pushed all the pieces off the board and onto my lap, and then got up and walked out of the tournament hall.

Things That Go Down Your Throat at a Chess Tournament

Question: What do you think is the best food to eat during a big tournament?

This is quite an interesting question! Many people eat all sorts of unhealthy things before an event, but should that change during it? I think the answer depends on the individual: Do you have blood sugar problems? Do you find that you can't think after a large meal and drift off or fall asleep? Or, are you more or less the same no matter what you consume?

Grandmaster Svetozar Gligorić ate chocolate during a game to keep his blood-sugar plodding along.

Bobby Fischer would sip apple juice to keep his brain zipping along, and I think many players do the same thing.

In the 1800s, top players would often bring a bottle of booze with them to the board and empty it during play. That doesn't happen anymore (since it would occasionally lead to the drunk player throwing the other player out the window, a real problem if you're several stories up), but many modern grandmasters and international masters get completely drunk after a game—often staying out all night at the local bar and somehow appearing the next day fresh and strong (or NOT). Then again, not all alcohol-loving players will wait to drink until *after* the game—there are many cases of titled players drinking before the game and appearing at the board in a state of near coma.

In the '60s and early '70s, some players gave drugs a try during tournament games. In general, LSD didn't work out too well for them (an unnamed International master wasn't able to make even one move, and sat at the board watching dinosaurs fly through the air until his flag fell on move one— sounds like fun). Others gave pot a try, others speed, and some opium.

Times have changed, especially when you consider that too much caffeine is now a FIDE offense, and if you're caught a couple times imbibing too many cups, you can be banned for a few years. That's quite a huge leap from the "exploration *uber alles*" mentality of the '60s!

Personally, I always had a serious sensitivity to sugar and in my youth, same as Gligorić, I would toss down chocolate bars during play— wouldn't it be wonderful if chocolate cured all diseases?—but would cause me to begin to fall asleep as the game progressed. I actually found myself waking up in several games with twenty to forty minutes having ticked off my clock! Later I would try juice, but even that level of sugar wiped me out and led to endless blunders as my brain melted and vision blurred. I finally gave high-quality ginseng a try, and it cured the problem—I would suck on a ginseng root throughout the game, and it kept my mind calmly chugging along.

Ultimately, you have to figure out what's right for your body. Knowing what foods and beverages work for you is extremely important. And, if you find coffee wakes you up and allows you to play at your usual level, or if cough syrup (banned by FIDE) is needed so you don't cough and disturb your opponent, go for it! Last I heard, coffee and over-the-counter cough syrup is legal in the real world, and personally, I would *love* it if my opponent glugged down forty cups of java. I can't understand why any chess organization has any say in such things. If some goon appears with a cup and demands a sample, spit on him and say, "There's your sample." Then pour a mouthful of coffee down your throat with one hand and several caps of cough meds with the other and, walk away.

I'm not condoning anything illegal, but I have no problem pointing a finger at raw stupidity.

Roller Coasters of Hell

> Question: Is it normal to have games that are good (like you control the squares, you play positional, you explore the roles on campsite) and ones that look like there is a monkey controlling your head? I'm asking because I have been studying chess (never forgetting the basics) by a book and by your articles, but my games keep being roller coasters of hell."

Everyone (including grandmasters) has good games and bad games, good days and bad days. I remember (long ago) playing in a New York Open and hanging pieces right and left. I was completely out of it. In fact, I might have had the same monkey you had controlling my head. Towards the end of the tournament I asked Grandmaster Edmar Mednis if there was any cure for the never-ending blunders. He said, "Yes, the next tournament."

A similar thing happened in San Francisco. I suffered through two horrific tournaments. Then I won the U.S. Open. We never know what the chess gods (or chess monkey) will give, or when they will take away.

Let's discuss why you're having so much trouble. Simply put, at your level there will be positions that you understand (which means you'll play well) and you'll get other positions that you won't understand (that's when the monkey will appear). It could be (and you don't realize it) that you need help in many areas. Nothing to be ashamed of since everyone has been there (myself included). You could just continue to play for the rush (which is fine), but there are ways to steadily improve.

Here are some suggestions.

- Many players create an opening repertoire and stick with it. That way (over time) you'll eventually understand your repertoire's pawn structures, typical tactics, situations where an attack is correct, and situations when positional understanding is the proper thing to embrace. Once you're well acquainted with all of that, move on to another repertoire which has different pawn structures and different needs. There are quite a few opening books that explain the ins and outs of those particular openings, and they will prove very helpful.

- Some people play ten-minute chess. If you like it, keep doing it. But also play thirty-minute or even one-hour games since those games will allow you the time to think deeply and, as a result, see what does and doesn't work in your game. Write down what you think you did right and wrong on paper or in a digital notebook, isolate your biggest weaknesses, and then (if you have the money or a benevolent chess coach) let an experienced voice lead you to the promised land.

Time Management

Question: I am playing online chess as preparation for an over-the-board tournaments, and I am focusing on slow games; I believe that at my level it is very important to reason through every move, trying to increase my board vision and analysis skills. However, I am thinking of introducing some fifteen-minute game chess tournaments, mainly for logistics reasons: I cannot play more than a couple of slow tournaments a year. In particular: do you think that trying to "remain hooked" to the opponent in terms of time is a good strategy (i.e. trying not to remain behind your opponent for what time is concerned, "mimicking" his time management strategy)?

The more games you play the better—there is no greater teacher than raw experience. Fifteen-minute chess is a relatively fast time control but it also allows for moments of actual though—of course, one-minute, three-minute, and five-minute games are all the rage and some chess addicts play online for as much as ten hours a night (Grandmaster Nakamura often powers back dozens of Red Bulls as one game ends and the next is set into motion in never-ending staccato fashion),

The first step to fifteen-minute success is to know your openings. If you use most of your time in the first moves, you'll drown in the complications when the real battle begins. On the other hand, if you don't know your opening but still toss out quick opening moves so that you have time "for later," you'll start the game with an awful position and all the time in the world won't save you.

I should add that "knowing your opening" doesn't just allude to the book moves. It mainly calls for a solid knowledge of the typical structures and plans and tactical ideas associated with the systems you play. That allows you to make quick but sensible moves deep into the middlegame and gives you a huge edge over most of the opposition (who won't know these things).

When the opening is over and done with and you've reached new and wonderful vistas, use your time to make sure you don't fall for silly tricks and to map out a logical plan. Once you have that plan, other moves will come fast and natural.

Never try to "remain hooked" (as the question put it) to the opponent! When you do that, you're not playing the game anymore. Instead you're stepping into some odd, self-destructive psychological bog that, quite honestly, won't end well. Your time is there to use when needed, and your goal in fifteen-minute is to use it intelligently. Moving fast because your opponent is moving fast isn't even chess, so please try and avoid it.

Let me add that in any time control, you should never pay attention to how much time your opponent uses. Worry about your moves, not his time! Don't get involved in his melodrama! Those who do pay attention to the opponent's time fall for all sorts of tricks.

I've witnessed players who, seeing that they are losing, deliberately let their clocks tick until they only have seconds left. The idea is that the opponent will employ the, "I don't want him to think on my time, so I'll move fast and prevent it" strategy. This "brilliant" idea effectively nullifies your advantage on the clock and leaves you tossing out moves so quickly that blunders are almost a given. It's a dead end philosophy that has left countless players sitting in a corner wondering how they failed to win an overwhelming position.

Simply put, when you play chess the idea is to make good moves, not quick ones!

Blindfold Chess

> Question: I wanted to know your take on blindfold chess for the improving player. How difficult is it to learn, and is it true that learning to play blindfold will really help improve your game and minimize blunders?

There is absolutely no reason to try your luck with blindfold chess, unless it's something you simply want to do for fun. Being able to play a game blindfold won't help you cure blunders, nor will it improve your overall strength. On the other hand, if you are giving a ten-board blindfold simultaneous exhibition, you'll find that the ladies really dig it.

I remember high school study hall in my early teens. The only reason I took study hall was to sleep, but once several other kids (all bored) found out that I was a chess player, they insisted I play them all blindfold at the same time. So study hall that year turned into me laying on top of a few desks, eyes closed and half asleep, while three or four kids would call out their moves and try to beat

"Alexander Alekhine, the Russian chessmaster, set a new world's record for simultaneous blindfold chess when he faced 26 players in an exhibition at the Hotel Alamac, New York city, on April 27, 1924. Alekhine started playing at 2pm and finished at 2am the next morning having won 16 games, lost 5, and drawn 5, without ever setting eyes on the boards." (Courtesy of the Cleveland Public Library's John G. White Collection.)

me. I found blindfold chess to be fairly easy, though I must admit to never playing more than five games at once.

Blindfold chess has been around for a very long time. It's said that Sa'id bin Jubair (665-714—a very, *very* long time ago!) was skilled at this form of chess. However, memory of Sa'id and others had dimmed by the 1700s, that when Philidor played blindfold against two men at the same time, that in 1782 it was touted by *The World* as, "A phenomenon in the history of man, and should be hoarded among the best examples of human memory, till memory shall be no more."

At the time, nobody could have guessed that this "amazing" record would one day be shattered by a little boy in study hall, or that it had been completely crushed long before the little boy was born by an avalanche of players:

Ladislas Maczuski (1838-1898) gave a ten board simultaneous exhibition in 1863, finishing with a score of +7, =2, -1. simultaneously;

Alexander Fritz (1857-1932) played twelve;

Zukertort played sixteen.

There were many more with similar numbers, and then blindfold aficionados really kicked it into high gear.

Harry Pillsbury gave many blindfold simultaneous exhibits, eventually reaching a record twenty-two games;

There followed **Richard Réti** twenty-nine;

Alexander Alekhine (1934) played thirty-two;

George Koltanowski played thirty-four (in 1960 he also played 56 consecutively though note this was *not* simultaneously!);

Miguel Najdorf (1947) forty-five (!!), and finally;

Janos Flesch, who in 1960 set the bar at fifty-two!

The definitive source on blindfold chess is, *Blindfold Chess: History, Psychology, Techniques, Champions, World Records, and Important Games* by Eliot Hearst and John Knott, over 400 pages and excellent in every way.

INDEX OF NAMES

Illustrations are indicated in ***bold-italic***.